Praise for

GRACE AND POWER

"[In] this prodigiously researched work . . . the reader is placed right there in the salons of Georgetown and upstairs at the White House, reveling in a dinner-party society that has largely disappeared."

—WILLIAM SAFIRE, *The New York Times*

"*Grace and Power* will be a runaway bestseller, deservedly so. The book is impressively well researched and smartly written. It is rich in character sketches, anecdotes and events. . . . [Smith] is in firm command of the vast Kennedy scholarship."

—*The Washington Post Book World*

"If we did not already know the ending, one might say this book reads like a novel."

—*Boston Sunday Globe*

"A gracefully written tell-all that really does tell a story worth reading . . . Smith is a compelling writer."

—*Los Angeles Times Book Review*

"Ravishingly readable."

—*Newsday*

"Smith writes neither to make idols nor to break them. She's unblinking but fair-minded in her assessment of the Kennedys and their friends, and she writes lucidly and engagingly. But what really sets this book apart from other Camelotery is the sheer density of revealing description and anecdote."

—*Houston Chronicle*

"[Smith] makes a marriage of sorts with her subject, devouring all details, sifting through the remains, the intentional as well as the concealed."

—*The Philadelphia Inquirer*

"This is a sensational portrait of the Kennedys in power—original in concept, exhaustive in research, judicious in approach and lovely in expression. . . . Such is the range of *Grace and Power* that it makes many of the memoirs, biographies and histories of the last 40 years now seem incomplete or incorrect."

—Toronto *Globe and Mail*

"With stylistic grace and authoritative reporting, Smith delivers what should stand for some time as the ultimate account of a marriage that, even with its secrets bared, remained veiled."

—New York *Daily News*

ALSO BY SALLY BEDELL SMITH

In All His Glory

Reflected Glory

Diana in Search of Herself

GRACE AND POWER

Grace and POWER

THE PRIVATE WORLD *of* THE KENNEDY WHITE HOUSE

SALLY BEDELL SMITH

RANDOM HOUSE TRADE PAPERBACKS
New York

2005 Random House Trade Paperback Edition

Published in the United States by Random House Trade Paperbacks,
an imprint of The Random House Publishing Group,
a division of Random House, Inc., New York.

RANDOM HOUSE TRADE PAPERBACKS and colophon are trademarks
of Random House, Inc.

Originally published in hardcover in the United States by Random House,
an imprint of The Random House Publishing Group,
a division of Random House, Inc., in 2004.

LIBRARY OF CONGRESS CATALOGING-IN-PUBLICATION DATA
Smith, Sally Bedell.
Grace and power : the private world of the Kennedy White House /
by Sally Bedell Smith.
p. cm.
Includes bibliographical references and index.
ISBN 0-345-48082-1
1. Kennedy, John F. (John Fitzgerald), 1917–1963. 2. Onassis, Jacqueline Kennedy,
1929–1994. 3. Kennedy, John F. (John Fitzgerald), 1917–1963—Friends and associates.
4. Onassis, Jacqueline Kennedy, 1929–1994—Friends and associates. 5. Presidents—
United States—Biography. 6. Presidents' spouses—United States—Biography.
7. United States—Politics and government—1961–1963. 8. Political culture—
United States—History—20th century. 9. Washington (D.C.)—Social life and
customs—1951– I. Title.
E842.1.S65 2004   973.922'092—dc22
[B]   2003060310

Printed in the United States of America

Random House website address: www.atrandom.com

9

Book design by Casey Hampton

Picture research by Susan Longacre

For Stephen, Kirk, Lisa, and David

My candle burns at both ends;
It will not last the night;
But ah, my foes, and oh, my friends—
It gives a lovely light!

—EDNA ST. VINCENT MILLAY,
"FIRST FIG"

THE KENNEDY COURT

JANUARY 1961

JOHN FITZGERALD KENNEDY, 43. President of the United States.

JACQUELINE BOUVIER KENNEDY, 31. First Lady.

JOSEPH PATRICK KENNEDY, 72. Father of the President. Principal architect of JFK's rise in politics.

ROSE FITZGERALD KENNEDY, 70. Mother of the President. Family organizer and White House hostess in Jackie's absence.

ROBERT FRANCIS KENNEDY, 35. Attorney General of the United States. De facto Vice President and confidant of JFK. Jack's proxy for conveying difficult messages and gathering information. His extroverted wife, *Ethel,* 32, an honorary Kennedy sister.

EDWARD MOORE KENNEDY, 28. Youngest Kennedy sibling. More outgoing than either Jack or Bobby. Elected to U.S. Senate from Massachusetts in 1962. His wife, *Joan,* 24, and Jackie often sought privacy from the Kennedy clan—Joan to play the piano, Jackie to paint.

PATRICIA KENNEDY LAWFORD, 36. Sister married to British actor *Peter,* 37. Lived in California where she and her husband entertained JFK at parties stocked with Hollywood actresses.

EUNICE KENNEDY SHRIVER, 39. Sister closest to JFK. Advocate for the handicapped and mentally retarded. Her husband, *Sargent,* 45, was JFK's first director of the Peace Corps.

JEAN KENNEDY SMITH, 32. Most demure of the Kennedy sisters, and closest to Jackie. Her husband, *Stephen,* 33, served as a key political operative for JFK and ran the Kennedy family business.

JOSEPH ALSOP, 50. Influential columnist for the *Washington Post* known for his erudition and hauteur. Famous Georgetown host and early booster of JFK. Advised Jackie on such matters as using power in Washington and handling female reporters she called "harpies."

JANET LEE AUCHINCLOSS, 59. Jackie's mother. Avid horsewoman and meticulous hostess. Like Rose Kennedy, frequently stood in for Jackie at official events. Her husband, *Hugh,* 58, Jackie's devoted stepfather, provided an idyllic upbringing in an old WASP setting.

LETITIA BALDRIGE, 34. Knew Jackie at Miss Porter's School and Vassar. As her first White House social secretary, orchestrated Jackie's official life in the White House for more than two years.

CHARLES BARTLETT, 39. Columnist for the *Chattanooga Times.* Friend of JFK from postwar years and of Jackie from her late teens, and played matchmaker between the two. Provided constant stream of advice and intelligence to JFK in the White House.

KIRK LEMOYNE "LEM" BILLINGS, 44. JFK's oldest friend. So ubiquitous at the White House that he kept a set of clothing in his own guest room. Eunice Shriver said Billings offered her brother "a complete liberation of the spirit."

MCGEORGE BUNDY, 41. National Security Adviser. Admired for a mind of "dazzling clarity and speed." So supremely confident it was said he could "strut sitting down." An influential voice on foreign policy.

BENJAMIN BRADLEE, 39. Washington bureau chief for *Newsweek.* Handsome, irreverent, and shrewd, he shared Kennedy's passion for political gossip. His wife, *Antoinette "Tony,"* 36, was a favorite of the President.

OLEG CASSINI, 47. Jackie's official couturier who also designed dresses for JFK's sisters. With his brother *Igor "Ghighi,"* 44 (Hearst gossip columnist *Cholly Knickerbocker*), frequented the Kennedy court, usually with an attractive woman to adorn the White House dinner table.

VIVIAN "VIVI" CRESPI, 33. Friend of Jackie's since childhood in Newport. Ex-wife of Marco Fabio Crespi, an Italian count. A glamorous presence at White House dinners and weekends in Hyannis and Newport.

CLARENCE DOUGLAS DILLON, 51. Secretary of the Treasury. Patrician Republican investment banker. Veteran of the Eisenhower years. Owner of Haut-Brion vineyard. Known for his rarefied tastes and homes filled with exquisite art and furniture.

PAUL "RED" FAY, 42. Under Secretary of the Navy. Friend of JFK from navy PT boat days. Referred to as JFK's "Falstaff" who was "full of the old malarky." Shared JFK's penchant for teasing and banter.

EVE FOUT, 31. Jackie's closest friend in the Virginia hunt country. Expert rider and astute judge of horseflesh. Along with her husband, *Paul*, 33, rode frequently with Jackie and oversaw care of her horses.

JOHN KENNETH GALBRAITH, 52. Harvard economist who served as ambassador to India. As JFK's adviser without portfolio, he traveled back to Washington a half dozen times in two years. Author of "impertinent cables" devoured by the President and First Lady.

DAVID ORMSBY GORE, 42. Britain's ambassador to the United States. Considered the eleventh member of the Kennedy cabinet. Soigné aristocrat related to JFK by marriage. Friend since college days. Had the effortless grace Kennedy prized, with brainpower that JFK felt exceeded even Bundy's.

LYNDON BAINES JOHNSON, 52. Vice President of the United States. Formerly Senate majority leader and Washington's most formidable power broker. Deeply resentful of Bobby Kennedy, who reciprocated the dislike. Wife, *Claudia "Lady Bird,"* 48, frequently filled in for Jackie at official events.

ROBERT MCNAMARA, 44. Secretary of Defense. Former "Whiz Kid" and president of Ford Motor Company. Famous for his bravura recitations of facts and figures. Favorite of Jackie, with whom she read poetry aloud.

RACHEL LAMBERT "BUNNY" MELLON, 49. Known for her rarefied taste and perfectionism, designer of the White House Rose Garden, creator of the East Garden, and quiet adviser on numerous matters of entertaining and style. A "very motherly figure" for Jackie. Wife of *Paul*, 53, enormously wealthy connoisseur of art and thoroughbreds.

MARY PINCHOT MEYER, 40. Lover of Jack Kennedy for the last two years of his presidency. Vassar graduate like Jackie. Ethereal artist with unconventional attitudes. Sister of Ben Bradlee's wife, Tony, a connection that provided convenient camouflage.

LAWRENCE O'BRIEN, 43. JFK's liaison with Congress. Son of a Massachusetts saloon keeper, highly regarded for keen political judgment. Bobby Kennedy said he could "talk the balls off a brass monkey."

KENNETH O'DONNELL, 36. White House Appointments Secretary. Supervisor of JFK's schedule, logistical organizer, and political sounding board. Known as the "Wolfhound," the "Cobra," and the "Iceman." Frequently abrasive, notoriously taciturn, and ferociously loyal.

DAVE POWERS, 48. The Kennedy court jester. Official White House greeter who entertained JFK with jokes and political lore. Often kept JFK company when Jackie was away, and would not leave until the President said, "Good night, pal, will you please put out the light?"

LEE BOUVIER RADZIWILL, 27. Jackie's younger sister and companion. Lived in London, but made frequent visits to the White House and Palm Beach and shared several long holidays with Jackie in Europe. Husband, *Stanislas "Stas,"* 46, was a colorful Polish prince who made a small fortune in London real estate.

JAMES REED, 41. Assistant Secretary of the Treasury. Friend of JFK from navy days in the Pacific. Yankee Republican who tramped through Civil War battlefields with JFK and shared his fondness for poetry of Emily Dickinson and Robert Burns.

FRANKLIN DELANO ROOSEVELT JR., 46. Under Secretary of Commerce. Fifth child of the thirty-second president. His campaigning helped turn crucial West Virginia primary to Kennedy. Former congressman whose drinking doomed his own political career.

ARTHUR M. SCHLESINGER JR., 43. White House gadfly, troubleshooter, and unofficial historian of the Kennedy years. Dubbed the "court philosopher" by *The New Yorker*. Pulitzer Prize–winning author and Harvard professor. Adviser to Jackie on everything from books for the White House library to foreign films for the screening room.

FLORENCE PRITCHETT SMITH, 40. Jack Kennedy's most important female friend. Vivacious hostess in New York and Palm Beach. Dated JFK in his bachelor days. Wealthy stockbroker husband, *Earl*, 57, was former U.S. ambassador to Cuba, friendly with Joe Kennedy as well as Jackie's family in Newport.

They certainly have acquired something we have lost—a casual sort of grandeur about their evenings, always at the end of the day's business, the promise of parties, and pretty women, and music and beautiful clothes, and champagne, and all that. I must say there is something very 18th century about your new young man, an aristocratic touch.

—BRITISH PRIME MINISTER HAROLD MACMILLAN ON JOHN AND JACQUELINE KENNEDY AND THEIR WHITE HOUSE CIRCLE

On November 29, 1963—a week after the assassination of President John Fitzgerald Kennedy in Dallas, Texas—his widow, Jacqueline Bouvier Kennedy, summoned presidential chronicler Theodore H. White to the Kennedy family compound in Hyannis Port, on Cape Cod in Massachusetts. She wanted White to write an essay about her husband for *Life,* the magazine that had celebrated the Kennedys in words and photographs for more than a decade.

Jackie Kennedy spoke for four hours, until just past midnight, with "composure," a "calm voice," and "total recall." It was a rambling monologue about the assassination, her late husband's love of history dating from his sickly childhood, and her views on how he should be remembered. She didn't want him immortalized by "bitter" men such as *New York Times* columnist Arthur Krock and Merriman Smith, the UPI White House correspondent. Well versed in the classics, she said she felt "ashamed" that she was unable to come up with a lofty historical metaphor for the Kennedy presidency.

Instead, she told White, her "obsession" was a song from the popular Broadway show *Camelot,* by Alan Jay Lerner (a JFK friend from boarding school and college) and Frederick Loewe, which opened only weeks after Kennedy was elected. The sentimental musical popularized the legend of the British medieval King Arthur, his wife Queen Guinevere, and the heroic knights of the Round Table. Jackie recounted to White that at night before going to sleep, Jack Kennedy listened to *Camelot* on his "old Victrola." "I'd get out of bed at night and play it for him when it was so cold getting out of bed," she said. His favorite lines were at the end of the record: "Don't let it be forgot, that once there was a spot, for one brief shining moment, that was known as Camelot."

White spent only forty-five minutes writing "For President Kennedy: An Epilogue," a thousand-word reminiscence for *Life*'s December 6 issue. With close editing by Jackie Kennedy (among her numerous alterations, she changed "this was the idea that she wanted to share" to "this was the idea that transfixed her"), the piece set forth the Camelot metaphor that has defined the Kennedy presidency for four decades. At an exhibit of Jackie Kennedy's designer clothing at the Metropolitan Museum of Art in New York, the John F. Kennedy Library in Boston, and the Corcoran Gallery in Washington in 2001 and 2002, the Lerner and Loewe tune played over and over, a soothing loop of background music.

As a child, Jack Kennedy would "devour [stories of] the knights of the Round Table," according to Jackie. As an adult he had been intrigued by tales of the martyrdom of folk heroes, from the ancient Greeks to Arthur in Britain and Roland in France. Given Kennedy's middlebrow fondness for show tunes, it was only natural that in May 1962 Jackie invited Frederick Loewe to a small dinner at the White House. At the President's request, the composer played the score of *Camelot* on the piano.

Still, many of Kennedy's friends, especially the intellectuals, have tried to dismiss or downplay the Camelot image as inapt and mawkish, suggesting that it would have made the cool and brainy JFK wince. Harvard economist John Kenneth Galbraith said Jackie regretted the Camelot association as "overdone." Historian Arthur Schlesinger Jr. called it "myth turned into a cliché. It had no application during President Kennedy's life. He would have been derisive about it." Jackie's conversation with Teddy White, he said, was "her most mischievous interview. The image was mischievous and legendary . . . Camelot itself was not noted for marital constancy, and it ended in blood and death."

For those very reasons, Jackie Kennedy might well have wished to retract her words. Although the Arthurian legend evoked battle-field bravery (King Arthur and his knights fighting to regain his kingdom) and idealism (the quest for the Holy Grail of perfection by the knights), it also, as Schlesinger pointed out, featured treachery (Arthur's nephew Mordred seizing his kingdom and taking the queen captive) and adultery (the love affair of Guinevere and Arthur's valiant knight Sir Lancelot).

But Jackie Kennedy never backed away from Camelot. What she wanted to convey was the "magic" of her husband's presidency—an interlude marked by grand intentions, soaring rhetoric, and high style. At the end of January 1964, in a letter to former British prime minister Harold Macmillan, she conceded that Camelot was "overly sentimental," but maintained it was "right" because those 1,036 days had been a "brief shining moment" that would not be repeated.

Two years after the assassination, in *A Thousand Days: John F. Kennedy in the White House,* the book that set the template for the Kennedy years, Schlesinger himself described the period's "life-affirming, life-enhancing zest, the brilliance, the wit, the cool commitment, the steady purpose." It was a view that remained undimmed for him, and for many others, despite forty years of tawdry revelations about JFK's reckless womanizing and his administration's decision to enlist the mob to assassinate Fidel Castro.

The picture of the Kennedy White House has been blurred by this competition between the Camelot mythology and the powerful impulse to tear it down. Thousands of books, articles, and television documentaries have created a fun-house mirror in which reflections of the Kennedys jump-cut from clarity to distortion. Hopes had been so high, the romance so strong, and the tragedy so great that the everyday reality of the Kennedy White House seemed insufficiently dramatic.

Because Jack and Jackie were such magnetic stars, their supporting players—and their complex interactions with the Kennedys—were often overlooked or given short shrift. But with the passage of time, emotions have softened, and members of the Kennedy circle, including many who have never spoken publicly before, discussed their years in the limelight with detachment and a sense of perspective. Fresh insights were also drawn from previously unavailable letters and personal papers. The story that emerges, recounted in this book, is more compelling than the Kennedy mythologies. It is a story of people selected by history—some with extraordinary talents, others blessed with the gift of loyalty—struggling to guide the United States through perilous times even as they wrestled with their own frailties and the temptations of power. From the remove of four decades, the Kennedy White House emerges not as a model of enlightened government nor as a series of dark conspiracies, but rather as a deeply human place.

The Kennedys may have been Democrats, full of compassion for the poor and dispossessed, but the image of Jack and Jackie as king and queen surrounded by their court had occurred to many people familiar with the administration. The British political philosopher and formidable Oxford don Isaiah Berlin—a guest at several private White House dinners—saw the Kennedys as "Bonapartist," finding parallels in Napoleon's brothers who, like Robert F. Kennedy as attorney general and Edward M. Kennedy as U.S. senator, held responsible positions in the government. Berlin found further similarities in the aides who served their leader: "devoted, dedicated marshals who liked nothing better than to have their ears tweaked." Kennedy's "men with shining eyes," Berlin observed, had a "great deal of energy and ambition" and were "marching forward in some very exciting and romantic fashion." David Ormsby Gore, the British ambassador during the Kennedy administration and one of the President's most intimate friends and advisers, likened the administration to a "Tudor Court."

Richard Neustadt, then a professor of government at Columbia University, mused that the Kennedy "court life," a cynosural arrangement last seen in the White House of Theodore Roosevelt, had the equivalent of "apartments at Versailles" and "latch keys for the weekends." The columnist Stewart Alsop complained after one year of the

Kennedy administration, "The place is lousy with courtiers and ladies in waiting—actual or would be." As with court life in earlier centuries, the Kennedy entourage made a stately progress: from the White House to expensive homes in the Virginia hunt country, to Palm Beach, Hyannis Port, and Newport—all playgrounds for the rich and privileged.

"Jackie wanted to do Versailles in America," said Oleg Cassini, her official dress designer and self-described "de facto courtier close to the king and queen." "She said this many times," Cassini added. "She had realized some very smart women encouraged a court throughout history." In particular Jackie admired Madame de Maintenon, who presided over a legendary salon before marrying Louis XIV, and Madame de Récamier, the early nineteenth-century hostess famous for the wit and intelligence of her gatherings.

Jackie organized her life in the White House according to what interested her, handing off many of the ritual obligations to others and delegating the paperwork to subordinates. "My life here which I dreaded & which at first overwhelmed me—is now under control and the happiest time I have ever known—not for the position—but for the closeness of one's family," Jackie wrote to her friend William Walton in mid-1962. "The last thing I expected to find in the W. House."

On any given day, President Kennedy would be managing what veteran Democratic adviser Clark Clifford called "the cockiest crowd I'd ever seen in the White House," a group of West Wing aides that National Security Adviser McGeorge Bundy likened to "the Harlem Globetrotters, passing forward, behind, sideways and underneath." At another moment JFK might be swimming in the White House pool (heated to 90 degrees for his ailing back) with his trusted factotum Dave Powers and a couple of fetching West Wing secretaries, or having a tête-à-tête lunch (grilled cheese, cold beef, consommé) with Jackie, or clapping his hands three times to welcome his three-year-old daughter, Caroline, into the Oval Office.

Jackie, meanwhile, might be at the long table in the Treaty Room on the second floor of the White House, smoking her L&M filtered cigarettes and scribbling memos on foolscap, or composing a letter to French culture minister André Malraux, one of her mentors. Perhaps she would be bouncing on the canvas trampoline on the South Lawn to relieve stress, or curled up with Marcus Cheke's *The Cardinal de Bernis: A Biography,* or ducking into the White House school in the third-floor solarium, where the squeals of children competed with the yelps of five dogs and the chirps of two parakeets: part of a menagerie that brought to mind Teddy Roosevelt's days in the Executive Mansion.

In the evening Jack and Jackie would typically host a dinner for eight—a collection of close friends with an imported New York artist or writer as a "new face"—as Italian songs played softly on the Victrola. The conversation, invariably informal and candid, might touch on the queen of Greece ("nothing but a busy-body . . . seeming to save the world [but] basically, building herself up," according to Jackie), the origin of the French ambassador's pin-striped shirt (Pierre Cardin, not Jermyn Street in London), the character of Richard Nixon ("nice fellow in private but . . . he seems to have a split personality and he is very bad in public," in Jack's view), or JFK's concerns about NATO ("Europe wants a free ride in its defense").

The Kennedys gave memorable private dinner dances as well—a half dozen in less than three years—where waiters carried large trays filled with such exotic mixed drinks as the Cuba Libre, a lethal combination of rum, Coca-Cola, and lime juice. "They served the drinks in enormous tumblers," recalled writer George Plimpton. "Everybody had too much to drink because they were excited." State dinners set new standards for culinary excellence (with menus in French for the first time) and cultural entertainments featuring Shakespeare's sonnets and Jerome Robbins's ballets. "It was Irish, which made it fun," wrote television correspondent Nancy Dickerson, "and blended with the spirit of Harvard and the patina of Jackie's finishing schools, the mixture was intoxicating."

Highbrow seminars brought in "great guns" to provoke "great thoughts" for a select group of friends and administration officials, in the irreverent view of Arthur Schlesinger's wife, Marian. "It was rather self-conscious though harmless," Marian said, "sort of like Voltaire at the court of Frederick the Great." Guest lecturers included noted historian Elting Morison on Teddy Roosevelt ("Not so," TR's daughter Alice Roosevelt Longworth periodically murmured in a stage whisper, a malicious glint in her eye) and philosopher A. J. Ayer on logical positivism ("But St. Thomas said," Ethel Kennedy twice interjected before her husband barked, "Drop it Ethel, drop it"). The sober atmosphere collapsed entirely during Rachel Carson's talk on "The Male Screw Worm" when Treasury Secretary Douglas Dillon's giggles caused the gathering to dissolve in laughter.

Such levity masked a more shadowy reality—a hedonism and moral relativism that anticipated the sexual revolution of the following decades. Behind the scenes, Kennedy engaged in private sexual escapades in the White House, Palm Beach, Malibu, Manhattan, and Palm Springs, activities that many in the Kennedy court heard as rumors, others refused to acknowledge, and a select few—primarily trusted White House aides Kenneth O'Donnell and Dave Powers, as well as inner-circle crony Charles "Chuck" Spalding—witnessed and sometimes abetted. Jackie knew what was going on, and confided as much to her sister, Lee Radziwill, several intimate friends, and even administration officials such as Adlai Stevenson. But publicly she stoically chose to ignore her husband's infidelities, which gave her greater latitude in pursuing her own rarefied life of foxhunting and hobnobbing with jet set friends in Europe.

Some, like her friend Eve Fout in Virginia, saw occasional evidence of Jackie's sadness and noticed that "she didn't have the easiest marital situation." Many assumed that Jackie simply shared the European aristocratic view that it was natural for husbands to stray. "All Kennedy men are like that," she once told Ted Kennedy's wife, Joan. "You can't let it get to you because you shouldn't take it personally." Jackie adored her father and her father-in-law, both of whom had been openly unfaithful to their wives. "She had made a bargain with herself," said her longtime friend Jessie Wood. "She discovered Jack was a real philanderer, but she decided to stick it out. I think she loved him."

Because of their youth, beauty, and social pedigree, along with their pursuit of fun and intellectual stimulation, Jack and Jackie Kennedy attracted a glamorous coterie of friends and colleagues—what Harold Macmillan characterized as the "smart life" (international socialites and Hollywood stars), "the highbrow life" (pundits and professors), and the "political life" (chosen aides and cabinet officers). Perhaps as never before, Washington was sharply divided between the "ins" and the "outs."

Washington society columnist Betty Beale, who observed from outside the circle, commented that Washingtonians invited to private parties at the Kennedy White House "adopted a comical air of smugness."

Within the court, "very few really had much in common with each other," said newspaperman Charles Bartlett, a Kennedy intimate. Some were accomplished athletes, others hopelessly uncoordinated. The socially prominent carried equal weight with those from modest backgrounds; neither Jack nor Jackie could be accused of snobbery.

Only two personal friends of the first Catholic president shared his religion, along with three of his close aides. A remarkable number in the inner circle—five personal friends and three members of the administration—were Republicans, not to mention Jackie Kennedy's entire family, including her stepsister Nina Steers, whose husband was active in GOP politics and later served as a Republican congressman.

Several Kennedy insiders were thought to be homosexual, although only one, the columnist Joseph Alsop, ever acknowledged it. Despite the macho image of the Kennedy administration, JFK was comfortable with homosexuals, perhaps, some friends believed, because he understood the tensions of having a secret life.

Most members of the Kennedy court were stars in their fields, lending what Kennedy biographer William Manchester called "an elegant, mandarin tone." They tended to be "cheerful, amusing, energetic, informed and informal," observed Kennedy's chief domestic aide Theodore Sorensen. Nearly everyone in the Kennedy court was attractive—and even those of lesser looks, such as the pockmarked artist William Walton, were clever and debonair.

Brainpower and a talent to amuse were the most highly valued traits. JFK "enjoyed . . . almost anyone from whom he could learn . . . communicating on the level of the Bundy brothers and the Cassini brothers," wrote Sorensen. Both Jack and Jackie abhorred the mundane. JFK said he "hated the suburbia-type existence" with its endless cocktail parties. Even as a teenager Jackie had confided to her sister a distaste for country club women who could converse only about monograms on guest towels and the progress of their children's teeth.

JFK expected "real ping pong in the communication," in the words of White House aide Fred Holborn. Katharine Graham, then the mousy wife of the *Washington Post*'s glamorous president and publisher, confessed that her "terror" of boring JFK "paralyzed and silenced" her. When Suzanne Roosevelt, the wife of Franklin D. Roosevelt Jr., hosted Jack and Jackie for dinner, she caught the President's attention by quoting Lincoln. "My God, I said something that interested him," she recalled thinking at the time.

Kennedy "hated dimness," said Isaiah Berlin. "Anybody who was dim, no matter how virtuous, how wise, how . . . noble . . . [was] no good to him." Nor was anyone with less than one hundred percent loyalty. "The Kennedys were pretty tough eggs," said Marian Schlesinger. "Either you were in or you were out. . . . I think the Kennedys really turned people into courtiers. . . . They manipulated and used people in a rough way."

Jack and Jackie Kennedy would quite literally command their courtiers to sing and dance. Paul "Red" Fay, who became friendly with JFK during World War II, routinely performed "Hooray for Hollywood," yelling out the lines as JFK doubled over with laughter. Oleg Cassini would launch into his "Chaplin walk" or the latest dance step from New York nightclubs. "Kennedy knew he was a potentate, and at a dinner for 150 he would point a finger at you and say, 'Talk,'" said Cassini. "Was I a performing seal? Yes, and it was a slightly naughty thing. He did it to a lot of people. In Palm Beach after a heavy lunch he told everyone to do pushups and everyone did, trying to impress him."

JFK had "to an exceptional degree, the gift of friendship," wrote Arthur Schlesinger. The foundations of his friendship were warmth, solicitude, and finely balanced flattery. Jack Kennedy compartmentalized his relationships, much as Franklin D. Roosevelt did. Kennedy's "friends came in layers . . . and each layer considered itself closest to the center. But Kennedy kept the layers apart and included and baffled them all," Schlesinger wrote. The President's intimates "each had a certain role we were cast into whether we knew it or not," said James Reed, a friend of Kennedy's since World War II. Kennedy even kept Theodore Sorensen, his intellectual "alter ego," off balance. "That man [Sorensen] never knows from one week to the next where he stands," said White House aide Ralph Dungan in mid-1963.

It seemed that Kennedy held something out on everyone. "No

one—no single aide, friend or member of his family—knew all his thoughts or actions on any single subject," observed Sorensen. Kennedy didn't talk about women with some of his friends, but he did with others—usually those with whom he wouldn't discuss intellectual matters. His closest political operatives were privy to Kennedy's ruthlessness, what Schlesinger called the "determined, unrelenting and profane" part of his personality that would have shocked his purely social friends. *Look* magazine reporter Laura Bergquist considered him "prismatic . . . He had many funny facets."

Kennedy disliked being alone, so he constantly surrounded himself with friends and family—a result, some friends thought, of growing up with eight siblings in a household that resembled a bustling hotel. But such relentless fellowship came at the cost of true intimacy, a distance that may have suited JFK. One or two people could claim special insight into his feelings, but most related to him superficially. "You'd never bleed in his presence nor would he in yours," said Bill Walton. "I'm not going to run around telling him when I'm hurt about something and God knows he's not going to tell me."

A close association with Jack Kennedy had clear rules. Charley Bartlett noticed that JFK "wasn't a cozy friend . . . somebody that you'd sort of slop around with on a Sunday. It was always . . . you'd arrange to take a walk . . . or do something that had been laid down." Chuck Spalding always knew that his time with Kennedy had limits: "He didn't like to be with the same people for forty-eight hours, if that long." Everyone in Kennedy's circle made himself available for a last-minute invitation, as well as phone calls at any hour, day and night.

Writing to his superiors in London, David Ormsby Gore noted that Kennedy created "his own private information network" that he used "to cross check about individuals and events." Instead of being put off, Kennedy's friends felt grateful to be on the receiving end of what James Reed called Kennedy's "consistent patter of asking people what they thought."

Jack Kennedy was most comfortable in the company of men. In this he was like his father, who once wrote to a friend, "Women never have any effect on our lives—we're men's men!" But several women were important members of the Kennedy court. Jack Kennedy had grown up with lively sisters, who combined girlishness and sophistication and who regarded men as authority figures. JFK viewed women primarily as sexual objects to be conquered; he was not much interested in falling in love, sharing feelings, or gratifying his partners.

But while he was a philanderer, Jack Kennedy was not a misogynist. He kept Jackie in what she herself called his "happiness compartment." "Whatever his waywardness may have been, even if there was no end of that," said Arthur Schlesinger, "he was very pleased and proud to be married to Jackie." Kennedy was fascinated by women—as lovers, amusers, comforters, pals, helpmeets of various sorts. He was intrigued by what women wore, how they looked, how they thought.

He had not been raised (nor did the times encourage him) to take women seriously enough to have them as advisers in his administration. "It drove him wild," his friend Bill Walton said, if a woman tried to "bend his ear." But he gradually learned to appreciate the quality of a woman's mind through exposure to Jackie's originality and intelligence, along with the ideas of a few women journalists, notably forty-six-year-old Barbara Ward, Baroness Jackson of Lodsworth, who wrote for *The Economist*. According to Arthur Schlesinger, Kennedy respected Ward's "capacity to state problems in a probing and persuasive way." Marian Schlesinger noticed other aspects of her appeal: "She was an intellectual, good-looking woman who dressed well and was a great expert who intrigued all those guys."

———

Jackie's own circle was smaller than her husband's. "I don't think she found it relaxing the way he did to have a lot of people around," said her sister, Lee. On her private phone line at the White House, "she did keep in touch with a handful of pals," recalled Tish Baldrige, Jackie's White House social secretary, "but not in long drawn-out conversations."

It has often been said—usually by women who had been rebuffed by her—that Jackie had little use for women and focused only on men. "She would cozy up to men with wine and cigarettes," said Pat Hass, who helped Jackie start the White House school. Jackie did find men more interesting than women—particularly during the White House days when there were so many bright, powerful, and appealing men around. (Before her marriage to JFK she had revealed to newspaperman John White her ambition to be "the confidante of an important man.") Most women of that era led confined lives that simply didn't appeal to Jackie. "She enjoyed the thoughts that were in men's minds," said Robert McNamara, JFK's secretary of defense.

Jackie Kennedy prized loyalty as much as her husband—especially in the White House, where she was reluctant to branch beyond trusted friendships forged early in her life. Since her childhood, she had selected her friends carefully, with a preference for offbeat characters. Most of the women she knew well had brains as well as style, humor, and imagination. "She didn't like empty-headed women who talked about manicures," said her longtime friend Solange Batsell Herter. Nor did Jackie care for any woman who was what she called a "pushy creature" or self-promoter. "She liked women who were feminine and who weren't just after what tough men were after," said Herter.

In the company of trusted friends, Jackie could be carefree and outgoing but not quick to confide. "Jackie didn't enjoy superficial relationships," said Deeda Blair, whose husband, Bill, served as ambassador to Denmark in the Kennedy years. "She wanted something a bit more." She had high standards of wit and intelligence, but she also had the capacity to draw people out, to make them feel important, as her husband could.

Yet those closest to Jackie were also aware that she "ran hot and cold," as Solange Herter put it—open and welcoming at one moment, distant and preoccupied the next. These "hermetic periods," as Oleg Cassini called them, sometimes perplexed her friends. "She would have enthusiasms, then the enthusiasm would wane," noted Baldrige.

It seemed to many around them that Jack and Jackie Kennedy were remarkably self-contained, with the result that no friend felt indispensable. Jack Kennedy "gave a great impression of affection and congeniality but he had immense reserve," an element of mystery that was "a source of his fascination and power," according to Arthur Schlesinger. Jackie, too, was "unto herself," said Baldrige. "She was self-sufficient." In Schlesinger's view, "Jack Kennedy enjoyed his friends and Bobby Kennedy needed his friends. Jack didn't dislike people, it's just that he didn't need them."

Schlesinger's view may have been affected by his tangential position at the White House. "I doubt life would have been any different for

[JFK] if I had not gone to Washington," he said. "I don't think I had much influence over Jack Kennedy. He liked talking to me." Others, including Sorensen, did have significant day-to-day influence—and knew it. In his role as speechwriter, "I was writing some things I hoped he would share," Sorensen said. "I had the opportunity to have some voice" in shaping Kennedy's views.

Both Jack and Jackie depended on the people close to them—for ideas, for approval, for help, for inspiration. Whether in dealing with the Soviet Union or choosing a fabric for the walls of the Blue Room, the President and First Lady constantly drew on the knowledge of trusted friends and associates, though far less so when it came to emotional matters. Their true intimates were family members, but even in a tightly bound clan, some were more inside than others. Most of their friendships were defined by strong bonds at crucial formative moments—for JFK in school, the navy, and political life, and for the much-younger Jackie in her childhood and school years. But there were newer connections as well, reflecting more recent social, intellectual, temperamental, and political needs.

Jack Kennedy subscribed to the "great man" theory of history, and the White House that he and Jackie presided over was a microcosm of that concept, filled with lively, smart, strikingly young, and strong-willed individuals who pushed ideas and policies, rather than being swept along by them. The Kennedys and their circle set out ambitiously, almost grandiosely, to create an America in their own image and according to their own tastes. To a remarkable degree they succeeded, leaving behind a more assertive nation, infused with a vision and an aesthetic that found its inspiration in Jeffersonian ideals. In the process, they cast aside the bland exertions of the 1950s, and set America on a higher path that combined the sophistication of the Old World and the vitality and power of the New. They were special people who intersected at a special time, a time when nothing seemed impossible.

GRACE AND POWER

ONE

"Where's Jackie?" asked Jack Kennedy, looking around his Hyannis Port home the day after his election as President of the United States. A dozen family members were organizing themselves for the formal victory photograph, but his wife had disappeared. Wearing low-heeled shoes and a raincoat with a green knitted cowl collar to ward off the early November chill, Jackie had gone for a solitary walk on the beach. Kennedy headed out across the grassy dunes to retrieve her. When the couple finally arrived in his parents' living room, the family hailed them with a round of applause.

It was a moment that captured the contrasting personalities of the forty-three-year-old President-elect and his thirty-one-year-old wife. On election day, the Kennedy clan had gathered at the compound on the shore of Nantucket Sound, the family's nerve center for thirty-five years. Throughout the day and into the night, as the returns fluctuated between hopeful and nail-biting, Jackie had stayed away from the commotion, keeping track of the results from her cheery white and yellow living room, with its chintz sofas, hooked rugs, Staffordshire lamps, heaps of patterned pillows, and what Lady Bird Johnson called Jackie's "pixie things"—droll watercolors and sketches of family and friends in the style of her artistic mentor Ludwig Bemelmans. (Norman Mailer once patronizingly observed that a "fairly important young executive" in Cleveland might be expected to own such a room.)

Jack, however, had restlessly shuttled among the three Kennedy homes: the cozy three-bedroom cottage he shared with Jackie; the home of campaign manager Bobby across the lawn that was a communications hub of news tickers and banks of telephones; and his father's seventeen-room white clapboard house with its wide veranda and commanding ocean views.

Besides his immediate family, Kennedy had sought information, reassurance, and amusement from the close aides and friends stationed in various places. The "Irish mafia"—Kenny O'Donnell, Larry O'Brien, and Dave Powers—along with Ted Sorensen, Kennedy's shadow for nearly four years of campaigning, shared the candidate's anxiety as he paced about, his ever-fidgety right hand tapping his teeth, or drumming tabletops. His childhood friend Lem Billings, a guest of Joe and Rose Kennedy, knew how to break the tension. Lem's mock weeping drew a wisecrack from JFK: "He's lost another state. His record is still minus one hundred percent. He's lost every county and every state of which he was supposed to be in charge."

The Washington artist Bill Walton had stayed over at JFK's house to keep Jackie company after a quiet dinner in their red-carpeted dining room. The closest to Jackie among JFK's intimates, Walton diverted her by talking about painting. When the returns looked promising at 10:30 p.m., Jackie turned to her husband, using her pet name for him, "Oh, Bunny, you're President now." "No," he replied. "It's too early yet."

Jackie went to bed before midnight; she was nearly eight months pregnant and dared not risk harming the baby by overextending herself. She had already lost two babies, one in 1954 after their first year of marriage. A daughter arrived stillborn in 1956, the result, Jackie's doctors said, of "the heat and crowds" at the Democratic convention in Chicago. She had borne another daughter, Caroline, in November 1957 after months of self-imposed rest and relaxation. Once again, she was taking no chances.

She had awakened when Jack turned in at 4 a.m., and he told her the outcome remained uncertain, but he was optimistic. As they both slept, Secret Service agents quietly infiltrated and secured the property. Seated on his bed in white pajamas at nine-thirty the next morning,

Kennedy learned from Sorensen that he had won. He emerged after breakfast to stroll along the beach, accompanied by a swarm of siblings and friends. An hour later, as family members tossed a football around on the front lawn, it was Jackie's turn to walk, and she typically slipped out of the house alone, unnoticed by her husband.

That afternoon they stood together on the platform at the Hyannis armory—as beautiful a couple as had ever entered the presidency. At six feet and 165 pounds, he looked bronzed and vibrant, with broad shoulders and a trim waist. Like a TV anchorman, he had a big head— his hat size was an "unusually large" 7⅝. His thick chestnut hair (a source of vanity, pampered by secretaries who routinely administered scalp massages) was carefully combed, his heavy-lidded gray eyes cool and impenetrable. Kennedy's warmth and magnetism came entirely from his gleaming, high-wattage smile.

Jackie, on the other hand, telegraphed every emotion through her extraordinary eyes—large hazel orbs fringed with black lashes—so melting that a Cape Cod reporter once wrote that "it would be unendurable—indeed actually impossible—to write anything uncomplimentary about anyone with such eyes." Her face was square and unusually photogenic, framed by dark brown hair teased high in a style that gave her "the look of a beautiful lion." Her eyes, she once wrote, were set "unfortunately far apart," and she had full dark brows, porcelain skin, a slightly pudgy nose, and a supple mouth above a strong chin. In deference to her pregnancy, she wore a "bouffant purple coat." Ordinarily, at five foot seven, she had the slender figure of a mannequin.

In different ways, Jack and Jackie had been preparing for this moment for years. They had taught each other a great deal, held the same ambitions, and looked forward to recasting their respective roles in the White House. They were both bright, inquisitive, and bookish, with enviably retentive memories. Each had a quick, ironic wit that sprang from high intelligence. Jack's humor was more deadpan. Asked to explain how he became a war hero, he responded, "It was involuntary. They sank my boat." Jackie usually wore a mischievous glint, like "a very naughty eight-year-old," observed Norman Mailer, and drew on a highly developed sense of the ridiculous. When a hard-boiled reporter once asked her to translate the French phrase spelled out in gold letters on her belt, "Honi soit qui mal y pense" (Evil to him who evil thinks), she said, "It means, 'Love me, love my dog.'"

The new first couple shared the Catholic faith, and came of age in a similarly wealthy and rarefied world—she in Manhattan, Paris, Easthampton, Newport, and Washington; he in Bronxville, London, Palm Beach, Hyannis, and the French Riviera. Jackie had the additional gloss of high WASP society through her mother's second marriage to Hugh D. Auchincloss II, a stockbroker from a venerable family. Jack and Jackie could each boast extensive travels as well. Jack had spent time in the Middle East and Asia, and had summered in Europe nearly every year since his adolescence. By her twenty-fourth birthday, Jackie had made five European trips. They had comparable academic bona fides as well: Choate and Harvard, Miss Porter's and Vassar. "The coat of arms for this Administration," quipped Jackie, "should be a daisy chain on a field of crimson."

She had broken an engagement to John Husted, a New York stockbroker with a proper social pedigree, after she began seeing Jack Kennedy. "All I ask is someone with a little imagination, but they are hard to find," she had told her sister, Lee, a year before her first evening with JFK. "It is having an open mind that counts." Their Newport wedding in September 1953 was a political and social extravaganza with 1,400 guests. But the marriage had nearly fractured in its first few years, as Jackie endured the political wife's persistent loneliness, aggravated by what Lem Billings described to Doris Kearns Goodwin, the authorized Kennedy family biographer, as the "humiliation she would suffer when she found herself stranded at parties while Jack would suddenly disappear with some pretty young girl."

When their relationship hit bottom in 1956, Jackie sat for a filmed interview in which she revealed her wounds. "You're pretty much in love with him, aren't you?" asked the interviewer in one of the outtakes. Jackie squinted, averted her eyes, laughed, and said, "Oh no." Returning her gaze to the interlocutor, she pondered and added, "I said, 'no,' didn't I?" In a retake she was asked the same question, only to reply, "I suppose so," adding, "I've ruined [the interview], haven't I?"

Jack was initially thrown by such moodiness, which "really drove him out of his mind," said Billings, and by Jackie's undisguised distaste for politics. Now, after seven years of marriage, they had come to understand each other's strengths and frailties with sophisticated objectivity. "She breathes all the political gases that flow around us, but she never seems to inhale them," JFK once said of Jackie. She kept that cheeky detachment, ultimately turning it to his advantage with her shrewd assessments and wry observations. She learned to devote herself to his interests but guarded her own strong character, refusing to be what she called "a vegetable wife . . . sort of humdrum [and] uninteresting."

Jack Kennedy responded to Jackie's cleverness, along with her passion for history, and her interests in what he called "things of the spirit—art, literature and the like." Comparing her to his sisters—"direct, energetic types"—he came to appreciate that Jackie was "more sensitive. You might even call her fey. She's a more indirect sort." Jackie adored his self-deprecation and his "curious inquiring mind that is always at work. If I were drawing him, I would draw a tiny body and an enormous head." She said she was "fascinated by the way he thinks. He summons every point to further his argument." In his political life, she admired his "imperturbable self-confidence and sureness of his powers."

Those who saw them privately sensed a deep connection when they "exchanged eyes," as Dave Powers described it. "Jackie was the only woman I saw him show affection to," said Vivian Crespi, a longtime friend of both. During the campaign a reporter from Louisiana named Iris Turner Kelso was "mesmerized" when she happened to witness Jack greeting Jackie with "a long kiss." "We loved them in every way that a woman loved a man," Jackie would write to Governor John Connally's wife, Nellie, after JFK was assassinated. "Our husbands loved us and were proud of us." Yet the intimate life of Jack and Jackie Kennedy puzzled even those closest to them. JFK's persistent womanizing was a mystifying trait, given the beauty, brains, and luminous style of his wife. It may have been that her capacity for love was greater than his, that "Jack's love had certain reservations but hers was total," in the view of Robin Chandler Duke, who knew him for nearly two decades.

Their manner together often seemed formal, mostly because each had been raised with the upper-class, boarding-school taboo against public displays of affection. "I would describe Jack as rather like me in that his life is an iceberg," Jackie would write to journalist Fletcher Knebel shortly after the election. "The public life is above water—& the private life—is submerged—I flatter myself that I have made his private life something he can love & find peace in—comfortable smoothly run houses—with all the things he loves in them—pictures, books, good food, friends—& his daughter & wife geared to adapt to his hours when he comes home." For Jackie in particular, life in the White House held the promise of a new togetherness, with the incessant years of campaigning behind them.

———

Looking pale, her chin raised slightly, Jackie watched her husband intently while he read his acceptance speech, holding sheaves of congratulatory telegrams with trembling hands. "My wife and I prepare for a new Administration and a new baby," he concluded, coaxing a slight smile from Jackie. "Hard-hearted Jack with tears in his eyes and his voice," journalist Mary McGrory reported to Teddy White, "the very first time I have seen the slightest display of emotion in the candidate and his team."

Flanking Jack and Jackie on the crowded platform were his parents, two brothers, and three sisters—"all made out of the same clay," the British aristocrat Diana Cooper once observed, "hair and teeth and tongues from the same reserves"—along with their handsome spouses. The eldest brother, Joe Jr., and a sister, Kathleen, both long dead, were ghosts of youthful promise in the family tableau. Absent, as always, was JFK's forty-two-year-old mentally retarded sister, Rosemary, who had been cared for by nuns since a failed lobotomy arranged nearly two decades earlier by her father. Joe Kennedy had intended to curb her aggressive behavior, but instead she was reduced to infantile incoherence. Rosemary's fate was known only within the family; for public consumption, she was a "childhood victim of spinal meningitis," an affliction, Joe Kennedy baldly asserted to *Time* magazine, that was "best to bring . . . out in the open."

Joseph Patrick Kennedy, the seventy-two-year-old family patriarch known by all as "the Ambassador," had himself come out in the open at the Armory. Almost twenty years earlier to the day, in November 1940, Joe had fled public life in disgrace after Franklin D. Roosevelt forced him out as the American envoy to Britain for advocating conciliation with the Nazis. As the mastermind of his son's political career—three terms in Congress, twice elected to the Senate—Joe had stayed behind the scenes, declining even to appear when Jack won the Democratic nomination the previous July. But this time Jack Kennedy overruled his domineering father, delaying the family's public appearance until the Ambassador joined them. On the platform, Joe Kennedy looked "grim and pale," and he balked when JFK tried to nudge him into TV camera range, an "awkward moment," observed Teddy White. The hesitancy belied Joe Kennedy's elation over his son's election. It had taken many years of hard work and iron determination, along with substantial infusions of money, to make Jack the first Irish Catholic president. His election was not only a triumph for the son, but also a personal vindication for the father.

TWO

At dinner the night after his election, Jack Kennedy was in an expansive mood. Once again Bill Walton dined with Jack and Jackie, this time joined by Ben Bradlee of *Newsweek* magazine and his wife, Tony, a fetching blonde. Excluded from their group was Lem Billings, who remained at Joe Kennedy's house. Billings's absence signaled not only his special status in the Kennedy clan, but also Jack Kennedy's compartmentalized approach to his friendships. Kennedy knew, as Bradlee put it, "Lem couldn't stand me, and I couldn't stand him." Walton regarded Billings simply as "a dud."

Catching sight of Jackie and Tony, both heavily pregnant, JFK cracked, "Okay, girls, you can take out the pillows now. We won." Although everyone laughed, the joke had originated with Jackie in an edgier form. Earlier in the year rumors had surfaced in Dorothy Kilgallen's gossip column that Jackie's newly announced pregnancy was a ploy by campaign handlers who feared voters would be turned off by the appearance of such a soigné creature on the hustings. "Do you think I should stuff a pillow under my dress to convince her?" Jackie had asked.

The President-elect rapidly moved beyond his quip, as he typically did, always impatient for the next topic. In a jovial tone he asked each of his guests to suggest an administration appointment. Bradlee said Kennedy should replace Allen Dulles, the director of the CIA for nearly a decade, and Walton made a comparable suggestion for FBI director J. Edgar Hoover, who had been in power for thirty-six years. Kennedy seemed to agree, and when the newspapers announced the following day the reappointment of both men, Walton and Bradlee were taken aback.

In the case of Hoover, Kennedy had little choice; the FBI director enjoyed extraordinary leverage over him that was tantamount to blackmail. For more than a year in the early 1940s, the agency had conducted surveillance of a lover of JFK's named Inga Arvad, who was a suspected Nazi spy. The statuesque Danish divorcée had kept company with Hitler and some of his deputies, writing afterwards that the Führer was "not evil as he is depicted by the enemies of Germany" and was "without doubt an idealist." Even after JFK had been alerted to the FBI bugs and wiretaps, he had continued his assignations. JFK's defiance was a measure of his penchant for personal risk, and the degree to which he was besotted by the sexiness of a woman four years his senior who once boasted, "He's got a lot to learn, and I'll be happy to teach him."

Kennedy knew that Hoover held the FBI dossier containing vivid accounts of his trysts with "Inga Binga." But JFK was unaware that the FBI had also been tracking his sexual adventures during the presidential campaign. Among his paramours was Judith Campbell (later Judith Exner), a former girlfriend of Frank Sinatra and now occasional mistress of the mobster Sam Giancana. Sinatra had introduced them in February 1960, during a campaign stop in Las Vegas, because he thought her resemblance to Elizabeth Taylor would appeal to JFK. By the fall of 1960, the FBI had not yet identified Campbell; informants had indicated only that he might have been "compromised" by a woman in Las Vegas.

Neither Walton nor Bradlee had a clue about any of this. Their audacious proposal to dismiss two icons of national security could only have been made by men confident of their closeness to Kennedy. Walton was nearly a decade older than Kennedy, and they had been friends since JFK first served in Congress in 1947. The son of an Illinois newspaper publisher, Walton had parachuted into Normandy on D-Day as a war correspondent. But he had quit journalism at age forty to become a painter. He was witty, cultivated, and a friend of Ernest Hemingway.

With his "gloriously florid" jug ears, his crooked grin, and a pock-marked face, Walton looked "rather like a clever and funny Hallowe'en pumpkin," wrote Hemingway's former wife Martha Gellhorn. Walton spoke in a languid baritone punctuated by warm conspiratorial chuckles. Kennedy loved gossip, and Walton always managed to have the most up-to-date intelligence. Walton was forthright and occasionally gruff, with a detached air—a sort of "been-there, done-that" manner. His wit was "glorious fun," wrote Gellhorn. "He hasn't a pompous bone in his body."

Bradlee had entered Kennedy's orbit early in 1959 during a Sunday afternoon walk in their Georgetown neighborhood. Bradlee had recently returned from a reporting stint in Paris and had been married for three years to Tony, his second wife. She was from the prominent Pinchot family and had left her husband for Ben after a love affair that began in a nineteenth-century chateau. Four years younger than JFK, Bradlee was a natural friend for an ambitious young politician. Bradlee's family mingled three centuries of Boston Brahmins and New York sophisticates (his mother's family included Frank Crowninshield, the founder of *Vanity Fair*). Like Kennedy, he was a boarding-school boy (St. Mark's) and Harvard graduate as well as a World War II navy veteran.

Their conversation invariably focused on "the private lives and public postures of politicians, reporters, and friends"—what Sorensen described as "nineteenth-century court gossip." Bradlee had a deliberately salty manner and an agile mind; he seemed to pluck his thoughts from the air without a trace of deliberation or predictability. He was unconventional enough to have a couple of tattoos: a snake entwined in his initials on his right buttock, and a rooster below his left shoulder. Bradlee exuded virility and prep-school cool, with his dark hair slicked back and parted with knife-edge precision. He embodied nearly all the traits Kennedy prized: high style, good looks, cheeky humor, worldliness, and self-assurance. As Bradlee recognized, "You had to have a light touch to get to Jack, to get through his defenses."

———

"I married a whirlwind," Jackie Kennedy once said. "People who try to keep up with [Jack] drop like flies, including me." In the ten weeks between the election and the inaugural, the Kennedy presidency took shape, as both Jack and Jackie laid the groundwork for the next four years by selecting key people and establishing themes and priorities. Instead of operating out of one command post, Jack Kennedy couldn't quite kick the campaign habit during the transition. He logged thousands of miles on the *Caroline,* the Kennedy family's private airplane, rarely staying in one place for more than a few days at a time: Florida, Washington, Texas, Massachusetts, and New York. He quizzed job candidates, met with dignitaries, tapped friends and "wise men" for advice, read one novel (Anthony Trollope's *The Warden*), gave interviews to reporters and columnists, swam in rough Florida surf, played touch football, cast for bluefish, digested memos and reports, spent hours on the phone checking references, sat through marathon meetings, played golf and tennis, held nineteen press conferences, saw a play (Gore Vidal's *The Best Man*), and gave a memorable speech to the Massachusetts legislature extolling government as "a city upon a hill" with "the eyes of all people . . . upon us."

His most awkward mission came in response to an invitation from the Vice President–elect, Lyndon Johnson, to visit his ranch in Texas. "We'll kill a deer," Johnson's wife, Lady Bird, said with a smile. Kennedy had indulged in grouse shooting in Britain as a young man, and more recently had shot quail, but he was a reluctant participant in blood sports. Johnson pressed him nevertheless as they waited in a carpeted blind for the deer to be driven toward them. When Kennedy brought down two bucks with three rounds, Johnson gushed that Kennedy was a "terrific shot." The President-elect couldn't help retorting, "Lyndon, I thank you for that, but I took a close look. That deer had rope burns on his legs."

———

The clashing sensibilities—a profound difference in tone and style— of Kennedy and Johnson would mark their relationship from beginning to end. They had been cordial but wary colleagues in the Senate, where Johnson had reigned as majority leader for five years, widely regarded as the second most powerful man in Washington after President Eisenhower. In Johnson's own vernacular, he was a "whale" and the junior senator from Massachusetts a mere "minnow." "To Johnson . . . [JFK] was the enviably attractive nephew who sings an Irish ballad for the company, and then winsomely disappears before the table clearing and dishwashing begin," wrote Harry McPherson, Johnson's longtime aide.

Kennedy and Johnson were by nearly every measure opposites. In his appearance, Johnson surpassed Kennedy only with his sheer size; four inches taller, he could stretch himself to a seemingly even greater height. His arms were disproportionately long, his hands like baseball mitts. Compared to the handsome President-elect, LBJ's face was powerful but irregular, with droopy dark eyes, a large nose, prominent ears, and a strong cleft chin.

Johnson had been born dirt poor nine years before Jack Kennedy; as a young man LBJ had picked cotton and worked in harness with mules on a road gang. While the serenely cerebral Kennedy was graceful and discerning, Johnson was moody, lumbering, and coarse. "Lyndon was a powerhouse who filled a room," said Ben Bradlee. "Jack was more demure." Johnson was overwhelmingly physical in his behavior: poking chests, grasping shoulders, leaning close. "He'd suck your guts out," said Orville Freeman, the governor of Minnesota who became Kennedy's secretary of agriculture. "He gave you the feeling that he was putting his tentacles around you."

Kennedy and Johnson were as different in speech as they were in manner. Kennedy was casually terse, sometimes stopping short of a finished sentence when he had made his point; Johnson was legendarily loquacious, repeating something a dozen different ways to make sure he was understood. It was, in a sense, a generational difference between speaking for television and addressing the crowds in a dusty Texas courthouse square. Johnson was a gifted storyteller who rarely read a book and tended to get his information from men he trusted. While many of Kennedy's acolytes underestimated LBJ's intelligence, JFK recognized the mental agility behind LBJ's simple words and colorful locutions. Like Kennedy, Johnson had an impressive memory—for facts, names, and situations.

Kennedy cringed at Johnson's public vulgarity—urinating in a sink in his office, scratching his crotch, picking his nose—and dismissed LBJ as "uncouth and somewhat of an oaf." Yet he admired Johnson's drive, cunning, and dedication, viewing him as a talented workhorse deeply knowledgeable about the intricacies of legislative politics. Since his election to Congress in 1936 at age twenty-eight as an ardent New

Dealer, Johnson had been building his base, cultivating allies, accumulating IOUs, flattering, and trading favors—in short, using every trick in the political playbook.

Kennedy's selection of Johnson as vice president had been crucial to the Democratic victory. While LBJ did not actively oppose Kennedy for the presidency in 1960, he maneuvered behind the scenes to gather delegates and strike alliances to deny Kennedy a first-ballot victory and emerge as a compromise candidate at the convention. The strategy failed, but Johnson still logged the second highest tally of votes by a significant margin. As liberals screeched that an old-fashioned conservative southerner besmirched Kennedy's message of youth and vigor, Kennedy told his aides that Johnson could deliver the South and take "the Catholic flavor off me." Joe Kennedy, the ultimate pragmatist, endorsed the choice as "the smartest thing" JFK ever did.

Kennedy also preferred to have Johnson as a "collaborator . . . than . . . competitor" on Capitol Hill. "I'm forty-three years old," Kennedy told his aide Kenny O'Donnell. "I'm not going to die in office. So the vice-presidency doesn't mean anything." To make the job appear important to Johnson, Kennedy assured him he would give him "significant assignments . . . especially in foreign affairs." For his part, Johnson figured that being majority leader under an activist president like Kennedy would be less palatable than under the more passive Eisenhower, because Kennedy would take credit for legislative success, and would blame Johnson for any failure. Somewhat chillingly, Johnson confided his rationale to journalist Clare Boothe Luce: "I looked it up," he said. "One out of every four presidents has died in office. I'm a gamblin' man, darlin', and this is the only chance I got."

———

While JFK traveled the country, Jackie stayed at home in Washington, but she kept herself busy. Her instinct was to surround herself with familiar and trusted staff, starting with her secretary Mary Gallagher, formerly employed by Jackie's mother as well as JFK at his Senate office. (That particular trust would prove to be misplaced, as years later Gallagher would write a spiteful memoir.) For her social secretary, Jackie selected Tish Baldrige, who not only had been three years ahead of her at Miss Porter's (often called Farmington, for the Connecticut town where the school is located) and Vassar but also was a friend of Jackie's family.

Baldrige had acquired discipline in grade school at a convent of the Sacred Heart—lifelong habits of diligence and organization that served her well when she worked as social secretary in the American embassies in Paris and Rome for two demanding women, Clare Boothe Luce and Evangeline Bruce. Having grown to six foot one at age thirteen, Baldrige developed a redoubtable but hearty personality; when a Greek newspaper described her as a "commando from the White House," she laughed and refused to take offense.

Baldrige's father had been a Republican congressman from Omaha, Nebraska, so her rightward political leanings were even stronger than Jackie's. Baldrige had initially opposed JFK for president, calling him "that floorflusher Kennedy" (she doubtless meant "four-flusher") and wearing a large "Vixen for Nixon" campaign button. But after Jackie offered the White House job following the Democratic convention, Baldrige was an instant convert. "Jack Kennedy has shown spunk and agility," she wrote to Clare Luce. "He deserves to win in November."

In the weeks following the election, Baldrige fielded a blizzard of handwritten memos (many illustrated with fanciful drawings) and a barrage of phone calls from Jackie, who was immersed in the intricacies of moving, selecting her wardrobe, planning White House cultural events, and mapping out what Baldrige called "a complete makeover of a tired, undistinguished, frumpy White House." (Jackie would call it a "restoration" based on scholarship because, she said, "redecorate" was "a word I hate.") "Jackie was suddenly on fire with plans for making her mark as an exceptional first lady," said Baldrige. "No detail . . . escaped her notice . . . down to the design of her official stationery."

As Jackie's de facto chief of staff, Baldrige embraced her boss's thinking with characteristic enthusiasm. At a press conference in late November, Baldrige told a gathering of "newshens," women from the society pages assigned to cover the First Lady, about Jackie's sweeping ideas for the White House: to highlight American performing artists and create "a showcase for great American art . . . even if it means hanging paintings in front of other paintings." Baldrige's remarks provoked a furor in the press, and anger from Jack and Jackie. They forgave her misstep but let her know that press relations were no longer her bailiwick. "I've learned lesson number one," Baldrige confided to Clare

Luce. "Keep the mouth SHUT at all times, *never* be myself, never relax, never *joke* with anyone about anything concerning the Casa Bianca."

The next day, JFK's press secretary, Pierre Salinger, introduced Baldrige to "a very inexperienced, beautiful young woman named Pamela Turnure." To Baldrige's amazement, this petite twenty-three-year-old had been designated as Jackie's press secretary, an innovation for a first lady. As a receptionist in JFK's Senate office, Turnure had applied for the White House job, telling Jackie she could "learn the duties gradually." Jackie had selected her instead of a "notably aggressive feminine reporter" recommended by Salinger.

The choice mystified both campaign aides and reporters, and not only because Pamela Turnure came from outside Jackie's tight circle. Turnure's landlady, Florence Kater, had tracked Jack Kennedy's comings and goings from her Georgetown house when Turnure was working for him. Kater documented his visits with a letter and photograph that she sent to news organizations. She even showed up at a campaign rally carrying a placard bearing the photograph, allegedly of Kennedy leaving Turnure's house after midnight.

But reporters at the time usually steered clear of the private lives of public officials, and they were especially protective of the popular Kennedy. "This lady claimed he was having a love affair and it was an immoral thing," said *Look* magazine's Fletcher Knebel. "I never paid any attention to it. I didn't care if he was screwing her or not. I just assumed he did his share of it."

Inside the Kennedy organization the attitude was less blasé. "The rumors were rampant," said Barbara Gamarekian, an aide to Pierre Salinger. "There was a debate among the Hill staff whether to take her to the convention because of the rumors. The former landlady was trying to get her story out, and we were aware of that." According to Chuck Spalding's wife, Betty, Jackie "asked me if I knew [Jack] was having an affair with Pamela Turnure. I said I didn't know, and even if I did, I wouldn't tell her." Whatever Jackie knew, her manner toward Turnure was invariably affectionate, akin perhaps to the eighteenth-century attitudes she so admired; after all, one of her "heroines," according to Lee Radziwill, was Louise de la Vallière, a mistress of Louis XIV.

Jackie evidently saw that Turnure could be useful to her. In an authorized biography of Jackie's White House years published in 1967, Mary Van Rensselaer Thayer described the cool and laconic Turnure as a "small, fine-boned brunette with the palest complexion and blue-green eyes which gazed unswervingly when she spoke" and who "seemed to understate her prettiness deliberately. Her poise was remarkable: She never raised her voice and remained unruffled under the most exasperating circumstances." Friends and associates couldn't help noticing a physical resemblance to Jackie; Mary Gallagher said Turnure "could almost be taken for Jackie's double."

She was also nearly as well bred: she was the daughter of the publisher of *Harper's Bazaar,* and a graduate of the Bolton School in Westport, Connecticut, and Mount Vernon Junior College in Washington. She was only nineteen, working as a receptionist at the Belgian Embassy, when she met JFK at the wedding of Jackie's stepsister Nina Auchincloss. In her job in JFK's office, Turnure "proved efficient as well as tactful," wrote Thayer. Equally important, according to Turnure's mother, Louise Drake, "Pam was always very quiet. It was hard to get much out of her."

Jack and Jackie spent Thanksgiving with Bill Walton in Washington. In the morning they went for a walk near Middleburg, Virginia, where Walton was completing negotiations on an estate for the First Couple to rent as a weekend escape. That afternoon the threesome had dinner that included caviar and champagne. Jackie's due date was still three weeks away, and JFK felt comfortable going to Palm Beach that night. While he was airborne, Jackie began to hemorrhage "because of all the excitement," she said later. The ambulance driver found her lying in bed, wearing thick white wool socks, a pink nightgown, and overcoat. "She was smiling and looked like a baby doll," he said. But her anxiety showed when she asked the doctor if she would lose her child.

The scenario was alarmingly similar to her circumstance four years earlier when she suffered internal bleeding and delivered a stillborn baby one month premature. Then, as now, she was alone for the ordeal. In 1956 she had returned exhausted to Newport from the Democratic convention, and Jack had gone on a Mediterranean cruise with his brother Teddy and some friends, including several women.

This time Walton managed to contact Kennedy by calling the airport in West Palm Beach, and JFK immediately flew back to Washington. After midnight on November 25, John F. Kennedy Jr. was born by cesarean section—an occasion marred only by an Associated Press photographer who snapped three flash pictures as Jackie left the recovery room. "Oh no, not that!" Jackie exclaimed. Secret Service agents seized the film and destroyed it.

The arrival of their second child gave Jack Kennedy a son and namesake, and put Jackie's role as a mother in the forefront. The presence of an infant and a precocious three-year-old daughter would add a lively dimension to White House life not seen since the presidency of Teddy Roosevelt, who had six children ranging from Alice the debutante to Quentin the toddler. But the Kennedy offspring would pose new challenges for parents seeking to balance a "normal" childhood with the growing demands of the press and public for information about their favorite new celebrities. Shortly before the election, in a TV interview with Sander Vanocur of NBC, Jackie had talked of her need to be with her children in the White House. "If you bungle raising your children," she said, "I don't think whatever else you do matters very much."

THREE

*D*uring her extended recuperation from childbirth, Jackie Kennedy methodically prepared herself for life in the White House. For two weeks she worked first from her bed at Georgetown University Hospital, and then from her bedroom at Joe and Rose's home in Palm Beach, where she stayed until two days before the inauguration. While Baldrige and other staff members dealt with logistics, Jackie steeped herself in the history of the White House and its interiors.

At 55,000 square feet, the President's House, as Jackie liked to call it, is imposing but not palatial. (By comparison, the Seattle home built by multibillionaire Bill Gates in the 1990s measures 65,000 square feet.) Completed in 1802 during the presidency of Thomas Jefferson, the White House had been burned by the British army during the War of 1812 and rebuilt by President James Monroe in 1817. It was Monroe who set the decorative standard for the modern White House by purchasing fine French Empire furniture.

Jackie consulted forty books from the Library of Congress along with assorted periodicals—including the January 1946 issue of *Gazette des Beaux Arts,* which described the pieces Monroe had ordered from Paris. After examining fabric swatches, blueprints, and photographs of White House rooms, she scribbled memos and letters on yellow legal pads to her interior designer, Mrs. Henry Parish II, known to all as "Sister." Jackie's collaborator on the Kennedy homes in Georgetown and Hyannis Port, Parish would be responsible for the first stage of work, a quick refurbishment of the private apartments on the second floor, using $50,000 designated by Congress. Parish was "a woman of quality and taste," said Tish Baldrige, "from the same social group," with "a tremendous sense of what was proper and refined."

The day she came home from the hospital, Jackie took a tour of the White House that showed how badly the place needed a major restoration. Room after room was filled with second-rate reproductions; curtains were "seasick green"; the ambiance was as cold as a hotel. Jackie was struck, she later said, that the Executive Mansion looked "so sad." She phoned Sister Parish immediately with her report. "Jackie did not have two big eyes," recalled Parish. "She had a dozen. Every room was observed, down to the last detail."

Although the White House lacked an overall decorative vision, a number of twentieth-century presidents and first ladies had made important improvements: Teddy Roosevelt added the West Wing and redesigned the ground floor; Calvin Coolidge's wife, Grace, created the "period room" concept with Federal-style furniture in the Green Room; Herbert Hoover's wife, Lou, added more original pieces; and the Trumans gutted the building in order to shore up its deteriorating structure.

But following that extensive refurbishment, Congress had refused to provide funds for antique furnishings, and neither Bess Truman nor Mamie Eisenhower showed much interest in sophisticated decor. Only a generous gift in 1960 from a group of interior designers—a collection of museum-caliber Federal-period furniture for the Diplomatic Reception Room—offered a hopeful precedent for Jackie's plan to enhance the historic integrity of the White House.

Jackie had grown up in an atmosphere of understated elegance in her family homes, Merrywood in suburban McLean, Virginia, and Hammersmith Farm in Newport. Gore Vidal, Jackie's relative by marriage, once described Merrywood as "a bit Henry Jamesian . . . deliberate quietude removed from 20th Century tensions." Jackie, he said, "tried to recreate Merrywood's heavenly ambiance." Good taste was in Jackie's bloodstream, along with a basic knowledge of historic periods in the decorative arts.

"Our background was influential in terms of knowing how things should be done," said Lee. Janet Auchincloss presided over her households with a disciplined formality. She was strict, proper, and old fashioned. "Every library . . . had chintz," Lee recalled, "very nice, but bland." Jackie incorporated her mother's sense of the appropriate with a more expansive imagination and a more relaxed style. Jackie was determined to bring history to life in the White House, but she also resolved to inject liveliness and informality. "I felt like a moth banging on the windowpane," Jackie said. "The windows . . . hadn't been opened for years." It was this balance of the casual and the grand that would redefine the look and feel of her new home.

Jackie was equally preoccupied with her personal image. After studying sketches and pages ripped from fashion magazines, she corresponded with fashion designer Oleg Cassini. Only days after her son's birth, Cassini met with her for nearly four hours in her hospital room. During the campaign, Jackie had been sharply criticized for her fondness for extravagant French clothes. *Women's Wear Daily,* which made a fetish of following her fashions, declared the Kennedys were running "on the Paris Couture fashion ticket." Jackie responded by showing reporters her maternity wardrobe from "a Fifth Avenue store" and issuing a stinging rebuttal: "A newspaper reported . . . that I spend $30,000 a year [the equivalent of $182,000 today] buying Paris clothes and that women hate me for it. I couldn't spend that much unless I wore sable underwear." Afterwards, she painted a watercolor of protesters marching with signs: "Put Jackie and Joan back in American clothes." But she understood that the way she dressed had political ramifications: The ladies' garment workers union was a key Democratic supporter that lobbied JFK for her to wear American-made clothing.

To head off further speculation by the fashion press that Jackie said had "gotten so vulgarly out of hand," she designated forty-seven-year-old Cassini as the designer of her official wardrobe. He would not be her exclusive supplier, although that was left unstated. In the authorized biography of her White House years, Jackie explained that she had wanted "a single person, an American and a man whom she had known for some years" so that "all information about her costumes could be controlled by a single source." Not only could she converse with

Cassini in French, his first language, he was steeped in the history, literature, and art of eighteenth- and nineteenth-century Europe. When she asked for a dress in "Veronese green" or "Nattier blue," he would instantly understand.

With his pencil mustache, pomade-glazed hair, deep tan, and courtly manner, Cassini was perfect for his role as official couturier—a first in White House history. He was the scion of a noble Russian family; when he was born in Paris, the doctor arrived in a top hat, white tie and tails, white gloves, and spats. Cassini's grandfather had served as Russian ambassador to the United States during Teddy Roosevelt's presidency, and Cassini's parents traveled in aristocratic European circles.

Cassini got his start in fashion through his mother, who built a successful dress-designing business that foundered during the Depression, prompting the family to emigrate to the United States. He became an American citizen and renounced his title of "Count Cassini." (He had taken the more illustrious family name of his mother; his father was Count Loiewski.) Cassini's career as a fashion designer took off in Hollywood when he began creating costumes for film stars such as Gene Tierney, whom he married, and Grace Kelly, to whom he was fleetingly engaged.

The *Washington Post* called Cassini a "wise-cracking ladies' man" when his new position was announced. During World War II his cavalry unit (which included multimillionaires Jock Whitney and Paul Mellon as well as Hollywood producer Darryl Zanuck) had what he called a "fantasy life" at officer candidate school in Fort Riley, Kansas, playing polo, foxhunting, and drinking cocktails with Gloria Vanderbilt and Claudette Colbert. In Palm Beach and Manhattan, Cassini became friendly with Joe Kennedy, whose table at La Caravelle Cassini would obligingly fill with models and society girls. The Ambassador not only blessed his friend's appointment by Jackie; he told Cassini, "Don't bother them at all about the money, just send me an accounting at the end of the year. I'll take care of it."

Jackie had strong views about fashion that complemented Cassini's approach, which was marked, she later noted, by "sophisticated simplicity" and the restrained use of "unusual materials." Since he was a family friend, Jackie could count on him to accept and incorporate her ideas. He in turn could feel comfortable applying his Hollywood approach, creating "fashion scripts" to evoke "a dramatic version of a look" so Jackie "would always be the same and there would be a discipline to the look."

Jackie had been intrigued by fashion since her adolescence, when she sketched ideas for dresses on the back of her exam papers. For nearly a decade she had been collaborating with her mother's dressmaker, Mini Rhea, to create her own clothing designs. During her senior year in college she had won the prestigious Prix de Paris at *Vogue* magazine on the strength of sophisticated essays that extolled the virtues of "excellent cut and unobtrusive color" in a suit, and the appeal of an orange skirt for evening that would "look delicious in front of the fire."

At a time when women wore big skirts, pinched waists, and puffy sleeves, Jackie favored the clean lines and slender silhouette of Givenchy and his mentor, Balenciaga. "Just remember I like terribly simple, covered up clothes," she wrote to Diana Vreeland, the legendary fashion editor of *Harper's Bazaar,* after the Democratic convention. Jackie's understated style was typical of upper-class fashion avatars such as socialite Babe Paley.

Yet Jackie brought her own youthful dash. The *New York Times* called Jackie "a pace setter who has worn sausage skin pants, streaked hair, chemise dresses and sleeveless tunics long before these became popular currency." Like Vreeland, Jackie embraced a sense of whimsy. In one of her *Vogue* essays she had described "a great dip brimmed black hat that makes you look like the femme fatale one takes to hear tangos at teatime," and she had imagined how even a humble turtleneck sweater could be enlivened by "gauntlet gloves and a beret and a walk with a swagger like D'Artagnan's."

During their hospital room conference Jackie and Cassini discussed for the first time using her official wardrobe to create the image of "an American Versailles" in the White House that would emphasize youth and elegance. But Jackie also intended, she told Cassini, to "continue to dress the way I like." In a letter to the designer summarizing her goals, she asked for designs "that I would wear if Jack were President of France—très Princesse de Rethy mais jeune"—a reference to the forty-three-year-old wife of King Leopold III of Belgium, who was admired for her refined style. Jackie wanted Cassini's assurance that her dresses would remain exclusive, so that she wouldn't see any "fat little women hopping around in the same dress." Above all, she asked that he keep the lid on publicity. "I refuse to have Jack's administration plagued by fashion stories of a sensational nature," she wrote, "& to be the Marie Antoinette or Josephine of the 1960s."

"Whenever I was upset by something in the papers," Jackie once recalled, "[Jack] always told me to be more tolerant, like a horse flicking away flies in the summer." But Jackie's dislike of the press would never subside; journalists covering her would always be adversaries who approached their work as a zero-sum game. "Mors tua vita mea est," she said to Cassini, explaining her view of their attitude: "Your death is my life." To some extent her animus was inbred. When the Kennedys invited journalists to Jack and Jackie's wedding in 1953, Jackie's mother, Janet Auchincloss, told Rose Kennedy that publicity would be "demeaning and vulgar."

Over the years Jackie had periodically spoken to reporters out of political necessity. Her remarks were by turns bland ("Women are very idealistic and they respond to an idealistic person like my husband"), artful ("I'd love to get to know exactly what to say in situations, like Noël Coward"), and irreverent. "I don't think Jack has changed much, I really don't," she said during the campaign. "He still thinks nothing of answering his door at home when he's wearing his shorts." During her campaign appearances she remained "skittish and edgy," observed *Look* magazine reporter Laura Bergquist, who once spotted her "curled up on the campaign plane, reading the Beatnik best-seller, Jack Kerouac's *Dharma Bums*." Before an appearance by JFK on *Face the Nation,* Jackie left notes on the reporters' desks saying, "Don't ask Jack mean questions." When Peter Lisagor of the *Chicago Daily News* did anyway, she sat in the studio "looking daggers" at him and afterwards said his questions were "absolutely horrible."

Those who had known Jackie a decade earlier might have been surprised by her hostility toward the press. After her graduation from college, she had worked for fifteen months as "The Inquiring Camera Girl" on the *Washington Times-Herald.* Armed with a bulky Graflex, she roamed the city, asking questions that were frequently droll, sometimes disconcerting, and invariably probing. "You could make the column about anything you wanted to," she said, "so I'd find a bunch of rough, salty characters and ask them about a prizefighter just so I could capture the way they talked."

She asked pretty young women if they would rather be "an old man's darling or a young man's slave," and at an elementary school in Virginia she inquired, "What makes little boys so bad?" She touched on issues of love and marriage: "Are wives a luxury or necessity?" "What didn't you give up after you got married?"

Since her girlhood, Jackie had loved writing; she had descriptive flair and a good ear for language. In her *Vogue* application she called Cecil Beaton's sets for the plays of Oscar Wilde "the candybox spillings of pinks and mauves." She told the *Vogue* judges that she had grown up with "vague little dreams of locking myself up somewhere and turning out children's books and *New Yorker* short stories."

Still, journalism was a raffish profession for a well-bred girl. Jackie found amusement in rewrite men and other newsroom characters, and savored that "there was no routine, no two days were ever the same." But Jackie didn't identify with the newspaper world, viewing herself more as a provocateur than a journalist. Mini Rhea said that Jackie regarded her job as a "field course in psychology," using her inquiries "to learn how people thought and reacted and what mistakes they had made in life and what they would do over."

As a reporter, Jackie had freely asked questions that she would never consent to answering herself. She used the excuse of her pregnancy to curtail much of her contact with journalists during the campaign. But she made an important foray into image-making that showed her skill as a "hidden hand." Within two days of Kennedy's election, Jackie began collaborating with Mary Van Rensselaer Thayer, a contributor to the *Washington Post* popularly known as Molly Thayer, on an authorized account of the new first lady's first thirty-one years. Molly Thayer was no ordinary journalist; she was a close friend of Janet Auchincloss and had known Jackie since her childhood in Long Island and Newport. "Molly was like her aunt," said Baldrige. "She adored Jackie. Molly was an obedient servant. She was poor and hungry and needed the money."

Jackie and Thayer agreed that Thayer would publish a three-part

series in *Ladies' Home Journal,* later to appear as a short book. Jackie gave
Thayer exclusive access to scrapbooks, photographs from her personal
collection, and family letters. "Jackie did a lot of the writing in bed, and
then Molly would take it over and rewrite it," said Mary Bass of *Ladies'
Home Journal.* Thayer sent the completed manuscript to Florida to be
edited by Jack as well as Jackie. The first installment arrived on the
newsstands on inauguration day, and the series was a "complete sellout." The biography, said Tish Baldrige, was "exactly how Jackie
wanted the world to see her."

It was an enviably rosy picture, complete with glowing tributes to
her mother and father, gently glossing over their bitter divorce when
Jackie was ten, after years of rancor over her father's womanizing,
drinking, and profligacy. Nor did Jackie mention the heartbreak of her
wedding day: after Janet excluded her former husband from the
rehearsal dinner, Jack Bouvier drank himself into a stupor and could
not escort his daughter down the aisle. A single sentence marked Bouvier's death at age sixty-seven, avoiding any mention of the cancer, alcoholism, reclusiveness, and financial reversals that darkened the end of
his life.

Jackie also paid homage to the Kennedy family. Bobby was "the best
legal mind" and "the one I would put my hand in the fire for," Eunice
"the most civic-minded," Pat "the smartest," Jean "the most domestic"
and the "closest" to Jackie, Teddy "the best natural politician," Rose
"the most devout," and Joe, the one Jackie said she adored.

The bumps in Jack and Jackie's marriage were invisible as well.
Jackie called her husband "a rock . . . I lean on him in everything. . . .
He's never irritable or sulky. He would do anything I wanted or give me
anything I wanted." Jack was said to be charmed by her "many-faceted
character" and to admire "her self-sufficiency in maintaining an inner
life of her own" that kept her "content, though not happy" when he was
away. Yet there was one crack in the facade, tucked into page 95 of the
book's 127 pages, that went unremarked on at the time.

It was an account of the evening in June 1951 when Jack and Jackie
were introduced at dinner by their mutual friends Charley and Martha
Bartlett. Jack Kennedy would take two years to propose after a sporadic
courtship. But that first night, as Jackie described it to Molly Thayer,
she "looked into Jack's laughingly aroused, intelligently inquisitive face

and knew instantly that he would have a profound, perhaps disturbing influence on her life." Jackie was "frightened" and "envisioned heartbreak, but just as swiftly determined such heartbreak would be worth the pain." Readers had no way of knowing that Jackie herself had written that touching and prophetic description as she was about to become the thirty-first first lady—words that illuminated the real nature of the Kennedy marriage.

FOUR

*J*ackie's arrival in Palm Beach on December 9 with baby John shifted the locus of activity away from Washington for more than a month. Jack still came and went, but he conducted many of his important deliberations in the fifteen-foot-square library of muted and perfectly proper chintz in Joe Kennedy's oceanside villa, La Guerida. The house, "long, white, vaguely Spanish and not unhandsome," as John Kenneth Galbraith described it, had been designed in 1923 by the resort's signature architect, Addison Mizner, in a style dismissed at the time as "Bastard-Spanish-Moorish-Romanesque-Renaissance-Bull Market-Damn-The-Expense." When Joe Kennedy bought it in 1933 at the bottom of the Depression, he added a wing created by the other premier designer, Maurice Fatio.

The property was hidden behind a high wall along North Ocean Boulevard. By Palm Beach standards, the house was not large, with only six bedrooms. It faced a wide lawn planted with palm trees down to the seawall. Off to the side were a swimming pool and tennis court, as well as Joe Kennedy's "bullpen," a wooden enclosure with benches where he sunbathed in the nude—slathered in cocoa butter, wearing a broad-brimmed hat—and conducted business on the phone, an instrument that he used "like a Stradivarius," said the singer Morton Downey.

Jack and Jackie's bedroom occupied a corner of the ground floor, with French doors opening onto a balcony overlooking the tennis court. After his election, JFK declined to move upstairs to a bedroom with an ocean view; he liked the room he had occupied since 1933 because he could get in and out quickly.

On the rear patio Lem Billings stretched his large frame in a chaise, sunbathing for hours each day and "relishing the mob scenes"—the constant parade of dignitaries, prospective appointees, staff, friends, and family. Billings's appearance was unobtrusive: square jawed and blue-eyed behind thick glasses in clear plastic frames (the same kind worn by McGeorge Bundy, Kennedy's new national security adviser, with whom he was frequently confused). But Billings had a loud raspy laugh—braying as he exhaled, honking as he inhaled—that was frequent, infectious, and so unusual that the TV talk show host Jack Paar claimed he could always hear his friend Lem "among hundreds of others in the studio audience." The Billings voice was similarly distinctive—deep, gravelly, and nasal.

Long before Zelig was invented by Woody Allen, Billings was ducking in and out of the picture, "a mystifying relic of JFK's youth," said Arthur Schlesinger. One moment he sat on an airplane with JFK sharing a sandwich and a bottle of milk en route to the Orange Bowl. Another time he might be spotted at mass on Sunday with the President-elect.

After the election, Fletcher Knebel was disconcerted to find Billings at the Kennedy home in Georgetown when he stopped by to retrieve Jackie's answers to a series of written questions about Jack for a profile in *Look*. With Jack in Florida, Billings was keeping Jackie company for several days. "I thought, 'Jesus, this is strange,'" Knebel recalled. "'This is not the middle-class way of living that I know. The guy goes off to Palm Beach with his cronies, leaving his pregnant wife at home with one of his good friends.'"

For nearly three decades, Billings had been an integral part of Jack Kennedy's life. He reminded Charley Bartlett of a "stable pony, relaxing, undemanding, peppy, and very vibrant." Jack and Lem met at Choate just after Billings's father, a physician, had died unexpectedly of a strep infection. Lem's mother was from a distinguished Pittsburgh family and had graduated from Farmington. The Billingses had lost most of their money in the Depression, forcing Lem onto the scholarship rolls. An Episcopalian descended from *Mayflower* Puritans and French aristocrats, Lem didn't switch from Republican to Democrat until Kennedy ran for president.

Lem and Jack had older brothers who were star athletes and students at Choate, creating an instant bond that fed their irreverence and incessant teasing. "Jack had the self-assurance of a sharp lyrical tongue," observed David Michaelis, who wrote about Billings and Kennedy in a book on famous friendships. "Lem had a Chaplinesque sense of situation." They had countless nicknames for each other, from "Leem" and "Moynie" to "Kenadosus" and "Rat-Face." Mostly the two were Billy and Johnny. Billings and Kennedy were also united in their dislike of Choate, which inspired them to form a subversive club called the "Muckers" that nearly got them both expelled. A poignant measure of Billings's adoration of JFK was his decision to repeat his senior year simply to be with his friend; Billings even pretended that he had been born the same year as JFK. Jack and Lem enrolled together at Princeton, although JFK had to withdraw because of illness and switched to Harvard the following fall.

After Billings's first visit to Palm Beach at Christmas in 1933 he became an honorary Kennedy brother. "Lem and his battered suitcase arrived that day and never really left," said Teddy Kennedy. Billings's full-time mission was to create laughter in his adopted family with amusing songs, wry observations, and tall tales filled with vivid details. "Lem had the ability to make you feel funny and clever," said Kennedy sister Eunice Shriver, who considered him her "best friend."

Joe Kennedy often subsidized Billings's expenses, including a European tour with Jack in 1937 when Lem was a walking Baedeker, tutoring JFK in the fine points of culture gleaned from studying art history at Princeton. After college Billings received an MBA from Harvard and pursued a fitful career in advertising, where his claim to fame was inventing "Fizzies," a carbonated beverage in tablet form that briefly became a national craze. Finally in 1960 he moved into the Kennedy office on Park Avenue and became an unofficial retainer, advising family members on real estate, art, and antiques. Whenever Jack called, Billings was at his doorstep with that battered bag, sometimes for weeks at a time. In the White House, Billings came and went as he pleased; he was so familiar to the Secret Service that he didn't even have an official pass.

Billings probably knew more about Jack Kennedy's relationship with Jackie than anyone else in the inner circle. Before Jack and Jackie were married, he cautioned her about her prospective husband's numerous romantic liaisons over the years, and how difficult it would be for him to settle down with one woman. Instead of being put off, she later told him, "I thought it was a challenge." After the wedding, "Lem was a bridge between them," said journalist Peter Kaplan, a younger friend of Billings. "She liked him but she didn't like him. He appreciated things. He had an aesthetic sense that she wanted Jack to have. But she got fed up with his ubiquitousness, and she made fun of him, although he did help her in various ways."

Because of Billings's giggling mannerisms and resolute bachelorhood, Jack's friends wondered about his sexual orientation. "I didn't see anything overtly gay about him; I think he was neutral," said Red Fay. Ben Bradlee regarded Billings as "idolatrous. The rest of Jack's friends felt great affection for Jack, but idolatry is not that male an attribute." The Kennedys tended to be homophobic, but in Billings's case, family members averted their eyes from any homoerotic hints in his personality.

Kennedy dutifully offered Billings three jobs in his administration: director of the Peace Corps, head of a proposed United States Travel Service, and ambassador to Denmark, all of which Billings turned down. "Can you imagine," Billings said, "my best friend becomes President of the United States and I spend his presidency *in Denmark*?" Instead, Billings preferred the singular role of "First Friend."

The Jack Kennedy who greeted visitors in Palm Beach was the picture of health, tanned and fit, an image crucial to his political success. During the transition, *Today's Health,* the magazine of the American Medical Association, issued an upbeat report on Kennedy's "superb physical condition" based on the opinion of his doctors, as related by Bobby Kennedy. The article acknowledged, almost in passing, the litany of health problems Kennedy had suffered since childhood, starting with the scarlet fever at age two-and-a-half that had separated him from his family for three months. In addition to standard ailments such as measles, mumps, and chicken pox, the magazine mentioned attacks of jaundice, malaria, and sciatica. According to the article, Kennedy had prevailed over these diseases with his "barb-wire toughness" and for more than a year he had been "singularly free of health problems."

The report was guilty of serious omissions, including his problems with colitis, cystitis, neuritis, gastroenteritis, hepatitis, and post-gonococcal and nonspecific urethritis, a venereal disease. Nor were there references to his periodic confinements at the Mayo and Lahey clinics for mysterious pains and fevers during his adolescence, or the nine times he was hospitalized—a total of more than six weeks—for a variety of gastrointestinal and urinary tract infections in his first term as a senator. Similarly ignored was the osteoporosis that severely weakened his lumbar spine—worsened by injuries on the Harvard football field and in the navy—and that led to three difficult operations. The second and third of these procedures, in 1954 and 1955, had kept Kennedy out of the Senate for nine months as he recuperated in Florida.

The most troubling evasion was Kennedy's affliction with Addison's disease, diagnosed when he collapsed during a trip to England in 1947. Addison's is a disorder in which the adrenal glands fail to produce two crucial hormones: cortisol, which regulates the immune system; and aldosterone, which maintains blood pressure. Many of Kennedy's symptoms over the years, including weight loss, fatigue, and a yellowing of the skin (which once moved columnist Joe Alsop to say JFK looked "rather like a bad portrait by Van Gogh"), were typical signs of a gradual adrenal gland degeneration. His critical illness in England—nausea, severe pain, weakness, fever, and vomiting—resembled a classic "Addisonian crisis."

Joe Kennedy had wept on hearing his son's diagnosis, because, as he told his friend Arthur Krock of the *New York Times,* he thought Jack was "doomed to die." Addison's meant Jack was highly vulnerable to infection as well as a potential breakdown of his circulatory system. But while Kennedy couldn't be cured, he could be treated with cortisone, which he took in varying forms—pellets inserted under his skin, injections, and pills—for the rest of his life. (Joe Kennedy even had supplies of the medicine placed in safe-deposit boxes around the world in case of emergency.) The medication eliminated the symptoms but had side effects including insomnia, restlessness, facial puffiness, and, depending on his hormone levels, heightened or diminished sexual desire. Equally dangerous was the fact that any severe stress, such as his back surgery, could trigger a potentially fatal Addisonian crisis. By the age of forty, Kennedy had been given last rites four times.

Today's Health dismissed accusations from Lyndon Johnson and his supporters before the Democratic convention that Kennedy had Addison's. (India Edwards, a former Democratic national committee-woman, had said Kennedy was so ill he "looked like a spavined hunch-back.") Instead, the doctors alluded only to a past "adrenal insufficiency" that required medicine "by mouth" to deal with "any possible after-math." Kennedy never admitted the truth about his disease, fearing it would harm his political prospects. (When Press Secretary Pierre Salinger asked about it, Kennedy said, "I don't have Addison's disease" and "I don't take cortisone.") But his personality and his relationships were affected by his poor health, brushes with death, and the throb of constant pain in his back as well as the "hard knot" in what Billings called JFK's "nervous stomach."

The only advantage to Kennedy's numerous confinements was that they fostered his interest in history and biography; family friend Kay Halle recalled seeing *The World Crisis* by Winston Churchill on JFK's hospital bed when he was fifteen years old. Otherwise, Kennedy's physical burdens tended to "set him somewhat apart from [his] ex-troverted and gregarious family," wrote Schlesinger, and invested him with a "peculiar intensity." He learned early to conceal his discomfort, rarely complaining, even to those closest to him. His friends and family saw what Bobby Kennedy described as "the face . . . a little whiter . . . lines . . . a little deeper . . . words a little sharper" as Jack had to reach for crutches or a cane. But in public, the President-elect managed to appear robust.

JFK's resilience took on almost mythic qualities that affected the way his intimates viewed him and the way he behaved. "I've always said he's a child of fate," Joe Kennedy wrote to Jackie. "If he fell in a puddle of mud in a white suit, he'd come up ready for a Newport ball." That kind of confidence helped fuel Kennedy's strength as a leader, but it also contributed to recklessness in his personal life—the sense that he could abide by his own rules and not suffer any consequences.

Jackie Kennedy had lived under the roof of her in-laws for extended periods, especially when she was caring for Jack during his illnesses.

Now, in Palm Beach, she had to conserve her strength in an atmosphere that afforded little privacy. "It was so crowded," she recalled, "that I could be in the bathroom, in the tub, and then find that Pierre Salinger was holding a press conference in my bedroom!"

She had arrived in a state of exhaustion after her tour of twenty rooms at the White House with Mamie Eisenhower. Jackie promptly collapsed, stayed in bed for five days, and then largely kept to herself, walking on the beach and catching some sun when she took a break from her children and her paperwork. During Ken Galbraith's visit, he noticed how quickly Jackie disappeared because "she was not feeling well." Occasionally she ventured out to watch Jack play golf, but she avoided fancy gatherings at the Bath and Tennis or the Everglades, the exclusive clubs where the Kennedys were members. Jackie once told French ambassador Hervé Alphand that she preferred Hyannis Port, "a sort of family home . . . similar to Colombey-les-deux Eglises [the bucolic village where French president Charles de Gaulle had a home] rather than Palm Beach . . . which I detest."

From the early days of her marriage, Jackie had declined to meld into the overpowering Kennedy clan, where "hey kiddo" was a standard greeting. The Kennedys had initially seen her "as a threat," according to Billings, who also viewed her as "a serious rival for [JFK's] time and affection." Kennedy had married late, at age thirty-six, and his family worried that "he'd be drawn away from them" by Jackie. The Kennedy sisters—whose long legs and great manes of hair reminded journalist Stewart Alsop of an "unbroken Shetland pony look"—"called her 'the Deb,' made fun of her babylike voice," said Billings, and tried to pull her into their high-intensity sports competitions. But Jackie resisted, figuring "why worry if you're not as good at tennis as Eunice or Ethel when men are attracted by the feminine way you play tennis?"

Jackie and the sisters eventually accommodated each other, but she felt the greatest kinship with her twenty-four-year-old sister-in-law Joan, who struggled to become a Kennedy. Joan was musically talented and beautiful, with a curvy figure and a cascade of blonde hair, but she could never shake her insecurity. "If only she had realized her own strengths instead of looking at herself in comparison with the Kennedys," Jackie lamented years later. Jackie revealed the depth of her affection for Joan as well as Teddy in a page-long unofficial "last will & testament" that she scribbled on a piece of hotel stationery during a vacation in Jamaica ten days after Jack announced his campaign for the presidency. On it she stipulated that if she and JFK were killed, Caroline should be raised by "Edward M. Kennedy and his wife Joan . . . as one of their own children."

Jackie's trickiest family relationship was with Rose Kennedy, the dainty (five foot three) matriarch who wore the latest Paris designs and took pride in her trim figure at age seventy. Their temperaments and habits were often at odds, although their respective marriages had discomfiting parallels. Bright and inquisitive, Rose had been thwarted in her ambition to attend Wellesley, forced instead by her father into strict convent schools run by Sacred Heart nuns where she wore a veil and disciplined herself with silent retreats of prayer and reflection. Decades later Rose called her missed educational opportunity her "greatest regret. . . . It is something I have felt a little sad about all my life."

Rose had raised her nine children like a team, organizing their lives with brisk efficiency, her office filled with card files containing vital information for each child. She was "great on self improvement," according to JFK. But by late middle age Rose had endured the profound sorrow of losing three of her first four offspring—two dead and one incapacitated. She had also withstood decades of her husband's philandering, including his flagrant two-year affair with Gloria Swanson. Rose's own father had been a womanizer, and she remained proudly stoic, never complaining, never confronting. To protect herself, Rose withdrew into her own interests, traveled extensively, and kept an emotional distance, even from her children. Jack, like his siblings, treated Rose respectfully, although he did complain to Bill Walton, "She was never there when we really needed her. . . . My mother never really held me and hugged me."

Catholicism offered Rose the deepest solace; she was a daily communicant, often sitting through two masses a day. Once, in urging Jackie to take a day-long religious retreat, Rose revealed, "I have spent a long happy life with a few baffling as well as tragic moments, and I have found that these spiritual signposts . . . have helped me tremendously." But when Rose tried to impose her piety, Jackie bristled. Jackie had been grounded in a more casual Catholicism. Her mother once told her Newport friend Marion "Oatsie" Leiter, "It might be noticed that Jackie could always be on a horse but not necessarily at mass." Jackie admired Rose's faith but struggled with her own beliefs, once admitting to Harold Macmillan the thought that "there was just nothing afterwards—or some great vague peace."

Jackie chafed under the regimented way Rose ran her own life: the daily ocean swims, four-mile walks, and nine holes of golf (usually by herself). By her own admission, Jackie liked "to live in a disorganized—or free way," focusing intensely on whatever task engaged her, but keeping a fluid schedule. She often slept late and thought nothing of declining when Rose asked her to join guests for lunch—habits that irritated Rose. When Rose pushed too far, Jackie would mimic her mother-in-law's tinny voice behind her back—irreverence that shocked Jackie's secretary, Mary Gallagher.

Jackie recognized the pressures of Rose's life even as she similarly endured her own husband's infidelity. Jackie once said she understood that Rose grew up—and indeed raised her son Jack—with the dictum "you don't reveal yourself. . . . Jack didn't want to reveal himself at all." By Jackie's analysis, "It must have been difficult for [Rose] to be married to such an extremely strong man . . . whose life was like a roller coaster zooming, accelerating, going up and down . . . having nine children . . . it almost took her breath away."

The cause of that angst, Joe Kennedy, also happened to be Jackie's favorite in the family. Like his wife, he had the vigor of someone a decade younger than his seventy-two years, with a tall and lean physique, fine features, and pale blue eyes by turns icy and mischievous. His personality was peppery and aggressive, which he leavened with a flashing smile and quick-witted charm. Jack Kennedy once called his mother "the glue" that held the family together while Rose described Joe as the "architect of our lives."

It was Joe's competitive ethos that conditioned his children. "We don't want any losers around here," Joe said. "In this family we want winners." His main forum was the dinner table where he forced his children to think quickly and defend their views. "He would drop a depth charge," said Kay Halle, "and watch the reaction." One houseguest compared the dinnertime experience to "living in an intellectual wind tunnel."

Few visitors to the Kennedy household wished to encounter Joe Kennedy's cold, disapproving stare. Once up in Hyannis Port, Joe shot "the look" Jackie's way when she arrived at lunch fifteen minutes late. Joe was in what Chuck Spalding called "one of his Emperor Augustus moods. . . . He started to give her the needle, but she gave it right back. Old Joe was always full of slang and so she told him, 'You ought to write a series of grandfather stories for children, like, "The Duck and the Moxie" and "The Donkey Who Couldn't Fight His Way Out of a Telephone Booth."'" The table fell silent as everyone anticipated an angry reaction, but instead Joe "broke into an explosion of laughter."

Perhaps because of Joe's unabashed outspokenness, Jackie could talk frankly to him. In her letters she always called him "Mr. Kennedy," and adopted a tone that varied from flirtatious to reverential. "I used to tell him that he had no nuances," she recalled, "that everything with him was either black or white, while life was so much more complicated than that. But he never got angry with me for talking straight to him; on the contrary, he seemed to enjoy it." Sitting together on the porch at Hyannis or the patio at Palm Beach, "they would talk about everything, their most personal problems," Bill Walton said. "She relied on him completely, trusted him, and soon adored him."

Joe Kennedy went out of his way to please Jackie, not only because he liked her, but because he knew she was an asset for his son. According to Oleg Cassini's brother Igor ("Ghighi")—the gossip columnist Cholly Knickerbocker whom William Manchester called "the Gibbon" of the Kennedy court—"Joseph Kennedy told me he had offered Jackie a million dollars not to divorce Jack" when the marriage was wobbly in the mid-fifties. There was no proof of such a transaction, nor could it be entirely disproved either. But on smaller matters, Joe Kennedy showed consistent generosity to Jackie.

When she wanted to buy a horse, Joe stepped up to pay for it, a gesture she accepted with care. Before proposing a "very quiet and beautiful" bay mare, she made numerous trips to Virginia and vetted twenty-three horses. "Honestly I can't see the point of saving a couple of thousand dollars and not having a winner," he wrote back. "You know all of us Kennedys don't like second prize. So get the horse you like and send me the bill."

With her customary insight, Jackie painted one of her Ludwig Bemelmans–style watercolors that captured Joe Kennedy's role in the family in one image: a horde of Kennedy family members cavorting on a beach, while overhead an airplane pulled a banner saying, "You can't take it with you. Dad's got it all." Joe proudly hung the painting in the Palm Beach villa.

FIVE

*J*ack Kennedy's appointment of his brother Bobby as attorney general was a brazen act of nepotism that would have been unthinkable by the standards of later presidencies. Bobby was just thirty-five and had meager legal experience. After graduating from the University of Virginia Law School, he had worked briefly in the Justice Department and then served as an investigator for two Senate committees, where he made a name for himself with his aggressive questioning. On the first of those committees, he was a protégé of his father's friend Republican senator Joseph McCarthy, during his witch hunts for communists in the federal government. Bobby also had a political imprint after running his brother's presidential campaign with a tough-guy style that made countless enemies, including Lyndon Johnson.

Yet with the exception of a few mild protests from legal scholars and editorial writers, the press and the Congress acquiesced in the appointment. Only one senator, conservative Republican Gordon Allott of Colorado, voted against confirmation. Washington reporters were so complaisant that Bobby had gathered nearly a dozen of them for dinner in a private room at the Occidental Grill to ask their advice on government postings, including his own appointment to the cabinet. Jack Kennedy was confident enough about his immunity from criticism that the night after the inauguration he would joke during the annual Alfalfa Club dinner, "I just wanted to give [Bobby] some legal experience before he practices."

Joe Kennedy suggested the move and urged it on both of his sons. By Joe Kennedy's reckoning, even the strongest personal and party loyalties were no substitute for blood fealty. Bobby at the Justice Department could protect Jack from FBI director Hoover and his compromising investigative files. Jack could speak candidly to Bobby in an atmosphere of complete trust; Bobby in turn could give his brother "the unvarnished truth, no matter what," as JFK put it.

Jack and Bobby were eight years apart, and until Jack ran for the Senate in 1952 they were not particularly close. Bobby had grown up small and scrappy, alternately ingratiating and sarcastic, with a brooding personality that inspired Jack to nickname him "Black Robert." While Jack enchanted people at first meeting, Bobby was an acquired taste. He often made a poor initial impression, playing with his sandy forelock, his pale blue eyes furtive, his manner abrupt, his shoulders permanently slouched. His salient trait was stubborn physical courage, most notably on the football field where he was usually overmatched. "He reminds me of a little donkey in the middle of the road, refusing to budge as a dozen autoists shriek their horns," wrote Joe Kennedy's cousin and political adviser Joe Kane.

As the seventh of nine children, Bobby struggled for the approval of a father who was focused on the achievements of his two eldest sons. "One had the impression that the family competition had been hardest on him, forcing him to scramble for everything," wrote Arthur Schlesinger. Joe Jr. was the superstar, and Jack, after scraping through Choate, graduated magna cum laude from Harvard with a thesis on Britain's inadequate preparation for World War II that became a bestselling book. Bobby muddled through a series of boarding schools and finished at Harvard without distinction.

Joe Kennedy was nearly sixty years old when Bobby graduated in 1947, with a fortune estimated in the hundreds of millions, the product of Wall Street speculation, liquor distribution, Hollywood filmmaking, and real estate. He had established trust funds worth $10 million for each of his children, making them financially secure. With the end of his own public life a bitter memory, Joe had shifted his sights to political office for the next generation. "I thought money would give me power, so I made money," he once said, "only to discover that it was politics—not money—that really gave a man power. So I went into politics." But Joe also believed in government service as a worthy calling. As Henry Luce, the flinty proprietor of Time-Life, observed, "It would take a very great dramatist-novelist . . . to mix the rhythm of earthy selfishness and higher loyalties that explained the motivation of Joseph Patrick Kennedy."

Joe Kennedy's grand political scheme had envisioned elective office for either Joe Jr. or Jack, but not Bobby (the Ambassador briefly thought of "buying *The Boston Post* for Bobbie to run"). With the death of Joe Jr. in 1944, the sole focus of Joe's ambition became Jack, "not because it was natural for him or that it was his desire," Joe explained to Massachusetts politician John McCormack, but because it was only right that Jack take up the eldest son's "obligations and desires."

It also followed that Bobby would be asked to help his brother at the appropriate time. He had finally attracted his father's attention by applying himself impressively as a Justice Department lawyer just as Jack began preparing for a difficult Senate contest. The campaign needed a strong and trustworthy manager, a job that suited Bobby's talents. When the call came, he earned the admiration of his father and brother with his fierce loyalty, hard work, and determination. The 1952 Senate race established the good cop/bad cop roles that the brothers would continue to play in subsequent campaigns and into the White House: Jack set a high tone while Bobby did the dirty work.

By the end of 1960, Jack Kennedy had assembled most of his "new generation of leadership" to direct the nation into the "New Frontier" of the coming decade, a terrain of "unknown opportunities and perils" as well as "unfilled hopes and unfilled threats." His team had an overtly bipartisan feel, and a self-consciously intellectual cast, with more egg-heads (including fifteen Rhodes scholars) than had been assembled by any president, including Franklin D. Roosevelt.

The close election results influenced the composition of the Kennedy administration: a plurality of only 112,881 ballots out of 68,832,818 total votes cast, which was the smallest victory margin (49.7 percent to

49.6 percent) in a century—"so thin as to be, in all reality, nonexistent," wrote Teddy White. "The election of 1960," White observed, was "totally devoid of cause or issue . . . nothing stirred Americans but the personalities of the candidates and the religion of one of them." Only anxiety about Soviet military strength resonated with voters, and both Kennedy and Nixon exploited that fear by asserting their ability to get tough with Soviet premier Nikita Khrushchev.

As president-elect, Kennedy understood that doubts about his experience lingered (during his fourteen years in the House and Senate he had been "just a member of the pack" who seized no great issues). Now he needed eastern establishment gravitas. As early as October, he had told *New York Times* columnist Cyrus L. "Cy" Sulzberger that he would emulate Franklin Roosevelt and Harry Truman, installing Republicans in important positions "in the interests of national unity." Kennedy relied heavily on the guidance of two of those Roosevelt-Truman Republicans, Robert Lovett and John McCloy, after they both rejected top cabinet positions for themselves. When Kennedy's longtime aide Kenny O'Donnell, probably the most liberal voice on his immediate staff, questioned the wisdom of such inclusiveness, Kennedy replied, "If I string along exclusively with . . . Harvard liberals, they'll fill Washington with wild-eyed ADA [Americans for Democratic Action] people. . . . I can use a few smart Republicans. . . . Anyway we need a Secretary of the Treasury who can call a few of those people on Wall Street by their first names."

Kennedy's three GOP choices—Robert McNamara, McGeorge Bundy, and Douglas Dillon—passed muster with his council of wise men. McNamara and Bundy were only nominally Republicans. Both had voted for Kennedy, and McNamara belonged to the ACLU and the NAACP, while Bundy had been a visible supporter of Kennedy since early in the campaign. Only Dillon was a partisan, having served Eisenhower as under secretary of state and contributed $26,000 to Nixon's campaign. But the three men fit the prerequisite Kennedy had mentioned to Sulzberger, with "basic thinking . . . close to his own." All would rapidly move into Kennedy's inner circle.

McNamara had been president of Ford Motor Company for only thirty-four days when Kennedy tapped him for secretary of defense in early December. McNamara was dazzled by Kennedy's winning personality and nimble mind, marveling at the "range of issues which [JFK] had thought and worked out in his head." Kennedy already knew that McNamara was a rare bird in the business elite—a wizard with numbers as well as a highbrow whose Ford colleagues once presented him with four volumes of Arnold J. Toynbee's *A Study of History*. Uncomfortable with country club socializing, McNamara refused to live in the posh suburb of Grosse Pointe, choosing instead more distant Ann Arbor, where he belonged to two book groups with University of Michigan professors. In keeping with Kennedy-style vigor, McNamara was a fearless mountain climber as well.

According to Schlesinger, McNamara had "striking gifts" that appealed to Kennedy, including an "inquiring and incisive mind," a "limitless capacity for work," and a "personality which lacked pretense." McNamara also projected the lanky athleticism of an outdoorsman that fit nicely with the New Frontier image. He was six feet tall, with a glossy pelt of dark hair brushed back from his forehead, and "the blotched pink complexion of one who has lain too long in a bathtub." He wore rimless glasses that gave him an academic air, and his superficially austere manner masked a temperament of intense emotions that occasionally made him unexpectedly tearful.

He was a year older than Kennedy and had grown up in modest circumstances in California, the son of an Irish Catholic sales manager for a shoe company. He graduated Phi Beta Kappa from Berkeley, majoring in economics with minors in philosophy and mathematics, then earned an MBA from Harvard. After serving as a statistical analyst during World War II, McNamara joined a cadre of ten men called the "Whiz Kids" at Ford, where he rose rapidly through management. "The things that most men have to turn to books and reports for, Bob is carrying around right in his head," said an unabashedly admiring Henry Ford II.

McGeorge Bundy exuded similar self-assurance and braininess behind a deceptively cherubic face defined by pink cheeks, thinning sandy hair, and "a faintly quizzical expression." The Bundys traced their roots back to the Pilgrims at Plymouth Rock, and his mother's family included Cabots and Lowells. "Mac" was the third son of five children in a household that prized serious discourse and clever one-upsmanship.

At Groton he was legendary for ostentatious displays of intellect, once delivering a lecture on the Duke of Marlborough from a blank sheet of paper.

Mac was the first student to matriculate at Yale with three perfect scores on his entrance examinations. The Yale literary magazine described him as "sly of wit and with a wicked gleam in his eyes." He wrote a column for the *Yale Daily News,* where he earned a reputation for political iconoclasm. His commentaries on national and world affairs, combined with his Brahmin demeanor, prompted the nickname "Mahatma Bundy."

By the time Bundy rose from a tenured professorship in American foreign policy at Harvard to become the university's dean of the faculty at age thirty-four, he had made an impressive list of connections, including Henry Stimson, FDR's secretary of war, Douglas Dillon, and Dean Acheson, Truman's secretary of state. Bundy's wife, Bostonian Mary Lothrop, was a relative of Ben Bradlee's, and Bundy's mother was close to Corinne Alsop, the mother of columnists Stewart and Joe. Bundy even had links to Kennedy. As a boy at the Dexter School in Brookline, he was two years behind JFK, and Bundy had been a wartime friend of Kathleen Kennedy, who asked him to serve as master of ceremonies on a quiz program she ran at an American Red Cross canteen in London. Bundy and Kennedy had renewed their acquaintance in 1957 when JFK was elected to Harvard's Board of Overseers. As early as 1959, Kennedy decided Bundy should be in his administration. Before he settled on national security adviser, JFK even considered him for secretary of state.

Douglas Dillon appealed to Kennedy because of his impressive portfolio of government experience. In addition to his service at Foggy Bottom, Dillon had been ambassador to France and was known as a committed internationalist with conservative economic views. Joe Kennedy may have been a longtime Democrat, but he told his son that "there weren't any Democrats who knew about money," recalled Charley Bartlett.

Although Dillon was eight years older than Kennedy, the two men had much in common. Both were sons of overbearing self-made men.

Dillon's paternal grandfather, a Polish Jew named Sam Lapowski, had emigrated to Milwaukee, where he set up a machine manufacturing business and changed his surname to Dillon, the maiden name of his French Catholic mother. Doug Dillon's father, Clarence, preceded him at Harvard, and was rejected by the university's exclusive "final" clubs, an indignity also suffered by Joe Kennedy as an Irish immigrant's grandson. Similarly, both JFK and Doug Dillon were admitted to Spee, an important badge of acceptance at Harvard, although a cut below the Porcellian Club.

Clarence Dillon moved from small business to Wall Street and made a $190 million fortune as the head of the investment banking firm Dillon Read. He used his largess to travel widely in Europe, where he bought the winemaking estate Château Haut-Brion on 104 acres in Bordeaux that had been owned by Talleyrand. Douglas Dillon was born in Switzerland and graduated second in his class from Groton, by then a virtual spawning ground for bankers with a commitment to public service. Tall and shy, he suffered like Kennedy from repeated bouts of poor health when he was growing up, including a ruptured spinal disc that forced him to work standing at a tall desk. In World War II he saw combat as a navy officer on Black Cat bombers and withstood kamikaze attacks. After the war he became chairman of Dillon Read. With six residences in the United States and abroad, Dillon lived like a Renaissance prince, with Renoirs on his walls and the finest Haut-Brion claret on his table.

It was only after he turned to government service that Dillon finally escaped the firm grip of his father. Kennedy and Dillon first took each other's measure at various Harvard gatherings and shared a "patrician reserve and almost British sense of understatement." Through Kennedy's membership on the Senate Foreign Relations Committee, he tapped Dillon's State Department expertise on international problems such as aid to India. They also had a mutual friend in Ben Bradlee, who had served as Dillon's press officer at the embassy in Paris.

Kennedy admired Dillon's quiet style, quick mind, and nondoctrinaire approach to economic policies. "We both had rather rapid minds," said Dillon, who noticed that Kennedy's decisions "were well taken. He wasn't pushed into doing things too rapidly." Dillon was particularly impressed with Kennedy's sense of history when he said during their initial meeting about the cabinet post, "Liberal governments have foundered on the reef of financial instability, and I will not let that happen to my government."

More than any other appointee, Dillon brought credentials that helped solve some urgent problems inherited by Kennedy as he prepared to take power. The U.S. balance of payments was precarious; investors were depleting U.S. gold reserves, which threatened to weaken the dollar, at least in part due to fears of a free-spending Democratic administration. Kennedy believed Dillon's appointment to Treasury would reassure the international financial community and stabilize the dollar.

"Kennedy was a deeply conservative fellow financially," recalled Dillon. "His father had tremendous influence on his background thinking." The preoccupation with the balance of payments was right out of Joe Kennedy's playbook. According to Arthur Schlesinger, Joe Kennedy believed that "lack of confidence" would drain America of gold, attitudes that were stamped on JFK and remained a preoccupation throughout his presidency.

Dillon's selection predictably disheartened the liberal wing of the Democratic party. No one was more disappointed than John Kenneth Galbraith, who had counted on influencing presidential policies since Kennedy first consulted him as a young senator mulling how to vote on economics legislation.

Canadian-born Galbraith was difficult to miss, not only because of his six-foot-eight-inch height, but also because of his trenchant views on economics. He had a "pacifist father" who bred livestock and instilled in Galbraith an urge to help impoverished people "on the edge of despair" during the Depression. Galbraith earned a doctorate at Berkeley and worked briefly in the Roosevelt administration before joining the Harvard faculty, the beginning of a sixty-year association with the university. He was a disciple of John Maynard Keynes, sharing his belief that increases in government spending could stimulate growth and ease unemployment.

Galbraith was one of the most prominent liberals to line up behind Kennedy in the campaign's Cambridge brain trust. He was the author of *The Affluent Society*, a harsh indictment of the impact of American advertising on consumer spending, and his ideas for the candidate ran at full throttle. "Along with people who like to hear themselves talk," he wrote to Kennedy, "there are unquestionably some who are even more inordinately attracted by their own composition. I may well be entitled to a gold star membership in both groups." Kennedy enjoyed Galbraith's drollery and didn't hesitate to fire back. When Galbraith objected that the *New York Times* described him as arrogant, Kennedy replied, "I don't see why. Everybody else does."

Kennedy's election thrilled Galbraith, who proclaimed "a government of the rich by the clever for the poor." There was talk that Galbraith might be named secretary of the Treasury or chairman of the Council of Economic Advisers. But Kennedy knew that Galbraith's views were too extreme for either of those jobs. Cy Sulzberger predicted "suicides on Wall Street" if Galbraith were named Treasury secretary. "They think Galbraith is mad." When Kennedy asked Lovett about Galbraith, the veteran investment banker deadpanned, "He's a fine novelist." (Ironically, Galbraith would publish *The McLandress Dimension* in 1963 under the pseudonym "Mark Epernay," a novel that skewered the Kennedy State Department as a fount of clichés and bad ideas.)

Less than a week later, Kennedy tapped Galbraith as ambassador to India, a prestigious post where he could do the least damage to the American economy. But Galbraith would not be silenced. With a stream of colorful letters and regular visits back home, he would continue pushing his views. To Dillon, Galbraith would be like a mischievous phantom darting around the edges of the administration's sober economic policies—a situation that Kennedy would find endlessly diverting.

Galbraith's Cambridge soulmate was Arthur Schlesinger. Together they were Kennedy's biggest egghead trophies, since both had been highly visible supporters of Adlai Stevenson, the liberal standard-bearer and twice-failed Democratic candidate for president. Just as Kennedy needed Republicans after his election, so were the "kinetic Democrats" (Schlesinger's term for progressive party activists) crucial to securing the nomination and energizing voters in the general election. Many liberals were wary of Joe and Bobby Kennedy's association with Joe

McCarthy. But the enduring misgiving centered on Jack. When the Senate censured McCarthy (67 to 22) for his abusive tactics in 1954, Jack was the only Democratic senator who failed to cast a vote.

Schlesinger was willing to accept JFK's flimsy excuse that he couldn't join the voting because he was recuperating from his back surgery. (Even from afar, Kennedy knew enough about the case against McCarthy to cast a vote, and he was accustomed to having staff members vote on his behalf, sometimes when they were unfamiliar with his precise position.) To Schlesinger, Jack was nearly infallible. They were exact contemporaries who first became friendly in 1946 when Schlesinger was teaching history at Harvard and Kennedy had just been elected to Congress.

JFK instantly understood the value of this twenty-nine-year-old who had just won the Pulitzer Prize for *The Age of Jackson*. As Kennedy began asking Schlesinger for ideas and advice, the ambitious academic was captured by his charm, his "skeptical mind," and "laconic tongue." Schlesinger grew to admire the "inward and reflective quality" of JFK's intelligence, and Kennedy used Schlesinger as a kind of liberal tuning fork whose perfect pitch enabled Kennedy to adjust his own position on the political scale as circumstances required.

Schlesinger was born in Ohio but lost all trace of the heartland (much like his friend Bill Walton) in the urbanity of Cambridge, where he grew up as the precocious son of Harvard's celebrated social and cultural historian Arthur Meier Schlesinger. Slightly built and bespectacled, with a wicked wit and writerly flair, young Arthur distinguished himself as a student and then a teacher at Harvard, though he never received an advanced degree. His great passion was Franklin Roosevelt and the New Deal.

While Kennedy was more politically conservative than Schlesinger, the two men shared a strong sense of irony, a playful regard for the vagaries of the human condition, and an openness to people and experiences. During the campaign, Kennedy took impish pleasure when his academic allies were thrown in with hard-bitten political veterans, described by *Time* correspondent Hugh Sidey as "brawling Irishmen." During a rally in Boston, Kennedy spotted Schlesinger and Galbraith in the crowd. Later, on the campaign plane, Kennedy asked Sidey, "Did you see Arthur and Ken trapped in the middle inhaling all the cigar smoke?" Said Sidey, "He enjoyed and respected them and their brains, but he understood the limits of intellectuals. He needed the stimulus but he needed the down to earth O'Donnells and O'Briens as well."

One after another of Schlesinger's suggested appointments for the Kennedy administration fell on deaf ears: Stevenson for secretary of state, former Connecticut governor Chester Bowles as ambassador to the United Nations, and Galbraith for Treasury. Recognizing Schlesinger's frustration, Kennedy tried to mollify him. "We'll have to go along with this for a year or so," JFK told Schlesinger. "Then I would like to bring in some new people." With that, Schlesinger began to grasp the dimensions of what he called Kennedy's "profoundly realistic mind."

Schlesinger's wife, Marian, believed that her husband "would have loved to have had Mac Bundy's job," but settled for a more nebulous designation as "special assistant," what Galbraith described as "a good address but no clear function." The notion of an adviser with no definable responsibility initially disquieted Schlesinger. "I am not sure what I would be doing as Special Assistant," he said. "Well," cracked Kennedy, "I am not sure what I will be doing as President either." Schlesinger took the job knowing, as he told Eleanor Roosevelt, "that no American historian has ever been privileged to watch the unfolding of public policy from this particular vantage point."

"In Jack's mind he must have perceived that Arthur was someone to evaluate his presidency," said William vanden Heuvel, who worked as an aide to Bobby Kennedy. "To give an inside role like that shows an aspect of Kennedy's self-confidence." As Kennedy himself explained it to O'Donnell, "I'll write my own official history of the Kennedy administration, but Arthur will probably write one of his own, and it will be better for us if he's in the White House, seeing what goes on, instead of reading about us in the *New York Times* and *Time* magazine up in his office in the Widener Library at Harvard."

Schlesinger's most burdensome task, one that originated early in the presidential campaign and continued in the White House, was as the middleman between Kennedy and Adlai Stevenson. "Adlai was not in the inner circle," said Schlesinger, "but Jack Kennedy always wanted to know what Adlai thought." Schlesinger never tired of insisting how compatible Kennedy and Stevenson should have been despite their seventeen-year age difference. Both had graduated from Choate, and Stevenson was a Princeton man. Their homes, Schlesinger observed, had the "same mood and tempo," they attracted "the same kind of irrelevant European visitors," had "the same gay humor" and "style of gossip," as well as "the same free and wide-ranging conversation about a variety of subjects" and "the same quick transition from the serious to the frivolous."

Despite such natural affinities, Kennedy and Stevenson were forever uneasy with each other: the slightly plump, balding elder statesman and the dashing usurper. In Kennedy's presence, Stevenson stiffened, and "became sort of prissy and overzealous," Schlesinger recalled. Kennedy "never saw Stevenson at his best . . . pungent, astute and beguiling." Behind Stevenson's back, Kennedy dismissed him as unmanly and weak. When criticizing the State Department, JFK once said, "They're not queer, but well, sort of like Adlai." Stevenson saw "a certain amount of arrogance in Jack Kennedy" that he found distasteful, according to Stevenson's sister Elizabeth Ives.

Neither Kennedy nor Stevenson forgot the slights they inflicted on each other during the presidential campaign. Kennedy lobbied hard through intermediaries, particularly Schlesinger, for Stevenson's support before the convention. As an inducement, Kennedy dangled the possibility of secretary of state, the job Stevenson coveted next to the presidency. "Had [Adlai] come out for Kennedy . . . he could have had anything he wanted," said Schlesinger. Four years earlier, Stevenson had encouraged Kennedy to make a bid for the vice presidential slot. Although Kennedy had lost narrowly, his prominence at the 1956 convention, followed by extensive campaigning, had set the stage for his own presidential bid.

But in 1960 Stevenson remained stubbornly neutral. He felt that he had provided the intellectual framework for Kennedy, who had used Stevenson's people and ideas to develop his own campaign. Stevenson still hoped for a draft by his diehard supporters, led by Eleanor Roosevelt. (Kennedy regarded the Stevenson followers with an amused curiosity, remarking to Charley Bartlett, "I don't have a cult. Why does Adlai have a cult?") Kennedy's youth and inexperience also gave Stevenson doubts. "I do not feel he's the right man for the job," Stevenson told British journalist Barbara Ward. "I do not really think he is up to it."

At the convention, Bobby Kennedy pressed Stevenson hard to nominate Jack. "You've got twenty-four hours," Joe Kennedy snarled to Stevenson aide Bill Blair. Not only did Stevenson refuse, he visited the convention hall on the eve of the balloting, provoking a "wild demonstration" that incensed Kennedy, who concluded that Stevenson had "behaved indecisively and stupidly."

Still, Stevenson pined to be secretary of state, and Schlesinger kept pressing his friend's case. But Kennedy didn't want a man with his own following that could form a separate power base. JFK was eager to run his own foreign policy, so he selected Dean Rusk, a Georgia poor boy turned Rhodes scholar known for his reliability and lucidity but lacking force and imagination.

The best offer Kennedy could make was ambassador to the United Nations, which he elevated to cabinet status to soothe Stevenson's injured pride. Stevenson initially rejected the overture, and complained that it was a "second-rate job," which irritated his friends as much as it did Kennedy. "You must never again say to anyone . . . that Jack gave you this appointment to 'get rid of you,'" Agnes Meyer, the wife of the *Washington Post* owner, wrote to Stevenson. "From now on you must play ball." Stevenson begrudgingly accepted the job, but his resentment remained, leaving Schlesinger resigned to his fate as intermediary for the next three years: "on the phone between the two of them, trying to translate one to the other."

SIX

"*Kennedys* were everywhere," wrote Arthur Schlesinger. "It was the first rally of the new frontier." The occasion was a party at the cream-colored home of Jack's sister Jean and her husband, Steve Smith, just three nights before the inauguration. The Smith residence at Thirty-first and O Streets in Georgetown was the epicenter of the movable Kennedy compound, with the rest of the family in rented houses down the street and around the corner. Jean and Steve put up a heated tent over their garden, where guests dined and danced to Lester Lanin. The evening "had all the glamour of a Hollywood premiere," the *Washington Post* reported.

The crowd was quintessentially Kennedy, a mixture of scholars, movie stars, and men who would hold top positions in the new administration. Robert McNamara arrived just after Milton Berle and Jimmy Durante. Frank Sinatra walked in with the wife of black singer Nat King Cole; when a reporter asked Sinatra if she was his date he snarled, "Where do you come from, Romania?" Eunice Shriver wore straw beach shoes with her evening gown because she had sprained her ankle earlier in the day. Her friend Deeda Blair, who had worked hard on the campaign, was astonished to be seated between JFK and Sinatra, while

Marian Schlesinger marveled at "the beautiful nymphets imported from New York."

The hostess, Jean Kennedy Smith, embodied what Ken Galbraith called "the agreeable enthusiasm of youth." She was thirty-two, the second youngest among the siblings. She had the family's strong jaw, but her blue eyes conveyed a slightly winsome look, and her manner was low key. A graduate of Manhattanville College, she had a sharp intelligence and quick wit that made her the Kennedy sister most compatible with Jackie. Both women had been pregnant during the campaign, and Jean had given birth to her second son in the fall.

Jean's husband, Steve, was educated by the Jesuits at Georgetown and worked at his family's tugboat company in New York. His Irish immigrant grandfather had been a three-term congressman from Brooklyn. Smith inherited political instincts as well as the sort of business acumen that the Ambassador felt the family needed. As Lem Billings said, "Listening to the Kennedy brothers talk about business was like hearing nuns talk about sex."

The chain-smoking Smith was handsome, wiry, and intense. He proved to be a resourceful strategist during the campaign. "He rowed to his objective on silent oars," said Jack Kennedy, remarking on his brother-in-law's famously taciturn but effective style. In the new administration, Smith would be assigned to the State Department as a troubleshooter.

Jack came alone to the Smith dinner dance because Jackie was still in Palm Beach, conserving her strength and waiting until the last moment to leave Caroline and John, who would stay at the Ambassador's home with baby nurse Luella Hennessey and nanny Maud Shaw while the private quarters of the White House were being redecorated. The President-elect was beaming and euphoric, urging his little brother Teddy to sing "Heart of My Heart" and his navy buddy Red Fay to perform "Hooray for Hollywood." But the performances fell flat, Fay recalled, because "people were having too much fun getting to know each other."

When Jackie flew north the next day, accompanied by Mary Gallagher and Pam Turnure, she slipped into town "almost unnoticed except by a small handful of waiting photographers, Secret Service men and fellow air travelers." Nobody came to the airport to greet the future first lady, who was driven away by a Secret Service man in a bright green Mercury. Jack was in Manhattan having lunch with Democratic elder statesman Averell Harriman. Jackie's mother, along with all the Kennedy "womenfolk," were busy at the National Gallery of Art standing in receiving lines to greet six thousand women. It was just the sort of gathering Jackie disliked, and that she had been told to avoid.

Her physician, John Walsh, had announced that she should "curtail her activities for about six months," which gave her a convenient excuse to duck any event she found tedious. In fact, her time in Palm Beach had hardly been restful, with the endless parade of visitors and the pressures to organize the move into the White House. As Jackie arrived at the three-story Federal-style Kennedy home on N Street near Thirty-fourth in Georgetown, conditions were no better. The place was swarming with visitors, cordoned off by the Secret Service, and surrounded by the press and curious onlookers.

For weeks Jack Kennedy had been working on his inaugural address, a statement of themes and goals to set the tone for his presidency. "I had heard it in bits and pieces many times," said Jackie. "There were piles of yellow paper covered with his notes all over our bedroom floor." Jack had solicited ideas from associates such as Schlesinger, Stevenson, and Galbraith (who would concede that the final version was "less daring" though "a lot wiser" than his own). Kennedy had also sought advice from prominent journalists, including Joseph Kraft and the dean of Washington columnists, Walter Lippmann, who suggested that Kennedy refer to the Soviet Union as the "adversary" rather than the "enemy." The membrane between politics and journalism was so thin in those days that such cozy cooperation was not only routine but a signal of eminence in the newspaper fraternity.

No one had more influence on Kennedy's words, however, than Ted Sorensen, the stiff and dour Nebraskan who had been his speechwriter and closest adviser since Kennedy's election to the Senate. The youngest of Kennedy's aides, only a year older than Jackie, Sorensen had a "square, wintry, bespectacled face" that seemed "carved from ice" and a "smile as spontaneous as a bank vault swinging open."

Sorensen was aptly described as Kennedy's "alter ego." They had the same retentive memories, mental and physical energy, intolerance for small talk, and directness of manner. In his eager self-effacement, Sorensen became a slavish extension of his boss.

After signing on with Senator Kennedy in 1953, Sorensen assumed JFK's broad Massachusetts inflections and chopping gestures, and abandoned his teetotaling to sip daiquiris and Heinekens, Kennedy's favorite drinks. Sorensen even developed a painful back, and for years Kennedy gave him advice on the latest remedy. "I could predict Jack Kennedy's thinking on most issues, and without his speaking of his emotions, I could read them," Sorensen recalled. Sorensen routinely used "we" instead of "I" to indicate that he and Kennedy thought alike. Yet paradoxically, "never have two people been more intimate and more separate," said Richard Neustadt, the Columbia University government professor who advised Kennedy on the transition.

Sorensen was neither sophisticated nor privileged. He had never seen a finger bowl until he first visited the Kennedys on Cape Cod, and he had never traveled much beyond the Midwest. His father, the son of Danish immigrants, was a crusading liberal lawyer in Nebraska, and his mother was an outspoken feminist of Russian Jewish descent. Ted was the third child in a family of five that thrived on spirited political discussions and a commitment to public service—perhaps Sorensen's only common ground with the Kennedy family.

When Sorensen joined Kennedy, he had scant Washington experience, but he was a Phi Beta Kappa graduate of the University of Nebraska and its law school. He also had sterling liberal credentials that seemed useful to Kennedy: membership in Americans for Democratic Action and a history of campaigning for Negro rights when few followed that path. A committed pacifist, Sorensen had registered for military service as a noncombatant, intending to serve as a medic if called.

Sorensen was impressed from the beginning that Kennedy "spoke easily but almost shyly, without the customary verbosity and pomposity" of politicians, and he was drawn to Kennedy's "insistence on cutting through prevailing bias and myths to the heart of a problem." Given his own deep reserve, Sorensen understood that Kennedy "disliked shows of emotion, not because he felt lightly but because he felt deeply." Although Kennedy was cautious in his politics, Sorensen considered his boss a "free man" with a "free mind" open to new ideas and arguments from the left.

Their remarkable intellectual compatibility led to controversy when Kennedy published *Profiles in Courage,* biographical essays on eight senators who endangered their careers by taking principled stands. Kennedy had many literary helpers, including several historians (among them Schlesinger) and Arthur Krock of the *New York Times,* who had moonlighted for years as an editor and ghostwriter for his friend Joe Kennedy (and at least once took a $5,000 retainer). They contributed research notes and wrote and edited drafts. Jack Kennedy wrote sections of the book and dictated some hundred pages of notes into a recorder. But it was Sorensen who worked full-time for six months to pull together a narrative that Kennedy polished.

When *Profiles* was published in 1956, Kennedy was listed as the sole author. In the preface, he gave a credit to Sorensen—"for his invaluable assistance in the assembly and preparation of the material upon which this book is based"—and to others who had helped him. It became a best-seller and won the Pulitzer Prize for biography in 1957, securing for Kennedy a national reputation as the thinking man's politician. At Joe Kennedy's request, Arthur Krock had used his considerable influence to "log roll" the Pulitzer Prize board into giving Kennedy the award, displacing their first and second choices, acclaimed biographies of Harlan Stone and Franklin D. Roosevelt. "I worked as hard as I could to get him that prize," Krock recalled. "Those are the facts. I don't take any pride in them."

Later in 1957, columnist Drew Pearson said in a TV interview that the book had been ghosted. The Kennedy family threatened a lawsuit and won a carefully worded retraction saying that JFK took "sole responsibility for [the book's] concept and contents." Enough doubt remained that when Robert McNamara first met Kennedy, he asked directly if the President-elect had written *Profiles.* "I am not sure precisely how he answered," McNamara said decades later. "But I came away with the firm conclusion that the book represented Kennedy's thinking, even if many of the words were written by Ted." McNamara recalled feeling abashed by his bold inquiry once he had a chance to see JFK "write prose of equal quality on many occasions in my presence."

Kennedy and Sorensen had been inseparable during the campaign as they barnstormed the country. Sorensen was the original workaholic, routinely staying up all night to write speeches. Other speechwriters failed to pass muster. When Schlesinger wrote remarks for Kennedy to deliver to the Liberal Party of New York (the progressive third party founded sixteen years earlier to counter the corruption and special interests of the mainstream Republican and Democratic parties), Sorensen observed that the language was vintage Stevenson and sounded false coming from Kennedy. As Schlesinger dryly observed, Sorensen "tended to resent interlopers."

Behind Sorensen's serious demeanor and formidable brain, Jackie detected vulnerability. "Ted is such a little boy in so many ways," she once said. "The way he almost puffs himself up when he talks to Jack. He hero-worships him." Sorensen was also deeply ambitious. Although Kennedy called him "indispensable," Sorensen now had to compete with others for the President-elect's attention. As JFK pulled his staff together, Sorensen insisted on being called special counsel to mark his seniority and to ensure that his role extended beyond writing. The title had added resonance because it had originated with Roosevelt and had last been used in the Truman administration. At first Kennedy didn't want any specific titles for his aides, but he finally relented. "Once Ted got the title of Special Counsel, he felt more secure and relaxed," said Richard Neustadt.

It would have been impossible to parse the inaugural address produced by Kennedy and Sorensen. By 1961 their writing styles were indistinguishable, and much of the rhetoric had been woven into previous speeches. They used the inversion known as chiasmus to produce a distinctive cadence: "Let us never negotiate out of fear, but let us never fear to negotiate." They stressed the need for renewal, self-sacrifice, conciliation, strength, and resolve to prevail in a "long twilight struggle" against "the common enemies of man: tyranny, poverty, disease and war itself." The tone sought to inspire, not polarize, containing nothing to upset the right or the left. The scope was international, with no mention of domestic issues such as unemployment, civil rights, or medical care for the aged. It was also the shortest address since 1944 because, Kennedy told Sorensen, "I don't want people to think I'm a windbag."

———

Kennedy carefully planned the inauguration festivities to evoke history as well as to emphasize the transfer of power to a new generation.

Instead of his predecessor's business suit, Kennedy decided to wear an aristocratic cutaway, pearl gray waistcoat, gray striped trousers, and silk top hat. "He recognized that even as the people would reject a king, their hearts tugged for the symbols of royalty," said Lem Billings. "For that reason, he deliberately decided to invest his inauguration with pomp and ceremony. He wanted to use the moment to appeal to the imagination, to raise the ceremony to a heightened level of feeling."

On Thursday, January 19, inauguration eve, a fierce storm imperiled the celebration. Nearly eight inches of snow fell, and stinging winds caused drifting that snarled traffic. Earlier in the day, while Jackie over-saw final preparations for their move, Jack transferred his command center to the other side of Georgetown, into Bill Walton's red-brick home at the corner of P and Twenty-ninth Streets. "If you stay in this house, I cannot move," Jackie told JFK. Walton didn't have much money and "camped out" in the spacious rooms, attended by a faithful housekeeper. Kennedy conducted meetings in Walton's faded red Vic-torian parlor furnished with threadbare pieces, while Walton typed up statements for the press on his rickety typewriter.

Kennedy met that day for the second time with President Eisen-hower. For his first meeting in early December he had been extensively briefed. A small task force including Adlai Stevenson and two of his associates, John Sharon and George Ball (soon to be under secretary of state), had prepared twenty pages of facts and a page of questions on each subject. Eisenhower, who had been dubious about Kennedy's readiness, afterwards remarked on Kennedy's "understanding of the world problems, the depth of his questions, his grasp of the issues and the keenness of his mind."

The pre-inaugural meeting at the White House lasted two hours. When Kennedy emerged, a reporter asked, "Aren't you excited?" Ken-nedy considered for a moment and said, "Interested!" His comment was vintage Kennedy cool, echoing a remark decades earlier during his bachelor days. Chiquita Cárcano, a South American friend, had asked him if he had ever been in love. "Not in love but very, very interested," he had replied.

By dusk the snow had piled up, and Kennedy called "Billy Boy" Walton to offer him a lift to the inaugural concert at Constitution Hall and the inaugural gala at the National Guard Armory. Jackie wore an elegant Cassini-designed white silk gown befitting a debutante; not only was white her favorite color, she considered it the "most ceremonial." Jackie once wrote that she dreamed of being "a sort of Overall Art Director of the Twentieth Century, watching everything from a chair hanging in space." She applied that theatrical sensibility to her first major appearance and each one that followed. Jackie had a profound sense of occasion, and she wanted to be noticed, but not in a vulgar way. White stood in brilliant contrast with the colorful gowns in the crowd on a winter night. She wore an emerald necklace, and a fabric rosette called a cockade accented her waist, a small tribute to the Gallic eighteenth century.

As the limousine carrying Jack, Jackie, and Walton crunched along deserted streets, "the night journey was eerie and exciting to the three isolated inside the heated car. During the ride they looked out the blurred windows and scarcely spoke. The street lights shone mistily on deep white drifts." Emergency road crews held up pink flares and torches, and Jack said to Walton, "Turn on the lights so they can see Jackie."

The gala, a fundraiser for the Democratic party, was an extravaganza produced by Frank Sinatra and Kennedy's brother-in-law, the English actor Peter Lawford. The performances ranged from Sir Laurence Olivier and Mahalia Jackson to Eleanor Roosevelt reading the words of Abraham Lincoln. The women ushers reflected the regal mood with their rhinestone crowns. Jackie returned home after the performance, while JFK and Walton went downtown to a party for three hundred at Paul Young's Restaurant given by Joe Kennedy. It was 3:48 a.m. when the President-elect finally returned to Georgetown.

Celebrities added dazzle to the new administration. Actresses such as Angie Dickinson had campaigned with Citizens for Kennedy along with baseball star Stan Musial, writer James Michener, and Arthur Schlesinger, who became Dickinson's lifelong friend. JFK had a direct link to Hollywood through Lawford, the husband of Patricia Kennedy.

Six years earlier, when Pat and Peter were both skimming thirty, they had married after a five-month courtship. Pat was tall and athletic, with auburn hair and lovely blue eyes. Like her sisters she had received a proper Catholic education in Sacred Heart convent schools, and had graduated from Rosemont College, a Catholic school in suburban Philadelphia.

The son of Sir Sydney and Lady Lawford, Peter had learned early to live by his wits and capitalize on his good looks after his family went broke during World War II and emigrated to Palm Beach. When he and Pat married, he had several successful films to his credit. The Kennedys were captivated by his glamorous connections, although his brother-in-law Sargent Shriver saw that he was a lightweight: "Peter was good fun, but he was not what you would call a power." The Ambassador was even more dubious, telling Oleg Cassini that English actors were "the worst kind."

Lawford compensated for his modest talent with an obsequious personality. He used his Kennedy connections to join forces with Sinatra, Sammy Davis Jr., and Dean Martin in the finger-snapping Rat Pack that had its apotheosis in the famous crime-caper film *Ocean's Eleven*. By the time of the inauguration, the Lawfords had three children, and Pat was pregnant for the fourth time. Pat and Peter seemed like a golden couple, but their marriage was crumbling, and both had sought solace in alcohol and extramarital affairs.

Jack Kennedy visited their Spanish-style 10,000-square-foot Santa Monica beachfront home whenever he passed through on the campaign. Their parties invariably featured an array of film stars for JFK's amusement. Kennedy's fascination with Hollywood originated with his father's stint as a movie producer during the twenties and thirties. The Kennedy family grew up watching first-run movies in the basement screening room at Hyannis Port, and they knew about the Ambassador's "friendship" with Gloria Swanson, who swept into the Compound in her Rolls driven by a chauffeur in wine-colored livery with puttees. After the war, Jack spent time on the West Coast, where he befriended a number of actors and actresses, including Lawford.

"Why did [Gary] Cooper draw a crowd?" Kennedy would ask his friend Chuck Spalding, then a Hollywood screenwriter. JFK "was always interested in seeing whether he had *it*—the magnetism—or didn't have it." Before walking into a party, Kennedy would tell Inga Arvad, "OK now it's time to turn on the BP—Big Personality," and she would watch "that great big grin . . . knock everybody out." As Gore Vidal once observed, Kennedy "enjoyed the game of pleasing others, which is the actor's art."

SEVEN

"We went to the ceremony on a snow plow," recalled Diana Vreeland of the sparkling Kennedy inaugural. "It was *so* cold that day . . . and the snow was *that* thick—there wasn't a branch that wasn't entirely encrusted with ice. And of course there wasn't a sound. The monuments of Washington stood out in this *white* white atmosphere. But what I remember best is the blue of the sky . . . Washington that day was so *clean,* and the dome of the Capitol stood out against this *blue* sky—blue like a china blue. I'll never forget that blue—or that day."

Bill Walton was on hand to watch proudly as the "shining young couple" left Georgetown for the White House. Jackie wore another Cassini design, a wool coat and pillbox hat perched on the back of her head. The color was "greige," a soft blend of gray and beige, with a circle of sable at the neck. She carried a matching sable muff that Diana Vreeland had suggested because "I thought she was going to freeze to death. But I also think muffs are romantic because they have to do with *history.*"

As with the evening before, Jackie had chosen her understated costume for dramatic effect, to stand out from the women around her, all of whom, the *Washington Post* reported, "were coated in mink." "I just didn't want to wear fur," Jackie said. "Perhaps because women huddling on the bleachers always looked like rows of fur bearing animals." In the 22-degree chill, JFK removed his overcoat before standing to take the oath of office, a strong message of youthful fitness—although he was protected by thermal underwear beneath his formal clothing. He projected commanding serenity as well, despite understandable jitters. Before he walked onto the platform in front of the Capitol's East Front, Nancy Dickerson watched as "he whistled and rocked back and forth on his feet."

Kennedy's address was preceded by an innovative contribution by eighty-six-year-old Robert Frost. The poet had agreed to read his famous verse "The Gift Outright," and had composed a special preface praising JFK for "summoning artists to participate in the august occasions of the state." Inviting Frost was the idea of Arizona congressman Stewart Udall, JFK's choice for secretary of the interior. Frost and Udall were friends, and when Kennedy met with Udall about his post in the administration, Udall reminded the President-elect that Frost had been an outspoken supporter during the campaign. Udall thought Frost could take part by preparing "a poet's benediction." Kennedy considered for a moment and shrewdly replied, "It's a good idea, but we don't want to be like Lincoln at Gettysburg. He is a master of words. We don't want him to steal the show. Let him read a poem."

Up on the podium, the white-haired bard faltered, however. The strong wind blew the pages of his preface, and the sun's glare obscured the words. After reading three lines, he stopped, and despite Lyndon Johnson's gallant effort to shield the podium with a top hat, Frost could not go on. Instead, he recited "The Gift Outright" from memory in a resonant voice. The symbolism of his appearance was important, and it was backed up by the presence of more than fifty other scholars and artists including Robert Lowell, John Hersey, W. H. Auden, and John Steinbeck. Kennedy had invited the cultural luminaries at the suggestion of Washingtonian Kay Halle, and he was happily surprised by the stir caused by their inclusion. Combined with Jackie's inchoate plans announced earlier by Tish Baldrige, the inaugural marked the first step in elevating the arts to new prominence in the Kennedy court.

Jack Kennedy took only sixteen minutes to read his address of 1,355 words. He spoke firmly, compared to the day a year earlier when "with shaking hands and in a voice that quavered" he announced his intention to seek the presidency. As he had hoped, his ideas caught the nation's imagination. The *New York Times* drew a comparison with King Henry V's summons to his troops before Agincourt, which was one of Kennedy's favorite passages of Shakespeare. The newspaper's chief columnist, James "Scotty" Reston, pronounced the speech "remarkable . . . a revival of the beauty of the English language." Jackie was rhapsodic, calling it "so pure and beautiful and soaring that I knew I was hearing something great." She predicted it would "go down in history as one of the most moving speeches ever uttered—with Pericles' funeral oration and the Gettysburg address." Harry Truman was more pithy but no less impressed: "It was short, to the point, and in language anyone can understand. Even I could understand it—and therefore the people can."

Jack didn't kiss Jackie on the podium, as she had watched Dwight Eisenhower buss Mamie's right cheek eight years earlier. In a series of feature stories for the *Times-Herald,* Jackie had written about the Eisenhower inaugural with an eye for droll detail, noting that "Mrs. Truman sat stolidly with her gaze glued to the blimp overhead," that the special seats in the presidential box were "old kitchen chairs" covered in gilt paint, and that a workman said Mrs. Eisenhower would be "a prisoner of the Secret Service for the next four years."

TV viewers wrote letters protesting the apparent slight by JFK, not knowing the First Couple's aversion to showing their affection in public. "I was so proud of Jack," Jackie later told Molly Thayer. "But I could scarcely embrace him in front of all those people, so I remember I just put my hand on his cheek and said, 'Jack, you were so wonderful!' And he was smiling in the most touching and most vulnerable way. He looked so happy."

———

Three District of Columbia transit buses bearing signs saying "KENNEDY FAMILY" whisked the clan around town, while the First Couple, along with Bobby and Ethel, rode in the inaugural parade. The most poignant moment occurred when Jack and Jackie's bubbletop limousine approached the reviewing stand in front of the White House. Joe Kennedy stood and doffed his top hat in a crisp salute to the new president, and Jack quickly returned the gesture. "It was an extraordinary moment," recalled Eunice. "Father had *never* stood up for any of us before. He was always proud of us, but he was always the authority we stood up for." In his exuberance, Joe Kennedy then similarly honored Bobby, the other members of the cabinet, and finally Harry Truman.

Also significant was the presence of the 11th Duke of Devonshire and his wife, Deborah ("Debo"), the youngest of the famous Mitford sisters—"the first members of British nobility to attend an American President's inauguration," according to Doris Kearns Goodwin. They served as vivid reminders of the lost Kennedy children. Kathleen Kennedy had married the duke's brother Billy, the Marquess of Hartington, in May 1944. Kathleen's choice of a Protestant, albeit an aristocratic one, had tormented her mother ("a blow to the family prestige," Rose had called it), although Joe had accepted it with barely disguised pride.

Three months later, Joe Jr. died when the plane he was piloting exploded over the English Channel on a mission to destroy the concrete bunkers hiding Hitler's deadly V-1 rockets. The following month, Billy Hartington was cut down by a sniper's bullet in Belgium. Kathleen chose to continue living in England, and in 1948 she too was killed in a plane crash over mountains in southern France. She was buried in her adopted homeland, at Chatsworth, the vast estate of the Devonshires, who remained close to the Kennedy family. On inauguration day, they had a privileged position in the reviewing stand, right next to the President.

———

JFK could scarcely contain his excitement as he watched the parade and greeted guests escorted by aides to his front-row seat. Forty marching bands provided the day's pageantry, along with the entire corps of the Naval Academy and West Point. Reflecting the intermingled themes of the inaugural address, the parade slogan promised "World Peace through New Frontiers" (one float had a blue and white replica of the United Nations building), even as army tanks, A-4D and F-4H navy jets, and an array of missiles (Pershing, Lacrosse, Nike Hercules and Nike Zeus) glided by in a mirror image of Red Square parades. Jack Kennedy did a double take when a cowboy on a buffalo (looking, as one observer put it, "like a beatnik on an avant-garde horse") headed for the reviewing stand at full gallop, paused to chat, then thundered away.

As the parade wound down and the sky darkened, the new president spotted a float carrying an eighty-foot-long PT boat painted to simulate

PT-109, the craft he made famous with a daring rescue during World War II. His heroism had resulted from a tragic accident on a "pitch black night" in the Pacific when the wooden patrol boat he commanded was rammed by a 2,000-ton Japanese destroyer steaming at top speed out of the gloom. Despite the force of the collision and the engulfing fireball, eleven of the thirteen men survived and swam to an island, with Kennedy pulling a badly burned crew member in his wake. They were marooned forty miles behind enemy lines for four days as Kennedy sought help by swimming to nearby islands. He finally succeeded after encountering two natives working for the Allies who suggested he carve a message into a coconut that they could carry to their superiors.

Kennedy's dramatic exploits made instant headlines and inspired an acclaimed article by John Hersey in *The New Yorker.* The story of Kennedy's bravery helped define his political persona and became a crucial element in his ascent to the presidency. Lost in the myth was the fact that if Kennedy and his crew had been equipped with radar or had been more vigilant, the collision might have been avoided. For a commander, it was an embarrassing incident. Inga Arvad recounted that JFK didn't know whether the navy would "give him a medal or throw him out." But no one could deny Kennedy's courage, leadership, determination, and resourcefulness in the aftermath. The famous coconut, encased in plastic, would soon rest on his Oval Office desk, a reminder of his valor to all his visitors.

When the PT boat display passed, Kennedy waved excitedly to his loyal crewmen and summoned his two closest friends from navy days down from the rear of the reviewing stand to join him in the front row. Each of those fellow officers, Red Fay and Jim Reed, reflected an aspect of Kennedy's personality.

Fay bristled with energy, always ready with the wisecrack. He came from a West Coast version of JFK's Irish Catholic family: six children dominated by a hard-driving Republican businessman—the politically conservative owner of a construction company—whom Fay referred to as "The Battler" and Kennedy called "the great industrialist." A graduate of Stanford, Fay was one year younger than JFK.

Fay inhabited Kennedy's world purely for pleasure and amusement. "Kennedy liked people who were brash, as long as they were not rude," said journalist Rowland Evans, a close friend of Fay. "He loved the banter, and Red Fay had that." Fay found Kennedy's sense of fun irresistible. "His laugh kind of exploded," said Fay. "It was not loud, but it was so contagious it was difficult to stop."

Shortly after his election, Kennedy had offered Fay a job as under secretary of the navy. But following an interview with Robert McNamara, whom Fay regarded as a "coldly serious man," the new defense secretary vetoed the proposal. Despite an agreement to give complete appointment power to McNamara, Kennedy overruled his decision, and Fay got the job. Kennedy knew McNamara was right. Fay lacked the necessary experience to be the second-ranking civilian in the navy; he had supervised around a hundred employees at the family firm and the navy employed more than one million.

But Kennedy wanted Fay in Washington as a boon companion, and Fay was Bobby Kennedy's friend as well. "It was the only appointment," recalled Roswell Gilpatric, McNamara's top deputy, that was "really forced. . . . We just designed the administration of the department around Fay . . . [who] was sort of carved out of the action." Fay's Republican label similarly suited Kennedy because, Fay recalled, "it was good to show the President was open to different points of view." Not incidentally, Kennedy also expected Fay to feed him intelligence. "You're my pal," he told Fay, asking him to "keep me informed" about people in the Pentagon.

———

Kennedy likewise enlisted Jim Reed for his administration, appointing him first as one of Bobby's deputies, then as an assistant secretary of the Treasury. Reed was a Harvard-educated lawyer with a busy practice in Springfield, Massachusetts. He had helped Kennedy in all his campaigns, and for several years had joined Kennedy as an investor in the *Narragansett Times,* a Rhode Island newspaper. But Kennedy's friendship with Reed wasn't an obvious match.

Reed was soft-spoken, unassuming, and from a modest background. "Jack had so many people, maybe he looked to Jim for normalcy," said Reed's wife, Jewel. Reed's family had deep roots in western Massachusetts. During the Depression, his mother had kept the family afloat by working as a housekeeper. Reed was an exceptional athlete, which earned him a scholarship at Deerfield, Choate's chief rival. There and later at Amherst, he was a football, baseball, and basketball star, attracting offers to play with the Boston Red Sox and New York Giants.

JFK admired Reed's athleticism, but their real affinity was a love of history and poetry. "We had enormous rapport," said Reed. "Jack Kennedy saw himself as a hero figure, but in a modest way." Reed was a Republican, a "Yankee Protestant, poised to dislike Jack Kennedy," he said. "Instead I was totally taken in by him." Reed was captivated by Kennedy's unexpected humility, a "willingness to listen" that gave Reed confidence. "If someone like Jack thought I was okay," said Reed, "I couldn't be so bad. I could go toe to toe with him in intellectual discussion." Reed felt the power of Kennedy's charm, although JFK "was never assertive, but rather quiet and a trifle shy, oddly enough." Nor did Kennedy ever needle Reed as he did other friends. A student of Robert Burns, Reed described Kennedy's ability to view himself with critical detachment by citing one of the poet's famous lines: "Oh wad some power the giftie gie us / To see oursels as others see us!"

Jackie left the inaugural parade at 3:27 in a state of exhaustion. After declaring, "I'm not leaving until the last man has passed!", her husband stayed until 6:12, an hour after sunset. Keeping him company were the Johnsons, the Robert Kennedys, and the Dillons. Inside the White House, friends and family members thronged the state rooms for a chaotic "high tea" that featured stiff drinks for the chilled and weary. Eunice and Pat arrived arm in arm with Lem Billings, who had been traveling around with the Kennedy entourage. As they entered the front door, Lem remembered a scene from *Gone with the Wind* when Mammy and Prissy walked with Scarlett O'Hara into her new mansion. Imitating Prissy's wide stare and baby voice, Billings exclaimed, "Lawzy, we sho' is rich now!"

The giddy mood continued throughout the afternoon. Lem and Eunice went to the Lincoln Bedroom and bounced on the massive bed with its eight-foot-high headboard carved with exotic birds and clusters of grapes. Downstairs, Teddy Kennedy, "who had drunk a little more than usual, was dancing crazily on a platform," observed French ambassador Hervé Alphand.

Jackie's family, the Auchinclosses and the Bouviers, were behaving more decorously. The only absentee was Jackie's sister, Lee, who had given birth prematurely in New York to a daughter the previous August; after months of serious illness, the baby had finally come home to London in late December. Jackie's mother and stepfather, Janet and Hugh Auchincloss, were included in the various parties and luncheons but remained virtually invisible compared to the energetic Kennedys— which suited Janet's sense of WASP propriety. "Janet never pushed herself in any way," said her friend Jane Ridgeway. "She never sought the limelight."

The Washington of Janet Lee Auchincloss was the haven of cave dwellers, what Bill Walton called "the guardians of tradition, revered social customs, and carefully manicured pedigrees." Janet Auchincloss was an old-fashioned snob typical of her generation and class. The irony was that her own forebears were no more illustrious than the Kennedys. Her Irish Catholic grandparents had fled the potato famine, but Janet feigned a link to the prestigious line of Robert E. Lee. Jackie was mostly amused by her mother's pretensions. "She is just lace curtain Irish," Jackie told her friend Jessie Wood. Publicly, however, Jackie chose to avoid her Irish ancestry as well. Yet Jackie was more of a free spirit than her mother, tending to judge others by talent or accomplishment rather than social bona fides.

Janet's father, James T. Lee, built a prosperous Manhattan real estate empire by pioneering the construction of luxurious apartment buildings. He was a tough-minded tyrant who practiced boxing every afternoon with a personal trainer. As a businessman, Joe Kennedy considered Lee "the smartest old rooster" and "the top of the pack." But Jim and Margaret Lee were deeply estranged, and the tensions of their arid marriage made Janet insecure, despite having every material advantage. A governess taught her to speak fluent French, she learned to ride skillfully at the family's summer home in Easthampton, and she received a correct education at Miss Spence's School in Manhattan, although she dropped out of Barnard College after only two semesters.

Janet had escaped her father's domination by marrying John Vernou Bouvier III, the rakish Yale-educated stockbroker sixteen years her senior who was known as "Black Jack" for his carefully cultivated tan. The Bouviers had their own fictitious posture of nobility that Jackie promoted in her official biography with Molly Thayer. In fact, the first Bouvier in America had been a carpenter for Napoleon's brother Joseph Bonaparte. Both Jackie and her mother were ardent Francophiles (Janet insisted that French be spoken at the dinner table), and the French connection offered Jackie a vivid romantic association with the eighteenth-century world she so admired.

When Jackie's mother married Hugh Auchincloss three years after divorcing Black Jack, she found financial security as well as prestige; she immediately became the chatelaine of Hammersmith Farm and Merrywood. "Uncle Hughdie" had been married previously to two unstable women, so Janet's conventional domesticity suited him perfectly. Like Jack Bouvier, he was a stockbroker and Yale man, but he had the cushion of a Standard Oil inheritance as well as a law degree. He had also served in the Hoover and Coolidge administrations. Amiable and kindhearted, he financed Jackie's many advantages and earned her loyalty with his sturdy dependability. If her father evoked Rhett Butler, "Unk" was Jackie's Ashley Wilkes.

Frequently disparaged as a dim-witted buffoon by his bitter stepson Gore Vidal, Auchincloss was actually a serious bibliophile, a nineteenth-century club man who took refuge in reading. It was in his library at Merrywood that Jackie steeped herself in stories of America's founders, especially George Washington, whose "human qualities" she came to appreciate, according to her stepbrother Hugh D. ("Yusha") Auchincloss III. She once told Yusha that he would "be famous" for loving Merrywood as his home "like Washington & Mount Vernon." While her fondness for French history was more well known, her knowledge of Americana through her stepfather prepared her well for her role as First Lady.

Jackie had notified the press that because of her recuperation, she would "take short rest periods after each inauguration activity." But she hadn't anticipated the extent of her fatigue when she returned from the parade. She and Jack had been invited to dine at the home of George Wheeler, a friend of JFK's from Choate, and his wife, Jane, who had been active in the Citizens for Kennedy group. But when Jackie tried to get dressed, "I couldn't get out of bed," she told Molly Thayer. "I just didn't have one bit of strength left." Dr. Janet Travell, JFK's official White House physician, prescribed dinner in bed and a brown Dexedrine tablet to revive Jackie for the inaugural balls.

JFK returned from the Wheelers' at nine-thirty to collect Jackie. Wearing white tie and tails, he puffed on a cigar in the Red Room as he waited. Finally she arrived "breathlessly, in a gentle flurry," and "stood in the doorway poised as if for flight." She wore a slender white sheath that she had designed, with a shimmering strapless beaded bodice veiled with an overblouse of chiffon—once more intended to set her off from the big skirts that were traditional for inaugural balls.

The Kennedys followed a royal progress from one ball to the next. Their elegance and charisma seemed to immobilize onlookers, who stared in admiration. As they were leaving the second of five balls, "I just crumpled," Jackie recalled. "All my strength was finally gone, so I went home and Jack went on with the others."

In Kennedy's restless enthusiasm, he was unable to quit when the last ball ended at 2 a.m. His next activity was a nightcap at the home of Joe Alsop at 2720 Dumbarton Avenue in Georgetown. Earlier in the week, Alsop had hatched the idea for a post-ball party with Manhattan hostess Florence Pritchett Smith and Afdera Fonda, the former wife of Henry Fonda. "If the lights are on in my house, there will be champagne to be drunk," Alsop had told the women, who spread the word.

Flo Pritchett had been a girlfriend of JFK during the postwar years and remained his good friend. "Over a long period of time, it was probably the closest relationship with a woman I know of," said Chuck Spalding's wife, Betty. After a humble upbringing in Ridgewood, New Jersey, Flo had become an expert in what her friend Robin Chandler Duke called "the fascinating people of New York—movie stars and people in social life."

Brown-eyed and slender, Flo had been a model, a clothing designer for Bergdorf Goodman, a fashion editor for William Randolph Hearst Jr.'s *New York Journal-American,* and a host of *Leave It to the Girls,* a popular radio show featuring a half dozen women trading witticisms. By the time of the inaugural, Flo was forty years old and married to a man nearly two decades older, Earl E. T. Smith, a wealthy and solidly Republican Wall Street banker from Newport. He had known Jackie since her childhood and was friendly with the Kennedys in Palm Beach. From

1957 until Fidel Castro's overthrow of Fulgencio Batista in 1959, Earl had been Eisenhower's ambassador to Cuba.

Kennedy was captivated by Flo's effervescent personality and an endless supply of gossip. She had closely studied men and their needs, and her views struck a chord with JFK: "Man is by nature a polygamous creature," she once wrote, "a sensualist, an adventurer. . . . He dreams of a life in which a woman dedicates her time to stimulating his senses." Although she had been "very keen" on JFK, according to Robin Duke, their relationship had been more companionable than romantic. She was one of the few women who made him laugh; on her twenty-seventh birthday she had scribbled in JFK's appointment calendar: "Send Diamonds!"

Flo grew close to JFK's sisters Pat and Eunice, and befriended Jackie as well. Jackie was the only person outside the Smith family to attend Earl's swearing-in as ambassador to Cuba. When Flo asked for ideas on literary classics to read in Havana, Jackie traveled to Manhattan to buy and ship 150 volumes that Flo proclaimed "the best collection of English literature of anyone I know—outside of Jackie herself."

———

As he was leaving the Statler Hilton in his limousine, Kennedy spotted Red Fay, who was escorting Angie Dickinson, along with Kim Novak and an architect named Fernando Parra. In a gesture typical of his private impulsiveness, Kennedy said, "Why don't you jump in here and come out to Joe Alsop's with me?" When Fay agreed, Kennedy suddenly had second thoughts about public consequences, saying he could "just see the papers tomorrow," with accounts of the new president "speeding into the night" with a couple of movie stars. "Well, Redhead, for a moment I almost forgot that I was President of the United States," Kennedy said. "It has its advantages and restrictions, and this is one of the latter. Good night." Fay drove Dickinson and Novak back to their hotel and continued on to the home of Bobby and Ethel Kennedy. In later years there were persistent rumors that Kennedy had a sexual assignation with Angie Dickinson at the Alsop home. "Neither Angie nor Kim Novak went to Joe Alsop's," said Fay, adding that Dickinson had told him the sexual tryst story "was a total lie." Bandleader Peter Duchin, who attended Alsop's party, also said "there were

no Hollywood stars there. Angie was a friend, and I would have noticed her."

Yet one Alsop guest had reason to wonder about Kennedy's behavior
that evening. Helen Chavchavadze, a twenty-seven-year-old brunette
divorcée with two young daughters, had been involved with him since
the previous summer. She was the first cousin of John Husted, the man
Jackie had thrown over to marry Jack, as well as a classmate of Jackie's
sister, Lee, at Farmington. Helen Husted had left Bennington College
after two years to marry David Chavchavadze, the son of a Romanov
princess who had grown up in the palaces of St. Petersburg. During
four years in Berlin, where David worked for the CIA, Helen had
become fluent in Russian and German. "She was just gorgeous," said
Ben Bradlee, "totally pretty, well educated, and interesting." She was
also unconventional in her attitudes, with a mother who had graduated
from Oxford and served as "a role model of freedom and rebellion."

Helen had met JFK in the spring of 1959 when Jackie invited her to a
small dinner party in honor of Lee. Jack took a keen interest in Helen's
knowledge of Russia, pelting her with one question after another, finding out about her life and her thoughts. "He was not at that point flirtatious," she recalled. A year later, in the summer of 1960, Chavchavadze
was teaching part-time and finishing her college degree at Georgetown
University when she got a call from Charley Bartlett inviting her to a
dinner party. It turned out that Kennedy, who was then only weeks
away from the Democratic nomination, had specifically requested her
presence. After dinner, as she was driving home to Georgetown in her
Volkswagen beetle, JFK pulled up beside her in his white convertible.
"He followed me home," she said. "I had an affair with Jack, and it
began then."

She saw him a few times, and he once sent her a note from the campaign scribbled on Butler Aviation stationery saying he had been unable
to reach her but planned to see her the following week. "One of the reasons is to discuss the education matter," he wrote. "There are, however,
other reasons." "A little innuendo," Chavchavadze recalled. "I was surprised that he pressed me, but I was up for it too." Once JFK was
elected, she figured the affair was over. But when she saw him at Joe
Alsop's, she was surprised that "he was cold and negative. I remember
feeling neglected. It was the first time I realized I might not be the only
clandestine affair." She figured that "he may have snubbed me because

he was having an assignation with someone else. It would not have surprised me if he had done that. It was typical of him."

Kennedy had not in fact given up on Chavchavadze. A few weeks after the inauguration, he walked into her house, which was across the street from his church in Georgetown, with Florida senator George Smathers. "By his appearance he was saying, 'I am a free man. The Secret Service are not going to stop me,'" she said. "He was paying a call. It was broad daylight, and it was a statement: 'I will be free to see the women I want to see in the White House.'" Kennedy would invite her from time to time for intimate evenings when Jackie was away, and Jackie would include Chavchavadze on the guest lists for their dinner dances and small dinner parties—the last of which was nine days before the assassination. "I never knew if Jackie knew, but I felt uncomfortable about her," said Chavchavadze. "I always felt ambivalent and wanted to end it. . . . I was never someone who had extramarital affairs. It was not my style, but it was irresistible with Jack."

It seemed highly unlikely that Joe Alsop would knowingly condone a sexual liaison under his roof, given his intense affection for both Jack and Jackie. Alsop was a full-blown eccentric—"almost an artifact, the way he got himself up, and the picture he presented to the world," said Teddy White's wife, Nancy. Although he was only seven years older than JFK, Alsop had the sensibility of an earlier era. He was balding, and wore flamboyant spectacles with perfectly round black frames that rested on a large wedge of a nose. With his bespoke wardrobe (Savile Row suits and waistcoats, Lobb's shoes, silk shirts sewn in Milan), he had a dandified elegance singular among his journalistic contemporaries. Philip Graham, president of the *Washington Post,* vividly recalled first encountering Alsop at age thirty in his Georgetown garden, eating breakfast and wearing a "weirdly shaped and more weirdly colored kimono."

Joe Alsop spoke in equally dramatic fashion, his patrician accent sprinkled with "dear boy" and "darling" as he drank scotch and waved his cigarette holder. Many acquaintances suspected what a select group knew: Alsop was homosexual. During a trip to the Soviet Union in 1957 he had been entrapped by the KGB and photographed in flagrante with a young man. The Soviets had failed in their attempt to blackmail him into espionage, but he had been forced to reveal his behavior to the CIA and FBI. J. Edgar Hoover had shared the details with top members of the Eisenhower administration, and by 1960 the secret had filtered out into the political and journalistic community. "Joe was gay, and Jack Kennedy knew all about that," said Ben Bradlee.

Alsop showed no visible disquiet, however; he was protected by the instinctive arrogance of what Bradlee called an "exaggerated WASP" background. Alsop proudly referred to "cousin Eleanor" Roosevelt, and a portrait of Teddy Roosevelt, his grandmother's older brother, adorned the front hallway of his home. Alsop was a product of Groton and Harvard, where he drank far too much in the salons of the Porcellian.

Alsop presided over the liveliest table in Washington. (He would add a hostess in February 1961 by marrying Susan Mary Jay, the widow of his close friend Bill Patten; she entered the marriage knowing it would be platonic.) With the eye of a theatrical director, he cast his dinners with a scrupulous mix of politicians, diplomats, and scholars, commanded "general conversation," and sat at the head of the table, his chin cupped in both hands, peering out with a mixture of hauteur and keen curiosity.

As a columnist in the thirties for the *New York Herald Tribune,* Alsop had written scathingly about Joe Kennedy's advocacy of isolationism and appeasement. Alsop had never liked the Ambassador, whose cowardice during the Blitz—spending many nights at his country estate during the London bombings—"made my flesh crawl," he said. Alsop's columns had caused "a mortal quarrel" with Joe Kennedy, but JFK could ill afford to hold such a grudge. "I am not like [Jack] who makes up to the people who attack him," Joe Kennedy once told a friend.

In his imperious way, Alsop had dismissed JFK as a playboy when they first met in 1947 after Kennedy's election to Congress. It was only when Alsop returned to Washington in 1958 after a year in Paris that he saw Kennedy's potential and became one of his most ardent boosters. Since 1945, Joe had teamed with his younger brother Stewart, and they had ranked with Walter Lippmann, James Reston, and Arthur Krock as Washington's powerful columnists. The Alsops were fierce anticommunists, although the Yale-educated Stewart was a more measured voice who restrained Joe's alarmist tendencies. Joe "wears gloom like a toga," noted *Time.*

But their partnership dissolved in 1958 when Stewart joined the *Saturday Evening Post,* and Joe on his own grew more shrill and less influential. Although raised a Republican, Joe became a relentless critic of the Eisenhower administration's foreign policy and "stuffy and self-satisfied attitudes." To Alsop, the Kennedys promised excitement, glamour, and much-needed change.

Hitching his fortune to Kennedy rejuvenated Alsop's career as he turned fifty. "Joe Alsop was a fawner," said Tom Braden, Stewart's closest friend. "He picked the Kennedys as his property, and in a sense they were. They came to dinner when asked. They did things which Joe was striving for, and he became the 'in' columnist." By cultivating Alsop, Kennedy could neutralize the sharp voice that had stung his father and solidify important links to the Washington establishment.

Mutual benefits aside, Alsop and the Kennedys genuinely enjoyed each other. Jackie was intrigued by Joe's outrageous personality, his impeccable taste (she recalled one of his luncheons as "a voluptuous daydream . . . reliving every sip and bite—noisettes & mushroom rice & caviar & champagne"), and his expertise in art and archaeology. Alsop assumed an avuncular role with Jackie, offering her all sorts of practical advice—"when to put a touch more brown sugar in the crème brûlée"—as well as guidance about the role of First Lady. "Jackie was a Bouvier and an Auchincloss, so Joe would be enchanted with that," said Ben Bradlee.

Kennedy relished Alsop's acerbic wit, insights into the Roosevelts, and provocative arguments, including the "missile gap" theory—the notion that the United States was vulnerable to attack by Soviet long-range nuclear rockets—that JFK exploited in his presidential campaign. Like other prominent journalists, Alsop used his entrée to offer views on candidates for top administration positions, recommending moderates such as Dillon and seasoned diplomats David Bruce and George Kennan.

Joe Alsop particularly appreciated that JFK "enjoyed pleasure. . . . It was one of his attractive traits," which was why the new president wished to carry his enjoyment "a little longer" after the official festivities ended on inauguration night. Alsop had caught a ride with Peter Duchin and his date for that evening, Pam Turnure, not long before Kennedy instructed his driver to head for the columnist's home. "All the lights on the outside were on," Alsop recalled, and "Flo Smith and Afdera Fonda [were] beating on my door knocker in a determined manner." Alsop barely had time to break out the champagne and start the fire before "an endless stream of guests" emerged from a line of limousines. When Kennedy arrived, he stood "in the bright light," his hair flecked with snowflakes, his manner ebullient. Appropriately enough, Kennedy looked "like something on the stage."

As the new President entered, everyone awkwardly rose until he "made a small, almost imperceptible downward motion with his hand." He was hungry, so Alsop offered a bowl of terrapin stew, rich with butter and redolent of sherry, which the President politely declined, although he did drink some champagne. Kennedy mingled for more than an hour before heading back to the White House at 3:21 a.m. Alsop was disappointed by Kennedy's rejection of "the greatest of American delicacies." Still, "it hardly mattered. I soon observed that what he really wanted was one last cup of unadulterated admiration, and the people crowding my living room gave him that cup freely, filled to the brim."

EIGHT

*T*he mantra of Jack Kennedy's presidential campaign had been "let's get this country moving again," an expression of the impatience of Kennedy and his "New Frontiersmen." "The atmosphere bubbles and sparkles like champagne," said Avis Bohlen, the wife of veteran diplomat Charles Bohlen, "All these young alive faces bristling with a desire to get started." Their arrival heralded a change in style and tone—a cool, finger-snapping approach akin to the Hollywood Rat Pack—but not the sort of radical reforms that the New Dealers had ignited three decades earlier.

Eisenhower left office with a somber warning that the "military-industrial complex" threatened to dominate America's economy and government. For most of his presidency, the nation enjoyed peace and prosperity, a period viewed by the Kennedy forces as one of sleep-walking complacency. The economy, however, had slid into a recession early in 1960, and unemployment stood near 7 percent. The Soviet Union had become a full-blown nuclear power, and cast a military shadow over Europe, as well as Laos and other Third World countries where Khrushchev advocated "wars of national liberation." Two years earlier, thirty-two-year-old Fidel Castro had led a communist takeover of Cuba.

While Kennedy's inaugural address had foreshadowed a "long twi-light struggle" on the world stage, his first months as president were de-fined by sunnier themes of renewal and hope. Ike was seventy-one when he left office, and now the nation seemed intoxicated by the youth-ful vigor and glamour of the Kennedy crowd. "The glow of the White House was lighting up the whole city," Schlesinger observed. "Wash-ington seemed engaged in a collective effort to make itself brighter, gayer, more intellectual, more resolute. It was a golden interlude."

Jack Kennedy had a deep distrust of bureaucracies, which he consid-ered stubborn obstacles to presidential authority. He believed his own intelligence and charm could crack any problem and win over any opponent. Jackie liked to call her husband "an idealist without illu-sions." He avoided abstract theories, preferring to meditate "on action, not philosophy," said Ted Sorensen.

The Eisenhower White House worked along a military model, with tight discipline, tables of organization, and lines of command that fun-neled decisions through a strong chief of staff. Because Ike was elderly and inarticulate, Kennedy and his advisers assumed that forceful subor-dinates such as Chief of Staff Sherman Adams and Secretary of State John Foster Dulles had made the decisions. "President Kennedy was under the mistaken impression that was shared by all the liberal Dem-ocrats around him that Eisenhower was not in charge," said Douglas Dillon. "That was 100 percent wrong. Eisenhower did not advertise the fact that he decided everything."

Kennedy took a distinctly improvisational approach to his "ministry of talent." He slashed the size of the White House staff and literally reinvented the wheel, situating himself at the hub, with numerous spokes radiating out to his men. "I can't afford only one set of advisers," Kennedy told Richard Neustadt, who counseled him on White House reorganization. "If I did that, *I* would be on *their* leading strings."

To maintain control, Kennedy grasped all the strings himself. The aim, said Neustadt, was "to get information in his mind and key deci-sions in his hands reliably enough and soon enough to give him room for maneuver." Kennedy often gave the same assignment to several people, "unimpressed," Neustadt noted, "by the emotional costs of duplication." Kennedy said he wanted the "clash of ideas" and "the opportunity for choice." In his compartmentalized fashion, Kennedy preferred to operate one on one, or in small "task forces" assigned to address specific problems. Not only did Kennedy insist on direct access to all his top advisers and cabinet officers, he felt free to dip into the bureaucracy and jump official channels to quiz experts on particular issues. He was the first president, said CIA official Richard Helms, to "deal up and down the line."

Such an ad hoc system placed a significant burden on Kennedy to set the agenda and ask the key questions. He also needed to exert "enormous energy to maintain these bilateral ties and [be] prepared to see a staggering number of people," said Walt Rostow, deputy special assistant for national security affairs. Kennedy had to "carry on endless guerrilla warfare with everyone around him to make sure they weren't closing out options that he wanted to keep open." According to Sorensen, on an ordinary day Kennedy would be "on the phone more than 50 times . . . with a large portion of the calls taking place in the mansion before and after his hours in the office."

Kennedy's belief in the "great man" theory of history helped shape his approach. JFK had studied the European and American past, including the writings of Winston Churchill and what Teddy White characterized as an "astonishing" list of American historians. As the author of *Profiles in Courage,* JFK considered himself an amateur historian as well. According to Jackie, Kennedy "read and reread" books on American statesmen: Henry Clay, John Calhoun, Daniel Webster, John Randolph, and John Quincy Adams. (The first book JFK gave to Jackie was *The Raven,* Marquis James's biography of Sam Houston.) Kennedy "was dubious about the theory of great historical tides that no person can change—economic, political or otherwise," said Ted Sorensen. As Schlesinger put it, "Kennedy felt individuals could make a difference for history, and within limits could make a great difference. He thought Churchill and Franklin Roosevelt were examples. He thought he would like to be like that."

———

Most of Kennedy's men clustered in the surprisingly modest West Wing, a warren of rooms with low ceilings and narrow corridors, although Bundy and Johnson worked out of spacious and airy quarters in the Executive Office Building next door. Arthur Schlesinger was dispatched to an office on the other side of the Executive Mansion amid Jackie's staff in the East Wing—a setting that reminded Galbraith of "the reception room in a Radcliffe dorm."

At lunchtime, the New Frontiersmen gathered in the White House Mess, a small dining room seating thirty-five in a corner of the basement. On white linen tablecloths set with silver cutlery and china rimmed in gold, they ate simple fare (Salisbury steak, omelettes, fish chowder—served by the quart) prepared by navy chefs. Each presidential adviser also had his own monogrammed silver napkin ring. The atmosphere was distinctly masculine, with nautical prints on the walls, lamps with eagle bases, and spare flower arrangements of daisies and fern in slender vases. Only two women had full privileges: Tish Baldrige, who occasionally appeared to "snow" a visitor, and Kennedy's longtime secretary Evelyn Lincoln, who was too busy to walk downstairs. She always ate at her desk, from a tray sent up by the navy men.

During the early days, Kennedy wandered through the West Wing maze to see where everyone was situated—at one point getting lost in a "complex little area when [he] kept going around in circles and . . . ending up in the same place." After an Oval Office meeting, he offered to take Galbraith to the mansion for a tour—and promptly marched "headlong into a closet."

For display in the Oval Office, Bill Walton found a model of the frigate *Constitution* and two paintings of the ship in battle. Kennedy spent time "hanging pictures of things he loved," recalled Jackie, and "setting out his collection of whale's teeth"—antique scrimshaw pieces, many of them chosen by Lem Billings. At Jackie's direction, JFK's office was transformed from "austere formality" to the ambiance of a "New England sitting room" with the arrangement of two sofas and a mahogany coffee table in front of the fireplace.

Even after he had been on the job for more than a month, Kennedy was "still restless," Salinger reported to Teddy White. "He paces all over the White House, up and down. He visits everywhere." Staff members were stunned to discover JFK one morning in the mail room "opening letters himself and writing instructions across them." Kennedy would stroll into the Rose Garden or drop by the press office, picking up books from desks along the way. When the President addressed press aide Barbara Gamarekian by name, she returned to her post "sort of floating on a little pink cloud."

Kennedy fostered an almost feudal loyalty among his top aides, all of whom remained with him to his death. John Steinbeck once asked Walt Rostow to explain "how Kennedy generated love." Rostow described a "repressed but powerful affection" among his aides that was "unspoken," "went both ways," and was "amusing, dry and understated" rather than backslapping and demonstrative. The Kennedys prided themselves on sticking with their friends and demanded 100 percent loyalty in return. In the White House the most stalwart loyalists were two men who had served with Kennedy the longest, David Francis Powers and Kenneth Philip O'Donnell.

Walking into the West Wing with the President for the first time "was like being Alice in Wonderland," recalled Powers. "He looked ten feet tall to me, and he seemed to grow every day." That unabashed admiration had taken root during Kennedy's first campaign for Congress in 1946. Stamped by his privileged background, Kennedy needed a well-connected "townie" to help him engage the man on the street, and Powers, the son of a coal miner turned dockworker, was perfect for the role.

Powers's parents had been born in County Cork; his father died when he was only two. To help support his mother and seven siblings, Powers went to work at age ten hawking newspapers at the Boston Navy Yard, putting in shifts before and after school. Following high school, Powers did census surveys for a publishing company, and during World War II he mapped bombing targets in China for the Flying Tigers commanded by Colonel Claire Chennault, for whom Joe Alsop served as an aide-de-camp.

Powers, who was described by *Newsweek* as an "irrepressible leprechaun," perched at a desk in the West Lobby, where visitors routinely arrived. The bald and ruddy aide put guests at their ease and escorted them to their appointments. Five years older than the President, he was part entertainer, part nanny, part valet. He knew nearly every detail of JFK's daily routine—what he ate, what he read, when he bathed.

By enlisting Powers, JFK was emulating his father, who "always had someone like a court jester around him," observed Rose Kennedy, "someone witty, light hearted; but faithful, loyal, and with sense enough to keep his mouth closed under all circumstances." While the Kennedy family may have recognized Powers's value, they underestimated his savvy. Behind his cheery facade, he was shrewd and resourceful, with a gift for sizing up character. In their first encounter, Powers astutely recognized that JFK was "aggressively shy," meaning that "he always got what he wanted," persistently but diffidently, through a series of questions.

It was no secret that Powers was on the White House staff only to make the President happy, and to be available for that purpose anytime. With his gentle voice—a lilting tenor with broad Bostonian inflections drawing out the last words of sentences for emphasis—Powers was a born raconteur. Whether soaking in his bath for "tub talk" or relaxing in his rocking chair, Kennedy loved to hear Powers's quips—the patrician Massachusetts Republican senator Leverett Saltonstall was "Irish on his chauffeur's side"—along with tales of Chinese peasants during World War II, the delights of the "Morning Glory" baseball league of Powers's working-class youth, an endless supply of sports statistics, and instant replays of elections and vote tallies.

Like Lem Billings, Powers had a dispensation from Kennedy to make outrageous comments that nobody else would attempt—announcing the Shah of Iran as "my kind of Shah." (Lem quite resented Powers, dismissing him as "a nice employee" that JFK "enjoyed," but he "wasn't as I was.") Powers called everyone "pal," and some White House aides were annoyed by the habitual humming that would signal Powers's arrival around the curve of the main West Wing corridor. "He was a perennial jokester," said Barbara Gamarekian. "It was almost demeaning to the President to find solace with someone like that." Even Jackie "thought he was crude," said Tish Baldrige, "although she couldn't be uncivil to him because he was popular." Jackie understood, as Tish explained it, that both Powers and Billings were "friends from the past who made Jack comfortable in the present."

Kenny O'Donnell was the flip side of Powers: a dour and intimidating presence who could often be found leaning against a wall, arms folded across his chest. O'Donnell had a hard face, his black eyes compressed into slits, his thin lips set impassively, his manner inscrutable. Few knew that he carried a concealed gun. He spoke sparingly, smiled fleetingly, and developed what William Manchester called "quiet almost fanatical devotion" to Kennedy. Joe Dolan, an aide to JFK, recalled encountering O'Donnell during the floor demonstration for Adlai Stevenson at the 1960 convention. "A lot of noise, huh?" Dolan remarked. Without bothering to shift his gaze from the crowd, O'Donnell said nothing, then finally growled, "Last gasp."

O'Donnell had come to JFK's 1952 Senate campaign by way of Bobby Kennedy, a football teammate at Harvard. Wiry and small like Bobby, Kenny was the superior athlete. He was the varsity quarterback and captain while Bobby was a scrappy benchwarmer. O'Donnell had grown up in Worcester, Massachusetts, the son of the football coach at Holy Cross College. He went to war at age nineteen after high school, serving in Britain as a bombardier in the Eighth Air Force, flying thirty missions.

When O'Donnell matriculated at Harvard in 1945, he was an authentic war hero. He and Bobby shared as much enthusiasm for debating as for football. O'Donnell was a mediocre student; only a photographic memory enabled him to slide through by cramming at the last minute. After Harvard, he halfheartedly studied law at Boston College, until the Kennedys lured him into politics.

"Kenny's genius was simply that his mind worked like a computer," said John Seigenthaler, an aide to Bobby Kennedy. "He never took notes, ever. It was all in his head." O'Donnell traveled everywhere with Jack, and helped organize campaign logistics with Bobby, who had become his closest friend.

It was a given that O'Donnell would assume a comparable role in the White House. Not only did the thirty-six-year-old assistant oversee Kennedy's daily schedule, he supervised the West Wing staff (which included access to the FBI's investigative files), coordinated all travel and security matters for the President, and functioned as an all-round political adviser.

O'Donnell took up a sentry position, "hovering, grim-faced," said Charley Bartlett, at his desk in an office just beyond the West Lobby, accessible to visitors through the West Gate on Pennsylvania Avenue. He was decisive and crisp, with little patience for small talk or courtesies. He spoke in grunts, "with his gut," said Nancy Dutton, a White House aide.

His door to the Oval Office was the main route to the President, but plenty of friends and aides subverted his tight grip by going through Kennedy's secretary Evelyn Lincoln, located on the other side of the

Oval Office—accessible by entering the White House through the East Gate. With her helmet of black hair, harlequin glasses, and prim shirt-waist dresses, Lincoln wore a deceptive mask of Nebraskan naïveté. But in her disarming fashion, she was also sharp-eyed and efficient, with a strong instinct for self-preservation. Years earlier Kennedy had tried to dismiss her (a task he always hated), but he had been so oblique in his message that she had simply appeared the next day anyway. "I thought I fired her, but she's still here," Kennedy told Sorensen. Lincoln bur-rowed in and made herself indispensable: she was one of the few who could read Kennedy's scrawl. O'Donnell considered Lincoln's access route an affront to his authority, but its flexibility suited Kennedy, so O'Donnell kept his resentment to himself.

Jack Kennedy held just one meeting of his White House staff "to talk about leaks to the press," recalled Sorensen. In Kennedy's view, staff meetings only stirred up trouble by allowing aides to air their dif-ferences. Following Neustadt's advice, Kennedy also did away with regular sessions of the National Security Council and disbanded the council's staff support groups—a move that eliminated a rich source of analysis from agencies and departments. Weekly cabinet meetings, which Kennedy considered "a waste of time . . . like bull sessions," also disappeared.

When Kennedy did call his cabinet together, he went through the motions, declining even to banter, much less ask advice. Four cabinet officials—McNamara, Rusk, Dillon, and Bobby Kennedy—saw JFK constantly. The remaining six formed an outer circle—Stewart Alsop called them "curious dim figures"—that had infrequent contact and felt frozen out. "We didn't even have clearance to see secret documents," recalled Stewart Udall, secretary of the interior. Udall called himself "the Gardener" and made the most of his opportunity "to work without adult supervision," developing initiatives that would stimulate the envi-ronmental movement of subsequent decades.

The White House atmosphere was what Sorensen called "hard driv-ing but easy mannered." With the exception of the notably formal Dean Rusk, who was "Mr. Secretary," and presidential secretary Evelyn Lincoln, who was "Miz Lincoln," Kennedy called everybody by their first names. Secretaries who had worked in the White House for years suddenly found themselves on a first-name basis with their bosses as well. Yet Kennedy had "enough of a remoteness about him," said Barbara Gamarekian, "that you didn't infringe on the fact that he was informal."

A handful of key aides—O'Donnell, Sorensen, Bundy, and Salinger—saw Kennedy several times a day, with no particular pattern to their contacts. Kennedy liked his advisers to be "quick, tough, laconic, decided people" who gave him fresh information and insights. He disapproved of anyone dull, prolix ("more than thirty seconds," said Marcus Raskin, an aide to Bundy, with only mild exaggeration), ideological, earnest, or emotional. His preferred time frame for meetings was fifteen minutes, and few lasted more than an hour, according to Sorensen. Although Kennedy promoted an informal ambiance, the White House "was terribly taut," said Isaiah Berlin. "Everyone was walking some kind of tightrope, and was very excited to do so. People were always terrified of slipping in some sort of way."

The British journalist Barbara Ward described Kennedy as "a stimulant. He wasn't a communicator. He was making up his own mind but he wanted to use everybody to the full . . . not to exploit them but just to get everything that was in their minds, get it absolutely clear to himself." Instead of a conversation, Kennedy would probe with questions at trip-hammer speed, often jumping to the next query before his interlocutor had finished the answer. "He often cut short others," said Sorensen, "no matter how important or friendly."

As a listener, Kennedy was simultaneously seductive and intimidating. He would "lean forward, his eyes protruding slightly," taking in every word. Having caught the drift quickly, he would betray his impatience by drumming his fingers or fidgeting with his tie. He sometimes asked "exactly what the words mean." He had little tolerance for grand pronouncements, persiflage, or loose talk. "Never even in conversation did he speak for the pleasure of hearing his own words and phrases," said Galbraith, and he was "impatient with wordy men," a "rare case," the economist added, of a politician applying rules "with equal rigor against himself."

Kennedy was careful to keep his own counsel, on the assumption that if he expressed his opinion he would inhibit the advice from his aides. He was open to "contrary arguments, sometimes very unpleasant ones," said David Ormsby Gore. As Kennedy confided to Gore, "One of the rather sad things about life is you discovered the other side really had a very good case." Kennedy listened until he was confident of his own views. "It was his habit," said Joe Alsop, "a very good habit for a political leader, not to make very grave decisions until they had to be made. He always left questions open until they were required to be closed."

Henry Luce once said Kennedy had a "beautiful mind"—and even Soviet foreign minister Andrei Gromyko described the President as "acute" and "penetrating." He had what Alsop called an "aptitude for facts" and an "interest in how things worked." Kennedy's curiosity was wide ranging, but he was not known for originality. As Gromyko put it, Kennedy was "a good catalyst and consumer of other ideas and thoughts." For that reason, he relied heavily on picking the brains of his advisers. One of his most memorable quips, that Washington was "a city of southern efficiency and northern charm," came from Amherst political science professor Earl Latham, an early member of JFK's "Academic Advisory Committee." Latham made the crack to Sorensen, who passed it to then-Senator Kennedy, who popularized it. "Kennedy's genius," said Sorensen, "was in recognizing that a line from an obscure source was accurate as well as deft and funny."

Kennedy had a remarkable memory, tossing out quotes and recalling tiny details. He kept a commonplace book—a small black leather volume filled with quotations that he began collecting before World War II. His apparent effortlessness resulted from calculated and determined application. "I'll read [an article]," Kennedy once revealed, "then I'll force myself to lie down for about a half hour and go through the total article in my mind, bringing to memory as much as I possibly can, analyzing the article, and then attacking it and tearing it down." He read voraciously (although not profoundly, as Joe Alsop would patronizingly point out), propping up a book on his bureau as he dressed or sometimes taking a volume to read as he walked.

But even his reading was purposeful, less for diversion, as Schlesinger explained, than for "information, comparison, insight, and the joy of felicitous statements." He habitually reached for biography and history—including such obscure texts as an exploration of economic dissent in Burma—although Henry Luce was once surprised to see him with one of Benjamin Disraeli's "two or three once-famous novels" that "probably a half dozen" people had read in the previous decade. Two of Kennedy's favorite works were by British writers: John Buchan's *Pilgrim's Way,* "a journal of certain experiences," and *Melbourne,* David Cecil's portrait of Whig England.

———

Richard Neustadt recalled that Kennedy "did not go out of his way to put people off balance," and exhibited "no sadism" as Franklin Roosevelt frequently did when pitting his men against each other. But Kennedy did promote creative tension among his staff. When he hired Dillon, for example, Kennedy explained that he also had to appoint Walter Heller, a liberal economist from the University of Minnesota, as chairman of the Council of Economic Advisers "to protect myself politically." Kennedy said he wanted to "give Heller more public exposure," while reassuring Dillon, "You are my chief financial adviser." At the same time, Kennedy was telling Heller that he was a necessary "counterweight" to Dillon's "conservative leanings." Kennedy was more candid with Dillon than with Heller. Dillon understood that "Heller was supposed to represent the left wing and make it appear that Kennedy was more interested than he was." Heller, however, never quite understood his role because he believed Kennedy when "he made Walter think he was going to be very important," said Dillon.

Kennedy wouldn't put up with complaining or overt displays of jealousy, so his inner circle had to present a facade of collegial bonhomie: "all the eggheads . . . in one basket," as Harold Macmillan put it. Merriman Smith, UPI's White House correspondent, once noted that Schlesinger walked slowly and tilted forward, while Bundy moved fast and leaned back: "When Bundy passed Schlesinger they formed in profile a perfect X." Sorensen and his deputy, Myer Feldman, even traded memos in rhymed couplets.

Below the surface, rivalries were inevitable. Ken Galbraith griped about the lack of "political buccaneers like Ickes," and Ambassador to Britain David Bruce pronounced Under Secretary of State Chester Bowles "an incompetent long-winded bore." Several months into the administration, veteran political adviser James Rowe told Teddy White that the White House staff "should be spanked" for its "loose talk about policy and colleagues." The intellectuals, he noted, were "giddy with power." Sorensen would later acknowledge that among the "aggressive individualists" surrounding Kennedy, there were "scornful references to political and intellectual backgrounds."

With his vague role and White House office in the equivalent of Siberia, Arthur Schlesinger encountered the most trouble fitting in. He had the "soft jackets and easy shoes" look of the intellectual, accented by a domed forehead and a pouty expression that seemed to suggest arrogance. "You have to understand that Arthur was over in the East Wing drinking tea with Jackie," said one White House aide. Jackie actually spent little time with her staff in the East Wing. But she did periodically enlist Schlesinger's help, and he was happy to oblige—which eventually gave him an enviable status.

Still, in February, Schlesinger told Galbraith that he was "unhappy and uncertain" in his job. "Arthur was always worried about his position," said Ben Bradlee. An assignment from Kennedy to study Latin America gave Schlesinger a new purpose, and he began to enjoy operating behind the scenes in an unrestrained fashion that kept him close to the power center. "There were frustrating moments," he said. "But I had great flexibility."

In the early evening, Schlesinger would make his way through the corridors and colonnades to the Oval Office to join other aides eager for the chance to have unstructured moments with Kennedy. It was Kennedy's favorite time, when he would sit with his two feet on the desk—what Mac Bundy called "bivouacking in his chair"—laid back and expansive, reflecting on the day's events with "that wonderfully spare, precise, coherent talk that was natural to him," recalled Walt Rostow. With Schlesinger present—and for that matter Sorensen and Rostow—Kennedy was consciously speaking for history. "They were meditations," said Schlesinger. "Jack Kennedy was a very impersonal man, objective and analytical, reviewing his own performance as if he were talking about someone else. He had a high degree of self knowledge, more than most people in politics."

NINE

While the family's second-floor quarters were being renovated, Jack stayed in the Lincoln Bedroom, and Jackie set up her headquarters in the Queen's Bedroom across the hall—a "dark and dreary" chamber she described as "the approximate size of a field in which we would turn Man O'War out to pasture." On the day after the inauguration, Kennedy brought Harry Truman upstairs for a visit after a courtesy call in the Oval Office. The two men found Jackie resting, "propped up in the enormous canopied bed, warmed by a pretty bed jacket, her hair covered with a frivolous little cap." An embarrassed Truman blurted out that when his mother stayed in that room, "the big bed scared her."

After the exertions of the inaugural events, "I couldn't get out of bed for about two weeks," Jackie recalled. She often made such remarks for dramatic effect. In fact, Jackie left her room frequently. Wearing a casual white shirt, jodhpurs, and low riding boots, she propped herself on a large desk to greet the entire White House staff. She took walks around the sixteen acres of grounds, poked through storerooms, removed "horrors" from the state floor, met with designers and consultants, and entertained friends. "We've got a lot of work ahead," she said with a "conspiratorial twinkle" to J. B. West, the Executive Mansion's house-hold manager, known as the "chief usher." "I want to make this into a grand house!"

With the children away until early February, Jackie was able to focus entirely on designing her new role. The previous August, when she had been despondent over "the conflict between what is properly private and the common demand to make every thing public," Joe Alsop had written her a long letter of advice, offering the example of Helen Taft as a first lady who had found "the most stylish and most effective solu-tion. . . . She did everything that could be useful and that involved no fakery or real loss of dignity. . . . As a result, she was a far greater polit-ical asset than any politician's wife I have known who was not a major active politician in her own right" like "Cousin Eleanor."

Jackie thanked him for his "very perceptive" counsel. "There is one more thing you have taught me," she wrote, "to respect power. . . . If things turn out right—I will welcome it—and use it for the things I care about." Despite her youth and what Arthur Schlesinger called her "veil of lovely inconsequence," Jackie was fully capable of acting on her words. "Her social graces," noted Schlesinger, "masked tremen-dous awareness, an all-seeing eye, ruthless judgment, and a steely purpose."

Nor was that determination anything new. Two years earlier, the tough-minded liberal columnist Doris Fleeson had expressed pity to Democratic activist Katie Louchheim that Jackie had been "caught in this maw of ambition, pushed into this role of wife to a ruthless man, this inexperienced girl brought up without preparation for the fate awaiting her, rich, shielded, so unarmed." But Louchheim understood that Fleeson had been fooled by the "disarming" manner of a "young thing," and that Jackie was "fully aware" of her "protective air of inno-cence" and knew "precisely what [she was] into and how to handle it besides." An early feminist, published poet, and "57-year-old grand-mother," as described by the New York Times, Louchheim was a savvy interpreter of the Washington scene. She had been educated at Choate's sister school, Rosemary Hall, spoke several foreign languages, and was married to a wealthy investment counselor. While not an intimate of the Kennedys, she counted many of their courtiers among her friends and kept a colorful journal of her observations.

Jackie was rigorously selective in her White House activities. "I was tired & I wanted to see my children," she confided to Bill Walton, "so I just told Tish—who nearly died from the shock—that I would NEVER go out—lunches, teas, degrees, speeches etc. For two months there was a flap. Now it is a precedent established." She had been advised that there were "ninety-nine things that I had to do as First Lady," and she later proudly boasted to her friend Nancy Tuckerman that she had not "done one of them."

What sounded like stubborn negativism actually allowed her to expand the First Lady's role beyond its traditional boundaries. She was fundamentally a conventional wife who knew, as she told Nellie Connally after JFK's death, "where a woman's place is—secondary to the man." Jackie said to Hugh Sidey that she felt "compassion for women who could not find enough in their husbands to stimulate them and interest them so that they themselves had to seek power and dominance."

Yet she was advanced in her tastes and attitudes. Since her girlhood she had been intellectually confident and mature beyond her years, conspicuous for her "great presence and control." At age sixteen, when Yusha Auchincloss, her eighteen-year-old stepbrother, told her she seemed conceited, she replied, "I really don't think I am better than other people, Yush—It just must be something I do that I don't know about." After spending her junior year in Paris, she had refused to return to Vassar, which she disliked, wishing she had gone to Radcliffe instead. She opted to finish her degree in the urban and coeducational environment at George Washington University because "I did not want to live like a little girl again."

"Jackie had a certain quality of mystery about her," said Oleg Cassini, "an aura she succeeded in maintaining. People did not usually know what she was thinking or what she was doing behind the scenes—and she wanted to keep it that way." As early as age fifteen she believed, as she advised Yusha Auchincloss, that once "you know every-thing" about a woman, "all your interest in her is gone." Jackie liked nostalgic clothes, she wrote in one of her *Vogue* essays, because they "make you feel quite secretly mysterious." Cassini saw her as "sphinx-like"—no accident, since the mythical figure was a crucial part of her identity.

Jackie's favorite statue depicts Madame de Pompadour as a sphinx—an image she arranged to have reproduced on a trompe l'oeil wardrobe in her White House bedroom painted with the beloved symbols of her life. "A sphinx is rather what I feel like when I go out with you," Jackie once told Adlai Stevenson following a week in which the UN ambassador squired her around New York. As Richard Avedon observed after photographing her for *Harper's Bazaar,* "She has a great deal in common with top movie stars. She knows when to hold herself back while everyone else you know gives too much of themselves at one time."

Both of Jackie's predecessors had embraced the official activities of the First Lady: obligatory functions with congressional wives and members of ladies' clubs. As a general's wife, Mamie Eisenhower had been particularly comfortable with large-scale formal entertaining, and had filled her spare time with TV soap operas and card games with friends. Bess Truman had defined herself in deliberate contrast to the politically active and opinionated Eleanor Roosevelt, saying "a woman's place in public is to sit beside her husband, be silent, and be sure her hat is on straight." Yet Bess also went home to Independence, Missouri, for months at a time and famously gave no interviews to the press—not even in writing. She was prickly but gracious, and emphatically set in her ways.

Bess Truman was the First Lady Jackie most admired, mainly because "she kept her family together in the White House regardless of the limelight that suddenly hits a President." But Bess also set a precedent for Jackie to go her own way—an approach even Janet Auchincloss applauded, noting that "it is very silly to try to behave as you think people expect you to, because then you become simply a colorless creature."

In her first weeks in the White House, Jackie spent time "organizing things as well as Field Marshal Rommel ever did" so she would have the "unfettered" life she preferred. The key to her success was finding the right people to deal with her unwanted chores, giving good direction, and then providing "overall unified supervision." The whole structure, Jackie told Bill Walton, showed her understanding of "the use of power that Joe Alsop used to lecture me about."

From the outset Jackie wanted to bring her oldest friend, Nancy Tuckerman, into the White House. Brunette and blue eyed but slightly mousy in both appearance and temperament, "Tucky" was to Jackie what Lem was to Jack: fiercely loyal and dazzled by Jackie's "charismatic presence." Tuckerman was a product of Manhattan and Southampton society, where she learned to play "all the accepted games competently." They had met at the Chapin School as nine-year-olds, when Jackie was known as much for her "distinctive looks and magnificent thick braids" as for her naughtiness.

Jackie and Tucky parted company when Jackie moved to Washington after her mother's remarriage, but the girls were reunited at Farmington, where they roomed together and formed what Tuckerman described as "a special bond of friendship." "Nancy knew everything," said Janet Felton Cooper, a friend of both women since childhood. "She knew all Jackie's feelings. There wouldn't have been anybody else but Nancy she would share that with." Quiet and somewhat withdrawn, Tuckerman was attracted to Jackie's "intelligence, wit, and sense of the ridiculous," she recalled. "You never could be bored when you were with Jackie, because you never knew quite what to expect from her."

Jackie was the provocateur, and Nancy the appreciative audience. At Farmington they would sneak off with a radio and cigarettes in a buggy drawn by Jackie's horse Donny. When Jackie decided to teach Nancy to ride—against school regulations—"she had me walk under Donny's belly 20 times a day," recalled Tuckerman, "to get over my fear of horses." They remained close in college and through the round of debutante balls and house parties as well as Jackie's marriage. When the Kennedy administration began, Tuckerman was working in New York as a travel agent. Jackie asked her to help with the White House restoration, but Tuckerman said she was happy where she was and couldn't leave. Jackie considered Nancy's response a temporary setback and continued to look for a suitable position.

It fell to Tish Baldrige to take on the most important of the First Lady's tasks. But Jackie also credited herself with having managed to "diabolically figure out" that Pam Turnure would be someone "who answers every question exactly as I would . . . so we don't even communicate for weeks on end." In drawing this velvet curtain across her life, Jackie gave explicit instructions to Turnure and never abandoned them during her tenure.

She told Turnure she had been chosen "for the very reason that you haven't had previous press experience" and for her "sense and good taste," unlike the "tub-thumping . . . highpowered girl" recommended by Salinger. She wanted Turnure to be "a buffer"—not to publicize but to "shield our privacy." Sensing that "you are rather like me," Jackie expected Turnure to be "fairly anonymous" and avoid interviews as well as stray comments in her private life. The credo would be "minimum information given with maximum politeness." Jackie left it to Turnure to explain away a promised press conference. "Just tell them it won't be for awhile," said Jackie, adding, "take lots of vitamins poor Pam."

In her new role, Jackie was able to impose her urbane sensibility on the national consciousness—serving as a model as well as a catalyst. As Diana Vreeland wrote, "Jackie Kennedy put a little style into the White House, and into being First Lady of the land, and *suddenly* 'good taste' became good taste. Before the Kennedys 'good taste' was never the point of modern America at all."

The White House restoration was the most obvious symbol of Jackie's reinvented role—"the stage on which the drama of the Kennedy Administration was played." Jackie had decided that the "President's House" would focus on 1802, when the White House was completed during Jefferson's presidency. She was enchanted by the Francophile third president because he "had such wonderful taste and selected per-fectly beautiful furniture. But the sad thing was that the War of 1812 came along and then everything was burned."

Obtaining high-quality antiques, art, and accessories was para-mount, and Jackie moved quickly to assemble a committee of wealthy collectors to help her—the Fine Arts Committee for the White House. Jackie's most important decision was to appoint eighty-year-old Henry Francis du Pont as chairman of the group—the suggestion of Wilmarth Sheldon "Lefty" Lewis, a noted collector of rare books and manu-scripts who was married to Uncle Hughdie's sister Annie. The Lewises lived in Farmington and had been intellectual mentors to Jackie when she was at Miss Porter's. Lewis was close to du Pont, and a trustee of Winterthur, the thousand-acre du Pont estate in Delaware whose man-sion had been turned into a museum with more than 175 rooms of Americana—the finest collection in the nation. The involvement of a prestigious connoisseur such as du Pont conferred instant legitimacy on Jackie's project.

Du Pont was shy and slightly deaf, but he didn't hesitate to "snap the whip," said Janet Felton Cooper, who served as secretary to the Fine

Arts Committee. Jackie's aides had to meticulously plan his visits from the minute he arrived in what he called "my cozy little Rolls." "He would leave and we would have our tongues hanging out," said Cooper. Du Pont initially agreed with Jackie's stylistic focus on the grounds that the decorative arts at the turn of the nineteenth century "reflect so eloquently the social, political and economic aspirations of the new, free country." He also concurred with her notion of making the White House "a symbol of cultural as well as political leadership." But after *Life* magazine weighed in with a critical editorial titled "Forward to 1802," Jackie began to sense that her approach was too confining.

Du Pont enlisted two scholars, Julian Boyd and Lyman Butterfield, to redefine the purpose of the restoration. They warned that a single style would be "monotonous" and recommended instead that the "present living character of the White House" would be better served by a selection of periods from the late eighteenth through the early twentieth centuries. Jackie embraced the new direction, and her collaboration with du Pont began in earnest. His letters "would come flying in 4 or 5 a week" and he would awaken her with phone calls at 7:45 a.m., when she "would have to pretend to be alert." Over nearly three years, they would exchange more than a hundred letters—always addressed to "Mrs. Kennedy" and "Mr. du Pont"—about questions of aesthetics and historical accuracy.

Despite their fifty-year age difference and their strongly held views, Jackie and du Pont communicated comfortably. His tone was invariably tactful and courtly, while hers was more outspoken and occasionally fretful: "That hall was getting so on my nerves I put anything decent I could find in it. It looks like a rather shabby shoproom now—but at least not like a hotel lobby."

Their Fine Arts Committee for the White House was not the formal organization it appeared to be: "purely a creation of my friends," Jackie said later, "and some people I did not know but whom I thought . . . would give donations!! We had about 2 meetings the whole time & I did all the work myself" one-on-one with each member. Jackie admitted she couldn't stand "ladies committee meetings" because she was too "autocratic."

"Jackie had everyone's number very well," said Janet Cooper. "Her cause was so important to her, and she knew how to go after the very wealthy." A New York doctor recounted how Jackie "talked with me for hours, showing me how sad and forlorn various White House rooms looked. She never once asked me to do anything about it, never asked me to give her anything. But when I left, I found myself promising her a mirror for which I had turned down a $20,000 offer."

Jackie would eventually pull in more than $1.5 million in three years (approximately $9 million at today's values), and she also obtained gifts of specific furnishings and artwork, including priceless portraits of Benjamin Franklin and Andrew Jackson, as well as a Thomas Jefferson by Rembrandt Peale. The Peale was her favorite, because it embodied "everything Jefferson was . . . aristocrat, revolutionary statesman, artist, skeptic and idealist, compassionate but aloof . . . The spirit of the 18th century is in Jefferson's face."

The Jefferson portrait meant even more because the donor was Rachel "Bunny" Mellon, one of Jackie's two close friends who served on her Fine Arts Committee. Bunny and her billionaire husband, Paul Mellon—renowned art collector, philanthropist, and thoroughbred breeder—were the twentieth-century equivalent of Edith Wharton's van der Luydens, who "stood above all of them" and "faded into a kind of super-terrestrial twilight": shy and gentle, the ultimate in discernment, seldom seen on the party circuit. "The Mellons didn't have to inhabit anyone else's world," said Oatsie Leiter, a prominent hostess in Washington and Newport. "Everyone had to come to them." By 1961, Paul and Bunny Mellon owned seven properties—in Upperville, Virginia; New York City; Osterville on Cape Cod; Washington (two brick Georgian Revival homes side by side, one of which held only an art collection); Paris; and Antigua—employing more than 250 people, as well as a private jet decorated with works by Braque, Klee, and Dufy.

Bunny and Jackie were bound by background and deep affinities. The daughter of Gerard Lambert of the pharmaceutical family ("the man who used to own Listerine," Rose Kennedy once said after a golf game with him at Seminole), Bunny was an heiress who had lived at Carter Hall, an eighteenth-century columned mansion on a large plantation in Virginia's Shenandoah Valley—a house "where girls didn't go to college." She was educated at Foxcroft, a southern version of Farmington. She had a pretty, fine-featured face kept defiantly unadorned, and she wore classic clothes—as well as outfits for gardening—created by Jackie's favorite designer, Hubert de Givenchy. "Bunny was kind of a star with absolutely faultless good taste," said the Duchess of Devonshire. "She lived in her own realm of beauty and perfection."

In 1948, Bunny married Paul, whose father's banking fortune had created the National Gallery of Art, after divorcing her first husband, Stacy Lloyd, a close friend of Paul. Paul's first wife, Mary, had died of an asthma attack while hunting, and Bunny had been "bewildered" by her husband's changed manner following his European service during World War II. "Having known each other so well for so long," Paul Mellon recalled with typical restraint, "we decided to marry." Observed Bunny, "We became partners to help one another, and we remained that." Both Paul and Bunny stayed close to Stacy Lloyd, who ran an equestrian magazine, *Chronicle of the Horse,* that the Mellons launched.

Paul Mellon was a gentleman farmer famous for his superb collections of English sporting art as well as French impressionism, which was Bunny's particular interest, an outgrowth of her passion for gardens and landscapes. Bunny had near-professional expertise in horticulture— she helped Joe Alsop devise the multileveled green garden with eight varieties of boxwood behind his Georgetown home—and sophisticated knowledge of the "interior landscapes" of architecture. The spacious and perfectly proportioned library she built in the middle of a field on the four thousand–acre Mellon estate in Virginia contained one of the world's best collections of botanical books and artwork. She spent her days studying her books, planting and pruning, and she filled her homes with beautiful flowers, starting with the small vase of buttercups and violets on her breakfast tray.

Shortly after the birth of Caroline, when Jackie was twenty-eight and Bunny was forty-six, they were introduced over tea by their mutual friend Adele Douglas, the wife of Kingman Douglas, who owned an estate next to the Mellons. The sister of Fred Astaire, "Dellie" had started as a vaudeville dancer, married Lord Charles Cavendish, brother of the 10th Duke of Devonshire, and returned to the United States after Cavendish's death during the war. "Marvelous woman, frightfully coarse," said the 11th Duke of Devonshire, recalling Adele's habit of "appalling language" that earned her the nickname "Lady Foulmouth."

"I loved your house, but I don't like mine," Jackie said to Bunny after their first meeting. Jackie worshipped Mellon's balance of elegance and comfort, and unabashedly relied on her new friend as a tutor on interiors and gardens. Oak Spring, the cheerful Mellon "farmhouse" in Upperville, with its pale palette, "natural shabbiness," and French accents, sparked Jackie's imagination. "I even loved the stale candies in the antique jars," she told Mellon. "It never bothered Mrs. Kennedy to show the leading lights that she didn't know all the answers and to ask would they help her," said James Roe Ketchum, who served as White House curator at the end of the Kennedy administration. "Bunny was pleased and flattered," said Tish Baldrige, "to have this beautiful young woman hanging on her every word."

Bunny shared Jackie's admiration for eighteenth-century France (she would be instrumental in restoring the king's vegetable garden at Versailles) and her fluency in the language. "I'm not scholarly myself," Bunny once remarked, "but I do like to talk to people with ideas." They were temperamentally compatible as well—controlled, soft-spoken, and instinctively private. "What appealed to Jackie was the easy way Bunny handled everything, and her peace of mind," said Lee Radziwill. Bunny appreciated that Jackie "was true to her self" and respected her "gift of insight into people and her dislike of false pretenses."

Less obvious was the model Bunny offered for a marriage with ample space for separate lives. In many ways the Mellons were a devoted couple who revered each other's intelligence and aesthetic sense, but their relationship was complicated. Although Paul was naturally reticent, his hobbies, particularly foxhunting and thoroughbred racing, kept him engaged in the outside world. Bunny became more remote and solitary, even as she indulged in frequent travels, especially to Paris. "She has a moat and drawbridge around her," said Baldrige. Both Paul and Bunny consulted Freudian psychoanalysts to help them deal with their emotional inhibitions.

When he was in Washington, Paul also sought the companionship of Dorcas Hardin, a prominent socialite who owned a high-end dress shop. Dorcas was a beautifully feminine vision of "fluffs and frills and adorable hats"—although rather hard of hearing. "At dinner they would talk and laugh," recalled Oliver Murray, the Mellons' butler. "She was cheerful and fun. Bunny was not bubbly like Dorcas." Washingtonians were aware of the relationship, as was Bunny, who was said to have told

1

On election day, November 8, 1960, Jack Kennedy watches the returns with (from left) William Walton, Pierre Salinger, Ethel Kennedy, Bobby Kennedy, Angie Novello (RFK's secretary), and campaign aide William Haddad. *"Oh, Bunny, you're President now."*

2

On November 9, Jackie takes a solitary walk on the beach at Hyannis Port while the Kennedy clan prepares for a victory photograph.

"She breathes all the political gases that flow around us, but she never seems to inhale them."

The Kennedy family gathers with the President-elect. Standing, from left:
Ethel Kennedy, Stephen Smith, Jean Kennedy Smith, John Fitzgerald Kennedy,
Robert F. Kennedy, Pat Kennedy Lawford, Joan Kennedy, and Peter Lawford.
Seated, from left: Eunice Kennedy Shriver, Rose Kennedy, Joseph P. Kennedy,
Jacqueline Kennedy, Edward M. Kennedy, and Sargent Shriver.
"All made out of the same clay—hair and teeth and tongues from the same reserves."

Joe and Rose Kennedy on inauguration day, January 20, 1961.
"We don't want any losers around here. In this family we want winners."

Newspaper columnist Charley Bartlett and his wife, Martha, at the inaugural. They had introduced Jack and Jackie at a dinner party a decade earlier.

"Nothing mattered to me more than to have Jack Kennedy succeed as president. It did compromise my role as a journalist."

Jack and Jackie Kennedy moments after he was sworn in as President.
"I could scarcely embrace him in front of all those people, so I remember I just put my hand on his cheek and said, 'Jack, you were so wonderful!' And he was smiling in the most touching and most vulnerable way."

The Kennedy entourage at an inaugural ball. Front row from left:
Joe and Rose Kennedy, Jack and Jackie Kennedy, Lyndon and Lady Bird Johnson.
Second row, center: Teddy and Joan Kennedy.
"I just crumpled. All my strength was finally gone, so I went home and Jack went on with the others."

Preeminent Washington columnist Joseph Alsop, a close friend of both Jack's and Jackie's, hosted the new President in his Georgetown home after the official inaugural festivities ended.

"[Joe] picked the Kennedys as his property, and in a sense they were. They came to dinner when asked. They did things which Joe was striving for."

Eunice Shriver (seated) and her husband, Sarge (standing), at an event in the White House East Room.

"Eunice and Jack were goddamn near duplicates in damn near every way, particularly in politics."

JFK with Stephen Smith in the Oval Office.

"He rowed to his objective on silent oars."

11

Bobby and Teddy Kennedy huddling with the President.
*"Bobby knew instantly what Jack wanted. They talked every day as pilot and co-pilot
in the same tank, rumbling through the country's problems."*

12

Bill Walton hangs a painting of the frigate *Constitution* in
the Oval Office as Jack Kennedy offers guidance.
*"He was at once the most indiscreet and most discreet man alive. . . . He knew with whom
to be indiscreet and whom to trust. He had a lot of secrets about everyone."*

13

Lem Billings in the White House, where he kept
his belongings in one of the guest bedrooms.
"He was like a stable pony, relaxing, undemanding, peppy, and very vibrant."

14

Chuck Spalding was a friend of Jack's for more than two decades.
*"Chuck got White House fever. He saw Jack leading a glamorous life and wanted to emulate it.
Chuck loved the glitz and was burned by it."*

15

Franklin D. Roosevelt Jr., Jack's friend despite the antipathy between
their fathers, helped JFK win the crucial West Virginia primary.
"He really had a sense of humor, he left himself wide open to be laughed at, and he was a very naughty boy."

16

Red Fay (left) and Jim Reed, friends of JFK's from his PT boat days.
"Jack had so many people, maybe he looked to Jim for normalcy."

JFK conferring with "alter ego" Ted Sorensen, his closest White House aide.

"I could predict Jack Kennedy's thinking on most issues, and without his speaking of his emotions, I could read them."

17

18

Jack Kennedy checking the morning's headlines in the office of
Evelyn Lincoln, his faithful—and ever vigilant—secretary.
"Kennedy takes printer's ink for breakfast."

Arthur M. Schlesinger Jr., Kennedy's "court philosopher," troubleshooter, and resident historian.

"It will be better for us if [Arthur]'s in the White House, seeing what goes on, instead of reading about us in the New York Times *and* Time *magazine up in his office in the Widener Library at Harvard."*

19

John Kenneth Galbraith, the Harvard economist who served as Kennedy's ambassador to India.

"Along with people who like to hear themselves talk, there are unquestionably some who are even more inordinately attracted by their own composition. I may well be entitled to a gold star membership in both groups."

20

Robert McNamara, Kennedy's "Whiz Kid" secretary of defense, left the presidency of Ford Motor Company after only thirty-four days to join the new administration.

"The things that most men have to turn to books and reports for, Bob is carrying around right in his head."

21

22

National Security Adviser McGeorge Bundy (right)
talking to FBI director J. Edgar Hoover.
"[Bundy] doesn't fold or get rattled when they're sniping at him."

23

Secretary of the Treasury Douglas Dillon was the most partisan
of the Republicans Kennedy chose for his cabinet.
"We both had rather rapid minds."

Lyndon Johnson relinquished his powerful post as Senate
majority leader to serve as JFK's Vice President.
*"Johnson remained a proud and imperious man of towering energies and passions.
Self-effacement was for him the most unnatural of roles."*

Onetime presidential contender Adlai E. Stevenson agreed to be JFK's ambassador
to the United Nations despite his belief that it was a second-rate job.
"Stevenson became sort of prissy and overzealous with Kennedy."

26

Dave Powers, Kennedy's longtime factotum, greeted
visitors in the West Lobby of the White House.
*"Someone witty, light hearted; but faithful, loyal, and with sense enough
to keep his mouth closed under all circumstances."*

27

Larry O'Brien, a veteran of three Kennedy campaigns,
worked as JFK's special assistant for congressional relations.
"O'Brien was the President's logical surrogate, spreading his ready affability across Capitol Hill."

Kenny O'Donnell, Kennedy's appointments secretary, was intensely loyal to Jack, but even closer to Bobby Kennedy, his football teammate at Harvard.

"[Kennedy] wanted an observer in the room who would follow the various arguments more or less objectively, without becoming involved or committed to any point of view."

Jackie chose fellow Farmington and Vassar alumna Tish Baldrige to be White House social secretary.

"I've learned lesson number one. Keep the mouth SHUT at all times."

Jackie selected European aristocrat Oleg Cassini as her official couturier—a first in White House history.

"I'm sure I can continue to dress the way I like—simple and young clothes as long as they are covered up for the occasion."

Pamela Turnure, Jackie's twenty-three-year-old press secretary, had been linked romantically to JFK while working as a receptionist in his Senate office.

"I am so glad you are doing it . . . for the very reason that you haven't had previous press experience—but you have sense and good taste."

Bunny Mellon advised Jackie on interiors and gardens, and redesigned both the Rose Garden and the East Garden at the White House.

"She lived in her own realm of beauty and perfection."

32

33

Jackie relied on Jayne Wrightsman's connections and knowledge of fine French furniture in her restoration of the White House.
"It was a cultural friendship."

her husband once on his return from Washington, "You don't need to shout anymore, Paul. You're home now."

With the arrival of Jackie at the White House, Bunny had a new mission that kept her more frequently in Virginia and Washington. Her signature contributions were redesigns of the Rose Garden and East Garden, but she was generous in an ongoing way, constantly on call for advice. "What does Bunny use to replace ghastly brass doorknobs?" Jackie asked in one of her numerous memos.

Bunny worked with Jackie on a new approach to floral design—loose arrangements of seasonal flowers such as anemones, tulips, freesia, and lilies of the valley in baskets and bowls that were inspired by Dutch still life paintings and informed by Bunny's seventeenth-century horticultural manuals—and helped set up a flower workroom. At Bunny's suggestion, the Eisenhower era's "lugubrious Victorian palms" gave way to "topiary trees in Versailles tubs." She often supplied blossoms for White House events from her own greenhouses, where she kept duplicates of the plantings she devised for the Rose Garden. The Mellons also had "six different sets of two hundred chairs," recalled Janet Cooper, that they provided for White House events. Oak Spring's carpentry and metal fabrication shops did work for the White House, and Bunny installed her favorite upholsterer on the Executive Mansion's third floor, where he lived for a year, working on the restoration.

Jackie's other mentor was a less intimate but comparably influential friend. Jayne Larkin Wrightsman had the same compulsion for privacy as Bunny Mellon, but while Jayne was supremely refined, she was also thoroughly self-invented. If Bunny preferred expensive simplicity, Jayne represented the "Louis Louis" opulence of ormolu, parquetry, and gilded boiseries. Like her husband, Jackie put her friends in compartments. In this instance, she looked to Mellon on pure matters of taste and to Wrightsman for rigorous scholarship. With Jayne, who was a decade older than Jackie, "it was a cultural friendship," said Marella Agnelli, wife of Fiat auto baron Gianni Agnelli, who knew Jackie and Jayne from the Riviera.

Jayne Larkin was a delicate brown-eyed beauty nicknamed "Little Egypt" as a teenager for "her dark hair in a pageboy, and her sophisticated use of makeup and eyeliner," according to New York writer

Francesca Stanfill. A midwesterner from modest circumstances who had worked as a shopgirl in Beverly Hills, Jayne had flair—an example was the "y" she added to her first name in high school—that attracted the attention of wealthy oilman Charles Wrightsman, described by Thomas Hoving, director of the Metropolitan Museum of Art, as "the most immaculate man I ever met. . . . He moved with a languorous grace as if participating in a minuet." A polo-playing ladies' man twice Jayne's age, Charlie had been educated at Exeter, Stanford, and Columbia. Although twenty-five-year-old Jayne lacked his pedigree, her ambition was obvious, and her attentiveness impressive.

After their marriage in 1944, Charlie and Jayne set out to conquer society as collectors of fine French furniture and objects, as well as old master paintings. With a net worth of at least $100 million, Charlie had plenty to spend. He drove Jayne relentlessly to learn about art and decor, and to master the French language. She read books and quizzed experts such as famed art critic Bernard Berenson. An exacting martinet, Charlie shocked antique dealers when he would bark, "Jayne, come over here and take some notes!" The photographer Cecil Beaton once observed that "her face twitches with anxiety when Charles is on a bait. . . . One wonders if it is worthwhile suffering for so much of her life."

Jayne's most important tutor was Stéphane Boudin, a Parisian interior designer with a prestigious clientele including the Duke and Duchess of Windsor, Gianni Agnelli, Pamela Churchill Harriman, and Lady Baillie, the glamorous Anglo-American owner of Leeds Castle. Boudin headed Jansen on the rue Royale, an antiques dealer as well as atelier that employed 650 craftsmen and designers. With Boudin's guidance, the Wrightsmans amassed a dazzling collection of eighteenth-century pieces, many created for French kings, that they would eventually donate to the Metropolitan Museum of Art. "Jayne consulted Boudin down to the slightest detail," said Boudin's New York partner, Paul Manno.

Jayne first met Jackie through Joe and Rose Kennedy, who lived north of the twenty-eight-room Wrightsman estate in Palm Beach. The Wrightsmans entertained the Kennedys in Florida as well as in the south of France, where they traveled every summer on a luxurious yacht. Typical fare at a Wrightsman dinner party would be a pound of caviar, cold pompano salad, and quail on toast. "Jaynie" once helped the

Kennedys find an artist to paint Kathleen's portrait, and when Joe was about to buy the *Caroline* for Jack's campaign in 1958, Charlie offered him advice on airplanes.

In 1959, Charlie Wrightsman, a committed Republican, asked Boudin if he would work with Jackie on her Georgetown house. Charlie advised that it could be useful to meet her because "who knows—she may some day be First Lady." During his visit that May, Boudin sold Jack and Jackie two antique rugs that they paid off at $100 a month. "I'm still in a glow over the day with him," Jackie reported to Jayne, pronouncing Boudin "an enchanting, brilliant man."

———

With Sister Parish, the ultimate in WASP chic, as her decorator of record, and American aristocrat Harry du Pont as her official consultant, Jackie seemed to have her team in place. But Jackie wanted Boudin's imprimatur as well. Having worked on the great houses of Europe, among them Buckingham Palace and Josephine Bonaparte's Malmaison, he was accustomed to grand historical settings. He could do "what no American decorator can do," Jackie later said, because he was "trained as an interior architect" with an "eye for placement and proportion" that she needed. As early as February 3—three weeks before the formation of the Fine Arts Committee—Boudin arrived at the White House for a secret four-day visit with Jackie. He suggested changes from top to bottom "to represent the United States in a bit more elegant and refined way."

After word of the visit leaked into the press two months later, Boudin emphasized that he was there only for "friendship," not professional reasons. Given Boudin's national origin, any overt role in the White House refurbishment would be politically awkward, so Jackie decided to keep his involvement from the public even as she considered him her "primary visionary." Chattering and sharing jokes in French, Jackie got along famously with seventy-two-year-old Boudin, who was diminutive, effervescent, and impish. On his visits to the United States, Boudin would bring his mistress; he was married to "a wife in name only," explained Manno.

Jayne Wrightsman's biggest gift to the White House was underwriting Boudin's design for the sumptuous Blue Room, a paragon of French-inspired taste. But she was also Jackie's co-conspirator in an elaborate minuet with Boudin, du Pont, and Parish, serving as liaison with Boudin and traveling frequently to Paris to scout for choice pieces for what she called "La Maison Blanche." Both Jayne and Jackie were skilled at presenting Boudin's ideas as their own, to avoid offending Parish and du Pont. (When Boudin had the brown stone mantels in the East Room painted with a faux finish of white marble, du Pont praised Jackie for her "stroke of genius.")

Even so, Parish threatened to quit several times when she sensed that Jackie was favoring Boudin's suggestions over hers. Parish's continuing role was vital, not least because she enlisted her friends—the John Loebs and Charles Engelhards—as large donors. At one point, Jayne had to write a ten-page letter from the Hotel Ritz in Paris imploring her to stay on. At another touchy moment, Jackie advised Janet Felton Cooper, "say this tactfully to Sister. I don't want to hurt her feelings."

Du Pont was irked by Boudin's preference for dramatic presentation over strict historical fidelity. "I shudder to think what Mr. Boudin would do with American furniture," du Pont once wrote. During his White House visits, du Pont would spend hours arranging furniture and artwork; he took placement so seriously that at Winterthur he pounded brass tacks into the floors—each stamped with a catalogue number—and instructed staff not to move pieces even an inch from the tacks without his permission. Boudin would arrive "fresh and vigorous" the next day to undo du Pont's scheme, and Jackie often rearranged items as well. "Mr. du Pont was rigid," recalled Joe Alsop's wife, Susan Mary, "but Jackie's charm made everything work."

Both Jayne and Jackie soothed du Pont with flattery: "You are a wonder man!" wrote Jayne, while Jackie praised "each 'little touch of Harry in the afternoon.'" "Mrs. Kennedy juggled everybody," recalled Jim Ketchum. "She felt certain people were able to handle certain points on the compass, and if she felt instincts and tastes would clash, she kept them in separate rooms." "As the elder statesman," du Pont "was always philosophical and appeared not to be unduly disturbed," noted his daughter Ruth Lord.

Jack Kennedy kept aloof from the internecine struggles, but he took a keen interest in the progress of the restoration. He had not been raised to appreciate the decorative arts, nor the visual and performing arts for that matter. The Kennedys had large houses with furnishings "that could survive the marauding swarms of children who wrought havoc there," recalled Oleg Cassini. Joe Kennedy bought antiques occasionally through Marie Bruce, a British friend, but only when she could find a bargain. "They didn't even own any paintings anywhere until very late," said Walton. The only counterbalance to the family's philistinism had been Lem Billings, whose passion for art and antiques had begun with his Princeton thesis on Tintoretto, a precociously sophisticated study.

When Jack married Jackie, "he really had no idea about how you should decorate a room, or what was the difference between a pretty house and an ugly house," said David Gore. At first, JFK resisted Jackie's insistence on "fancy stuff," but according to Gore, "gradually he came to appreciate good taste" and to admire Jackie's "instinct for excellence." It was Jack who selected their Georgetown house because "he liked the door knocker," said Jackie. During one of Jackie's series of redecorations there, JFK surveyed the muted shades on the walls, sofas, and curtains and asked, "Do you think we're prisoners of beige?"

JFK grew to admire the impressionists, especially "paintings of water and sky." At Jackie's urging, he even took up painting for a brief spell during their first year of marriage. Wearing surgical scrubs bought by Jackie, he set up his easel and "did a lot of terrible paintings, but he was enjoying himself," said Walton, who served as his teacher. JFK quit after admitting "he had no gift," but Jackie hung one colorful canvas—a Riviera scene he did from memory—in their Hyannis Port living room.

He remained eager to learn, and "he was really very visual minded," said Mary Lasker, the philanthropist and renowned collector. Kay Halle recalled her astonishment during one of her Georgetown dinner parties when Kennedy crawled under an Adam table and announced, "You can tell by the boards what its age is, whether it's a reproduction or whether it's of the period." Halle was impressed that the "one thing that really caught him" was her highest-quality piece.

Jack Kennedy's love of history converged nicely with the artistic appreciation nurtured by his wife. The White House restoration also proved a political boon, as the public and the press reacted with enthusiasm. "Furniture classes sprung up all over town as young women studied the difference between Sheraton and Queen Anne, and between

Lowestoft china and Chinese export," wrote Nancy Dickerson. JFK took to stopping by the White House Curator's Office on the ground floor to see the latest acquisitions. When two dust-covered side chairs originally made for President Monroe arrived, Kennedy was so delighted that he asked that they be wrapped and tied with bows so that he could present them to Jackie himself.

Almost from the beginning, Kennedy had his own project to complement Jackie's work in the White House: influencing the design of the city of Washington. Kennedy had acquired an interest in public architecture, and he knew Washington intimately after living there on and off for nearly two decades. As a result, "John F. Kennedy's feeling for Washington was probably deeper than any president since Jefferson," wrote Bill Walton. "He deplored its ugly areas and schemed, as president, to help make the capital a far more beautiful city than he had found it."

In the earliest days of his administration, JFK called Walton "every morning for something." One day he asked Walton over to talk about the Eisenhower administration's plan to raze historic buildings near the White House in order to build much-needed modern offices. The first target was the Executive Office Building (officially known as the State, War and Navy Building), a massive six-story granite pile of pediments and columns topped by an ornate mansard roof sprouting chimneys, medallions, and dormers. It was a nineteenth-century extravagance, but Kennedy thought it deserved to survive.

Together Walton and Kennedy gazed out at Lafayette Square, where a number of buildings were also endangered by the bulldozers—homes that had been occupied by such famous nineteenth-century figures as Stephen Decatur and Dolley Madison. Walton convinced Kennedy that the structures had to be saved and offered his help. (Walton's wasn't an original idea; a Citizens Committee to Save Lafayette Square had formed in 1960.) To give Walton official status, Kennedy appointed him to the Commission of Fine Arts, which was charged with preserving the cultural and architectural heritage of the capital. But ever mindful of practical concerns, Kennedy warned Walton, "I want you to remember one thing: Don't ever get me out on a limb that I can't support what you're doing . . . I have a limited amount of political capital to spend, and I can't spend it all on your projects."

TEN

The thing that broke me up was this snowman . . . He was wearing a big floppy Panama hat, like Frank Lloyd Wright A.D. 1920 or somebody . . . It seems to me there is an awful lot of formality around this new house of mine. Maybe you have noticed a certain look in my eye . . . like I have an independent streak. Well I do . . . I intend to have a fine time for myself.

—BY CAROLINE KENNEDY AS TOLD TO THOMAS WOLFE, FEBRUARY 5, 1961, *WASHINGTON POST*

The make-believe description of three-year-old Caroline's arrival at the White House after nearly two months in Florida offered an early glimpse of the satirical talents of Tom Wolfe before he began exposing the foibles of American society in his journalism and novels. Unlike the sober reports of his competitors, Wolfe captured the mischievous spirit that the Kennedy children unleashed in the Executive Mansion.

Jackie had prepared well for the arrival of her children, having recruited and trained her staff and put everyone on notice about the way she planned to operate in private and public. Jackie structured her life to allow her to spend as much time with Caroline and John as she wished.

The Kennedys enjoyed the luxury of an English nanny named Maud Shaw, who had been with the family since Caroline was eleven days old. Shaw lived in a spartan room between the two children's bed-rooms on the second floor. "She won't need much," Jackie cracked to J. B. West, the chief usher. "Just find a wicker wastebasket for her banana peels and a little table for her false teeth at night." Red-haired and droll, Shaw oversaw daily logistics, reinforced Jackie's emphasis on good manners, and, according to Jackie's secretary Mary Gallagher, was the principal disciplinarian who "with words alone . . . could master the situation." With her starched white uniform, Shaw was "a little puffed up with herself," recalled Anne Truitt, whose daughter Mary was a playmate of Caroline's, "but she was a very competent nanny."

Jackie's involvement with her children was striking for a woman of her class, where formality and emotional distance were the rule. (Sig-nificantly, she was "Mommy," not "Mummy.") "She usually had her youngsters in tow," recalled James Ketchum of the Curator's Office. "Mrs. Kennedy had the kids more than Miss Shaw, which was a great shock to me. I assumed she turned them over to Miss Shaw as her responsibility." In Georgetown, Jackie had participated in a playgroup that several mothers took turns hosting at their homes. "She was a remarkable mother, the way she spoke and engaged the children," said Sue Wilson, who had also known Jackie at Vassar.

Jackie declined to "talk down" to children. As a surprise for Jack, she taught Caroline at age three to memorize Edna St. Vincent Millay's "First Fig" and "Second Fig," two short poems with more sophisti-cated language than standard nursery rhymes. Yet Jackie also had what Ketchum called "a tremendous sense of play." "Let's go kiss the wind," Jackie would exclaim to Caroline. Watching her with Caroline and John on the South Lawn, J. B. West observed that she was "so happy, so abandoned, so like a little girl who had never grown up." Jackie valued the imagination of children—"a quality," she noted, "that seems to flicker out in so many adults."

In her quest to shield Caroline from prying eyes, Jackie asked the playgroup mothers—who included Jane Saltonstall, daughter-in-law of the Republican senator from Massachusetts, and Cathy Mellon Warner, daughter of Paul Mellon and wife of lawyer John Warner, the future

Republican senator from Virginia—to move their gatherings to the White House. "Jackie thought it would be more natural for Caroline," said Sue Wilson, "to demystify the place, to make it less cold and formidable, to have kids scampering in the long hallways."

The mothers at first feared that publicity would violate their privacy. But JFK promised that the names of the seven children would be tightly guarded, so Pat Hass organized the group as a cooperative, with the parents paying all expenses for equipment and staff. For the first four months, Anne Mayfield, a graduate of Bank Street College of Education, supervised the group informally. The following fall she was joined by Jaclin Marlin, who had a master's from the Harvard Graduate School of Education. Marlin and Mayfield ran the White House nursery school—expanded to twelve children—for four mornings a week during its first full year. Jackie worked with child development specialists to design a playground on the South Lawn and a schoolroom in a third-floor solarium—a sun-filled space with a panoramic view of the capital.

JFK routinely saw his children at breakfast and before their bedtime, spending as much time with them "as the average medium- to high-income man," observed *Time*'s Hugh Sidey. But unlike most organization men, he lived "above the store," which afforded glimpses of Caroline and John at lunchtime and when he took breaks in his schedule to sit on a bench next to the playground. Compared to the previous five years, when he had been either on the road campaigning or in the Senate chamber many evenings, the White House, for all its abnormality, forced him into more normal family rhythms.

JFK lacked the exuberance of Teddy Roosevelt, known for wild pillow fights with his sons Archie and Quentin. Still, "Jack Kennedy with children was pure fun," said Anne Truitt, recalling his three-clap summons into the Oval Office. He was the patriarch of his generation who took an active interest in the children of his siblings. In Hyannis Port, with the family golf cart loaded with nieces and nephews, he would zoom to the local candy store, looking like Toad in *The Wind in the Willows*. While riding on the *Caroline*, Walt Rostow watched Kennedy settle a rambunctious swarm of children one by one—"a man who all his life was at home with women and kids and human situations."

Like Jackie, JFK spoke to young people in a straightforward fashion;

when arts adviser August Heckscher brought his teenage son to the Oval Office, Kennedy let the boy sit in on the meeting, listening to sensitive discussions. Charles Heckscher was struck, he amusingly wrote afterwards, that Kennedy addressed him "with an air of businesslike equality."

Kennedy also knew that his children showed the human side of his presidency and welcomed "photo ops" with them for publications such as *Look* and *Life*—publicity that Jackie tried to restrict. Some of the most enduring images of the Kennedy years—"John John" peeking out from underneath his father's Oval Office desk, Caroline eating chocolates in Evelyn Lincoln's office—were organized by their father while Jackie was out of town. "I always heard back from the First Lady," wrote Tish Baldrige, recalling Jackie's annoyance.

———

To the press and the inhabitants of the West Wing, Jackie was like "a slender butterfly flitting through the corridors of power." She continued to keep irregular hours, awakening as early as eight or as late as noon, depending on the previous night's activities. "She was determined to have her own time, and not change her life," said Baldrige. Jackie had breakfast on a tray (orange juice, toast and honey, coffee with skimmed milk), surveyed the morning papers, and played with John on her bed.

After pushing John in his pram, she liked to take a brisk walk, play tennis, usually with her favorite Secret Service agent Clint Hill, or jump on the canvas trampoline that she surrounded with seven-foot holly trees for privacy. She avoided the White House pool because the ninety-degree temperature was too warm for her taste, although she did train with light weights in the adjacent fitness room. Long before people understood the effect of endorphins, she believed that she would be more alert if she exercised before settling down to work. At first she had toyed with the idea of an East Wing office. But like her predecessors, she chose the seclusion of the private quarters, sitting either at her father's small Empire-style slant-front desk in the living room, or in a green velvet armchair at the large table in the Monroe Room, which she refurbished and renamed the Treaty Room.

In remarkably short order, Jackie brought a homey elegance to the second floor reminiscent of the rambling Manhattan apartments of her youth—eleven rooms including a newly constructed "President's Dining Room" and kitchen. (On the third floor were six additional guest bedrooms, two sitting rooms, two solariums, offices, and servants' rooms, as well as a terrace and greenhouse.) The second floor was dominated by a wide but dark hall running the entire length from east to west that Jackie tried to soften with arrangements of sofas and chairs, and groupings of nineteenth-century American Indian portraits. Still, Arthur Schlesinger groused that "an average Park Avenue tycoon" would regard the apartment as "claustrophobic."

On the eastern end were the formal historic rooms—the famous Lincoln Suite, Queen's Suite, and Treaty Room. At the west end Jackie created a comfortable living room—known as the "West Sitting Hall"— enclosed by a wall with tall wooden sliding doors topped by a fanlight. On the other side of the living room was a large lunette window that overlooked the majestic Executive Office Building, Rose Garden, and West Wing. New built-in bookcases contained Jackie's favorite volumes (identified by her specially designed Tiffany bookplates), and paintings by Maurice Prendergast, Winslow Homer, and John Singer Sargent complemented period furniture. A door on the north side of the living room led to the new dining room with views of Pennsylvania Avenue and historic Lafayette Square.

The Kennedys had their own bedroom suites, in keeping with the upper-class practice of the day. Jackie's was the larger, accessible through a doorway on the living room's south side. The main entrance to Jack's, also on the south side, was from the Center Hall, opposite the children's bedrooms, which faced Pennsylvania Avenue. Jack and Jackie's bedrooms were connected by a dressing room that Jackie fitted with a stereo system for her husband's nighttime listening. The immediacy of the First Couple's most intimate quarters sometimes startled visitors, especially when they were directed to use the President's bathroom. Many dinner parties wound down in JFK's bedroom, as he walked around "without the slightest embarrassment," noted Ben Bradlee, removing his socks and trousers and unbuttoning his shirt as "the last guests [were] bidding one another witty farewells"—not exactly an eighteenth-century levee, but close enough.

Also on the south side was the high-ceilinged Oval Room that had initially shocked Jackie with its starkness—"like the Lubianka!" she said, referring to an infamous Soviet prison. It soon became her favorite work in progress. She painted it yellow—"a way of letting sunlight in," she explained to Sue Wilson—and envisioned it as "the heart of the White House," a sitting room that would exemplify the Louis XVI style loved by Madison and Jefferson, not to mention Jackie. With its commanding views of the South Lawn and Washington Monument, this was the room where the Kennedys would entertain friends and state visitors alike.

Jackie usually spent several hours in the late morning ploughing through folders neatly stacked in a straw basket by Tish Baldrige, writing memos and personal letters in her refined, rounded hand, and dictating instructions on household matters to Mary Gallagher. (While she left an extensive epistolary trail of her tenure as First Lady, she never kept a journal: "I want to live my life, not record it.") She had a light lunch of broth and a sandwich, often with her husband, and rested after her maid Providencia Paredes had changed the sheets from the previous night.

Since her teen years, Jackie had followed a meticulous beauty regimen that included sprinkling cologne on her hairbrush ("fifty to one hundred strokes . . . every night"), glistening her eyelashes with a pinch of skin cream, and applying powder before and after lipstick ("should stay on through . . . corn on the cob"). Jackie was disciplined about her weight—120 pounds, according to Oleg Cassini. "She was very slim, and had great muscle tone," he recalled. "She had no extra fat." Jackie watched the scale "with the rigor of a diamond merchant counting his carats," said Tish Baldrige. If Jackie added just two pounds, she would fast for a day, then confine herself to a diet of fruit while increasing her exercise time with more hours on the tennis court or trampoline.

Jackie was, however, hopelessly addicted to the filtered L&Ms that she kept in a barrel-shaped gold cigarette case containing a small lighter—a gift from her brother-in-law Stas Radziwill. "She was always smoking, ever since I can remember," said Vivian Crespi, "even if she would take a few puffs and put it down, she sort of needed it. She smoked all through her pregnancies, but we didn't know at the time that it was harmful." (The landmark surgeon general's report on smoking and health would not be released until the autumn of 1963.) Few outside the Kennedy circle were aware of her habit—which averaged nearly a pack a day—a badge of sophistication since Farmington. When Jackie was agitated, Mary Gallagher observed that "newly lit cigarettes

were being stubbed out in the ashtray on her desk, one after the other."
On the campaign trail, Larry O'Brien used to hold her cigarettes so that
she could "take furtive puffs from time to time."

Afternoons for Jackie were given over to reading, painting watercolors on an easel in a corner of her bedroom, or to outings with the children in her blue Pontiac station wagon. Camouflaged by a head scarf
and an old trench coat over her jeans and sweater, she moved about the
city unrecognized, taking her children to the circus or theater, with several Secret Service agents unobtrusively nearby. Even at Caroline's ballet recitals, "she had a way of rendering herself anonymous," recalled
Anne Truitt.

Jackie rarely held a staff meeting and was a stranger in the East Wing,
choosing instead to drop in on the ground-floor Curator's Office, the
hub of the restoration work that absorbed most of her mental energy
and gave her the most pleasure. "For others she insisted upon order,"
said J. B. West. "For herself she preferred spontaneity." West discovered early that Jackie would take advice, but only when she sought it.
"She strongly resisted being pushed," he said. "The trick was to read
her correctly . . . not to oppose her . . . sometimes she was so subtle she
needed a translator." Lady Bird Johnson, an astute judge of character,
"never saw her dealing with an opponent, but I sensed she could be difficult if faced with one. 'My antenna' just felt it so to speak."

With her irrepressible enthusiasm, Tish Baldrige never accepted
Jackie's self-imposed limits, constantly pressuring the First Lady to do
more until, as arts adviser August Heckscher observed, she would have
her "ears pinned back" by Jackie. Establishment Washington was sometimes dismayed by Jackie's unconventional ways. Ymelda Dixon, a
Washington Star society columnist and daughter of a veteran congressman, recalled that Jackie mostly avoided the annual lunches for wives
and daughters of senators and congressmen. "The President came. *He*
cared," she said. "But Jackie got away with it."

Even when Jackie made a commitment, she could easily duck out,
confident that Baldrige would find an instant substitute from a group of
women "on call" that included Janet Auchincloss, Rose Kennedy, Ethel
Kennedy, Lady Bird Johnson, and JFK's sisters. Lady Bird cheerfully
assumed the last-minute duty more than anyone, earning the nickname

"Saint Bird" among Jackie's staffers. Jackie's "little-girl quality made you want to help her—to be 'on her side,'" said Lady Bird. Rose Kennedy frequently volunteered to fill the breach, although Jackie bristled whenever Rose tried "to reinvent the White House social agenda," recalled Baldrige.

Barbara Gamarekian of the press office remembered the times when Jackie canceled "meet and greets" with visitors. Once when Ethel Kennedy was filling in, Gamarekian heard that Jackie was playing tennis on the White House court. "I was lying through my teeth, saying Jackie wasn't feeling well," recalled Gamarekian. "I had visions of someone walking along the Ellipse, where the tennis court was visible, visions of being caught in a lie, and I resented being put in that position if I had said she was indisposed." From time to time Jackie got caught "playing hooky"—as she did to Kennedy's embarrassment when he told June Havoc and Helen Hayes that she was ill, only to have the newspapers disclose that Jackie had been riding in Virginia with the tony Orange County hunt instead.

For all of Jackie's surface serenity, at age thirty-one she periodically felt swamped. "She gets pressured very easily," JFK told Baldrige. "I want Jackie to feel protected, not persecuted." Janet Auchincloss pointed to Jackie's "stiffness, even shyness. It's not that she's frightened of people, but she's not outgoing." Those close to Jackie saw the external evidence of her stress: the nails that she would pick and gnaw, the circles under her eyes after a sleepless night. "She would get terribly down," said Baldrige. "I would know it because she would swallow repeatedly. That was a sign of great tension. To be queen of the world was overwhelming to her at times. She thought about it a lot and lost her energy."

It took vigorous physical activity—the trampoline, riding at full gallop—to invigorate Jackie and relieve her stress. For all her cosmopolitanism, Jackie had depended on the restorative powers of the countryside and seaside since her girlhood roaming on Uncle Hughdie's estates. She savored the woods, the Potomac River view, and "great steep hills" of Merrywood, as well as "the green fields and summer winds" of Newport's Hammersmith Farm, where she could "watch the water like bits of broken glass in the sun." "I love them both, whichever I'm at—just as passionately as I loved the one I left behind," she told Yusha Auchincloss as a teenager.

In a ritual that began during her childhood when her mother decamped each summer first to Easthampton, then to Newport, Jackie spent more than three months—two in Hyannis Port followed by nearly six weeks at Hammersmith Farm—away from Washington in the summertime. "It was a Washington pattern," said Jim Ketchum. "People would pull up stakes at the end of June and return after Labor Day." Jackie had also become accustomed to staying for as long as a month at a time in Palm Beach at Christmas and Easter. Jack would join her for weekends, and at Newport for his vacation of several weeks.

———

With the help of Bill Walton, Jackie secured her own nearby refuge— "the most private place I can think of to balance our life in the White House"—at Glen Ora, the four hundred–acre estate the Kennedys rented from Gladys Tartière in Middleburg, Virginia. (Jackie preferred the verdant hunt country to Camp David, the rustic mountaintop presidential retreat in Maryland.) The early-nineteenth-century six-bedroom home of beige stucco was "comfortable and unpolished," said Ken Galbraith, "in the trim countryside of the farming and non-farming rich." Jackie and Sister Parish organized a quick makeover of N Street furnishings as well as those of Mrs. Tartière, with new slipcovers, rugs, and curtains, along with repainting and repapering. The Secret Service fortified the estate with gates and guardhouses, and built a heliport. Jackie belatedly discovered that the property was also a pig farm, so she had to wait until the stalls had been cleared before she could stable her horses, Bit of Irish, a frisky bay gelding, and the more seasoned piebald Rufus.

Unlike the White House, where tourists peered through fences at the First Family's activities on the South Lawn, and waiters served the children hamburgers on silver trays, Glen Ora offered the illusion of down-to-earth freedom. "Jackie wanted her kids to have what she grew up with, and to make their lives normal and fun," said Eve Fout. "She applied effort and ingenuity to that." Within the spacious boundaries of Glen Ora, Caroline rode her pony, Macaroni, Jackie took the children on picnics in a cave, and in the evenings she enjoyed "giving them baths & putting them to bed—reading—the things I have no chance to do in the W. House."

The unencumbered life in Virginia was crucial to Jackie. She could buy a cup of coffee in town without being gawked at, slip over to Bunny

Mellon's for a visit, or grill steaks in the fireplace at the home of Eve Fout and her husband, Paul. "I do not consider myself a part of the Hunt Country life," she told Eve. "I appreciate the way people there let me alone."

Most Thursdays Jackie would leave for Virginia with Caroline and John, not returning to the White House until Monday afternoon. Accompanied by friends, Jack would join the family for Saturday and Sunday. The two weekdays gave Jackie the opportunity to ride her horses, either in solitude on Glen Ora's trails or at the front of the field with the exclusive Orange County Hunt—a way "to be out with people, but not too much so," said Eve Fout. Jackie had been spending her weekends riding for many years. As she once explained to Joe Kennedy when Jack was in the Senate, "There isn't anything to do in Washington but ride . . . and I can go down & hunt & one feels so much better when one exercises."

Jackie was passionate about horses and foxhunting, which appealed to her romantic spirit and allowed her to lose herself in the excitement of galloping behind baying hounds in pursuit of their elusive quarry. "There is a kind of religious cultish thing about the world of horses," said Oleg Cassini. "It's a world apart. Horse people see life differently, because the animal plays such an important role." Jackie was a fine and fearless rider, "very, very good," said Janet Whitehouse, whose husband, Charlie, hunted with Jackie for more than four decades. "She would jump anything and go very fast." Once when Jack was a senator, Jackie was riding with the Piedmont Hunt when her horse stepped in a hole and threw her to the ground. She landed on her head, was "knocked unconscious . . . swallowed her tongue and was turning blue" when a fellow rider resuscitated her.

The Fouts were Jackie's quintessential country friends. Jackie had known Eve since she was a teenager, when Eve attended Miss Hall's, a girls' boarding school in western Massachusetts, and they competed on the horse show circuit. Eve grew up in Warrenton, the heart of the Virginia hunt country, and became a well-regarded sporting artist after apprenticeships with several prominent painters of equine portraits. *The Chronicle of the Horse,* the magazine founded by Bunny Mellon's first husband, published Eve's artwork on its covers, which helped launch her career.

Eve and her husband, Paul, also built a business training horses, including one of Jackie's. Direct and brusque, Eve jealously guarded Jackie's privacy, declining even to tell close friends when she was going riding with the First Lady. Paul was somewhat irreverent, teasing Jackie that "she walked like a duck." Eve sponsored Jackie for the Orange County Hunt during the presidential campaign, which led to criticism in the press. Jackie thanked Eve for "sticking your neck out for me," and wondered why "the mass of people" couldn't understand that hunting was not "a cruel sport of the idle rich" but instead tended "to bring out the best in people—love of animals, each other, nature, sport, happiness etc."

Jackie did not withdraw from her duties when she was away. "She liked homework; she was on the phone all the time," said Baldrige. "When she was at Glen Ora she was working," said Ketchum. "The stuff came back in spades in memos." Jackie told Eve that spending time by herself in the country "freshened her up to go back to Washington" and "re-enthused" her about her work.

Jack Kennedy, however, barely tolerated the countryside and what Ben Bradlee described as the "hunt country hangers-on." JFK liked to visit the Mellons and Adele Astaire Douglas, but otherwise he spent his time taking long naps and playing backgammon with Lem Billings, who came along most weekends to keep him company while Jackie was riding. The two old friends would often escape boredom by driving around the countryside to look at old houses and check out where various people lived.

Kennedy welcomed having a place to entertain friends away from the White House, but he far preferred to sit with them on the fantail of the ninety-two-foot presidential yacht, *Honey Fitz,* in Nantucket Sound. "The whole reason for Glen Ora was to be nice to Jackie," said Paul Fout. "He agreed to have the house here to appease her. He had no interest in foxhunting." At the beginning, Jackie tried to entice her husband to ride, and outfitted him with a jacket and jodhpurs from Miller Clothing in New York. "He looked like Ichabod Crane with his legs flying," recalled Ben Bradlee. "I think he liked the idea of it, but didn't know what he was doing." Amazingly, Kennedy sustained no injury, and his bad back gave him an excuse to stop.

JFK's life necessarily revolved around the vast responsibilities of his office, but less obviously his schedule included unusual accommodations to his myriad ailments. His principal physicians, Janet Travell and Admiral George Burkley, worked in a room on the ground floor, and he had an array of specialists in regular contact by telephone that included an allergist, endocrinologist (for his Addison's disease), gastroenterologist (for colitis), urologist (for urinary tract infections resulting from venereal disease), and orthopedist (for his degenerative spine).

JFK's regimen of strong medications required strict oversight and constant calibration, especially the corticosteroids for his Addison's. To treat his chronic back pain, Travell gave him daily injections of the local anesthetic procaine. Kennedy also routinely took cytomel (for thyroid deficiency); Lomotil, Metamucil, paregoric, phenobarbital, and Trasentine (to control the diarrhea from his colitis); testosterone (to increase energy and boost weight following bouts of colitis); penicillin (for urinary tract flare-ups); Fluorinef (to increase his ability to absorb salt, which Addison's depleted); Tuinal (for insomnia, a side effect of the cortisone); antihistamines (for an array of allergies); vitamin C; and calcium supplements (to substitute for milk products, which exacerbated his colitis). As a precaution against triggering an Addisonian crisis, JFK's doctors boosted his cortisone when he faced stressful situations such as speeches and press conferences.

Kennedy's day began at seven or seven-thirty—often before Jackie had awakened. After tackling his first batch of newspapers (the *Washington Post, New York Times, New York Herald Tribune, Baltimore Sun,* and *Wall Street Journal*) in roughly fifteen minutes, he would slip into his frayed tan bathrobe and take "a short soak in a long tub." He ate a hearty breakfast of orange juice, lean bacon, toast and marmalade, two four-minute-eggs, and coffee with cream and sugar. One morning when Ken Galbraith joined him, Kennedy finished what was left on the economist's plate after polishing off his own serving. Following a round of phone calls and a quick visit with Dr. Travell, Kennedy reached the office by 9 or 9:30 a.m. "He was a slow starter," said Walt Rostow. "He would gather speed in the morning."

For the sake of his health, Kennedy typically left the Oval Office from one until four, first swimming in the warm indoor pool for a half hour—a ritual he would repeat after work in the early evening. "It was part of his therapy," said Dave Powers, who did the breast stroke along-side JFK, the better to keep up his entertaining patter. The swimming would "help the pain in his back, and . . . help him relax and think bet-ter." Most of the time, Kennedy dispensed with swimming trunks—a perfectly natural choice for someone shaped by all-male boarding school, college, military service, and clubs.

After Kennedy's lunch on a tray in the private quarters, his black fifty-three-year-old valet George Thomas closed the bedroom curtains. Since Kennedy entered Congress in 1947, Thomas had been looking after him. Cherubic and amiable, Thomas now lived in a room on the third floor, usually slept less than six hours a night, and had acquired "the stumpy walk of a man who has spent a lot of time on his feet."

After changing into a nightshirt, Kennedy climbed under the covers—usually with a hot pad to soothe his back—and read until he dozed off. He stayed in bed at least forty-five minutes even if he could not sleep. Taking a nap after lunch "changed Jack's whole life," Jackie told Lyndon Johnson. "He was always sick, and when we got to the White House he did it every day."

To support his unstable spine, JFK wore a stiff corset and needed a firm mattress specially made from cattle-tail hair, because he was extremely sensitive to horsehair and horse dander. (He could be near horses only in the open air; once when Jackie took him to an indoor horse show, he had to leave early when he developed an allergic reac-tion.) A bed on Air Force One was fitted with a similar mattress, and JFK brought along still another for use in the accommodations where he stayed on his travels. Heads of state had to concern themselves with ensuring that a double-sized frame would be available for Ken-nedy's use.

Kennedy's famous rocking chair was also intended to help manage his back pain. "Such a chair," Dr. Travell told the press, "provides gentle constant exercise and helps prevent muscular fatigue." Sometimes JFK instructed aides to bring it along when he went out to dinner. He seemed to need the rocker to discharge tension—or so it appeared to a number of his visitors. Teddy White's wife, Nancy, speculated that Kennedy's constant rocking indicated a "most restless man who's able probably to work it off in simple ways." Whether it was a side effect from medica-tion or a symptom of one of his illnesses, Kennedy's agitation couldn't be missed—what William Manchester described as a right hand that "seems to have a life of its own": tapping, scratching, tugging, snapping, and seldom still.

Kennedy stoically declined to discuss his persistent pain, but it was evident in "his gingerly walking and sitting," said Sorensen, "in not carrying anything, and when his jaw would tighten and he would become more quiet and less animated." Hervé Alphand, the French ambassador, was shocked when Kennedy couldn't "bend to pick up a match" on one occasion, and another time "asked me to pick up a cup of tea for him" on a low coffee table. Even Tony Bradlee was taken aback when Kennedy asked her to crack some crabs for him at dinner. Friends became accustomed to seeing him periodically on crutches or using a cane—aids that he hid from the public.

While watching movies, he assumed "strange sitting positions," shifted around, and usually had to walk out because of discomfort. Since Kennedy loved movies, this was a source of terrible frustration; finally he instructed that a bed be moved into the White House theater so that he could watch comfortably, propped up by four pillows. He was similarly incapable of completing a round of golf, a game he enjoyed thoroughly. Most of the time, he barely made it through nine holes.

Kennedy had modest personal habits, and was fastidious about his custom-tailored clothes, changing his shirt three or four times a day as he moved through his routines of work, exercise, and rest. In the evenings JFK would unwind by sipping a bottle of beer, a scotch and water (no ice), or a daiquiri. His major indulgence was a slender Upmann cigar. He would smoke one or two after dinner, and he liked to have one lit during ocean cruises. "He could chain smoke cigars when the spirit moved him," recalled Ben Bradlee. Kennedy enjoyed small-stakes gambling on backgammon and golf with friends like Billings and Earl Smith—purely to sharpen the competition—but they rarely collected the wagers.

Although JFK was determined to keep his social and work lives separate, he never fully relaxed. When the Kennedys had dinner parties, he customarily stood up at ten or eleven, suddenly announcing, "I've got some reading to do." But he rarely fell asleep until well after midnight, frequently reaching for the phone to call his father and Bobby. "All our family are light sleepers," Joe Kennedy explained to William Manchester. "Of course he is preoccupied. It would be a miracle if he weren't."

ELEVEN

To a degree not seen before or since in the presidency, Jack Kennedy had an extraordinarily close relationship with the press and co-opted most of the reporters who covered him. He considered himself a journalist manqué. Before turning to politics, Kennedy had flirted briefly with a newspaper career, covering the United Nations Conference and British elections in 1945 for the Hearst chain, and he had briefly owned a newspaper with Jim Reed. When he was a senator, his byline had appeared on articles in the *Atlantic Monthly, New Republic,* and *New York Times Magazine,* although the writing had been done primarily by Sorensen. "Kennedy takes printer's ink for breakfast," said James Reston of the *New York Times.*

JFK read so many publications—delving into the Washington, New York, Baltimore, Boston, Chicago, Philadelphia, and St. Louis papers each day plus *Time, Newsweek,* the *New Republic, New Yorker, Sports Illustrated,* and even Britain's *Times, New Statesman, Spectator, Economist,* and *Manchester Guardian Weekly* "as though they were his household papers," said aide Fred Holborn—that he frequently astonished reporters and columnists by citing information from deep within their stories. After Laura Bergquist had written a piece for *Look* on Generalissimo Rafael Trujillo Molina, dictator of the Dominican Republic, Kennedy slyly asked, "What happened to Snowball?"—a reference to one of the dictator's torture experts, "a notorious Negro dwarf" who specialized in "biting off men's genitals."

Kennedy also liked to "play editor," suggesting topics for stories, as well as lines of inquiry. He constantly prodded Ben Bradlee to pursue leads about political adversaries ("You ought to cut Rocky's ass open a little this week") and gave him tidbits for profiles on members of the administration and the Kennedy family. JFK could "read leaks," scanning the front page of the *New York Times* to "spot special prejudices" and "unerringly identify the sources," said *Time*'s Hugh Sidey. More often than not, JFK himself was the disguised source. "The American ship of state is the only ship that leaks at the top" was the common joke.

Journalists and authors also frequently submitted material to Jack and Bobby Kennedy for corrections and comments before publication. "That's a great thing, that right of clearance," JFK told Bradlee. While he was writing *The Making of the President 1960* early in 1961, Teddy White asked Bobby to review the "thumbnail sketch of the present Attorney General of whom I am so fond and whom I do not want to hurt."

Cabinet officials and White House aides had the same free and easy rapport with the press as their boss—unlike the Eisenhower White House, where access had been carefully monitored by Press Secretary James Hagerty. Kennedy's men circulated through the Georgetown dinner party circuit, buffing his image, advancing his cause.

But one staff member went further than Kennedy would have wanted, acting in a subversive way that JFK, for all his skill at reading between the lines, didn't detect. Fred Dutton served as a liaison between the Irish mafia and the eggheads in the West Wing and considered himself a hybrid of the two camps, an "intellectual politician." But he was also more of an ideologue than most. When he became annoyed that Kennedy's policies were too middle of the road, he secretly began writing for the liberal syndicated columnist Doris Fleeson, known as "God's angry woman," whose opinions were guaranteed "to make [JFK] growl." "Fred didn't do it on purpose at first," recalled his wife, Nancy. "Doris was sick for a couple of weeks during the transition, and she said, 'I can't write my column today,' so Fred wrote it. Then when he was in the White House and frustrated, he would write a liberal attack on the President." While Kennedy never found out, one day he did buttonhole Dutton, who, he knew, was friendly with Fleeson. Slamming the editorial page of the *Washington Star* on Dutton's desk, Kennedy exclaimed, "Can't you control this woman?" Recalled Nancy, "It was a column Fred had written."

———

Because Kennedy was in effect his own press secretary, his official press chief—"the court publicist"—assumed a secondary role. With his bushy eyebrows, plump physique, and ubiquitous cigar, thirty-five-year-old Pierre Salinger was a comic figure known more for his jocular manner than his professional expertise. He ran a chaotic West Wing office of nine people in quarters so cramped that he kept the teletype machines in his bathroom, with one of his "girls" assigned to dash in and out to clip wire service bulletins announced by insistently ringing bells. "In the tradition of TV mysteries," David Wise of the *New York Herald Tribune* wrote admiringly, "he has not one but three blonde secretaries."

Salinger confined himself mainly to routine briefings and the flow of information. "Pierre would poke his head into the Oval Office and be startled to see a reporter talking with the President," recalled Hugh Sidey. The Irish mafia, especially O'Donnell, disliked Salinger's flamboyance and self-promoting ways. "Kenny thought he was a foppish guy," said John Reilly, an aide to Bobby Kennedy.

Still, JFK was amused by Salinger, who left himself open to numerous japes. "Get back into long pants," Kennedy once exclaimed. "You haven't got the legs for shorts." Underneath the banter, Kennedy appreciated Salinger's ability to divert and soothe reporters lacking special access to the top. Salinger also enjoyed a cultural cachet. Growing up in San Francisco as the son of a French Catholic mother and an American Jewish father, he had been a child prodigy pianist, an accomplishment that occasionally earned him a spot on Jack and Jackie's guest list. But while Salinger saw Kennedy often in the course of a day, he remained outside the inner circle.

Salinger did have one great idea that helped define the Kennedy presidency: he pushed JFK to conduct his news conferences live on television. Sorensen, Bundy, Rusk, and others objected. "It's really crazy," Sorensen said. "Suppose he makes a mistake? It'll get around the world." But Kennedy liked the opportunity to present himself directly to the people, confident that he had the ability to get his message across.

For the most part, Kennedy's formal encounters with the press were friendly and bore little resemblance to the adversarial exchanges of later presidencies. Reporters asked softball questions and laughed heartily at Kennedy's jokes. "We were simply there as props," said Peter Lisagor of the *Chicago Daily News*. "I always felt we should have joined Actors' Equity."

It took a few sessions for Kennedy to find his footing; he was initially judged as "elaborately serious." But his formidable memory, rapid quips, and knowledge of arcane facts resulted in bravura performances. It didn't much matter, as the *New York Herald Tribune* noted, that Kennedy "sometimes gets lost in a fog of words," or, as ABC's Howard K. Smith observed, "It was hard to find a verb." JFK was telegenic and skillful at debate after years of training at his father's dinner table.

"He was always in control," said Robert Pierpoint of CBS. "I don't think Kennedy ever really gave us or very seldom gave us the answers we were looking for. But he was clever in handling the non-answers." As Kennedy told Ken Galbraith during a preparation session with a group of aides for a press conference, "When it comes to evasion, I don't need help. I can do that myself."

JFK had been tutored in media manipulation by his father, who was advised in 1944 by his cousin, the political sage Joe Kane, "Our presidents are selected more or less by newspapers, radio commentators and magazine writers." While Joe Kennedy's credo was "remember, reporters are not your friends," he taught his sons how to coddle and flatter them—for instance, by sending notes of thanks for any "kind reference"—and to use influential contacts to place stories in national magazines. When *Life* was about to run a cover story on Jack, Jackie, and baby Caroline in April 1958, Joe predicted to a friend that it would be "of great political import."

JFK had also seen the power of his father's checkbook during the 1952 Senate race when the Ambassador made a $500,000 short-term loan to the *Boston Post* to reward the cash-strapped publisher for switching his endorsement from Lodge to JFK. "You know we had to buy that paper," JFK told Fletcher Knebel of *Look* in 1960. Knebel instinctively protected Kennedy by omitting the damaging quote from his article.

JFK spun journalists with greater finesse than his father, primarily because he understood them and found their company intellectually stimulating. "It was studied and calculated, but still [JFK] liked reporters," said Democratic senator George Smathers of Florida. While Kennedy's predecessors in the Oval Office seldom saw the press in private, he went out of his way to do so. Not only did he brief influential Washington insiders such as James Reston and Walter Lippmann, he regularly scheduled lunches with out-of-town editors and publishers. Otis Chandler of the *Los Angeles Times* recalled that Kennedy "was fascinated that I had been Republican and that I was changing to independent."

In parceling out his leaks, Kennedy tried to make each newsman feel he was receiving special treatment. "Protect me," JFK once told Cy Sulzberger of the *New York Times*. "Don't let Reston or any of those other fellows know you have seen me." (Unbeknownst to Sulzberger, Kennedy had already arranged to meet Reston for a similar briefing two days later.) Sulzberger's status as a member of the powerful family that owned the *Times* enhanced his access to Kennedy and members of his circle. Although he was based in Paris, Sulzberger traveled regularly to the United States and kept a detailed journal.

Kennedy inspired nearly as much awe in journalists as he did in his own staff. "I always had the feeling," said Rowland Evans of the pro-Republican *New York Herald Tribune,* "when I was writing about President Kennedy that he was standing right there behind me, watching the words come and waiting to bore in."

JFK granted reporters interviews that would run beyond their scheduled time, keeping cabinet officials and other aides waiting. He thought nothing of talking to reporters in his bedroom or while taking a swim in the nude. When Hugh Sidey joined him for several swims, "both of us were naked," Sidey recalled. "Later all the *Time* editors wanted a reading on the President's private parts. He wasn't abnormal in any way." On another occasion, Stewart Alsop recounted that "typically, when Jackie surprised [JFK] and two other men swimming bare ass in the White House pool, the other two were reporters."

Kennedy's most effectively ingratiating technique with the press was his "unbelievable private candor"—indiscreet revelations, outspoken opinions about individuals—that virtually bound his listener to keep the confidence. At various times, Kennedy told Ben Bradlee that the vice premier of Laos was "a total shit" and that French president Charles de Gaulle was a "bastard," and he revealed precisely how much tycoons J. Paul Getty and H. L. Hunt paid in income taxes ($500 and $22,000, respectively), adding it was "probably illegal" for him to know, much less tell a journalist. Bradlee duly noted these explosive comments in his journal, but like his colleagues, printed none of them. Sometimes Kennedy stipulated an "off-the-record" remark; more typically he would place the onus on the reporter. "He put you on your mettle," said Henry Brandon, Washington correspondent for the *Sunday Times* of London. "He left it entirely up to you . . . In the end one was more careful than one should have been."

In addition to supplying material for JFK's speeches, journalists vied for his attention by giving him policy recommendations—Cy Sulzberger suggesting talking points for de Gaulle, Teddy White arguing for the admission of Communist China to the United Nations, CBS correspondent David Schoenbrun analyzing the situation in Morocco. Kennedy was always "playing the game of making us feel that we were big people and very helpful to him," said Pierpoint.

———

Kennedy's closest journalistic *consigliere* was Charley Bartlett, a columnist for the *Chattanooga Times*. JFK had met Bartlett late in 1945 in Palm Beach, when JFK was poised to run for Congress and Bartlett was an aspiring newspaperman. Bartlett had served with the navy in the Pacific as an intelligence officer specializing in radio eavesdropping. They were both Catholics, and they had in common Joe Kennedy's editorial factotum Arthur Krock, who had recommended Charley to Arthur Hays Sulzberger, publisher of the *New York Times,* for a reporter's job on the family's newspaper in Tennessee.

Bartlett came from what Krock called the "Chicago industrial aristocracy," solid Republicans with conventional values and attitudes. The family had made a fortune from a headache remedy, and Charley's father, Valentine Bartlett, was a successful stockbroker. Charley went to Yale, like five previous generations of Bartletts. His wife, Martha, was the granddaughter of a founder of U.S. Steel and had a slightly stern manner. As a couple they were "kind of classy," observed Katie Louchheim after a dinner party, noting that they didn't "condescend" or "snoot."

Affable and quick-witted, Bartlett spoke in a rapid-fire mumble and laughed in a "cosy, conspicuous way." Charley instantly fell for the Kennedy magic—what he once described as a "kind of cheerful lightning [that] touched us all." The two men "had the same view of life and people," said Bartlett, "warm but rather critical. We both saw the same elements of humor, and we were both deeply interested in politics. It was a very chemical relationship, for me a very easy relationship, and I think for him too."

Like Walton, Bartlett had a separate connection to Jackie—coincidentally through Arthur Krock, who knew her through his friend Hugh Auchincloss. Bartlett, who was four years younger than JFK and eight years older than Jackie, had dated her briefly when she was a college junior—an "intellectual beau," said Yusha Auchincloss. She had viewed Bartlett as well meaning but straitlaced, and had mildly resented his warnings not to consort with "foreigners."

Of the three journalists in Kennedy's inner circle—Bradlee, Alsop, and Bartlett—it was Bartlett who most overtly abandoned his journalistic principles for his friendship with Kennedy. Pierre Salinger felt that as a result, Bartlett's writing "became so dull" during the Kennedy years. Bartlett later admitted that "nothing mattered to me more than to have Jack Kennedy succeed as president. It did compromise my role as a journalist. My respect for the reading public is great, but it didn't match my feeling to do what I needed to have Jack succeed, not just as a friend but as a citizen. I made a cold decision on that. . . . It was not possible to be a good newspaper man and be a close friend of the President. . . . I felt I would protect anything he told me. He had reason to trust me because it didn't blow onto him."

For professional as well as personal reasons, Bartlett and Ben Bradlee were openly at odds. Because Bradlee often put morsels from his dinner table talks with Kennedy into the pages of *Newsweek,* Bartlett considered him disloyal. "Ben had a different approach," said Bartlett. "He put *Newsweek* ahead of his relationship with Kennedy." Bradlee said he used material from his friendship with Kennedy "without embarrassment," although he never resolved the "conflicting loyalties" he

felt. Bradlee believed that Bartlett "got pleasure and reward out of giving Kennedy advice. Charley was more of a sounding board. They were
fellow wonks together."

Yet Bradlee was not immune to counseling JFK either. Early in the
presidential campaign he had written a long memo on LBJ's performance and prospects. His verdict: As a campaigner Johnson "could
never make it. . . . He's somebody's gabby Texas cousin . . . hard to take
seriously." But Bradlee had presciently warned Kennedy that LBJ was
"to be feared not as a potential winner but as a game-player" who could
"try to maneuver you right out of" the convention.

The real source of the rivalry between Bartlett and Bradlee, as often
happened with old boarding-school boys, was St. Mark's, where they
had been classmates in the mid-thirties. Bartlett had disapproved of
Bradlee's irreverence and ambition. "I am a little stuffy," Bartlett admitted, "Ben was always tough." Bradlee, who had been a keen athlete
before being paralyzed at age fourteen for a number of months during a
polio epidemic, recalled dismissing Bartlett for his lack of athletic talent
and for being "a dweeb."

As a Washington journalist, Bartlett "cast no shadow at all," said
Bradlee. Bartlett's reports by definition had a limited audience in Washington, although he did have the prestige of a Pulitzer Prize he won in
1956. Bartlett had written a series examining the links between Eisenhower's secretary of the air force, Harold E. Talbott, and a Manhattan
consulting firm doing business with defense contractors. Bartlett had
been helped in his probe by Bobby Kennedy, whose contacts unearthed
Talbott's client list, clinching the story and prompting the secretary's resignation. As he was writing the series, Bartlett discussed it with
JFK, who told him to "make it tough." Bartlett believed that Arthur
Krock worked to secure his Pulitzer, much as he would assist Jack a year
later.

Throughout his presidency, Kennedy was frequently on the phone
with Bartlett, who routinely sent him memos—what JFK called
"Bartlettisms"—offering ideas on policy, personnel, and even matters of
health (once advising a "Spartan diet" to help JFK's ailing back) and
image (When Charley suggested JFK wear a more folksy herringbone
overcoat instead of navy blue on a campaign trip to Wisconsin, JFK
snapped, "Are you trying to change my personality?"). "I'd shoot things
in to Jack that I thought were important to his situation," said Bartlett.

"I functioned, let's face it, as his eyes and ears. I was very helpful to him because you see as a newsman what you don't see in the White House."

Jack Kennedy relied on Bartlett, ex-journalist Walton, and other key allies in a sub rosa intelligence network to serve what JFK called his "need to know something about the people I have to deal with." "We told him everything," said Bill Walton, who, like Bartlett, regularly reported back what he had heard at dinner parties. During one such evening at the home of Walter Lippmann, Walton paid close attention to CIA director Allen Dulles, whom he "detested." The next morning, Walton called Kennedy at dawn to confide that Dulles "started boasting how he was still carrying out his brother Foster's foreign policy." Recalling his own words the night after the election, Walton said, "See what I mean? You should have fired him," to which Kennedy replied, "God damn it, did he really say that?"

———

Some reporters resisted Kennedy's allure. Stewart Alsop called himself "Mr. Facing Both Ways" to emphasize his effort to be evenhanded. Hugh Sidey kept his identity as a "guy from Iowa" and refused to get "swept into the Kennedy social circles" that made him "uncomfortable." But the most vexing to JFK was *New York Times* political columnist Arthur Krock, who was seventy-four when Jack was elected and had known him since he was a little boy.

William Manchester observed that the "impeccable Arthur Krock . . . appears and reappears in the Kennedy saga, like a benign linking character in a Henry James novel." It was Krock who had suggested Jackie for a job at the *Times-Herald,* as he had Kathleen Kennedy a decade earlier. Long before lobbying the Pulitzer judges for *Profiles in Courage,* Krock had been an early mentor of Jack; one of JFK's Harvard roommates, James Rousmanière, called Krock "the single major influence" during the Harvard years. Krock had seen the commercial potential of Jack's senior thesis, suggested the title *Why England Slept,* and helped "work over" the book for publication. Krock even "gave [JFK] my house man," George Thomas, who would remain with Kennedy throughout his presidency—the only black Kennedy knew more than casually.

A close contemporary of Joe Kennedy, Krock admired the Ambassador's blunt, hard-charging personality, his talent as a political strategist, and his "natural conservatism." When Joe had harbored his own presidential ambitions in the late thirties, Krock had written favorable columns speculating about his potential candidacy. Although Krock was Jewish, he remained loyal when Joe was charged with anti-Semitism following his ouster as ambassador. Krock had accepted his $5,000 retainer from Joe to ghostwrite a booklet called *I'm for Roosevelt.* But he had refused the Ambassador's offer of a car one Christmas—"a kind of bribe," Krock recalled.

Krock had long recognized JFK's ability, but during the 1960 campaign he took strong exception to the Democratic platform as too liberal, especially on "the racial question," which Krock feared would "exclude the rights of the majority." Krock knew that his views mirrored those of the Ambassador, but his coverage of Jack was so disparaging that Joe Kennedy rebuked him for it. When Krock did not finally "come out for Jack," Joe ended their friendship of more than twenty-five years. Krock reflected later, "Probably he never liked me at all, but found a use for me. . . . I happened to be in a position of value to him."

Jack was careful to maintain cordial relations with the influential "Mr. Krock," although he did urge Bradlee to criticize the columnist in *Newsweek.* "Bust it off on old Arthur," said Kennedy. "He can't take it, and when you go after him he folds." In the first few months of his presidency JFK socialized with Krock a couple of times—once at the White House in the company of Arthur Schlesinger, Sam Rayburn, Alice Longworth, LBJ, and William Fulbright, where Kennedy preserved "his easy domination of the evening"—as well as at a small dinner at Krock's Georgetown home arranged by Charley Bartlett. But Kennedy flashed his pique over brandy and cigars when he joked, "How does such a benign-looking fellow write such mean bullshit?" Krock continued to "jab" the President, and JFK kept fretting about it. "It was very very hard on Jack," said Lem Billings. "Jack always read everything he wrote and always felt badly and just couldn't understand why he was doing it."

According to Sorensen, Kennedy "rarely saw" those he considered "hopelessly unfriendly" in the press, but he "kept trying with *Time*" because it was the most influential American publication of the day, with a circulation of nearly three million. "I read that damn magazine,"

Kennedy told Hugh Sidey, "and I don't care where I've been in the world, I go into the Ambassador's office, and he says, 'As I was reading in *Time*.'" Kennedy also believed that no other publication had such sway with the "swing opinion" that decided elections. In its depth of analysis, colorful texture, historical details, erudition, and overall comprehensiveness, *Time* far surpassed the coverage of even the best daily newspapers.

Time, like its founding editor, Henry Robinson Luce, was Republican in its outlook, but Jack Kennedy had strong connections to Luce, sixty-two, and his beautiful fifty-seven-year-old wife, Clare. Harry Luce had been a classmate of Hugh Auchincloss at Yale, and a friend of Joe Kennedy for several decades. Clare Luce, a mesmerizing journalist, playwright, diplomat, and congresswoman, had an even closer relationship with Joe. Writing in her diary, Clare once hinted that she and Joe had been lovers ("JPK in bedroom all morning"), but Tish Baldrige, who worked for Clare for four years, insisted that it was a "political power relationship," defined by spirited talk on issues and personalities. "Give me a half an hour's conversation," Joe once wrote to Clare, "I will know more than I will reading twenty magazines." Rose also appreciated Clare's sophisticated intelligence, particularly her talent for the "devastating remark which is both comic and still pregnant with meaning."

At Joe Kennedy's request, Harry Luce wrote a glowing foreword to *Why England Slept,* which gave the book an important boost. When Jack made his vice presidential run in 1956, the Luces were houseguests of the Kennedys on the Riviera, and Harry cabled his editors to expand *Time*'s coverage of Jack as a "considerable national figure." Both *Time* and *Life* gave the Kennedys extensive play in their pages, and in 1960 Luce told Joe his publications would look favorably on Jack as long as he held a tough line on communism. *Life* gave Nixon a tepid endorsement, and Luce welcomed Kennedy's victory. Putting his Republican principles aside, Luce knew a Kennedy presidency would be a dynamic story for his publications. He also knew that Kennedy as chief executive would be more cautious than his rhetoric.

"He seduces me," Luce said, when asked to explain his attraction to Jack Kennedy. JFK was equally fascinated by Luce—"like a cricket, always chirping away"—as an individualistic self-made man who reminded him of his father. Clare admitted to falling for young Jack's charms—"no doubt my feminine weakness," she told Baldrige—and gave him a "sacred medal" for good luck in the navy. As time went on, JFK and Clare became scratchy. "They liked each other in the way that two tigers like each other," said Sorensen. When Kennedy was president, Clare didn't hesitate to write what Lem Billings called "mean and bitter" articles in various magazines and newspapers (not *Time* or *Life*) expressing her disappointment.

The Kennedys excluded the Luces from their inner circle (contributing at least in part to Clare's venom), yet JFK remained obsessed with *Time*. He and his top aides, especially Bobby, gave continuous access to Sidey, at age thirty-three one of the younger journalists covering the White House. Each Sunday night JFK received the latest issue of *Time* by special messenger directly from the printer. Most weeks Kennedy would call Sidey at home to complain "in cheerfully profane style." With his folksy midwestern personality, Sidey was difficult to dislike, so Kennedy railed that the editors "who lived in Greenwich and ate at '21'" twisted the Washington reporting. (Kennedy once told Bradlee that *Time*'s reporters "file the Bible . . . and the magazine prints the Koran.") Sorensen was even more outspoken, decrying *Time* as "slanted, unfair . . . inaccurate."

Although *Time* was more consistently critical than *Newsweek*, it did not lose to its smaller rival on important stories. Despite Bradlee's social access, *Time* editors "never worried about *Newsweek*," said managing editor Otto Fuerbringer. A dozen times during his presidency, Kennedy summoned Luce to the White House to needle him about *Time*'s coverage. Luce would hold his ground while attempting to keep the peace, but would not direct Fuerbringer to change his approach.

"We were never anti-Kennedy by any means," said Fuerbringer. "We were critical when there was something to be critical about, or if he did something for political reasons." Kennedy "took all praise as his due and reacted with anger to any criticism." (When *Time* made JFK "Man of the Year" at the end of 1961, the Kennedys asked Sidey, "Has anybody been Man of the Year eight times in a row?") Still, after Dwight Eisenhower, who didn't read *Time*, Luce and company were pleased to have a president who "paid attention to everything, knew about everything, and cared about everything going on, policy and serious matters and also gossip," said Fuerbringer. "It was one of the liveliest presidencies to cover. It was more fun, more interesting than any other."

The fact was, Kennedy's admirers and critics alike enjoyed playing the game with him. Visiting the Oval Office a couple of months after Kennedy took office, Teddy White was tickled by the President's appealing informality. Kennedy stood in his underwear as they spoke while his tailors fitted him for a suit. Yet White also saw that beneath the bravado, the new president "was groping . . . strangely uncertain"— until Kennedy shifted gears and began spouting foreign policy ideas, showing his "sense of the reporter's craft," even asking White if he should write a letter to Mao Tse-tung and Chou En-lai about problems in Southeast Asia. White couldn't help feeling pleased, knowing that Kennedy was "saying what he felt I needed for a toga clad portrait."

TWELVE

*E*arly one evening after the Kennedys had been in the White House for a few months, the phone rang at the home of Franklin D. Roosevelt Jr. in Washington's Spring Valley neighborhood. The Kennedys felt like chatting. "Here they were in that house that wasn't their home, and they had the evening off, so they were calling their friends, just to talk on the phone," recalled Suzanne Roosevelt. "That really got to me because of the circumstances. They were in the White House."

Jack and Jackie never lost their eagerness to stay connected to people and events beyond what Harry Truman called the "Big White Prison." "Jack missed things," said longtime friend Vivian Crespi. "He was always saying, 'What's going on out there?'" In part, he wished to be diverted, but Kennedy knew, as Marian Schlesinger observed, that "historians are great gossips at a high level." He used information about personalities to take the measure of both enemies and friends, and to understand the ebb and flow of human relations, all with a slightly sardonic eye.

JFK "took the opinion of everyone within range," said Joe Alsop—from Pat Hass, the mother of one of Caroline's friends, whom Kennedy quizzed about "what people were thinking at the Safeway," to Jackie's New York hairdresser Kenneth Battelle, who could report on the chitchat among ladies under the hair dryers. "It was light, but not idle," recalled Kenneth. "He was interested, he wanted answers." Kennedy even "liked to meet friends of his friends," Bradlee recalled, "provided they were involved in vital fields—'out there on the cutting edge,' he once called it."

Kennedy tapped certain friends for Manhattan gossip, and others for the latest Hollywood news or Palm Beach tittle-tattle. When Solange Herter reported that "Liz Taylor would scream four-letter words out the chalet window" in Gstaad, "Jack loved that," Herter recalled. He dutifully inquired about the business world where he had few contacts and about which he knew precious little. But discussing journalists was another matter. It was one of Kennedy's "all-time favorite subjects," said Ben Bradlee. "It is unbelievable . . . how . . . clued in he was to their characters, their office politics, their petty rivalries." Kennedy's interest in foreign leaders was similarly voracious—from policy to peccadilloes. "Who does Castro sleep with?" Kennedy asked a disconcerted Laura Bergquist of *Look*. "I hear he doesn't even take his boots off."

Jackie's approach to gossip was more selective. With Pat Hass she would speculate about Washington insiders such as Frances Scott "Scottie" Lanahan, the daughter of F. Scott Fitzgerald, who had snubbed Jackie when she was a Senate wife. "Jackie would say disparaging things—so and so is not very sexy," recalled Hass. "For that time she could be fairly raunchy. These were women who had kind of hurt her feelings." Jackie was also intrigued by figures in fashion and the international jet set. "She liked to hear things, but not to the same extent as Jack," said her sister, Lee. "It was always with humor."

Jackie arranged their White House social life in tiers from the least to the most formal. Like President Franklin Roosevelt, JFK craved variety. The Kennedys' intimate dinners—with one to three other couples—were usually hatched late in the day after Jackie had assessed her husband's frame of mind. "He was seldom sure in the morning what his mood would be in the evening," she said. Jackie would signal Evelyn Lincoln to phone the invitations, sometimes as late as 6 p.m. The atmosphere at these get-togethers was so nonchalant that Bill Walton took to calling the White House "the pizza palace on Pennsylvania Avenue."

Still, they were invariably command performances, often requiring

quick rearrangements of schedules by invited guests. Despite the impromptu nature of such evenings, Jack and Jackie paid close attention to
the social mix, recognizing the fault lines within their circle of friends.
For example, Bill Walton, Red Fay, and Ben Bradlee were never invited
with Lem Billings. Charley Bartlett would not share a table with Ben
Bradlee, nor would Walton socialize with Fay. "There was underground
jealousy among these people," said Laura Bergquist. "There was an
orbit, like the sun with the planets, and the planets each had their
own place."

Every ten days or so, Jackie would organize one of her elaborate dinner parties for eight or more guests that would include "stimulating
people"—diplomats, artists, actors, writers, summoned from as far as
California and Europe, the names often supplied by Arthur Schlesinger, Oleg Cassini, and other well-connected insiders. Jackie preferred such gatherings to the "social treadmill" of cocktail parties for
which she had "no esteem." The small dinner could be "awfully valuable," in Jackie's view, because "men can talk to each other afterwards. . . . The French know this. . . . If you put busy men in an attractive
atmosphere where the surroundings are comfortable, the food is good,
you relax, you unwind, there's some stimulating conversation. You
know, sometimes quite a lot can happen, contacts can be made. . . . It's
part of the art of living in Washington."

Jack Kennedy brought an "intense concentration" and a "gently
teasing humor" to the dinner table, along with what Katharine Graham
called his habit of "vacuum cleaning your brain." Marian Schlesinger
felt that exchanges with Kennedy had a "hit-and-run" quality: "You
were intimate one minute, and then it was over." Oleg Cassini thought
of the Kennedy courtiers as "social samurai" participating in "the conversational equivalent of athletic competition." Ben Bradlee observed
that more often than not, "the conversation jumped around" in a "relaxed but scattered" fashion. Among some close friends, Kennedy lapsed
into navy talk. "He used 'prick' and 'fuck' and 'nuts' and 'bastard' and
'son of a bitch' with an ease and comfort that belied his upbringing,"
said Bradlee. "Somehow it never seemed offensive, or at least it never
seemed offensive to me"—mainly because such language came just as
easily to Bradlee. Yet Kennedy scarcely swore in the presence of Charley
Bartlett or Jim Reed.

As a hostess, Jackie reminded William Manchester of "an eclectic blend of traditionalism and *ton*" who evoked "memories of young Edwardian ladies briefing themselves before a party by writing conversation topics on the sticks of a fan." Yet she created an illusion of utter spontaneity.

Jackie discouraged "gen con"—general conversations focused on meaty issues of the day—and consciously sought to mute what Chuck Spalding called Jack's "extremely sensitive and high-strung" nature by setting a casual tone. "She conceived it right to try and avoid serious conversation when [Jack] was supposed to be relaxing, and rather deliberately made fun of serious topics—would sometimes, I think, quite deliberately make a foolish remark about the political situation just to see him explode," recalled David Gore. "It was this sort of light-hearted approach while he was away from work which I think she thought was very important for him, and I think it intrigued him and was very valuable to him."

From time to time Jackie invited Flo Smith to the White House "to talk about parties," recalled Flo's son Earl. Flo was a fount of arcana— "sybarites in ancient Egypt wore little gloves on their tongues between courses so that they could enjoy flavors to the fullest"—as well as ideas for entertaining that she eagerly shared. Among the suggestions Jackie took to heart: "Have pretty women, attractive men, guests who are *en passant,* the flavor of another language. This is the jet age, so have something new and changing."

"Old-fashioned Washington was put on the side," said Elizabeth Burton, a member of the city's old-line establishment. "With the Kennedys, the Europeans came to Washington. Who had known about Agnelli in Washington before the Kennedys?" Gilbert "Benno" Graziani, an Italian photographer for *Paris-Match* and unofficial "historian of *le tout monde,*" became a coveted White House guest who "wouldn't think twice about flying from Paris for a party," said Oleg Cassini. Another favorite was Arkady Gerney, a wealthy Swiss American who had attended Harvard with JFK and had known Jackie from Paris days. A longtime bachelor, "Arkady was very close to Jackie," said Solange Herter. "He was concerned about things like what shoes Jackie wore so her feet wouldn't look so big." (Jackie had cause for concern: she wore a size 10A.)

Still, the most popular extra man at the Kennedy court was Bill Walton, who took on a role akin to the nineteenth century's Henry Adams.

Walton wrote about Adams's "niche" as "stable-companion to states-men," exchanging visits in the "tight little world" of Theodore Roosevelt's White House and the homes of his friends on Lafayette Square across the street. "Adams managed to be on the edge of great events, to stay near the seat of power, and to know intimately most of the great political figures of his time," wrote Walton, who could easily have been speaking about himself.

While Walton had known JFK longer, he was just as close to Jackie, who had met him when she worked at the *Times-Herald*. Fresh out of college, she had seen Walton as the epitome of worldliness, but he was also infinitely sympathetic, shrewd about people, and affectionate. His eccentricity amused her. He wore work shirts and blue jeans ("a size too small," she teased him in a telegram) long before such attire was fashionable. Walton's mid-career shift into painting appealed to her aesthetic side and to her fascination with nonconformists.

Most women, Jackie included, found Walton "charmingly ugly," in the words of Senator Claiborne Pell's wife, Nuala. Jackie once sent Walton a Valentine comparing him to the sexy Marlboro man: "against a million smiles on the faces of a million handsome models, this face would stand out." Walton became a "walker" for Washington's grandes dames. He played bridge with Katharine Graham and Stewart Alsop's wife, Tish, and savored the bons mots of Alice Roosevelt Longworth in her "slightly crumbling mansion near Dupont Circle." His confiding manner made him popular with men and women alike. "He was at once the most indiscreet and most discreet man alive," said Nancy White. "You could absolutely trust him. He knew with whom to be indiscreet and whom to trust. He had a lot of secrets about everyone. He knew which things to reveal."

Many Washingtonians assumed that Walton was, as Ben Bradlee put it, "gay as a goose." But other than platonic friendships with numerous women, there was no evidence for that assumption as there was with Joe Alsop. Walton had gone through a searing divorce that left him with a son and daughter to raise by himself. Whenever the subject of matrimony came up, he slipped into an impenetrable silence.

It was no accident that Walton had been included in the Kennedys' first small dinner party, held two nights after the inauguration. It was a lively if haphazard evening. The furniture was draped with swatches left by Sister Parish, everyone feasted on ten pounds of fresh caviar (a gift from a Palm Beach acquaintance) in an "enormous gold bucket as big as a milk pail," consumed Dom Pérignon champagne, ate a dinner of turtle soup, filet mignon, and profiteroles, and watched films of the inauguration in the White House movie theater.

Walton shrewdly brought as his date Mary Russell, a fifty-something widow of a *New York Herald Tribune* reporter. The daughter of Russian aristocrats, Mary promised good value for Kennedy. She was knowledgeable about the Soviet Union and fluent in Russian, lively and attractive, one of the most popular women in Washington. The other guests were Joe Alsop and the Franklin D. Roosevelt Jrs.

The presence of the Roosevelts that evening was particularly significant as a gesture of both gratitude and solace by the Kennedys. The third of FDR's four surviving sons (another namesake boy had died at seven months), Franklin Roosevelt Jr. had known JFK since Harvard days, when he was a senior during Jack's freshman year, and both were famous for being speed demons behind the wheel. They also had overlapped for four years as congressmen. Young Roosevelt had been the son who seemed destined for a successful political career after Groton, Harvard, University of Virginia Law School, and naval service during the war, when he participated in the invasion of North Africa. As a girl, Jackie had been smitten with Franklin, and was caught peeking from behind a curtain to watch him in his ensign's uniform at Newport dances.

FDR Jr. had his father's strong good looks, radiant smile, and gregarious personality but sadly lacked his focus and grit. After three terms in Congress, he had lost to Averell Harriman—the candidate of the Tammany Hall machine—in his 1954 bid for the gubernatorial nomination in New York. "He didn't do his homework," recalled Sue, who was his second wife. "Franklin didn't have much self-discipline. He was terribly bright and able, and he would start off like a house afire, then he would lose his confidence and start drinking and do things like not get up and go to work." Like his siblings, Franklin also had a turbulent love life; the five Roosevelt children would log twenty marriages, and Franklin would account for five of them.

As a scion of twentieth-century America's great WASP political family, FDR Jr. intrigued Kennedy, who also recognized his strategic value.

Jack Kennedy was an admirer of FDR's political skills, which he had studied carefully. Yet undercurrents of tension existed between the Kennedys and Roosevelts stemming from FDR's firing of Joe Kennedy as ambassador to Britain. FDR took a dim view of Joe Kennedy; four months after Joe had left public life, Roosevelt called him "a little pathetic" for worrying that his family would be "social outcasts," and dismissed him as "thoroughly selfish."

Roosevelt's widow shared FDR's disdain, which spilled over into skepticism about Jack—a "cold and calculating person," in her view, who succeeded only through "a kind of meretricious charm and money." During JFK's campaign for the presidency, Eleanor Roosevelt had been a persistent scold, accusing Joe of buying his son's Democratic nomination. After her ardent support of Adlai Stevenson at the 1960 convention, Arthur Schlesinger urged her to make peace with Jack. Kennedy "did a lot to win her over, but she didn't like him," said Charley Bartlett. According to Walton, "Jack honestly didn't like her particularly."

But Jack and Jackie got along well with FDR Jr., who was "huge fun," recalled Bartlett. "He really had a sense of humor, he left himself wide open to be laughed at, and he was a very naughty boy." Early in 1960, Franklin had broken with his mother to support Jack's candidacy, and Joe Kennedy persuaded him to join the primary campaign in heavily Protestant West Virginia, where the Roosevelt name was revered. "In a certain sense he was almost God's son coming down and saying it was all right to vote for this Catholic," recalled Charles Peters, a Kennedy campaign aide. Under intense pressure from Bobby Kennedy, Roosevelt unfairly portrayed JFK opponent Hubert Humphrey as a draft dodger, which helped push the electorate to Kennedy.

It was the turning point that helped seal Kennedy's nomination—for which both Jack and Jackie would always feel indebted. Kennedy tried to return the favor by asking Robert McNamara to name Roosevelt secretary of the navy, a sentimental choice because FDR had held the same job. But McNamara rejected him as unqualified, mainly because of his drinking problem. It was clear that FDR Jr. was hurt deeply, although he said nothing at the time. "Jack Kennedy owed Franklin," said Sue Roosevelt. "But he had to be careful not to put him anywhere where he could be embarrassing to the administration by making a mistake." Eventually Kennedy appointed him under secretary of commerce, where "he couldn't get into too much trouble," said Sue Roosevelt.

The signature events of Jackie's social calendar—formal only in their requirement of black tie and gowns—were her elegant private dinner dances. The Kennedys "didn't dare give one for themselves," wrote Ben Bradlee. To make such frivolous occasions "more publicly acceptable," the trick was finding "beards"—friends or relatives whom the Kennedys could "honor" with a party. The first of these honorees were Jackie's sister, Lee, and her husband, Stanislas, popularly known as Prince and Princess Radziwill—a sixteenth-century Polish title that his British citizenship invalidated.

Four years younger than Jackie, Lee was just twenty-seven as the Kennedy administration began. She had been married to forty-six-year-old Stas (pronounced "Stash") for two years—a shotgun wedding that produced a son, followed a year later by a daughter born three months early. Stas had a bulky build, a black mustache, and tanned skin as smooth as polished stone. "Why he is nothing but a European version of your father!" exclaimed Janet Auchincloss when she first met Stas, which Lee said "made me love him all the more." Lee was a more classic beauty than Jackie, with high cheekbones, delicate features, and eyes that Truman Capote described as "gold-brown like a glass of brandy . . . in front of firelight." At five foot six, she was an inch shorter than her sister, but just as slender.

Jackie and Lee (who called each other "Jacks" and "Pekes") were typecast early by their parents: Jackie the intellectual, and Lee the one Janet said would "have twelve children and live in a rose-covered cottage." Jackie was also "strong and athletic," while Lee was, by her own admission, "soft and chubby." Horses frightened Lee, but Jackie pleased their mother by equaling her talent as an equestrienne. In part because Jackie resembled her father (and carried a feminine form of his name), Black Jack Bouvier favored her as well. He relied on her cleverness as a way of ingratiating himself with his own father, Grampy Jack, a scholar of Greek and Latin who prided himself on his erudition and demeaned his son as an intellectual lightweight. Grampy Jack picked Jackie as his star, applauding her poems and literary interests.

Both girls received plenty of encouragement from their parents—accolades for achievements, as well as exhortations to work hard, use their talents, and "be the best." Their mother prodded them to create birthday and holiday gifts—either drawings or poems—and every Christmas Eve they performed a play in her honor "where she cried incessantly," said Lee. Janet was taut and nervous, with a quick temper, and she often assumed the role of enforcer, sharply reprimanding her daughters for lapses in comportment and appearance—a crooked seam in a stocking or a dangling coat button. "She was overbearingly proper," said Solange Herter, "and not very warm." Still, Jackie "was always grateful to her," in Lee's view, and "felt she had intentionally enlarged our world. . . . She was always far more grateful than I was."

Jackie and Lee particularly adored their roguish father, a "life enhancer" who indulged them with treats and amused them with daring excursions to casinos, racetracks, and boxing matches. He warned them that "all men are rats," urging them to "play hard to get" and "never be easy." They thrilled to his dramatic impulses, although they lamented the nasal laugh that he passed on to both of them. His sense of style deeply impressed them—the crisp gabardine suits adorned with his Society of the Cincinnati boutonniere—not to mention his completely hairless chest. "To be with him when we were children meant joy, excitement and love," Lee recalled.

Jackie and Lee were caught in the crossfire of their parents' acrimonious divorce, which embarrassingly played out in the pages of the *New York Daily Mirror* with photos of Black Jack's girlfriends. Lee was hit especially hard by the withering remarks their mother and father made about each other; she became anorexic when barely a teenager. Jackie coped by developing what Lee called the ability "to press the button and tune out."

Jackie's resilience was severely tested by her lonely and bitter father as his fortunes declined and his personal life fell apart. He was reduced to giving Jackie and Lee dinner on a card table in front of the fireplace in his one-bedroom Manhattan apartment, because his tiny dining room served as a bedroom for the girls. (He did manage to help cover their school and travel expenses, although Hughdie paid a significant share.) Insecure and sensitive to any slight, whether imaginary or real, Jack Bouvier repeatedly complained that both girls neglected him, but Jackie bore the brunt. "If I didn't come in for as much praise as Jackie," Lee recalled, "I also didn't receive the same amount of criticism as she did." In angry letters, her father accused Jackie of selfishness, arrogance, intolerance, and carelessness with money.

Surrounded by luxury and wealth, but lacking fortunes of their own, both Lee and Jackie became preoccupied by the need for financial stability. "They were like little orphans," said Helen Chavchavadze. "Jackie and Lee were very fused, the way sisters are when they haven't had much security." They also shared a mocking humor. Their mother had a soft, husky voice, and each of the girls spoke in such a similarly whispery fashion that Janet "could never tell us apart on the phone," said Lee. Neither sister was loquacious like Janet, whose "galloping tongue" prompted their ridicule. Rather, Jackie and Lee had what Cy Sulzberger, who spent time with the sisters on a European holiday, described as "the odd habit of halting consistently" while talking, "a kind of pause rather than a stutter."

Lee followed Jackie to Farmington, and after graduation Jackie took her on a European trip that they turned into a whimsical book written by Lee and illustrated by Jackie. Their observations were laced with self-deprecation ("My voice cracked like a sick rabbit") and a sense of the world's absurdity ("We jitterbugged to 'Wave the Green for Old Tulane' underneath the Flemish primitives") that carried into adulthood.

Lacking Jackie's intellectual drive, Lee dropped out of Sarah Lawrence after only three terms and went to work as an assistant to Diana Vreeland at *Harper's Bazaar*. By the age of twenty she was married to twenty-seven-year-old Michael Canfield, the dazzlingly handsome adopted son of New York book publisher Cass Canfield. (Michael was rumored to be the bastard child of the Duke of Kent.) Canfield was a heavy drinker, and after the couple moved to London, the marriage foundered.

One evening in 1957 at the American Embassy, where Canfield worked, his fellow attaché James Symington, the well-connected son of Democratic senator Stuart Symington of Missouri, gave a party attended by three couples: Michael and Lee, Stas Radziwill and his wife Grace, and the Earl of Dudley and his wife Laura. Within two years, the three couples had reconfigured like partners in a grand gavotte: Stas married Lee, Eric Dudley married Grace Radziwill, and Michael Canfield married Laura Dudley. "I often thought to myself, 'What was I serving that night?'" recalled Symington.

Stas had an outsized personality, by turns genial and intense. His aristocratic confidence often made him dismissive, but he was big-hearted and full of fun, an extravagant and gracious host. He was difficult to miss in London, tearing around in his Cadillac, living unapologetically beyond his means.

During the presidential campaign, Stas had helped by addressing Polish-American groups in their native language, nearly fainting from anxiety before each speech. Jack and Jackie enjoyed entertaining Stas at the White House, where he played backgammon with JFK and filled him in on British gossip. Jackie had great affection for her brother-in-law, whose quirks she understood better than Lee. "In a way, Jackie was a confidante to Stas," recalled Marella Agnelli.

Jackie pulled Lee even closer during the White House years—"the one person with whom she could relax and pour out her feelings," wrote Mary Gallagher. Letters flew back and forth, they talked frequently by transatlantic phone, Lee came for extended stays, and the sisters took vacations abroad. "Lee wanted to be at the White House all the time," said Tish Baldrige. "Jackie was kind and good to her, making time for Lee to get her into the loop, but Lee also meant escape for Jackie from her official life." The two sisters often lapsed into their schoolgirl roles, whispering together, sharing jokes, "banging around their mother to each other," said Baldrige, who took offense that Janet would be maligned unfairly.

"There was drama in Jackie and Lee," said Oatsie Leiter, who had observed them growing up in Newport. "The way they moved and spoke and greeted people." But friends could see pronounced differences in style and temperament. Jackie was warmer than Lee, and more off the cuff; Lee tended to be insecure and guarded. Lee also had more refined taste than Jackie, and cared even more about fashion. At Jackie's request, Lee combed the Paris couture showrooms for fashion ideas, and inspected antiques suggested by Boudin. When Lee arrived at the White House, she usually had a sheaf of black-and-white photographs for Jackie to review as she played the willing lady-in-waiting at the Kennedy court.

After being apart for more than four months, Jackie and Lee embraced when they were reunited at Washington's National Airport in early

March 1961. Both women looked tanned and healthy, Lee from a vacation in Jamaica, and Jackie from more than a week at the Wrightsman home in Palm Beach. Accompanied by two Secret Service agents, Jackie had flown commercial, occupying five seats at the front of the plane, where she sketched dress designs, read *Madame de Genlis* (a biography of the French mistress of Philippe d'Orléans), and stunned a stewardess by recounting her honeymoon trip to Acapulco and San Francisco.

Jackie and Lee arrived at the White House shortly after the departure of Lem Billings, who had been keeping JFK company during Jackie's absence—the First Friend's second week-long visit in two months. Lee occupied the Queen's Bedroom and Stas the Lincoln Bedroom. To the delight of the press, the Kennedys and Radziwills popped up repeatedly—at a White House reception for Latin American diplomats; at a performance of the Comédie Française followed by a party given by the French ambassador; in Middleburg, where they played golf and shot skeet; and in Manhattan, where Jackie and the Radziwills rode in a black limousine with the license plate "JK 102," dined at Jayne Wrightsman's and Diana Vreeland's, and attended the New York City Ballet with Adlai Stevenson.

Jackie brought ten suitcases to New York and spent four days with Lee touring antique shops and galleries, as well as selecting clothes presented by Oleg Cassini in the privacy of the Kennedy apartment, a duplex on the top two floors of the Carlyle Hotel. Jack and Jackie's Manhattan aerie was decorated with Louis Quinze furniture and paintings by artists ranging from Romare Bearden to Mary Cassatt. It was said that the owner of the Carlyle would purchase whatever book the President was reading and leave it opened to the correct page for Kennedy's arrival.

The capstone of the Radziwill visit was the White House dinner dance on Wednesday, March 15. These parties were "very precious" to Jackie, said Tish Baldrige. "The guests all had to be beautiful. She said it was for Jack's sake, but it was for her sake as well." Jackie always made a point to include single beauties from New York and Washington such as Mary Meyer, Helen Chavchavadze, Robyn Butler, Fifi Fell, and Mary Gimbel, often seating them next to her husband. "Jackie was in charge," said Helen Chavchavadze, "choosing his playmates. It was very French."

Besides friends, family, administration insiders, and favored journalists ("no *New York Times,* no Luce—very hurt feelings," noted Stewart Alsop), the list of seventy invitees that spring included such exotic
personalities as the Aga Khan and Ludwig Bemelmans. "From that
moment the city's official society tote boards began to be changed,"
wrote Hugh Sidey. ". . . There were no obligatory guests. These were
the people the Kennedys wanted around for a long gay evening."

Guests mingled first in the East Room for cocktails and hors d'oeuvres
before drifting into the Red Room and State Dining Room, where nine
round tables for eight were covered in yellow linen with white, embroidered organdy top cloths, and decorated with low vermeil baskets of
spring flowers. After a dinner of *saumon mousseline à la normande, poulet
à l'estragon,* grilled tomatoes, mushroom *aux fines herbes,* and casserole
marie-blanche, everyone danced in the Blue Room to Lester Lanin's orchestra until 3 a.m.—an astonishing hour for midweek.

Lee wore a red brocade gown, and Jackie looked ravishing in a
"dramatic white sheath." Jackie danced just once with the President,
who typically felt uncomfortable on the dance floor. Instead, Kennedy
"moved from one group to another, a glass of champagne in his hand,"
wrote Arthur Schlesinger. "Never had girls seemed so pretty, tunes so
melodious, an evening so blithe and unconstrained." Stewart Alsop
observed that with "champagne flowing out of every available crevice,"
the evening had a "slight speakeasy quality since the whole thing was
supposed to be kept quiet because of Lent."

One scene offered a revealing glimpse into the politics of the Kennedy White House. Lyndon Johnson had Bobby Kennedy cornered in
the Blue Room, pressing him about a judicial candidate that Bobby was
resisting. Stewart Alsop witnessed the "full Johnson treatment, right
down to the knee rub and the lapel pull," which Bobby countered with
his "wolfish grin" and "cutting wisecracks," leaving a humiliated Johnson to retreat "in confusion—first time I've ever seen it happen." The
Vice President, noted Alsop, "seemed a bit sad."

Even more revealing, although only in retrospect many years later,
was the choice of Jack Kennedy's two dinner partners, which made "the
Beautiful People from New York seethe with disbelief," according to
Ben Bradlee. Sitting on either side of the President were the famous
Pinchot sisters, Tony Bradlee and her sister Mary Meyer, two of Wash-
ington's most alluring women. Tony already knew that Jack Kennedy

was attracted to her, because he had made several unsuccessful passes. "Jack was always so complimentary to me, putting his hands around my waist," she recalled, "I thought, 'Hmmmm he likes me.' I think it surprised him I would not succumb. If I hadn't been married maybe I would have." (At the time, Tony told neither her husband nor her sister about JFK's advances.) Kennedy was equally drawn to Mary, but it would be some months before he would instigate their clandestine affair. On that evening in March, when "the sense of possibility had its gayest image," Kennedy was in a lighthearted mood as he chatted during dinner. Afterwards he linked arms with Mary and Tony, and when they entered the Blue Room he exclaimed, "Well, girls, what did you think of *that*?"

$\mathscr{T}$he "girls" Kennedy entertained in the State Dining Room were the least of his dalliances in the spring of 1961. His complicated amorous life included Judith Campbell, Helen Chavchavadze, and further out on the periphery, Marilyn Monroe, with whom he had been linked since they were seen during the Democratic convention dining at Puccini's, an Italian restaurant in Beverly Hills. JFK also had a lover on the White House staff whose identity was revealed to Hugh Sidey only months after Kennedy's inauguration.

Sidey was working late in the *Time* bureau when he was interrupted by a colleague named Billy Brammer, a colorful thirty-one-year-old Texan who had written an astute political novel called *The Gay Place* inspired by Lyndon Johnson. As Sidey recalled it, "Billy said, 'Hugh, this is the darnedest thing,'" and recounted that a young woman he was dating, a "beautiful girl" named Diana de Vegh, was also having an affair with Jack Kennedy. "Billy said he asked her why she did it. 'Nothing will come of it,' she said. 'But he has a hold on me.'" The attraction, she confessed, was "power."

Several months later, Brammer disclosed more details in a letter to a friend back in Texas: "Jack Kennedy is down in the back, and this has apparently limited his roundering," Brammer wrote, "for he does not often call to bug his teenaged mistress to whom I am secretly engaged. Very late on a recent evening a voice that was unmistakably our Leader's reached me on the phone, inquiring of 'Diaawhnah.' (I started to say she'd gone to 'Cuber' for a week and a hawrf.) I informed him that she was in the bawrth, tidying herself, and he rang off rather abruptly."

JFK's involvement with de Vegh, a twenty-two-year-old Radcliffe graduate, was known among West Wing aides as well as members of the press. "You heard there was a special relationship with her," said Barbara Gamarekian. "She was very classy." De Vegh had arrived in Washington before the inauguration, working first in a job Kennedy arranged on Capitol Hill and then as a member of the National Security Council staff. She was a striking brunette (like Jackie, Helen, Judith, and Pam), and an upper-class New Yorker descended from John Jay (as was Joe Alsop's wife, Susan Mary) and related to Civil War hero Robert Gould Shaw (in a strange coincidence, also a great-great-uncle of Mary Meyer and Tony Bradlee).

She and Kennedy had met during his 1958 Senate campaign at a political dinner in Boston when she was a twenty-year-old college junior and he was forty-one. "There was an empty place next to me," she recalled, "and he came and sat down and . . . asked . . . who was I and what was I doing . . . I was just thrilled." When Kennedy visited Boston, he would send Dave Powers or his longtime driver Muggsy O'Leary to collect her at her Radcliffe dorm. The Kennedy aides were matter-of-fact, inquiring only if she had an interest in politics. Mac Bundy, then dean of the Harvard faculty, heard about de Vegh and became alarmed, not only because Kennedy was on Harvard's Board of Overseers, but because de Vegh's father sat on visiting committees at Harvard for rare books and economics. "Bundy said to Kennedy, 'You have to stop it,'" said Marcus Raskin, one of Bundy's assistants in the White House. Kennedy ended the dorm pickups, but continued to see her.

Over a ten-month period, de Vegh and JFK got together a half dozen times in a platonic relationship as he sought her views on his performance as a politician. "We would have dinner," she recalled. "He was looking for a mirror, someone who would keep reflecting back that he was fascinating and amazing. . . . Eventually it became a love affair." After de Vegh graduated, Kennedy's placement of her on Bundy's staff was "a way to get even," said Raskin. "She was put to work for me. . . .

Bundy said to me, 'Well, I have a present for you.' I knew something was going on." Her work involved doing research and writing reports about the Trust Territories—a genuine if marginal job.

Once she was installed in the Executive Office Building, Kennedy invited her to the private quarters when Jackie was away. They would usually dine with Powers or O'Donnell, and afterwards JFK and de Vegh would retire to the Lincoln Bedroom—a place sacred to Jackie for "the kind of peace . . . you feel when going into a church," its high carved bed "like a cathedral," where she'd find herself "sort of . . . talking" with the great Republican president.

During his time with de Vegh, Kennedy gave away little, never talking about his parents, siblings, or his immediate family. Their conversation focused on the events of the day, and he joked about other politicians. "I never did experience John Kennedy in a moment of reflection or pain or sadness," she recalled. To make herself more interesting, she purposely took views contrary to his, which amused him. By keeping the tone superficial, Kennedy was a man "of his time," de Vegh said. "He was limited . . . He was caught in privilege."

For Kennedy, de Vegh's appeal was that she was impressionable, pretty, and adoring. She had a good brain and brought him information that diverted him. He displayed no guilt, nor did she. De Vegh settled for an emotionally barren and lopsided arrangement mainly because she was programmed by her background to cater to a handsome, powerful, charismatic, and important man. Their common ground was a fascination with Jack Kennedy.

———

De Vegh's niche was by no means unique. Kennedy had a need for the company of attractive and wellborn women half his age. "There were a couple of the girls who worked on the White House staff who had also worked on the campaign and who had a pretty close relationship with the President," said Barbara Gamarekian. "The thing that amazed me so was that these . . . girls were great friends . . . and gathered in corners and whispered and giggled, and there seemed to be no jealousy between them, and this was all one great big happy party, and they didn't seem to resent any interest that the President or any other men might have in any of the girls. It was a marvelous example of sharing, which I found very difficult to understand as a woman!"

The most conspicuous among these female staff members were Priscilla Wear, known as "Fiddle," who worked for Evelyn Lincoln, and her close friend Jill Cowan ("Faddle"), an assistant in Salinger's office. Both women were twenty years old and had left college to work in the Kennedy campaign, winding up with the staff who assembled at the family compound on election day. "The President said to Fiddle and Faddle on the night of the election, 'If I win I'm going to give you jobs in the White House,'" recalled Phyllis Mills Wyeth, who shared a house with the two women in Georgetown. "Fiddle was so lovely. He said, 'I want you in my front office.' He lived up to the promise."

The presence of Fiddle and Faddle in the White House prompted speculation at least in part because, as Gamarekian observed, "these girls would go on presidential trips but not do the work. There was not animosity but a great deal of curiosity." Both young women, for example, were seen in the Oval Office "doing his hair"—massaging gel into Kennedy's scalp. The first time Bundy and White House aide Myer Feldman witnessed this unusual pampering, they were taken aback. "I said I didn't think this kind of thing was sufficiently dignified for the Oval Office," recalled Bundy. Kennedy stared at their balding pates and cracked, "Well, I'm not sure you two *plan* your hair very well."

Wear and Cowan were "long-legged, tawny coltish kinds," said Gamarekian. "They were kind of the same, like Pamela, like Jackie. They all had the veneer of good breeding, a little money, the right schools and the attitude of the world is your oyster." Wear had gone to Farmington, and Cowan was related to Alfred Bloomingdale of the department store family. They had a "joking, warm, easygoing relationship" with Kennedy, said Wendy Taylor, who worked as a White House intern and knew Wear from Farmington.

Cowan answered phones and clipped the wire copy for Salinger, while Wear helped Lincoln with typing and perfected JFK's signature on photographs sent to well-wishers. But mostly they were known for joining Kennedy and Powers for the midday or early evening swim. "They would go off to the pool and come back with wet hair," said Gamarekian.

There has been no firsthand evidence that Kennedy's co-ed pool encounters with women on the White House staff (including, from time to time, Pamela Turnure) were anything more than what Gamarekian called "swimming and cavorting." "We swam in borrowed bathing suits, and Dave Powers was sitting there near the side of the pool," said Taylor, who took the plunge with two other interns after repeated invitations from Powers. "The President came in wearing his bathing suit. We didn't know he was coming. He came walking in with a big grin. He was amused by these young things, and he swam around with us, chatting to us about our jobs. He or Dave asked that they bring in a tray with glasses of wine. We were sipping wine while swimming, and all the while Powers was on the sidelines. . . . I remember thinking President Kennedy was tall, with a dramatic scar on his back."

Jack Kennedy's preoccupation with sex had been evident since he began confiding his raw thoughts about masturbation and sexual intercourse ("that gal needs a red hot poke") in letters to Lem Billings as an adolescent. With Billings in tow, Kennedy lost his virginity with a white prostitute in a Harlem brothel at age seventeen, the beginning of his relentless pursuit of women. Kennedy "was a sensuous man," said Arthur Krock. "He loved sex . . . enjoyed the sexual conquest. He was an amorist." At a party in the late forties in Manhattan with Bill Walton, Kennedy said, "Look around and see how many women there you have laid." Recalled Walton, "I gave him a true count, and he said, 'I envy you.'" Walton told Kennedy, "I was here earlier than you were"—the advantage of being eight years older. "I'm going to catch up," Kennedy replied.

As Kennedy began his presidency, his attitude about women reflected his generation's view that men were inherently more important and more interesting. JFK prized a beautiful face and lovely figure, and he saw women as subordinates whose role was to cater to men, although he had little patience for empty-headed ornaments. "Jack wanted more than looks," said Oleg Cassini. "He wanted courage, accomplishment. He wanted a champion, a star." He preferred women who were lively, amusing, sophisticated, and clever in conversation—but not engaged in serious issues. These sentiments pervaded his subordinates as well. Even Ted Sorensen, the son of a feminist and a father who supported women's suffrage, flatly declared to Katie Louchheim, "Most women have no influence whatsoever."

Kennedy appointed few women to executive positions: longtime labor organizer Esther Peterson as head of the "women's bureau" in the

Labor Department, and Katie Louchheim to the State Department as a special assistant to arrange activities for women visitors from overseas. His unease with women in a professional setting was evident when Lyndon Johnson brought his assistant Liz Carpenter to an early cabinet meeting. "I was the only woman in the room," recalled Carpenter. "I was seated next to the Vice President, and Kennedy swung his chair around away from me. You could feel the tension, the discomfort in the room."

Around the same time, in mid-February, Kennedy had lunch with Ken Galbraith, his wife Kitty, and Barbara Ward, the English writer with a voice "compounded of grit and soft soap" who was known for her expertise on Africa. During World War II, Kathleen Kennedy had promoted Ward as "the girl for Jack," describing her as "pretty," with "tremendous charm," and extolling her as "a leading Catholic speaker . . . what a brain." Kennedy had befriended Ward, but as a woman she was too high powered for his tastes.

At lunch with her in the White House, Kennedy's manner betrayed his conflicting intellectual and emotional impulses. As Ward spoke eloquently and specifically about problems in Ghana and the Congo, Kennedy listened attentively. "As usual, he was absolutely after the facts," recalled Ward. Once Kennedy had extracted the information he wanted, he shifted the tone to regale his guests with "one of the rare and unexpected pleasures of his post," which was reading the FBI reports on his appointees. According to Galbraith, Kennedy revealed that "no one could imagine how many seamy things were reported about even the most saintly of his men."

Ward had no illusions about her ability to influence Kennedy in those early days, jokingly calling herself a "vivandière." "On the whole he had little empathy for the trained intelligent woman," said Ward, who knew Kennedy's type well in her native land. Writing to JFK about her own fondness for such Englishmen, his sister Kathleen had once observed, "They treat one in quite an offhand manner and aren't really as nice to their women as Americans, but I suppose it's just that sort of treatment that women really like. That's your technique, isn't it?"

In his guilt-free promiscuity and chauvinistic views, Kennedy did take more of a European approach. JFK "vibrated sympathetically," in the words of Arthur Schlesinger, to the cosmopolitan hedonism portrayed in David Cecil's *Melbourne*. Whig society strove "to make the most of every advantage, intellectual and sensual," Cecil wrote. "Good living gave them zest, wealth gave them opportunity . . . [they] threw themselves into their pleasures with an animal recklessness. . . . The conventions which bounded their lives were conventions of form only. . . . They took for granted that you spoke your mind and followed your impulses."

Kennedy could be cavalier in his approach to women, sometimes neglecting to learn even the names of his fleeting sexual partners; he'd often just call them "kiddo" and "sweetie." "The chase is more fun than the kill," he told Vivian Crespi. Former lovers remarked on his disregard for preliminaries. According to Judith Campbell and several other women, Kennedy preferred to be supine while making love because of his bad back. George Smathers, the Florida senator who frequently prowled with Kennedy during their time together on Capitol Hill, dismissed JFK as a "lousy lover" because he took too little time. Yet as Smathers was quick to point out, many of Jack's girls remained fond of him nevertheless. "He was such a warm, lovable guy," said Smathers, "a sweet fella . . . It was very rare you'd see him get all tough and hardboiled."

To Helen Chavchavadze, "Jack was caring. I don't feel he ever moved away from me, although I tried in every way to get away from him." Throughout the Kennedy years, she had serious romances with other men that she sought to make permanent. She looked to her infrequent trysts with Kennedy for amusement—the electric charge when Evelyn Lincoln called to say, "The President would like you to come for dinner," followed by the appearance of Dave Powers or Ted Reardon, another Kennedy factotum, in the White House car. Over dinner, Powers would tell Irish jokes that would have Kennedy "falling out of his chair with laughter," after which Helen and Jack would retire "to the privacy of his room."

Chavchavadze's involvement with Kennedy "was kind of a game," she recalled. "I was not into Jack in a serious way. To this day I don't know exactly what I got out of it. It wasn't for the sex. It was more that he was very charismatic, and I loved to have dinner with him and Dave or Ted because it was so much fun." Still, she said, "I was capable of being hurt if I didn't hear from Evelyn Lincoln for months."

She and Kennedy never talked about their relationship. Unlike Diana de Vegh, Chavchavadze did not consider JFK narcissistic. "He wanted to know about you," she said. "Jack had a lot of social insecurities. He liked to have women of a certain class. I didn't feel any disrespect." Nor did Kennedy ever discuss Jackie. "He was very loyal, very compartmentalized," Chavchavadze said. At White House dinner parties, she noticed that "he was filled with admiration" when he looked at Jackie. "He prized her artistic and social ability, and her ability to look beautifully coiffed and dressed." Chavchavadze concluded that his "incorrigible promiscuity" had less to do with sex than "having his own secret life. Maybe it was performance, to keep proving himself, maybe it was that he was rebellious about being locked into a dreary and stressful life. Those little clandestine adventures enabled him to deal with it. He needed a lot of women in his life, and playing with fire was part of his nature."

Still, the extent of Kennedy's philandering was remarkable, and many friends blamed his father's example. Both Charley Bartlett, who took his marriage vows seriously, and Chuck Spalding, who strayed from his wife under Jack's influence, called Joe Kennedy's womanizing a "disease." "It tears at the human fundamentals," Spalding said.

Despite his fondness for Jackie, Joe appeared indifferent to JFK's sexual peccadilloes. "I haven't seen those beautiful girls. . . . Maybe when Jack arrives . . . he'll find them," the Ambassador had written to Teddy before JFK arrived for a vacation on the Riviera in 1955. Not even the presidential campaign gave Joe cause for concern, as Arthur Krock discovered. "I think Jack had better watch his step," Krock told the Ambassador in August 1960. "He keeps taking the young girls to El Morocco and so on and so forth, and I think it might hurt him." Replied Joe, "The American people don't care how many times he gets laid." Reflecting back, Krock said, "He was right. That was his reply, cold as you could imagine, no concern."

Jack and his siblings had long rationalized stories of their father's behavior with the defensive jocularity that was a conspicuous Kennedy trait. Commenting on a 1944 article in a London "scandal sheet" when Joe Kennedy was fifty-six, Kathleen had expressed her delight that "there's a lot of life in the old man of ours if he can start being a playboy at his ripe old age!" But Jack Kennedy was well aware of the truth. "He was totally open about what a wicked old man [Joe] had been," said Bill Walton. "I thought it was amusing. He didn't defend him in any sense. . . . It may have rendered [Jack] as being more promiscuous himself as a result of this pattern but . . . none of us has enough evidence to know what caused that."

With its combination of powerful men and their mostly young female secretaries, the Kennedy administration was known for an "underlying sexual tension that made the West Wing a titillating place to work," said Barbara Gamarekian. "It was a discreet but sexually charged White House." Marriages unraveled (Salinger, Sorensen, and Schlesinger most prominently) and illicit liaisons flourished. Among the Kennedy courtiers, there was a division between those who recognized and embraced Kennedy's behavior and those who either willfully ignored it or chose to suspend judgment.

The clearest example of what Marian Schlesinger called "license in the air" was the love affair of Fred Dutton and his secretary, Nancy Hogan, a graduate of Manhattanville, the Catholic alma mater of Jean, Joan, and Ethel Kennedy. When asked once about rumors of JFK's extramarital activities, Dutton replied, "There are more votes in virility than fidelity." Dutton unabashedly admired Kennedy's behavior, years later telling biographer Richard Reeves that Kennedy was "like a God, fucking anybody he wants to anytime he feels like it."

The romance between Dutton and Hogan began during the campaign, and she had moved on to work in his West Wing office, even as she was carrying his child. Dutton had a wife and family who came to Washington in March, and Hogan didn't know about her pregnancy until two months after that. "Fred and I were both wearing blinders," said Hogan. "We were on dangerous ground."

As she grew from size ten to fourteen, few people knew about their affair, much less the pregnancy. "She kept getting heavier, and she had always been a little pudgy," said Barbara Gamarekian. Eventually the press office learned the truth, and White House reporters as well. "No one touched it," said Gamarekian. "Fred had a lot of friends in the press." The lid nearly blew when Salinger's office received an anonymous letter saying that at JFK's next press conference he would be asked how he could rationalize having on his staff a married man who had impregnated his secretary. Salinger informed JFK, who "was very careful about whom he called on that day," said Gamarekian. Shortly afterwards, Kennedy transferred Dutton to the Department of State, but the affair continued. Hogan left to have the baby and returned a month later to work in Dutton's new office. It would be more than a decade before Dutton would divorce his wife and marry Hogan.

Censuring such staff behavior was difficult, given the predilections of the commander in chief. The prevailing view of Jack Kennedy's infidelities among the White House staff and press corps was that "the rich are different." As Hugh Sidey observed, Jack and Jackie's "nomadic lives, their separateness—a phenomenon of great wealth—was not fully understood by the public, which clung to its older ideas of married life." JFK felt free to operate by his own code and didn't mind if staffers followed his lead. "While in the White House, on several occasions, President Kennedy encouraged me to take a lover, an obvious sign he also had some himself," said Pierre Salinger.

The stories about JFK and women spread from Washington and Hollywood to Manhattan and the capitals of Europe. "Kennedy is doing for sex what Eisenhower did for golf," said the Duke of Devonshire to his sister-in-law Nancy Mitford, who also told a friend early in Kennedy's tenure that "if the First Lord doesn't . . . every day he has a headache" and that "Jackie doesn't like it that often." Even Joe Alsop couldn't resist telling Oatsie Leiter (a lively Washington figure who once wore a black fur hat and black-and-white body suit to symbolize "integration" at a costume party), "Magnolia, you're the only woman in Washington who has not been in bed with the boy!"

New York publishing executive Thomas Guinzburg (who years later would employ Jackie as an editor) was surprised late one night while sleeping with his girlfriend when Kennedy called from the White House. "The President made a request as to whether this lady wouldn't like to go down to Palm Beach the next day for a weekend," recalled Guinzburg. The woman—"a marvelous lady"—flew to Florida as requested and "had an extended romance" with Kennedy, according to Guinzburg.

Among White House insiders, Douglas Dillon, like Mac Bundy, had personal knowledge about Kennedy that he chose to disregard. The Treasury secretary knew from his daughter Joan that JFK was intimate with a friend of hers, a "decent person" who kept "very very quiet." Dillon concluded that Jack and Jackie "had a different kind of relationship than I had with my wife." Years later the writer Louis Auchincloss asked Robert McNamara, "Didn't you know all about Jack's women in the

White House?" "Yes," McNamara replied. "But we didn't know that there were that many!"

Arthur Schlesinger took the more active role of trying to squelch rumors about his boss. During the campaign he had written to Adlai Stevenson, insisting that "the stories in circulation are greatly exaggerated," adding that while Kennedy had strayed earlier in his marriage, once he began to "prepare himself for the presidency" he abandoned his hedonistic ways. "Even if such stories were true, I do not see how they bear essentially on Kennedy's capacity to be President, especially when one considers the alternative." Stevenson's sister, Elizabeth Ives, was not mollified by Schlesinger, telling Adlai that fellow Democrat Gay Finletter said Kennedy was "just a bull. He's after every woman." Ives told her brother that while he could refer to Kennedy as "a brilliant man . . . don't call him a good man."

Schlesinger's wishful thinking was shared by others close to Kennedy. After his election, Kennedy sat on Charley Bartlett's terrace and assured his friend, "I'm going to keep the White House white," a pledge Bartlett stubbornly believed throughout the presidency. Bill Walton clung to deep denial, once writing that "a President is watched too closely to have a secret life." For all his worldliness, Ben Bradlee also chose to ignore Kennedy's philandering. "Like everyone else, we had heard reports of presidential infidelity, but we were always able to say we knew of no evidence, none," recalled Bradlee. Even Lem Billings, who knew more details than anyone else about Kennedy's sexual conquests over the years, decided to avert his eyes. "Lem didn't want to know about Jack Kennedy's infidelity in the White House," said Peter Kaplan. "He wanted to believe in that marriage. He wouldn't let Jack discuss it with him. He turned it aside. He heard about it because he hung around with Sinatra and others, but he was never a co-conspirator."

Kennedy had no lack of choices among insiders willing to collude in his assignations—not only Powers and O'Donnell, but longtime friend Charles Spalding. When JFK saw Gore Vidal's *The Best Man* before his inauguration, the playwright observed Kennedy's flash of self-recognition in the promiscuous politician onstage. Kennedy "looked quite nervous," Vidal recalled. "He gave a lightning look at Chuck Spalding and sat lower down in his chair."

Kennedy had first met Chuck Spalding, a six-foot-five beanpole with a bad complexion and engaging personality, during the summer of 1940 on the Cape. One of Kennedy's neighbors, Nancy Tenney Coleman, said Spalding "wasn't that attractive, but he had a Cary Grant kind of manner. He was debonair."

As a young man, Spalding was legendary for his comic gifts. The son of a stockbroker, he came from a wealthy family in Lake Forest, Illinois, and went to the Hill School and Yale, where he wrote witty satire for the *Yale Daily News*. During the war he turned out *Love at First Flight,* a best-selling book lampooning his experiences at navy flight school. Spalding's wife, the former Betty Coxe, was six feet tall and had a forceful personality that earned her the nickname "Brune" for Brunhilde. She grew up on Philadelphia's Main Line and graduated from fashionable St. Timothy's boarding school. A championship golfer and keen sailor, she had been close to both Eunice and Kathleen Kennedy before her marriage to Spalding.

Kennedy appreciated Spalding's ironic humor, but they also shared intellectual interests, and both were Anglophiles. Spalding was bowled over by Kennedy—"the most engaging person" he had ever met. "He was so determined to wring every last minute that he just set a pace that was abnormal," Spalding said.

By the time Kennedy entered the White House, Spalding had tried his hand at several professions—screenwriting in Hollywood (including projects for Gary Cooper), advertising at J. Walter Thompson, and finally a small venture capital company in New York. Spalding declined Kennedy's offer of a job in the Defense Department because he wanted "to keep a totally abnormal situation reasonably normal." Spalding, then forty-two, and Betty, forty, lived in Greenwich, Connecticut, with their six children, and he would escape to Washington whenever Kennedy called, sometimes with her, more often without her.

"Betty was in Greenwich, and Chuck was off having fun," said Nancy Coleman, Betty's closest friend. Betty had little in common with Jackie, although she later claimed she had been close enough to Jack when he was a senator that he "would talk to me about his sex life with Jackie and ask me about women and marriage. . . . We had a very kind of brotherly, sisterly long association." Yet when JFK became president, Betty preferred to remain aloof—"always on the outside a bit," said her son Dick Spalding. Betty was neither stylish nor glamorous, and she lacked any social aspirations. "She was not given to airs," said Nancy Coleman. "People would kill to go to the White House, but Betty could take it or leave it."

Spalding, however, "got White House fever," said Charley Bartlett. "He saw Jack leading a glamorous life and wanted to emulate it. Chuck loved the glitz and was burned by it." Since Spalding's days in Hollywood when Kennedy had joined him for "hunting expeditions," the two men had pursued women together. "Chuck would serve as a beard for him in situations," said Betty, "so he had that kind of relationship with him."

Kennedy was almost serene in his approach to sexual trysts. "He knew how to take precautions, and he did," said Spalding. "He certainly wasn't naïve." With its cordon of security, the White House was Kennedy's most protected venue. When he expected female guests, JFK gave his staff the evening off after they had prepared food and drinks. They would leave the meals in warming containers so that the President and his guests could serve themselves. (The *Washington Post* once noted charmingly that JFK "has even been known to take dinner guests into the kitchen while he ladles out their soup from the stove.") Secret Service agents rarely ventured to the second floor. They kept guard downstairs and covered for Kennedy, alerting him when they received word from Jackie's detail that she was en route home.

Only after the first public revelations about Kennedy's womanizing in the mid-seventies did various members of the White House staff give their own accounts of his indiscretions, most famously Traphes Bryant, the White House kennel keeper. He claimed to have seen Kennedy skinny dipping with female visitors, and to have spotted a "naked blonde office girl" running into the West Sitting Hall one evening after Bryant mistakenly opened the elevator door onto the second floor.

JFK also misbehaved in a less secure setting at the Carlyle apartment in Manhattan. Just once, shortly before the inauguration, the public had a tantalizing glimpse of Kennedy's nocturnal habits in a *Time* report that New York City policemen had checked his bedroom at midnight only to discover "a slightly mussed bed" and a "discarded Kennedy shirt." *Newsweek* further revealed that Kennedy had escaped down the back stairs and not returned until after 3 a.m.

Kennedy and his guests could come and go through elevators and stairways with access to both levels of the duplex: the two bedrooms and two baths on its upper floor, and a living room, dining room, library, and kitchen on the lower floor. What's more, the hotel was connected through a network of tunnels to other hotels as well as apartment houses on the Upper East Side, offering the ability to move around undetected. "It was kind of a weird sight," Spalding recalled. "Jack and I and two Secret Service men walking in these huge tunnels underneath the city streets alongside those enormous pipes, each of us carrying a flashlight."

Kennedy had little fear of disclosure either from the press or the women who passed in and out of his life. Between the tradition of privacy and the bonds he had with journalists, Kennedy did not seem to consider his behavior reckless. "The fact is a lot of reporters were very keen to spend time with him," observed Diana de Vegh. "I think he assumed they would not turn him in, and they didn't."

Reporters covering the President not only deflected plausible tips about Kennedy's love life, such as Florence Kater's letter about Pamela Turnure, they also disregarded their own eyewitness experiences. During a trip to Palm Beach, Robert Pierpoint of CBS saw JFK and a young woman emerge from a cottage early one morning and enter a waiting limousine where "the woman disappeared into the President's arms and the inside car light went out." Pierpoint didn't publicize the incident. "The affairs that I knew about, it seemed to me were private, personal and had no real relationship to his presidency," he said.

Other journalists pointed to the absence of proof. Hugh Sidey insisted he was stymied because "it was hearsay, no confessions, no documents. The rumors were there, and circumstantial evidence." Sidey's boss, *Time* managing editor Otto Fuerbringer, had his own tantalizing encounter after an early evening interview with Kennedy in April 1961. Fuerbringer had left his hat on a chair in the private quarters, and when he returned to retrieve it, "there sitting on the sofa was a striking blonde, about thirty-five years old, wearing a short black dress and pearls. Jack handed me my hat, and I left."

Even the few women covering Kennedy kept mum. "We knew

about his affairs and his—well, scandals," recalled syndicated columnist Ruth Montgomery, "but we didn't write about it." Like their male
counterparts, both Laura Bergquist and Nancy Dickerson were flattered by Kennedy's attentiveness, and tickled by his gossip about the sex
lives of public figures and journalists. Bergquist admiringly called him a
"very swinging sexual animal" who "saw others in his own light." Dickerson knew that Kennedy "entertained other women" at the White
House in Jackie's absence, but persuaded herself that "he was extremely
discreet about it."

Both Jack and Jackie insisted on absolute loyalty from their friends, yet
JFK's profound disloyalty defined their marriage. While she would cut
friends who violated her trust, Jackie feigned ignorance about her husband's behavior. Arthur Schlesinger said many years later that he believed the Kennedys had exercised "reciprocal forbearance," and that
for the sake of harmony, "Jackie didn't press" her husband. Still, she
had great antennae and was far more aware of his activities than she let
on. Janet Auchincloss once remarked that Jackie had "marvelous self-
control" and concealed "certain inner tensions" but "always felt very
intensely about things."

Jackie confided in Lee when she was upset, and Lee made an effort
to intervene, but to no avail. "I knew exactly what [Jack] was up to
and would tell him so," Lee told her friend Cecil Beaton. "And he'd
have absolutely no guilty conscience and say, 'I love her deeply and
have done everything for her. I've no feeling of letting her down because I've put her foremost in everything.'"

Around the White House, Jackie used different strategies, some
subtle, others more overt, to cope with her husband's behavior. She
may have avoided direct confrontation, but Jackie telegraphed displeasure through her deliberate refusal to show up at official events, which
made her husband momentarily uncomfortable or vexed. These inflic-
tions of mild embarrassment were small victories—and reminders of
her strength.

Sometimes she took oblique aim at targets of her disfavor, such as
the morning she came into Pierre Salinger's office looking for a tennis
game when her usual opponent, Secret Service agent Clint Hill, was
unavailable. Salinger's assistant, Jill "Faddle" Cowan was conscripted

"in her bare feet because she had no tennis shoes" to "give a command performance," said Barbara Gamarekian.

On another occasion, Jackie was taking a reporter from *Paris-Match* on a White House tour. Jackie "walked into Mrs. Lincoln's office and said hello to Mrs. Lincoln, and Priscilla [Wear] was sitting there," recalled Gamarekian in her oral history at the Kennedy Library. "Mrs. Kennedy turned to him and said, 'This is the girl who supposedly is sleeping with my husband' in French."

Afterwards, the reporter asked Gamarekian, "What is going on here?" She was equally dumbfounded. "I think he thought she said it somewhat facetiously and sort of threw it away," said Gamarekian. "And of course my reaction too was, 'No matter how little French you know'— and I knew Priscilla knew some—'I certainly would recognize a few words like "sleep" and "girl" and "my husband!"' I'm sure Priscilla must have realized what Mrs. Kennedy said."

Taking a page out of French court customs, Jackie relied on a pretty but completely trustworthy close friend to entertain JFK. Vivian Stokes Crespi was two years older than Jackie and had grown up with her in Newport, where she visited with her maternal grandparents, the Fahnestocks, during the summers. Their mothers were friendly as well—"creatures of their time," recalled Vivian, "who criticized us a lot." Vivian also had a "naughty" father who was "a blond Jack Bouvier." Jackie's friendship with Vivian was open and playful. "Vivi, you have curves," Jackie would say when Crespi put on weight.

Vivian had attended "ten different schools in five different countries" where she learned Italian, French, and German, but never went to college. At eighteen she married Henry Stillman Taylor, the twenty-six-year-old son of the president of Standard Oil, who introduced her to Jack Kennedy during the war. "Jack and I were great pals," said Vivian. "He tried everything but I was never interested, because he wasn't my type, but we always stayed very close friends. When he married Jackie I couldn't believe he had the brains to choose her." Vivian's marriage fell apart quickly, and in 1950 she married Marco Fabio Crespi, a handsome Italian count. By the early sixties they had separated, and Vivian was living in New York.

The free-spirited Vivian enjoyed Jackie's "zany quality" as well as her depth and loyalty. "She was like a tomb," said Vivian. "I would tell the most intimate things to her." They did not discuss JFK's infidelity, however. Like other Kennedy intimates seeking to explain away Kennedy's behavior, Vivian viewed it as "recreational, not emotional. Men of that type need a release." Nevertheless, Vivian could speak bluntly to JFK: "I said to Jack once, 'How does Jackie put up with you the way you carry on?' He said, 'I guess she loves me.' 'You don't know how lucky you are,' I said."

During the White House years, Jackie and Vivian talked on the phone several times a week (sometimes in French), and Vivian came to dinner dances, small parties, and vacations in Hyannis and Newport. Jackie knew Vivian could be counted on to amuse JFK with jokes and "salty stories," especially about her friendship with Tammany Hall boss Carmine DeSapio and his "swinging soirees at Sheepshead Bay" with cabaret singers and Democratic leaders from Brooklyn and the Bronx. At Jackie's urging, Jack and Vivian would take cruises together on the *Honey Fitz,* the presidential yacht. "Alone on the boat he could talk freely," said Vivian. "He could relax. We would laugh and laugh." Afterwards Jackie would tell Vivian, "When he comes back he is in such a good mood." So was Jackie, who knew that for a few hours her husband had been in safe female company.

———

The idea of taking her own lovers had crossed Jackie's mind when Jack was in the Senate. "She told me she knew Jack had affairs," said Tony Bradlee. "She was pondering maybe doing it herself. I don't think she did, but she seemed a little sad at that point." Once her husband became president, the risks of such behavior escalated. "She was very dignified, she took her job very seriously and she didn't want to make some scandal," said Benno Graziani. Instead, Jackie sought friendships with some of JFK's closest advisers. "The men she liked were all affectionate, all with humor, all wanting to help and be as supportive as they possibly could," said Lee.

Robert McNamara periodically had dinner with Jackie, and she introduced him to the work of Gabriela Mistral, the Chilean Nobel laureate who wrote passionate poems about love and nurturing. The First Lady and secretary of defense read Mistral's poems together, including Jackie's favorite, called "Prayer," which implores God to forgive the sins of a man with imperfections. McNamara sensed that the poem resonated deeply with Jackie, with such lines as "You say he was cruel?

You forget I loved him ever. . . . To love (as You well understand) is a bitter task." Jackie admired McNamara because "he was very quick and very affectionate," said Lee. There was also something vaguely romantic about the hint of torment behind his crisp smile. "Men can't understand his sex appeal," Jackie said. "She was flirtatious," said McNamara, but she was mostly interested in hearing his ideas. McNamara came to understand that Jackie "was much brighter, with a broader intellect than people have given her credit for."

Handsome and urbane New York attorney Roswell Gilpatric, McNamara's deputy secretary of defense, developed a friendship with Jackie that would turn romantic after JFK's death. During the White House years, they often talked about books that they recommended to each other (she once thanked him for an "insidious slim little volume"), and Gilpatric fielded her questions on power, ambition, and loyalty among the men at the Pentagon. She told Gilpatric that she admired his combination of "force and kindness"; after spending a day with him at his Maryland farm, she was "happy for one whole week," she wrote.

Intriguingly, given her husband's uneasy dealings with him, Jackie also sought the company of Adlai Stevenson, who was old enough to be her father. He frequently escorted her to the ballet and opera in New York, entertained her at his New York apartment, and called her "my little friend Jackie." For Valentine's Day one year she gave him a painting she had made in his honor. "There was real rapport between [Adlai] and Jackie," said Stevenson aide John Sharon. "There was genuine affection. . . . They always kissed each other whenever they met." Stevenson's sister, Elizabeth Ives, believed Jackie "had troubles that she liked to discuss" with Stevenson. "He saw a great deal more of her informally than he ever saw of the President."

Kennedy was mystified by the appeal Stevenson had for women— not only Jackie but a coterie of ardent admirers such as diplomat Marietta Tree, Katharine Graham and her mother, Agnes Meyer, and Marella Agnelli. To satisfy his curiosity, JFK once queried newsman Clayton Fritchey, who worked for Stevenson at the United Nations. "Look, I may not be the best-looking guy out there, but for God's sake, Adlai's half bald, he's got a paunch, he wears his clothes in a dumpy kind of way," said Kennedy. "What's he got that I haven't got?"

With surprising alacrity, Fritchey replied, "While you both love women, Adlai also likes them, and women know the difference. They all respond to a kind of message that comes across from him when he talks to them. He conveys the idea that they are intelligent and worth listening to. He cares about what they're saying and what they've done, and that's really very fetching." Joked Kennedy, "Well, I don't say you're wrong, but I'm not sure I can go to those lengths."

———

Jackie's most unusual relationship with a man outside her marriage was completely secret—and therapeutic in its purpose. "I always push unpleasant things out of my head on the theory that if you don't think about them they won't happen," Jackie told Ros Gilpatric. But denial worked only up to a point; Jack's promiscuity caused her anxiety and depression, and she needed to talk about it. Because of her position, Jackie could not seek professional counseling, so she managed to find help through a serendipitous encounter with Dr. Frank Finnerty, a friend and neighbor of Bobby Kennedy in McLean, Virginia. Finnerty was a thirty-seven-year-old cardiologist and professor of medicine at Georgetown University—good looking, charming, and Catholic.

In the spring of 1961, during a visit to Bobby's home at Hickory Hill in Virginia, Jackie got lured into one of the family touch football games that she usually avoided. While trying to catch a pass, she tripped and sprained her ankle. Bobby asked Finnerty to treat her, and Jackie was taken with his warm and straightforward manner. When she called the following week to report on her progress, "she startled me by asking if I would mind if she called me once in a while, just to talk, to get an independent opinion," recalled Finnerty.

Thus began an unusual sub rosa friendship conducted solely by telephone over the next two years. Calling an average of twice a week for fifteen minutes or so at a time, Jackie spoke intimately about her marital difficulties, the frustrations of her role, and problems in her relationships. "I was like a therapist for her," said Finnerty. "Here was a guy nobody knew in her circles. She could say anything to me, and it would go no further. . . . I was useful to her . . . I played the role she wanted." Their conversations yielded practical advice and offered her "a period of escape, of raising her self-confidence."

To ensure confidentiality, Jackie used her private line at the White House, and she initiated all the calls to Finnerty's office. If someone else answered, she would hang up and call back, sometimes making four or five attempts before Finnerty would be able to pick up the phone. "I would play by her rules," he said. "I let her completely structure the conversation. She would ask questions, and I would answer." From Finnerty's standpoint, "it was a thrilling relationship. I was amazed, surprised, delighted. . . . Very few men knew her as I did, which was good for my ego."

In her whispery voice Jackie concentrated initially on her concerns about JFK's infidelity. "She wanted me to know she was not naïve or dumb, as people in the White House thought," said Finnerty. "She did know what was going on. This conversation shocked me." She said the Secret Service was covering up for her husband, and she was bothered that many people, especially reporters, "thought she was strange and aloof, living in a world of her own."

Jackie took more of an analytical approach to problems—what Lee called her "man's mind"—than most people realized. "Jackie seldom talked without having something pertinent to say," said Finnerty. "I did not get the impression she was mad or obsessed, she was just telling me the facts." She reeled off the names of JFK's various women, none of whom Finnerty recognized with the exception of Marilyn Monroe, who "seemed to bother her the most."

Jackie said she didn't know the identities of many others, nor was she certain JFK even remembered most of them. "She was also sure that Jack felt no love or any kind of affection" for these women. "He was just getting rid of some hormonal surge," she said. "She was not a jealous girl," said Finnerty. "She would say he treats all women like that." Jackie felt incapable of stopping her husband's activities, which were "an intrinsic part of his life," a "vicious trait" he had "undoubtedly inherited" from his father.

Eventually Jackie acknowledged that sex with JFK was unsatisfactory because "he just goes too fast and falls asleep," and she wondered if she had somehow failed him. Using clinical words he feared would offend her, Finnerty offered specific advice about helping Kennedy to make sex more enjoyable for her by engaging in foreplay. "Nobody had ever talked to her this way," said Finnerty. Together they scripted an approach she could use with JFK to discuss their sex life without offending his masculinity. She would portray herself as being "left out" of the sexual experience and talk in a factual way about how he could help her.

As planned, Jack and Jackie had the conversation over dinner, and she reported to Finnerty that their sexual relations became more satisfying as a result. (Several months later, Bill Walton would confide to Gore Vidal that JFK had started calling Jackie "the sex symbol.") When Kennedy asked how she could speak so authoritatively, she told him a priest in confession had recommended she consult her obstetrician, who had suggested several books. "Kennedy never thought she would go to that much trouble to enjoy sex," said Finnerty. "This impressed him." JFK didn't abandon his womanizing ways, but Jackie no longer had reason to believe that their difficulties with sexual intimacy had been her fault.

FOURTEEN

*J*oe Kennedy's role in the 1960 campaign had demonstrated how smoothly and silently he operated the levers of power. As Ted Sorensen observed, "The Ambassador was never present, but his presence was never absent." While JFK gathered support in the primary contests—the first time a candidate used primaries so effectively—Joe Kennedy worked the political bosses.

Joe had entertained Democratic power brokers at Hialeah racetrack and phoned them frequently to make certain their delegations, particularly in the Northeast industrial states, went for his son. "If Jack had known about some of the telephone calls made on his behalf," said Kenny O'Donnell, ". . . [his] hair would have turned white." There were numerous reports that Joe Kennedy spread large sums around during the primary and general campaign to buy support, even enlisting the aid of the Mafia in Chicago, where he had substantial business interests, although he typically left no written record. "Joe Kennedy would use indirection," said Carmine DeSapio, the Tammany Hall leader in New York City. "He would have one of his people approach a fella and get him some business. There would be money involved, but it was a matter of exchanging courtesies."

After the election, Joe was shrewd enough to create an impression of distance from Jack. An article in the *New York Times* before the inauguration recounted that while the elder Kennedy had grown more conservative, JFK had grown more liberal. Joe Kennedy would not be a "tyrannical old man running the nation through an obedient son-President." The article repeated what Jack had told *Time* magazine the previous July: "Our disagreement on policy is total. We never discuss it. There is no use because we can't agree." On many issues, especially in foreign policy, that statement held true, but in some crucial areas, mainly economic matters, the Ambassador's influence remained strong. Joe Kennedy and the new president talked by telephone, as Joe later revealed to William Manchester, "sometimes four or five times a day."

The Ambassador remained firmly in charge of the family's political operations. JFK's election created a vacancy in his Senate seat that needed to be filled until the term ended in 1962. "It was another one of the old man's fiats," said Charley Bartlett, "that Teddy would go for the Senate."

The baby of the Kennedy family was too young—just twenty-eight—and unseasoned to be appointed as a replacement, so Jack insisted that the outgoing Democratic governor of Massachusetts, Foster Furcolo, keep the seat warm by naming Benjamin A. Smith, the mayor of Gloucester, who had roomed with JFK at Harvard. Kennedy chose Smith over Massachusetts congressman Torbert Macdonald, another Harvard roommate and longtime friend who assumed he would get the nod.

The ruggedly handsome Macdonald had been a college football star and PT boat hero before marrying the actress Phyllis Brooks. He graduated from Harvard Law School and won a congressional seat in 1954. Kennedy and Macdonald shared a bantering sense of humor and, more conspicuously, "they were tailhounds together," said Ben Bradlee. Macdonald "chased everything, drank a lot and got into fights," said his congressional aide Richard Krolik. For those reasons, Joe Kennedy vetoed Macdonald for the Senate seat, and JFK kept him at arm's length once he became president. "Torb was quite conscious he had been passed by," said Krolik.

Nothing was said publicly about the family's plan for Teddy, although JFK confidentially tipped the *Boston Globe*'s political reporter

Bob Healy, who wrote that "the latest backroom word" was a possible run by the youngest Kennedy. Almost immediately, Joe Kennedy took command of the new campaign, arranging a job for Teddy as an assistant district attorney in Massachusetts and orchestrating an extensive speaking schedule throughout the state.

Teddy had been a garrulous charmer since his boyhood; at age twelve on a train trip from Florida he slipped away to the observation car to tell the fortunes of two women, a skill he had just learned. Jack "used to say he wished he were like Teddy," said Dorothy Tubridy, an Irish friend of the family, because Teddy was "so full of life" and "easy to talk to." JFK also often remarked that "Teddy on the hoof was the best politician of the family."

But Teddy had also stumbled more than the others. He had a fondness for alcohol and a tendency toward boisterous behavior that earned him a reputation as "the scapegrace younger brother," in Schlesinger's words. After he was kicked out of Harvard for cheating on a Spanish test, his father straightened him up by making him spend two years in the army. Teddy eventually graduated from Harvard and followed Bobby to the University of Virginia Law School. The Kennedys began talking up his political prospects as early as the mid-fifties. JFK "would mention him in a very casual way," recalled Tom Winship, longtime editor of the *Boston Globe*.

Like his older brothers, "Ted had no real choice" about his political destiny, said his wife, Joan. During the presidential campaign, JFK put Teddy in charge of the western states as a way of giving him more exposure. As president, Jack continued to help Teddy in quiet ways, sending him off to Africa on a fact-finding trip to enlarge his experience.

With his Ben Smith maneuver, Kennedy managed to alienate an important power broker in Washington. Edward J. McCormack, the attorney general in Massachusetts, had wanted the interim appointment as a platform for his own Senate run. JFK's choice created a considerable strain with McCormack's uncle John, the House majority leader, whose support Kennedy needed for his legislative program.

An even more important hindrance to Kennedy's relations with Congress was his decision to marginalize Lyndon Johnson. LBJ entered office in a precarious position despite his undeniable contribution to the Democratic victory. ("Without Johnson," said Schlesinger, "Kennedy would have lost Texas and perhaps South Carolina and Louisiana.") LBJ and Bobby Kennedy were already at loggerheads—a mutual mistrust that had begun when RFK served as a staff lawyer in the Senate, and Johnson had dismissed him as little more than a clerk. At the Democratic convention Bobby had tried to talk Johnson out of the vice presidency after he had accepted—a display of contempt that made Johnson tearful and "sealed their enmity," said LBJ aide George Christian.

With JFK's narrow election victory, the Democrats forfeited real control of the legislative branch with the loss of twenty-three seats in the House. On paper, Democrats held majorities (262–174 in the House and 65–35 in the Senate). But the Eighty-seventh Congress was dominated by a powerful coalition of southern Democrats and Republicans. The southerners controlled half of all the committees in the House and nine out of sixteen in the Senate. Left to their own devices, these conservative forces were poised to defeat every progressive New Frontier initiative Kennedy presented.

Although Johnson had been dismissed as a retrograde Texan by Kennedy's professorial brain trust, he had pushed through the Civil Rights Bill of 1957 when he was Senate majority leader, and he instinctively favored New Deal–style government spending more than Kennedy did. With his experience, his contacts, and his temperament, Johnson was well positioned to help pass Kennedy's program.

Johnson took office believing he could carve out a unique role that would perpetuate his power in the Senate. Montana senator Mike Mansfield—a "likable man" who resembled "an amiable exhausted monk"—had been Johnson's whip and dutiful subordinate. When Mansfield was elected the new majority leader, the Vice President proposed that the Democratic senators reelect Johnson as the chairman of their caucus. In effect, Johnson would continue to function as majority leader. Johnson told his longtime aide Bobby Baker that he could do JFK the most good in the halls of Congress, "the place I know best," because Kennedy's associates "don't know any more about Capitol Hill than an old maid does about fuckin'."

Mansfield supported the plan, but Johnson's old enemies, including Albert Gore of Tennessee and Joseph Clark of Pennsylvania, argued that it would be unconstitutional for a member of the executive branch to supervise his party's legislators whenever they formally conferred. When Mansfield said he would resign if Johnson were not elected, the caucus assuaged their leader by endorsing Johnson with a vote of 47 to 17. But the unexpectedly large number of negative votes had a chastening effect, convincing Johnson to attend caucus meetings only in a token capacity. "The steam really went out of Lyndon, didn't it, when they wouldn't let him in," Kennedy said later.

The second rebuff to Johnson's ambition came when Kennedy named Lawrence O'Brien as his special assistant for congressional relations—the chief advocate and horse trader for the legislative agenda. At that point, "Johnson beat an angry and humiliating retreat," recalled Sorensen. O'Brien was "tactful and courteous" with Johnson, said LBJ aide Liz Carpenter, pointedly including him in strategy sessions with Mansfield. But Johnson mostly limited himself to his required ceremonial role of presiding over the Senate and injected himself in the legislative process only when asked by O'Brien or JFK.

———

In Jack Kennedy's Irish mafia, Larry O'Brien was the canny counselor, a graduate of Northeastern University known for his people skills and common sense. Bespectacled and plain-featured, O'Brien had a russet crew cut, gravelly voice, and the "ovoid torso of a bouncer." He first worked for Kennedy in the 1952 Senate campaign. Kennedy recruited him in part because O'Brien and his father were well connected in the Democratic power structure of Springfield, the largest city in western Massachusetts.

Both of O'Brien's parents had emigrated from County Cork, and he had been born six weeks after JFK. Larry O'Brien Sr. had operated a rooming house as well as a number of rental properties before the Depression wiped him out. He leased a saloon in a property he had once owned and put his son to work behind the bar at age eighteen. Larry developed a bartender's cordiality, an ability to chat up even the most sullen customer.

During the 1952 campaign, he proved a master at registering voters, deploying campaign workers efficiently, and getting out the vote on election day. O'Brien admired Kennedy's "audacity" in taking on the seemingly invincible Republican Henry Cabot Lodge. O'Brien was also delighted by the young congressman's engaging inquisitiveness. "Once he came to my cafe and tried his hand at drawing beer from the taps," said O'Brien. "Next he wanted to know where beer came from. . . . Nothing would do but that we go . . . for a guided tour of the walk-in cooler where we kept our barrels of beer . . . [which] led . . . to a detailed discussion of the profit margins on each glass of beer sold."

Since Kennedy's first days in Congress, he had shown little appetite for political persuasion, so O'Brien was the President's logical surrogate, spreading his ready affability across Capitol Hill, from the most obscure small-town representative to influential party leaders. On weekends he and his wife, Elva, threw Sunday brunches at their Georgetown home for congressmen, administration officials, and reporters.

Adversaries as well as allies appreciated his "winning mixture of blarney, candor and political insight." O'Brien was a committed New Deal liberal and a member of Americans for Democratic Action. But he was also a realist, and recognized the need to follow Kennedy's lead. JFK found his low-key style more attractive than Johnson's full-throttle cajolery.

Politicians, journalists, and scholars often wonder what might have happened if Kennedy had turned over his congressional operations to Johnson. Galbraith observed that Kennedy "always used less power than he had in dealing with the Congress and dealing with the public; Lyndon Johnson, in contrast, with a better understanding of power, always used slightly more than he had." But for all Johnson's legislative talents, Kennedy felt he had to keep the Vice President in check. If Johnson had been unleashed, "he would have found it hard to refrain from running the whole show," said his aide Harry McPherson.

Instead, Johnson entered the political wilderness, a "frustrated force of nature," in Joe Alsop's words, whose loss of influence was agonizingly conspicuous. After running the Senate, now he could only carry out orders—a supernumerary confined to "powerless obscurity." Johnson was "a proud and imperious man of towering energies and passions," wrote Schlesinger. "Self-effacement" was "unnatural."

Kennedy was elaborately courteous to LBJ in what Schlesinger called "a doomed relationship," issuing edicts that the Johnsons be included in all official ceremonies, state dinners, and even the private dinner dances. But Johnson sometimes seemed awkward in those glamorous settings. At the dance in March, Jackie placed the Vice President next to Vivian Crespi, who watched in amazement as he piled portions of both choices of entrée—chicken and fish—on his plate. Observing "the young beauties exuding sex, exhibiting their wares," Lady Bird was heard to drawl, "does remind you of Scott Fitzgerald, doesn't it?"

Both Johnsons knew about JFK's sexual wanderings. A womanizer himself, LBJ could hardly be shocked. Dating back to the Senate, Johnson had shown a wistful admiration for Kennedy's prowess with the opposite sex. Harry McPherson recalled an evening when he noticed Kennedy and George Smathers standing at the back of the Senate chamber. "They were laughing and joking," said McPherson, "waiting for a vote. Every once in a while Smathers and Kennedy would glance up at the balcony where there were two gorgeous women. Then the vote was taken at 10 p.m., Smathers looked up at the balcony and signaled, and he and Kennedy disappeared. Suddenly I felt a large hand on my shoulder. It was Johnson: 'Now where are those sons of bitches going?'"

Once Kennedy was president, Johnson mused about his apparent recklessness. "You know what he does at night?" Johnson told McPherson. "He gets in a convertible and he drives to Georgetown to see one of his girlfriends." LBJ added that Kennedy's prowling was "driving the Secret Service crazy. They are right behind him."

McPherson suspected that Johnson's information had come from J. Edgar Hoover, who had been cozy with LBJ for years. "J. Edgar Hoover has Jack Kennedy by the balls," Johnson told some reporters at *Time*. "Johnson said he was waiting for someone to blow the whistle on Kennedy," recalled CBS president Frank Stanton, a close friend of the Vice President. "But the press was completely in Kennedy's hands and Johnson knew that. Johnson didn't criticize Kennedy. It was only that he knew he was getting away with it."

In small doses JFK seemed to enjoy LBJ's company, "poking fun at him in a gentle way," recalled Ros Gilpatric. During a visit in Palm Beach, the President invited his Vice President for a cruise, where Gilpatric observed them sitting on the fantail as JFK "spent two or three hours going from state to state and just dredging out of Johnson every bit of the latest political gossip and lore he could elicit."

Among his friends, Kennedy called Johnson "Riverboat Gambler" and "Landslide"—referring to his election to the Senate in 1948 with a margin of only eighty-seven votes. JFK "really likes [LBJ's] roguish qualities," wrote Ben Bradlee in his journal. "But there are times . . . when LBJ's simple presence seems to bug him." Kennedy could laugh about Johnson because he was "a strange figure," said Joe Alsop. "The President used to say [he] wasn't like anyone he'd ever known . . . somewhat monstrous . . . larger than life . . . [with] a comic side." At least once, in a conversation with Bradlee, JFK expressed concern about LBJ's honesty, saying he was "not on the take since he was elected [VP]. Before that, 'I'm not so sure.' "

In Joe Alsop's view, Kennedy treated Johnson better than he did Adlai Stevenson, "whom he loved to tease and held really in contempt. . . . He didn't have any contempt for Johnson." Kennedy assigned LBJ to tasks that seemed to invest him with greater importance than his predecessors: supervising the space exploration program, chairing the President's Committee on Equal Employment Opportunity, and frequently traveling abroad. (During his time as vice president, Johnson visited thirty-three countries and made more than 150 speeches.) But these responsibilities were tangential, his overseas trips seen by the press as mere "errands." In the view of Johnson aide Lloyd Hand, "Johnson would have to be seen as one of the least utilized vice presidents in terms of what he could contribute."

LBJ's demeanor in meetings only exacerbated the situation. "I can't stand Johnson's damn long face," Kennedy told George Smathers. "He just comes in . . . with his face all screwed up, never says anything. He looks so sad." Whenever Johnson was asked his opinion, he would say, "I agree with the President." "I know he didn't do that when the President called him privately," said Joe Alsop, but "he didn't want anyone to hear him disagree with the President."

JFK assigned Kenny O'Donnell to be LBJ's "handler." O'Donnell kept in daily touch with Johnson's staff, but he was sometimes high-handed with the Vice President. Once LBJ came into O'Donnell's office to ask the status of a nomination he had submitted. "Oh that," O'Donnell said, pulling open his file drawer an inch or so. "That's where it is, right there." After slamming the drawer shut, he snapped, "That's where it's going to stay, Lyndon." Dumbstruck, Johnson stalked out.

The chilly indifference of Bobby Kennedy—who called Johnson's vice presidency "gilded impotence"—was particularly obvious. "Bobby saw him as a manipulative force," said William vanden Heuvel. "He dismissed LBJ as vice president, and LBJ knew it. But he would always have people watch Johnson, who he saw as a counterforce." To his allies, Johnson called Bobby "that little shitass" who had supplanted him as Kennedy's second in command. Their incompatibility "was a kind of chemical thing," in Joe Alsop's view.

Like her husband, Jackie flinched at Johnson's crudity; she was shocked when she heard that LBJ described Stevenson as a man who "squats to piss." But she was also tickled by Johnson's colorful mannerisms and extravagant gestures, and touched by his contribution to her restoration project. Responding to her pleas, he cut red tape to arrange the transfer of a crystal chandelier from the Senate to the White House, where she installed it in the upstairs Treaty Room.

Jackie had fun with Johnson. Since her husband disliked dancing, she often took to the floor with LBJ. She also expressed compassion for the Vice President, as she did for Adlai Stevenson—two men whose power was diminished by the Kennedys. She told Johnson "the greatest act of a gentleman" was his willingness to relinquish his influential position to serve under her husband. Johnson would later say that Jackie "was always nicer to me than anybody in the Kennedy family. . . . She just made me feel like I was a human being."

Jackie found little common ground with Lady Bird, a shrewd businesswoman who owned radio and television stations in Texas, critiqued her husband's speeches, and offered political advice that was beyond Jackie's ken. Yet the two women established a good rapport. Acknowledging the number of times she requested a stand-in for official events, Jackie told LBJ how much she appreciated Lady Bird's "willingness to assume every burden—She assumed so many for me."

———

With Johnson out of the mix, Kennedy adopted an incremental approach to domestic policy. "It was a disappointment to many liberals who had expected a fighting President who would appeal to the people over the head of a stuck-in-the-mud Congress," wrote British diplomat David Gore. JFK relied heavily on Douglas Dillon to pursue what Gore called "the unadventurous path of waiting to see if the economy would recover without radical changes of policy." Early on, for example, Dillon convinced JFK to reject Walter Heller's proposal to spend $1 billion on a public works program as an anti-recession measure.

Behind the scenes, Kennedy and Dillon had quietly agreed on the need for reduced taxes to stimulate the economy. First would come a 10 percent investment tax credit to encourage business investment in plant and equipment. The second stage would be a cut in the personal income tax. Marginal rates in 1961 were 91 percent, which Dillon viewed as "one of the greatest obstacles to growth." By dropping the rates to 77 percent, consumers would have more money to spend.

Both men were also willing to embrace Keynesian principles and run a deficit to stimulate the economy—a break from the Eisenhower administration's commitment to balanced budgets. While Dillon believed in keeping a tight rein on federal expenditures (compared to Galbraith, who wanted to use spending, not reduced taxes, to prime the economy), the Treasury secretary could see the usefulness of a deficit when the economy was operating below capacity. Still, neither Kennedy nor Dillon wanted to risk defeat on Capitol Hill, so they decided to wait for a more favorable moment to introduce their tax policy.

Instead, Kennedy focused on more anodyne goals. He secured a modest increase in the federal minimum wage and an extension of unemployment benefits, but declined to take the lead on health insurance or, more pointedly, civil rights. Black voters had contributed significantly to Kennedy's victory, but he had no appetite for taking a stand in Congress for desegregation against the dominant southerners of his party. Kennedy did introduce a bill providing federal aid to education, which Congress promptly defeated. "I think Kennedy is trapped," longtime Democratic adviser James Rowe wrote to Teddy White that March. "He leads a country divided exactly in two, with horrible apathy on each side."

———

Kennedy sought to create the impression of momentum with a pair of high-profile foreign policy initiatives that captured the progressive spirit of the New Frontier. In the Cold War, a major point of contention was whether recently decolonized countries in Africa, Asia, and Latin America would choose democracy or communism. "The Soviets were on the move," said Walt Rostow, financing "wars of national liberation." Castro's victory in Cuba directed the spotlight to Latin America, where the United States was eager to prevent similar communist takeovers. Kennedy's response, announced in March, was the Alliance for Progress, which sought to support democracy in Latin America through trade and financial assistance.

The Peace Corps, the most emblematic new program of the Kennedy administration, was unveiled the same month. In the last days of the campaign, Kennedy had floated a proposal to create a government agency employing young Americans to be "ambassadors of peace" to win hearts and minds in Third World countries. In its final form, the Peace Corps consisted of volunteers rather than paid employees, an idealistic cadre of fresh-faced men and women who tried to help poor people help themselves by living "at the same level as the citizens of the countries which they are sent to, doing the same work, eating the same food, speaking the same language."

Kennedy named Robert Sargent Shriver, his forty-five-year-old brother-in-law, as the first director of the Peace Corps, and Shriver moved quickly to put his imprint on the program. "Jack never uttered more than thirty words to me about the Peace Corps," Shriver recalled. "He delegated to me the organization." It was Shriver who decided on unpaid volunteers, and who pushed to make the corps an independent agency within the State Department. His zealous advocacy also led to congressional approval of a budget by a large margin.

As with Bobby's appointment as attorney general, JFK humorously deflected charges of nepotism, saying that if the Peace Corps failed, "it would be easier to fire a relative than a political friend." While Shriver wasn't as close to Kennedy as Steve Smith, he occupied a special position as the husband of thirty-nine-year-old Eunice, JFK's kindred spirit among his sisters.

Eunice was the only sister with superior academic achievement—a Stanford degree in sociology that included a year at Radcliffe—along with professional ambitions. After the war she had worked in the Justice Department on juvenile delinquency and other problems of criminal justice, once spending several weeks inside a women's penitentiary to immerse herself in the issues. Her great cause, prompted largely by her sister Rosemary's affliction, was mental retardation, an interest that expanded during the Kennedy administration into promoting research and better care for the mentally ill.

Lanky and freckled, with a wide mouth and bright blue eyes partly

obscured by a thick curtain of brown hair, "Eunie" had what Diana
Cooper described as a "wild originality of countenance." In her restless
mannerisms—she would think nothing of standing up and wandering
around in the middle of a conversation—taut style of speaking, inquisitive intellect, and ironic humor, Eunice closely resembled JFK. They
shared an intense friendship with Lem Billings, and she was even diagnosed with a mild form of Addison's disease. "Eunice and Jack were
goddamn near duplicates in damn near every way, particularly in politics," said Sarge Shriver.

George Smathers used to quote the Ambassador: "If that girl had
been born with balls she would have been a hell of a politician." Since
JFK's first congressional race in 1946, Eunice had been an avid campaigner, delivering forceful speeches, helping with organization, and
reviewing her brother's performance. "Eunice can hardly wait to get on
that platform and talk to the voters," Rose reported to Jackie as the presidential campaign began. Eunice idolized JFK, but "she was direct with
him about important things," said her friend Deeda Blair. "Jack took
Eunice seriously. She is perhaps the least frivolous person I know." As
Dave Powers observed, Eunice could "make Jack laugh" but "also bawl
him out."

It took Sarge seven years of what Charley Bartlett called a "fantastically dogged" courtship to win Eunice's hand. "It was not an easy
sales job," said Shriver. The handsome scion of a socially prominent
Catholic family from Maryland that had been hit hard by the Depression, he had been educated at Canterbury and Yale. After stints as a Wall
Street lawyer and a journalist at *Newsweek,* he had run Joe Kennedy's
real estate enterprises with a combination of charm, efficiency, and reliability. Shriver considered "Mr. Kennedy" a genius, and he was smitten
with Eunice from the start. Behind their bustling personalities, both
Sarge and Eunice shielded themselves with opaque reserve. Probably
their strongest bond was their devout faith; like Rose, they attended
mass every morning.

Sarge and Eunice were married several months before Jack and
Jackie in a wedding extravaganza at St. Patrick's Cathedral. They moved
to Chicago, where Sarge immersed himself in civil rights and school
reform. Eunice continued her work with juvenile offenders and developed a reputation for chaotic domesticity—inviting friends for dinner
and then showing up late for her own party. Sarge became the perfect

foil for his hard-driving wife: earnest and idealistic (JFK called him a "boy scout"), a man of "unruffled courtesy" and "easy amiability," in Schlesinger's view, famous for his loyalty and honesty.

As head of the Peace Corps, Sarge was the poster boy for all the virtues the organization espoused. He threw himself into the job, building a successful program that would grow in two years from 500 volunteers to 5,000 in 46 countries. But while JFK admired Shriver's executive ability, "you never get the feeling that Sarge is close in," said Charley Bartlett. Nor was Shriver, by his own admission, "a person capable of penetrating Jackie's domain." Neither Sarge nor Eunice was privy to the secrets of the Kennedy White House, which suited them both. "I never saw Jack act very worried," said Eunice. "He would just move on. When what was done was done, it was over, and on to the next."

FIFTEEN

The public euphoria of Kennedy's first hundred days masked concerns in the West Wing over communist encroachments in Southeast Asia and Cuba. The first flashpoint was tiny (population an estimated two million) Laos, which, according to Schlesinger, occupied more of Kennedy's time than anything else during his first months in office. After the expulsion of French colonial forces from Southeast Asia by the communists in 1954, Laos had survived as a weak neutralist kingdom, bolstered by $300 million in American aid over five years. Now, with Pathet Lao guerrillas (backed by both the Soviet Union and North Vietnamese leader Ho Chi Minh, the victor over the French) poised to overrun the country, Kennedy was developing plans to intervene with the U.S. military.

Events in Laos also affected neighboring South Vietnam. Communist Viet Cong guerrillas, who relied on North Vietnam for men and materiel, would benefit greatly from unfettered supply routes through Laos. "The President was watching this thing," recalled Walt Rostow. "He knew that he had inherited a disintegrating situation." If the pro-Western governments in both Laos and South Vietnam fell, according to the prevailing "domino theory," the communists could gain control of Southeast Asia before extending their reach to India and possibly the Middle East.

Among those Kennedy consulted in his deliberations was Sir William David Ormsby Gore, a man little known in Washington who would become a de facto member of JFK's cabinet—a shadow counselor who had "a special relationship within a special relationship." Bobby Kennedy believed that his brother would "rather have [David's] judgment than almost anybody else's."

If Ted Sorensen was Kennedy's intellectual alter ego, the President's beau ideal was forty-two-year-old David Gore, later the 5th Baron Harlech. Tall and lean, with a bold nose and sharply receding hairline, Gore had qualities of aristocracy, public service, and intelligence that Kennedy found compelling. When Harold Macmillan spoke of Kennedy's three lives—fashionable people, highbrows, and politicians—he also observed that "David belonged to all three."

They had first met when Joe Kennedy was ambassador to Britain, and Jack and David were students at Harvard and Oxford. Not only was Gore's father a baron, his mother, Lady Beatrice "Mima" Gascoyne Cecil, was the daughter of the 4th Marquess of Salisbury, a prominent Conservative politician. David's first cousin was Billy Hartington, Kathleen Kennedy's husband, and David's sister Katie married Maurice Macmillan, Harold's son. David Gore's uncle David Cecil wrote one of JFK's favorite books, the biography of Lord Melbourne. To complete the family circle, Billy Hartington was also the nephew of Harold Macmillan's wife, Dorothy.

JFK admired Gore as an exemplar of what Schlesinger described as "English political society, with its casual combination of wit, knowledge and unconcern." Like Kennedy, Gore started out as a rebellious playboy with a fondness for fast cars. (At Oxford, Gore lost all his teeth in an auto crash.) They shared a sense of the ridiculous, and an impatience with long-winded or self-important bores.

Both men were sons of dogmatic fathers, and were touched by the tragedy of losing a beloved older brother in his youth. Kennedy and Gore gave the appearance of being laid-back and unemotional in the stereotypical English manner. Recognizing aspects of himself in Kennedy, Gore observed, "I think he had deep emotions, but he very much disliked the display of them"—an echo of Ted Sorensen's own self-reflective view of his boss.

Kennedy and Gore had traveled in the same London pack with Kathleen and Billy Hartington that included Gore's future wife, Sylvia

"Sissie" Lloyd Thomas. As they matured, the two friends recognized the extent of their political and intellectual compatibility. A member of Parliament since 1950, Gore was a Tory—but of the "wet" or liberal variety, an advocate of the sort of policies Kennedy supported.

In 1954, when Gore was in New York as part of a UN delegation, he and JFK began to see each other more frequently. As a diplomat Gore had become an expert in the technically intricate field of arms control. Kennedy liked to pick Gore's brain on the subject, and at JFK's request, Gore sent him a memo on nuclear test-ban negotiations and nuclear disarmament in the autumn of 1959 in preparation for the presidential campaign. "He took a very keen interest," said Gore. "I know it did have some effect on his subsequent opinions."

During the campaign, Gore attended events wearing his *PT-109* tie clip. When Gore met with Kennedy late in 1960, the President-elect had a simple message for his friend, that he "must come to Washington as ambassador." By that time Gore had become "Uncle Harold" Macmillan's minister of state for foreign affairs. Macmillan readily agreed when Kennedy requested Gore's transfer to Washington.

"David fitted exactly between Uncle Harold and Jack Kennedy," said the Duchess of Devonshire. "They were all completely out of the same hat." With such unusual access and insight, Gore was "ideally equipped to interpret or even predict" the reactions of Kennedy and Macmillan, noted Sorensen. Although the appointment would not take effect until the autumn of 1961, Gore made himself available whenever Kennedy called.

In that spirit, Gore and JFK had dinner in late February at the White House. "Speaking with the bluntness of an old friend," wrote Schlesinger, Gore "offered a caustic picture of American policy in Laos." The British government opposed military intervention, advocating instead a cease-fire negotiated by an international commission. But Kennedy leaned nevertheless toward using American troops to keep at least part of Laos in friendly hands.

A month later, in a state of "deepest anxiety," Kennedy sought advice directly from Harold Macmillan in a hastily convened meeting at Key West, Florida. With his trim mustache, smart bespoke suits, and silver hair, Macmillan had the appearance of a "languid Edwardian," but he possessed "a sharp, disillusioned mind," wrote Schlesinger, and "a vivid sense of history." Kennedy had been impressed by the "elegance, information and style" in Macmillan's letters to him.

At age sixty-six, Macmillan was close to Eisenhower, a contemporary whom he had known since World War II. He and Eisenhower had "common experiences," Macmillan said at the time. "Now there is this young cocky Irishman. . . . How am I going to deal with him?" Macmillan disliked Joe Kennedy and feared the possibility of his malevolent influence. The British prime minister had also been alerted by Eisenhower's ambassador to Britain, Jock Whitney, about JFK's flaws. "Kennedy must be a strange character," Macmillan wrote in his journal after Whitney's post-election briefing. "Obstinate, sensitive, ruthless and highly sexed."

Counteracting those misgivings was David Gore's fondness for the Kennedys, along with Dorothy Macmillan's kinship with Billy Hartington. When Kennedy and Macmillan met for the first time in Florida, "I 'fell' for him," Macmillan later told Jackie. "But (much more inexplicably) he seemed to warm to me. . . . We seemed to be able (when alone) to talk freely and frankly to each other (as if we had been lifelong friends) and to *laugh* (a vital thing) at our advisers and ourselves."

Not surprisingly, Kennedy and Macmillan admired each other's intelligence, patrician bearing, and political instincts, but their shared irreverence provided a level of comfort neither man had anticipated. "They were astonished by each other although they were poles apart," said the Duchess of Devonshire. "They were certainly dependent on each other." Kennedy's bond with Macmillan was his most important among America's allies, and he would repeatedly tap the elder statesman's judgment in international crises. They would meet seven times in three years.

Macmillan didn't prevail in their Key West meeting, however, as Kennedy insisted on keeping the military option open in Laos. The President had already made a tough televised statement and moved troops and warships into position. JFK's plan was to secure the Laotian capital of Vientiane with several battalions of American soldiers joined by troops from regional allies such as Pakistan and Thailand. Although Kennedy "pressed very hard," Macmillan couldn't offer British forces, explaining that he needed cabinet approval for such a commitment. "Kennedy obviously thought this was an excuse," said Henry Brandon,

Washington correspondent for London's *Sunday Times*. Against his better judgment, Macmillan agreed that Kennedy might have to take action out of political necessity "in order not to be 'pushed about' by the Russians."

Privately, Kennedy assured dovish aides such as Schlesinger that his maneuvers were more theatrical than real—bluffs intended to convince the Soviets to support a cease-fire. Kennedy thought Laos was not "worthy of engaging the attention of great powers," Schlesinger wrote. But the hawks on his staff believed Kennedy intended to proceed. In Walt Rostow's view, "Kennedy was ready to fight in Laos to hold the Mekong Valley"—the strategic linchpin of the country.

A crucial factor in Kennedy's thinking had nothing to do with Southeast Asia. By late March he was immersed in plans for an American-backed invasion to overthrow Fidel Castro—the infamous landing at Cuba's Bay of Pigs. The scheme had been hatched during the Eisenhower administration by the CIA, which trained Cuban exiles in Guatemala for what was known as Operation Pluto.

The numerous mistakes Kennedy made in authorizing and directing the ill-conceived invasion resulted from inexperience and overconfidence. In dismantling Eisenhower's national security apparatus, Kennedy had intended to broaden his sources of information for decision-making. Yet the ultimate irony of the Bay of Pigs was that Kennedy limited himself to advice that he couldn't test or analyze. "He tried to keep it very secret, and he succeeded too well," said Douglas Dillon. JFK's susceptibility to a covert preemptive operation also hearkened back to themes in *Why England Slept,* in which he argued that the cautious nature of democracy could hamper a nation's response to totalitarian aggression.

Having taken a stand as an anti-communist fighter committed to oust Castro, Kennedy considered several options. The simplest was to help a small cadre—perhaps several hundred men—infiltrate Cuba to strengthen an indigenous resistance movement. The most ambitious was a full-scale invasion including American troops, which was unacceptably imperialistic. JFK compromised on what Macmillan called "a complete muddle"—an amphibious landing of 1,400 men that was expected to provoke a popular uprising against Castro. Disguised

American planes piloted by Cuban exiles would neutralize Castro's air force, enabling the invaders to entrench themselves in a key region of Cuba. As originally conceived, the operation was slated for the port of Trinidad, adjacent to mountains offering a haven for escape if necessary. But Kennedy wanted a quieter scheme, so the planners shifted to the more remote Bay of Pigs, which, as it turned out, was fatally hemmed in by impassable swamps.

Among Kennedy's closest advisers, only Bundy and McNamara participated fully in deliberations that included a tight group of officials from the military, CIA, and State and Defense departments. Both men embraced the plan, relying on the expertise of the masterminds from the military and intelligence communities. "Boss, it checks out one hundred per cent," Bundy told JFK. But as McNamara ruefully noted later, "We were led to believe the cost of failure would be small."

Arthur Schlesinger expressed skepticism in several memos, although he later reproached himself for declining to speak up in meetings in the "curious atmosphere of assumed consensus." Rusk seemed dubious but never voiced strong reservations. More outspoken dissenters were Under Secretary of State Chester Bowles and Arkansas senator William Fulbright.

Kennedy had serious doubts from the start; he questioned the likelihood of mass uprisings, for example. "He couldn't quite bring himself to trust his own sense," wrote Stewart Alsop. But a greater concern was that he would seem the appeaser—the ghost of his father's legacy—if he derailed the plan, handing the Republicans "the issue forever," said Rostow. "The President was quite passive, quite deferential to the brass and the CIA," said Ted Sorensen, who did not participate in the decision-making. "He was indecisive and vacillating. He made decisions on a piecemeal basis."

Kennedy and George Smathers had visited Cuba together at the end of 1957, scarcely a month following the birth of Caroline, when Jackie was still recovering from a cesarean section. The Cuba trip was "frankly for a vacation," said Smathers. They stayed at the U.S. Embassy as guests of Kennedy's longtime friends Ambassador Earl Smith and his wife, Flo. On December 23 the two senators were honored at an embassy Christmas party, followed by gambling at the Sans Souci casino.

Kennedy also went sailing, played golf, and visited various nightspots. "Kennedy wasn't a great casino man," said Smathers, "but the Tropicana nightclub had a floor show you wouldn't believe. . . . Kennedy liked Cuba. He liked the style."

Many in the State Department dismissed Earl Smith as a light-weight, but Kennedy gave him more credit. "He loved Earl Smith, who was a great personality," said Charley Bartlett. "Earl had a very sharp mind, was a very good investor, a bit of a gambler. Earl had good judg-ment and was shrewd." A graduate of Yale who was fluent in three lan-guages, Smith had been visiting Cuba since 1928 and had made many friends there before arriving in Havana as ambassador in July 1957, seven months after Castro landed with a guerrilla force he had trained while exiled in Mexico.

For the next eighteen months, Smith tried to manage an increas-ingly explosive situation as Castro gathered strength and Fulgencio Batista, Cuba's longtime president, tightened his dictatorial grip. Un-like Smith's predecessor, Arthur Gardner, who was friendly enough with Batista to play canasta with him several times a week, Smith kept his distance and reached out to an alternative "anti-Batista element" in the intelligentsia, middle class, and Catholic Church. Smith recognized early that Castro was an avowed Marxist, which the State Department and influential reporters such as Herbert Matthews of the *New York Times* ("Castro's own boy," according to Charley Bartlett) chose to ignore.

Shortly after Batista fled on New Year's Day 1959 and Castro seized power, Earl and Flo returned to the United States. Within the next year, Castro declared himself a communist and ally of the Soviet Union, prompting the Eisenhower administration to impose economic sanc-tions. The U.S. government viewed the close proximity of a Soviet client state as a significant military threat, not only to Latin American countries but to the United States as well. While Smith's warnings about Castro were vindicated, State Department mandarins continued to belittle the former ambassador.

In February 1961, Kennedy named Smith ambassador to Switzer-land, but the Swiss government, which represented U.S. interests in Cuba, objected to the appointment because of Smith's strong stance against Castro. Smith quickly withdrew his name, telling Kennedy, "the pro-Castro elements have succeeded in creating a tempest over my appointment. I don't believe that you should longer be burdened with this problem."

Kennedy spent the long Easter weekend in Palm Beach, where he had more than three hours of private meetings with Smith at his friend's beachfront home. The topic, according to Earl Smith Jr., was the proposed attack on Cuba. "My father said they were talking about how could one remove the threat without an all-out military exercise," said Smith. "Kennedy said, 'What happens if we get bogged down?' My father said, 'Don't undertake it unless you do it 100 percent.' Jack Kennedy said, 'There are things at hand you are not aware of.'"

When he returned to Washington on April 4, Kennedy didn't disclose the substance of his Florida discussions. But Mac Bundy and Schlesinger detected a toughening of Kennedy's attitude and suspected that Joe Kennedy, Earl Smith, and Smathers were responsible. On April 5, JFK approved the CIA plan. Bundy was not yet comfortable enough in their relationship to say to the President, "What the hell has happened to you on the weekend?" Bundy recalled. "But I didn't say that. I said, '*Yes, sir.*'" By the time JFK entertained Chuck Spalding at Glen Ora on April 9, he appeared confident when he revealed the plans to his old friend. "He told me . . . he expected a success. . . . He didn't expect any troubles," recalled Spalding. Ben and Tony Bradlee, who were also weekend guests, got no whiff of the plans.

Although there had been a surprising number of press accounts on the CIA training in Guatemala, journalists were strikingly timid on reporting the invasion plans. With the assistance of Arthur Schlesinger, Kennedy managed to kill a story about the operation in the *New Republic* after convincing the editor, Gilbert Harrison, that publication would endanger the national interest. A similar article in the *New York Times* was watered down after JFK leaned on publisher Orvil Dryfoos.

Charley Bartlett had the story as well, and censored himself. Bartlett had been tipped by no less than Ernesto Betancourt, Castro's representative in the United States who had just returned from Florida. "In Miami everyone is talking about the invasion, Bay of Pigs," Betancourt told Bartlett. "It will be a disaster." Bartlett refrained from telling Kennedy because "I thought, 'Why add to his burdens?'" Instead, Bartlett told Allen Dulles, director of the CIA, who denied the account. "I had a lot of detail," Bartlett recalled. "As a newspaperman I should have broken the story." Years later, declassified documents confirmed that the KGB had been alerted on April 8 about an imminent invasion, but the message "did not land on Khrushchev's desk." However, neither the Soviets nor the Cubans knew the precise location of the attack.

On Saturday, April 15, two days before the invasion, Kennedy authorized the first of two air strikes. Out at Glen Ora, he appeared anxious and restless. Jackie attempted to divert him by organizing an outing to the Middleburg Hunt races with Steve and Jean Smith and Paul and Eve Fout. JFK arrived between races, "striding suddenly into the paddock at a Tennessee walking-horse pace." He was too impatient to wait for the next race, although on the way out he emerged from his car to watch the steeplechase for a few minutes from a distant hill. Otherwise, he passed his time hitting golf balls in the Glen Ora pasture and taking long walks.

The initial air assault went badly, managing to destroy only a handful of the thirty or so planes in Cuba's air force. A CIA cover story claimed the pilots were defectors from Castro's air force. When the Cuban government protested at the United Nations, Adlai Stevenson insisted the United States was not involved. He lied unintentionally because he had been inadequately briefed by Schlesinger and CIA official Tracy Barnes. When the cover story collapsed and Stevenson learned the truth, he was furious that his integrity had been jeopardized and threatened to resign. Shaken by Stevenson's plight and filled with second thoughts, Dean Rusk urged Kennedy on Sunday to cancel the second air strike, which was slated for dawn on Monday the seventeenth, the scheduled time for the amphibious attack.

At 2 p.m. on Sunday, Kennedy gave the green light for the invasion. As he pondered Rusk's request, JFK tried to distract himself by whacking golf balls, first at Glen Ora with the Smiths, then at Fauquier Springs Country Club, where Lem Billings joined them for three holes. It was a truncated game typical of Kennedy, with lots of topped balls—"menacing the field mice," as singer Bing Crosby once described JFK's weakness with his long irons.

Late that afternoon, following a long talk with Rusk on the phone, Kennedy canceled the second air strike. He hung up the phone and, Schlesinger wrote, "sat on in silence for a moment, shook his head and began to pace the room in evident concern, worried perhaps less about this decision than about the confusion in the planning: what would go wrong next? Those with him at Glen Ora had rarely seen him so low."

Kennedy had doomed the invaders even before they landed, leaving them vulnerable to attack by air. "Kennedy understood part of the plan, but he never understood that the navy planes were essential to the plan," said Douglas Dillon, who had been involved in the Cuba operation under Eisenhower. After a day of fighting, the refugee force was surrounded by 20,000 Cuban troops, and more than 1,000 were taken prisoner. It was a humiliating rout—and the biggest failure of Kennedy's life.

On Tuesday night the eighteenth, Jack and Jackie hosted a gala reception for members of Congress. Wearing a Cassini-designed sheath of pink-and-white straw lace, a feather-shaped diamond clip in her hair, and "an impish look," Jackie twirled around the dance floor with LBJ, while the President greeted guests at one end of the East Room. After the First Couple left a few minutes before midnight, Kennedy shed his white tie and tails and hurried to the West Wing to meet with his top aides until 2:46 a.m. Then, as Salinger and O'Donnell watched, Kennedy slowly paced the Rose Garden for nearly an hour in the dark.

The next day, he had a seven-hour meeting with top aides, during which he smoked "his normal quota of two cigars" and "showed no signs of anguish," according to *Time*. He also had lengthy phone conversations with his father and Bobby. Jackie later told Arthur Schlesinger that during lunchtime JFK described his sorrow over the men dying on the Cuban beaches. As Jackie sought to comfort him before his nap, he embraced her. That night, after the Kennedys dutifully attended a dinner at the Greek Embassy given by Prime Minister Constantine Karamanlis, Jackie confided to her mother-in-law that JFK had been "so upset all day and had practically been in tears."

The following weekend at Glen Ora with Chuck and Betty Spalding, Kennedy labored to shake the gloom. "That's the only time in all the time that I knew him that he was really beside himself over a mistake," recalled Spalding. "He had this golf club and six or seven balls. Once in a while he'd just take a wild swing at a ball and knock it into the cornfield. We just walked and walked all over the place, and he couldn't talk about anything else. . . . We just had to let him talk himself out."

Reaction around the world ranged from harsh condemnation to expressions of regret. Khrushchev called the botched invasion "a crime which has revolted the whole world." French politician Jean Monnet told David Bruce that Kennedy had "suffered heavily in prestige." Harold Macmillan privately expressed disappointment; he and Kennedy had met twice in the weeks before the decision—first in Key West, and then in a series of wide-ranging discussions during the prime minister's visit to Washington in early April—and Kennedy had neither sought his advice nor revealed any details. Macmillan believed that Kennedy "should have committed U.S. air power to support the landings rather than let it fail, or should not have accepted the CIA plan in the first place." In all likelihood, even air strikes couldn't have saved the over-matched invaders, who would doubtless have been crushed in the end by Castro's far more numerous forces.

The press offered the predictable dissections. *Time* described the "sour fog of failure" that enveloped the administration, but James Reston portrayed a "sadder and wiser young President." Reston also pointedly mentioned that Kennedy had proceeded "against the advice of Rusk and Bowles," and that Arthur Schlesinger "had serious misgivings and expressed them."

Charley Bartlett sent Kennedy a memo with suggestions for an inquiry into the landings. "I think a public panel of three outstanding men would be best," Bartlett wrote. "From a public relations standpoint, I would love to see the thing launched in the Sunday papers." Instead, Kennedy appointed only one outsider, retired Army General Maxwell Taylor, along with Bobby, Allen Dulles, and Admiral Arleigh Burke, the navy's representative on the Joint Chiefs, considered by JFK an "admirable, nice figure without any brains." The composition of the commission was unfortunate, since the presence of two Bay of Pigs planners forever cast doubt on the group's conclusions.

In his public statements, Kennedy appropriately took full responsibility for the debacle, and the American press and citizenry were in a forgiving mood. Two weeks after the Bay of Pigs, Kennedy's approval rating registered at 82 percent. "It's just like Eisenhower," Kennedy cracked to Schlesinger. "The worse I do, the more popular I get." (Richard Nixon bitterly observed that if he had been in charge, "I would have been impeached.")

But the Bay of Pigs snapped the Kennedy spell and altered the course of his presidency. "Before the Bay of Pigs everything was a glorious adventure, onward and upward," Spalding said. "Afterwards it was a series of ups and downs with terrible pitfalls, suspicion everywhere, [with him] cautious of everything, questioning always."

Contrary to his public protestations, Kennedy assigned blame and meted out punishment. He never again listened so credulously to the military chiefs or assumed, as Joe Alsop put it, "that the odds would break for him." After a decent interval, he would fire Allen Dulles as well as Richard Bissell, the chief CIA strategist for the invasion. Kennedy turned on Chester Bowles for leaking ("somewhat deviously," *Time* noted) his opposition to the press. JFK already considered Bowles a "soft" Stevenson man and found his windy style irritating.

Reston's mention of Schlesinger caused no harm, although Kennedy couldn't resist tweaking his unofficial historian for a memo "that will look pretty good when he gets around to writing his book on my administration." Rusk lost favor for failing to weigh in more vigorously with his objections—the beginning of a "certain mistrust" of Rusk that "lasted through the rest of Jack Kennedy's administration . . . on his part and on Bobby's part," said State Department official Richard Davies.

Despite their support for the invasion, neither Bundy nor McNamara suffered any damage. McNamara emphatically concurred with Kennedy's view of the principal lesson to be learned: don't take the advice of the experts at face value and "do your intellectual home-work." According to Ros Gilpatric, McNamara "became so disenchanted with the military advice, he insisted on examining basic data himself." Stricken with guilt, Bundy tendered a resignation letter that Kennedy rejected. If anything, Kennedy pulled Bundy even closer, moving his office from the Executive Office Building to a hideaway in the West Wing basement, where Bundy also established a "Situation Room" that would combine messages from military, diplomatic, and intelligence sources. Kennedy also reconstituted some of the National Security Council oversight and analysis groups he had scuttled, and he revived NSC meetings.

Even more consequential was Kennedy's immediate expansion of the duties of Ted Sorensen and Bobby Kennedy, placing them at his side for all further foreign policy deliberations. Bobby had appeared at an early briefing on the Cuba plan two days after the inauguration and again five days before the scheduled landing, but otherwise he had been out of the loop. "I need someone who knows me and my thinking and can ask me the tough questions," Kennedy told Sorensen, who recognized that Bobby would be the President's equal and Ted the subordinate. According to Lem Billings, JFK knew that "Bobby *was* the only person he could rely on to be absolutely dedicated. . . . From that moment on, the Kennedy presidency became a sort of collaboration between them."

Bobby's entry into foreign policy had a disturbing downside, however. Beneath the radar, the United States had been engaged in murkier schemes against Cuba since August 1960, when Richard Bissell had hired Mafia operatives to assassinate Fidel Castro. Before Batista was overthrown, American organized crime had run extensive gambling interests in Havana, so the Mafia operatives had useful connections on the island. Among the men recruited for the job was Sam Giancana, the Chicago mob boss who was also having an affair with Judith Campbell, JFK's occasional mistress.

According to Richard Bissell, the Kennedy administration planned an assassination attempt to coincide with the Bay of Pigs operation. As Smathers said in an oral history in 1964, Kennedy had asked him a month before the invasion whether "people would be gratified" if Castro were eliminated. Talking to historian Michael Beschloss nearly a quarter century later, Smathers asserted that JFK had been "given to believe" by the CIA that "someone was supposed to have knocked [Castro] off and there was supposed to be absolute pandemonium" as the exiles landed.

Instead of shutting them down, JFK put his brother in charge of these "black" operations, which took on a life of their own as Operation Mongoose, a series of subversive plots to unseat Castro. Before the Bay of Pigs, JFK had both mistrusted and underrated Castro. In a pre-inaugural interview with *Look*'s Laura Bergquist, a veteran reporter on Cuba, he had asked "some very naïve questions," she recalled. "He seemed baffled about Castro's appeal. . . . I think he was cocky about him, didn't take him seriously." For all the sober lessons of the Bay of Pigs, the Kennedy brothers, and Bobby in particular, came away with a deep grievance against the Cuban leader. "Bobby became very anti-Castro," said Richard Davies. "He was determined to get after this villain who had damaged his brother's start as president. . . . Bobby was extremely protective and resentful."

There was no denying that Castro was a repressive dictator with designs on other Latin American countries, but the architect of the botched plot had been the U.S. government. Castro had won an easy victory against a superpower, which emboldened him as well as his patron, the Soviet Union. In a prescient memo to JFK on April 19, Bobby stated a legitimate concern: "If we don't want Russia to set up missile bases in Cuba, we had better decide now what we are willing to do to stop it." The trouble was, Bobby's clandestine schemes for a "showdown" ran risks equal to or greater than the Bay of Pigs. Besides assassination attempts, Operation Mongoose envisioned what Bobby described as "espionage, sabotage, general disorder," even creating an incident such as a bogus air attack on the U.S. military base at Cuba's Guantánamo Bay and claiming Cuban responsibility to justify American armed intervention.

The first major reverberation from the Bay of Pigs was in Southeast Asia. Macmillan worried that "the failure of the covert action in Cuba might lead to the Americans insisting upon overt action in Laos." In fact, the opposite reaction occurred. "I was ready to go into Laos," Kennedy told Hugh Sidey. "Yes, we were going to do it. Then because of Cuba I thought we'd better take another look at the military planning for Laos." Kennedy still believed, as he told Lem Billings, that if the communists prevailed in Laos, "Vietnam would be next. Then Thailand, et cetera." Yet when "we began to talk about maybe going into Laos," Kennedy recalled, "all the generals and other people disagreed about this, and you don't know whom to believe and whom to disbelieve."

Kennedy was asking those generals tougher questions than he had before Cuba, and the unsatisfactory answers steered him away from intervention—mainly because he realized the United States lacked enough conventional troops to win. "I just don't think we ought to get involved in Laos," Kennedy told Richard Nixon, citing the possibility of fighting "millions" of troops "in the jungles." Moreover, said Kennedy, "I don't see how we can make any move in Laos, which is 5000 miles away, if we don't make a move in Cuba, which is only 90 miles away."

JFK's skepticism was reinforced by Bobby, as well as Sorensen, who favored a peaceful resolution. For public consumption, Kennedy continued to make warlike noises, keeping 10,000 marines in readiness on Okinawa. But he also pushed a face-saving political alternative—a cease-fire followed by the creation of a coalition government including the Pathet Lao, with the country's neutrality guaranteed by an international conference.

By early May the Pathet Lao comfortably controlled half of Laos. The Soviets helped organize a cease-fire, and a conference convened in Geneva to work out the terms of a newly configured neutralist Laos. The solution was expedient and flawed, placing communists in numerous government positions and failing to prevent the Pathet Lao from continuing to quietly secure more territory. It seemed unlikely that Laos would achieve independence, but at least the United States couldn't be accused of abandoning the country to outright communist rule.

Legendary Parisian interior designer Stéphane Boudin was Jackie's "primary visionary," although she kept his involvement in the White House restoration a secret.

"In France, you are trained as an interior architect, really. Boudin's eye for placement and proportion was absolutely right."

Jackie chats with Henry F. du Pont (standing, behind the settee), her official adviser on the White House restoration, during the first meeting of the newly formed Special Committee for White House Paintings, whose chairman, James Fosburgh, sits beside her. Other notables on the paintings committee include Susan Mary Alsop (seated next to Fosburgh) and Babe Paley (standing behind Alsop).
"Mr. du Pont was rigid, but Jackie's charm made everything work."

Jackie with Caroline Kennedy in the third-floor classroom of the White House school organized by the First Lady and a group of mothers from her Georgetown playgroup.

"Jackie thought it would be more natural for Caroline to demystify the place, to make it less cold and formidable, to have kids scampering in the long hallways."

36

37

Jackie leads Caroline on Macaroni at the Apple Barrel Pony Show
in Middleburg, Virginia, where the Kennedys rented Glen Ora,
a four-hundred-acre estate, for weekend escapes.
*"I go to Glen Ora to be alone with my husband and children . . . giving them baths &
putting them to bed—reading—the things I have no chance to do in the W. House."*

Stas and Lee Radziwill at the Half Moon Hotel in Jamaica, shortly before their first visit to the White House in March 1961.

"Lee wanted to be at the White House all the time. Jackie was kind and good to her, making time for Lee to get her into the loop, but Lee also meant escape for Jackie from her official life."

Jackie (far right) riding with the Piedmont Hunt in Virginia
in November 1961, with (from left) Paul Mellon; Edward R. Stettinius,
son of the former secretary of state; and Eve Fout.
*"If the mass of people knew how great people who like hunting are . . .
they wouldn't imagine it as a cruel sport of the idle rich."*

Tony Bradlee's sister Mary Meyer, whose affair with Jack Kennedy lasted from January 1962 to his death.

"Mary sought attention the way a nymph rises to the surface of a stream. Wherever she went, she attracted it, and that gave her pleasure."

40

41

Jack and Jackie with Ben and Tony Bradlee in the West Sitting Hall on the second floor of the White House. Jackie doctored the photo by adding ink to lengthen her skirt because she worried that too much of her legs showed.

"You had to have a light touch to get to Jack, to get through his defenses."

Helen Chavchavadze (with her daughters Marusya, left, and Sasha), a first cousin of Jackie's onetime fiancée John Husted, was JFK's lover for most of his presidency.

"I never knew if Jackie knew, but I felt uncomfortable about her. . . . It was not my style, but it was irresistible with Jack."

42

43

JFK at the Middleburg Spring Races on Saturday, April 15, 1961, shortly after he authorized the first of two air strikes to support the Bay of Pigs invasion. To the left is Jackie's friend Eve Fout.
"The President . . . appeared at the races that April afternoon, striding suddenly into the paddock at a Tennessee walking-horse pace."

Jackie at Versailles with French president Charles de Gaulle (center) and French minister of culture André Malraux, June 1, 1961.

"De Gaulle leaned across the table and told Kennedy that his wife knew more French history than most French women."

44

45

JFK greeting Soviet premier Nikita Khrushchev on June 3, 1961, in Vienna, moments after Kennedy had received an injection laced with amphetamines to relieve his severe back pain.
"Out of the residence door, like a bronco-buster sprung from his chute, bounded John Fitzgerald Kennedy."

Jackie with Harold Macmillan in London before her husband's conference with the British prime minister to discuss Kennedy's difficult Vienna summit meeting with Khrushchev.

"Our friendship seemed confirmed and strengthened."

46

47

JFK conferring with Joe Alsop (left) and David Ormsby Gore, the newly appointed British ambassador to the United States, in London at a christening party for Stas and Lee's daughter.

"He didn't really face up to the appalling moral burden that an American president now has to carry until Vienna."

JFK hobbling out of a Washington ballroom after
giving a speech on foreign aid in mid-June 1961.
*"I think he is suffering a good deal from his back.
Certainly it is more serious than he admits or wants to admit."*

Out on Joe Kennedy's cabin cruiser, *Marlin*, off Hyannis Port in early
July 1961, JFK discusses Soviet threats against Berlin with (from left)
General Maxwell Taylor, his newly appointed personal military adviser;
Defense Secretary Bob McNamara; and Secretary of State Dean Rusk.
"We need a man like Taylor to give things a cold and fishy eye."

Jack and Jackie during a
cruise on the *Honey Fitz,*
the presidential yacht, in
the late summer of 1961.

"He never relaxes in the house,
just gets out of it on the boat—
or else takes a nap."

In the summer of 1961, Martha Bartlett poses with her godson,
eight-month-old John F. Kennedy Jr., along with Jackie and Lem Billings.
"Children have imagination, a quality that seems to flicker out in so many adults."

David Ormsby Gore and his wife, Sissie, who arrived at Washington's British embassy in October 1961.

"David fitted exactly between Uncle Harold [Macmillan] and Jack Kennedy. They were all completely out of the same hat."

52

53

Janet Auchincloss and her husband, Hugh, sailing off Newport, where they lived at Hammersmith Farm.
"I think Jackie was always grateful to her because she felt she had intentionally enlarged [her] world."

Peter Lawford stepping out in
Palm Beach with Flo Pritchett
Smith, a girlfriend of Jack's
in his bachelor days who
became a good friend.

*"Have pretty women, attractive men,
guests who are* en passant, *the flavor of
another language. This is the jet age, so
have something new and changing."*

54

55

Jackie and Jack at Washington's International Horse Show on October 27, 1961,
with Alice Roosevelt Longworth (seated on JFK's right), Bill Walton (behind
Longworth), Eunice Shriver (behind her brother), and Eve Fout. Gore Vidal
was also with the group, which had earlier dined at the White House.
"Jackie dragged us all to the horse show. Jack didn't want to go. He was fuming over it."

Flo's husband, Earl E.T. Smith, was a close friend of Jack's and Jackie's who was serving as U.S. ambassador to Cuba when Fidel Castro seized power in 1959. Smith is seen standing on the patio of Joe Kennedy's home in Palm Beach with JFK, who is wearing his special brace—visible only in private—to ease his back pain.

"He received us dressed in shorts, his back encased in a peculiar little white corset. . . . He got dressed with difficulty."

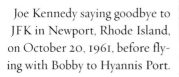

Joe Kennedy saying goodbye to JFK in Newport, Rhode Island, on October 20, 1961, before flying with Bobby to Hyannis Port.

"Joe Kennedy would use indirection. He would have one of his people approach a fella and get him some business. . . . It was a matter of exchanging courtesies."

58

JFK, Jackie, and Bobby at St. Mary's Hospital in West Palm Beach on
December 19, 1961, after visiting Joe Kennedy, who had been
debilitated by a massive stroke the previous day.
*"Old Joe had had several small strokes before and planned to go off suddenly. . . .
He had been given decoagulants at that early stage and had chucked them away."*

59

Jackie and John Kenneth Galbraith, the U.S. ambassador to India,
in New Delhi, March 12, 1962, with Lee Radziwill following.
"He makes Tish look reticent. He is always darting out to give briefings."

India's seventy-one-year-old prime minister, Jawaharlal Nehru, applies vermilion powder to Jackie in New Delhi on March 21, 1962.

"We never talked of serious things. . . . Jack has always told me the one thing a busy man doesn't want to talk about at the end of the day is whether the Geneva Conference will be successful or what settlement could be made in Kashmir or anything like that."

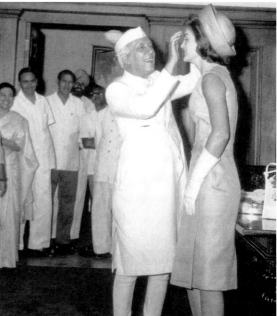

60

61

Jackie and Lee atop a camel in Karachi, Pakistan, in March 1962.
"Oh! It makes an elephant feel like a jet plane."

Bobby Kennedy
with Peter Lawford
and Frank Sinatra,
who was banished by
Jack Kennedy in
March 1962 at his
brother's insistence.

*"[Sinatra] blamed Peter for
not standing up for him."*

62

63

Jackie with Oleg Cassini (right) and Benno Graziani, a photographer for *Paris-Match*.
*"Benno was the historian of le tout monde. . . .
He wouldn't think twice about flying from Paris for a party."*

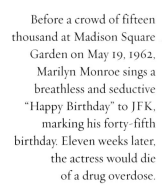

At the White House dinner honoring forty-nine Nobel laureates in April 1962, JFK chats with Ernest Hemingway's widow, Mary.

"Your friend Mary Hemingway is the biggest bore I've had for a long time."

Before a crowd of fifteen thousand at Madison Square Garden on May 19, 1962, Marilyn Monroe sings a breathless and seductive "Happy Birthday" to JFK, marking his forty-fifth birthday. Eleven weeks later, the actress would die of a drug overdose.

"You think, 'By God, I'll sing this song if it's the last thing I ever do.'"

$\mathcal{T}$wo weeks before the Bay of Pigs defeat, William Shannon wrote in the liberal *New York Post* that Kennedy was like "a lithe young diver on the high board bouncing conspicuously but never quite taking the plunge." With his foreign adventure ending in a belly flop, Kennedy sought new ways to make a more graceful impression. On May 25, JFK effectively started his presidency all over again, giving what he called his "second State of the Union address," speaking for forty-seven minutes to a joint session of Congress and a national television audience. As before, he presented a laundry list of domestic and foreign initiatives.

This time Kennedy grabbed attention with a bold proposal to spend nearly $700 million ($4.2 billion today) as the first step in a $9 billion ($54 billion today) effort to put a man on the moon by the end of the decade. Space exploration, he declared, could "hold the key to our future on earth." Previously, Kennedy had viewed the space program as an unnecessary expense, although Lyndon Johnson, whom Kennedy had designated his point man on space issues, had long been a forceful advocate.

Kennedy changed his mind in April after Russia successfully sent a manned spacecraft into orbit around the earth for ninety minutes.

Three weeks later the United States conducted its own space launch, televised live for maximum effect by Kennedy's order. Astronaut Alan Shepard Jr. soared 115 miles into the upper atmosphere, then emerged safely after his capsule landed 302 miles out in the Atlantic. It was a risky enterprise—scientists had estimated a 75 percent chance of success—but it paid off handsomely for Kennedy. "With Shepard rode the hopes of the U.S. and the whole free world in a period of darkness," *Time* observed. The Soviets still held the technological lead, so Kennedy's moon exploration plan was a guaranteed crowd pleaser.

Otherwise the speech failed to register as resoundingly the second time around—only eighteen interruptions for applause compared to thirty-seven times during his forty-three-minute address in January. While diplomats and cabinet members filled the galleries, members of the Supreme Court were otherwise occupied. So, most conspicuously, was Jackie, who had left for Glen Ora the night before.

A more promising effort to jump-start the Kennedy presidency was his first official trip overseas. In early April he announced a visit to Paris to confer with French president Charles de Gaulle; in mid-May he added Vienna to the itinerary for a meeting with Nikita Khrushchev. These consultations, and the pomp surrounding them, would be a major part of Kennedy's aggressive image-making.

The prospect of a Paris visit caught the public imagination instantly. Press accounts speculated that Jackie would serve as her husband's translator. Kennedy had a middling knowledge of French, telling Nicole Alphand, wife of the French ambassador, that he understood "about one out of every five words but always the words 'de Gaulle.'" The White House hastened to clarify Jackie's role, saying that instead of translating, she would be "tied up in other official good will duties." But Jackie's special French expertise—her linguistic fluency, Bouvier heritage, sojourns in Paris, knowledge and affinity for the history and culture—offered unmatched opportunities to burnish the image of the United States.

Jackie's view of the French was both subtle and amusing. During her junior year in Paris, she had remarked on the "strange Frenchmen in their shiny suits and squeaking shoes" who seemed "much too stuffy" but nevertheless introduced her to "the little hidden places." Her favorite was the Kentucky Club, "an Existentialist night club" that

by day was "dark and smoky" with "jazz . . . blaring," its inhabitants—
"Negroes and Chinese and unwashed boys with long hair"—"leaping
around or necking frantically in the booths." Jackie had evolved from
her initial "drunken dazzled adoration" to an "easy going & healthy
affection" for the city. She was intrigued, she told her sister, that one
could "come out of a museum, walk down the street where Voltaire
lived—and bang go into a little dive and be back in the present."

De Gaulle had been a source of special fascination for Jackie since
World War II, when she had named her poodle Gaullie because her dog,
like the French general, was "straight and proud with a prominent nose,
and a fighter," her stepbrother Yusha recalled. Later she read de Gaulle's
Mémoires in French; during a primary campaign swing in Wisconsin,
she had appeared with volume two at her side. When Jackie and de
Gaulle finally met, at a garden party at the French Embassy in 1960, he
had declared, "The only thing I want to bring back from America is
Mrs. Kennedy."

To prepare for her return to the City of Light, Jackie brushed up her
language skills with a tutor from the French Embassy, read briefing
papers prepared by the State Department, and organized a wardrobe
of continental sophistication. She hewed to the now celebrated—and
widely imitated—"Jackie look" of classic, simple tailoring, with an emphasis on what Oleg Cassini described as "sumptuous fabric, unusual
color and distinctive details" to please the Parisian cognoscenti. For one
appearance, she chose Cassini's "jonquil yellow silk suit" intended to
shimmer in the daylight. "She didn't plan to outshine the President,"
said Robert McNamara, "but she certainly gave thought to what her
impact would be and how to plan her behavior and actions in a way that
was supportive and compatible."

With Jackie in charge of the stagecraft, JFK focused on the substance. To Kennedy, de Gaulle was a "great and gloomy figure"—the
hero of the French resistance during World War II, and as president
since 1958 the apotheosis of French national pride. Kennedy knew, according to Sorensen, that the seventy-year-old de Gaulle could be "irritating, intransigent, insufferably vain, inconsistent and impossible to
please." After France had been driven out of Southeast Asia, de Gaulle
opposed American military intervention there—a "bottomless military
and political quagmire," he called it. He was also working to build a

French nuclear capability—both to achieve superpower status and to ensure an independent defense against the Soviets. In April, France tested its fourth atomic bomb.

JFK had clashed once with the French before his presidency, when he gave his farsighted 1957 speech promoting independence for their colony in Algeria. The French establishment was "wild with fury." Over a quiet lunch, Ambassador Hervé Alphand had admonished Kennedy for interfering in France's efforts to resolve the situation. "He promised me not to pursue the question," Alphand recalled. "He kept his promise." When Kennedy fretted that he would suffer domestic political consequences for his position, his practical father assured him, "You'll be out of the woods on the Algerian statement long before the people vote."

Kennedy readied himself for de Gaulle by ploughing through history books and contemporary analyses. He studied a translation of the de Gaulle memoirs so he could cite pertinent passages, and he was briefed in the Oval Office by Raymond Aron, the contrarian political philosopher and critic of de Gaulle. Bundy and Sorensen counseled JFK to lead his discussion with de Gaulle by asking questions. In a confidential memo, *New York Times* columnist Cy Sulzberger urged the President to "prepare a favorable atmosphere" beginning with areas of agreement, then progressing to more thorny issues.

Kennedy relied mostly on advice from Macmillan, who took a philosophical view after a long history with his imposingly tall French counterpart, whom he nicknamed "the little pinhead." On Kennedy's behalf, Macmillan wrote to "my dear friend" de Gaulle, advising him to "talk to [Kennedy] very frankly and set out your views fully." The Englishman well understood de Gaulle's "pride, his inherited hatred of England," and "his intense 'vanity' for France." Macmillan cautioned Kennedy that "conversations with de Gaulle are quite difficult to conduct" because the Frenchman "sometimes puts his thoughts in a rather elliptical way."

Far more challenging to Kennedy was the summit with the sixty-six-year-old Khrushchev, whom Kennedy had met fleetingly when the Soviet leader visited the Senate in the fall of 1959. At that time, Khrushchev had pegged Kennedy as a man on the rise. The first overtures for a summit meeting had come just weeks after Kennedy's inauguration, but the Bay of Pigs seemed to scuttle all prospects until Khrushchev surprisingly issued an invitation less than a month later. In one of his first forays into foreign policy as a back-channel operative for his brother, Bobby Kennedy met secretly with a Russian intelligence agent named Georgi Bolshakov, who led him to believe that Khrushchev might be ready to discuss a possible ban on nuclear weapons tests.

The nuclear menace lay at the heart of relations between the United States and the Soviet Union. The Soviets tested their first atomic bomb in 1949, but the magnitude of that threat took on new meaning in 1957, when they launched the *Sputnik* rocket into space and served notice that they could deliver nuclear weapons across the oceans in a half hour. JFK fanned American fears by harping on the "missile gap" during the presidential campaign. In fact, each superpower then possessed significant "overkill"—18,000 nuclear weapons in the U.S. arsenal and a smaller but still substantial amount on the Soviet side.

Even as the two superpowers raced to amass nuclear arms, they (along with Britain) had voluntarily suspended atomic weapons tests since 1958 and had also engaged in arms control talks in Geneva. But in May 1960 the Russians shot down an American U-2 spy plane, which sabotaged a planned summit between Eisenhower and Khrushchev, and cooled the atmosphere for negotiations on nuclear issues. Spurred on by David Gore, JFK remained a believer in the test ban as a first step toward nuclear disarmament. The possibility of engaging Khrushchev on arms control seemed a worthy goal for the Vienna summit.

Kennedy had no shortage of tactical advice on ways of approaching the Soviet leader. From India, Ken Galbraith relayed Prime Minister Jawaharlal Nehru's warning that the Soviet premier was "a man of exceedingly fast responses." Walter Lippmann, who had recently returned from the Soviet Union, observed that Khrushchev used deceptively simple language to connect with the average Russian, sometimes speaking in fables to make his points. CIA analysts warned that Khrushchev (who had shocked the world the previous year by brandishing his shoe during a speech at the United Nations) "is more aggressive when he's tired." Sixty-nine-year-old Averell Harriman, a former ambassador to the Soviet Union, cautioned against taking Khrushchev's pugnacity too literally or trying to debate him. Rather, Kennedy should try to deflect the Soviet leader's bluster with humor.

Both Kennedys followed a hectic schedule in the month preceding the European trip. Jackie went into overdrive on the White House restoration project, working with Harry du Pont on the legal framework for donations as well as vetting and accepting donations. She visited Winterthur with Jayne Wrightsman and philanthropist Mary Lasker, tramping through 120 rooms of American furniture; on the return flight to Washington, Lasker gave Jackie $10,000, the first cash contribution to the Fine Arts Committee for the White House.

Jackie's decorating sensibility had evolved to embrace the Empire style of Monroe and its antecedents in the France of Napoleon and Josephine. The French aesthetic of the late eighteenth and early nineteenth centuries was infused with the motifs of classical Greece that had long fascinated Jackie. A French flavor even appeared in the wallpaper she chose for the Diplomatic Reception Room and second-floor President's Dining Room covered with American scenes. Designed in nineteenth-century France, the murals featured people who looked "more Parisian than American."

Jackie once told Adlai Stevenson that as a neophyte first lady she seemed to spend her time "under a hair dryer getting ready for the next appearance." At their first state dinner, for pint-sized President Habib Bourguiba of Tunisia, Jackie wore a dramatic "Nefertiti" one-shoulder gown of pale yellow organza. For entertainment, she organized a flood-lit full-dress parade under the stars by five hundred men from the four armed services.

A few weeks later Prince Rainier III of Monaco (nicknamed "Prince Reindeer" by Tish Baldrige) and his wife, the former Hollywood actress Grace Kelly, came for lunch. There had been rumors during the fifties that JFK and the exquisitely beautiful Kelly "had nurtured crushes on each other," said Baldrige. When Kelly—who was four months younger than Jackie—was briefly engaged to Oleg Cassini, Joe Kennedy had propositioned her—a tale that "never failed to amuse" JFK, according to Cassini. Jackie had enjoyed her own joke at Kelly's expense, when she persuaded the actress to dress as a night nurse to surprise JFK in the hospital after his back operation. "I suspect [Jackie] got Grace into a nurse's uniform so the actress would not look nearly as smashing as she did in a French designer original," said Baldrige.

The small White House luncheon included the Franklin Roose-velts, Claiborne Pells, and William Walton. JFK engaged Princess Grace in light banter, correctly guessing that she was wearing a dress by Hubert de Givenchy. But while the prince was expansive, the princess appeared subdued. As Walton later explained, "She was so scared of coming to the luncheon that she had two double Bloody Marys and was bombed."

For Jack's forty-fourth birthday on May 29, Jackie conspired with Paul Fout to create a three-hole golf course at Glen Ora—"rather long & difficult ones—so it will be a challenge to play & not just so easy that one gets tired of it." To further amuse Jack, she asked that the holes have Confederate flags that would "not be visible from the road." The Bradlees visited Glen Ora on May 20 for a birthday celebration, and Ben and JFK inaugurated the course, which had grown to four holes on "9,000 square yards of pasture, filled with small hills, big rocks, and even a swamp," Bradlee recalled. JFK "shot the course record, a thirty-seven for four holes."

In mid-May the Kennedys also spent a restorative weekend at the Wrightsman estate in Palm Beach with Chuck and Betty Spalding. With its seventeenth-century parquet floors from the Palais Royal in Paris, Louis XV furniture, and eighteenth-century Chinese wallpaper in the large salon, Charlie and Jayne's home offered a far more opulent setting than Joe Kennedy's La Guerida. JFK could swim in the large saltwater swimming pool heated to 90 degrees; a staff of fourteen servants inside, a half dozen outside, and Jules, "the giant French chauffeur," could cater to every need—an experience Cecil Beaton likened to "bathing in the milk of luxury."

For four straight days, Jack and Chuck played partial rounds of golf on three different courses—the Palm Beach Country Club near the Kennedy estate as well as the Breakers and the exclusive Seminole—with Betty joining them for one game. But the pressure and pace of official activity had taken its toll on Jackie. Although she had begun her telephone talks with Dr. Finnerty, and she exercised as much as she could manage, she couldn't banish her anxieties as she approached her first state visit at the age of thirty-one. "I think she realized how im-portant she was to the world, and it was terrible pressure," said Tish Baldrige. "She was not moody, she was on steady ground, but she would wake up with huge circles under her eyes because she hadn't slept one bit."

In Palm Beach, Jackie's complaints of a severe migraine drove her husband to summon Dr. Max Jacobson, a Manhattan physician to the rich and famous, who was called "Dr. Feelgood" for his mysterious injections laced with amphetamines. A disheveled figure with fingernails darkened by chemical stains, Jacobson had a strong German accent and a direct manner. He operated at the fringe of medical practice, and his loosely regulated stimulants produced feelings of exhilaration and clarity, although little was yet known about such side effects as agitation, grandiosity, lingering depression, and even psychosis.

Among Jacobson's patients were Oleg Cassini; Mark Shaw, a *Life* photographer admired by Jackie; and Chuck Spalding, who suggested the doctor's services to JFK during the presidential campaign. Several days before his first debate with Nixon, JFK had secretly visited Jacobson's office for an injection to relieve symptoms of fatigue and muscle weakness that "interfered with his concentration and affected his speech," according to an unpublished account by Jacobson. Afterwards Kennedy told Jacobson "he felt cool, calm and very alert."

Now Kennedy wanted Jacobson's help for Jackie's "periodic depression and headaches," the doctor recalled. After receiving Jacobson's injection, "her mood changed completely." Kennedy had no need for treatment during this visit, as his vigorous golf schedule indicated. He had been adhering to the swimming fitness program prescribed by Janet Travell in February, along with her daily procaine shots in his back. Still, according to Dr. Travell's records, since taking office Kennedy had been intermittently afflicted with gastrointestinal problems, urinary tract discomfort, fevers, and insomnia. Kennedy gave little evidence of these ailments, although during one meeting Ken Galbraith noticed that JFK was so "bone tired" that when he offered the ambassador a cup of tea, he instead "absentmindedly filled the cup with milk and sugar."

As a warmup to their transatlantic trip, the Kennedys made a two-day visit in mid-May to Canada. It was a ceremonial success, as "normally blasé" citizens of Ottawa thronged the streets to hail the Americans: out of a population of 280,000, an estimated 70,000 turned out. Jackie smiled sweetly as JFK struggled through his arrival speech in French and wryly noted the "unfortunate division of labor" that compelled her to remain silent. Even after she canceled a television interview due to fatigue, Jackie scored what the press called a "major triumph" with Canada's leaders and citizens, who were thrilled simply to watch her excitement over equestrian drills by red-coated Mounties.

The President wrenched his back on the first day when he and Jackie attended a tree-planting ceremony at the governor general's residence. While Jackie politely turned three "tiny" spadefuls, JFK heaved his shovel repeatedly into the earth around the red oak sapling. He felt stabbing pain, but thought it would disappear. Two days of hitting golf balls with Ben Bradlee on the Glen Ora "course" the following weekend doubtless aggravated the injury, leaving JFK to hobble on crutches at home and in the privacy of the Oval Office.

On Tuesday, May 23, Kennedy sneaked Max Jacobson into the White House for four days of amphetamine shots "to relieve his local discomfort" and "provide him with additional strength to cope with stress," recalled Jacobson. His treatments coincided with the "second State of the Union address" that Thursday, during which Kennedy ignored many passages in the text and interjected new language. Jacobson noted that Jackie was in "comparatively good spirits," but she too received the treatments before leaving Wednesday night for five days of rest and relaxation at Glen Ora. Concerned about the impact his injury could have on his stamina in the Paris and Vienna meetings, Kennedy asked Jacobson to join him for the trip.

JFK had to deal with one domestic crisis before his departure when a mob of more than a thousand whites attacked a busload of Freedom Riders in Montgomery, Alabama. The victims, black and white members of the Congress of Racial Equality, had traveled from Birmingham to challenge a whites-only policy at the Montgomery bus station. Days earlier, when another bus had been set afire between Anniston and Birmingham, Kennedy had focused primarily on the propaganda value Khrushchev could find in American racial conflict. "Can't you get your goddamned friends off those buses? Stop them!" Kennedy lamented to Harris Wofford, his civil rights adviser.

Faced with a second group of Freedom Riders determined to go to Montgomery, JFK had authorized Bobby to send in U.S. Marshals if necessary. The Montgomery riot on Saturday the twentieth—the very day Kennedy was sinking putts near Confederate flags on his new golf course—brought out the U.S. Marshals as well as national guardsmen. One of the injured was Bobby's deputy at the Justice Department, John Seigenthaler, who was clubbed from behind as he tried to help a white girl escape the mob. Days later, Bobby urged the protesters to take time to cool off, and the crisis subsided. As martial law ended in Montgomery on the eve of JFK's departure, he exuded confidence, proclaiming that he would "not retreat a single inch" in his meeting with Khrushchev.

From the moment Parisians caught their first glimpse of the American president and his wife, they were enchanted by the Kennedys' beauty, youth, and glamour. The chants of "Zhack-ee" and "Kenne-dee" and the massive turnout—estimated at half a million—far surpassed the enthusiasm of the Canada trip. In his public appearances Kennedy was witty ("I am the man who accompanied Jacqueline Kennedy to Paris") and refreshingly informal, bolting from his police escort to plunge into crowds of well-wishers. The French press judged him "serene," "relaxed," and "intelligent." Jackie was equally impressive, fielding questions from reporters in English and "very commendable" French for forty minutes.

Only Jackie, his physicians, and closest aides were aware of Jack's constant pain. At every opportunity, he slipped into a gold bathtub to soak in hot water for relief as he chatted with Kenny O'Donnell and Dave Powers. Kennedy had arranged for Max Jacobson and his wife to fly on an Air France charter—a strange journey, since they were the only passengers on the plane. Even as Kennedy was being treated by Drs. Travell and Burkley, Jacobson would sneak into the President's quarters to administer his injections to Jack and Jackie. When Ted Sorensen asked, "Why is he here?" he was told "it was for Jackie, for nerves, tension." Tish Baldrige regarded Jacobson as a "slimy person," but she felt the shots "didn't have an impact" on the Kennedys. "I couldn't notice any difference in their behavior."

Through two days of talks with de Gaulle, Kennedy established bonhomie but failed to dislodge the Frenchman from his insistence on what *Time* called his "do-it-yourself nuclear arms development." Even when Kennedy promised that the United States would defend its European allies with nuclear weapons, de Gaulle refused to believe that if the Soviets invaded Western Europe, Kennedy would risk a Soviet nuclear counterattack on American cities. JFK was struck, he later told Cy Sulzberger, that de Gaulle's "anti-American feeling and suspicions go way back and are very deep rooted."

Kennedy rebuffed de Gaulle's requests for support of France's nuclear program and his attempt to make his country an equal partner with the United States and Britain—a tripartite "directorate"—to oversee strategic planning for Europe. When de Gaulle declined to give Kennedy any help with Laos—a "fictitious" country, in the Frenchman's view—Kennedy expressed his "fear of communist contamination of the entire Southeast Asia region." De Gaulle did offer Kennedy some insights into Khrushchev, calling him "méchanceté," which means "wickedly malicious." "I can't really translate this for you," de Gaulle said. "You had better ask your wife to elaborate."

Despite the lack of progress on substance, de Gaulle was impressed with Kennedy's "intelligence, lucidity and grasp of international affairs." The Frenchman considered Kennedy his most agreeable presidential interlocutor. "Roosevelt and [de Gaulle] had hated each other, he despised Truman, and with Eisenhower . . . problems were never studied in detail," noted Hervé Alphand. As de Gaulle and Kennedy wrapped up their talks, the French leader said, "I have more confidence in your country now."

The old general was transfixed by Jackie, who conversed with him in her "low slow French" over lunch in the Elysée palace on the first day. De Gaulle scarcely touched his food as they discussed "Louis XVI, the Duc d'Angoulême and the dynastic complexities of later Bourbons," inspiring de Gaulle to tell JFK that Jackie "knew more French history than most French women," according to Schlesinger. Jackie further endeared herself by giving de Gaulle a letter from George Washington to Vicomte de Noailles that Jayne Wrightsman had purchased for $90,000 (half a million dollars today). "There is tremendous value in Mrs. Kennedy's fluent French and charming youthfulness," veteran diplomat Charles Bohlen observed. "De Gaulle was visibly in a very good mood."

As Jackie toured the city's historic and cultural sights, her cicerone was André Malraux, the celebrated writer who was the French minister of culture. Only days earlier, Malraux's sons had died in an automobile accident, and Jackie was touched that the Frenchman rose above his sorrow to carry out his duty. Jackie had been intrigued by Malraux, a French resistance fighter, since she first heard about him from her close friend from Vassar days, Jessie Wood. Jessie's mother was Louise de Vilmorin, an elegant but eccentric Parisian hostess and poet whose lovers included Orson Welles and Aly Khan. One member of de Vilmorin's salon was Malraux, who first encouraged her to become a writer.

Jackie was well versed in Malraux's work, having read his novels *Man's Fate* and *Man's Hope*. She and Malraux clicked immediately, not only with their shared literary and cultural interests but because they amused each other. "What did you do before you married Jack Kennedy?" he asked Jackie. "J'ai été pucelle (I was a little virgin)," she replied. Tish Baldrige thought Jackie had an "intellectual crush" on Malraux, who became her "greatest mentor. She listened to him and wrote to him. Malraux was her prize. He advised her on various things."

After escorting Jackie through the Jeu de Paume's impressionist painting collection (her favorite was Manet's provocative reclining nude, *Olympia*), Malraux took her to Malmaison, the home of Empress Josephine. When Malmaison's conservator told Jackie that Josephine had been "extremely jealous" of Napoleon, the First Lady laughed and replied in French, "She was quite right, and I don't blame her." Jackie was particularly interested in Malmaison because Stéphane Boudin had done some restoration work there. To Jackie, the house was the epitome of the French Empire style that influenced the design scheme for the Red and Blue Rooms in the White House. Napoleon and Josephine had employed the artisan Bellangé to make carved and gilded furniture similar to the suite he created for President James Monroe.

De Gaulle lavishly entertained the Kennedys—and members of their inner circle as well. The entourage included Lee Radziwill, Lem Billings, Eunice Shriver, Tony Bradlee (with press credentials secured by Ben, who was covering the trip), Rose Kennedy, and what *Time* called a "bevy of lesser ladies in waiting." Jack had initially resisted including his mother, but according to Billings, "There wasn't anything he could do about it because Mrs. Kennedy was determined to be in on everything."

Pam Turnure and Tish Baldrige, toting two thick black notebooks, kept Jackie on her schedule and smoothed logistics, counting their bruises after encounters with the surging press corps. Jackie escaped just once from the liveried footmen and Second Empire opulence of her "Queen's Chamber" in the Quai d'Orsay state apartments. For forty-five minutes a lone Secret Service escort drove her around at dusk on the second evening to see the Paris she had known as a college girl.

The highlight of the visit was the final dinner in the candlelit Hall of Mirrors at the Palace of Versailles, where 150 guests ate a six-course dinner on Napoleon's gold-trimmed china. Jackie regaled de Gaulle and periodically interpreted for her husband. Afterwards, they watched the Paris Opera Ballet perform in the newly restored Louis XV theater. Surrounded by the trappings of eighteenth-century French style and culture that she adored, Jackie proclaimed, "I thought I was in heaven. I have never seen anything like it."

In honor of her hosts, Jackie wore a dazzling gown by Givenchy of white silk embroidered with multicolored flowers and a bell-shaped skirt. Parisian stylist Alexandre arranged her hair with "four diamond flame clips" to give her "a fairy-like air." She earned raves (*Charmante! Ravissante!*) from the French press for her carefully chosen outfits and stylistic flashes such as a topknot evoking a "Gothic Madonna" from the fourteenth century. As David Bruce observed, Jackie proved herself "more valuable to United States prestige than ten divisions."

The mood of their two days in Vienna was as grim as the cold hard rain that greeted them on Saturday morning, June 3. Jack and Jackie brought Rose, Lem, and Eunice along; JFK counted on Eunice's humor, Lem said, "to make the atmosphere at this meeting more pleasant." Dave Powers was also available to jolly the President during their "tub talk."

The Kennedys had barely a half hour to settle into the American ambassador's residence before JFK's first meeting with Khrushchev. Almost immediately, Max Jacobson was directed to Kennedy's room. "The meeting may last for a long time," JFK told him. "See to it that my back won't give me any trouble when I have to get up or move around." Jacobson administered his injection, and a tanned and youthful Kennedy was next seen bounding out of the front door "like a bronco-buster sprung from his chute" and dashing down the steps "to meet his bald, fat guest," wrote *Time*. Whatever it took, Kennedy was determined to present a vibrant image. "I was damned if I was going to use my crutches with Khrushchev," JFK told Douglas Dillon's daughter Joan several weeks later.

After nearly five hours with the Soviet leader, Kennedy was in a state of shock. He was particularly unnerved, he later told Schlesinger, by Khrushchev's "combination of external jocosity and internal rage." Khrushchev had no intention of discussing a test ban, and he spent most of the time haranguing Kennedy and luring him into debates about Marxism—the very snare JFK's advisers had urged him to avoid. In his preparation, Kennedy had focused on the Soviet leader's character and personality, but had not steeped himself in communist philosophy.

In a "quiet and understated" fashion, Kennedy gamely tried to press important points—his concern about the possibility of war by miscalculation, the need to find common ground while respecting each other's vital interests. But the Soviet leader continued his verbal pummeling, managing even to trap Kennedy into admitting that the Bay of Pigs "was a mistake." Khrushchev was "intent upon . . . gaining the psychological upper hand," said Richard Davies of the State Department. "He got the psychological upper hand."

That evening during a banquet at Schoenbrunn Palace, Khrushchev ogled Jackie "like a smitten schoolboy," and she responded coquettishly. She·wore a figure-hugging "mermaid dress," in "shimmering pink-silver" designed by Cassini, who called it "subtly seductive." She tried to discuss the folkways of nineteenth-century Ukraine, but when Khrushchev began a pedantic comparison of contemporary education to life under the czars, she exclaimed, "Oh, Mr. Chairman, don't bore me with statistics." Khrushchev guffawed and launched into his favorite jokes. Jackie worked diligently to please, and at one point, according to a newspaper account, "she threw back her head and laughed hard."

Jackie later told Arthur Schlesinger that Khrushchev reminded her of the slapstick comedians Abbott and Costello, and that at times he seemed "almost cozy." In his own recollections, Khrushchev downplayed any mesmerizing effect on the part of the First Lady. "She didn't impress me as having that special brilliant beauty which can haunt men," he wrote. "But she was youthful, energetic and pleasant." He also perceptively noted that Jackie was "quick with her tongue. . . . She had no trouble finding the right word to cut you short if you weren't careful with her." Chillingly, he concluded, "I couldn't care less what sort of wife he had. If he liked her, that was his business—and good luck to them both."

Khrushchev's chummy interlude with Jackie clearly had no impact on his bullying manner with Kennedy. During their meeting the next day, Khrushchev hardened his attack. The crux of his message was the status of Berlin, which Khrushchev called a "bone in my throat." After their victory in World War II, the Allied powers had formally agreed to share the supervision of Germany, with the United States, Britain, and France overseeing the western sector, and the Soviet Union the eastern. The four nations similarly divided the capital city of Berlin, which lay 110 miles inside East Germany. It was understood that the Western powers would have unimpeded access through the Soviet zone to West Berlin, which functioned as a state of West Germany.

There had also been a commitment among the victors to the reunification of Germany with democratic elections. Instead, the Soviets sought to consolidate their hold in East Germany, and in 1948 Moscow abruptly cut Allied land routes to Berlin. The Allies responded with the Berlin airlift, which ferried supplies to the isolated city for eleven months until the Soviets yielded. Since 1958, Khrushchev had been threatening to sign a formal treaty with the hard-line communist government of East Germany that would automatically end all Western occupation and access to Berlin.

Now Khrushchev announced his intention to complete the treaty before the end of the year to officially recognize the existence of two German entities and shore up his country's relationship with East Germany. Kennedy said such unilateral abrogation of the surrender terms after World War II was unacceptable, and the Soviets would be violating the principles of unification and self-determination for Germany. Khrushchev countered that if the West responded with force, he would take military countermeasures. "If the United States wants war, that's its problem," said Khrushchev. Replied Kennedy, "Then, Mr. Chairman, there will be war. It will be a cold winter."

None of the news accounts fully conveyed the gravity of Kennedy's exchanges with Khrushchev. James Reston's *New York Times* dispatch came closest by emphasizing the "split on Berlin and key arms issues" and the "hard controversy" that ended the meeting. Reston described Kennedy's "solemn, although confident mood," and wrote, "there were no ultimatums and few bitter or menacing exchanges." In fact, Reston knew better, having heard a far more candid version of events from Kennedy only minutes after the meetings broke up. The "worst thing in my life," Kennedy told the newsman. "He savaged me." Kennedy also conceded that the Soviet leader "did it because of the Bay of Pigs. I think he thought anyone who was so young and inexperienced as to get into that mess could be taken. And anyone who got into it and didn't see it through had no guts." But Reston, like Joe Alsop when faced the next day with similar revelations—that Khrushchev had "asked him for surrender and threatened war."—chose to protect Kennedy from his alarming disclosures.

Khrushchev actually had a more favorable impression of Kennedy than he let on—although he shaded his views for different audiences. To his aide Fyodor Burlatasky, he declared Kennedy "too intelligent and too weak." U.S. Ambassador Llewellyn Thompson heard that the Soviet premier had found JFK "a modern man not cluttered up by old formulas. Kennedy had done his homework well and never once had to turn to an adviser for information." Khrushchev told Cy Sulzberger he considered Kennedy "a worthy partner" who "formulates his own ideas" and "has a much broader outlook" than Eisenhower.

The last stop for the Kennedys was an overnight visit in London cloaked as a social call for the christening of Stas and Lee's daughter, Anna Christina, at Westminster Cathedral. Jack and Jackie stayed at the Radziwills' Georgian home on Buckingham Place in the less than fashionable Victoria neighborhood of central London. Kennedy still had Max Jacobson in tow. The doctor entered the Radziwill home through the garden, and made his way through the Victorian sculptures in the foyer to treat the President and First Lady in a second-floor bedroom. On his way out, Jacobson encountered Stas—"a handsome man dressed in tails"—who would join his roster of patients.

For Kennedy the visit was primarily an opportunity to talk intimately and frankly to Macmillan. On his arrival, Kennedy appeared "ebullient" and "fit" to David Bruce, but Macmillan saw a different man. Kennedy was "stunned" and "baffled" by the "offensive and even brutal" line taken by Khrushchev. JFK said he regretted being drawn into an ideological debate, and he conceded that "no progress was made on any issue." Macmillan later told the queen that Kennedy had been "completely overwhelmed" by Khrushchev. The prime minister felt that Kennedy had overreacted to Khrushchev's tactics "like a bull being teased by the darts of the picadors." Kennedy had built a political career on his engaging persuasiveness, but "for the first time in his life," Macmillan noted, the President had "met a man wholly impervious to his charm."

In honor of Jack and Jackie, the prime minister and his wife, Lady Dorothy, organized "a very gay luncheon" with "lots of nice men and pretty women." Macmillan was "encouraged by the President's buoyancy" and tried to distract him with humor. Nit-picking a newspaper article about Jackie, Kennedy said, "How would you react if somebody should say, 'Lady Dorothy is a drunk'?" Said Macmillan: "I would reply, 'You should have seen her mother.'" The prime minister warmed to Kennedy's openness, noting afterwards, "Our friendship seemed confirmed and strengthened." Kennedy later told Henry Brandon, "I feel at home with Macmillan because I can share my loneliness with him. The others are all foreigners to me."

JFK flew back to Washington after a dinner given by the queen at Buckingham Palace on Monday, June 5, while Jackie remained behind in London for a holiday with Lee. Still wearing his tuxedo, he boarded Air Force One close to midnight, accompanied by Bundy, Rusk, O'Donnell, Powers, and other aides as well as Eunice. Kennedy stripped down to his shorts, but he was unable to sleep, so he summoned Hugh Sidey for a talk. Sidey noticed that the President looked haggard as he hugged his bare legs and "shifted stiffly in his seat to ease the back pain." "He remembered little things," Sidey recalled, "like what [Khrushchev's] hands looked like." Trying to be upbeat, Kennedy insisted the trip was "invaluable," the future "grim but not hopeless."

Sizing up both Khrushchev and de Gaulle face-to-face "helps me make up my mind when the moment for decision comes," Kennedy told Cy Sulzberger. "You have to know the men themselves in order to be able to evaluate their words." Vienna, more than the Bay of Pigs failure, was the real turning point for Kennedy—the first time, Joe Alsop observed, that JFK faced "the appalling moral burden" of the presidency.

SEVENTEEN

*H*aving shed her official duties, Jackie spent the day after her husband's departure shopping and socializing with Lee. When they emerged from a private tour of the Grosvenor House antique show, the sisters were "surrounded by enthusiastic bobby-sockers," reported David Bruce. That night they attended a small dinner party at the home of Jakie and Chiquita Astor, longtime friends of Jack's. Society photographer Cecil Beaton recorded in his journal that Jackie was "outspoken and impolitic, telling of the rough talk between Jack and Mr. Khrushchev." Beaton, who was known for his disparaging remarks about the appearance of famous women (Audrey Hepburn: "a huge mouth, flat Mongolian features . . . a long neck, but perhaps too scraggy"), had an axe to grind with Jackie. The previous fall she had postponed and then canceled his photo shoot for *Vogue,* choosing instead Richard Avedon for the pages of Diana Vreeland's *Harper's Bazaar.*

Predictably, Beaton took caustic note of Jackie's "affected" manner, as well as her "huge baseball-player shoulders and haunches, big boyish hands and feet," "somewhat negroid appearance," and "suspicion of a moustache." He did concede the beauty of her "receptive eyes," capable of "looking roguish or sad," and the "slight hesitancy" of her speech that made her appear "modest and humble." He also noted that Jackie criticized the queen's dress from the previous evening and her "flat hair style." The First Lady "seemed to have no fear of criticism. She enjoys so many aspects of her job, and takes for granted the more onerous onslaughts of the press."

The next morning Jackie and Lee took off for eight days in Greece as the guests of Prime Minister Constantine Karamanlis. Since the Greek leader lived in a small apartment in Athens, he asked his friend Marcos Nomikos, a shipping tycoon, to lend Jackie and Lee his seaside villa at Kavouri, as well as his 125-foot yacht, the *North Wind,* for a four-day cruise of the Greek islands. The sisters were joined by Stas and several friends: John Mowinckel, an official from the American Embassy in Paris, and his wife, Letizia ("Jackie invited us and said 'Don't tell any-body,'" recalled Letizia. "Secrecy was part of her nature"), as well as extra man Arkady Gerney, Jackie's friend from Paris days. Although the trip was private, Tish Baldrige was on hand to help out, getting the villa ready and organizing itineraries and cultural events.

All appeared serene as Jackie and Lee toured ancient ruins, sun-bathed, and swam. Behind the scenes, however, they had reverted to the wisecracking "Jacks" and "Pekes" who had roared around Europe exactly a decade earlier, but now they were turning on Baldrige and arbitrarily changing schedules. "I could only describe it as mean-spiritedness I had not seen before," Baldrige recalled. "There was whispering behind my back, and conspiratorial giggling." Baldrige compounded the problem by complaining to the President, mainly because she had security concerns, putting her in the position of "chief tattler."

The sisters' behavior was the first overt sign of Jackie's growing resentment of Baldrige's strong-willed management of the First Lady's office. "Jackie was a very complex person," said Letizia. "She was not manipulative, but she had her own way, her own likes and dislikes. . . . She didn't like to be told what to do, and Tish would say, 'You must do that,' which got on Jackie's nerves." In Letizia's view, "There was already a campaign against Tish, and Lee didn't help. She was blowing on the fire. . . . She had a lot to do with Jackie's behavior toward Tish." Baldrige preferred to excuse Jackie's actions as "a momentary lapse of selfishness going back to her school days of doing what she wanted, being independent, and stamping her foot."

As Jackie's trip wound down, her activities began drawing potentially embarrassing headlines such as "First Lady Dances Till 1." After dinner one evening, she insisted—against the wishes of the Secret Service—on visiting a nightclub, where she danced the Kalamatianos with a group of Greeks. She was also spotted whizzing through the countryside "in a Mercedes with young Crown Prince Constantine at the wheel."

These reports presented an unfortunate juxtaposition with her husband's situation. Within days of his return to Washington, the press had been filled with reports on his badly injured back. Having watched his agony in Paris, Vienna, and London, Jackie was fully aware of his condition, and during her vacation she kept in touch with the White House. "She was on the phone every night, in long conversations with Jack," said Letizia Mowinckel.

Yet Jackie declined to cut her vacation short, prompting Pierre Salinger to fib twice to the press, first saying she had gone to Greece without knowing of JFK's injury, then asserting that in London he mentioned "in passing" his back pain. According to Salinger, she only realized the severity when she read about it in the newspapers. She had offered to return home, Salinger said, but JFK had recommended she remain on holiday.

Kennedy's back problems had deteriorated once he reached the White House, and he was forced to use crutches all the time, even to greet visiting dignitaries. When his doctors ordered him to Palm Beach for "complete rest" for four days during the second week of June, Salinger disclosed the tree-planting incident in Canada. The crutches were necessary, Salinger explained, "to rest the strained muscle." Kennedy needed to soak in the Wrightsmans' hot saltwater pool, so he returned to their estate, which by then had been closed for the season and looked rather eerie with its furniture protected by dustcovers.

Kennedy was accompanied by Chuck Spalding as well as Janet Travell, White House chef René Verdon, and staff members including Priscilla Wear and Jill Cowan. Travell "kept a sharp vigil over her patient," who slept nearly twelve hours, relaxed in his pajamas, and swam in the rain. He also consulted with an orthopedist flown in from New York.

One evening, Kennedy invited Hugh Sidey to join him for dinner on the terrace with Spalding, Wear, and Cowan—"a weird night," by Sidey's recollection. Kennedy wore white flannels and despite his infirmity was full of jokes. As Frank Sinatra tunes played in the background, Kennedy and his guests sipped daiquiris and ate "fish in the bag" prepared by Verdon. Kennedy told a wild tale about a small nuclear bomb that had been smuggled piecemeal into the attic of the Soviet Embassy on Sixteenth Street—only blocks away from the White House. Sidey dismissed the story as improbable and declined to pursue it. (Years later, he would learn that the Defense Intelligence Agency had for two decades believed such a bomb existed.)

Kennedy's willingness to regale Sidey that way showed his confidence that the journalist would keep the President's remarks—as well as his behavior—"off the record." As dinner ended, Sidey offered Fiddle and Faddle a ride back to their quarters at the Palm Beach Towers, where the press and White House staff usually stayed. Wear and Cowan assured Sidey they had their own car. As the awkwardness grew, they rose to leave with Sidey. But once in their car, they said it wouldn't start, explaining they had to return to the house to call for help. "I said to myself, 'Hugh, you stupid guy,' as they went back in," recalled Sidey. "That was as close as I got. I think it was a therapy session of sorts. It was reckless of him, but he called it right. He knew I wasn't going to write about it."

———

The President's journey home from Florida couldn't have been more dramatic. Unable to climb the steps to his airplane, he resorted to a cherry picker to lift him aboard. When he arrived at the White House, he hobbled across the South Lawn on crutches—a sight that was "just a bit upsetting . . . to a good many Americans," *Newsweek* observed. He had to be helped into his rocking chair, and he conducted meetings from his bed and even his bathroom. Ken Galbraith had to sit on a stool while Kennedy soaked in the tub, turning on the hot water with his foot. "I think he is suffering a good deal from his back," Galbraith noted in his journal. "Certainly it is more serious than he admits or wants to admit."

Harold Macmillan was so concerned that he asked a British physician, Sir John Richardson, to travel to Washington and investigate Kennedy's condition. Richardson's confidential report said that JFK had a "badly formed" back—"one or more vertebrae" that "never grew properly"—which was aggravated by injuries as well as unwise back surgery. "This is why he has rather a stoop and is inclined to hold his arm close to his body," Richardson concluded. Although Richardson predicted that Kennedy's immediate strain would subside, his back "would continue to be a source of irritation and intermittent pain."

JFK was driven to National Airport just before midnight on Thursday, June 15, to meet Jackie's arriving flight, but he couldn't get out of the limousine. Jackie debarked looking "tanned and radiant," reported *Time,* while cameras caught her in an unusual public embrace with Jack. According to *Newsweek,* she "flew into the arms of her husband, waiting for her in his car with his crutches at his side. As photographers clicked away and a crowd of 200 cheered, the First Couple kissed and chatted excitedly until, a trifle embarrassed, the President commanded his driver: 'Come on, let's go.'"

The next afternoon they went to Glen Ora for the weekend, but Kennedy wasn't well enough to attend Paul and Bunny Mellon's debutante party at Oak Spring for their daughter Eliza, so Bill Walton served as Jackie's escort. Jackie arrived late, looking "very fresh, gay and beautiful," recalled Ken Galbraith. The all-night dance was held in a specially constructed ballroom designed as a replica of a French village square bustling with a country fair. In a nearby field tents flying flags served as quarters for male guests. Count Basie's orchestra alternated with a popular dance band, and a fireworks display lit up the night sky. "Someone said an entire vintage year of Dom Pérignon was consumed that night," wrote Katharine Graham.

After Paris, Vienna, and London, Jackie was "a huge star," said Baldrige. "All the men are in love with Jackie," Stew Alsop wrote to a friend that June. Jackie naturally enjoyed the adulation of the crowds and savored the opportunities for adventure that came with being first lady. "She liked the excitement," said Martha Bartlett. "She was eager to taste and test everything." As Jackie had vowed to Joe Alsop a year earlier, she was now fully committed to deploy her influence "for the things I care about." Susan Mary Alsop observed that Jackie had learned to "use power with tact and reticence."

But as Charles de Gaulle perceptively observed, Jackie was able to enhance the Kennedy presidency "without mixing in politics . . . she played the game very intelligently." Nor did Jackie have any illusions about her own position. "I was an observer (not a participant as [Jack] didn't wish his wife to be that way)," Jackie later told Harold Macmillan. "He knew I did not miss much—and that I was so aware of all that he was doing. He was proud that I knew."

JFK counted on Jackie's insights into those he did business with—from foreign leaders to garden variety politicians—her "deeper purpose," in Ken Galbraith's view. Jackie "would observe, hear and render judgment," observed Galbraith. "She distinguished sharply between those who were serving him and those who were serving themselves, and especially those who concealed imperfect judgment behind a display of personal importance—the accomplished frauds. Her wise and astringent analysis was especially important to Jack Kennedy."

Both Kennedys took away a renewed appreciation for the potency of ritual and historical ambiance that they had witnessed in France. Back in Washington, Jackie applied her new perspective to the state dinner the administration was planning for Pakistani president Mohammad Ayub Khan. Because Ayub had been such a staunch ally, agreeing to send five thousand of his troops to Laos, JFK wanted to treat him to a special celebration.

Earlier in the year, Charles Cecil Wall, the director of Mount Vernon, had notified Jackie that George Washington's historic plantation overlooking the Potomac would be "at your disposal" for a "little special entertaining." He noted, according to Tish Baldrige, that the location was "fabulous in the early evening with the setting sun and the beauty of the river." Jackie replied to Baldrige, "Remind me if we have a state visit or some VIPs this spring."

The arrival of President Ayub on July 11 offered the perfect opportunity for some pageantry at a great American shrine. In less than a month, Jackie, Baldrige, Turnure, and platoons of staff pulled together one of the most memorable dinners in White House history—a "native *fête champêtre*," in *Time*'s words, on the lawn at Mount Vernon. Designers from Tiffany's and Bonwit Teller decorated the thirty-two-by-fifty-two-foot dining marquee set up near the mansion's colonnaded terrace—the guy ropes disguised with artificial greenery, the chandeliers hung with garlands of flowers. Bunny Mellon and her resident horticultural expert arranged the centerpieces of seasonal flowers in small vermeil cachepots on yellow tablecloths to match the buttercup yellow interior of the tent. Bunny also lent black wrought-iron garden chairs to accommodate 138 guests. Dinner would be prepared by chef René Verdon at the White House and trucked to army field kitchens on the Mount Vernon grounds.

The weather was clear as four boats, each with its own trio of musicians, ferried the guests on an hour-long cruise fifteen miles down the Potomac. High officialdom—cabinet members, congressional leaders, senior White House aides—dominated the guest list, which also included the Stephen Smiths and Sargent Shrivers, the Jim Reeds, Franklin D. Roosevelts, Harry du Ponts, and Fifi Fell, a Manhattan beauty often invited by the Kennedys as an extra woman guaranteed to provide lively gossip. ("Not Jack's type," Vivian Crespi observed, "more for the salon than the boudoir.") Also on the guest list was Maurice Tempelsman, who three decades later would be Jackie's lover and constant companion until her death. At the time, he was a Democratic party supporter with an extensive diamond business in Africa.

Jackie wore a sleeveless dress with rows of narrow white lace over white organza, accented by a sash and stole in "Veronese green" that Cassini designed for a "romantic antebellum look" to evoke the "pillared elegance" of the setting. All the men sported white dinner jackets except the President and Bobby, who wore more formal black. The guests sipped mint juleps (George Washington's own recipe) from silver stirrup cups and watched the Continental Fife and Drum Corps in red coats and tricorn hats perform military drills. At the conclusion, the corps fired blanks from their muskets directly at the scrum of sixty reporters across the lawn. When a cameraman waved the white handkerchief of surrender, JFK and President Ayub convulsed with laughter.

Following the dinner, there was a concert by the National Symphony Orchestra of selections from Mozart and Gershwin. The evening was very much in the tradition of Washington's own lavish entertaining style. "It was done meticulously to evoke a real aristocrat," said Tish Baldrige. But the event did draw criticism as being "too fancy and costly for a democratic country." The most biting comment came from the *New York Herald Tribune,* which compared the dinner unfavorably to the "grandeur of the French court at Versailles." Although that was precisely what Jackie had in mind, she bristled nevertheless, and conveyed her displeasure to *Tribune* reporter David Wise.

The four-day visit by the "starchy strongman" with the "grey guards-man's mustache" was judged a success. Beforehand he had expressed concern that the Kennedy administration favored India over Pakistan. Although he failed in his request that the United States end military aid to India, he came away reassured of Pakistan's value to American inter-ests. He also landed one jab at rival Nehru, telling Kennedy, "People think he's thinking. Actually, he's just in a trance." At the end of his visit, Ayub was so taken with Jackie that he invited her to visit Pakistan.

———

Jackie had come back to Washington for the state dinner from the Kennedy compound on Cape Cod, where she had gone with Caroline and John on June 30. With the exception of a few brief trips home in September and October, she would not return to the White House full-time until the third week in October. Jack would join her every weekend, usually arriving on Friday evening and departing Monday morning. Lem Billings was usually on the scene, although he was ab-sent for more than two weeks at the end of the summer, escorting Eunice and Jean around Europe. While in Poland, they dined in an eighteenth-century palace that formerly belonged to the Radziwills, and Billings stole a silver place setting with the family crest that he later presented to a tearfully grateful Stas. JFK was furious about the prank, but predictably forgave Billings.

Throughout the summer, various friends—Oleg Cassini, the Spald-ings, Bill Walton, the Bartletts, and the Roosevelts among others—came to stay at JFK's cottage in Hyannis. The routine was unvarying—cruises in good weather and bad on Joe Kennedy's fifty-two-foot cabin cruiser, the *Marlin,* often with a water-skiing display by Jackie; an early evening trip to the Hyannis Port candy store by the President in his pale blue golf cart with up to eighteen children hanging on—and sometimes toppling off; tennis matches; swimming in the Ambassador's pool, followed by a baking in the Finnish sauna; dinners with family and friends; movies in the Ambassador's screening room. (Joe and Rose had gone to the Riviera for the summer.)

During that first summer both Jack and Jackie realized that their cottage was too cramped for a presidential entourage. "He never relaxes in the house," Jackie told her mother, "just gets out of it on the boat—

or else takes a nap." Jack's natural habitat was the ocean. "It was curiously moving to see that attractive young couple wearing gay colours, shooting off across the grey-green 'Boudin' sea, followed and preceded by armoured coastguard cutters," observed Noël Coward.

Jackie found the weekends "almost as exhausting as a week in Washington." Weekdays were a halcyon time, however, playing with her children, painting as she listened to chamber music (the better to concentrate and avoid distractions), reading, and sunbathing. Jackie even took golf lessons from the pro at the Hyannis Port Club; wearing large sunglasses and a kerchief, she would play only when the course was nearly empty. During one demonstration of her progress, JFK watched patiently as Jackie struggled to hit her ball out of a sand trap on the seventeenth hole.

On Arthur Schlesinger's recommendation, she read Henry Adams's classic Washington novel, *Democracy,* and declared herself "enthralled" as well as grateful that she had waited to read it, as "I wouldn't have loved it as much as I do now." She traveled incognito (wearing a wig with blonde braids) to Provincetown to see Shaw's *Mrs. Warren's Profession* with Gore Vidal and Bill Walton. Vidal told his biographer that at his motel Jackie "bounced up and down on the bed in playful, semi-anonymous pleasure."

Jackie periodically visited Bunny Mellon, who lived in Oyster Harbors, an exclusive enclave on the Seapuit River in nearby Osterville; once she went to Boston with the Mellons and Adele Astaire Douglas to see *Sail Away,* a comedy by Noël Coward, Paul and Bunny's close friend. They dined first at the Ritz, and after the show, Jackie "was sweet to the whole company," Coward recalled.

Jackie "liked Hyannis Port because it was her down time," said Joan Kennedy. "She had privacy and quiet to pursue her interests. I didn't bother her unless she called me." When she and Joan were together, they talked of family and cultural interests, skirting personal matters and politics. "She could relax with me," said Joan. "Jackie didn't say a lot of stuff. She liked having me because I didn't say a lot either."

Jackie stayed in almost daily contact with her White House staff, while others took on her official duties. After returning from Greece, an exasperated Tish Baldrige had tried to quit, but the President persuaded her to stay on and braced Jackie about managing Baldrige more carefully. "She was wonderful again," said Baldrige, "but it wore off."

Baldrige kept pushing Jackie to assume new activities, and Jackie continued to resist, even when it was a pet project such as the series of young people's concerts on the South Lawn. For the inaugural concert that August, the President welcomed the young performers as his wife's representative.

From afar, Jackie oversaw the accumulation of furniture, paintings, and objects for the White House, even as she steered clear of conflicts among her various advisers on decor. Lorraine Pearce, the first White House curator, was as rigorous as Baldrige in her own fashion—a meticulous scholar trained at Winterthur who favored Harry du Pont's views rather than those of Boudin. When Jackie hired Pearce in March, she called her "brilliant and full of energy and charm . . . as excited as a hunting dog." After only four months on the job, Pearce found herself in a "difficult situation," Metropolitan Museum curator James Biddle wrote to Harry du Pont, reduced to serving as "coordinator of a variety of decorating whims."

Among the patrons who signed on that summer were Douglas and Phyllis Dillon, who donated exquisite Empire furniture for the Red Room, and Bernice Chrysler Garbisch, who gave what Jackie described as a "van load of treasures" including Sheraton settees for the Green Room. "I feel a bit the way I did when my son was born and I couldn't see him for four days," Jackie wrote breathlessly to Bernice Garbisch and her husband. Sister Parish also enlisted her friends John and Frances Loeb to finance Jackie's Louis XVI plan for the Yellow Oval Room on the second floor. Through the legerdemain of Jackie and Jayne Wrightsman, Parish incorporated the ideas of Boudin, yet maintained her pride of authorship. Jackie praised Loeb's generosity by inquiring, "Shall we have a little statue of you on the mantelpiece?"

During the summer Jackie also worked on an article for *Life* on the White House restoration in collaboration with Hugh Sidey. The idea had been percolating since the spring, and Jackie kept postponing her deadline. Sidey even traveled to Hyannis several times, only to find that Jackie was elsewhere. "One time I sat for three days in the rain," recalled Sidey. In late August he was back in Iowa when the call came that the manuscript was ready. He found Jackie "in a skimpy bikini, all greased up, lying on a chaise and eating grapes. Oleg was there, a model named Robyn Butler, a bunch of others. I remember thinking there was a whiff of decadence." Jackie gave him the manuscript "rolled up like the Dead Sea Scrolls, written on papers from yellow pads." The article was unfocused and had to be rewritten under Sidey's byline.

Life for Jack in Washington was as fraught as Jackie's in Hyannis was idyllic. The European trip had enhanced his image, but it accomplished little of substance. Not only had Kennedy been unable to produce any progress on banning nuclear weapons tests, he now had Khrushchev's dark ultimatum on Berlin to worry about. Although he flashed a hint of humor to Billings—dealing with the Soviet leader, JFK said, "was like dealing with Dad—all give and no take"—Kennedy couldn't shake his distress over the encounter in Vienna.

"For weeks after he returned he talked about little else," recalled Ben Bradlee. "He carried excerpts from the official translation of his talks with Khrushchev around with him wherever he went, and read chunks of them to me several times." After the military estimated that seventy million Americans could die following a nuclear exchange, JFK shared his anguish with Bobby. "Tears came into his eyes," Bobby recounted to Hugh Sidey. "He was sitting on his bed and he said, 'Bobby, that is just incomprehensible.'" Bobby told Sidey, "It was the only time I've seen him cry." In meetings, Kennedy was uncharacteristically distracted; according to one White House staff member, "he sometimes ceases to listen as he stares into space—apparently searching for an answer to some nagging problem." Even Billings found him "suddenly . . . hard to get close to."

Kennedy's first instinct was to reach for the most hawkish Democrat he could find: Dean Acheson, Truman's highly respected secretary of state. The sixty-eight-year-old diplomat was known for his brilliant mind and intimidating eloquence, not to mention his withering criticisms. "Whoever is flailed by him will long remain sore," David Bruce once remarked. With his close-clipped mustache and crusty manner, Acheson was the quintessential establishment man. Kennedy had consulted him on cabinet appointments and had followed his advice on Rusk for State and Dillon for Treasury.

Yet Acheson had an uneasy relationship with the Kennedys, including Jackie. Her displeasure stemmed from his 1958 book, *Power and Diplomacy,* in which he took JFK to task for his speech on Algeria, declaring "this impatient snapping of our fingers . . . was a poor way to treat an old and valued ally." Not long after the book came out, Acheson encountered Jackie on a train making its way slowly to Washington in a blizzard. As they settled into the parlor car together, she turned from soft-spoken ingenue to protective tigress, sharply rebuking Acheson for unfairly attacking her husband. Acheson attempted to deflect her by proposing that since they faced a long journey they should avoid arguing. Jackie agreed to be pleasant but sulkily declined to say much. Days later, Acheson received a letter from Jackie fiercely inquiring "how one capable of such an Olympian tone can become so personal when attacking someone for political difference." Replied Acheson, "The Olympians seem to me to have been a pretty personal lot."

JFK followed the axiom that "in politics you don't have friends, you have allies," and he needed Acheson's gravitas to help craft a muscular response to the Soviets. The recommendations Acheson forcefully presented on June 29, however, pushed too close to the brink of nuclear war for Kennedy's comfort: an intense buildup of military might, including the deployment of several divisions in West Germany; the declaration of a national emergency; and a call-up of the reserves. In the following weeks, Kennedy spent much of his time studying his "Berlin Book," a black looseleaf notebook in which he collected position papers responding to the Acheson plan.

Schlesinger, who had previously told JFK he considered Acheson to be "consumed in vanity and bitterness," judged the elder statesman's analysis "rather bloodcurdling" and offered a five-page memo outlining diplomatic options. Galbraith similarly weighed in from India, castigating those "asking only that we advertise our willingness to risk a deep thermonuclear burn." Sorensen offered an argument that especially resonated with his boss: "We should not engage Khrushchev's prestige to a point where he felt he could not back down from a showdown." As he did before with Laos, Sorensen nudged Kennedy toward exploring a peaceful solution.

During a cruise on the *Marlin* in early July, Kennedy quizzed Rusk, McNamara, and General Maxwell Taylor, the newest member of the White House staff. At Bobby's urging, Kennedy had designated the hawkish Taylor his personal military adviser. Taylor was a handsome and confident intellectual fluent in Japanese, German, Spanish, and French—a prototypical New Frontiersman. "We need a man like Taylor to give things a cold and fishy eye," Bobby said.

At Sorensen's suggestion, Kennedy decided to make a televised speech about his policy on Berlin. The President's July 25 address stopped short of Acheson's state of emergency but included an addition of $3.45 billion ($20.7 billion today) to the defense budget—nearly $1 billion less than Acheson had recommended, but a significant increase at a time when military spending totaled $47.5 billion. Defense spending represented 9 percent of the gross domestic product, compared to 3.4 percent four decades later under George W. Bush.

This measure was JFK's first step toward implementing a "flexible response" in American military strategy that he had been considering since the presidential campaign when he first read about it in *The Uncertain Trumpet* by Maxwell Taylor. Instead of the Eisenhower administration's doctrine of massive nuclear retaliation in a confrontation with the Soviet Union, Kennedy wanted more options than "holocaust and humiliation." Following Taylor's framework, Kennedy approved a progression of responses—from covert operations through counterinsurgency guerrillas to engagement by an enlarged army, navy, and air force—that would meet a range of threats. It was Kennedy's hope that beefing up conventional forces in Europe could deter Soviet forces from making any hostile moves.

In strong language Kennedy asserted the Allies' legal right to be in Berlin and declared that "an attack upon that city will be regarded as an attack upon us all. . . . We do not want to fight, but we have fought before." But Kennedy also signaled a willingness to negotiate a formula for Germany's unification and self-determination. In his peroration, Kennedy used ideas suggested by Max Freedman, Washington correspondent for Britain's liberal *Manchester Guardian,* asking Americans for patience because in the battle with communism "there is no quick and easy solution."

Khrushchev's response barely three weeks later shocked the world, but not Kennedy and his men. They had long been aware that East German refugees—many of them well-educated professionals—were fleeing to the West through Berlin. The outflow had been accelerating over the summer—nearly thirty thousand in the month of July—which sharpened Kennedy's awareness of Khrushchev's problem. "Kennedy wasn't the type to feel someone else's pain," said historian Philip Zelikow, "but he spent a lot of time thinking in cold clinical terms how Khrushchev would see a situation and react."

In the first days of August, Kennedy was walking along the colon-

nade to the Oval Office when he said to Walt Rostow, "The Russians
are going to block off access to West Berlin from the East, and there is
not a damn thing we can do about it." Kennedy explained that the
"brain drain" to the West was imperiling Khrushchev's position not
only in East Germany but in all of Eastern Europe. While the United
States could go to war to defend West Berlin, Kennedy told Rostow,
"We won't go to war to keep East Germany from bleeding to death."

By various winks and nods, through private emissaries as well as
public utterances, Kennedy indicated to Khrushchev the sentiments he
expressed to Rostow. When asked about the refugee problem at an
August 10 news conference, Kennedy said the United States had no
position on the issue. Three days later, East German soldiers backed
by Soviet troops erected barbed-wire barricades between East and
West Berlin; within weeks the wire was replaced by an imposing concrete wall.

The wall was an egregious affront to freedom, but Kennedy knew
that it effectively neutralized the crisis that began in Vienna. "Why
would Khrushchev put up a wall if he really intended to seize West
Berlin?" Kennedy said to Kenny O'Donnell. ". . . This is his way out of
his predicament. It's not a very nice solution but a wall is a hell of a lot
better than a war." Khrushchev stopped making noise about Allied
rights of access to West Berlin, and well before the end of the year
dropped his threat to sign a separate peace treaty with East Germany.

Kennedy flexed American military muscle only once—in part for
Khrushchev's benefit but mostly to reassure anxious West Berliners.
Five days after the first appearance of barbed wire, Kennedy ordered
1,500 troops to West Berlin in a convoy through East Germany, and he
sent Lyndon Johnson to meet them. Addressing 350,000 West Berlin
citizens, Johnson pledged, "This island does not stand alone!"

It was a singular moment in the spotlight for Johnson. In May,
Kennedy had sent him on a fact-finding tour of Asia—the sort of trip
Johnson welcomed. "It was where he was in charge of his life," said Liz
Carpenter, "a way to establish himself and have his own persona." But
while Kennedy had assigned Johnson the serious task of preparing
a report on South Vietnam, the tour had been noteworthy mainly
for the comic relief of Johnson's encounter with a camel cart driver in
Pakistan. "Come and see us, heah?" Johnson had said to Bashir Ahmed.

At the instigation of a Karachi newspaper columnist, Bashir surprisingly accepted the invitation to visit the United States the following October.

Johnson got the full measure of praise for his Berlin visit, but he exercised no influence during the crisis deliberations. He had sided with Acheson's hard line, showing what Walt Rostow called "conventional toughness . . . without really seeing all the complications." Johnson had better luck with his other responsibilities. Taking advantage of Kennedy's new emphasis on space exploration, the Vice President helped engineer the choice of Houston for the new $60 million command center for the National Aeronautics and Space Administration.

After navigating several crises, Kennedy had not fundamentally changed the way he made decisions. "He is sort of an Indian snake charmer," a disappointed Dean Acheson wrote to Harry Truman. "He toots away on his pipe and our problems sway back and forth around him in a trance-like manner, never approaching, but never withdrawing. . . . Someday one of these snakes will wake up; and no one will be able even to run."

But Kennedy was learning which of his men were reliable, which theories were reasonable, and what machinery was most effective. In Douglas Dillon's view, JFK was discovering "who made sense. He spent less time listening to anybody and everybody. He listened partly to keep people and groups friendly, not just for decisions. He would listen and massage everyone while deciding. He would listen and build support, and in his questions he wanted to be sure you thought through and understood the implications of your recommendations. He wasn't ever argumentative. He was trying to find out so he could better understand."

As national security adviser, Mac Bundy was responsible for pulling foreign policy opinions and data together and offering his analysis to Kennedy. Before the Bay of Pigs, Bundy had only rudimentary contacts throughout the government bureaucracy, which impeded his effectiveness. Now his new basement West Wing office had become a clearinghouse for intelligence.

Kennedy admired Bundy's capacity for "a tremendous amount of work." The President could also communicate easily with Bundy in "rapid fire shorthand." After Kennedy had left the room, Bundy knew his boss's thinking well enough to accurately convey what needed to be done. "He doesn't fold or get rattled when they're sniping at him," Kennedy observed. Yet a colleague lamented Bundy's "iron faith in the definitiveness of his yes or no," and his ability to "make everything he says sound plausible that . . . scares the hell out of me."

Bundy's confident approach tended to overshadow Dean Rusk, a quiet and controlled man who became known as "the Buddha" for his impassive demeanor. "Rusk plays his cards so close," observed Dean Acheson, "he can't see them himself." Bundy was "very correct" with Rusk, said Arthur Schlesinger, "but he always presented the State Department position better than the State Department."

Dillon enjoyed both professional and social intimacy with Kennedy. Not only were he and his lively wife, Phyllis, major donors to Jackie's cause, they were among the handful of insiders who entertained the Kennedys at home. Their stucco villa in Washington's fashionable Kalorama neighborhood was like "one of those Italian palaces on a small but perfect scale," noted Jewel Reed. "The opulence is a rare thing in this day and age, and yet it is so understated that it couldn't possibly be out of keeping with the New Frontier."

On economic policy, Dillon's cautious positions continued to win favor with Kennedy. In the days before JFK's Berlin speech, Bobby Kennedy, backed by McNamara, Johnson, and Rusk, had proposed an income tax increase to help finance an expanded military budget. Dillon argued that such a hike would dampen the economic expansion that was beginning to pull the country out of recession, and Kennedy promptly rejected Bobby's idea. Appraising Dillon's rising status, Stew Alsop called him "a brilliant bureaucratic infighter."

Even Ken Galbraith, who initially regarded Dillon as an "obdurate Republican," concluded that the secretary of the Treasury was an "excellent operator." Galbraith kept pressing his economic agenda at every opportunity. "Galbraith would come back and see Kennedy and tell him how terrible everything was because we were not spending enough money," Dillon said. "Kennedy would ask me questions Galbraith had posed, and I would answer them. Nothing ever had any effect." Once, when Dillon thought Galbraith was in India, Kennedy asked "a particularly exotic question about the economy," recalled Dillon. "I said, 'Mr. President, I'll look into that. By the way, is Galbraith back in town?' The President laughed and laughed and said yes."

Galbraith was more successful in getting Kennedy's attention with his assessments of the situation in India, Vietnam, Laos, and China. By the fall of 1961, Galbraith's missives across the ocean—what he called his "Indo-Talleyrand Series" with a nod to the French diplomat and politician—were part of Jack and Jackie's routine reading. The envoy's efforts to avoid "tedium" resulted in some eye-catching observations. "Saigon," Galbraith reported, "has the most stylish women in all Asia. They are tall with long legs, high breasts, and wear white silk pajamas and a white silk robe, split at the sides to the armpits. . . . On a bicycle or scooter they look very compelling."

Bob McNamara solidified his position through an unusual mixture of brainpower, loyalty, and dexterity. Before a meeting of the National Security Council to discuss Berlin, Kennedy gathered several top aides in his office. When Kennedy asked McNamara for his opinion, the defense secretary "gave the most brilliantly argued and authoritatively documented case for a national emergency that you could imagine, all with no notes," recalled Ted Sorensen. Other aides weighed in, and Kennedy responded with a cogent rationale against a national emergency, which he viewed as unduly alarmist. The group then moved into the formal NSC meeting, and once again, Kennedy said, "What do you think, Bob?" at which point McNamara delivered what Sorensen remembered as "the most dazzling and authoritative argument on why we should not declare a national emergency."

In his own quiet fashion, Sorensen had become as close to a chief of staff as Kennedy could tolerate. He parsed and synthesized arguments as he exercised power with formidable reserve. He spoke softly and often paused deliberately, a psychological ploy that commanded attention while creating an aura of maturity. "Ted can look at you in silence better than any man I know," noted Teddy White. "He can play with silence like a tool until you crack." Idle chatter was anathema to Sorensen, and he struck many as peremptory. "I probably was abrupt," he recalled. "But it was not aloofness or arrogance, although it might have been reticence. It was more the unbelievable volume of work. I suffered from sleep deprivation. I probably cut people off from time to time."

Bobby Kennedy used his influence more flamboyantly. Social life at Hickory Hill, the home he shared with his thirty-two-year old wife, the former Ethel Skakel, their seven children and collection of pets, occupied the opposite pole of the Kennedy court life. Most of the inner circle frequented Hickory Hill, with the Dillons and McNamaras topping the list of particular friends. Bobby named one of his children after the Treasury secretary and on Saturdays would arrive unannounced at the Dillon home with several from his brood, seeking company for a movie matinee.

Jack and Jackie's White House may have condoned strong drinks, smoking, and dancing until the early morning hours, but the party scene at Hickory Hill was notably uninhibited. Ethel set the exuberant tone that her socially uneasy husband tolerated. The sixth of seven children, Ethel had a madcap "anything goes" quality, concocting pranks such as unleashing a live chicken on the dining table and pushing presidential advisers (Arthur Schlesinger most notoriously) into her swimming pool in their evening clothes.

Jack and Jackie seldom appeared, nor did Ethel and Bobby socialize much at the White House. Once when they did come to dinner, Mary Gallagher observed the sharp contrast between Jackie's "subdued" manner and Ethel's "peppy" personality. Bobby's intensity was an obstacle to socializing with his brother. Bobby "never seemed to need any release" from the issues of the day, observed Chuck Spalding, "whereas the President obviously did." "With Bobby there were no belly laughs, as there were with Jack," said Red Fay.

Bobby's prevailing mood was suspicion. He could be a rough and tactless presence around the White House, which JFK found more useful than irksome. Once after fielding a difficult phone call, Kennedy told Ken Galbraith, "Bobby would just tell him to cut the crap. I'm more polite." Bobby was known for retreating into discomfiting silences or subjecting people to aggressive inquisitions. "He was like a human drill," said Douglas Dillon's daughter Joan. As Harry Hopkins was for FDR, Bobby served as his brother's "Lord Root of the Matter," empowered to get to the heart of issues with "devastating questions that coming from the President would have had a more explosive impact," said Arthur Schlesinger.

It was clear, as Bobby's aide Jim Symington said, that "Bobby knew instantly what Jack wanted. They talked every day as pilot and co-pilot in the same tank, rumbling through the country's problems." Many observed the brothers' almost telepathic communication, anticipating each other's thoughts, flashing signals with looks and gestures. As soon as Kennedy heard that the Berlin wall was going up his first command was, "Get Rusk on the phone. Go get my brother."

Yet JFK knew his brother's weakness—his tendency to react too fiercely, and to judge everything as either black or white. "Jack has traveled in that speculative area where doubt lives," said Chuck Spalding. "Bobby does not travel there." JFK could—and did—overrule his brother because, as Walt Rostow pointed out, "He didn't have to be nice to Bobby."

Bobby's most conspicuous assignment came when Jack was in Paris and Rafael Trujillo, dictator of the Dominican Republic, was assassinated with machine guns supplied by the CIA. With Dean Rusk en route to Europe, Under Secretary of State Chester Bowles was technically in charge. Bobby, however, set up a command post on the seventh floor of the State Department and ordered U.S. Navy ships close to the island. Their purpose was to show support for the anti-communist faction trying to take control, but Bowles objected when Bobby—with McNamara's backing—tried to send in marines as well. In his post–Bay of Pigs caution, JFK agreed with Bowles, although he didn't disapprove of Bobby's effort to poach on Bowles's turf.

By summer's end Jack seemed to have recovered from his back injury, although it would be many months before he could pick up a golf club again. The most effective treatment was a new exercise regimen to strengthen his abdominal muscles prescribed by Dr. Hans Kraus, a specialist in rehabilitative medicine from New York. But unknown to either public or press, Max Jacobson remained in the picture, operating as a sort of court wizard, offering Kennedy his injections with surprising regularity. According to Jacobson's expense records, from June through October 1961, he saw the President thirty-six times. When Dr. Eugene Cohen, the endocrinologist responsible for managing Kennedy's Addison's disease, learned of Jacobson's role, he wrote JFK a stern warning: "You cannot be permitted to receive therapy from irresponsible doctors like M.J. [Jacobson]. . . . With such injections [patients] may perform some temporary functions in an exhilarated dream state. However, this therapy conditions one's needs almost like a narcotic" and "is not for responsible individuals who at any split second may have to decide the fate of the universe." Kennedy still declined to cut Jacobson loose, although he would rely on his services only inter-mittently in the following two years.

Not long after Billy Brammer declared in mid-July that the President's "roundering" had been curtailed by back problems, Kennedy was seeing other women again. On two Tuesday nights in late August and early September, he went out on the *Honey Fitz* for three-hour cruises down the Potomac with George Smathers and Bill Thompson, a rail-road executive from Florida, and several comely women including Helen Chavchavadze. "Jack would just take them out on the boat and hug and kiss a little bit," Smathers told Robert Kennedy biogra-pher Evan Thomas several decades later. "It was very innocent really." Chavchavadze recalled the cruises as "lighthearted. Jack let off steam. He had people around he could be himself with, to get away from the serious business of the presidency. He may have been in the back of the cabin with someone else, but it wasn't me, not at that juncture, not in that place."

For several weeks in September, Otto Preminger was in Washington filming *Advise and Consent,* Allen Drury's political thriller. The stars included Henry Fonda, Charles Laughton, Walter Pidgeon, Burgess Meredith, Franchot Tone, and Peter Lawford, as well as Farmington graduate Gene Tierney, who played a Washington hostess. Lawford came to dinner at the White House frequently, sometimes accompanied by a young woman to amuse the President. One such evening im-probably surfaced in the *New York Times,* offered as a "Cinderella story" about twenty-one-year-old Susan Perry, who worked in the office of Republican senator Jacob Javits. The "pretty young receptionist" "at-tracted the attention" of Lawford and "blushingly accepted" the actor's invitation to dine with Kennedy at the White House.

With his Hollywood fascination, Kennedy kept close tabs on the film's progress. "He got so excited he kept calling them to find out what was going on," said *Look*'s Laura Bergquist. "He didn't want to be left out." Kennedy tried several times to schedule dinner with the cast. They finally came to the White House for lunch with Jack and Jackie in late September. Also in attendance was Frank Sinatra, who was "show-ing off, being quite objectionable," said Helen Chavchavadze, who filled out the distaff side along with Eunice, Jean, Ethel, Mary Meyer, and San Francisco newspaper heiress Nan McEvoy—all known for lively company as well as good looks.

Dave Powers continued to serve as a beard for women visiting Kennedy in the evening. Powers jokingly referred to himself as "John's other wife" when he assumed his customary "night duty" on the second floor at the White House. In Jackie's absence, JFK would summon Powers to keep him company to relieve his "solitary confinement." It was assumed that Powers would have dinner, chat with JFK if he liked, or amuse himself as Kennedy did paperwork. Sometimes JFK would play his favorite records on the stereo, dance tunes from the thirties and forties such as "Beyond the Blue Horizon," "The Very Thought of You," "Stardust," and "Stormy Weather." Only when Kennedy turned in would Powers drive home to his wife, Jo, and three young children in McLean, Virginia.

For the last ten days in September, Jack joined his family for a vacation at Hammersmith Farm while Janet and "Unk" traveled in Europe. The sprawling gray nineteenth-century shingled home, with its red roof and "pepper-pot tower," was situated on seventy-five acres overlooking Narragansett Bay, offering greater privacy than Hyannis. The pace was far more leisurely as well, with long cruises on the *Honey Fitz*. Jack held court on the fantail from his brown leather chair bolted to the deck, Bill Walton buzzed around with his movie camera, and FDR Jr. "stood on deck like an old sea dog, surveying the water."

Each day an airplane from Washington brought a pouch of official papers and intelligence briefings that JFK read "a lapful at a time," and he had access to the White House by a specially installed phone link, although he took few calls. Instead, he reread Alfred Duff Cooper's *Talleyrand*—"a great book," said JFK. For the first time since he assumed the presidency, Kennedy was able to genuinely relax. "We sit for hours on the terrace just looking at the bay and drinking in the beauty & all one's strength is renewed," Jackie wrote to her mother. "You would never guess what this vacation has done for Jack. He said it was the best he ever had."

EIGHTEEN

$\mathcal{J}$oining Jack Kennedy for drinks on October 3, the day after the President's return to the White House, Cy Sulzberger noted that he "seemed extremely well, suntanned and fit, but his face is a bit puffy"—a common observation that only those closest to JFK could link to cortisone treatments. (Because of his medication, Kennedy's appearance varied significantly; ten days later, Molly Thayer would observe that the President "has grown thinner" and "lost the jowly look.") Kennedy spoke again of Khrushchev, but more dispassionately, noting that the Soviet leader had seemed "much softer" of late. The President also ingratiated himself with Sulzberger by dismissing rival journalist Walter Lippmann as "very confused."

That night, with Jackie scheduled to return from Newport the following afternoon, Jack Kennedy had his first known private visit from Mary Meyer. As she would do on thirteen documented occasions in the following two years, Meyer signed in to see Evelyn Lincoln and was admitted to the White House residence. (She may have entered anonymously at other times, as the second person in "Dave Powers plus one.") Meyer was also a conspicuous presence at all six of the Kennedys' dinner dances, and she was included in another half dozen small lunch and dinner parties given by Jack and Jackie. Meyer's confidante

Anne Truitt does not believe that her intimacy with the President began as early as October 1961, but their friendship was already well established.

Mary Pinchot Meyer and her younger sister, Tony Bradlee, had been raised in upper-class refinement in Manhattan and Grey Towers, a 3,600-acre estate in Pennsylvania, with the sort of advantages—horses, French governesses, elite private schools—Jackie had enjoyed. Both Pinchot sisters had even preceded Jackie at Vassar. But instead of Auchincloss propriety, the atmosphere of the Pinchot household was distinctly bohemian. Nude sunbathing was de rigueur, while weekend guests included writers, artists, and New York political activists.

Mary had first encountered Jack at a Choate dance in 1935 when he was graduating and she was finishing her sophomore year at the Brearley School in New York. Reminiscing twenty-eight years later with William Attwood, Mary's escort that evening, Kennedy "happily recalled having cut in on her on the dance floor." Mary went on to work as a reporter before marrying Cord Meyer, a Yale-educated war hero who lost an eye to shrapnel as a marine lieutenant. (His memoir of wartime experiences won the O. Henry Prize in 1946.) Cord came from a socially prominent New York family and was considered one of the golden boys of his generation along with JFK, with whom he was featured in a magazine article about future leaders.

As an idealistic advocate of world government (he would head the United World Federalists), Cord attended the UN conference in San Francisco in 1945 with Mary, who was covering it for United Press. There they encountered JFK, also working as a reporter; Jack and Cord took an instant dislike to each other that would never diminish. Back in Washington, Cord joined the CIA while Mary raised their three boys and took up painting. Their marriage began unraveling in the early fifties and collapsed several years later after their second son was struck by a car and killed.

Mary moved to Georgetown, where she began an affair with "color field" painter Kenneth Noland, whose artistic style she admired. "She was probably affected by my work," Noland recalled. "She wasn't a professional painter, but she was a good painter, and she had ambitions." Mary worked hard at her art and developed a minimalist style of vibrant circular themes. She also underwent psychotherapy, first briefly with a disciple of Wilhelm Reich in Philadelphia who also treated Noland, then with a Washington therapist.

When Tony and Ben Bradlee returned to Washington from Paris in early 1959 and befriended the Kennedys, Mary joined their social group. She was by all accounts a luminous presence, with loosely styled blonde hair and bright blue eyes—the sort who reduced a cocktail party to a hush with a dramatic entrance. "She was extremely feminine as was Tony, in a quiet way," said Ben Bradlee. "Mary was very earthy and really lovely looking, and she had no airs at all."

Like Jackie, Mary had an elusive quality. But Mary also exuded a frank sexuality, alluringly draping herself in her clothes in a manner that suggested spontaneity and independence, compared to Jackie's rather armored and meticulous persona. Since adolescence, Mary had been aware of her power over men. "She had an eager charm," said Anne Truitt. "She liked to give it a run. Mary sought attention the way a nymph rises to the surface of a stream. Wherever she went, she attracted it, and that gave her pleasure." In Truitt's judgment, "Mary lived to give and take pleasure." Like Jack and Jackie, she operated as she pleased. "The secret to Mary's personality was she didn't care about conventions," said her close friend Cicely Angleton, the wife of the CIA's legendary chief of counterintelligence James Angleton.

It is unclear precisely why Mary showed up at the White House on October 3. Since her privileged appearance at the White House dinner dance in March, she had been largely invisible until she moved onto JFK's radar at the *Advise and Consent* luncheon two weeks earlier. Her appeal to Jack, in Ben Bradlee's view, was that "she was a little out of reach, a different example of the species." For all the starlets, models, and socialites in Kennedy's orbit, he was intensely drawn to bright and original women—Jackie, Mary Meyer, Helen Chavchavadze, Diana de Vegh, even Marilyn Monroe. "Jack Kennedy once said to Mary, 'What does Kenneth Noland have that I don't have?' and she said, 'Mystery,'" recalled Cicely Angleton. "The President was duly taken aback."

The Washington social whirl hit top speed in the autumn. The newest star in town was David Ormsby Gore, who finally arrived in late October to present his credentials as ambassador. Jackie was more finicky than ever about the social ambiance she created. "She crawled on the floor among diagrams as she arranged the complex seating. She went over menus minutely," wrote Hugh Sidey. Her judgments could be severe, as when she rejected Tish Baldrige's plea to include Scottie Lanahan, the daughter of F. Scott Fitzgerald, in a state dinner. "The 2 times I've seen Scotty [sic] she has gotten quite tight & really made a slight spectacle," Jackie scribbled on the guest list. "Some other time."

"Standing is determined by entree to the White House," Stewart Alsop told a friend, "and of course the final cachet is conferred by the descent of the roi soleil on a maison particulière." The Kennedys ventured out less than they had a year earlier, but the "maison particulière" where they were likely to turn up was Joe Alsop's home on Dumbarton Avenue. One December weekend when Jackie was at Glen Ora, Jack went there in typically impromptu fashion after returning with Dave Powers from a speechmaking trip through Palm Beach and Miami. The Alsops' guests of honor were the Duke and Duchess of Devonshire, who were planning to lend their collection of old master drawings to the National Gallery for an exhibit the following year.

The Alsop dining room was packed with eighteen guests. As Susan Mary, Joe's wife, was talking to the President about the National Gallery, he suddenly decided to show the museum to the Duchess of Devonshire. "Let's go," JFK said to John Walker, the museum's director, who hastily made the arrangements. Kennedy and the Duchess arrived at the National Gallery before midnight, somewhat improbably joined by Dave Powers for the tour. "Our arrival caused great excitement," said the Duchess of Devonshire. "I don't think the President went to exhibitions as a rule the way Jackie did." Kennedy and Powers didn't return to the White House until 1:16 a.m.

Out at Glen Ora, Jackie frequently rode with both the Piedmont and Orange County Hunts. In November, her frisky mount, Bit of Irish, tossed her over a post and rail fence. Her fall was captured by a local photographer and would later be splashed across two pages of *Life*. At the hunt breakfast following the meet, no one knew about the First Lady's spill. "Jackie didn't look the least disheveled or shaken up," recalled her hostess, Kitty Slater. Jackie arrived with Eve Fout, shed her cork-lined velvet cap and riding coat, and stood in her shirtsleeves and canary vest, sipping Dubonnet on the rocks. "She was easy, natural and gracious," Slater recalled. Jackie complimented her hostess on "this lovely old house," and before leaving, Jackie asked to borrow a book called *Fifty Years of White House Gossip.*

Jackie now began to put her strong cultural imprint on state occasions, arranging a Shakespeare performance on a new East Room stage for President Ferik Ibrahim Abboud of the Sudan, and a concert by cellist Pablo Casals for Governor Luis Muñoz Marín of Puerto Rico. In response to a White House request for "red meat" after dinner, the Shakespearean excerpts included the murder scene from *Macbeth* as well as passages from comedies; among the guests was Helen Sandison, Jackie's professor of Shakespeare at Vassar. The presentation evoked "the polite drawing room evenings of Shakespeare commanded by Queen Victoria," the *New York Times* reported.

The Casals evening inspired similarly royal allusions, with *Time* comparing it to "a concert led by Haydn at the court of the Esterhazys." The 153 guests included major American composers as well as prominent conductors in white tie and tails. "English royalty entertains movie stars," said composer Gian Carlo Menotti. "Our president entertains artists." Wearing a chartreuse beaded gown by Cassini, Jackie presided over the evening like "a willowy medieval princess who had stepped down from a painting, with her top knot of hair interwoven with black velvet and pearls."

Lee came on November 7 for an extended stay. As they had the previous March, the Kennedys decided to throw a dinner dance "in honor of" Jackie's sister as well as Giovanni "Gianni" and Marella Agnelli, who were visiting from Italy. The Kennedys had met the Agnellis during trips to the south of France and at the Wrightsman home in Palm Beach. They also had a connection through Franklin Roosevelt Jr., who was the American representative for Fiat, Agnelli's automotive empire.

Not only was Agnelli a powerful and enormously wealthy industrialist, he was a famous playboy, and Marella was one of Europe's most stylish women. Gianni and Jack greatly enjoyed each other's company. "In some things they were similar," said Marella. "They had vivid curiosity about everything, and also being easily bored. Both Gianni and Jack Kennedy always if they were in one place wanted to be in another." Jack was equally enchanted by Marella. Some days later at a party at the Shrivers', Nancy Dickerson watched JFK's "intense conversation with the beautiful wife of Giovanni Agnelli," a scene Dickerson found "titillating." To Marella, Jack "looked to me extremely like

Carlo, my brother. He was charming and easy to be with," and Jackie was "very warm, and she wanted to have fun."

The black-tie candlelit dinner dance for eighty on Saturday, November 11, offered perhaps too much fun. The women "had spent hours and days on their dress and with remarkable results," observed Ken Galbraith. "This and youth made for sensational effect." Lester Lanin played, and Oleg Cassini introduced the twist, the hip-gyrating dance sensation that was sweeping the country. The twist, which originated at New York's Peppermint Lounge, was considered so improperly suggestive that Pierre Salinger denied it had been part of the evening's festivities. Charley Bartlett, a self-confessed prude, afterwards urged JFK to ban the dance at the White House. "That crowd has been getting along for years on champagne and the fox trot, and they won't need the twist to keep them stirred up," Bartlett wrote. "It's bound to get out, and it doesn't seem to me to be worth the price however small."

The champagne flowed until 4 a.m., and many partygoers got hopelessly drunk. Lyndon Johnson fell on Helen Chavchavadze as they were dancing. "He slid to the floor and lay like a lox," recalled Mary Bailey Gimbel, a guest from Manhattan who had known Jack and Bobby since school days. New Yorker Heyward Isham had to hoist LBJ to free Helen. During an after-dinner toast to Lee, Franklin Roosevelt mistook Oleg for Stas (both men sported mustaches), as Kennedy buckled over with laughter. In the West Wing the next day, a severely hung over Ken Galbraith watched as a wobbly Mac Bundy "went over his desk three times in search of a paper we were there to discuss, failed to find it and finally asked me why I had come in." For others, though, the consequences were less amusing.

One of the more dyspeptic guests was Gore Vidal, Jackie's distant relative by marriage. Although Jackie had not known Vidal until she was in her twenties, she and Jack were impressed by his talents as a writer and amused by his company; he was "filled with charm and malice," wrote Schlesinger. After an unsuccessful run for Congress in 1960, Vidal had penned an admiring piece about JFK for the *Sunday Telegraph* in London. The Kennedys had entertained him in Hyannis Port and at the White House; only two weeks earlier, Vidal had joined Jack, Jackie, Eunice, and Bill Walton at the International Horse Show. During dinner that Friday evening, Jackie had announced to her guests, "We are old-fashioned observant Catholics," as she produced a tub of Beluga caviar. "Jackie dragged us all to the horse show," Vidal recalled. "Jack didn't want to go. He was fuming over it."

Vidal's conversations with Kennedy skittered from politics to sexual gossip to culture. A proud libertine, Vidal was delighted that Kennedy enjoyed Fellini's *La Dolce Vita,* the antithesis of Anglo-Saxon puritanism. According to his biographer Fred Kaplan, Vidal "admired the President's pragmatic intelligence, his powers of cold analysis, his self-serving ruthlessness" as well as his promiscuity. But Vidal and Bobby Kennedy grated on each other. Vidal considered RFK to be "rigidly Catholic," grudge bearing, and intolerant. He sensed, correctly, that Bobby took a dim view of Vidal's homosexuality.

Vidal sat down at dinner next to Sue Roosevelt for what he later described as a "Mad Hatter evening." Wandering into the Red Room, he exchanged sharp words with Janet Auchincloss, whom he detested. In the crowded Blue Room, he spotted Jackie sitting with a group of people. Leaning down to chat, he rested his arm against her back and shoulders. At that point Bobby Kennedy arrived. "He had been working late and he was feeling frustrated," recalled Sue Roosevelt, who said he charged over to Vidal and removed his arm from Jackie's back. Vidal followed him out of the room and growled, "Don't ever do that again," adding, "I've always thought that you were a god-damned impertinent son of a bitch." Depending on the version, the two men told each other either to "get lost" or to "fuck off." Vidal had an equally nasty spat with Lem Billings, who rebuked him for failing to attend an arts council meeting. "Gore went after him" with a string of insults, said George Plimpton. To cap off the evening, Vidal told Jack Kennedy, "I'd like to wring your brother's neck."

Arthur Schlesinger recalled that "someone . . . perhaps Jacqueline Kennedy, asked me whether I would get [Vidal] out of there." With the help of Galbraith and Plimpton, Arthur transported him back to the Madison Hotel. "Gore was having a terrible time," said Plimpton. "He knew the die had been cast." Although what Plimpton called "the bad Bobby, oversensitive and rude," had been in evidence, Jack and Jackie pinned the blame on Vidal for all three contretemps. Vidal tried to justify himself the next day to Schlesinger, figuring he would be writing a history of the Kennedy years. Nevertheless, Schlesinger noted that Jackie was sufficiently "irritated" by Vidal's behavior that she "resolved not to have him in the White House again."

Jack Kennedy had spent much of the evening strolling around, drinking minimally as usual, conversing with friends and family. (Only the Ambassador, Teddy, and Joan were absent; Joe Kennedy avoided such events, while Rose couldn't get enough of them.) Anne Truitt's husband, James, then a reporter for the *Washington Post,* said Mary Meyer later told him that sometime during the dance Jack Kennedy had propositioned her but that she had rebuffed him.

The Kennedys' most intriguing official visitors in the fall of 1961 were Jawaharlal Nehru, India's seventy-one-year-old prime minister, and his forty-three-year-old daughter, Indira Gandhi, who would become prime minister in 1966. As the prickly leader of a neutralist nation, Nehru was too cozy with the Soviet Union to suit Kennedy. The two men had previously met during JFK's Asian tour in 1951, when Kennedy judged him "very intelligent" but "rather rude" and was irked by his vague answers. ("It's like trying to grab something in your hand," Kennedy said, "only to have it turn out to be just fog.")

Educated at Harrow and Cambridge, the widower Nehru had governed for nearly a quarter century with his only child as his hostess and confidante. Indira, who had gone to Oxford, was already an ambitious politician. Two years earlier she had been elected president of the Indian National Congress. Ken Galbraith had established good rapport with father and daughter, and had brought a message from the prime minister in late October inviting Jackie to visit India. Just before Nehru's arrival in America, the Kennedys announced that Jackie would take up the invitations of both Ayub and Nehru to visit Pakistan and India at the end of November. At Jackie's insistence, Lee would also make the trip.

Nehru had asked that his first meeting with the President be informal, so Kennedy arranged a luncheon at Hammersmith Farm. While the two leaders talked policy, Jackie dined separately with Indira and Lem Billings. Nehru briefly showed "interest and vivacity" in Jackie's presence, but he was remote and monosyllabic with Kennedy. Both Jackie and Billings found Indira surprisingly engaging; she avoided politics and spoke about her upbringing, even making jokes about herself. Afterwards, however, she acted grumpy and seemed resentful that she had been excluded from her father's meeting. "Jack Kennedy did see

Nehru at his worst, as a weary cynical man, and Indira was bitter and spiteful," said Schlesinger.

Flying from Rhode Island to Washington on Air Force One, Indira incongruously flipped through *Vogue* while Jackie read Malraux. Subsequent meetings between Kennedy and Nehru turned into "a brilliant monologue by the President," said Galbraith. It took Jackie and Lee, who flanked Nehru at the White House dinner, to produce "the light of love in his eyes," but afterwards Jackie told Galbraith she wished to postpone her trip. Indira continued to alienate various lunch and dinner partners with "wobbly and fuzzy leftist remarks about the United States." Kennedy told Arthur Schlesinger his meetings with the prime minister were "a disaster . . . the worst head-of-state visit I have had."

JFK did manage to inject some humor into the gloom, however. Lem Billings had considered his lunch with the prime minister's daughter a success, so he was flattered when he received a flurry of phone messages from her while he was staying at Steve and Jean Smith's in Georgetown. But every time he tried to reach her at Blair House, the President's guest house near Lafayette Park, she was unavailable. Only later did Billings learn that "Madame Gandhi's passion for his company" had been invented by Kennedy with the complicity of the White House switchboard.

Once tensions over Berlin lessened after the construction of the wall, Kennedy faced a new international problem provoked by the Soviet Union's resumption of atmospheric nuclear tests on September 1. In Vienna, Khrushchev had promised Kennedy he would not undertake any tests unless the United States did so. "That fucking liar," Kennedy said to Steve Smith when he heard the news. Throughout the fall, the Soviets tested one atomic bomb after another—the most massive and dirty series ever—and Kennedy knew the United States had to resume testing as well.

Yet Kennedy was actually feeling more sanguine about the relationship with the Soviets despite bluster on both sides about military dominance. The reason was an unusual correspondence Khrushchev had initiated in late September. Beginning with a twenty-six-page discursive letter sent through back channels, the secret correspondence would continue until Kennedy's death—more than three hundred pages in all. Kennedy showed the contents only to a few top aides—Bundy, Rusk, and Bobby primarily. The letters did not modulate tough positions on either side, but they conveyed moods and intentions, and maintained an open channel intended to avoid misunderstanding or miscalculation in times of crisis.

South Vietnam began to weigh on Kennedy as well. On returning from his Asian swing the previous May, Johnson had recommended significant U.S. aid and the use of American military personnel to train the South Vietnamese, although he balked at sending American troops. His observations about South Vietnamese president Ngo Dinh Diem's aloofness from the populace were astute, but his overall report was too optimistic. Weeks later, during JFK's talk with James Reston in Vienna, the *Times* correspondent noted that, almost as an afterthought, Kennedy spoke of a need to show American might to Moscow. "We have to confront them," Kennedy said. "The only place we can do that is in Vietnam. We have to send more people there."

In the fall, Kennedy dispatched Maxwell Taylor and Walt Rostow on a second fact-finding mission. They reported that despite problems, the South Vietnamese army showed promise, and they recommended that American soldiers be deployed. Kennedy heard plenty of advice to the contrary. In a two-page single-spaced letter after a trip to Vietnam, Teddy White told the President that the situation there was "a real bastard to solve. . . . To commit troops there is unwise." The President quoted White's observations during a National Security Council meeting "much to the irritation of the Joint Chiefs of Staff," Arthur Schlesinger happily recounted. Galbraith issued another in a series of jeremiads, calling Vietnam "a can of snakes," with the political situation in "total stasis" and Diem beyond hope of reform.

For a variety of reasons—innate skepticism, the memories of French futility from his visit to Vietnam in 1951, a warning from General Douglas MacArthur against "a ground war in Asia," the caution of such aides as Schlesinger and Galbraith—Kennedy decided to increase the number of military advisers instead of committing troops. Kennedy felt he couldn't retreat in Asia, wrote Schlesinger, but he needed to buy time. Over the next eighteen months, incursions by Viet Cong guerrillas became less frequent, prompting Bob McNamara and other American visitors to report South Vietnamese progress. "Kennedy was stringing out Vietnam, hoping it would go away," said Sidey.

Later that fall Kennedy shook up his administration for the first time since the Bay of Pigs. In October he replaced sixty-eight-year-old Allen Dulles as director of the CIA with fifty-nine-year-old John McCone, a tough-minded Republican industrialist from California who had been under secretary of the air force in the Truman administration. The following month, Kennedy took aim at Chester Bowles—a marked man since his self-aggrandizing comments after the Bay of Pigs. During the summer Kennedy had tried to shift him out of the State Department by planting stories with Charley Bartlett and Joe Alsop that Bowles was in trouble. But Bowles alerted liberal allies who leaked word that "the first head to roll after the Cuban affair is the head of the man who opposed it." Kennedy kept his man in place, "furious" at Bowles's "very smart counterploy to keep his job. . . . The long knives are gleaming," Stew Alsop told a friend.

Since then, Bowles had found himself "more and more out of things," wrote Galbraith in early November. "Bowles cannot make his decisions stick." In a Thanksgiving weekend shuffle, Kennedy replaced Bowles with fifty-one-year-old George Ball, a lawyer with expertise in international economics, and gave Bowles the lofty-sounding title of "special adviser." As usual, Kennedy couldn't bring himself to fire Bowles, so he dispatched Ted Sorensen to tamp his anger and soothe his hurt feelings.

Kennedy persisted in thinking the State Department was the weak link in his administration. Dean Rusk, fifty-two, displeased the President for failing to take firm stands on policy. To buttress Foggy Bottom's "force and fertility of thought," Kennedy moved in forty-five-year-old Walt Rostow as head of policy planning. Rostow was a dedicated hawk, and such a strong proponent of counterinsurgency guerrillas that some called him "Chester Bowles with machine guns." The plump and balding former MIT professor had fit in well as Mac Bundy's deputy. But given his intellectual exuberance, Rostow wanted out from Bundy's shadow, even if it meant leaving the West Wing.

Fred Dutton, whose romance with his secretary was becoming awkward, was also transferred to State, as was Richard Goodwin, a fast and eloquent speechwriter who vexed Sorensen. Finally, as proof that the "vigah" of the Kennedy crowd wasn't defined by years, the President appointed Averell Harriman as assistant secretary for the Far East. At age seventy, the former ambassador to the Soviet Union and Britain was so eager to have a role that he settled for a relatively low-ranking job. In part, Harriman was being rewarded for negotiating the still-shaky Laos neutrality agreement. But the veteran diplomat also got on well with Kennedy because of his "instinct for the care and feeding of presidents," said Schlesinger.

Kennedy remained "the supreme centre of power," David Gore reported to Macmillan. The President was surrounded by "first class men," but they were "clearly not yet able to take from his shoulders a single part of his tremendous burden"—in large measure because Kennedy didn't want them to. Kennedy's men were no longer "giddy with power" as they had been when the year began. Having "peered over the brink at nuclear warfare," the British ambassador observed, they now seemed "less cavalier." They were far from lugubrious, though, thriving on the hectic pace of their professional and social lives.

One symbol of the Kennedy administration's combination of intellectual liveliness and reflexive conviviality was the launching in November of the Hickory Hill seminars. Inspired by two weeks Bobby and Ethel had spent at the Aspen Institute during the summer of 1961, these sessions reflected Bobby's earnest devotion to self-improvement. RFK appointed Arthur Schlesinger to organize the seminars, and from the fall through the spring, the group met nearly every month, rotating among the participants' homes. Regulars included the Dillons, McNamaras, Ormsby Gores, Bundys, Shrivers, Rostows, and Gilpatrics. Three seminars (led by historians David Donald, Arthur Schlesinger Sr., and Isaiah Berlin) took place at the White House. Jackie attended several others, and both the President and First Lady liked to receive texts of the talks that they missed. Debate was spirited, with Ethel and Eunice "particularly undaunted questioners," said Schlesinger.

Alice Roosevelt Longworth viewed the seminars skeptically at first, dismissing them as "precious," but she decided they were "all sorts of fun." Arthur's wife, Marian, called them "a sort of intellectual quick fix . . . no doubt a harmless exercise, but so Kennedyish . . . the whole of Western thought in eight hour-long seminars, sort of silly." The meetings turned out to be good publicity for the administration, as Princeton's David Donald discovered after his discussion at the White House on the Reconstruction period. With considerable perplexity, he reported to Ros Gilpatric that he had fielded a phone call several days later from *Washington Star* reporter Mary McGrory, "who seemed to have an extraordinarily detailed knowledge of the questions the President asked and the comments he made." Replied Gilpatric, "How word of such affairs gets out remains a mystery to me."

The Kennedy insiders were also diehard club men who believed in the informal exchange of information while dining at a long table, followed by brandy and cigars in large leather chairs near the hearth of a capacious sitting room. The hub of these gentlemanly transactions was the Metropolitan Club, only blocks from the White House, and, to a lesser extent, the Cosmos Club on Embassy Row. Like New York, Boston, and other big cities, Washington had exclusive women's clubs, but the all-male bastions were the centers of power—and of controversy as well. Not only did they exclude women, they also shunned blacks and other ethnic minorities.

Such restrictive policies created a brouhaha in September when Republican George Lodge, the son of Henry Cabot Lodge, was censured by the board of the Metropolitan Club for bringing a black man to lunch. Lodge's guest was George Weaver, an assistant secretary of labor in the Kennedy administration. Lodge resigned in protest, and Bobby Kennedy swiftly followed suit, releasing his resignation letter to the press. "It is inconceivable to me," RFK wrote, that privileges in the Metropolitan Club "would be denied to anyone merely because of his race."

Charley Bartlett also resigned, as did Assistant Attorney General for Civil Rights Burke Marshall and Ambassador to Denmark Bill Blair. But a more significant number of prominent men kept their memberships: Adlai Stevenson, Hugh Auchincloss, Stuart Symington, Dean Acheson, Claiborne Pell, Arthur Krock, Rowland Evans, and Joe Alsop among them. Mac Bundy actually joined the Metropolitan Club right after the furor broke, even as his brother Bill, a State Department official, left the club. Although the President declined to speak publicly about the matter, it was assumed that Bobby represented his viewpoint. According to the *New York Times,* JFK left the decision "up to the consciences of his aides." Privately, JFK liked to bait his national security adviser about his membership, which discomfited Bundy more than he admitted.

What Bundy didn't know was that JFK maintained his own membership in the Brook, New York's most exclusive men's club, which at the time had no black members. Through his friendship with Earl E.T.

Smith, Kennedy had joined in 1957, when he had been a senator for four years. (JFK was rankled, he once told Red Fay, that it was "impossible for an Irish Catholic to get into the Somerset Club in Boston"— that city's equivalent of the Brook.)

Soon after he became a member of the Brook, he took Evan Thomas, an editor at Harper & Row, to lunch. "This is the first and probably the last time I will have visited this club," Kennedy said, feigning embarrassment. But Kennedy visited whenever he could and even held a strategy session there during the presidential campaign. In his compartmentalized fashion, he was able to serenely enjoy the comforts of one men's club while chiding his top aide about membership in another. Bundy would eventually resign from the Metropolitan Club in the fall of 1963, prodded by Kennedy's "persistent and not always gentle needling." "I always felt sorry for Mac Bundy," said Charley Bartlett, recalling that after Kennedy's assassination, Bundy said repeatedly, "I never had a chance to tell the President." At the time of his death, Kennedy was still a member of the Brook.

After his setbacks in domestic and foreign policy, Kennedy seemed poised to begin 1962 on an upbeat note. He and Jackie made a quick goodwill tour ("more a schmalzfest than a bold adventure," cracked *Time*) to Puerto Rico, Colombia, and Venezuela, drawing huge crowds chanting "Viva Miss America" to Jackie. In two days of talks in Bermuda before Christmas, Kennedy pressed Harold Macmillan for permission to use British territory in the Pacific for atmospheric nuclear tests. While Kennedy was "moved" by Macmillan's passion for disarmament, he insisted on the tests, and the prime minister finally agreed to present the proposal to his cabinet.

The two leaders enjoyed a deep mutual trust, abetted by David Gore, who felt that "it was almost like a family discussion when we all met together." Kennedy showed Khrushchev's secret correspondence to Macmillan and confided his irritation with de Gaulle. Macmillan observed that Kennedy was more efficient on specific problems while "on the wider issues he seems rather lost." The British leader also detected Kennedy's sensitivity—"very easily pleased, and very easily offended. . . . He likes attention."

Kennedy evidently felt so at ease with his British counterpart that he

confided his sexual proclivities—already revealed to Macmillan by Jock
Whitney two years earlier. "I wonder how it is with you, Harold?"
Kennedy said. "If I don't have a woman for three days I get a terrible
headache"—an assertion Nancy Mitford had heard from friends in
Venice five months earlier and passed along to her sister the Duchess
of Devonshire. According to biographer Alistair Horne, to whom
Macmillan disclosed this conversation with Kennedy three decades
later, "the sixty-seven-year-old monogamous Prime Minister was non-
plussed." Macmillan was hardly naïve, however, as he had for years
endured his wife Dorothy's affair with fellow Tory member of Parliament Robert Boothby.

Before arriving in Bermuda, Kennedy had hurt his back again.
Macmillan duly observed JFK's discomfort and restlessness that made
it "difficult to sit in the same position for any length of time" or to "pick
up a book or paper off the floor." Oddly enough, only four days later,
after a physical exam, Kennedy's doctors declared him in "excellent
general health," his back improved after several months of Dr. Kraus's
exercises.

Overshadowing Kennedy's trip to Bermuda, and indeed the end of
his first year as president, was the sudden and debilitating illness that hit
Joe Kennedy. On the way home from South America on December 18,
Jack and Jackie had stopped in Palm Beach. Jackie was settling in with
the children for an extended Christmas holiday at an eight-bedroom
Regency-style home on loan from friends of the senior Kennedys,
Colonel Capton Michael Paul, a wealthy former Cossack cavalryman,
and his equally rich wife, Josephine, the head of Kidder and Company,
the Wall Street brokerage. The Paul estate—four hundred feet of beach,
a heated pool, Gothic tapestries, a loggia filled with exotic tropical
plants—was a mile south of La Guerida. Jack had planned to touch
down only briefly, but after developing a heavy cold and earache during
his trip, he decided to spend a day resting in the sunshine before returning to the White House.

Dressed in shorts and a sports shirt, Joe brought Caroline to say
goodbye to Jack at the airport the next morning. The Ambassador
seemed chipper before heading out to play golf with his niece Ann Gargan. As he was teeing off on the eighth hole, Joe felt faint and asked Ann
to drive him home, where he briefly encountered Jackie and Caroline
on their way to take a swim. Heading to his room to rest, he spoke his

last words: "Don't call any doctors!" When Ann looked in and discovered that he could neither move nor speak, she alerted Rose, who summoned an ambulance. That afternoon, Jack and other family members rushed to Palm Beach.

Joe had suffered a massive stroke, technically an intracranial thrombosis, or blood clot in an artery of the brain. After several days in the balance, he regained consciousness, but there seemed little hope his faculties could be restored. When Richard Cardinal Cushing reported that his old friend had spoken, hospital sources gently explained that Cushing "might have hopefully interpreted" the stream of garbled sounds that were all Joe could manage. Other than "nooo" or "yaaa," the Ambassador would never talk intelligibly again, although he retained the capacity to understand.

It turned out there had been prior indications that all was not well with Joe. The Kennedy clan had gathered as usual for Thanksgiving at the compound in Hyannis. Lem Billings was with them, and Red Fay and his family were staying at Bobby and Ethel's. Jack and Jackie opted to eat dinner in their own house ("Jackie probably likes to be alone for a change," Rose noted in her diary. "She has a crowd so much"), but afterwards everyone gathered at the Ambassador's for a jolly evening. As the President smoked a cigar, Fay reprised "Hooray for Hollywood," Teddy danced (with his "big derrière," Rose observed, "it is funny to see him throw himself around"), and Jackie, wearing a pink Schiaparelli pantsuit, demonstrated the twist "to the jungling-rumbling music of Joan." But Joe Kennedy was uncharacteristically quiet. He had sustained what Rose called "an attack" ten days earlier. He "complains about a lack of taste in his mouth & feels blah," Rose recorded.

As Jackie recounted later to Cy Sulzberger, Joe had suffered a series of small strokes, had been given anti-coagulants and "had chucked them away." He had planned, she said, "to go off suddenly"—perhaps her explanation for Joe's injunction against calling doctors. Three days after Joe was stricken, the *New York Times* also cited a family source who said Joe had received several warnings of "the possibility of a stroke" and had refused to take his medication.

If Joe Kennedy was depressed, he gave little evidence. Frank Waldrop, the former editor of the *Washington Times-Herald,* later said that during a conversation that fall Joe had confessed, "I get awfully blue sometimes." But less than a week before he fell ill, Joe was engrossed in his latest project in presidential image-making, a film of *PT 109*, the laudatory new book about Jack's wartime heroics in the Pacific. Jack Warner, the head of the Warner Brothers studio, had told Joe: "The President will have the final approval of everything . . . not only the person who will portray him but the story itself." Joe had replied enthusiastically that he would make the necessary arrangements when Jack arrived for his Christmas holiday.

Jack and Jackie visited Joe at the hospital each day. On Christmas Eve they spent an hour, leaving before midnight. They saw him twice on Christmas Day, and received communion in the hospital chapel. Otherwise, life went on pretty much as usual. Jack held meetings with Ted Sorensen, Doug Dillon, and other advisers, Jackie entertained the family for Christmas dinner, and the First Couple took cruises on the *Honey Fitz* with family and friends (Oleg Cassini, Fifi Fell, Lem Billings). One evening Jack stayed at Earl and Flo Smith's from 11 p.m. until 1:30 a.m.

The loss of Joe's everyday presence was an immeasurable blow to the young president. The Ambassador had been a practical-minded sounding board and a boundless source of moral support. Jack could no longer call for advice, as he once did at 3 a.m., and hear his father bark, "Holy cow, fella, call me in the daylight!" Jack continued to check in with his father regularly, dutifully describing events and people as Joe grunted acknowledgment. For Joe Kennedy, long accustomed to power and control, the fate of being trapped speechless inside a largely immobile body was especially cruel. It was an irony not lost on the son who had confronted his own mortality more deeply than most men his age. "Old age is a shipwreck," Jack Kennedy told Charley Bartlett, with a sad shake of his head.

$\mathcal{C}$harlie and Jayne Wrightsman treated the Kennedys and a large crowd of their friends to a New Year's Eve dinner dance with music by Lester Lanin, Krug 1929 champagne, and exquisite food. The tony gathering turned raucous after midnight, as Oleg Cassini and his brother, Ghighi, performed a combination of the twist and the Russian Kazatsky dance, while Bobby, Teddy, Steve Smith, and Peter Lawford played touch football in the living room, breaking glasses and spilling drinks on the Savonnerie carpet. According to Oleg Cassini, "a rare signed pair of antique chairs was demolished," and local millionaire Stephen "Laddie" Sanford "almost drowned in the reflecting pool, only 35 inches deep, which faced the living room. He was rescued, along with a goldfish that was stuck in his pocket."

Jack and Jackie prolonged their stay in Palm Beach until the end of the first week of January so that they could continue to spend time visiting the Ambassador. Several days later, Kennedy gave his State of the Union address as Jackie sat in the gallery with Martha Bartlett, Tony Bradlee, and the wives of White House aides. Jackie "rarely took her eyes off him during the more than 45 minutes he spoke," observed the *Washington Post*.

Kennedy sought support for Medicare, aid to education, tax cuts, and loosened restrictions on international trade. The President still faced obstacles in Congress, where House Republicans and conservative Democrats maintained their stranglehold. But he did benefit from popularity ratings that had held steady at over 75 percent throughout his first year in office. When JFK was named *Time*'s "Man of the Year," the cover article was full of praise for his "wiser, more mature" leadership after a difficult first year. Jackie, *Time* noted, had "managed to stay very much herself," refusing to be "falsely humble." The *New York Times* offered a different sort of endorsement, declaring that Jackie had "made the world safe for brunettes" and transmitted "upper-crust habits" to the "common woman."

On Monday, January 15, 1962, Jackie took the unprecedented step of appearing in front of eight television cameras from CBS for nearly seven hours, taping a tour of her White House restoration that had been aided by a hundred donors and lenders. The hour-long program had been in the works since October, when Blair Clark, a network executive who had known JFK since Harvard days, persuaded Jackie to cooperate with CBS as she had earlier with *Life*.

Months of arrangements had preceded the taping. CBS producer Perry Wolff signed up his friend Franklin J. Schaffner, an up-and-coming Hollywood director (his later hits would include *Patton* and *Papillon*), along with debonair correspondent Charles Collingwood, a former Georgetown neighbor of the Kennedys. "I thought a couple of handsome men would help," said Wolff. Jackie and curator Lorraine Pearce worked out which objects she would highlight and what she would say. Jackie committed all the facts to memory and followed CBS's "guide script" that allowed her to improvise as she went along.

On the day of the taping, Jackie had only her New York hairdresser, Kenneth Battelle, and Pam Turnure in attendance, and CBS brought a crew of forty. Deferring to "Mr. Schaffner" about where she should walk and turn, Jackie clearly admired the Hollywood director. She made small talk with Collingwood, confiding that Nehru had tried to teach her yoga, "but I had to rest my feet against the wall." Collingwood was taken with her "shy manner, even a sort of shy way of moving . . . youthful yet quietly assured, though not arrogantly so." Her demeanor was ladylike but aloof with Collingwood, who made the mistake of overfamiliarity, inviting her to join him and his wife for a drink at their hotel. Jackie gave him what Farmington girls called the PBO—polite brush off.

The First Lady was a disciplined performer. She rehearsed each take, including the questions Collingwood would ask in the conversational format. "She knew her stuff," said Wolff. "Nobody was cuing her. No curators were there feeding her. That was how meticulous she was with language. She was a combination of sophistication and ingenuousness, almost childlike, and it was so winning."

Between takes "she smoked all the time," said Wolff. "She kept missing the ashtray and flicking the ashes onto the expensive silk covering of the bench she was sitting on. I knew there was tension there." Despite the strain, she maintained her energy throughout the demands of the day and even had to be reminded to eat lunch. The taping concluded in the second-floor Treaty Room, which Jackie described for the cameras as a "chamber of horrors" because it was a work in progress. She said the room would eventually be a comfortable place for the men "who now sit in the hall with the baby carriages going by them. So they can sit in here and have a conference around this table" while waiting for the President. By prearrangement, Jack joined Jackie at the end to offer his own brief comments. He quickly memorized the prepared script and hurried through it for the cameras.

Jackie was exhausted by the taping, but she nevertheless entertained Joe and Susan Mary Alsop for dinner that evening. At the Kennedys' request, Wolff screened some of the rushes in the White House theater. Instead of the sculpted bouffant for the cameras, Jackie's hair hung straight down, and she sipped on a big glass of scotch. After the screening, everyone applauded. "When the lights went up, the President looked at her with adoration and admiration," Wolff recalled. "There was an emotional connection in that couple, I have no doubt. It was a real look of love. He was so proud of her, and she was so happy that he was proud." Yet Kennedy was displeased with his own stilted performance, so he asked to do a retake the next day at a more measured pace.

One Thursday evening that winter the Kennedys threw a small dinner in honor of the Russian-born composer Igor Stravinsky. The guest list, drawn from London, Paris, New York, and Chicago, included Leonard

Bernstein, Lee Radziwill, Vladimir Nabokov and his cousin Nicholas, and Helen Chavchavadze, who was seated near the maestro. Amid all the "Russian kissing," Bernstein heard JFK saying, "How about me?," a plea the conductor found "endearing and so instantly unpresidential . . . at the same time never losing dignity." The guests were disappointed when Stravinsky had to leave early, "weary" from a day of rehearsals, the White House explained to the press. In fact, Stravinsky had gotten so drunk that his assistant Robert Craft had to carry him out.

Jackie had Lee as company for long stretches of January and February. To all appearances, the sisters had never been closer. Lee and Stas had been spending more time apart, and their marriage was shaky, aggravated by the difficult birth and five-month-long hospitalization of their daughter,Christina, just a year after the arrival of their son, Anthony. There were submerged tensions with Jackie as well. After lunch with Lee in New York on Friday, February 9, Truman Capote reported to Cecil Beaton, "My God, how jealous she is of Jackie. I never knew . . . Her marriage is all but finito."

That evening, Lee and Stas were together in Washington at another festive White House dinner dance, this time for Steve and Jean Smith, who were moving to New York. With Joe Kennedy's incapacity, it fell to the son-in-law with the business acumen to oversee the vast Kennedy family fortune. Their send-off, JFK told Ben Bradlee, was the best yet of the three private dances. Because the Kennedys were obliged to invite nearly a hundred guests to dinner, the Bradlees, Bill Walton, Mary Meyer, and other regulars dined at private homes before joining the dance at 10 p.m. "We were so out," Bradlee recalled, "that we were in. . . . The Kennedys couldn't afford to snub anyone . . . except their really good friends."

Once again, the twist held center stage in the East Room, as Oleg Cassini performed a solo, and Jackie and Lee instructed both Bob McNamara and Averell Harriman, "much to the distress of John Kennedy, who tried to stop us," McNamara recalled. During another twist demonstration, *Washington Post* publisher Phil Graham left the dance floor with a six-inch rip in his trousers.

Jackie, wearing a white satin sheath, danced nearly every dance and stayed until 4 a.m. Shortly before midnight, JFK found time to tip Bradlee that Francis Gary Powers, the pilot of the U-2 spy plane shot down by the Soviets in May 1960, was being exchanged for a Soviet spy held by the Americans. *Newsweek*'s deadline had passed, so Bradlee, with dance music playing in the background, dictated the story to its sister publication, the *Washington Post*. Kennedy slipped away from the party at 2 a.m. to check with Berlin to make sure Powers was safe, then rejoined the festivities and didn't leave until 4:30 a.m., after the band stopped playing. "By that time," Bradlee recalled, "Tony and I both agreed that he seemed a bit high—one of the very rare occasions we'd seen him in that condition."

Rehashing the evening's events on the phone the next day, Kennedy brought up Bradlee's sister-in-law. "Mary would be rough to live with," JFK said, "not for the first time." Bradlee agreed, "not for the first time." "Mary was not easy because she had so much attention, effortlessly like a tide," said Cicely Angleton. "The husband would be left out in the cold. That is what Kennedy meant." Unknown to Bradlee, JFK's offhand remark concealed his latest clandestine entanglement.

Less than three weeks earlier, while Jackie and the children were in Glen Ora with Lee and her son Tony, Mary and Jack had begun their affair at the White House on a wintry Monday evening. Although she was as free a spirit as her friend Helen Chavchavadze, Meyer became more deeply enmeshed with Kennedy from the outset. Unlike Chavchavadze, who kept her liaison secret, Meyer confided in Anne Truitt a couple of months after the affair began—and later that year to Anne's husband, James. "She told me she had fallen in love with Jack Kennedy and was sleeping with him," Anne recalled. "I was surprised but not too. Mary did what she pleased. She was having a lovely time." Anne was a safe confidante, too polite and "incurious" to probe, and disinclined to pass judgment.

Bill Walton was Meyer's frequent escort when the Kennedys called, and he served as Helen Chavchavadze's designated date as well. Despite Walton's sophistication, Kennedy kept him in the dark about the nature of his relationships with Meyer and Chavchavadze. "Bill was a friend of the marriage," said Chavchavadze. "For Jack he was a cover. Jack always arranged for Bill to bring me to White House dinner parties. Bill was very romantic about the marriage, perhaps too romantic."

Meyer had other lovers during her involvement with Kennedy. "She and Jack understood each other. Mary didn't want to marry anyone," said Anne Truitt. "In that sense the relationship was superficial. Jack and his wife were joined together, in the same business. Mary also liked her privacy. They were two very sophisticated people who formed a friendship with no intention of it being forever. It was for mutual friendship and pleasure and enlightenment. It was a matter of lifting each other."

Truitt characterized the affair as an "amitié amoureuse," a romantic friendship. "He saw that she was trustworthy," Truitt said. "He could talk to her with pleasure, without having to watch his words. Mary brought him a whiff of the outdoors, the quick interchange of light-heartedness. He needed entertainment of various sorts. Mary was very entertaining."

Mary and Jack betrayed nothing in the company of others—including Tony and Ben, who had no idea. "I think the real key to Jack was his love of risk," Bradlee said. "How could he be fucking her and inviting her to dinner with Jackie?" Kennedy once told Charley Bartlett that he thought Mary was a "great woman," Bartlett recalled. "Normally he didn't talk to me about girls, so that comment gave me a few suspicions." Characteristically, Bartlett kept his hunch to himself. In the East Wing, "we knew Mary was a pal," said Tish Baldrige, "and she was invited to dinner often. Jackie was accepting, didn't complain. She was as cool as a cucumber always."

On Valentine's Day, America fell more in love with Jackie Kennedy than ever, as both CBS and NBC broadcast her White House tour to an estimated 46.5 million people in prime time—about 75 percent of the viewing audience. (ABC would show the program the following Sunday afternoon, adding 10 million more viewers.) Jackie wore a red dress, but neither that nor the beautiful hues on upholstery and curtains could be seen by viewers since the show was shot in black and white. For a solid hour (the networks ran no commercials) the American audience heard a history of the White House as Jackie and Collingwood chatted while strolling from room to room.

She filled her narrative with piquant anecdotes and characterizations as well as factual details. Charles Dickens called the White House an "English clubhouse," and when funds ran low it was known as the "public shabby house." In the Green Room, Jackie noted that Thomas Jefferson gave dinner parties where he introduced such exotic foods as "macaroni, waffles, and ice cream." She conscientiously explained the periods represented by each room, pointing out the Egyptian touches that Napoleon brought to the Empire style, wryly recalling President Grant's "ancient Greek and Mississippi riverboat" version of the East Room, and pausing in the State Dining Room to marvel at the "architectural unity" of the 1902 era.

The presentation was thoroughly beguiling, from Jackie's bow-legged walk down a corridor toward the camera to her soft, low voice with its hint of breathiness. Her accent was distinctly upper-class New York—"mahvelous" and "rawther" and "hahbor"—yet her style was unaffected. As she spoke of her favorite acquisitions, she enthusiastically arched her eyebrows, and her eyes sparkled with a suppressed merriment. She cleverly mentioned by name such prominent donors as the Walter Annenbergs, Henry Fords, and Marshall Fields.

That evening, Jack and Jackie had the Bradlees for dinner with Max Freedman and Fifi Fell. Afterwards they watched the program in the Lincoln sitting room, as Bradlee recalled, "impressed with Jackie's knowledge and poise." Even after redoing his part, Kennedy was unhappy with the way he came across. (Tony told her husband later that she sensed JFK might have been jealous of his wife.) Among those calling with congratulations was Charley Bartlett, who said the program had moved him to tears, prompting JFK to crack that he had cried too—"over my performance." Moments later when Eunice called and asked to talk to Jackie, the First Lady "shook her head," Bradlee recorded in his diary. Inexplicably tearful, Jackie went off to bed.

In a page-one review the next morning, Jack Gould, the respected television critic of the *New York Times,* raved about the program, praising Jackie's evident "verve and pleasure" and declaring her an "art critic of subtlety and standard." In the three days following the broadcast, the White House was swamped with 6,300 pieces of fan mail for the First Lady. But several months later, Norman Mailer scorched Jackie in *Esquire* with what *Newsweek* called a "scathing neurotic attack." Mailer, who had tried early to ingratiate himself with the Kennedys, had turned on them when they excluded him from White House gatherings. Her "odd public voice" reminded him of a "weather girl," and she moved "like a wooden horse," a "starlet who is utterly without talent." Jackie, in Mailer's view, was "a royal phony."

Jackie's critics frequently assumed that her breathy voice—"so

gentle," said Hervé Alphand, "as if she were continually astonished"—
was a manufactured mannerism, but friends like Jessie Wood, who had
known her since adolescence, insisted it was genuine. Her voice became a liability because it led people to underestimate her intelligence.
Cy Sulzberger's wife, Marina, found herself expecting platitudes, and
was pleasantly surprised to hear "really intelligent things. . . . One sits
there open mouthed and . . . completely entranced." To women such as
Vassar acquaintance Sue Wilson, "it was a voice that kept you a little
away from her. It wasn't a voice that said 'kick off your shoes and join
me and relax.'" Yet George Plimpton felt Jackie's whispery quality "was
part of her intimacy. From the time she was a girl she talked that way
to me." Those who found her quiet tone inviting often detected the
accompanying glint in her eye that carried a hint of mischief.

The White House restoration was only partly finished in February
1962. Jackie was working on new decorative schemes for the Blue and
Green Rooms with Boudin and Jayne Wrightsman, which increased the
strain with curator Lorraine Pearce, whose loyalty remained with Harry
du Pont. Despite feeling that Pearce was "too full of herself," Jackie assigned her to write the first White House guidebook. Jackie considered
the guidebook "desperately important," not least because she needed its
revenue to help pay for White House furnishings.

    "She wanted a story," said Jim Ketchum, "concentrating on the
people in the White House and the objects in their time." Jackie spent
many hours on the guidebook, working on the layout with staff from
National Geographic, who donated their time, and editing the text prepared by Pearce. Jackie felt satisfied with Pearce's work, but in mid-
February she asked Arthur Schlesinger to add "some stirring phrases"
and "beautiful words."

    By then Schlesinger had become a versatile intellectual factotum for
both the President and First Lady. He had solidified Kennedy's loyalty
after the Bay of Pigs by flying to Florida to mollify angry Cuban exile
leaders. From time to time Kennedy heeded Schlesinger's periodic
memos on foreign and domestic policy, most notably when he took into
account his aide's admonition against playing "chicken" with the Soviets over Berlin. Yet Kennedy ignored much of Schlesinger's political

advice—to push a recalcitrant Congress forcefully for a liberal agenda, for example, and not to appoint Republican John McCone as head of the CIA.

Schlesinger freely exchanged information with favored journalists such as Ben Bradlee, who "relied on him a lot" for historical perspective. "He was pulling strings all the time," said Jean Friendly, who had known Schlesinger since the late forties.

In addition to his role in the Hickory Hill seminars, Schlesinger proposed August Heckscher, a New York cultural critic, to serve as the first White House consultant on the arts, an appointment that Kenny O'Donnell viewed with undisguised hostility. As a part-time film reviewer for *Show* magazine, Schlesinger would also alert the Kennedys to new releases for the White House theater—Jackie seemed to like his selections more than Jack. The President found *L'Avventura* so slow paced that he asked to skip to the final reel, and he walked out of *Last Year at Marienbad* after twenty minutes. Jackie loved "the puzzle aspect" of *Marienbad,* said Schlesinger. "She felt it was a mysterious, stylized movie." She even asked Cassini to design an evening dress similar to the "chanelish chiffons" in the film.

For Jackie, Schlesinger's most important role was as unofficial consultant on the restoration project. "I am sorry to impose on you," she wrote to ask his assistance on the guidebook. "But you are the only person who can do it—and the only one who is always kind enough to help me with whatever project I need help with." Once he had burnished Pearce's text, Jackie pressed him to rewrite the introduction. Jackie considered Pearce's version too long and pedantic: "ghastly," she told Schlesinger, "uncoordinated and conceited."

JFK suggested that Jackie write a short introduction herself. In a lengthy memo to Schlesinger, she outlined her objectives for the book: to give visitors "something to take away," to describe the meaning of the White House in American history, and to explain the effort to furnish the mansion in a historic way "without making one sound conceited." She also needed a "marvelous closing sentence worthy of Euripedes."

Schlesinger complied with four elegant paragraphs, touching on the "imperishable memories" evoked by the White House, and the recent restoration work to "bring back old and beautiful things" that would remind us of our nation's "rich and stirring past." It was only when Jackie tried to prod Schlesinger into writing a White House guide to the presidents that he drew the line. She envisioned pithy profiles that were "lively, even controversial." Significantly, she gave Schlesinger a book about Versailles to help inspire him. "If you can do all this I will carve your name on the Blue Room mantelpiece," she wrote.

Schlesinger gently reminded Jackie that he had "certain jobs to do for her husband that had priority," and he promised to find another historian for the task. While she didn't take offense, the project would languish for more than a year until Schlesinger's choice, Harvard historian Frank Freidel, took on the job.

Jackie and Lee's goodwill trip to India and Pakistan had been postponed three times since it was first planned for the end of November. The final delay, announced less than a week before their scheduled arrival in New Delhi on March 4, was blamed on Jackie's "low-grade sinus infection" which had been causing her "intermittent low fever." Only the day before the announcement, Jackie and Lee had given a lively water-skiing demonstration for friends aboard the *Honey Fitz* in Palm Beach, and several days later Jackie was back in Glen Ora, riding with the Orange County Hunt. *Time* speculated that the postponement had more to do with "John Kennedy's pique at an intransigent Nehru," who had recently invaded the tiny Portuguese territory of Goa.

It turned out that Jackie's second thoughts were the real reason. At a dinner party the night after her televised White House tour, Jackie had been in high spirits, dancing the twist with Joe and Susan Mary Alsop, diplomat Chip Bohlen and his wife, Avis, the Ros Gilpatrics, and Joan Braden, the wife of former CIA official turned newspaper publisher Tom Braden. "Jackie now hates the idea of going to India, but JFK insists that, having made the commitment, she must go for state reasons," Stew Alsop revealed to a friend. "She kept insisting that she needed Joan along as a companion and general cheerer-upper."

Jackie was hardly an intimate friend of Joan Braden, a diminutive and feisty mother of seven who switched from Republican to Democrat because of JFK. Joan had worked in a variety of government posts, and during the campaign she had ghosted a homespun weekly column for Jackie called "Campaign Wife." In addition, Joan had served as an informal press secretary, fending off requests from reporters as well as overeager campaign aides. "She has a remarkable talent for being a close personal friend of the great," Stew Alsop observed, "a unique combination of charm and brass."

Jackie called her "that little freckle-faced girl" and wondered why Jack and Bobby were "forever asking her opinion." Joan and Tom Braden had what would later be called an "open marriage," in which they gave each other "total freedom—just enough rope," as Joan put it, to have extramarital affairs. Joan's most noted liaison was with Nelson Rockefeller, the Republican governor of New York who was a leading candidate to oppose JFK in 1964. (In later years her lover would be Robert McNamara.) Still, Jackie felt comfortable with Joan, so Jack announced that Pierre Salinger would "fix it up" for a magazine exclusive on the First Lady's trip. Stew Alsop arranged Joan's "inside story" for the *Saturday Evening Post,* to be written in a "gay chatty style."

On her way to the subcontinent, Jackie spent several days in Rome, where she was greeted with shouts of "Che bella!" (How beautiful!). She was scheduled to have a private audience with Pope John XXIII, which had been secretly sought to help Lee secure an annulment of her first marriage to Michael Canfield. As Roman Catholics, Lee and Stas had been compelled to marry in a civil service—five months before Tony was born. Now, despite the cracks in their relationship, Stas still wanted a religious service, which an annulment would permit.

Jackie saw the pope alone, and they talked in French for an unusually long time—more than a half hour, compared to the usual fifteen to twenty minutes. Afterwards, Jackie consulted with Cardinal Cicognani, the pontifical secretary of state, who had originally discussed the annulment during a White House visit the previous November. The Kennedys had deep connections at the Vatican: one of Joe Kennedy's oldest friends was Enrico Pietro Galeazzi, a top papal aide and chief architect of the Holy See, and for her motherhood and good works Rose Kennedy had been named a "Papal Countess" by Pope Pius XII.

Jackie and Lee arrived in New Delhi on Monday, March 12, 1962. During what Jackie called the "most magic two weeks in my life," they made a few dutiful visits to such locales as a hospital and a home for "maladjusted and vagrant boys." The focus was far more on beautiful sights—the Taj Mahal by moonlight, a marvel, Jackie said, of "mass and symmetry"; the Shalimar Gardens in Lahore; the dramatic Khyber Pass, where Jackie wore Ayub Khan's Astrakhan hat at a rakish angle and mused about Alexander of Macedon. The sisters stayed in a 900-room palace and partied with maharajahs and maharanis. One night in Jaipur, Jackie was up until 3 a.m. after a post-midnight tour of the city's flood-lit pink buildings. In New Delhi, Jackie expertly completed a riding and jumping course with the mounted bodyguards of the Indian president. In Pakistan, Ayub gave her a bay gelding named Sardar, and Jackie excit-edly took her new mount through three "fantastic gaits."

After some initial unease, Jackie grew increasingly relaxed. She un-abashedly smoked as she settled into her box at Pakistan's national horse show. When Bashir Ahmed, the famous camel driver befriended by LBJ, offered her a ride, she merrily dragooned Lee into joining her and announced that a camel "makes an elephant feel like a jet plane." "Both the First Lady and her sister were as natural and unaffected as they were as very young girls before political lightning changed their lives," wrote Molly Thayer.

Nehru was so bewitched that he insisted Jackie and Lee vacate the guest house that the Galbraiths had carefully prepared and move into his residence. He showed them a snake charmer and treated them to sumptuous feasts with elaborately costumed dancers. Each day in New Delhi, Jackie and Lee walked for an hour or so with Nehru in his gar-den. "We never talked of serious things," Jackie told Joan Braden. "I guess because Jack has always told me the one thing a busy man doesn't want to talk about at the end of the day is whether the Geneva Confer-ence will be successful or what settlement could be made in Kashmir or anything like that." Instead, "they talked about what they were reading, about people, and about some of the insanities of foreign policy," Gal-braith recalled. "Nehru was a lonesome man who loved the company of beautiful and intelligent women."

Jackie also clicked with Ayub, a military man—"magnificent" in his uniform, she said—educated in England like Nehru. Harold Macmil-lan considered Ayub a man of "fine character . . . easy to talk to." Jackie thought the Pakistani president was "like Jack—tough and brave and wants things done in a hurry."

Jackie and Lee created a tableau of splendid outfits, mostly designed by Cassini, in sherbet colors that were intended to complement their surroundings. "There will be a lot of sun, a lot of light," she had said to Oleg, stressing that she wished to avoid anything "subdued." In the evenings she often wore what Galbraith called "queenly white." Her lavender dress in Benares, the ambassador noted, conformed to her "excellent sense of theater" and "could be picked out at any range up to five miles." The sisters brought sixty-four pieces of luggage, and in the first six days Jackie wore twenty different ensembles. During one shopping expedition, Jackie dropped nearly $600 (the equivalent of $3,600 today) in five minutes on purses embroidered with rubies and emeralds as well as yards of silk brocade. She was mildly irked at Ken Galbraith for misleading her into thinking she was paying far less. "Only an economist could make such a mistake," she told Joan Braden.

Jackie and the Galbraiths got along well, although she confessed to Jack in a letter that the ambassador turned out to be a publicity hound. "He makes Tish look reticent," she wrote. "He is always darting out to give [the press] briefings." Galbraith noted in his journal that the President "told me that the care and management of Mrs. Kennedy involved a good deal of attention, and he is quite right."

As with the previous year in Greece, Jackie and Tish Baldrige were quietly at odds. Baldrige had knocked herself out with logistics and had avoided burdening Jackie with details. (One hundred pages of typed notes included diagrams showing where Jackie would stand.) At Baldrige's suggestion, the Galbraiths had even imported provisions from Beirut so that their Indian chef could prepare grilled cheese for the First Lady that would be "exactly like a drugstore sandwich at home."

Above all, Baldrige had adapted to the First Lady's shifting plans. Jackie wouldn't accept early morning appointments, and she insisted on time each afternoon for a nap. "One must be adamant," Jackie later told a friend, "or they will run you into the ground." "It was not easy for me," Baldrige recalled. "It was the same behavior again. It was Lee's fault, but it was also Jackie's fault. She should have been more sensitive to the role I was playing." Midway through the trip, Baldrige fell ill and was flown to London to recuperate with the Bruces.

Before Jackie's departure, Galbraith had been concerned about her exhaustion, and a "slightly alarming report on her health" from a local doctor. But stopping in London for a few days en route home, Jackie bounced back at a party given by Lee and Stas with Oleg Cassini, Benno Graziani and his wife Nicole, Cecil Beaton, and the actress Moira Shearer. They consumed large quantities of caviar and vodka, danced the twist, and learned "le hully gully" from Graziani and Cassini. The two friends draped themselves in oversized Indian necklaces, Graziani perched a pot on his head, and Cassini fashioned a towel into a turban to do an impression of a Moghul potentate—jackanape routines they would repeat several weeks later for the President at a White House dinner party attended by the French ambassador.

Jackie's trip had no specific political impact, but Galbraith told Kennedy that she "took all the bitterness out of our relations with India." Nehru spoke of "the charm of her personality" that deepened the "psychological pull" between the two nations. Even Indira Gandhi melted. On a visit to New York afterwards, she said "everyone loved" Jackie, and Indira's mood brightened that much more when JFK met with her privately in the Oval Office. True to form, Kennedy couldn't resist making political sport with Jackie's activities. On hearing that she had taken an elephant ride in India, he told the press, "She gave him sugar and nuts, but, of course, the elephant wasn't satisfied."

TWENTY

*W*hile Jackie was overseas, her husband enjoyed his tomcat freedom. The day after he bade her goodbye on March 8, he headed off for a Miami weekend with two of his partners in prowling, George Smathers and Bill Thompson. The following week Jack spent an evening in the White House with Mary Meyer, meeting her only hours after Caroline and John returned from a stay with their grandparents in Palm Beach.

On Thursday, March 22, precisely two months to the day since his affair with Meyer began, Jack Kennedy sat down for lunch with FBI chief J. Edgar Hoover. Kennedy knew about Hoover's old dossier on Inga Arvad, and he was aware that the FBI was keeping tabs on him. But now Hoover decided to share for the first time his knowledge about Kennedy's trysts with "freelance artist" Judith Campbell since early 1960, citing phone calls she had made to Evelyn Lincoln's office. The reason for Hoover's disclosure was the FBI's evidence that Campbell was also having affairs with Chicago mob boss Sam Giancana and his associate Johnny Roselli, who had been involved in the CIA's assassination attempts against Fidel Castro. That afternoon, Kennedy called Campbell for the last time and broke off the relationship.

The next day, Kennedy flew to California to speak at Berkeley and inspect military facilities. Over the weekend he stayed with Dave Powers in Palm Springs at the luxurious home of Republican crooner Bing Crosby. Kennedy had been scheduled to stay at Frank Sinatra's estate, but he had canceled the visit on the recommendation of Bobby Kennedy. RFK had known of Hoover's information on Campbell and the mob since late February, including the fact that Sinatra, a good friend of Giancana, had described her as "shacking up with John Kennedy in the East."

Sinatra's relationship with the Kennedys had been uneasy since Jackie strongly objected to his involvement in the presidential campaign. Through Lawford, the singer served as the impresario of the inaugural gala, but Sinatra was offended that "he got in to see Jack only once alone" at the White House, according to Tina Sinatra, a fierce defender of her controversial father. The reason, Tina wrote, was that her father "personified a page of history that [the Kennedys] would rather have erased." During the campaign, according to Tina, Sinatra had been a go-between for Joe Kennedy and Giancana: Joe had needed Giancana to get the support of "mob-infested unions" for the West Virginia primary, but since the Ambassador couldn't risk approaching the mob boss directly, he asked Sinatra to do it instead.

After Kennedy's election, Bobby launched a vigorous campaign against the Mafia that included surveillance of Giancana and his associates. "Dad was stunned when the Administration began to prosecute the very people it had enlisted for help just the year before," wrote Tina. Under those circumstances, Bobby wanted his brother to keep his distance from Sinatra, who had hired workmen around the clock to prepare accommodations for JFK's late March visit to Palm Springs. When Lawford brought the bad news only days before the President's scheduled arrival, Sinatra was enraged. With the end of his White House connection, Sinatra "blamed Peter for not standing up for him" and cut off his friendship with the British actor, whose Hollywood career declined as a result.

On the weekend of March 24 and 25, while Jackie was visiting the Khyber Pass and riding on Bashir Ahmed's camel, her husband had a rendezvous with Marilyn Monroe at Bing Crosby's home, courtesy of Peter Lawford. Kennedy had seen the actress only intermittently since they disappeared together during the Democratic convention. But for all her status as the ultimate Hollywood sex symbol, Monroe was now on a self-destructive spiral—mentally unstable and addicted to drugs and alcohol.

The Monroe liaison was the most vivid example of the personal risk-taking that Kennedy's closest aides couldn't square with his public caution. In his public life, Kennedy was reckless only when it came to Cuba. Ted Sorensen had said on television in early January 1962 that the Bay of Pigs taught Kennedy "something about the difficulties in a democracy of conducting a covert operation." Yet the following spring, Operation Mongoose, the brain warp of Bobby Kennedy, was firmly in place. None other than Johnny Roselli—Justice Department investigations notwithstanding—was still engaged in conspiracies to eliminate Castro.

Richard Helms, then the CIA's deputy director for plans, later referred to these plots as "nutty schemes," although he declined to say explicitly what the President knew. "There was nothing Bobby did that Jack didn't want him to do," said Helms. "I think Bobby made his contributions but he did what Jack said in the end. . . . What interests me about Bobby Kennedy is that in all those phone calls and meetings, Jack was driving him to get rid of Castro. Nobody but Jack could do that. Bobby couldn't get away with doing it on his own."

The Cuban intelligence service was concerned enough about covert American activity to raise the prospect of an invasion. Castro transmitted these fears to Khrushchev, who was already worried about various indirect signals—articles in the American press, speeches by various administration officials—that emphasized U.S. military superiority and suggested the possibility of a preemptive nuclear strike against the Soviets. Kennedy's resumption of atmospheric nuclear tests on April 25—itself a response to the series of Soviet detonations—seemed designed to further reinforce American dominance over Moscow.

These shared apprehensions drew Khrushchev and Castro together in the spring of 1962 to devise a plan to put nuclear missiles in Cuba. The maneuver had the potential to protect Cuba from the United States, enable the Soviet Union to force the Allies out of Berlin, and equalize the U.S.-Soviet nuclear balance. For all its obvious risks, the Cuban missile scheme seemed reasonable to Khrushchev, who equated it with the recent American deployment of nuclear warheads in Turkey on the Soviet border. Khrushchev had also seen Kennedy back down before—at the Bay of Pigs, in Laos, and in Berlin—so he had reason to believe the President would do so again. Khrushchev and Kennedy may have been exchanging ideas in their secret correspondence, but the Soviet leader failed to calculate the intensity of the President's feelings about a nuclear threat inside the Western Hemisphere.

Jackie marked her triumphant return from India and Pakistan on Thursday, March 29, by issuing a subdued, almost melancholy statement: "It feels unnatural to me to go on such a long semi-official trip without my husband," she said. "I have missed my family and have no desire to be a public personality on my own." Jack entered the cabin of the *Caroline* so that they could have a private reunion. Waiting on the tarmac to greet Jackie were the ambassadors from India and Pakistan, as well as Ken Galbraith, who received an unexpected kiss that he happily noted was "well-televised and widely reported."

Galbraith and the Schlesingers joined Jack and Jackie on Sunday at Glen Ora for dinner. It was a relaxed evening as they watched an NBC special on the trip with a running commentary from Jackie and Galbraith. JFK expressed his admiration for Jackie's "general political grace and style," Galbraith said. Schlesinger recalled that she offered "acute observations about Nehru."

Galbraith detected that Jackie seemed "a bit tired" but found her "handsome and compelling without benefit of makeup or hair-doing." In fact she was exhausted, telling Janet Cooper that she couldn't face any questions about the White House restoration for at least a week. "I don't even care if the White House burns down!" she wrote. Jackie assured Cooper that she would see her "when I recover. Think it may be smallpox."

That Monday, Jackie flew from an airfield in Virginia with Caroline and John for eight days in Palm Beach to recuperate. She had scarcely returned to Washington when she was off once more to Florida with her family for a nine-day Easter holiday at the Paul estate. After her three-week absence from the White House in March, Jackie was away an equal amount of time in April. The President had to serve as solo host at a luncheon for twenty-four in honor of the Duchess of Devonshire, as well as a state visit by the president of Brazil. In his spare time he approved the script and screened rushes of *PT 109* starring Cliff Robertson as a young JFK, and he tossed out the first baseball of the season at a new $24 million stadium in Washington, with Dave Powers at his side.

The ambiance of Kennedy's twice-daily swims with Powers improved considerably that month. Jackie considered the White House swimming pool drab and institutional, so she commissioned French artist Bernard LaMotte to decorate three of its bare walls (the fourth was mirrored) with vistas of St. Croix in the Virgin Islands. The murals depicting a cerulean Caribbean harbor bobbing with sailboats were a gift in Joe Kennedy's name, echoing scenes at his favorite New York restaurant, Le Pavillon. To ensure that moisture wouldn't peel off the paint, the Ambassador's funds also paid for a special new exhaust system. JFK watched in fascination as the paintings slowly took form. At one point, LaMotte, working on a special platform, reached too far, lost his balance, and landed in the water.

In April, Jackie periodically swooped into Washington to preside over selected high-profile events—a congressional reception, a youth concert on the South Lawn, a state dinner for the Shah of Iran and his wife, and a celebratory evening for forty-nine Nobel Prize winners, known as the "brains dinner" among the East Wing staff. The Shah's wife, Empress Farah, wore "blindingly impressive" jewelry, including a tiara and necklace with huge emeralds and twenty-carat diamonds, while Jackie was the picture of simplicity with only diamond drop earrings and a diamond sunburst pin nestled in her "brioche" topknot. For entertainment Jackie brought in Jerome Robbins's *Ballets USA* featuring jazz dancers in sweatshirts and sneakers, which she had seen in Europe and New York.

Even with 175 guests, the Nobel dinner struck a surprisingly informal note—"one of the most stimulating parties ever" at the White House, according to the *Washington Post*. The host and hostess had nut brown tans, and Jackie wore a long dress of pale green jersey, pleated and draped like a Greek statue. Arthur Schlesinger "appeared to be self-conscious," writer Diana Trilling observed, "as if borne down by his official White House connection." During the cocktail hour, "a stupendous amount of liquor was flowing around," wrote Trilling. Her "pleasantly looped" husband, Lionel, consumed six martinis and was overheard telling Jackie, "When you were at Vassar you weren't much of a student but always personable."

At dinner JFK sat next to Ernest Hemingway's widow, Mary, who contributed one of the evening's three readings by actor Fredric March: a chapter from an unpublished novel by her late husband about a young American fighting Nazi submarines from his fishing boat. According to Diana Trilling, Hemingway's prose was "so poor that one was pained for the man who had written it." His widow "was having a tough time, poor woman," Trilling observed, prompting Kennedy to do "something nice. He squeezed her arm comfortingly."

The President's gesture was that much more magnanimous given his genuine feelings. During dinner Mary Hemingway had managed to irritate Kennedy profoundly by lecturing him about how to deal with Castro. Kennedy later told Walton she was "the biggest bore I've had for a long time." But the elderly widow of George Marshall, seated on his other side, tickled the President by telling him, "I am so happy to get out of my briar patch and come here for dinner." Rising for his remarks, Kennedy "at once had the place in his hands," noted Trilling, when he said, "This is the most extraordinary collection of talent, of human knowledge, that has ever gathered together at the White House, with the possible exception of when Thomas Jefferson dined alone."

As the official entertainment wound down, the Kennedys invited about a dozen guests upstairs to continue the party—"Jackie's personal part of the evening," Diana Trilling recalled, "her turn to have fun." The Yellow Oval Room "was filled with cigar smokers and their lady companions," William Styron wrote. "One would have thought the entire Nobel dinner had been arranged to produce this fragrant climax." JFK sat in what Jackie described as his "health rocker" with a lit Havana, "wreathed in smoke," wrote Styron, "relaxed and contented."

Oblivious to the mild insult about her Vassar days, Jackie was intent on probing Lionel Trilling's insights as a distinguished literary critic. They debated the merits of *The Rainbow* and *Women in Love* by D. H. Lawrence, prompting Jackie to find her copy of British novelist Compton Mackenzie's memoirs to locate a pertinent passage. "Jackie spoke very openly and unpretentiously . . . very sure of herself and reliant on her own wit," wrote Diana Trilling. At twelve-thirty, Bobby Kennedy squeezed the Trillings, Robert Frost, and other guests into the elevator. With mock horror of the perils of overcrowding, Jackie said, "Think of the headlines tomorrow morning, with all these distinguished people dead at the bottom of the shaft!" "Hold on, Mr. Frost!" said Bobby, as he closed the grate and Jackie waved goodbye.

By the time of the Nobel dinner, Jack Kennedy's biggest domestic worry had been safely resolved, but only after a major blowup resulting from what the President viewed as a double cross. Since the previous September, Kennedy had been cajoling the steelworkers union and the steel industry to reach a noninflationary settlement on wages that would help hold the line on prices. Kennedy's lingering fear for the economy—one legacy of his father's training—continued to be the specter of inflation. During the first week in April, both sides agreed to a two-year contract with an acceptable increase of 2.5 percent—all in fringe benefits, with no wage increase. Roger Blough, the chairman of United States Steel, told Douglas Dillon it was "the best settlement . . . in twenty years."

Kennedy's dealings with the business and financial communities had always been edgy. With the exception of Thomas J. Watson, president of IBM (who married JFK's onetime girlfriend Olive Cawley), the President had few friends prominent in the business world. Even the businessmen in his inner circle were atypical: McNamara the maverick and Dillon the investment banker who had spent most of his career in public service. JFK's father had been an independent operator detached from a wide range of business practices and attitudes. He had, as Ros Gilpatric put it, "only one slant on things."

Because Gilpatric mingled with tycoons through his New York legal practice, Kennedy frequently quizzed him on his experience. "Many of his questions were very naive because of what he'd learned from his father," said Gilpatric. "He couldn't understand what made businessmen tick."

On Tuesday, April 10, Roger Blough arrived in the Oval Office to announce that his company would hike prices by 3.5 percent, or $6 a ton—the first rise since 1958—with other steelmakers expected to follow suit. Kennedy was furious. "They kicked us right in the balls," JFK fumed to Ben Bradlee. Kennedy felt particularly betrayed because he had carefully cultivated Blough for months as the chairman of his business advisory council. "My father always told me that all businessmen were sons-of-bitches, but I never believed it till now," Kennedy told one aide after another—a characterization that was widely circulated in the business community.

But Kennedy had not been completely blindsided. The previous Friday, Hal Korda, a New York public relations man close to U.S. Steel executives, had tipped his friend Charley Bartlett about the company's intentions. Bartlett had immediately alerted Kennedy, whose advisers could find no confirmation. After Blough's announcement, Bartlett (drawing on his connections to U.S. Steel through his wife's family) played a key role as an intermediary and adviser to Kennedy. On Wednesday morning, Kennedy called Bartlett to ask whether he should take "a stiff or conciliatory line." Bartlett counseled him to "play it rather straight . . . scare them a little but do not overdo."

Kennedy chose to overdo, denouncing the steelmakers in a televised statement for their "irresponsible defiance of the public interest." His anger barely contained, his voice hard, Kennedy threw every threat in his power at the steelmakers: anti-trust and price-fixing investigations by Congress, the Federal Trade Commission, and the Justice Department, as well as shifts of lucrative military contracts to steelmakers who kept prices stable.

Bobby Kennedy rashly dispatched FBI agents to seize documents from steel company officials, threatening to prosecute them for income tax violations. Federal agents even woke up reporters in the middle of the night to interrogate them about statements made by steel officials. "It was highly overdone," said Charley Bartlett. Bobby would later concede that "it was a tough way to operate, rather scary, but we couldn't afford to lose it."

"The steel people made a terrible mistake," said Dillon. "Kennedy quite rightly thought he had been double crossed. He blew up and Bobby blew up." On Wednesday night as the Kennedys were entertaining the Shah of Iran, Korda called Bartlett to say that U.S. Steel was "ready to make peace." Bartlett alerted Kennedy, who immediately agreed to negotiate. With Korda and Bartlett handling the logistics, the administration began a series of meetings with U.S. Steel executives.

Kennedy enlisted Washington power broker Clark Clifford as his representative because, he told Bartlett, the lawyer "understood the workings of a politician's mind and . . . the position that the politicians had to protect." For public consumption, Kennedy continued the bluster, telling Ben Bradlee on Friday, "We're going to tuck it to them and screw 'em." As the secret talks proceeded that day in New York, Bethlehem Steel, the second largest producer, announced a price rollback, and U.S. Steel quickly followed.

After only three days, the crisis was over, the investigations ceased, and Kennedy turned conciliatory. He met with Blough, who recalled that Kennedy "began to realize that there are two sides to this coin." According to Bartlett, Kennedy believed that if Blough "had been smart enough to wait until summer" he could have slipped in a price increase. The problem, said Bartlett, was "the juxtaposition of the increase with [the wage] settlement." Bartlett felt Kennedy was "very undoctrinaire" and understood that the steel industry was "entitled to an increase." A year later when the steel companies moved to raise prices to cover their costs, Kennedy would voice no objections.

Kennedy's stance played well with the public, as his approval rating held at 77 percent. But what *Time* called the administration's "almost totalitarian" tactics against the steel industry caused a breach with the business community that Kennedy never repaired. Even Harold Macmillan looked askance, sympathizing with Blough as a "modest and intelligent man" subjected by Kennedy to "a certain amount of blackmail."

Kennedy tried to retract his "sons-of-bitches" comment, claiming he meant to aim it only at the steel industry. In a speech to the U.S. Chamber of Commerce, he proclaimed his interest in helping business, not harming it. Continuing his singular role as sub rosa counselor, Bartlett "watched him work over that speech and discussed it with him." But the audience responded coolly and continued what Bartlett called "this fixation" that the President was "out to cut the throat of business."

During the last weekend of April, Kennedy and Macmillan sat down together for talks—their fifth meeting in little over a year. JFK valued the opportunity to vent in his sessions alone with Macmillan. "He seems to want advice," Macmillan noted. "At the same time it's all very vague, and when we come down to brass tacks, we don't make much headway. . . . He is *very* secretive and suspicious of leaks." Macmillan was surprised by the "bitterness of his feeling . . . against the French."

Kennedy complained about "de Gaulle's rudeness to Rusk" and the French leader's "being cynical in his policy." Macmillan thought that JFK suffered for not taking "the same humorous view of this sort of treatment as we are willing to do."

On Sunday the two leaders had lunch at the White House with Jackie and the Gores. Much of their conversation focused on *The Guns of August,* by Barbara Tuchman, about the series of blunders that led to World War I. Kennedy had just finished the book, which reinforced his belief that war usually was the result of misunderstanding and miscalculation, a view that he had shared the previous year with Khrushchev. JFK had already urged his top advisers, especially in the military, to read the book, and he presented a copy to Macmillan.

More than ever, Macmillan recognized the importance of David Gore's unique relationship with the President. David and Sissie made an easy foursome with Jack and Jackie, keeping each other company over dinner and on weekends in the country. A statuesque beauty with porcelain skin and black hair who resembled "a Plantagenet, with a strong face," Sissie was as graceful on horseback as Jackie. Sissie had a fey, fawnlike manner, and her strong Catholicism gave her "a certain puritan streak," recalled British politician Roy Jenkins. "But if she disapproved of Jack, she kept it under wraps."

Jackie considered the early part of May "the worst two weeks of the year—morning, lunch, tea and dinner official things" that she could not escape. She endured lunches in her honor given by the Senate Ladies Red Cross and the Congressional Club, where she occupied herself by mouthing the words to *Kismet* and other show tunes sung by Broadway star Alfred Drake. She gave a tea for nearly two hundred Farmington students, faculty, trustees, and alumnae, including Lem Billings's mother, and she christened a nuclear-powered submarine with a hearty "Je vous baptise Lafayette!"

On the way to the ceremony in Groton, Connecticut, she stopped in New York to see Joe Kennedy, who was settling into Horizon House, a rehabilitation facility at New York University Medical Center. "While the others pretended not to notice the side of his body that was affected by the paralysis, she always held his deformed hand and kissed the affected side of his face," wrote the Ambassador's nurse Rita Dallas.

"Her lack of fear helped him overcome his." During her two-hour visit, Jackie pushed him in his wheelchair, read to him from that day's front page, talked of her children, and told him "the little blunders the President would make while he was at home. . . . Her visit . . . was done in a whisper, and when she left, he was completely calm."

Before the social season ended, the Kennedys hosted their memorable dinner for Frederick "Fritz" Loewe, in which the composer played selections from *Camelot* and *My Fair Lady* on the baby grand piano in the Center Hall of the second floor. The Bradlees and Spaldings joined Jack and Jackie, along with Bill Walton and Helen Chavchavadze. Since JFK had been friendly with lyricist Alan Jay Lerner since Choate, he already knew a fair amount about his work. With Lerner's collaborator Kennedy was a relentless quidnunc: "How do you go about writing a piece of music?" "Do you write the music first?" Loewe explained that he always wrote music "for a purpose" and demonstrated the complex process of composing, which transfixed the President.

The Kennedys also gave one more dinner dance that spring, this time in honor of Ken Galbraith. Just thirty-five guests made the cut, including Mary Meyer and Helen Chavchavadze. The McNamaras, Bundys, Schlesingers, and Earl Smiths were there, as well as bachelors Bill Walton, Arkady Gerney, and Walter Sohier, a handsome favorite of Jackie's who had lived for some years next to Merrywood. Galbraith pronounced himself satisfied with the "good and sometimes sultry looks" of the women, particularly his dinner partners, a "Swedish-French actress" and Lilly Pulitzer, with "a rich Palm Beach suntan and admirable shape." This time the champagne-fueled dancing didn't break up until 5 a.m. Galbraith claimed to awaken four hours later with "a remarkably clear head."

Far more important to Jackie was the dinner in mid-May for 168 luminaries in honor of André Malraux that she had been planning since January. As Malraux had done for her at the Jeu de Paume, she first took him on a tour of the National Gallery, although he had already announced, "I know the National Gallery by heart. The most haunting painting in it—here, I'll write it for you, 'La Balayeuse' by Rembrandt." He predictably "strode through" the gallery "expounding freely on the history and impact of some of its masterpieces."

Jackie welcomed the French statesman by giving him two rare nineteenth-century books of political caricatures from Uncle Hughdie's library. Only later did she learn that they were worth $2,000—the equivalent of $12,000 today. She wore a luminous strapless gown in pink silk shantung designed by Christian Dior, once again crowning her leonine hairdo with a diamond sunburst.

To match Malraux's varied experience as a novelist, art critic, philosopher, and resistance fighter, she filled the guest list with artists and writers, among them Tennessee Williams, Saul Bellow, Elia Kazan, Geraldine Page, Archibald MacLeish, Andrew Wyeth, and George Balanchine, who nearly was turned away because he arrived by taxicab wearing a shabby raincoat. Jackie also included such patrons of the arts as the Wrightsmans and the John Loebs. JFK insisted on some "great Americans," namely the reclusive Charles Lindbergh and his wife, Anne, who surprisingly accepted and stayed in the White House. Kennedy particularly liked the idea that Lindbergh had "landed in France." "This is becoming a sort of eating place for artists," Kennedy quipped in his toast to Malraux, "But they never ask us out."

Malraux spoke little English, so Jackie placed Walt Rostow's wife, Elspeth, a history professor who was fluent in French, on his other side to translate for playwright Arthur Miller. The previous year, Miller had been divorced from Marilyn Monroe, whose allure for JFK was known to Jackie—and who barely a week later would be the headline act in a birthday tribute to the President. Malraux, a dapper sixty-year-old with sleek black hair, "wanted to talk to Arthur Miller more than he wanted to talk to the President's wife," said Rostow.

It turned out that Miller's French was workmanlike, so Rostow became "the unnecessary third party." Jackie remained unruffled by Malraux's disregard for dinner party protocol. "Her manners were perfect," said Rostow. From time to time, Malraux turned to Jackie, and she murmured to him in French, at one point confiding that German chancellor Konrad Adenauer was "un peu gaga." As the evening came to a close, Malraux confirmed his pleasure by promising that France would lend the Mona Lisa to the National Gallery.

Some months later, Kennedy told Cy Sulzberger that he had difficulty communicating with Malraux and wasn't much impressed with him "above all on political or diplomatic matters." Yet over lunch at Glen Ora at the end of the Frenchman's visit, the President was keen to hear Malraux's theories about the endurance of mythology in contemporary society. When Malraux wondered whether ideologies such as capitalism and socialism were the real issues, Kennedy ventured that "the management of industrial society" had superseded ideology, and that most problems had become administrative and technical questions. It was a theme he would repeat two weeks later in an economic conference at the White House, and the following month in a commencement address at Yale designed to encourage innovative thinking about the economy. Business, labor, and government, Kennedy maintained, had "to look at things as they are, not through party labels."

Kennedy's speeches on the economy were also intended to win over the business community. Dillon had been working for many months on a decidedly pro-business investment tax credit providing incentives to buy new equipment, but Democratic senator Harry Byrd, chairman of the Senate Finance Committee, had termed the credit a "give-away" and stalled the bill.

Throughout the fall of 1961, the economy had been growing, and in December the stock market had hit an all-time high of 734.91. But January brought a slowdown that deepened with the steel crisis. According to Dillon, business felt that "the government was going to try to control prices generally, which, of course, was never the President's idea." As confidence dimmed, a slide in stock prices began to feed on itself. Finally, on Monday, May 28, the market dove from 611 to 576, the largest one-day point drop since 1929.

Kennedy immediately called Galbraith, the self-proclaimed "Thucydides of the 1929 crash," who was vacationing in Vermont. The President's first instinct was to go on television to "calm fevered nerves." Galbraith opposed Kennedy's plan, arguing that "he would put his prestige on the line" and make the situation seem more grave than it was. Bundy, Dillon, and other aides agreed with Galbraith. Dillon believed the plunge was "a psychological occurrence largely motivated by excessive fear, and . . . would work itself out." The Treasury secretary made a careful public statement emphasizing the fundamental soundness of the economy and characterizing the market drop as a necessary correction. He pointed out that inflation had been quelled, and that stable prices would mean a rising economy.

When Jack Kennedy turned forty-five the following day, the stock market rewarded him by rallying to 603.96, signaling an end to the momentary panic. Kennedy kept his focus on a push to pass the investment tax credit bill in 1962, and at a press conference on June 7 he announced that in January he would introduce his long-promised legislation to reduce taxes across the board.

The President celebrated his birthday on the twenty-ninth at Glen Ora with Jackie, Lem, Jean, Bobby, Ethel, Sarge, and Eunice. Chef René Verdon prepared a chocolate cake with fudge icing that was transported to Virginia by helicopter. The President never saw the extravagant white and yellow flower-covered rocking chair sent by Frank Sinatra. In a final insult to the banished singer, the gift was donated to Children's Hospital shortly after it arrived at the White House.

The more memorable birthday event had occurred ten days earlier at a nationally televised Democratic fundraising rally in Madison Square Garden. Kennedy delighted in performances by the likes of Maria Callas, Harry Belafonte, Ella Fitzgerald, and Jack Benny, who cracked, "The amazing thing to me is how a man in a rocking chair can have such a young wife." The President allowed that his father's "all businessmen are SOBs" maxim didn't apply to show business.

The showstopper of the evening was Marilyn Monroe. "The figure was famous," wrote *Time*. "And for one breathless moment the 15,000 people in Madison Square Garden thought they were going to see all of it. Onto the stage sashayed Marilyn Monroe, attired in a great bundle of white mink. Arriving at the lectern, she turned and swept the furs from her shoulders. A slight gasp rose from the audience before it was realized that she was really wearing a skintight flesh toned gown." Kennedy grinned as Monroe sang a breathy and seductive "Happy Birthday." "I can now retire from politics," he announced, "after having had Happy Birthday sung to me in such a sweet wholesome way." But the suggestive performance raised eyebrows. Columnist Dorothy Kilgallen called it nothing less than "making love to the President in the direct view of forty million Americans."

Afterwards, Kennedy attended a gathering of about a hundred people at the home of United Artists head Arthur Krim on East Sixty-ninth Street, where a photographer caught Jack and Bobby in the library hovering over Monroe dressed in what she called "skin and beads." "I didn't see the beads!" Adlai Stevenson wrote to Mary Lasker, describing his "perilous encounters" with the film star that evening, "only after breaking through the strong defenses established by Robert Kennedy, who was dodging around her like a moth around the flame." Bill Walton (who later insisted that Monroe "was not the mistress of any Kennedy. Never") recalled that he and JFK stood on a staircase and watched as "Marilyn started making passes at Bobby, and backing him up against the wall. . . . He didn't know what to do or where to look. . . . We're upstairs rocking with laughter."

Arthur Schlesinger said both he and Bobby met Monroe that night for the first time. Schlesinger was "enchanted by her manner and her wit, at once so masked, so ingenuous and so penetrating. But one felt a terrible unreality about her—as if talking to someone under water." Given her weakness for dangerous combinations of alcohol and pills (she had attempted suicide a number of times, most recently the previous month), Monroe was probably high that evening—at least judging by behavior witnessed by Walton. "She was an exhibitionist," he said. "I caught her . . . in a darkened bedroom, standing before a window, making a naked erotic dance for guards who were on the rooftop of an adjoining building."

Jackie had wisely avoided the Marilyn Monroe spectacle by remaining in Virginia, where she competed as a "surprise participant" in the Loudoun Hunt Horse Show. She took third place in one of three classes, riding Minbreno, a horse she owned jointly with Eve Fout. Jack had debated the political wisdom of letting her participate in such a fancy public event (unlike her hunting, which was private), even asking Mac Bundy for advice. His national security adviser replied with some doggerel:

> It is a sign of pride—a horse,
> But not a thing to hide—a horse,
> Assuming you provide—of course,
> A brave and lovely lady who can ride.

> For voters dare to admire the fair,
> And voters crave to honor the brave;
> Only the rich are likely to bitch,
> But which rich itch for us anyway?

So smothering doubts the President shouts,
"I who decide say, 'Let her ride!'"

As the summer holiday approached, Jackie wrapped up the latest additions to her restoration project. In May the Rose Garden redesign by Bunny Mellon was completed. It was, in fact, more Jack Kennedy's inspiration than Jackie's. He had enlisted Bunny the previous August during a picnic at the Mellon beach house in Osterville. Inspired by gardens he had seen during his European visit, he wanted a landscape "to appeal to the most discriminating taste, yet . . . hold a thousand people for a ceremony." Kennedy had also read Thomas Jefferson's garden notes and told Mellon he "hoped for flowers used in Jefferson's period."

Mellon brought in Perry Wheeler, a highly regarded landscape architect, as her collaborator. Throughout the fall she had pondered design ideas. At the Pablo Casals dinner in November, JFK gazed at her across the table and said, "Bunny, where is my garden plan?" It was still in her head, and shortly afterwards she committed the scheme to paper—the four bare corners of the new garden anchored by magnolia trees, and a broad lawn defined at either side by what Mellon described as a "tapestry of flowers that would change with the season," accented by the garden's signature roses. The beds would be shaded by ten flowering crab-apple trees and bordered by lines of low boxwood hedges.

Mellon dug up the old garden in March and had it ready two months later. The President designed the steps and platform for ceremonies outside the doors of his office, and he constantly monitored Mellon's progress. He drew the line, however, at her vision of a "gaily striped pavilion" at the east end of the garden: "Too exotic," he told her. Mellon often worked in the late afternoons "changing and pruning plants" as she watched Kennedy at his desk. "I was aware of and touched," she recalled, "by the serious tranquility of this scene."

Jackie unveiled both the new White House library and Treaty Room in June. With its soft palette of colors and suite of Duncan Phyfe furniture, the library was intended to capture the classical period of Jefferson and Adams, two of the most "bookish" presidents. The room bore the strong imprint of Harry du Pont, although Boudin advised Jackie on the paint color and antique Aubusson rug. The 2,500 volumes still needed to be assembled by a committee of scholars including Arthur Schlesinger—a "working library," said Jackie, not a collection of price-less editions for "a frozen assemblage in a museum display."

The Treaty Room was discernibly Victorian, Jackie's least favorite period, but she recognized its value as what she called "the most his-toric room in the White House," filled entirely with authentic presi-dential furniture of "rather ugly charm." Most of the ponderous relics dated from Lincoln and Grant. Jackie covered the walls in flocked dark green wallpaper trimmed in a red diamond–patterned border copied from the room where Lincoln died—a dramatic design conceived en-tirely by Boudin. To emphasize the room's purpose as a setting for his-toric events, Jackie hung reproductions of famous treaties signed when the cabinet met there regularly in the second half of the nineteenth century.

On the same early summer day that Jackie opened the Treaty Room, she received the first copies of the new White House guidebook. Stand-ing in the West Wing's Fish Room, the President read aloud from Jackie's foreword, which she had rewritten in a more conversational style than Schlesinger's elegiac version. She told of expanding her orig-inal idea of aiming the book at children to include "adults and scholars also . . . on the theory that it never hurts a child to read something that may be above his head." In keeping with Jackie's wish not to seem "conceited," she included only one image of herself, sitting in the East Room audience as Pablo Casals played the cello.

TWENTY-ONE

During his second summer in the White House, Jack Kennedy experienced a sharp drop in his approval rating. By September it reached a new low of 62 percent—not as bad as Eisenhower's 56 percent in September 1958, or Truman's 43 percent at the same time in 1950. Still, given Kennedy's 79 percent approval as recently as March, the plunge was unnerving.

Kennedy failed even to get much of a bounce from a splashy three-day trip to Mexico at the end of June. The Kennedys drew a tumultuous welcome from more than a million people in Mexico City. Once again, the people and press were enchanted by Jackie's beauty, and her Cassini-designed dresses in shimmering "sun colors" of pink, azure, yellow, and green.

For all the regal aspects of the quick tour, it was Jackie's down-to-earth manner that caught the emotions of Mexicans. At a luncheon given by President Adolfo López Mateos, she delivered from memory a short speech in impeccable Spanish. Betraying slight nervousness, she rubbed her hands occasionally as she spoke of "the underlying values" of the Mexican culture, "the profound faith in man's dignity" shown in the country's art and literature. The *Washington Post* detected no shift in the Mexican-American political equation but a "change in the attitude on the part of government and people" in America's southern neighbor.

Only days after the Kennedys returned to Washington, Jackie left for a summer holiday that would again last more than three months. For greater privacy and security, the Kennedys rented a seven-bedroom home in Hyannis owned by tenor Morton Downey, a longtime family friend. It was on Squaw Island, a half mile from the family compound and connected to the mainland by a short causeway. Teddy and Joan's house was across the road.

During the summer of 1962, Jackie was more detached from her official duties than she had been the previous year—in part because she had reached so many of her goals in the White House restoration, but also because she wished more than ever to escape the pressures of her role. Like Bess Truman before her, Jackie considered her time away from Washington sacrosanct. When the president of Ecuador came for a state visit, it was Rose who accompanied JFK to the capital, and when the wives of bankers from the International Monetary Fund met at the White House for tea, Janet Auchincloss flew down from Newport to be their hostess.

Instead of talking to her staff on the phone, Jackie began taping instructions on Dictabelts that were sent to Washington by the Army Signal Corps. "She became more remote," said Janet Cooper. "I felt it was because of Tish, who was very demanding, telling Jackie to do things, and Jackie didn't want to hear it." Still, Jackie was "very organized. She had the memos down pat. She asked a million questions, wanted to know thoroughly what everything was. She was very much on top of things."

In his press conferences and other public appearances, Kennedy was unvaryingly upbeat despite bouts of severe back pain. Summoned to the White House after the steel crisis, Max Jacobson found JFK "tense and apprehensive." Following a treatment, Jacobson recorded that Kennedy "smiled and said, 'Now I can go downstairs to shake hands with several hundred intimate friends.'" In May the President's special bed had appeared for the first time in the White House screening room to enable him to watch films in greater comfort. A month later he needed to take one of his rocking chairs to a dinner party in the garden of Jean Smith's Georgetown home. In midsummer Stas Radziwill told Cy Sulzberger that Kennedy's "back still bothers him, and he can't play golf."

Under those circumstances, Kennedy's stamina in meetings was remarkable—a phenomenon witnessed by his closest advisers, but only revealed publicly decades later with the disclosure of a secret taping system that he installed on July 28 and 29 in the Oval Office, Cabinet Room, and "study/library" (probably the Treaty Room) on the second floor of the Executive Mansion. Kennedy recorded just those conversations and meetings he wished to preserve by the flip of a switch.

The existence of the system was known only to its technicians, members of the Secret Service, Evelyn Lincoln, Bobby Kennedy and his secretary Angie Novello, and possibly Kenny O'Donnell. Vice President Johnson remained in the dark until he became president, when he decided to expand the system and tape far more extensively. Richard Nixon would install an even more elaborate voice-activated system for his presidency.

Kennedy kept his rationale for the recording system to himself. He doubtless was thinking of his own memoirs and the needs of future historians. Much of what he recorded cast him in a favorable light, displaying his ability to move seamlessly from one issue to the next across the day, and to immerse himself in each topic with commendable mastery. But the whirring tapes captured moments of profanity, pettiness, and temper. He also chose to begin the recordings when his popularity was at a low ebb, the economy was stalled, and he faced growing crises in foreign policy.

Only two weeks earlier, *Newsweek* had written that critics on both the right and left were castigating him simultaneously for being "a power-drunk dictator" (for his performance in the steel crisis) and an "ineffectual rhetorician" (for his legislative quagmire). Despite JFK's efforts to placate the business community and signs that the stock market was gaining strength, business investment continued to lag, unemployment was rising, and Kennedy's economic advisers were privately worrying about a recession. Congress had defeated Kennedy's "cherished" Medicare legislation by 52 to 48, and influential columnists like Walter Lippmann were pressing him for a "quickie" tax cut to kick start the economy. After lying dormant for nearly a year, Berlin had re-emerged as an issue as well, with intermittent Soviet harassment in the air corridors to West Berlin and distant rumblings from Khrushchev about signing the peace treaty that would expel the Allies from the city.

Kennedy's singular success was the completion of the Geneva Accords on Laos toward the end of July—more than a year after tortuous negotiations began following the cease-fire arranged by the United States and Russia. The shaky coalition government was now buttressed by international agreement, and its neutrality was guaranteed. Still, Kennedy worried that the Pathet Lao would violate the agreement, and wondered how the United States should react.

The first day of taping in the White House on Monday, July 30, showed that Kennedy's closest advisers had grown comfortable enough in his presence to joke as well as express firm opinions. When Kennedy started to denounce diplomats who "don't seem to have cojones," especially one who didn't "present a very virile figure," Dean Rusk disagreed. But Kennedy persisted, railing against "languid" American diplomats who didn't seem "hard and tough" compared to the new Soviet envoy, Anatoly Dobrynin, who appeared "assured and confident." Mac Bundy laughingly dismissed the Russian as an "aircraft engineer" and sided with Rusk to defend American diplomats, saying "the appearance is somewhat deceptive." Kennedy ended the conversation by resurrecting the memory of his father's counselor in London, Herschel Johnson, "an old lady if you ever saw one . . . He used to call my father Jeeves, which drove my father mad."

Such moments of recorded levity were rare, as Kennedy kept the focus on details and pressed for new ideas. Later that day he shifted from an hour-long meeting on the economy to an intricate two-hour discussion of a nuclear test ban that included myriad technical details of monitoring seismic signals from underground explosions. Faced with disagreement among his men about the number of on-site inspections to request from Khrushchev, Kennedy effectively synthesized their arguments as the meeting drew to a close. His temporary solution was to bring in wise men Robert Lovett and John McCloy for further discussions.

That night, following an off-the-record interview with investigative journalist Clark Mollenhoff, Jack entertained Mary Meyer and railroad executive Bill Thompson. It was hardly a tranquil interlude, with interruptions for phone calls from Dean Rusk, Lee Radziwill, Jackie (twice), Peter Lawford, and Pierre Salinger. The first phone conversation JFK had the next morning was with Helen Chavchavadze, whom he had seen ten days earlier during a Potomac cruise on the *Sequoia*.

Meyer showed up on the White House entry logs five evenings in the summer of 1962—once in June, twice in July, once in August, and once the Wednesday after Labor Day weekend. Jim Reed, who had separated from his wife, Jewel, in June, recalled attending one of those dinners along with Ben and Tony Bradlee. Reed thought Meyer had "a lovely way about her. . . . She was quiet, very much of a lady." Although Jack and Meyer were "very friendly," Reed saw no hint of intimacy.

"It was mostly Ben and the President talking," said Reed. "I couldn't get a word in." Ben was baiting JFK about Frank Morrissey, a longtime retainer for Joe Kennedy who was a municipal court judge in Boston. The previous year Kennedy had tried to appoint Morrissey to the federal bench, but had backed away when bar associations found him unfit. "Bradlee was critical, and Jack defended it," said Reed. "It was lively and interesting."

James Truitt later claimed that during Meyer's visit on July 16, she and the President smoked marijuana together—an allegation that was never independently corroborated. Truitt made his revelation to the *National Enquirer,* which published an article in its March 2, 1976, issue about JFK's affair with Meyer. Truitt had been suffering from alcoholism and mental illness since the early sixties, and he sold his story to the newspaper for $1,000. He said his information came from notes he made of conversations with Meyer during the Kennedy presidency.

Meyer did confide in James Truitt, but not until late in 1962, some six months after she told Anne about the affair. During that period, said Anne Truitt, James was often "drunk and out of control." Like others in the art world, Mary experimented with marijuana. "Mary was a risk taker," said Kenneth Noland. "She was quite curious about a lot of things." But Noland—and the Bradlees, for that matter—knew nothing of such behavior with Jack Kennedy. Nor did Meyer tell Anne about drug use in the White House.

Ben, Tony, and Anne all read a diary kept by Meyer that the Bradlees found after her death in 1964. In later years much was made of the supposedly explosive information about Kennedy that the diary contained. The diary's disclosure of an affair with JFK stunned the Bradlees, and

Tony "was devastated," said Ben. But the "little notebook with a pretty cover," as Anne Truitt described it, consisted mostly of jottings about Mary's art, and paint swatches on otherwise blank pages. Only about ten pages were devoted to Kennedy, who was never mentioned by name.

Anne, who had been told about the diary by Meyer, was "just floored" to find it was "nothing, nada, a series of scrawls and notes, not in order, no chronology, no real facts." Tony considered it "very cryptic. You had to sort of interpret. It wasn't a fascinating look at the whole situation at all. It was more like putting images that were in her mind, the atmosphere when she saw Jack." Said Ben Bradlee, "No entry was more than twenty-five words. They were tiny little things. There was nothing about dope in the diary at all." Still, "it was perfectly obvious that Mary was describing the affair," he said, "and that it was obviously the President of the United States. There were phrases like, 'At the party the other night,' and it was obvious which party it was."

After James Truitt's interviews with the *National Enquirer*, Tony decided to destroy the diary. She called Anne Truitt (by then divorced from James), who lived across the street in Washington, and they watched the notebook burn in Tony's fireplace. "Everyone thought it was full of all kinds of gossip which it wasn't," said Tony. "I think I burned it because there was interest in the diary, and I didn't want the kids to get into it."

In June 1962, Jack Kennedy gave a television interview to Eleanor Roosevelt about his Commission on the Status of Women. By way of example, he singled out graduates of Radcliffe, whose "curve of academic excellence . . . is higher than it is at Harvard." He expressed regret that these young women "get married, many of them become housewives. . . . I wonder whether they have had the full opportunity to develop their talents, and as the Greeks said, the definition of happiness is full use of your powers along the lines of excellence. And I wonder whether they have had that opportunity."

Kennedy's special Radcliffe friend, Diana de Vegh, could find little comfort in the Greek credo. After more than a year on JFK's staff, she was having difficulty dealing with their occasional surreptitious meetings. From time to time she saw other men socially; besides Billy Brammer, she went out with Mary Meyer's former husband Cord, then forty-two, who also dated Jill "Faddle" Cowan. At age twenty-four, de Vegh was feeling disillusioned about her work and thought Kennedy seemed indifferent to her.

De Vegh was unaware of Mary Meyer and Helen Chavchavadze, nor did she detect the appearance of a still younger woman on Kennedy's radar that summer. She was nineteen-year-old Marion "Mimi" Beardsley (later Mimi Fahnestock), who came to the White House for an internship after her freshman year at Wheaton College in Massachusetts. As the editor of the newspaper at Farmington, she had originally asked Tish Baldrige to help arrange an interview with the First Lady for a profile of the school's most famous alumnus. Baldrige provided background material and arranged Beardsley's visit to Washington in 1961. While she was in the White House, Beardsley "was brought over and met with the President," said Barbara Gamarekian. The young woman also met Farmington graduate Priscilla "Fiddle" Wear. A year later, at Wear's invitation, Beardsley came to work in Pierre Salinger's office. In June 1962, shortly after her arrival at the White House, Beardsley began what she later described as "a sexual relationship" with JFK.

"She wasn't in the office very long before the press began to ask why she was there," recalled Gamarekian. "Mimi had no skills. She couldn't type. . . . She was a bright girl. She could answer the telephone and she could handle messages. . . . But she was not really a great asset to us." Customarily the assignments for presidential trips rotated among the office girls. In the summer of 1962, however, Mimi "made all the trips!" said Gamarekian. "She loved the summer job, so she didn't want to go back to school." Finally, at the insistence of her family, Beardsley returned to Wheaton that autumn.

Diana de Vegh's father had died in the spring of 1962, and three or four months later, she confided her unhappiness to Marc Raskin on the NSC staff. Her colleague was aware of the romance with Kennedy "in this way that people know things around the White House," Raskin recalled. But when she spoke of her sadness, he urged her to escape. She went to Mac Bundy to say she was leaving. He inquired about her plans, and she told him she intended to live in Paris. Jack Kennedy also asked what she wanted to do, and said he hoped to see her again. After living in France, she returned to the United States and became an actress, eventually joining the cast of the daytime television drama *All My Children*. Along the way she earned a master's in social work at

Columbia University, worked at a liberal think tank in Washington, and found her métier as a psychotherapist.

As Diana de Vegh was escaping, Marilyn Monroe was falling apart. Following her performance for Jack Kennedy's birthday, Monroe began telling people in Hollywood that she and the President were having an affair. JFK cut off contact with her, but she started calling Bobby Kennedy's office, presumably asking for his intercession. "Phone records show conversations," said RFK biographer Evan Thomas. "She was a very troubled woman." Bobby became involved in "damage control" and, according to Thomas, "saw her on four occasions," although Thomas doubted the allegations that Bobby slept with her too.

Fearful that the Monroe stories would surface in Hollywood gossip columns, JFK asked George Smathers for help. The Florida senator later said he dispatched a friend to persuade Monroe to stop talking. In her last interview, with Richard Meryman of *Life* magazine in midsummer 1962, Monroe said nothing incriminating about the President. Instead she confessed to stage fright before singing "Happy Birthday": "You think, 'By God, I'll sing this song if it's the last thing I ever do.' "

She seemed downbeat but impressively lucid about the "special burden" of fame. "You kind of run into human nature in a raw kind of way," she said. "It stirs up envy, fame does. . . . It warms you a bit but the warming is temporary." Twice she echoed comments Jackie had made earlier, saying, "I've always had too much fantasy to be only a housewife" and "I just hate to be a thing"—not unlike Jackie's observation at the inauguration: "I felt as though I had just turned into a piece of public property."

Meryman's interview was published on Friday, August 3. The next day, Monroe called Peter Lawford, who was sufficiently alarmed by her slurred speech to alert the actress's manager. Assured by Monroe's housekeeper that she was fine, the manager did nothing. On Sunday the fifth, Monroe was found dead. Lawford notified JFK, who had spent a sunny afternoon on a five-hour cruise with his family aboard the *Patrick J,* a sixty-four-foot navy yacht—Jack lounging in the cockpit, Jackie water-skiing behind a small speedboat. Kennedy made no public comment on the superstar's death.

The *Washington Post*'s banner headline on Monday reported: "MARILYN MONROE IS FOUND DEAD: SLEEPING DRUG OVER-

DOSE IS TENTATIVELY BLAMED." That morning, moments after alighting from his helicopter on the South Lawn, Kennedy jovially greeted a group of teenage performers on hand for the fourth of Jackie's concerts by young people. Throughout the hour-long performance, he kept the Oval Office door open so that he could hear the music. He met at midday with Arthur Schlesinger and August Heckscher, took a swim, and retired to the second floor for lunch. He didn't return to the office from the Executive Mansion until nearly 5 p.m. His last meeting of the day was with Wilbur Mills, where he learned that the powerful chairman of the House Ways and Means Committee opposed a "quickie tax cut." After an extended discussion the President agreed with Mills to stay on course with his plan to introduce tax reduction and reform legislation early in 1963. Forty-five minutes after Mills left the West Wing, Mary Meyer arrived in the mansion for the evening.

When Jack Kennedy said goodbye to Jackie and Caroline in Hyannis on that morning of August 6, it was his last glimpse of them for nearly a month. The next day mother and daughter left for a holiday on Italy's Amalfi coast with Lee, Stas, and their two children. The Kennedys flew on a commercial flight, in a specially prepared bedroom converted from a four-seat section of the first-class cabin.

They stayed in Villa Episcopio, a nine hundred–year-old home in Ravello, perched on a cliff 1,200 feet above the Bay of Salerno. On the evening of their arrival, the town illuminated its main square with hundreds of red, green, blue, and white decorative lights. Jackie took in the scene from her villa's high terrace a block away. Lee and Stas invited an assortment of friends including Gianni and Marella Agnelli, who stayed for a week; Arkady Gerney; Lee's close friend Sandro D'Urso; and Benno and Nicole Graziani, who were with Jackie for the entire vacation. "We went sightseeing and sailing," recalled Marella. "The conversation was extremely light. Benno made them laugh, which was a great advantage. Jackie and Lee were on very good terms. It was a real vacation in a different place."

For several days, Jackie and her party joined the Agnellis on cruises aboard their eighty-two-foot yacht, the *Agneta,* with its distinctive brown sails. They took one overnight trip to Capri, prompting Caroline to make "angry faces" when she was left behind in Ravello. Dining at the villa of the Agnellis' friend Irene Galitzine, Italy's top fashion designer, they were serenaded by three singers with guitars. Afterwards they danced at Number Two, Capri's most fashionable nightclub, until the early morning hours. On their return trip, they giddily sang "Volare." When the group returned to their beach house at Conca Dei Marini the next afternoon, Jackie, wearing a light blue blouse and white slacks, sat barefoot on the deck while the canvas sails billowed behind her.

Over the years, a number of accounts suggested that Jackie had gone off alone with Gianni that night. But Marella was also aboard, along with several other friends and Clint Hill, Jackie's chief Secret Service agent, who also attended the dinner in Capri. Nevertheless, one report decades later in *Vanity Fair* said that Jackie's cruise with Agnelli "was notable for a fair amount of kissing, caught on film by the paparazzi." That sort of public display of affection was entirely out of character for Jackie, and indeed no such photographs have ever turned up.

There are images of Jackie and Gianni walking along the dock, dining in cafes, relaxing on the yacht, and picnicking on a beach. Some pictures are artfully framed to suggest Jackie and Gianni were alone, but they were always in the company of friends and family. The raciest image shows Jackie in a black-and-white bathing suit holding a small bottle of suntan lotion in her right hand as Gianni bends over, his face touching her left forearm while he holds her wrist. Behind him is a woman in a bikini, looking down, and a man sunbathing beside her.

"There was nothing between Gianni and Jackie," said Benno Graziani, Gianni's closest friend. "We were with them the whole time." Added Lee Radziwill, "Obviously there is no truth in it whatsoever." Noted Countess Marina Cicogna, an intimate friend of both Agnellis, "It was not like Gianni" to have an affair with Jackie. "He didn't want to be involved in things that were complicated, and that would have been complicated. Also I'm not sure Jackie was the type he was attracted to."

Jackie wrote her first letter to "Dearest dearest Jack" on her third day in Italy. Her tone was wistful, her emotions slightly at bay. "I miss you very much," she began, "which is nice though it is also a bit sad— because it is always best to leave someone when you are happy & this was such a lovely summer." She noted that Caroline had fit in more readily with the Italian routines than she had, "but then I think of how

Marion "Mimi" Beardsley, a nineteen-year-old White House intern who began what she later described as "a sexual relationship" with JFK in June 1962.

"Mimi had no skills. She couldn't type. . . . She was a bright girl. . . . But she was not really a great asset to us."

66

67

In June 1962, artist Bernard LaMotte finishes painting scenes of St. Croix on the walls of the White House swimming pool, where JFK swam twice a day, often in the company of women on the West Wing staff.
"The President . . . swam around with us, chatting to us about our jobs. . . . We were sipping wine while swimming, and all the while Powers was on the sidelines."

Jackie with her sister, Lee, and Gianni Agnelli on August 14, 1962,
walking toward his yacht, the *Agneta*, for a cruise along the Amalfi coast.
*"I am having something you can never have—the absence of tension—no newspapers every day to
make me mad. I wish so much I could give you that. . . . But I can't give you that. So I give you
every day while I think of you—the only thing I have to give & I hope it matters to you."*

Jackie with Marella Agnelli at the base of one of the Greek temples
at Paestum during a cruise on the *Agneta* on August 15, 1962.
*"The conversation was extremely light. . . . Jackie and Lee were on very good terms.
It was a real vacation in a different place."*

JFK on the Coast Guard yacht *Manitou* in Narragansett Bay with Countess Vivian Crespi (left) and Nuala Pell (far left), September 2, 1962.

"Jack and I were great pals. He tried everything but I was never interested, because he wasn't my type, but we always stayed very close friends. When he married Jackie I couldn't believe he had the brains to choose her."

70

71

Jack Kennedy with his brother Teddy and a swarm of Kennedy children at the family compound on Cape Cod, September 3, 1962.
"This was a man who all his life was at home with women and kids and human situations."

Robert McNamara
and Deputy Secretary
of Defense Roswell
Gilpatric, both
favorites of Jackie.

*"Men can't understand
[Bob's] sex appeal."*

Adlai Stevenson escorts Jackie
to lunch in the delegates' dining
room at the United Nations on
February 7, 1963.

*"There was real rapport between
[Adlai] and Jackie. There was genuine
affection. . . . They always kissed each
other whenever they met."*

Jackie arrives at the National Theater with Alice Roosevelt Longworth and Bill Walton for a benefit performance of *Mr. President*, the Irving Berlin musical, on September 25, 1962.

"It was an evening to remove any remaining doubts that the magnetism of the Kennedys has become the hub of the social universe."

74

75

Jackie taking a jump while riding with the Middleburg Hunt in the autumn of 1962.

"I do not consider myself a part of the Hunt Country life. I appreciate the way people there let me alone."

Jackie with André Malraux at the National Gallery of Art on January 8, 1963, to open the exhibit of the *Mona Lisa,* which the French minister of culture had promised to her the previous May.

"She listened to him and wrote to him. Malraux was her prize."

Jackie at the *Mona Lisa* opening with the French ambassador, Hervé Alphand, and his wife, Nicole, only days before Charles de Gaulle rebuffed United States policies on nuclear weapons and British membership in the Common Market.

"The French have now been consigned to the deepest recesses of the doghouse by the President."

JFK with Paul Fout at Wexford, the new Kennedy home in Virginia, designed by Jackie, in the spring of 1963.

"It was a joke, that house. Jack didn't want it. What was he going to do there?"

At her farewell party on May 29, Tish Baldrige dances with J. B. West, the chief usher at the White House.

"When the President said goodbye to me in his office, he told me I was the most emotional woman he'd ever known."

79

80

Jack, Jackie, and Janet Auchincloss attend a dance performance by Caroline's class in the third-floor hallway outside the White House schoolroom on JFK's forty-sixth birthday, May 29, 1963.
"When people spoke [the Kennedy children] listened. They did not interrupt their elders."

JFK's forty-sixth birthday party, a dinner cruise on the Potomac aboard the *Sequoia* on May 29, 1963. To the left of JFK: Martha Bartlett, Lem Billings, Anita Fay, Teddy Kennedy, and Hjordis Niven. To the right of JFK: Fifi Fell, Bobby Kennedy, and Enüd Sztanko. In the foreground: British actor David Niven.
"[Jack] chased me all around the boat. A couple of members of the crew were laughing. I was running and laughing as he chased me."

Jack Kennedy opening his birthday presents on the *Sequoia*.
To the right of JFK: Red Fay, Jackie, and Fifi Fell (leaning over).
To the left of JFK: Ethel Kennedy and Lem Billings (back to camera).
"Kennedy ripped the wrappings of his presents with the speed and attention of a four-year-old child."

Jackie's thirty-fourth birthday on July 28, 1963, celebrated aboard the
Honey Fitz in Hyannis Port with friends and family, including (from left)
Lem Billings, Steve Smith, Jean Smith, and Chuck Spalding.
Two days earlier, JFK had announced agreement on a nuclear test-ban treaty.
"I think you would like the novel I gave Jackie called The Fox in the Attic.
It . . . has a haunting quality about it."

On Sunday, August 4, 1963, in Hyannis Port, JFK relaxes on the *Honey Fitz*
with Red and Anita Fay. The previous day they had learned that Phil Graham,
president and publisher of the *Washington Post*, had committed suicide.
"Jack was as upset as everyone else, but we couldn't dwell on it."

Jackie on the *Honey Fitz* on August 4, 1963. Three days later she would give birth prematurely to Patrick Bouvier Kennedy, who would die of complications from hyaline membrane disease after thirty-nine hours.

"It is so hard for Jackie. After all the difficulties she has in bearing a child, to lose him is doubly hard. . . . It would have been nice to have another son."

Jackie's longtime friend Nancy Tuckerman (left), Tish Baldrige's replacement as social secretary, and Pamela Turnure, Jackie's press secretary, bring flowers to the First Lady at the Otis Air Force Base hospital following the death of Patrick Kennedy.

"[Nancy] was the opposite of me, quiet, soft-spoken, not a zealot. . . . Obviously Jackie welcomed a change from the overly strong dose of managing I had given her."

Jack and Jackie leave the Otis
Air Force Base hospital on
August 14, 1963.

*"The President's anguish for
his wife and their dead son gave
August a melancholy cast."*

87

88

Joe Kennedy celebrating his seventy-fifth birthday in Hyannis Port with his family
on September 6, 1963. JFK is to the left. To the right: Sarge Shriver, Jean Smith,
Bobby Kennedy, and Pat Lawford. Later in the evening, JFK sang "September Song."
*"That was a killer, the old man in a wheelchair, the son singing.
You almost felt Jack knew he wasn't going to see old age."*

JFK with (from left) Tony Bradlee, Ruth Pinchot, and Mary Meyer in Milford, Pennsylvania, on the front porch of the Pinchot home, September 24, 1963.

"He was easy with both of us. There was no sexual thing evident. I always felt he liked me as much as Mary. You could say there was a little rivalry."

89

90

Jackie greets JFK on his arrival at Hammersmith Farm on September 12, 1963, to celebrate their tenth wedding anniversary.
"Without Jack as her husband, she told Charley, her life would have 'all been a wasteland, and I would have known it every step of the way.'"

On October 1, 1963, Jackie escorts the Ethiopian emperor, Haile Selassie, to a meeting with JFK in the Rose Garden, accompanied by Caroline (left) and a friend. The First Lady is wearing the full-length leopard coat that Selassie has just given to her.

"See, Jack! He brought it to me! He brought it to me!"

91

92

Jackie cruising the Aegean in October 1963 on the *Christina,* the luxurious yacht owned by the controversial Greek shipping tycoon Aristotle Onassis (standing, center). Franklin D. Roosevelt Jr. is seated to the right.

"I don't think Jack wanted Jackie to go. I think he was appalled by it."

Lem Billings with Jack, Jackie, and John Jr. at Wexford on Sunday, October 27, 1963—Billings's last weekend with the Kennedys.

"I got the feeling at the end that Jackie was trying to close Lem out."

93

The President and First Lady reviewing a
performance by the Black Watch Regiment of
bagpipers on the South Lawn, November 13,
1963—eight days before their scheduled
fundraising trip to Texas, Jackie's first
foray into the 1964 campaign.

*"She wanted to take a 'pass' on the Texas trip, citing the
advice of her doctors. But Jack wanted her at his side."*

On November 22, 1963, the presidential motorcade
makes its slow progress through the streets of Dallas,
Texas. Governor John Connally and his wife, Nellie,
are in the presidential limousine with the Kennedys.

"Mr. President, you can't say Dallas doesn't love you."

Charley Bartlett escorts Evelyn Lincoln
from an elevator at the Naval Medical
Center in Bethesda, Maryland, to join
other friends and Kennedy family members after JFK's assassination.

*"The Washington landscape seemed to me
to be littered with male widows."*

Jackie flanked by Bobby and Teddy Kennedy at the
Arlington National Cemetery grave site of Jack Kennedy.
"I really believe in God, I believe in heaven, but where has God gone?"

lucky I am to miss you—I know I exaggerate everything, but I feel sorry for everyone else who is married."

Jackie went on for ten pages to describe her activities. She lamented having missed JFK's calls, which couldn't get through the little Ravello switchboard. "I waited till 3 AM for the call—then they said it was an imposter . . . that happened again at 6 AM," she wrote. "I would love to talk to you—& if you have called & haven't gotten me please know I have waited 3 hours each time & then been told they 'lost connection.'" (He eventually got through—several times at 3 a.m.) She expressed relief at not having to worry about tax cuts and other pressing issues. "I am having something you can never have—the absence of tension—no newspapers every day to make me mad," she continued. "I wish so much I could give you that—I never realized till I got to another country how the tension is—But I can't give you that. So I give you every day while I think of you—the only thing I have to give & I hope it matters to you."

After two weeks, Jackie was enjoying her escape so much she decided to stay nearly two weeks more. "Jackie was very quiet, very nice, gentle and serene," said Benno Graziani. "She was cooking spaghetti for Caroline. She bought sandals in Capri. She took pictures. She was more simple, less sophisticated than when she was first lady. In Italy she was only a tourist." Jackie spoke expansively, telling Cy Sulzberger, a guest for several days, that she adored Lee, considered Bobby an "immensely ambitious" man who would never feel satisfied "until he has been elected to something, even Mayor of Hyannis Port," and thought that astronaut John Glenn (who six months earlier had been the first American to orbit the earth in space) was "the most controlled person on earth." Her own "highly self controlled" husband, who could "relax easily and sleep as and when he wishes," seemed "fidgety and loose" by comparison.

By the end of her sojourn, Jackie had been inducted as an honorary citizen of Ravello, and the Conca Dei Marini beach where they swam each day had been renamed by the town council "the Jacqueline Kennedy Beach." She and Caroline were reunited with Jack and John Jr. (who had spent the month with his grandmother Auchincloss) on the last day of August in Newport. Still unready to return to Washington, Jackie would remain with her children at Hammersmith Farm until early October.

Her exuberant behavior abroad sparked some carping in the American press, especially over the paparazzi pictures of her with Gianni Agnelli. "JACKIE'S BIG NIGHT IN PIRATE'S DEN," ran a headline in New York's *Daily News* on a story recounting her nightclub exploits. Katie Louchheim, by then a deputy assistant secretary of state working to promote cultural and educational programs overseas, was irked that Jackie's behavior would reflect badly on American women. Writing to a friend, Louchheim wondered "why Mrs. Kennedy had to go get herself all this daily exposure in bathing suits and pants, and was it to keep Caroline, as she always insists, from publicity that she took this voyage?" But, overall, the coverage was adoring, and Jackie's popularity didn't suffer.

Jackie knew all too well the impossibility of an "absence of tension" for her husband. His anxieties about world problems rose steadily while his wife was overseas. In early August, Kennedy had sent a message to Khrushchev through Georgi Bolshakov, Bobby's back-channel Soviet intelligence officer, asking that the Soviet leader put the Berlin matter "on ice" until after the congressional elections in early November. When Khrushchev made no immediate reply, Kennedy prodded his aides to prepare contingency plans to meet a provocation in that strategic city—including the possibility of using tactical nuclear weapons. He also asked Congress to authorize a call-up of 150,000 reservists to signal U.S. resolve to Moscow.

In late August, Cuba finally emerged as a significant problem—three months after Khrushchev and Castro concocted their nuclear missile plan. Bobby Kennedy's Operation Mongoose had accomplished little more than spying, and CIA chief John McCone was eager for the group to be more assertive. But during a review of Mongoose activities on August 20, Mac Bundy's main concern was avoiding any embarrassment "if it became known the Attorney General was running dirty tricks in favor of the counterinsurgency committee, which is essentially an overseas enterprise."

Two days later, McCone briefed Kennedy on the cause of his concern about Cuba: an ominous influx of Soviet military materiel and personnel arriving by merchant ship. McCone was convinced that the Russians intended to build a ballistic missile base on the island. Bundy and Rusk insisted to their boss that Khrushchev would not take such a risk. Nevertheless, Kennedy asked his advisers to explore strategies for dealing with a nuclear-armed Cuba, including a blockade ("an act of war," he noted) or invasion. "No one would desire more to see Castro thrown out of there," Kennedy said. "But throwing Castro out of there is a major military operation." Kennedy also requested a review of the fifteen Jupiter nuclear missiles installed in Turkey earlier in the year. "I will say that the Soviet Union exercises some restraint in some areas," JFK reminded his advisers. "We did as I say put missiles in Turkey with nuclear warheads, and they didn't take action."

On August 31 aerial reconnaissance ordered by Kennedy confirmed the presence of surface-to-air (SAM) missiles on Cuba. McCone considered these defensive weapons a mere prelude to missiles aimed at the southern United States. As Republican senator Kenneth Keating accused Kennedy of withholding information about a Cuban buildup, the President and his closest advisers worked out a statement cautioning the Soviet Union that the "gravest issues would arise" from any installation of offensive weapons.

Bobby had pressed his brother to issue the warning and had pushed for tough language as well. "We've got the Monroe Doctrine, and they've spit in our eye," Bobby sputtered. Rusk worried about "creating a kind of panic," while Dillon advised against "making a threat." As they debated the wording, JFK snapped at his brother, "You have to understand we're going to have to redo this." In the end, Rusk prevailed with softer language in the passive voice. Khrushchev responded through various messengers including Ambassador Dobrynin and back-channel man Bolshakov that the Soviet Union was only helping Cuba with its defense.

It wasn't until mid-September that Kennedy finally got a reply to his early-August message about Berlin. Stewart Udall had been in Moscow with his friend Robert Frost for a meeting with Russian poets when Khrushchev summoned both men to his Black Sea hideaway. In a two-hour discussion with Udall, Khrushchev revived his menacing ultimatum to "go to war or sign a peace treaty. . . . We will not allow your troops to be in Berlin." But, he added, "we won't do anything until November." Frost also had a long conversation with the Soviet leader. Speaking to reporters afterwards, the eighty-eight-year-old poet recounted that Khrushchev said Americans "were too liberal to fight." It was a statement JFK considered so unforgivable he would sever his relationship with the man whose words had helped set the tone for the Kennedy presidency.

———

The press picked up nothing about the contingency plans on Berlin and Cuba brewing in the White House. Kennedy appeared, as *Time* put it, the hard-working "summer bachelor . . . retiring to the deserted White House at dusk with sheaves of work under his arm." The President visited his twenty-one-month-old son only once at Hammersmith Farm during Jackie's trip to Italy. Kennedy insisted on staying in what his mother-in-law described as an "absolutely boiling hot" guest room. "He never complained," she recalled. "He would come off the boat about 3 o'clock in the afternoon . . . and then he would sit there and work."

In mid-August he took a long weekend in Maine to sail on several large Coast Guard craft with a crew including Red Fay, Chuck Spalding, Jim Reed, and Peter Lawford. They stayed at the home of former world heavyweight champion Gene Tunney, a family friend, on John's Island across from Boothbay Harbor. With Kennedy at the tiller, they sailed as far as Dark Harbor, some fifty miles away.

JFK's friends played their designated roles. Fay and Spalding supplied comic relief. Reed, now working as one of Doug Dillon's deputies, provided substance as Kennedy quizzed him on the investment tax credit bill making its way through Congress. With so many problems to face, Kennedy appeared to enjoy talking about legislation that seemed certain to lift the economy.

The following weekend Kennedy made a quick speechmaking jaunt out west, where he spent two afternoons at Peter Lawford's place in Santa Monica. Bored with the tranquility of the Lawford pool, Kennedy suddenly bolted through the gate and onto the beach. He was surrounded by women as he plunged into the surf. ("They swooned when he swam," wrote *Time*.) Just as Jackie was skimming across the Mediterranean waters "in perfect form on a single red and white ski," her husband was photographed dripping wet in his bathing trunks with adoring fans clutching his arms. Kennedy "likes pleasure and women," Hervé Alphand noted in his journal that week. "His desires are difficult to satisfy without causing concern for scandal and its use by his political adversaries. That might happen one day, since he doesn't take sufficient precaution in this puritan country."

When Jackie rejoined her husband, Newport swarmed with friends on a succession of balmy September weekends—Vivian Crespi, Bill Walton, the Reeds, Gores, Roosevelts, and Fays. While in Ravello, Jackie had planned the guest lists, telling Jack, "if you want more special [sic] I can arrange it." The one prominent absentee was Bradlee, who had irritated Kennedy with his comments to Fletcher Knebel for a *Look* magazine article in August about the President and the press.

Bradlee had cited a phone call from JFK about a *Newsweek* story on the Morrissey federal judgeship nomination. "It's almost impossible to write a story they like," Bradlee told Knebel. "Even if a story is quite favorable to their side, they'll find one paragraph to quibble with." Bradlee's candor about the Kennedy family requirement of "110 percent from their friends, especially their friends in the press" put him on ice for three months—from "dinner at the White House once and sometimes twice a week, and telephone calls as needed in either direction, to no contact."

Kennedy managed to carve out ten days in Newport starting in mid-September. The centerpiece of his holiday was the series of America's Cup races that the Kennedys and their guests watched from the deck of the *Joseph P. Kennedy Jr.* destroyer. Although Jim and Jewel Reed were separated, they showed up together "to present the semblance of a marriage," said Jewel. Jackie spent a long time one afternoon talking to Jim, which irked the Fays. "They were pumping Jim to find out what he and Jackie were talking about, but Jim was coy," recalled Jewel.

Ben Bradlee made a cameo appearance in a conspicuously nonsocial role when Kennedy summoned him to Newport for a "scoop." A rumor had been circulating for more than a year that before meeting Jackie, JFK had been secretly married to a Palm Beach socialite named Durie Malcolm. Over the summer several right-wing periodicals had promoted the story, so Kennedy offered Bradlee FBI files that he could use on background to debunk the story and those who were disseminating it. Bradlee wrote his article, and Kennedy approved it, yet the chill persisted. David Gore spotted the *Newsweek* man and asked if he was coming to the races. "No," Kennedy curtly interjected. "He's not coming."

Dressed in a blue yachting blazer with brass buttons, Jack Kennedy

peered through his binoculars at the twelve-meter sloop *Weatherly* de-
feating the America's Cup challenge from Australia's *Gretel,* while back
in Washington the centennial of the Emancipation Proclamation was
being celebrated in front of the Lincoln Memorial. Not only did Kennedy's absence from the ceremony fail to raise eyebrows, it was consistent with his hands-off approach to civil rights.

His point man on the issue, Bobby Kennedy, sat on the platform with
Arthur Schlesinger and Adlai Stevenson, who addressed the crowd of
three thousand, calling individual freedom "the great unfinished business of the world today." In a recorded message transmitted through
loudspeakers and broadcast on nationwide radio and television, JFK
sounded the same note as Stevenson, praising blacks for their "quiet
and proud determination" and rejection of "extreme or violent policies" in their efforts to secure equality.

On Monday, September 24, the last day of Jack's vacation, he and Jackie
hosted a lunch for Pakistani president Ayub Khan at Hammersmith
Farm—as they had the previous year for his Indian counterpart. That
evening Jackie flew with her husband to Washington for a two-night
visit. Tuesday night featured a performance at the National Theater of
Mr. President, a new Irving Berlin musical inspired by the Kennedy
administration, with the $70,000 proceeds benefiting two mental retar-
dation charities in memory of Jack's brother Joe. The crowd numbered
1,600 of what the *New York Times* called "the political and social elite of
Washington and New York." Among the administration luminaries
hosting pre-theater dinner parties were the Dillons, McNamaras, and
Johnsons, who had the front of their house decorated to resemble a
theater marquee. At the White House, the Kennedys entertained Rose,
Bill Walton, Alice Longworth, and Carlos Sanz de Santamaria, the Co-
lombian ambassador, and his wife.

The real "Mr. President" was well aware that the musical starring
Robert Ryan and Nanette Fabray had bombed during its Boston tryout.
While Jackie and their guests went to the theater, Jack stayed behind to
watch a heavyweight boxing match between Floyd Patterson and Sonny
Liston on closed-circuit television. Broadway producer Leland Hayward delayed the curtain by a half hour as JFK's new contoured red
leather rocker sat empty in the presidential box. Kennedy didn't show

up until intermission at ten-thirty. He seemed to spend more time studying his program than watching the stage, turning at one point to ask Bill Walton, "Was the first act as bad as the second?" With a twist dance number, a song titled "The Secret Service Makes Me Nervous," and a first lady riding a white sequined elephant, the show fell flat for the rest of the audience as well. "Dismal, corny, and hopelessly dated" was David Bruce's verdict.

The fun came after the final curtain, at a lavish midnight champagne supper dance for six hundred at the British Embassy, its terrace covered by a huge white silk tent decorated with gold braid, gold medallions, and ropes of hemlock and pine entwined with tiny white lights. Jack and Jackie sat at a table next to the dance floor with the Gores, Alphands, and de Santamarias.

"Everyone ogled everyone," Katie Louchheim recalled. A diamond tiara adorned Sissie's hair, and Jackie wore an exquisite gown made of pink and gold brocade that had been given to her by King Saud of Saudi Arabia. She chose Hervé Alphand as her first dance partner, only to have Charlie Wrightsman cut in. Jack wandered and chatted as usual, although he took to the dance floor twice—with Eunice and Natalie Cushing, Fifi Fell's daughter. David Bruce observed that both the President and First Lady "danced vigorously."

Even as Jack Kennedy's standing with the electorate had dropped, "it was an evening to remove any remaining doubts that the magnetism of the Kennedys has become the hub of the social universe," declared the *Washington Post*'s influential Maxine Cheshire. Jackie seemed eager to stay all night, but her husband took her hand at 2 a.m. They finally left thirty-five minutes later as many others "were still hot footing." "The only thing that had intruded on a memorable night," noted *Time,* "was that miserable play."

TWENTY-TWO

$\mathcal{S}$carcely a week after the Emancipation Proclamation Centennial, Kennedy was forced to face the violent undercurrents of race relations in America. The trouble stemmed from the efforts of twenty-eight-year-old James Meredith to register as the first black student at the defiantly segregationist University of Mississippi. Meredith's case had been winding through the legal system for nearly two years before a federal court ruled in his favor in September 1962. For four days in a row, starting on Tuesday, September 25, Meredith tried to register at the Ole Miss campus in Oxford and was turned back by forces directed by Governor Ross Barnett. In response, the Fifth Circuit Court of Appeals declared Barnett guilty of contempt.

At that stage, JFK canceled his scheduled weekend in Newport with his family and took charge. For the next forty-eight hours, Jack and Bobby reviewed various stratagems, even giving their approval to sneaking Meredith into the registration center so Barnett could save face by claiming he had been tricked. But 2,500 segregationists armed with guns, rocks, iron spikes, and Molotov cocktails stymied the plan by encircling the Lyceum, the school's administration building that was protected by federal marshals. (Unbeknownst to the mob, Meredith was safe in a dormitory, surrounded by armed guards.) As JFK gave a televised speech on Sunday night saying that Meredith would register unhindered the following day, a riot broke out. By the time the U.S. Army arrived near dawn on Monday morning to restore order, more than two hundred people had been injured and two men had died, including a French journalist.

To oversee the tense situation, Kennedy gathered his closest domestic advisers—O'Donnell, O'Brien, and Sorensen, who left the hospital bed where he had been confined for a week recovering from an ulcer attack—along with Bobby and aide Burke Marshall. They shuttled between the Cabinet Room and Oval Office for more than six hours on Sunday night starting at 10:40 p.m., sustained by milk, beer, and cheese snacks served by Evelyn Lincoln.

The atmosphere was chaotic as they communicated by telephone alternately with Barnett and Justice Department officials in the Lyceum. They heard reports of shootings and dealt with false rumors such as a bulletin from Bobby that Meredith's dorm was under siege. "You don't want to have a lynching!" exclaimed O'Donnell. Yet the deep camaraderie between Kennedy and his men was evident in their intermittent bursts of jocularity.

"Where is Nick? [Deputy Attorney General Nicholas Katzenbach, posted inside the Lyceum] Is he up in the attic?" asked JFK amid laughter. "He's in the pillbox," said Sorensen. Later Kennedy chuckled and observed, "I haven't had such an interesting time since the Bay of Pigs," to which Bobby replied, "The Attorney General announced today he's joining Allen Dulles at Princeton University."

Kennedy frequently fretted about reported injuries. "Did he break his back? Did it break his back?" JFK urgently inquired when told that a state trooper had been wounded. But despite the attacks by rioters, the President opposed a return of fire by the marshals. As the hours slipped by, Kennedy and his men grew angry over the army's slow progress from Memphis, Tennessee, to Oxford. O'Donnell growled, "I would think they'd be on that fucking plane in about five minutes. . . . I have a hunch that Khrushchev would get those troops in faster." Yet moments later, O'Donnell had the group laughing when he told a story about a *Boston Post* reporter calling the governor to say, "Your daughter's car has been found cracked up on the Cape. Do you have any statement?" "Certainly," the governor replied. "The thief must be apprehended."

Although Kennedy was often exasperated, he and his men maintained a calm detachment. "If you ever made a chronological listing of the reports we've gotten over that phone in the last three hours, it wouldn't make any sense at all," said Sorensen shortly before 2 a.m. Yet Kennedy paid no political penalty either for the mayhem in Mississippi or the federal government's miscues and haphazard response. The evening after the all-night ordeal, Kennedy was relaxed enough to entertain Mary Meyer and Bill Thompson for dinner. With the protection of some five thousand national guardsmen and soldiers, James Meredith enrolled at Ole Miss, and the crisis was soon overtaken by world events.

The First Lady, Caroline, and John finally came home on Tuesday, October 9. In the aftermath of an eight-part *Washington Post* series on her White House restoration project in September, Jackie faced some unanticipated challenges in pursuing her plans. The series by Maxine Cheshire had hit within days of Jackie's return from Ravello. It was filled with praise for her effort to "transform the White House into a dazzling showcase of Americana." Cheshire emphasized Jackie's reputation as a "terrible tightwad" with taxpayer money, and her skill in raising an unprecedented hundreds of thousands through her "soft sell" with private donors. Yet Cheshire also highlighted the extravagance of some expenditures—"$28,000 [$166,000 today] for weaving special gold and magenta fabrics in an exclusive design" for the Red Room.

The worst part was Cheshire's revelation that a much praised Baltimore desk in the Green Room was a fake—a disclosure that embarrassed its donor, Mrs. Maurice Noun of Des Moines, Iowa, as well as Jackie, who had singled out the desk during her televised tour. The *Post* series also unmasked the secret role of the "mustached and dapper" Stéphane Boudin, and the shopping expeditions in France by Jayne Wrightsman. Cheshire predicted that under Boudin's influence, the Green Room would become chartreuse and the Blue Room's walls a white striped silk—"Boudin's Boudoir," in Harry du Pont's words. She described the effort to evoke Malmaison in the Red Room even as the White House sought to "play down the French influence in the White House today." The notion of such a dominant role for a non-American designer using European furniture, fabric, and objects offered opportunities for mischief to Kennedy's political opponents.

The series caught Jackie completely off guard. Cheshire usually wrote favorably about the Kennedy administration, but like other "news-hens" covering the East Wing, she met with undisguised disdain from Jackie. Once, when liberal columnist Doris Fleeson appeared at a White House luncheon for women journalists, Jackie said, "Oh, Doris, what in the world would you be doing here with these others?" in a voice audible to all the "others" nearby in the receiving line. Laura Bergquist recalled that Jackie "wouldn't even recognize [the] existence" of Helen Thomas and Frances Lewine, the famous "harpies" in Jackie's journal-istic demonology.

From the deck of the *Joseph P. Kennedy Jr.* during the America's Cup, Jackie had scrawled a twelve-page letter of "seething indignation" to Harry du Pont about the Cheshire series. "If you were appalled," wrote Jackie, "multiply your reaction by 1,000,000 & you will have mine." Jackie viewed Cheshire as clever but one of the "more malicious of the charming female press who do so much to make the children and my lives a pleasure." JFK had been incensed about the Baltimore desk in particular: "He told Bill Elder that it was criminal to have let Mrs. Noun be placed in such a humiliating position." Jackie declined to blame Elder, a "diligent, dedicated & un-temperamental man—a joy to have as curator." (Elder had been appointed after the resignation of Lorraine Pearce at the end of the summer.) His only failing was inexpe-rience and naïveté "about the fierce white light that is always trained on the W. House." Jackie's big regret was not learning of the series soon enough to have "handled it correctly—with the *Post* editors."

Jackie fretted that if the articles were to create a political brouhaha, she would have to cease work on the Green and Blue Rooms. "Messrs Scalamandré & Jansen will just find themselves with a lot of unused material on their hands," she wrote, "and Maxine Cheshire can just have that on her conscience the rest of her life." The lesson, Jackie said, was that "if we are to complete something that is *so* important—the silence of the tomb is necessary. . . . Why are some people so avid for publicity—when it poisons everything. I hate & mistrust it & no one who has ever worked for me who liked it has been trustworthy."

Jackie's alarm subsided as she engaged in skillful damage control that enabled her to proceed as planned with the restoration. She directed Pam Turnure to vet a *Newsweek* cover story on the restoration, excising such references as a "chartreuse" Green Room and the prospect of a white Blue Room. "The room will remain blue," Turnure told *News-week*'s Charles Roberts. "No decision has been made for fabric for walls." Months earlier Jayne Wrightsman and Jackie had indeed chosen a white on white striped silk with a blue fabric border to carry out Boudin's idea of evoking a tent room at Malmaison.

One particularly happy development on Jackie's return from Newport was the arrival from Paris of a trompe l'oeil wardrobe for her dressing room. On its doors were images by turns obvious and enigmatic, designed by Boudin and painted on canvas by artist Pierre-Marie Rudelle, representing what Jackie called "mes objets adorés." The idea for the wardrobe came late in 1961 from Bunny Mellon, who had a similar trompe l'oeil of her own life in a gallery between her greenhouses in Virginia.

Jackie's wardrobe featured books written by Jack (*Profiles in Courage, Why England Slept,* and a collection of speeches titled *The Strategy of Peace*); a photo of six-year-old Jackie with her father at a horse show; the *Life* spread of Marshall Hawkins's picture of her flying off Bit of Irish across a fence; a nineteenth-century engraving of the White House; paintings by jeweler Fulco di Verdura and Philippe Julian; a book about the Roosevelt family; Fabergé clocks; Jackie's sculpture of Madame de Pompadour as a sphinx; a piece of coral that Jack kept as a souvenir from his shipwreck during World War II; and *Les Fleurs du mal,* nineteenth-century poet Charles Baudelaire's intensely evocative and somewhat decadent collection. In her *Vogue* essay at age twenty-one, Jackie had described Baudelaire and Oscar Wilde as "poets and idealists who could paint their sinfulness with honesty and still believe in something higher."

Jackie immediately thanked Boudin for the "miracle" he had produced. "I am flabbergasted!!!!!" she wrote, calling the wardrobe "more beautiful than all my adored objects, and I am in heaven when I am there." She said JFK liked it so much that he wanted to move it to the Blue Room. She also professed concern that her husband would appear at her door with a visiting dignitary to see the wardrobe, "so I am always coiffed and wearing a peignoir from Worth." As for Boudin's Treaty Room, Jackie said JFK now preferred to sign bills and treaties in that historic setting rather than the Oval Office. She slyly added that if her husband were to move his office upstairs and "receives his visitors in my bedroom, I will tell you it will restrain him a bit."

With Caroline approaching her fifth birthday, her parents needed to place her in kindergarten that autumn. Jackie wanted to keep her in the White House for another year, so she created a fully professional school. The previous spring, the two preschool teachers Anne Mayfield and Jackie Marlin had decided to leave—in Marlin's case, because she was pregnant. Marlin had told no one of her condition, so she was astonished after Easter break when the First Lady exclaimed, "Jackie, you're pregnant!" "She saw the look on my face," Marlin recalled. "Don't worry," the First Lady said, "I have a sixth sense. I can always tell when someone is pregnant."

To accommodate all the children of varying ages already enrolled, the First Lady hired two experienced teachers for separate nursery and kindergarten classes, enlarged the size of the school from fourteen to twenty, and expanded the schedule to five mornings a week. She also enriched the curriculum with instructors for twice-weekly lessons in music and dance.

The two new teachers, Alice Grimes, who taught Caroline's class, and Elizabeth Boyd, who took charge of the younger group, were typically "safe" in their backgrounds. A graduate of Sarah Lawrence (where Lee had studied briefly), Grimes had been teaching kindergarten at the Brearley School in New York. Grimes recruited Boyd, who had graduated from Farmington (where she had known Lee) and Vassar and was a kindergarten teacher at the Potomac School outside Washington.

Jackie knew she could count on both women to keep the school's activities and participants secret. Grimes received several press inquiries in the beginning but understood that "it was a given" to refer everything to the press office. "We were very private people," said Boyd. "At Potomac we were taught you do not discuss your children at social occasions outside the school. In Washington you whisper, and everyone knows everything."

Still, before the school year began, the White House itself breached the confidentiality rule for political reasons. On the eve of the Emancipation Proclamation Centennial, the press office had announced the enrollment of the son of Deputy Press Secretary Andrew Hatcher, one of three black officials (with George Weaver in the Labor Department and Carl Rowan at the State Department) in the Kennedy administration. Five-year-old Avery, the youngest of seven Hatcher children, was meant to be an important symbol of Kennedy's belief in integration at a particularly charged time.

On Wednesday, October 10, only one night after Jackie's homecoming, she and Jack gave the season's first full-fledged dinner party, which turned into an unusual high-wire act for Jack. On the guest list were Najeeb Halaby, head of the Federal Aviation Administration, and his wife; James Truitt, now working as Phil Graham's deputy at the *Washington Post,* and Anne, whom Jackie knew from the White House school; Bill Walton; architect John Warnecke; and Mary Meyer—the first time she had been part of an intimate gathering in Jackie's presence since the *Advise and Consent* luncheon a year earlier.

Walton had brought Mary (who had last seen JFK nine days earlier), but his link that evening was more with Warnecke. Since the early days after the inaugural, Walton had been working to save Lafayette Square. His initial efforts had met little success, and both he and Kennedy had resigned themselves to the destruction of the nineteenth-century homes on the square's edge—until Jackie forcefully intervened in the spring of 1962. "The wreckers haven't started yet," Jackie said to the two men. "Until they do, it can be saved." By coincidence, Red Fay brought Warnecke, a friend from San Francisco, to visit Kennedy, who asked the architect's help with the square. Kennedy was an admirer of Warnecke, a handsome former football star at Stanford nicknamed "Rosebowl" by Fay.

Warnecke came up with a compromise design that retained the townhouses on the east and west sides of the square, with modern brick buildings of eight to ten stories set back behind them. The scheme, in the view of Kennedy arts adviser August Heckscher, indicated the President's "conservative taste." It also captured Jackie's preference for buildings neither too contemporary nor resembling "some State School for the Deaf" from the nineteenth century.

Jackie twice found JFK and Walton on the floor working over models of the square with paper facades. But it was Jackie, Walton later said, who "played a key part. . . . She kept us at it." As a member of the Commission of Fine Arts, Walton remained the Kennedys' personal advocate for the project.

Warnecke had come to town in October 1962 to unveil the plan for Lafayette Square to the press, and the White House dinner was intended to celebrate the victory for historic preservation. James Truitt was included because he had put Warnecke together with Nathaniel Owings, the architect selected by Jack Kennedy to plan another pet project, the redevelopment of the dilapidated stretch of Pennsylvania Avenue running from the White House to the Capitol.

Yet for both Jack and Jackie, the evening came at an inconvenient moment. She was dealing with the details of her reentry, and he was more preoccupied than usual with domestic and foreign problems. At a hastily scheduled meeting with John McCone that day, the President had learned that Soviet Ilyushin-28s, bombers with a range of around 1,500 miles, were now in Cuba—the first sign of weapons with an offensive capability. Kennedy had been so rattled by the news that he had told McCone to conceal it from other members of the administration.

Kennedy was also concerned about the coming midterm elections. Against the advice of some of his advisers, he had begun campaigning for Senate and congressional candidates. Schlesinger in particular had warned him that his prestige would suffer if the Democrats fared badly on election day—as the party in power usually did at midterm. But Kennedy was determined to push for more northern moderate Democrats to tilt the balance on Capitol Hill in his favor. To help the campaign, he had committed to speak for fifteen minutes at a rally in Baltimore that evening. As a result, he could just stay for cocktails until eight and return after dinner to join the group for coffee.

As the guests gathered in the Yellow Oval Room, only Anne knew about Jack's affair with Mary. Anne recalled that the two lovers were "polite and plain," exchanging no telling glances. Standing on the Truman Balcony to see the landing of the helicopter that would transport Kennedy to Baltimore, "it was the only time I felt sheer power," said Anne. After some pleasantries with the President, they all watched him take off from the South Lawn.

When Kennedy returned, Anne Truitt began to feel that just being there was a mistake. "I think I was corrupt," she recalled. "I knew the President and Mary were having an affair. I should never have put my feet under Jackie Kennedy's table."

———

By October, Jackie had made most of her major decisions for the White House restoration. Custom silk fabrics for the Green and Blue Rooms were being woven, and the furniture and art had been acquired. She looked forward to having everything installed by mid-January.

Her newest project, conducted in even greater secrecy than her work on the Executive Mansion, was a country house in Virginia. Using Paul Fout as a front man, she and Jack had paid a bargain price of $26,000 for thirty-nine acres of prime land on Rattlesnake Mountain between Middleburg and Upperville, near a tiny crossroads called Atoka. For Jack, it was a grudging commitment—even when Jackie christened the property "Wexford" after the Kennedys' county of origin in Ireland. After nearly two years, he had grown no fonder of life in the hunt country. Back in July, Stas Radziwill had reported to Cy Sulzberger that Kennedy "hates Virginia and Glen Ora, detests horses."

During the summer, JFK had spent his first weekend at Camp David and "rather liked it, primarily because it's in Maryland and not Virginia." Situated on 125 wooded acres, the official presidential hideaway (originally named Shangri-La by FDR) atop the Catoctin Mountains was a compound of cabins with names like "Aspen" and "Hickory." The camp had a pool, skeet-shooting range, stables, a playground, and miles of hiking trails. Yet Jackie was dismissive of the retreat's "motel shacks with their bomb shelters churning underneath."

Although Kennedy routinely brought pals to Virginia, he found weekends there tiresome. "I always knew he would call me Sunday at Glen Ora, at noon promptly. He was bored," Labor Secretary Arthur Goldberg told Katie Louchheim. Kennedy's aversion was so widely known that when he and Jackie attended the French play *A Shot in the Dark* that autumn, the audience roared when one of the characters said, "I myself do not like the country. It is my wife who likes horses and the hunt."

But Jackie was determined to build a house on a piece of land where both her own Orange County Hunt and Paul Mellon's Piedmont Hunt could gallop across the rolling countryside. She chose the property for its seclusion: its former owner, local newspaper publisher Hubert Phipps, controlled a thousand surrounding acres, and the Mellons owned the four hundred acres of adjacent land. The nearest road was two miles down a winding driveway.

Jackie sketched out on graph paper a 3,500-square-foot ranch-style dwelling with three sides around an enclosed courtyard—seven bedrooms, five and a half baths, spacious living room and dining room, library, small den, and breakfast room. The exterior would be pale yellow stucco and fieldstone, the backdrop volcanic rocks and thick woods, with a panoramic view of the Blue Ridge Mountains. There would be a swimming pool, commodious terrace, stables, and a pond where the children could fish.

To keep the project quiet, Jackie chose as her architect Keith Williams of nearby Winchester, Virginia, and instructed Paul Fout to conceal her name from him. "She wanted a practical house," said Fout. "Jack had a huge bathtub in his bathroom for his back." The interior would be simple, even stark, but with the highest quality materials. Bunny Mellon, who had an expert architectural eye, was an invaluable consultant.

Construction began in October, causing the White House to announce the project officially. The estimated cost was $45,000, but everyone assumed it would be closer to $100,000 ($600,000 today). Fout became Jackie's general contractor, paid by a Kennedy family company managed by Steve Smith in New York. "Jackie was immersed in the details, and I was delighted because she was good," said Fout. On weekends she would sit in Fout's office and "draw stuff on the floor. The plan got changed so many times. She was smart. She would think of things you wouldn't think she could think of."

Monday, October 15, 1962, was a day of pageantry, mischief, and sentiment in the Kennedy White House. The President had just finished a weekend of successful campaigning in New York, New Jersey, and Pennsylvania, having arrived home shortly before 2 a.m. He had also been buoyed by two important legislative victories. Several days earlier, he had signed the trade expansion act, which enabled him to dramatically cut tariffs, and the Senate had sent him a revised investment tax credit bill—two key building blocks in his economic program.

That morning Kennedy greeted Algerian premier Ahmed Ben Bella in a South Lawn ceremony featuring a twenty-one-gun salute. As the military men barked their commands, the assembled dignitaries heard youthful echoes from the third-floor balcony outside the White House schoolroom: "Attention!" the children shrieked. "Forward march!" "Boom!" Kennedy glanced upwards, but couldn't spot the culprits. A mortified Alice Grimes instantly sent a letter of apology. Telling her not to worry, Jackie replied, "It was really charming and not embarrassing at all." The President "was probably the most amused of all."

Later in the day Joe Kennedy came to the White House for a week-long visit—the first since his stroke nearly a year earlier. In her customary meticulous fashion Jackie had prepared for every eventuality, issuing instructions to J. B. West about obtaining a hospital bed, a lift for the bathroom, and other medical equipment. Jackie even detailed the contents of a drink tray at Joe's bedside and on a suitcase stand in the dining room: gin, tonic, Coke, ginger ale, rum, scotch, ice, cock-tail shaker, lemon juice, and sugar syrup in a jar, although she noted that the Ambassador had only "make-believe cocktails." Joe would stay in the Lincoln Bedroom, his niece and full-time companion Ann Gargan in the Queen's Room, and three nurses in the third-floor guest rooms.

While Joe was visiting with the President and his family on Monday evening, Mac Bundy was hosting a party at his Partridge Lane home in honor of Charles "Chip" Bohlen, who was about to leave for Paris to be the new U.S. ambassador. Across town in Kalorama, Robert McNamara was presiding over a Hickory Hill seminar on cybernetics with a professor of neurology and psychology from the University of California. All afternoon, analysts at the CIA had been scrutinizing a batch of photos shot over Cuba the previous day by a U-2 spy plane. Shortly before 6 p.m. they discovered images of medium-range missiles capable of hitting the nation's capital—clear proof of the dangerous offensive weapons McCone had been warning about.

Both McNamara and Bundy learned about the evidence that evening. Elspeth Rostow, whose husband was in Berlin, later said that McNamara betrayed nothing and politely offered to drive her home. "There we all were, listening to cybernetics, and the Cuban Missile Crisis was about to start," she recalled. As national security chief, Bundy had the responsibility to inform the President. Mindful of Kennedy's fatigue after "a strenuous campaign weekend," Bundy declined to call JFK. "It was a hell of a secret," the national security aide explained later to Kennedy. Bundy decided to wait until morning, figuring that for the President, "a quiet evening and a night of sleep were the best preparation" for the days ahead.

TWENTY-THREE

*T*he thirteen days of the Cuban Missile Crisis in October 1962 brought out the best in Jack Kennedy, but some less attractive traits emerged as well. Making policy on the fly, Kennedy calmly juggled conflicting viewpoints, anticipated problems, moved cautiously, and kept his focus. He settled on a graduated course of action that offered him the greatest flexibility and gave Khrushchev plenty of leeway to back down, then held his ground against stiff challenges from his advisers, often amid contentious and confusing debate. He tightly controlled the operation, using Bobby as his proxy—not only in meetings that he didn't attend, but also in back-channel overtures to the Soviet government. The successful outcome hinged on a grand deception that eight of Kennedy's men kept secret for several decades. To help maintain that fiction, Kennedy deliberately undermined an old rival and exploited the loyalty of an unwitting old friend.

Throughout the crisis Kennedy repeatedly relied on his uncanny ability to compartmentalize his life. For the first seven days, JFK and his top aides deliberated in extraordinary secrecy, excluding foreign allies as well as congressional leaders. At the same time, Kennedy carried out his public duties as if nothing were amiss, greeting dignitaries and stumping for congressional and Senate candidates in the East and Midwest.

From beginning to end, he moved smoothly from the high tension of West Wing meetings to the light banter of dinner parties. (He was helped, according to historian Robert Dallek, by "increased amounts of hydrocortisone and testosterone . . . to control his Addison's disease and increase his energy.") Instead of shutting down their social life, Jack and Jackie intensified it, drawing in both close friends and diverting acquaintances.

At 8 a.m. on Tuesday, October 16, Bundy showed JFK the photographs of missiles and sites still under construction in Cuba. Kennedy quickly convened his top foreign policy advisers—a handpicked group that would be known as the "Ex Comm"—the Executive Committee of the National Security Council. Besides JFK, the dozen core members were Lyndon Johnson, Dean Rusk, Robert McNamara, Douglas Dillon, Bobby Kennedy, John McCone, George Ball, Roswell Gilpatric, Maxwell Taylor, Llewellyn Thompson, Ted Sorensen, and McGeorge Bundy. Others inside the administration, along with outside experts such as Dean Acheson, Robert Lovett, and arms negotiator John McCloy, would join the discussions when needed. Jack Kennedy chose to secretly tape-record most of the deliberations.

His initial instinct was for a quick surprise attack before the missiles could be operational. "We're going to take out these missiles," he said— either with an air strike or an invasion. But he invited arguments from his advisers and expressed his own concerns and doubts. From the start he worried that Khrushchev would counter a U.S. strike on Cuba by moving on Berlin—although JFK suspected that "he's probably going to grab Berlin anyway." Kennedy was also constantly aware of Khrushchev's anxiety over the recently installed Jupiter missiles in Turkey. "The only offer we would make, it seems to me, that would have any sense, according to him, would be our Turkey missiles," said JFK on the third day of debate.

In the first week, Robert McNamara had the greatest impact, pushing the group toward a blockade. A cordon of navy vessels would show American resolve while buying time and preventing additional offensive weapons from reaching Cuba. Bundy's voice was surprisingly muted, posing questions rather than framing arguments or setting the agenda. The NSC adviser initially favored doing nothing, fearful that any action would result in a Soviet takeover of Berlin, which could trigger a nuclear war. Rusk also urged caution. He seemed able to step back and take the long view, occasionally relying on historical references, including Kennedy's touchstone book, *The Guns of August.*

Sorensen (who continued to be plagued by his ulcer) said little, occasionally asking for detail or clarification, preferring to confer with Kennedy one-on-one. JFK frequently turned to former ambassador to Moscow Llewellyn Thompson to interpret Khrushchev's thinking. Thompson was the first to piece together the Soviet leader's scheme to reveal the fully installed missiles after the November elections, using Russia's new leverage to gain control of Berlin.

Several participants likened a surprise attack to Pearl Harbor. "Just frightens the hell out of me," said Marshall Carter, deputy director of Central Intelligence, on the first day. Two days later George Ball declared that a strike without warning was "the kind of conduct that one might expect of the Soviet Union," and Rusk predicted the United States would carry "the mark of Cain" as a result.

"I am depending on you to pull this group together," Jack told Bobby. RFK "kept the discussion moving," said one colleague. "He kept it from going back over the same ground 50 times." As he shifted between goad and conciliator, Bobby took intermittent notes, keeping tabs on everyone's position with what Ros Gilpatric described as a "score sheet" or "rating card." Bobby started out hawkish. At one point he proposed a Mongoose-style clandestine maneuver to provoke the Cubans, much as the explosion on the battleship *Maine* had ignited the Spanish-American War. After four days of debate, Bobby agreed that a surprise attack was "not in our traditions."

By Thursday evening, Kennedy and most of his advisers had settled on a blockade, which the President defended Friday morning to his deeply skeptical Joint Chiefs. Kennedy didn't flinch as air force chief Curtis LeMay compared the blockade plan to "appeasement at Munich." But when LeMay observed, "You're in a pretty bad fix," JFK shot back. "You're in there with me. Personally."

The hawkish views of the military men gave JFK second thoughts, which were reinforced when Bundy switched overnight to favoring an air strike. Before leaving on a campaign trip to the Midwest, Kennedy asked Bundy to elaborate on his proposal. When Kennedy rejoined the Ex Comm on Saturday afternoon, the "Bundy plan" had the full backing of the military men. But once again the consensus spurned a "Pearl Harbor" attack. Contrary to subsequent mythology, McNamara—not

Adlai Stevenson—was the most ardent dove, lobbying for a blockade linked to negotiations.

To get the missiles out of Cuba, McNamara said the "minimum price" would be removal of nuclear missiles from Italy as well as Turkey. Sorensen favored McNamara's approach, as did Adlai Stevenson. But the UN ambassador also suggested that the United States consider proposing the "evacuation of Guantánamo," the U.S. naval base in Cuba. Kennedy "sharply rejected" Stevenson's additional concession as a sign of American weakness. "You have to admire Adlai," Kennedy mused afterwards as he, Bobby, and Sorensen stood on the Truman Balcony. "He sticks to his position even when everyone is jumping on him."

JFK ultimately ruled out making any opening offers to the Soviets. Instead, he approved a more muscular blockade—labeled a quarantine at Rusk's suggestion—backed by a threat of military attack if the missiles were not removed. Kennedy would announce the blockade and ultimatum in a televised address on Monday night. The advocates of this two-step approach were Bobby and Thompson, as well as Dillon and McCone, both of whom had originally favored a swift air strike. Throughout the discussions, Kennedy pointedly and repeatedly conceded the possibility of removing missiles in Turkey and Italy "at an appropriate time" in the future. He understood that the Jupiter land-based missiles had become militarily obsolete and could be replaced by new Polaris nuclear-armed submarines in the Mediterranean.

Maintaining normal routines during these deliberations was vital, Kennedy said, "so that we don't take the cover off this." Several times the group met in the elegant Yellow Oval Room, with participants whisked into the Executive Mansion by different routes. On the afternoon of Tuesday the sixteenth, Kennedy appeared at a State Department foreign policy conference where he spoke briefly, took questions, and departed in whirlwind fashion. "Not a happy man," observed Katie Louchheim.

That evening Jack and Jackie attended a dinner party at Joe and Susan Mary Alsop's for Chip and Avis Bohlen. Phil and Katharine Graham, Bobby and Ethel, Mac and Mary Bundy, Hervé and Nicole Alphand, and Isaiah and Aline Berlin also sat around the table. It was a warm Indian summer night, and during cocktails Kennedy walked deep into Joe's leafy garden with Bohlen, where their intense conversation lasted so long Susan Mary feared her roast would be ruined. Kennedy was urging Bohlen to postpone his departure for France and join the Ex Comm talks, but the envoy argued that a delay might arouse suspicions.

Once at the table, JFK was "in a jolly mood," Berlin recalled. "The sangfroid which he displayed . . . on a day on which he must have been extraordinarily preoccupied, was one of the most astonishing exhibitions of self-restraint and strength . . . as if there were not a cloud upon his brain." Kennedy playfully said to Berlin, "You must go and sit next to Jackie. She wants to bring you out." Feeling "greatly honored and rather excited," the British professor found Jackie "infinitely easier to talk to" than her husband.

The men gathered after dinner for brandy and cigars in Joe's "garden room," where Kennedy pressed Berlin, an expert in Russian history and politics, with questions about how Russians reacted "when their backs were against the wall." Berlin felt he answered inadequately, but he couldn't help admiring Kennedy's skill "as a cross examiner." Ironically, Kennedy reminded Berlin of Lenin, "who used to exhaust people simply by listening to them."

In the following days, Jack "sought [Jackie's] company at meals normally devoted to business," wrote Sorensen, "and on walks around the South Lawn." She too kept her schedule by attending the press conference unveiling the Lafayette Square plan, traveling to New York on Wednesday the seventeenth to receive a citation for her role in the arts, and taking the children to Glen Ora on Friday. Other spouses remained in the dark, although Adlai Stevenson confided in his close friend Marietta Tree.

Charley Bartlett's keen eye saw through Kennedy's facade on Wednesday during a campaign trip to Connecticut. When Bartlett asked him a question about Latin America, "his shoulders sort of caved," Bartlett recalled. "His face took on lines and he said, 'Boy, Charley, do I have problems down in that region.'" As the crisis developed, Jack unburdened himself to intimate friends such as Lem Billings and Chuck Spalding. "He'd find me, wherever I was, and call me up in the middle of the night," said Spalding, "just to relieve his tension, I guess. He would talk about anything from Voltaire to girls, always warm and funny." Between Ex Comm meetings, Jack and Jackie had a final dinner with Joe Kennedy on Thursday evening. The next day the Ambassador left the White House for Hyannis as Jack headed to Cleveland and Chicago for long-planned appearances at political rallies.

Finally, on Saturday morning, Bobby signaled to JFK that it was time to make a decision. "A slight upper respiratory infection," Salinger explained to the press, prevented the President from making further speeches and required him to rest at home. Jackie returned from Glen Ora with the children, and Lyndon Johnson was also summoned back from a political trip to Hawaii. On a stopover in Los Angeles, LBJ briefed his friend Lloyd Hand about the situation, adding, "If you tell I'll shoot you between the eyes." By this time, the secret was beginning to seep out. Bobby Kennedy arrived three hours late for Red Fay's Potomac cruise on the *Sequoia* and "couldn't hide his anguish," observed Hervé Alphand.

Reporters and columnists buzzed with rumors during a twenty-fifth anniversary dance on Saturday night given by James Rowe and his wife. The word from the *Washington Post* newsroom was "they think it's Cuba." Stevenson admitted to his friends Katie and Walter Louchheim that a "mean" crisis had been brewing since Tuesday. "The President did *not* have a cold," Katie told a friend. Kenny O'Donnell called the White House from the party with the news that both the *New York Times* and *Washington Post* were preparing stories.

As he had done before the Bay of Pigs, Kennedy phoned *New York Times* publisher Orvil Dryfoos, who killed the article being written by James Reston. The President was less successful at the *Washington Post*. When Kennedy called Phil Graham, the publisher "would probably have taken out the story completely, but the paper wouldn't let him," said Katharine Graham. A modified version ran on Sunday under the headline "MARINE MOVES IN SOUTH LINKED TO CUBAN CRISIS." Both publishers agreed to hold off further stories until after Kennedy's speech.

In meetings with his advisers and a briefing for congressional leaders on Monday, October 22, Kennedy lucidly described the rationale for action and outlined the next steps. He warned Ex Comm members not to let on that they had ever contemplated a surprise attack. "I can't say that strongly enough," he said. The senators and congressmen drilled Kennedy with queries and objections. He told them that a military strike could invite a nuclear retaliation, and "doing nothing . . . would imperil" both Berlin and Latin America. Only the blockade offered "flexibility." "There's no use in waiting, Mr. President," concluded Georgia Democrat Richard Russell, the most powerful force in the Senate. "The nettle is going to sting anyway." That session, Bobby said later, was his brother's "most difficult meeting," creating "tremendous strain."

Kennedy's seventeen-minute speech to the nation included an implicit repudiation of his father's pro-appeasement stance when he was ambassador to Britain. "The 1930s taught us a clear lesson," JFK said. "Aggressive conduct, if allowed to grow unchecked and unchallenged, ultimately leads to war." Shortly afterwards, he had the first in a series of evening conversations with Macmillan—mostly monologues with occasional words of encouragement from the prime minister, who "often sounded rather vapid." Given his age and experience, Macmillan soothed Kennedy simply by listening. He had earlier urged the President to negotiate, but now he leaned toward taking action. Khrushchev's duplicity rankled Kennedy more than anything. He "played a double game," said JFK, "to face us with a bad situation in November . . . to squeeze us on Berlin."

To divert her husband, Jackie hastily organized a dinner party with Benno and Nicole Graziani, Oleg Cassini, and Lee, who had flown to Washington that weekend and moved into the Queen's Bedroom. The White House also belatedly phoned Bill Walton. His designated date was Mary Meyer, but he decided instead to bring Helen Chavchavadze. Helen watched the speech with Bill at his Georgetown home, and they raced to the White House, arriving on the second floor just before the President.

As Kennedy was telling Walton that he was "just listening and praying," an aide informed Chavchavadze that if a Soviet attack was imminent, she would have to go with the group to the presidential shelter at Camp David. She began to sob, begging to be sent home to be with her two daughters. Only after the aide reassured her that an evacuation was highly unlikely did Chavchavadze calm down.

"Jackie tried to be cheerful and upbeat," Cassini recalled. "But it was a tense evening." Bundy interrupted several times, and when Kennedy left to take a phone call, Cassini walked out with him. Kennedy "refused to seem depressed or overwhelmed by the immensity of the moment," recalled Cassini. Puffing on his cigar, Kennedy ruminated on the possibility of "being obliterated." It was an example, Cassini said, of Kennedy's "elegant fatalism."

———

In a series of meetings on Tuesday the twenty-third, the Ex Comm discussed how to impose the quarantine and analyzed Khrushchev's initial bellicose reply. At the United Nations, Adlai Stevenson made a dramatic presentation using several of the spy satellite photos as evidence. JFK gave a background briefing to Harry Luce and *Time*'s managing editor, Otto Fuerbringer, promising them full access to the surveillance photographs for the following week's issue of the magazine. As they talked in the Oval Office, Kennedy tapped the coffee table in front of him with two fingers. "Our troops are ready in Florida," he said. "If there is any reason to go in, they are going to go in. Khrushchev is not going to get away with this." Luce later observed that Kennedy was "emotional . . . deeper than any ordinary emotion, because the President evidently felt that the situation was very serious and that the worst could happen."

Meanwhile, Bobby dispatched two trusted emissaries to meet separately with his KGB contact, Georgi Bolshakov: Charley Bartlett and Frank Holeman, a *New York Daily News* reporter who had introduced the Russian to the attorney general and had helped set up their secret meetings. Each newsman carried the same sub rosa message: a willingness to trade the removal of missiles from Turkey and Italy for the weapons in Cuba. Bolshakov dutifully relayed these proposals in a cable to Moscow that included an important caveat from Holeman: "The conditions of such a trade can be discussed only in a time of quiet and not when there is the threat of war."

At 7:10 that evening, following a meeting in the Cabinet Room, Bobby reported to his brother that Bartlett and Holeman had seen Bolshakov. But in the brothers' telepathic conversational style, the attorney general offered no details, making unclear the President's involvement in the overture. With the tape recorder running, the Kennedy brothers carefully avoided saying anything beyond simple confirmation of the contacts with the Soviet agent. Perhaps more noteworthy was Kennedy's call to Charley Bartlett at 7:50 p.m.—his last conversation before leaving the Oval Office at 8:06.

The Kennedys were dining again with friends, but the President was in no mood for socializing. His talk with Bobby had come moments after ringing off with Jackie. "Oh Christ, about the dinner tonight," Kennedy said with annoyance. "She's invited somebody and I invited somebody." In a gesture of reciprocal hospitality, Jackie had asked the Maharajah and Maharani of Jaipur to stay for two days at Blair House, the official presidential guest house across Pennsylvania Avenue. They were invited to dinner along with Lee, Oleg Cassini, and the Grazianis—the remnants of a dinner dance originally planned in honor of the distinguished Indians. Jack, in turn, had invited the Duke and Duchess of Devonshire, newly arrived in town for the opening of an exhibit at the National Gallery of old master drawings from their Chatsworth estate, David and Sissie Gore, and several other British friends in town for the exhibition.

The dinner was held on the state floor, in the smaller of the two official dining rooms. With "unfailing good humor," Kennedy "kept everybody else calm and in a good mood," recalled David Gore. As the evening wound down, Kennedy and Gore disappeared to talk privately. Jackie wandered upstairs to see what had become of the two men, and found them both "squatting on the floor, looking at the missile pictures. . . . I had to rush backwards and forwards, to keep the party going."

Kennedy was disappointed in the lukewarm European reaction to his speech. To help build the American case, Gore suggested that instead of selectively showing the surveillance photographs to the press, Kennedy should release a batch of pictures immediately. Together, the two men chose the images that illustrated the situation most clearly. (*Time* was still able to run its "big spread" of dramatic exclusive photos.) Gore also recommended that Kennedy reduce the quarantine perimeter from eight hundred to five hundred miles outside the Cuban coastline. "The Soviet Union had some very difficult decisions to take," Gore recalled. "They had to climb down as gracefully as they could. . . . Every additional hour that could be given them might save us from a dangerous episode." The President immediately phoned McNamara with the new instructions.

Kennedy had earlier dispatched Bobby to meet with Soviet ambassador Anatoly Dobrynin. Shortly after 10 p.m., Bobby joined JFK and Gore upstairs. Bobby's mood was glum. He had greeted Dobrynin "in a state of agitation," bursting with angry accusations over Soviet betrayal, and warnings that the United States was serious about stopping the ships. Unlike his emissaries, Bobby had said nothing about Turkish missiles.

Meeting with the Ex Comm on Wednesday morning the twenty-fourth, Kennedy received word that a Soviet submarine had approached a U.S. aircraft carrier on the cordon. McNamara described the options for an American response as JFK endured what Bobby later called "the time of greatest worry. . . . His hand went up to his face & covered his mouth and he closed his fist. His eyes were tense, almost gray, and we just stared at each other across the table." Moments later, the group heard that Soviet ships were turning around, prompting Dean Rusk to whisper to Bundy, "We are eyeball to eyeball, and I think the other fellow just blinked." Still, when Kennedy called London, he asked Macmillan "straight out, the 64 thousand dollar question. 'Should he take out Cuba?' "

Jack invited Charley and Martha Bartlett for dinner. "I think the pressure of this period made him desire more to have friends around," said Bartlett. "Just small groups which he would break up about nine-thirty and go back to the cables." Bartlett was encouraged that Soviet vessels weren't testing the blockade. "I should think you'd feel like really celebrating," Bartlett said. "You don't want to celebrate in this game this early," Kennedy replied. "Because anything can happen." On the way home the Bartletts went to Bill Walton's for a nightcap. Shortly before midnight, as Charley and Martha were getting into bed, Kennedy called to say, "You'd be interested to know I got a cable from our friend. He says that those ships . . . are coming through tomorrow." Recalled Bartlett, "On that kind of a note, he had to go to sleep."

Kennedy responded to Khrushchev's threatened challenge to the blockade with a brief and blunt reply sent at 2 a.m., reiterating his displeasure over Soviet deception and implying that the United States would take action soon if the missiles were not removed. The *Washington Post* sent quite a different signal on Thursday morning in a Walter Lippmann column suggesting publicly for the first time that the United States trade its missiles in Turkey for the withdrawal of missiles in Cuba. It was a leak, most likely from George Ball—a trial balloon aimed directly at Moscow.

Throughout that day's meetings, Kennedy and his men debated block-

ade enforcement. Turning hawkish, McNamara wanted to strengthen
the blockade by stopping ships carrying products besides offensive
weapons. Kennedy gently restrained his defense secretary and permitted selective enforcement of the quarantine to avoid confrontation.
Late in the day, Adlai Stevenson challenged Valerian Zorin, Soviet ambassador to the United Nations, in a televised Security Council meeting. As Zorin evaded, Stevenson dramatically announced, "Don't wait
for the translation—yes or no? . . . I am prepared to wait for my answer
until hell freezes over." Watching with Kenny O'Donnell, Kennedy
said, "I never knew Adlai had it in him."

Nearly four decades later, in December 2000, the feature film *Thirteen Days* would place O'Donnell, played by Kevin Costner, at the center of the Cuban Missile Crisis deliberations. The portrayal stretched
the truth, leading many irritated participants to dismiss his importance
entirely. Ethel Kennedy sent a spoof valentine to her friends saying,
"Roses are red, Violets are blue, You've got 13 days dear to figure out
what Kenny O'Donnell would do."

But O'Donnell did serve a key function for JFK during those
days. While he may not have joined any strategy deliberations of the
Ex Comm, JFK asked his longtime aide to sit in on all meetings he
attended. The President wanted him "to watch and listen," O'Donnell
wrote, ". . . so that he could talk with me later about what had been said
and compare his impressions and conclusions with mine. He wanted
an observer in the room who would follow the various arguments more
or less objectively, without becoming involved or committed to any
point of view."

On Friday the twenty-sixth, Kennedy shifted his full attention to removing the weapons on the ground in Cuba. Reacting to large crowds
of peace demonstrations in Britain, Harold Macmillan was pressing
Kennedy to avoid military action, drop the blockade, and negotiate—a
position that diminished the prime minister's usefulness as an adviser.
(Hervé Alphand would remark later on Macmillan's "hesitant and
frightened attitude" compared to de Gaulle's unequivocal support.)
Stevenson was urging the same course, with a guarantee of Cuba's
"territorial integrity" as well as a willingness to disarm the missiles in
Turkey and Italy if asked. Pounding the table with his fist, McCone
exclaimed that the Cuban missiles were "pointed at our hearts. . . . *That
threat must be removed before we can drop the quarantine.*"

Continuing surveillance had revealed accelerated work on the Cuban sites all week; by Friday the medium-range missiles were ready for use. Kennedy also learned in a noon intelligence briefing that the Soviets had deployed tactical nuclear weapons for battlefield use. An invasion, McCone warned, would be a "much more serious undertaking. . . . It's very evil stuff they've got there."

At the same time, Kennedy received two promising feelers, first from Acting UN Secretary-General U Thant, and later from ABC journalist John Scali, who had been approached by a KGB agent. Both men said that the Soviets would consider dismantling the missile sites in exchange for a pledge from the United States not to invade Cuba. Early that evening, a long, rambling private message from Khrushchev clattered across the Teletype, offering the same terms to resolve the crisis.

On that hopeful note, Jackie and the children drove to Glen Ora the next morning. She had bowed out of two events in Washington that day, the Washington International Horse Show and a dinner and preview of the Devonshires' exhibit. Of far greater interest to Jackie was riding in the opening meet of the Orange County Hunt on Saturday afternoon. As she was chasing the hounds over the top of Rattlesnake Mountain and through the fields near Wexford, her husband was struggling to avoid full-scale war in the face of disturbing new developments.

Khrushchev had followed his private overture with a public demand for a Cuba-Turkey missile trade, forcing Kennedy and his advisers to scramble for the correct response. Not knowing about the Bartlett and Holeman approaches, the advisers concluded that the Lippmann column had suddenly emboldened Khrushchev. They spent hours trying to address both messages while concentrating on the terms Khrushchev had outlined in the first one. ("It's too complicated Bobby," Bundy said after several iterations.) In the middle of the debate, the Duke and Duchess of Devonshire arrived for a half-hour chat with Kennedy in the Oval Office. "A lot of Jack's close advisers were surprised to see my wife and me," the duke recalled.

Kennedy was unwilling to risk going to war in Cuba and Berlin over outmoded rockets in Turkey. Yet he recognized that a public quid pro quo would seem like a sellout of Turkey, leading to what Bundy called "a radical decline in the effectiveness" of the NATO alliance. Eventually the group finessed the problem by deciding to answer only the first letter. It was known as "Bobby's formula," but Bundy had initiated the idea. Sorensen, Thompson, and McCone had reinforced it, and Bobby refined it. It would soon be known as "the Trollope ploy," after an incident of similarly selective interpretation in one of Anthony Trollope's novels.

The whole plan nearly came unstuck when a U-2 plane was shot down on Saturday afternoon by a surface-to-air missile over Cuba, killing the pilot. McNamara pushed to "take out that SAM site," while McCone insisted on issuing a "violent protest." Kennedy held them both at bay. O'Donnell was struck by "the uncertainty many of [Kennedy's advisers] showed under pressure, the inability of some to make a thoughtful judgment and stick to it."

After nearly eight hours of meetings, the Ex Comm crafted a reply— removal of the Soviet missiles in exchange for an American noninvasion pledge—that Bobby would deliver to Dobrynin at the same time it was publicly released. Kennedy invited Rusk, McNamara, Bobby, Ball, Gilpatric, Thompson, Sorensen, and Bundy to join him in the Oval Office to devise Bobby's oral explanation to accompany the letter. It was there that Dean Rusk outlined a second deal to be kept confidential: the United States would dismantle the Turkish missiles but only after all offensive weapons had been removed from Cuba and the crisis had passed—the very message Holeman had given to Bolshakov. If either side betrayed the secret, the deal was off.

Ex Comm members excluded from the briefing on the clandestine plan—either by happenstance or reasons that never have been made clear—were Dillon, Taylor, McCone, and the Vice President, who had been a silent presence during most of the missile crisis deliberations. Only on that Saturday, particularly when Kennedy was out of the room, did LBJ assert himself with heated objections to any Cuba-Turkey trade.

After Bobby returned from the Soviet Embassy, the Ex Comm met at 9 p.m. Saturday night to discuss contingencies for an invasion on Monday or Tuesday, as well as an interim occupation government in Cuba. "I'd like to take Cuba back," Bobby mused. "That would be nice." "Suppose we make Bobby mayor of Havana?" cracked another participant. "That's something you're going to have to get done tomorrow," said Dillon.

Many of Kennedy's advisers anxiously remained in their offices overnight. Dave Powers stayed with the President in the Executive Mansion. "Dave, are you sure your wife doesn't mind being alone at home at a time like this?" Kennedy asked Powers. "Of course she minds," Powers replied, "but she's used to it." After a late dinner of broiled chicken, JFK and Powers went down to the White House theater to watch one of the President's favorite movies, *Roman Holiday*. The romantic comedy features Gregory Peck as a raffish newspaperman and Audrey Hepburn as a willful European princess who kicks over the traces to secretly spend an adventuresome day in Rome with him. From her fondness for quoting Keats to her mischievous humor, Hepburn's wide-eyed "Princess Ann" bears more than a passing resemblance to Jackie.

On Sunday morning, October 28, Khrushchev accepted the terms of Kennedy's letter. By doing so, the Soviet leader could claim, as McCone had pointed out the previous day, "I saved Cuba. I stopped an invasion." "Today was the day of the doves," said Bundy. While he and the others were jubilant, JFK presided over the Ex Comm meeting "without a trace of excitement or even exultation," noted Sorensen. Kennedy's strongest injunction was against public gloating of any sort. After lunch, Kennedy and Billings took the chopper to Glen Ora to join Jackie and the children for lunch.

No one could explain Khrushchev's retreat, although documents released in the 1990s after the collapse of the Soviet Union shed some light. The discovery of the missiles had taken Khrushchev by surprise, and he feared an American invasion of Cuba. When Kennedy responded instead with the more modest quarantine, a relieved Khrushchev rejected a proposal from Dobrynin that the Soviets retaliate by blockading Berlin—"fuel to the conflict," in the Soviet premier's words.

Kennedy's unanticipated firmness about removing all offensive weapons from Cuba, coupled with intelligence reports of heightened American military activity, ended up persuading Khrushchev to back away from a potential nuclear war. He was also influenced by the Lippmann column and the private overtures through Bolshakov, although Khrushchev blundered by demanding the Cuba-Turkey trade publicly. The secret deal may have been duplicitous, but it shrewdly allowed Khrushchev to eliminate an irritating problem in nearby Turkey.

Negotiations over the withdrawal of Soviet weapons from Cuba took several weeks, and the blockade ended on November 20. A month later Khrushchev finally abandoned his efforts to dislodge the Allies from West Berlin. By the following April, the fifteen Jupiter missiles in Turkey were removed quietly. The Soviets kept the secret, and so did the nine American officials.

Those out of the loop inadvertently diverted attention from the secret deal with their own accounts of the crisis. "When the crunch came . . . at the end of the week," said Rostow in an oral history, Kennedy "firmly excluded using the Turkish bases for bargaining. . . . He was right." In his memoirs, Harold Macmillan admits perplexity over the "mystery": "Why did [Khrushchev] suddenly abandon the Turkey-Cuba deal?"

Kennedy worked hard to ensure that the press had no glimmer of the swap. *Time*'s cover story on the missile crisis called Khrushchev's negotiating ploy "a cynical piece of statesmanship." *Newsweek* noted that politically a trade "would be hard to accept," while acknowledging that the Polaris submarines were a more effective deterrent than the Jupiters. Several weeks later, Kennedy told Cy Sulzberger that Khrushchev "could not have thought of really getting us to dismantle Turkey," adding that he "simply could not understand" the Lippmann column.

But the most cunning piece of disinformation was in a *Saturday Evening Post* analysis of the crisis by Stewart Alsop and Charley Bartlett. On Monday the twenty-ninth, the day after Khrushchev caved, Bartlett told Kennedy of his plan to collaborate with Alsop. "It occurs to me," Bartlett wrote, "that I could inject the warm feeling that [Alsop] tends to lack and hopefully avert the little hookers that he intends to include. . . . I feel strongly it should be written without involving you directly."

Kennedy encouraged Bartlett to proceed and gave the two journalists carte blanche for background briefings. The duo talked to everyone involved in the crisis deliberations except McNamara. "It obviously was going to entail conflict, and it was McNamara's policy to stay out of instant history," recalled Bartlett. "He didn't want to get involved." Their biggest nugget came during lunch with Mike Forrestal, a member of the National Security Council staff. "He gave us a story about Adlai Stevenson going soft," said Bartlett. After checking with both Bobby and Jack, they decided to run with it.

When they had finished their chronicle of the crisis, Bartlett and

Alsop gave it first to Kennedy's military aide Ted Clifton to check for accuracy. Clifton made no changes, "so I gave the manuscript to Jack," Bartlett recalled, "and he wrote in some changes." The article "had Kennedy's prints all over it," said Bartlett. Alsop wanted to keep the manuscript as a memento, but Bartlett "threw it in the fire at Stewart's house to protect Kennedy."

Despite his secret role as an emissary to Bolshakov on the Cuba-Turkey trade, Bartlett was offended by Stevenson's stance. "He was ready to give in," Bartlett muttered to Katie Louchheim at a dinner party in late November. "It will be better for the President in '64 if Adlai is not in his present post." Louchheim detected no venom in Bartlett's remarks, "just a friend looking after a friend who happens to be President."

But when the three-page article appeared in early December, the portrayal devastated Stevenson—and nearly ruined his career. The central assertion was that Stevenson had challenged the consensus of the Ex Comm and was the only adviser to advocate trading missiles in Europe for those in Cuba. Stevenson "wanted a Munich," said an anonymous source—in fact, Forrestal. "Stevenson was strong during the UN debate," a photo caption added, "but inside the White House the hard liners thought he was soft."

Stevenson charged that Alsop and Bartlett were "wrong in literally every detail." He appeared on the *Today* show to defend himself, accurately pointing out that he had "emphatically" approved the blockade and had correctly predicted that the Soviets would ask for a trade. The depiction was indeed unfair, because McNamara had been the leading advocate for negotiations, and Kennedy himself had frequently raised the prospect of a missile exchange. Most members of the Ex Comm had shifted their positions in the course of their debate. But Stevenson had made himself vulnerable by suggesting one concession too many (Guantánamo) and advocating a suspension of the quarantine during negotiations.

The article triggered a burst of speculation, led by Joe Alsop, that Stevenson would resign his post. In a strong defense of Stevenson, *Time* observed that "it was promptly and widely assumed that Kennedy himself had instigated the accusation" in the *Post* piece. Recognizing that he needed to backpedal, Kennedy called Stevenson press aide Clayton Fritchey and said, "All right, cease fire. We'll both put down our arms."

Kennedy insisted to Federal Communications Commission chairman Newton Minow, a close friend of Stevenson, "I had nothing whatever to do with that article." In a private letter to Stevenson, Kennedy repeated the denial. "The fact that Charley Bartlett was a co-author," he wrote, "has made this particularly difficult for me. . . . In this case, I did not discuss the Cuban crisis or any of the events surrounding it with *any* newspaperman. . . . I am certain that the quotations . . . did not come from the White House." Kennedy placed all blame on the impulse of journalists to "delight in stirring needless controversy."

A publicly released version of the letter made no mention of Bartlett and offered Kennedy's "regret" over the "unfortunate stir," his praise for Stevenson's role in resolving the crisis, and his "fullest confidence" in the ambassador's continued work at the United Nations.

Stevenson stayed in his job but never got over his feelings of bitterness at the way he had been treated. By fingering Stevenson in the *Saturday Evening Post,* Kennedy made sure that no one would trace to him the idea of a missile trade. It took Charley Bartlett twenty-five years to realize he had been a pawn in Kennedy's scheme. "We had the illusion that it was just Mike talking too much," Bartlett recalled. "But Jack had planted the story on us through Forrestal, because when I told Jack that I had it, he was delighted." Bartlett "came to the conclusion that we were sort of used. It is dismaying, but I guess the presidency involves a lot of maneuvers."

TWENTY-FOUR

*E*lection day on November 6 resoundingly advanced Joe Kennedy's dynastic dreams. Even though he had no political experience, thirty-year-old Teddy Kennedy vaulted into the U.S. Senate with 54 percent of the vote, beating George Cabot Lodge, the son of the man Jack Kennedy beat in 1952. Publicly, the President had kept a discreet distance from the race. But his team had been heavily involved in the campaign, and JFK had closely monitored his baby brother's progress.

The first challenge for JFK and his aides had been to deal with the little-known fact that Teddy had been expelled from Harvard for cheating. "The family could not quite figure out the most helpful way from their point of view that it should come out," recalled Tom Winship, editor of the *Boston Globe*. Winship sent his political editor Bob Healy to discuss the matter with Bobby. JFK wanted to have the incident mentioned as part of a major profile of Teddy, but Winship suggested handling it as a straight news story.

Mac Bundy "gave more than a little thought to this problem plaguing the family," Winship recalled, and persuaded Kennedy that the *Globe* would treat the subject judiciously. The resulting article on March 30 was tame indeed. It "ran fully for one day," said Winship. "That was the end of the incident."

Less than a month later, JFK organized a secret strategy session in Washington that included Boston politicians traveling under aliases to avoid detection. As the campaign got under way, Ted Sorensen supplied material for Teddy's speeches, and other aides drilled the neophyte candidate before press conferences and debates. The Kennedy family also underwrote polls that tracked Teddy's progress.

When Massachusetts Democrats met in June to register their preference, Steve Smith orchestrated Teddy's easy win over Edward McCormack with 70 percent of the delegates. Ben Bradlee was covering the event, and the President called him repeatedly from the White House (where he was dining with Jackie, Bill Walton, and Tony Bradlee) for reports on the balloting. Jack even correctly predicted the lead of Ben's story: "For fledgling politician Edward Moore Kennedy . . . the First Hurrah rose from a steaming, smoking auditorium in Springfield, Mass., at 12:25 a.m., June 9, 1962." Teddy's margin in the September primary was equally impressive—67 percent of the vote.

Teddy was one of six new Democratic senators. Two incumbents lost, which gave the administration a net gain of four senators. In the House, the Democrats lost four seats but still held a healthy majority there as well. It was a solid result for a midterm election, although it didn't overturn the controlling conservative bloc of southern Democrats allied with Republicans. Still, Kennedy's popularity surged to 76 percent in the aftermath of the missile crisis, giving him added leverage with recalcitrant legislators.

On Thursday, November 8, Jackie assembled a dozen friends for a dinner party to celebrate her husband's recent victories. When she called to invite Arthur and Marian Schlesinger, she asked him to recommend additional guests who would "keep the evening light." He combined levity with intellectual depth by nominating Isaiah Berlin as well as humorist S. N. Behrman, while Jackie added *Look* magazine publisher Gardner Cowles and his wife, and Joe and Susan Mary Alsop, who asked to bring along their houseguests, Cy and Marina Sulzberger. Mary Meyer rounded out the guest list as a last-minute substitute for Lee, who was unavailable.

Cy Sulzberger found the evening "extremely informal. The President looked well, calm and relaxed." Cocktails were served in the Yellow

Oval Room, complemented by caviar and crabmeat, as soft music played in the background, and Caroline wandered nearby in her nightgown. The *New York Times* columnist took note of Mary Meyer as a "very pretty young blonde," but also observed that Kennedy "made only rudimentary efforts to converse with the ladies at dinner and none before and after." For all Jackie's intentions, Kennedy "wanted to talk only about politics and foreign policy," wrote Sulzberger.

The President's conversation bounced from topic to topic: progress on disarming Cuba, a rant against the "excesses" of the press, and frustration over France's unwillingness to supply enough troops to NATO, as well as a lament about Joe Kennedy's poor health. "It is better to 'go' fast," Kennedy concluded. Seated on the President's left, Marina Sulzberger—"as excited and nervous as a debutante"—was content simply to bask in his presence. A zestful but plain woman, Marina thought JFK "the sexiest and most irresistible man on earth. . . . I would have given my right hand to seduce him. He loves or makes love or talks politics. Nothing between. . . . Just to listen to him talk is irresistible."

As he had at the Alsops' several weeks earlier, Isaiah Berlin was discomfited in the presence of Kennedy, who glowed with "absolute happiness . . . a state of triumph and satisfaction after the second Cuba." Once again, Berlin felt "cross examined about subjects about which I was conceived to know." Cy Sulzberger observed that Jackie seemed "a little ill at ease." The reason, according to Schlesinger, was Sulzberger's presence at the party. "Cy was very deaf," said Schlesinger. "He had a heavy conversational style, and as a result the evening lacked the light touch Jackie intended."

Promptly at 11 p.m., Kennedy announced that he was off to bed, and the "exciting tension" created by his presence disappeared. In a more easygoing mood, Jackie tried to brighten the atmosphere by playing phonograph records, including the new hit song "PT 109." "Jackie seems to know the words by heart and loves it," Sulzberger observed. After another half hour, the guests took their leave.

The next night the Kennedys threw their fifth dinner dance, a welcome home for Ambassador James Gavin and his wife, who had been replaced by the Bohlens in Paris. Sixty guests came for drinks in the Yellow Oval Room followed by dinner in the Blue Room, and another dozen arrived at 10 p.m. to join the dancing. Most of the inner coterie turned up, including the Bradlees, newly released from social purgatory. Their rehabilitation had begun on election day when Jackie invited Tony for a movie and supper with their children. During a brief stop in the Oval Office, John Jr. and Marina Bradlee had performed a "special dance" for the President as Arthur Schlesinger gamely held their lollipops. Three nights later at the Gavin party, Tony and Jack "had a long session about the difficulties of being friends with someone who is always putting everything he knows into a magazine," Bradlee noted in his journal. "Everybody loves everybody again."

Among the decorative women on hand was Mary Meyer but not Helen Chavchavadze. One noteworthy newcomer was a friend of Chavchavadze's, a blonde twenty-six-year-old Hungarian emigré who taught English as a second language with Helen at Georgetown. Her name was Enüd Sztanko, and she was "extremely pretty," recalled Chavchavadze. "Enüd was quite an amazing person, very strong, self-contained and reserved."

Sztanko had left Hungary during World War II when her father, a professor of internal medicine, was conscripted to teach medicine in Germany. After the war, her family fled first to West Germany, then to the United States. At age fifteen Enüd entered Manhattanville College of the Sacred Heart (where she overlapped with Joan Kennedy), and she received a master's in linguistics and languages at Georgetown.

During a dinner party at Chavchavadze's in October 1962, Sztanko was introduced to Walter Sohier, one of Jackie's favorite extra men. Early one evening several weeks later, Sohier called Sztanko to invite her to a small White House dinner. He explained that Mary Meyer was supposed to be his date, but she had to cancel because her son was ill. Sztanko was still polishing her nails as Sohier drove her to the White House gate.

At dinner Sztanko was seated on JFK's left, with Susan Mary Alsop on his right. "I hope you're not a spy. Walter said you might be," JFK said to Sztanko. "If you must know, there's a microphone under the table," she replied, which the President found amusing. "From the first day to the last I was never nervous with him," she recalled.

An invitation to the Gavin party followed quickly, and Sztanko became a regular at second-floor dinner parties and formal dances, where she and JFK would "sit down in the corner, and no one would disturb anyone talking to the President." He queried her about religion, existentialism, and political matters such as the admission of Hungary to the United Nations. Kennedy was fascinated by her life story, and he even helped arrange to have her father transferred from a veterans hospital in West Virginia to one in Tampa.

When JFK made advances, she "made it very clear that I would not get involved with him sexually." Sztanko knew Kennedy was having affairs and she was "almost obsessive about not wanting to be part of that. I think I would have been hurt if I had been one of his many women. I was protecting myself, and I think I became more interesting to him as a result."

After raising his dosages of cortisone to compensate for acute stress during the missile crisis, Kennedy suffered a flare-up of his gastrointestinal problems in the following weeks, prompting his doctors to order a special bland diet. His back problems also worsened, forcing him once again to watch movies in the screening room from the bed in the front row. Most worrying of all, in early December Kennedy appeared unusually depressed, a mood shift Jackie attributed to prescription antihistamines.

Kennedy was certainly under no extraordinary strain. He spent the second weekend of December relaxing at Bing Crosby's estate in Palm Springs with Powers and O'Donnell. On Sunday morning they were joined by Pat Lawford, who accompanied them to mass at the Sacred Heart Church and hitched a ride back to Washington after midnight on an Air Force One red-eye flight. Only later did a journalist tell Barbara Gamarekian that he had caught sight of former White House intern Mimi Beardsley, by then a college sophomore, who had flown out to Palm Springs on one of the air force "backup" planes.

On Monday evening, December 10, Jack and Jackie hosted a Hickory Hill seminar with Isaiah Berlin lecturing on nineteenth-century Russian literature. Berlin was more nervous than ever, knocking over an antique tabouret that Kennedy managed to catch before it crashed to the floor. At dinner the professor tried to amuse Kennedy with a story about Lenin and an illicit lover. But instead of being titillated, Kennedy reacted angrily. "Not at all a way to treat a great man," Kennedy told Berlin with a frown. Berlin gave his talk after dinner as Kennedy listened quietly in his rocking chair. But Berlin was taken aback when

Kennedy asked only one question—about the fate of Russia's writers and artists after the communist revolution in 1917—and then left abruptly.

The next day, JFK's gastroenterologist, Dr. Russell Boles, prescribed an anti-psychotic drug called Stelazine. Kennedy took two one-milligram tablets that Tuesday, and two more doses on Wednesday. His mood rebounded quickly, and Kennedy stopped the medication. By Thursday evening at dinner, Ken Galbraith found Kennedy to be "tanned and brisk and in the best of form. Talk was varied and gay."

Jackie showed periodic evidence of tension as well. Before her speech at a fundraising benefit for the National Cultural Center at the end of November, Arthur Goldberg noticed that "she was trembling." Despite her numerous appearances as first lady, Goldberg concluded that she was "scared to death" of crowds. "These people adore you," he told her. "All they want is a chance to meet you." Two weeks later as she left the White House for the Christmas holidays in Palm Beach, Jackie had tears in her eyes when she said goodbye to her secretary, Mary Gallagher.

Staff as well as friends detected heightened friction between Jack and Jackie over money. At dinner with the Bradlees in mid-November, the First Couple openly squabbled about her $40,000 (the equivalent of $240,000 today) in department store bills that he had been "boiling" about all day. While Jackie was scrupulous about getting good prices for the White House restoration project, she had been personally extravagant since adolescence. Even her indulgent father had frequently criticized her spendthrift habits, enumerating her expenses at Bloomingdale's and Saks, pleading with her to think twice before buying something she didn't need.

The residue of her "poor relation" status in the Auchincloss family was an impulse to spend lavishly on herself whenever she had the opportunity. "She didn't shop all the time," said Tony Bradlee, "but whatever she got was expensive, and Jack thought so too." Jackie had a weakness for costly clothes, antiques, and paintings. "If Jackie liked something, she ordered it and coped with the bills later," according to Mary Gallagher.

While the Ambassador paid for her Oleg Cassini wardrobe, Jackie bought European clothing surreptitiously through "clothing scouts"— Lee in London, Letizia Mowinckel in Paris, Irene Galitzine in Rome, and a friend named Molly MacAdoo in New York. Jackie had "art scouts" as well in Manhattan and London. In the autumn of 1962, Jackie splurged on a custom-made black double-breasted mink coat that even her husband admitted was "terrific."

But by the end of his second year in office, Jack said her habits were getting out of hand. In 1962, Jackie's spending had climbed to $121,461 ($750,000 in current dollars, or $62,000 a month), an increase of 15 percent over the previous year—and more than JFK's annual presidential salary of $100,000, all of which he gave to charities such as the United Negro College Fund, National Association for Retarded Children, and the Boy Scouts. With trust funds worth an estimated $10 million (some $60 million today) Kennedy could certainly afford Jackie's purchases, but he was careful with money and disliked the appearance of financial excess.

As she had many times before, Jackie promised to economize, and Jack backed off. Whether out of guilt or indulgence, Jack invariably "would agree with almost anything to please her," said Gallagher. Lem Billings believed that Kennedy was simply trying to prevent Jackie from sulking, which he couldn't bear. For Christmas JFK bought his wife a drawing of two nude women by Renoir and a painting by Maurice Prendergast. Jackie's gift to Jack would be a piece of scrimshaw etched with the presidential seal by artist Milton Delano, who spent 240 hours carving and polishing the sperm whale's tooth.

For all the strains of the preceding months, the latter part of 1962 signaled new beginnings for Jack and Jackie. On weekends they excitedly showed various intimates—Charley and Martha, Lee, Lem, and Bunny—the progress of their Virginia country house even as the costs continued to climb. And within weeks of Caroline's fifth birthday and John Jr.'s second at the end of November, Jack and Jackie conceived another child.

———

It was only a matter of time before a comedian sent up the Kennedys for a national audience. *The First Family,* a phonograph album by twenty-six-year-old impersonator Vaughn Meader, was a runaway hit by the year's end. In a series of skits, Meader and an ensemble of players captured such family mannerisms as Jackie's whispery voice and Jack's broad Bostonian accent ("you drive a haaaad baaagain"), as well as Kennedyesque foibles ("Good night, Jackie; Good night, Bobby; Good night, Ethel . . ."). Jackie took a dim view of the album, objecting to its cover photograph of the fake presidential family in front of the White House as one of the comedian's "cheap jokes." Jack quite enjoyed the mockery, laughing about various sketches over dinner with the Bradlees.

Kennedy himself remained the master of self-deflating humor. When a reporter queried him that December about his surge of interest in the performing arts (he and Jackie had recently ventured out to performances of the Bolshoi and American Ballet Theatre, as well as a French farce at the American National Theatre), JFK deadpanned that his support was modest compared to that of leaders in the past. Pressed for an example, he mentioned Louis XIV, who entertained his courtiers in the seventeenth century by wearing brightly colored tights and flying across the stage in a production called *Furious Roland*.

Turning to more somber matters, Kennedy sat down on Saturday, December 15, in the Oval Office for an unprecedented interview with correspondents from all three television networks for broadcast two nights later. While noting that the superpowers were "far out of contact" before the missile crisis, making no mention of the still-secret correspondence with Khrushchev, Kennedy expressed cautious optimism that a "long period of peace" could result if Khrushchev "would concern himself with the real interests of the people of the Soviet Union."

JFK also briefly mentioned his opposition to Skybolt, a long-range nuclear missile that could be launched from the wing of a jet. Within days, that seemingly benign reference erupted into a full-blown crisis that imperiled the government of Harold Macmillan and threatened Kennedy's relationship with his closest ally. The United States and Britain had invested some $375 million (out of a projected $2.5 billion) to develop Skybolt, which turned out to have numerous technical problems. With a tin ear for political implications, Bob McNamara decided to scrap the missile to save money and move on to more modern and reliable weapons.

For the United States, Skybolt was only one among a range of nuclear armaments, but Britain was counting on the missile as its sole strategic deterrent—a symbol of its prestige as a nuclear power. Losing such an essential element of its foreign policy posed what Macmillan biographer Alistair Horne called potentially "lethal damage" to the conservative government.

With a long-scheduled conference in Nassau between Kennedy and Macmillan set to begin on December 19, the President hastily summoned his advisers for two days of marathon meetings to solve the problem. David Bruce responded to the "urgent summons" by arriving "in tweeds and muddy jodhpur boots" to find McNamara, Gilpatric, Ball, Bundy, and others in Kennedy's "admirably furnished" Treaty Room.

They decided to offer the Polaris missile instead, which was actually a better weapon—with a range twice the distance of Skybolt—at a lower cost. But the missile could be fired only from the new American Polaris submarine, a vessel that would take years for the British to build. The quid pro quo for the deal would be a willingness by Britain to join in a multilateral sea-based nuclear force (MLF) using sailors from NATO countries but giving full control over the weapons to the United States. The purpose would be to check nuclear proliferation by urging individual countries—France and Britain in particular—to scrap their own independent nuclear capability. In that spirit, the United States would offer the Polaris missile on the same basis to France.

All parties arrived in Nassau on Tuesday, December 18. The aides were assigned rooms in the exclusive Lyford Cay Club, while Macmillan and JFK each had a luxurious villa. The atmosphere was tense for nearly two days of talks until Kennedy and Macmillan agreed on terms. David Bruce observed that JFK was "acute, quick and comprehensive," with an ability "to catch every slip or specious argument." By contrast, Macmillan was "almost hesitant at times in speech, at others eloquent, sentimental and where he wishes steely." Ultimately the tight bonds of the "special relationship" prevailed. The outcome, David Gore wrote, was "a compromise which I feel sure no other ally of the U.S. could have achieved."

When Kennedy was leaving Nassau on Friday afternoon, Mimi Beardsley quite literally popped up again. "As the entourage of cars pulled up in front of the house to pick up the President," Barbara Gamarekian recalled, Pierre Salinger and his aide Chris Camp "saw the top of a little head over the door" and "thought there was a little child sitting in the front seat of the car. Chris said to Pierre, 'Who could that child be?' and they walked over and looked in the car, and here seated on the floor was Mimi! She was sitting on the floor of a car so she wouldn't be seen by anyone. She'd been [in Nassau], apparently for several days. They took one look and sort of backed away and didn't say anything."

It turned out that Kennedy had also asked Enüd Sztanko to accompany him on the trip. "What in heaven's name would I do in Nassau?" Sztanko exclaimed. "He got embarrassed," she recalled. "He said, 'I'd like to have you along and see you and talk to you.'" She told him the idea was "foolish for him because it would be noticed."

Kennedy arrived at the Paul estate in Palm Beach to join Jackie and the children for more than two weeks of relaxation leavened by meetings with his advisers. Besides the daily cruises on the *Honey Fitz,* the President enjoyed poolside manicures, shopping on Worth Avenue, and sketching sessions with Elaine de Kooning for a portrait to hang in the Truman Library. Unlike the gray soggy weather of their Christmas holiday the previous year, the days were warm and brilliantly sunny. Billings was a constant presence, along with the Radziwills, Gores, and Agnellis, who were staying with the Wrightsmans. One day the *Honey Fitz* voyaged up the inland waterway to Lantana for a lunch at the Vanderbilt estate that included George Plimpton, Leland and Pamela Hayward, and Loel and Gloria Guinness.

Hervé and Nicole Alphand came aboard for an afternoon cruise on Saturday the twenty-ninth, in part because the French ambassador wanted to discuss the Polaris offer. The Frenchman immediately observed Kennedy's "peculiar little white corset," noting that he "got dressed with difficulty." At the beginning, Nicole joked with the President in the rear of the yacht while Hervé spoke French with Lee. During lunch, Hervé sat next to Kennedy and talked to him throughout the meal. The President "was very agitated, always preoccupied by a new thought, sometimes phoning, sometimes asking the most diverse questions on all subjects," Alphand noted in his diary.

One reason for Kennedy's excitement may have been the event he had attended that morning. With Jackie, Lem, the Radziwills, Pat, and Eunice, he had flown by helicopter to the Orange Bowl in Miami Beach. There he addressed 50,000 Cubans to welcome the arrival of 1,113 veterans of the Bay of Pigs invasion who had just been released from prison by Castro. Departing from his prepared text, Kennedy told the crowd that the United States would neither impose a regime on Cuba nor return the island to its former status—in essence affirming his earlier pledge not to invade. Jackie pleased the crowd by giving brief remarks in Spanish.

The price for the prisoners' freedom was $53 million worth of drugs, baby food, and medical equipment that Bobby Kennedy had organized through New York attorney James B. Donovan. Jack had approved a ransom made more palatable in goods than cash, although he emphasized that the donations came from "private committees." Still, Bobby and his men "all but ordered drug and chemical companies to kick in with 'donations' of their own products," *Time* wrote. Their reward came in tax deductions and anti-trust exemptions.

The Wrightsmans threw their annual New Year's Eve bash for the Kennedy crowd. "You knew from the moment you walked into their orchid-filled house that everything was going to be perfect and delicious," recalled Lee Radziwill. Salinger was on the guest list, and so was Ted Sorensen, one of the few occasions that Kennedy invited his dour aide to a social event. Sorensen left shortly after midnight—hours before the party broke up. "I don't know that my social skills were as highly developed as they should have been," Sorensen recalled. "I would not have been altogether comfortable in those circles. It was discomfort, not awe."

Jack and Jackie stayed until 3:40 a.m. While nothing appeared in the newspapers about the party, Hugh Sidey took note of the generally licentious atmosphere and sent a titillating off-the-record memo to his bosses in New York. "Not since the fall of Rome has there been such a scene," Sidey began. He went on to describe Salinger "in the bushes breathing heavily" with a married woman, and to recount the disappearance of Andy Hatcher (father of seven) to Jamaica with some models. Sidey even joked that one journalist had been assigned to be Rose Kennedy's "gigolo." "It was a paragraph," said Sidey, "tongue in cheek."

A couple of months later, Bobby got a copy of the memo and braced Sidey about it. "He was shaking he was so angry," said Sidey. RFK zeroed in on the innuendo about his mother, for which Sidey promptly apologized. But the *Time* man was unrepentant about the rest. "I didn't make this up," he told Bobby. "This was what was going on, and it was not a pretty picture."

After only two years, the Kennedy administration had suffered a large number of marital casualties. Couples like Arthur and Marian Schlesinger remained together, but with increasingly visible fissures. Marian became accustomed to being left "more or less at the front door" during Washington parties. "Arthur is not one of my favorites," Katie Louchheim wrote in her journal. "Rumor has it he is mean to [Marian] and outdances [sic] the pretty ladies around while she lingers forgotten—a 'lech' they say." Marian kept her equilibrium—"a natural, winning person," in Louchheim's view. "I didn't mind," said Marian. "I'm rather a voyeur. I like to watch the passing show. . . . The time had an anything goes quality, and Arthur was drawn to power and glamour."

Salinger's antics were most well known, and his wife, Nancy, was the most long suffering. During the missile crisis he had moved into the Claridge Hotel near the White House. "He was in the hotel with a French reporter," recalled Barbara Gamarekian. "I had two numbers at the hotel where I could reach him. Pierre wasn't discreet about any of it. Pierre had a lot of liaisons."

That autumn Jewel Reed had returned with her family to western Massachusetts, and Chuck Spalding had moved to Bedford, New York, leaving Betty and the six children in Greenwich. The Spaldings showed up together at the dinner dance for James Gavin, but that was an exception. "Without the White House, Chuck and Betty's marriage would have gone on," said Betty's friend Nancy Coleman. "Chuck being caught up in the power web changed everything."

Betty turned bitter, and her problems with Chuck "colored her view" of Kennedy and the White House, according to Coleman. "She saw such a weakness with the men. It was like Louis XIV and his court." Chuck's "White House fever" reached delirium when he made a play for Lee Radziwill. "She said, 'You must be kidding,'" recalled Charley Bartlett. "The whole thing was so irrational."

Lee's marriage had been precarious for more than a year. *Time* had inadvertently hit a nerve in September 1962 with a cheeky profile of Stas and Lee called "Unhitching Post." The magazine impudently described the connubial merry-go-round that led to the Radziwill marriage—a portrayal so infuriating to JFK that he summoned Harry Luce to the Oval Office for a dressing-down. "The President was bitter as he pointed out the hurt feelings that would be caused by this story," Luce recalled. When the Time Inc. chief emerged from the White House, he said to Sidey, "I think I need a drink."

In fact Lee had increasingly been going her own way. Besides frequently traveling between London and the United States, she had been writing articles for *McCall's* and *Ladies' Home Journal* about style and fashion. (Her coverage of Parisian couture shows was a bonus for Jackie, who got an early glimpse of the latest trends.) Lee had also been looking for romance outside her marriage. Marella Agnelli described Lee's Ravello companion Sandro D'Urso as "a little flirtation and friendship." In 1963, Lee would begin an affair with controversial Greek shipping tycoon Aristotle Onassis. His vast wealth was alluring to Lee, but she was equally intrigued by his odd combination of magnetism and ugliness.

Ted Sorensen's marriage crumbled in the Kennedy years as well. Sorensen may have worked harder than anyone else in the White House, routinely putting in twenty-hour days. When Tish Baldrige teased him once about his punishing habits, he gravely told her that "frankly there wasn't anything he would rather be doing." That commitment contributed to his ulcers as well as wrenching back pain. Tom Sorensen, who worked in the State Department, told Hugh Sidey he feared his brother would collapse from exhaustion because he was "ill half the time."

With three rambunctious sons under ten years old, Ted's wife, Camilla, had little time for socializing. Only months into the Kennedy administration Ted and Camilla were estranged. Sorensen's friend Katie Louchheim noted that he was "a genius," but "not a fond husband type." Before long Ted was showing up at dinner parties on his own, and then with a string of women. "Sorensen, [James] Rowe reports, has an 18-year-old girl and Pierre is on the loose," Louchheim recorded in her journal in January 1963. "Well, if they will lower the age limit for the power set, these things will happen."

Sorensen's dates included a young Englishwoman ("shy with perspiring palms"), a budding society columnist named Cissie Miller ("a winning blonde who stood too tall"), and future feminist writer Gloria Steinem. But even Sorensen's favorite, a petite woman with vivid blue eyes named Sally Elberry, got fed up and moved to Boston.

"He never lets me feel he cares," she told Louchheim. "I was lonely in Washington."

Early in 1963, Camilla fled to Nebraska with the boys, and a divorce followed in October. "It was very sad to have a family splinter and children move away," Sorensen said. "It was very sad, but I don't regret what I did for Jack Kennedy."

JFK had only a vague notion of Sorensen's travails. "He apologized once," Sorensen recalled. "I said, 'It is not your fault.' He lumped me with Chuck Spalding. I knew nothing about Chuck Spalding's marriage. I said, 'There is nothing for you to apologize about.' But he did apologize. I am not easily surprised, but I suppose it was unusual for him to do that."

TWENTY-FIVE

"I am taking the veil," Jackie announced to Mary Gallagher on Friday, January 11. In a memo to Tish Baldrige that day, Jackie declared her intention to significantly curtail her activities as first lady and devote more time to her family. The Kennedys had returned three days earlier from their extended vacation in Palm Beach. Jackie had been there for nearly a month, and Jack for seventeen days. After endless hours of yacht cruises, snoozing, and reading in the sunshine, husband and wife were tanned and rested.

Gallagher and White House maid Providencia Paredes suspected the pregnancy, but Jackie was determined to keep her condition a secret as long as possible. Responding to written questions from Helen Thomas, she said Caroline and John were now "at an age" where it was "important that their parents be with them as much as possible." When Arthur Schlesinger asked Jackie about a possible White House ceremony for a new medal of science, she suggested he consult with JFK. "All I beg of you is, whatever is decided, make it stag, as I am trying to uncrowd my schedule," she wrote.

Scarcely a month later, on February 20, the White House announced that Tish Baldrige would leave at the end of May. Baldrige didn't know yet that Jackie was expecting, but she understood that her forceful style no longer fit with Jackie's plans. The White House "genius in joviality," as David Bruce called Baldrige, had contributed enormously to Jackie's success. At large social gatherings, Baldrige was "adept in elevating the shyest to ease," wrote Bruce, and was "omnipresent introducing the wayfarers to the cavedwellers in a medley of tongues." She had also earned the appreciation of West Wing operatives such as Kenny O'Donnell for the public relations value of the "social stuff" they had initially dismissed.

By early 1963, Baldrige had endured having her "ears pinned back" by Jackie one too many times. "It was a change in the climate," said Baldrige. "The laughing and familiarity and funny jokes stopped." Baldrige felt overworked and underappreciated, suffered spasms in her neck and dizzy spells. Baldrige knew, she wrote later, that Jackie had begun "to resent press clips that mentioned my influence on the entertaining after dinner, on the youth concerts on the White House lawn."

Jackie confided to Bill Walton that her mother and Baldrige "prefer frenzy, but that's all they have to fill their lives." Publicly, Jackie had nothing but praise for Baldrige. "Their relationship had frayed to an extent," said White House curator James Ketchum. "It didn't hit a brick wall. Tish was too professional to let that happen. Jackie was too sensitive to let that happen to Tish."

Before Joe Kennedy's stroke, he had said to Baldrige, "You need to learn about the business world, and to know about more than hors d'oeuvres and jewelry and whipped cream." He gave her an open-ended job offer at his Merchandise Mart in Chicago, which she now embraced to exit the White House.

As soon as Janet Cooper heard that Baldrige was planning to leave, she called Jackie and said, "Nancy is ripe to come and work for you." Nancy Tuckerman had tired of her job in New York at Frew Hill Travel and was open to a new challenge. She had occasionally helped her mother, Betty, who ran a business in Manhattan planning debutante parties, but otherwise Tuckerman had no exposure to the demands of the White House social secretary. "She was the opposite of me," Baldrige noted, "quiet, soft-spoken, not a zealot, and a person with no international diplomatic experience. Obviously Jackie welcomed a change from the overly strong dose of managing I had given her."

Jackie had remained in close touch with Tuckerman and had periodically invited her to White House events and Virginia getaways. Before one weekend, Tuckerman had archly asked Jackie whether she should bring blue jeans or a "cotillion ball gown." Between their shared humor and total discretion, Jackie and Tuckerman were compatible professionally as well as personally. Jackie told Tuckerman about her pregnancy and "convinced Nancy that after her child was born, life would be quiet," said Ketchum. "Jackie would take time off, and J. B. West would run interference." Tuckerman could also rely on help from Anne Lincoln, whom Jackie had recently shifted from Baldrige's assistant to chief housekeeper. "Linky" was another veteran of Park Avenue and Vassar who helped Jackie organize the household, its events, and its financial accounts. "She knows how I want cigarette boxes placed," Jackie told West.

———

Before Jackie eased into her quieter life, she had numerous prior commitments to discharge in the winter months of 1963. The night of their return from Palm Beach after the Christmas holidays, the Kennedys attended a dinner at the French Embassy in honor of André Malraux. Jackie's favorite Frenchman had come to Washington to open the exhibit of the *Mona Lisa* he had promised her the previous May. Jackie wore a strapless mauve chiffon dress in Empire style designed by Cassini to evoke Empress Josephine and "show off" the First Lady's shoulders and neckline. The preview at the National Gallery for 1,200 guests turned into a chaotic crush that shocked Malraux and angered the President.

John Walker, the director of the gallery, wrote Kennedy an apologetic letter, and Jackie replied soothingly: "You mustn't brood and make it worse in your mind. It was a fantastic evening. It is as Malraux said, part of the magic of the *Mona Lisa,* almost an evil spell. . . . So please don't ever have a backward thought again, and just think how beautifully you have hung the picture."

Several days later she displayed her new mink coat at Kennedy's State of the Union address, sitting in the gallery with her mother and Lee. Jack had invited the Bradlees to dinner afterwards with Bobby and Ethel, which prompted a flurry of concern from Jackie about ill will between Bobby and Ben. "I don't want a fight to start," Jackie told Evelyn Lincoln. "The President said they can get along some way," Lincoln jotted in her diary, "so they all came."

That week Jack and Jackie attended the annual "inaugural salute" fundraising dinner followed by a show at the Washington Armory. The Johnsons threw an after-party at their house, and the Kennedys didn't return to the White House until nearly 3 a.m. The next night Jackie and Lee pulled one of their schoolgirl stunts by impulsively inviting some of the gala entertainers—George Burns, Carol Channing, and Kirk Douglas—to dinner upstairs at the White House. "You girls must be crazy," Jack told Jackie and Lee. "But I guess there isn't anything I can do now."

In late January, Jackie unveiled her new Green Room as an authentic "Federal parlor" of the early nineteenth century, and her Blue Room in Monroe's American Empire style furnished with gleaming Bellange chairs. After all the fuss the previous fall over the cream-colored walls in the Blue Room, the refurbishment drew accolades. Each room had newly stained dark walnut parquet floors, a Boudin-inspired treatment that Jackie also used to dramatic effect in the Yellow Oval Room. Hanging prominently in the Green Room was *Nocturne,* by James McNeill Whistler, a gift from Averell and Marie Harriman. Jackie loved the "mysterious" painting, she told the Harrimans. "Think of people seeing it generations from now," she wrote. "It will be like seeing a Poussin (a picture from a century earlier than the one you live in) given by Talleyrand—our Talleyrand!"

———

Jack and Jackie were socializing with friends outside the White House with a frequency equal to their first months in office. During January and February the Kennedys dined at Franklin and Sue Roosevelt's, danced at Doug and Phyllis Dillon's, and attended an elegant dinner party at Joe and Susan Mary Alsop's for Lady Diana Cooper, the seventy-year-old widow of British diplomat Duff Cooper—the onetime lover of Susan Mary. A former actress and one of Britain's celebrated beauties, Lady Diana had recently published her witty memoirs.

Despite their twenty-five-year age difference, Jack and Lady Diana were, as David Bruce put it, "mutually attracted." She considered JFK a "vigorous animal," and Kennedy could only exclaim, "What a woman!" after parrying with her all evening. "I found Jackie more beautiful than I had expected and a hundred times more of a personality," Lady Diana wrote. (It helped that Jackie told Cooper she had read all her books and "remembered a lot.") Cooper had heard rumors of Jackie's "near-divorce mood" over JFK's "preoccupation with anything or anybody but her," but now the British aristocrat observed that Jackie's manner "had turned to connubial comfort. It is said that she has the whip hand as she cares not a jot for what people say."

Cecil Beaton had caught the same whiff of dismissiveness in Jackie two years earlier, and her determination to go her own way had only deepened with time. "If you are in political life you must get used to people who don't like you saying things," she told Harry du Pont that winter. "And you must never let it upset you as life is too short."

While the bulk of Jackie's restoration work was now complete, she continued to scout New York galleries and antique shops for treasures. During the first week of February, she and Lee settled into the Carlyle for some extended socializing and shopping. Their first night in town, Adlai Stevenson threw a party in Jackie's honor. Throughout his missile crisis travails, Jackie had remained loyal to Stevenson. He saluted her friendship by putting together a glittering group that included Bill and Babe Paley, Charlotte Ford, Marietta Tree, Teddy and Nancy White, Jason Robards, Mary Lasker, George Plimpton, and the cast of *Beyond the Fringe* (Peter Cook, Jonathan Miller, Dudley Moore, and Alan Bennett), the satirical revue that had recently opened on Broadway after a sellout run in London.

Jackie's presence proved so unnerving that one guest called Teddy White "Jackie," and Stevenson introduced Babe Paley as "Mr. Paley." At the end of the evening, the British cast performed several sketches from the revue. The next day Jackie thanked Stevenson for an evening that "ran the gamut—comedy, drama and for me abandoned delight . . . the gayest happiest evening imaginable." She gave her friend a picture she had drawn on the plane to New York, "with much love."

Later in the week Jackie and Lee had lunch with Stevenson and UN Secretary-General U Thant in the delegates' dining room. Jackie told Stevenson that she had been fascinated by the "undercurrents and tension and excitement" of the United Nations, and that she and Lee were "dreaming of intrigues in the delegates lounge." But Jackie also worried that the pressures of Stevenson's job were taking a toll on his health.

Jackie, Lee, and Stas were joined by JFK and Chuck Spalding for the weekend. They made a merry band, hiking up and down Park Avenue for lunch at Voisin and dinner at Le Pavillon, followed by a performance of *Beyond the Fringe* and a party at Earl and Flo Smith's that lasted until nearly 2 a.m. On their return to Washington on Sunday, February 10, Jack and Jackie surprised onlookers by stopping their limousine at the corner of Constitution Avenue and Seventeenth Street to walk across the Ellipse to the White House.

Jackie was at the delicate six-week mark in her pregnancy, and on Monday she slept the entire day, declining to appear for dinner and a movie that evening with Ben and Tony. (Jackie had also slept for twelve hours the previous Friday and had missed a birthday party for Adlai Stevenson.) Jack, however, was bursting with energy. Ben Bradlee noticed that in their dinner conversation Kennedy was "relaxed but scattered." After taking his friends on a tour of the Blue and Green Rooms, Kennedy insisted on a midnight walk around the Ellipse "in the cold, pouring rain." Noted Bradlee, "Counting all the Secret Service men, we made up a task force, but no one recognized the president."

Reporters speculated that Kennedy's visible displays of vigor were linked to the "fitness fever" he had stirred up at the beginning of February by resurrecting an executive order written by Teddy Roosevelt that challenged all marine officers to march fifty miles in twenty hours. Ordinary Americans took up the call along with New Frontiersmen. On the weekend JFK was tramping around New York with Jackie, Bobby managed to march fifty miles up the Chesapeake & Ohio Canal—all the way to Camp David—while four companions dropped out from exhaustion.

JFK could hardly be expected to follow his brother's example. Visiting Kennedy in the White House on February 20, David Bruce noted that while the President "always looks well . . . the cortisone, or whatever drug he takes for his ailments, seems to have thickened his face to the extent that he is almost jowly, and there is a slight protrusion of his eyeballs." Nor had Kennedy's back problems abated. One day late that winter, Dr. Hans Kraus was summoned to the White House for a 9 p.m. appointment; the following night at dinner with Ben and Tony, Kennedy described the pain "he felt at that minute in his back" and wondered if he might prefer the intense pain of childbirth because "he thought he could stand any kind and any amount of pain, provided he knew that it would end."

Yet Kennedy could take vicarious pleasure in watching his friends prove themselves. During Christmas in Palm Beach he had bet Stas and

Spalding $1,000 that they would be unable to finish the fifty-mile walk. (The wager would be donated to charity.) They accepted the challenge, provided they be given two months to train. Stas "looked as if he hadn't seen a locker room for thirty years," Ben Bradlee observed. But Stas practiced diligently every day, walking up and down Park Avenue for fifty blocks "with a look of fierce determination on his face and a stone in each hand to keep his fingers from swelling," according to Lee.

Kennedy scheduled the hike for the final Saturday in February during a long weekend at the Paul estate in Palm Beach. Accompanying Stas, forty-eight, and Chuck, forty-four, was Dr. Max Jacobson, who had last treated JFK at Glen Ora during the University of Mississippi crisis the previous September. In June 1962, Bobby had submitted samples of Jacobson's serum for examination by the FBI. The analysis showed no trace of narcotics—Bobby's principal concern—but there were evidently no tests done for amphetamines. When Bobby nevertheless cautioned Jack against the shots, the President replied, "I don't care if it's horse piss. It works."

In his unpublished memoir, Jacobson made no mention of administering shots for the fifty-mile trek, although he acknowledged giving pure oxygen to Stas every five miles when his leg muscles turned wobbly. The men set out at 2:05 a.m. on Saturday the twenty-third, with Jackie and Lee following in a station wagon stocked with orange juice for Stas and raw steak for Spalding. Jack broke away from a cruise on the *Honey Fitz* to check their progress at the thirty-five-mile mark in Pompano Beach. Worried that the exertion might endanger Stas's heart, JFK told his brother-in-law he could quit, and the $1,000 would still go to charity. Stas continued the walk, marching "like an English grenadier, his bent arms swinging rhythmically." For the last fifteen miles, Stas walked on blistered bare feet.

They reached the finish line in Fort Lauderdale at 9:35 p.m. A limousine returned them to Palm Beach, where Kennedy hung paper medals around their necks. Jackie immortalized the event with one of her watercolors: the two men striding in profile against a green background, with plump Stas behind lanky Spalding. As a tiny joke, Stas's visible left foot was clad not in one of his Tyrolean hiking boots, but a black tasseled loafer.

Jackie remained in Palm Beach to rest for another week while Jack flew back to Washington with Stas and Lee. The following Sunday, Jack and Charley Bartlett spent a sunny afternoon sightseeing like a couple of eager tourists. They walked up the Mall, visited the Lincoln Memorial, hopped into the limousine, and drove to Arlington National Cemetery. They wandered among the graves and toured the Custis-Lee Mansion, the pillared home of Robert E. Lee perched on a hill with a direct sightline to the Lincoln Memorial. Jack loved the view across the river so much that he joked, "Maybe we'd better move the White House over here." The two men also discussed where Jack would be buried. "He said, 'I guess I'll have to go back to Boston,'" Bartlett recalled. "I remember arguing for the national cemetery. We left it sort of up in the air."

The Kennedy crowd was badly jolted early in 1963 by the mental collapse of Philip Graham, the influential president of the *Washington Post*. Graham had met JFK in the late 1950s through Bill Walton and had fallen hard for the young senator. Phil and Katharine Graham were fixtures on the Kennedys' White House guest lists and joined them at Georgetown dinner parties. Phil would offer advice to Kennedy from time to time, including the suggestion shortly after JFK's election that David Bruce would be "a strong and wise London ambassador."

Ben Bradlee considered Phil a "natural friend for Kennedy" because of their "shared humor, understanding of the uses and abuses of power, charm, common goals for America, and much more." To Katharine Graham, her husband and the President were "friends of a certain kind. They were very funny with each other." Yet Graham never became part of JFK's inner circle. The primary reason for their lack of intimacy was Graham's manic-depressive illness, which "cut him off terribly," said Anne Truitt, who knew about Graham because her husband worked as his assistant.

In his manic phases, Graham plunged into "erratic, often brilliant activity" that alternated with "debilitating depressions," Bradlee observed. As recently as the summer of 1962, Graham had "seemed well and in balance," Katharine later wrote. But that autumn, Kennedy had asked Graham to head COMSAT, a public/private company charged with operating communications satellites. As Graham threw himself into organizing the new company, he became "out of control, hectic, unhinged," Arthur Schlesinger recalled. "A life enhancer became a life destroyer."

Graham turned abusive to colleagues, employees, and even the President. When JFK called him in November, Graham unleashed an angry outburst that Kennedy patiently endured. Walt Rostow was impressed that in a White House meeting several weeks later when Graham was "quite wild," Kennedy "did the best to treat him with dignity but calm him down."

During a trip to Paris late in 1962, Graham met a young Australian reporter named Robin Webb in the *Newsweek* bureau there. Graham became infatuated with Webb and brought her back to New York, where they moved into a suite at the Carlyle. His mood aggravated by excessive drinking, Phil confronted Katharine with his affair and walked out in mid-January. He and Robin flew out west, ending up in Phoenix, where a group of newspaper publishers and editors on the Associated Press board were having a conference at the Biltmore Hotel. Graham "was in a high mood, cursing a lot," recalled Otis Chandler, the *Los Angeles Times* publisher who took the cottage next to Graham's.

On Thursday, January 17, Graham called the Oval Office at 7:30 p.m. Arizona time—three hours after JFK had left the office—and spoke with Evelyn Lincoln. Graham "wanted me to ask Curtis LeMay to call him," Lincoln noted in her diary. "He said he was in love with Robin Webb and was going to get married to her as soon as he got a divorce. He sounded drunk to me."

That evening Graham went to dinner with the newsmen. As soon as Ben McKelway, editor of the *Washington Star,* the *Post*'s rival in the capital, stood up to speak, Graham walked to the lectern, seized the microphone, and began shouting insults at various publishers in the room. Chandler made his way to the podium and escorted Graham back to his cottage, where Webb tried to settle him. Well past midnight Graham called Jack Kennedy to continue his tirade. Banging on Chandler's door, Graham implored him to talk to "his buddy" the President.

By then Chandler had reached the president of the *Washington Post* television stations, also in Phoenix for a meeting, to report, "Phil is out of control. You'd better get him out of here." The *Post* executive called Katharine Graham. She desperately contacted James Truitt, who phoned Jack Kennedy. The President immediately dispatched Phil's psychiatrist to Phoenix in an air force plane.

In later years, there were persistent rumors that Graham had shocked the gathering by telling them "who in Washington was sleeping with whom," including Kennedy and his "favorite," Mary Meyer. Yet two men in the audience could remember no such revelation. Bernard Ridder, publisher of the *St. Paul Pioneer Press*, vividly recalled Graham's "rude and critical" remarks, and Otis Chandler remembered that "Phil was roaming from one subject to another, and he was not making sense. There was stone silence in the room. He didn't talk that long. Phil's utterances were of nonconnecting thoughts and four-letter words."

After being tranquilized and restrained by physicians, Graham was hospitalized for several weeks and resigned from COMSAT. In a letter of gratitude to Jack Kennedy, Katharine wrote that her husband "would die at the thought that he might have hurt you in any way. I hope he didn't—too much." The reference had to do with Graham's conduct rather than any specific statement. "No one present that night has ever told me exactly what happened or what Phil said," Katharine Graham wrote years later. She knew only that her husband's "wild remarks" had attacked individuals, but she never heard any mention of Mary Meyer.

"We heard Phil flipped out," said Ben Bradlee. "All the drama was Phil going crazy. Mary Meyer wasn't talked about, not at all. If Tony had heard that, she obviously would have talked to Mary." Added Anne Truitt, "James would have told me if Phil had mentioned Mary. It would have worried him terribly." Katie Louchheim, who had few inhibitions about passing along the latest scuttlebutt, wrote to a friend only that Phil Graham was "the story of the week," describing his behavior but saying nothing of sexual allegations about JFK. Eleven days after Graham's breakdown, Meyer was at the White House for the evening while Jackie was at Glen Ora.

Graham had barely been released from the Chestnut Lodge psychiatric hospital when he was back in New York at the Carlyle with Webb. Shortly after JFK arrived in his thirty-fourth-floor suite on Saturday, February 9, for the weekend with Jackie, Lee, Stas, and Spalding, he stopped by Graham's suite for twenty minutes. When he returned to his apartment, Kennedy inadvertently left behind his briefcase—a reflection of what one author called his lifelong habit of "peculiar absentmindedness . . . always leaving clothes, briefcases or papers behind in hotels or airports or on trains."

In a burst of grandiosity, Graham told friends that he had seen classified papers. When Tony Bradlee asked about Graham's claim, JFK explained that it was "hardly a briefcase of 'national crises' . . . just a "bunch of documents." Holding his thumb next to his forefinger, JFK said, "The line is so damn narrow between rationality and irrationality in Phil. . . . He has been good to me and good to this country, and I want to help him out." Graham was beyond anyone's help by then. Shortly after his visit with Kennedy, he and Webb took off on a trip to the Caribbean and Europe, not to return until early summer.

Jackie betrayed no change in attitude toward the Bradlees to signal she knew about Jack and Mary. The only hiccough in their relationship occurred in March when Ben revealed to the Kennedys over dinner that he had been keeping a journal of their conversations. He had not intended to tell them, but Tony forced him to. Ben assured JFK that he "would not write anything about him as long as he was alive without his permission." Kennedy was unfazed. "He insisted that he was glad that someone was keeping some kind of a record of the more intimate details without which the real story of any administration cannot be told," Bradlee recorded that evening. "I am not convinced he knows how intimate those details might get, but I suspect Jackie does."

On Friday, March 8, the Kennedys had their sixth and what would be their final dinner dance at the White House. The honoree was Eugene Black, the director of the World Bank, who didn't understand his role as front man and insisted the Kennedys invite a large group of his friends. As a result, the Kennedys had to "uninvite" old friends as they had done previously when their dinners were oversubscribed. Once again, the Bradlees, Bill Walton, Arkady Gerney, and Mary Meyer were among those who had to dine elsewhere before the 10 p.m. dance.

During dinner in the Blue Room, a dozen violinists played "gently and wildly Viennese and Hungarian music," Adlai Stevenson told Marietta Tree. The Red and Green Rooms were illuminated by fireplaces and soft lighting, and when the Blue Room was cleared for dancing to Lester Lanin, "the lights were shut off and the gayety [sic], enhanced by a large number of younger people who arrived after dinner, proceeded far into the morning lit by only a few candles around the walls."

Ninety-four guests consumed "only" thirty-three bottles of champagne and six bottles of hard liquor, Kennedy later reported. But spirits were giddy nevertheless. The girlfriend of Godfrey McHugh, Kennedy's soigné air force aide, was reported to have taken a swim at midnight and to have jumped on the bed in the Lincoln Room—a story Jackie recounted several days later and Jack didn't deny. Lyndon Johnson "spent a large portion of the evening floating in the capacious embrace" of New York beauty Lilly Guest. At 3 a.m., Stevenson was surprised to encounter Marian Schlesinger "quite high and *very* affectionate." In the car on the way home he witnessed "curiously daring behavior by Phyllis Dillon in a dim corner of her car."

Kennedy had a comical run-in with the Earl of Arran, a journalist known as "Boofy" Gore who was a cousin of the British ambassador. (Gore was famous in the House of Lords for advocating the rights of homosexuals and the protection of badgers, proclaiming, "I want to stop them from badgering the buggers and buggering the badgers.") He made the mistake of bringing up the Skybolt imbroglio, causing Kennedy to shout, "Where's McNamara?" "A simply terrifying-looking man came up," the journalist later wrote. McNamara assaulted him with facts and figures, and when he stopped, Kennedy took over. "It was like a Greek chorus," wrote Gore.

Although Kennedy appeared to be in a "lighthearted mood" at the dance, something went awry with Mary Meyer that night. Her date for the evening was Blair Clark, JFK's old friend from Harvard. Despite the chill in the air, Meyer decided to wear a wispy dress that had belonged to her great-grandmother, which she instantly realized was a mistake. At some point in the evening, Meyer "simply disappeared for a half hour," Clark told author Ralph Martin six years after James Truitt disclosed the Kennedy-Meyer affair. "Finally I went looking for her. She had been upstairs with Jack, and then she had gone walking out in the snow. So there I was, 'the beard' for Mary Meyer."

Tony Bradlee remembered "people talking about 'Where was Mary?' It was long enough so you would notice her absence." Later Meyer told Anne Truitt only that she had been "unhappy," and that when she came inside she couldn't find Clark. Bobby Kennedy called a White House limousine, put her in the back, and sent her home. "Mary said Bobby had been nice to her," recalled Cicely Angleton. "She was upset, and he saw that she got home safely."

Whether Kennedy tried to break it off with Meyer that night is unknown. But a stray remark he made to Bradlee may offer a clue. Surveying the "females imported from New York," Kennedy said, "If you and I could only run wild, Benjy." Jackie startled Adlai Stevenson, her dinner partner, by confiding that she and Lee had "always talked about divorce as practically something to look forward to," and that "I first loved you" when she and Stevenson met back in Illinois just after she and Jack were married. Jackie may have been indulging in her known tendency to exaggerate for effect. But, more revealingly, she told Stevenson, "I don't care how many girls [Jack sleeps with] as long as I know he knows it's wrong, and I think he does now. Anyway that's all over, for the present."

———

Kennedy's amorous adventures were becoming more widely known within the intelligence community. In addition to the likelihood that J. Edgar Hoover was passing information to LBJ from the growing FBI dossier on JFK, there were rumors in later years that CIA spymaster James Angleton had learned about Kennedy's affair with Meyer by tapping her phones. His widow, Cicely, dismissed that notion as "the nuttiest thing." Although Cicely was one of Meyer's closest friends, she was unaware of the affair with Kennedy. "I took it for granted that as a wonderful charming woman naturally she would be going to the White House," said Cicely. Yet Richard Helms said James Angleton had "indicated a knowledge of Mary Meyer and Jack Kennedy. I don't know how or where he got it. He had no capacity to tap her phone."

Helen Chavchavadze had also come under scrutiny, and by March 1963, she began to suffer the consequences. Since 1961 she had been studying for her master's degree in Russian at Georgetown and earning money by teaching English as a second language there. She had completed her master's thesis in the fall of 1962 and was accepted at the Foreign Service Institute as a supervisory linguist. But although she had graduated at the top of her class and received glowing recommendations, she was unable to start work because her security clearance had not come through.

In January 1963 her interviews began with State Department security officers. "They were interrogating me about my life, asking questions about abortions I had had," she recalled. "They had a dossier, and they were asking if I believed in free love. I had two children to support, and I couldn't get a security clearance." Chavchavadze soon began to sense that her house was under surveillance. She knew that Jack had to be the key factor in her problems; when she lived in Berlin, she had received a security clearance as a contract translator for the CIA, where her then husband worked.

Chavchavadze went swimming at the White House with Jack at lunchtime one day in early 1963. "You look like a frightened rabbit," he said to her. "I was about to crack," she recalled. "I was paranoid about all those interviews." A day or so later, a limousine arrived at her Georgetown home, and a chauffeur handed her an envelope containing $500 in cash (the equivalent of $3,000 today). "It was obviously from Jack," she said. "He did something. It wasn't much. He was worried for me."

Kennedy interceded with the State Department to grant Chavchavadze permission to start work in April. But her lack of a clearance prevented her from attending meetings, which she found humiliating. She became depressed, unable to concentrate or read, and she quit. Shortly afterwards she had a nervous breakdown and checked herself into the new psychiatric ward on the seventh floor of Washington's Sibley Hospital.

She was surprised to have regular visits from Ted Sorensen, whom she had met at the home of Washington hostess and health care activist Florence Mahoney. "I think he was interested in me as a woman," Chavchavadze recalled. "But I sort of wondered if he was concerned that I might be saying something too." She had lost her house, and her two daughters had been sent to live with their grandmother on Cape Cod. But the greatest pressure was what Chavchavadze called "the conspiracy of silence"—her inability to discuss her affair. "It was one of the many aspects that were the cause of my crack-up," she later said. "It was stressful, on top of the whole thing with the clearance."

———

As Jackie's pregnancy advanced, her official appearances dwindled. In March she attended just two White House functions—a noontime White House reception for the American National Theatre and Academy, and a state dinner for dashing young King Hassan II of Morocco.

Both Jack and Jackie were enchanted by Hassan, who gave the President a gold sword encrusted with fifty diamonds. Jackie wrote the king a five-page letter in French and told the Bradlees that if she could visit anywhere in the world, it would be Morocco.

Jackie dropped a few tantalizing hints among friends about her condition. At the Eugene Black dinner she had rattled Tony Bradlee by announcing "my bust is bigger than yours, but then so is my waist." Three weeks later at dinner Ben had asked Jackie if she was expecting. She denied it, but the Bradlees remained unconvinced. Jackie's unwillingness to confide in them upset Tony, though less so when she learned that Janet Auchincloss had also been kept in the dark.

With riding horses out of the question, Jackie devoted herself to decorating Wexford, mostly with furniture she had used in the Georgetown house. By April 1 the family had moved out of Glen Ora. Until the new house was ready, they spent their spring weekends at Camp David. Jackie used the presidential retreat as a jumping-off point for two excursions to Civil War battlefields—first in Jack's convertible to Gettysburg with Paul and Anita Fay, and a week later to Antietam by helicopter with Lem Billings, Jim Reed, and Ralph "Rip" Horton, a Choate friend who was serving as special assistant to the secretary of the army.

When the group returned to Camp David that Sunday, Reed and Jackie had a deeply personal conversation. "I was getting divorced from my wife, and Jackie asked me all kinds of questions: why I was divorcing Jewel, what did I think of Jewel, probing questions," Reed recalled. "She knew I knew that Jack was doing various things he shouldn't have done. That wasn't the issue. We were talking about intimacy. She was forthright with me about her relationship with Jack. They did have a sex life. She talked about that intimately with me. She loved him dearly, and I felt they were getting much closer together." Reed was neither shocked nor judgmental about Jackie's frankness. "I rather enjoyed it," he said. "I knew her pretty well. I never got any girls for Jack, and she felt I was not contributing to the delinquency of the President." Reed was struck, however, that "Jackie was genuinely sorry I was going through [the divorce] experience. There was a lot of kindness and gentleness in Jackie."

The following Wednesday, Jackie and the children flew to Palm Beach for Easter vacation at the Paul residence. When JFK arrived the next day with the Fay family, the press had an unusual glimpse of the closeness between Jack and Jackie that Reed had detected. Jackie "waited for her husband at a spot well out of the range of news cameramen," the *Washington Post* reported, "and gave him a big hug and kiss when he stepped from the jet."

On Worth Avenue, JFK bought Lilly Pulitzer dresses for Jackie and Caroline, and he interrupted a *Honey Fitz* cruise on the afternoon of Easter Sunday to flag down a catamaran called *Pattycake*. With Fay at his side, Kennedy jumped aboard and asked if he could take the tiller. Dressed in his sporty red trousers, the President stood barefoot on the deck, clamped a cigar between his teeth, and sailed the craft around Lake Worth.

The next day, Monday, April 15, Jackie announced that she would have a baby at the end of August. The birth would be the first for a presidential couple since Marion Cleveland was born in 1895. Jackie would cease her official schedule and spend most of her time away from the White House, remaining in Palm Beach for ten more days and moving to Cape Cod at the end of May. As so often happened in the fecund Kennedy family, Jackie was not alone. Joan was expecting her third child in August and Ethel was preparing for her eighth in June.

TWENTY-SIX

Jack Kennedy's upbeat mood in the early months of 1963 was rooted in more than happiness over the prospect of a third child. For the first time in two years, he felt optimistic about the world situation. His new tone came through clearly in his State of the Union address on Monday, January 14. Sitting in the gallery, Katie Louchheim thrilled to the "theatrical quality of grandeur" and the vision of Kennedy as a "hard-muscled man with a neat hero's look, and a way of taking it in but not letting himself be taken in by it." She watched him glance at John McCormack and Lyndon Johnson "not with deference but with political respect." The President's reading was "flat," yet he communicated "beyond words. . . . He leaves it to you, and so you listen carefully."

The centerpiece of his address was the proposed $13.5 billion tax reduction to stimulate economic growth and reduce unemployment, which had exceeded 5 percent in sixty-one of the previous sixty-two months. But his words also highlighted a receding Soviet threat following the missile crisis. In Kennedy's first State of the Union, he had solemnly declared that "the tide of events has been running out and time has not been our friend. . . . The news will be worse before it is better." Now he proclaimed the United States had "the tides of human freedom in our favor . . . We have every reason to believe that our tide is running strong." Specifically, the possibility of peaceful compromise with the Soviet Union seemed within reach. James Reston concluded that in two years Kennedy had turned from pessimistic to "buoyantly hopeful."

Not even a dyspeptic blast from Charles de Gaulle that morning could dim Kennedy's sunny posture. The French leader had rejected the Nassau offer of the Polaris missile—which effectively scuttled the proposed multinational nuclear force—and vetoed Britain's entry into the European Common Market. Kennedy saw neither development as a major setback for American interests. "From a strictly economic view-point," he told Schlesinger, British integration into Europe actually posed problems for the United States. Nor was Kennedy enthusiastic about the multinational force, which was murky in its details. He had reluctantly recognized that France could not be dissuaded from going its own way to develop nuclear weapons. When Ben Bradlee asked about the multinational force's future during dinner a few weeks after the State of the Union address, Kennedy "gave an evasive answer which translated meant to me that he was not terribly serious about it."

Kennedy declined to confront the French, but he was privately irri-tated with de Gaulle for his obstructionist attitudes. "What can you do with a man like that?" Kennedy would ask his aides. Kennedy "had con-tempt for the spitefulness of official French pronouncements," wrote Schlesinger. In a National Security Council meeting several days after de Gaulle's rebuffs, the President acknowledged "we have to live with" the French leader while recognizing that de Gaulle's emphasis on French nationalism ran contrary to American interests. By early March, Hervé Alphand recorded in his journal, "During official dinners I get the cold shoulder. President Kennedy has his brother Bobby tell me that for the moment it's best that we don't meet."

Alphand was also deeply jealous of David Gore's closeness to JFK. Cy Sulzberger concluded that the French envoy had become "bitter and emotionally anti-British, rather anti-Administration." Alphand told the New York Times correspondent that British propaganda against France was so ingrained at the White House that Mac Bundy had come to sound like Gore: "He even uses the same phrases." Gore well under-stood his advantage. "The French," he told Macmillan, "have now been consigned to the deepest recesses of the doghouse by the President."

Despite the missteps over Skybolt, Kennedy's bond with Gore had tightened—"a remarkable position," Macmillan noted that spring, "an intimate and trusted friend. It is most fortunate—and almost unprecedented—for a British ambassador to have this position." The principal British-American goal was obtaining a treaty banning the testing of nuclear weapons—"the most important step we can take towards unraveling this frightful tangle of fear and suspicion in East-West relations," Macmillan wrote Kennedy on March 16.

Throughout the first six months of 1963, Kennedy and Macmillan exchanged secret correspondence with each other and with Khrushchev about terms for the proposed treaty. Kennedy had been interested in nuclear disarmament for years, but Macmillan felt a "very deep personal obligation" to achieve a ban "before it is too late." The British leader made it his mission to stiffen JFK's resolve against the "rats" in the Kennedy administration who urged a more timid course. Yet for all Macmillan's pushing, the negotiations hit an impasse over "on site" inspections to verify a ban on underground tests. When Khrushchev appeared willing to accept three such inspections a year, Kennedy said no fewer than eight or ten would suffice.

Britain's elder statesman was in serious political trouble in 1963. Coming on top of Skybolt, the Common Market rejection was a "devastating blow" for Macmillan—"the gravest failure of all his policies." In late March, Macmillan's situation worsened with the disclosure that John Profumo, the secretary of state for war, had been linked to Christine Keeler, the mistress of a Soviet military attaché. Macmillan had known since late January that Profumo had socialized with a "girl of doubtful reputation." Schlesinger, just back from England (where David Bruce's office had been closely monitoring the revelations), filled in Kennedy by telephone the day after the story broke on March 21. Kennedy said little, asking only for a description of the scandal, and whether the woman was a spy. Schlesinger replied that Keeler was a "sort of fashionable London call girl," and that "espionage hasn't been suggested."

Several days later, Schlesinger elaborated on Macmillan's plight, writing that the impression created by the Profumo case was of a "frivolous and decadent" government where everything was "unraveling at the seams." Schlesinger praised Harold Wilson, the newly named leader of the Labour party, for his "intelligence, self-control . . . and cool political skill," slyly noting that criticism of Wilson's ambition mirrored "what people were saying about Kennedy in 1960." Added Schlesinger, "Wilson's footwork is fancy, and it is hard to lay a glove on him." Kennedy was suitably impressed, telling Bradlee it was "the best memo he had ever received—bar none . . . especially on the shadow Prime Minister Harold Wilson."

In the view of Ken Galbraith, Schlesinger had settled nicely into his gadfly role. "The papers have rather forgotten that he was meant to be the whipping boy," Galbraith had noted in his diary at the end of 1962. Galbraith, however, was restless. Kennedy had asked him to extend his leave of absence from Harvard for another year. But the envoy to India was well aware that Dean Rusk continued to regard him as "a major inconvenience in an otherwise placid organization." Rusk was so irritated by Galbraith's "high and mighty ways of presenting his views to Washington" that for Christmas he sent him a cable saying, "Happy Birthday."

Galbraith had also grown disillusioned with Kennedy's economic policies. After reading a speech JFK had prepared for the Economic Club of New York in December 1962, Galbraith despaired that it was "full of Republican clichés," including the notion that "taxes were handicapping investment and undermining incentives." Galbraith couldn't reconcile himself to the fact that these "Republican" notions were Kennedy's fundamentally conservative economic beliefs. He tried to change the speech, but "it was beyond retrieval and I effected little improvement."

It came as no surprise when Kennedy announced that Galbraith would be the first member of his inner circle to leave the administration. He would return to the United States in June to work on some projects for the President and resume teaching at Harvard in the fall. "What is interesting about Ken Galbraith is I don't think he was taken in by the Kennedys to the extent the others were," said Marian Schlesinger. "Ken is such a colossus. He wouldn't care."

As Jack Kennedy was happily cruising in Palm Beach on his Easter vacation, the first big crisis of the third year of his presidency was unfolding in Birmingham, Alabama. Kennedy had finally submitted his civil rights legislation in February 1963. Once again he took an incremental approach, focusing only on voting rights. For civil rights leaders, the measure didn't go far enough.

On April 3 the Reverend Martin Luther King Jr. and other black leaders launched a campaign of civil disobedience in Birmingham. Blacks staged sit-ins at lunch counters that refused to serve them, and picketed department stores where blacks and whites had to use separate water fountains and toilets. Over a period of three days in the middle of April, police arrested hundreds of demonstrators, including King. Kennedy helped arrange King's release and sent Bobby's deputy, Burke Marshall, to negotiate with local business leaders.

King changed his tactics in a controversial but highly effective way. When few adults agreed to march again, King enlisted thousands of schoolchildren for a protest in early May. Many were arrested, and Birmingham police commissioner Eugene "Bull" Connor ordered his men to turn powerful fire hoses on the young protesters and unleash fierce attack dogs. Evening newscasts and the front pages of newspapers showed affecting pictures of the brutality, including a German shepherd lunging at a teenage boy.

While Kennedy pressed for a negotiated settlement, the unrest continued. Finally on Sunday evening, May 12, Kennedy made a brief television address calling on the citizens of Birmingham to "maintain standards of reasonable conduct" and announcing that he had put federal troops on alert near the city to preserve order if necessary. But the images of violence had shifted national perceptions toward greater sympathy for racial equality. Kennedy's aides, Bobby in particular, were pushing him to exert moral leadership by introducing a comprehensive civil rights bill.

Jack Kennedy happened to have his legacy very much on his mind at that moment. The previous day he had toured Boston and its suburbs by helicopter and car to inspect possible sites for his presidential library. He had already met with John Warnecke, his favorite architect, to discuss possible design schemes.

Since the beginning of the year, Arthur Schlesinger had been pressing Kennedy in a series of memos about obtaining an official record of "major episodes in your administration." The way Kennedy made decisions was contrary to the orderly processes admired by historians: he disliked organized meetings, and preferred to make policy in private, often one-on-one, after meetings had ended. This executive style, in the view of James Reston, "made the gathering of history extremely difficult."

Schlesinger cautioned—seemingly with unintended irony—that a "house historian could become a nuisance if he tried too zealously to record things as they happened." Kennedy agreed, and shot down the idea of an official historian as well as Schlesinger's proposal to import "ad hoc specialists" to write up specific events. Kennedy also rejected taping conversations after "major episodes" to capture the details before memories had faded. "I plead for you to consider this," wrote Schlesinger.

But Schlesinger's appeals went nowhere, perhaps because JFK believed his secret taping system would provide a sufficient historical record. Kennedy knew that Schlesinger, Sorensen, and probably Bundy at the very least would write their own accounts of his administration, and his view of their efforts seemed ambivalent. When Charley Bartlett once asked Kennedy about rumors that Emmet Hughes, who had written a book on the Eisenhower White House, was coming to work for Kennedy, the President replied, "Don't worry, I have enough biographers around here already." In conversations with Bradlee, Kennedy referred to contemporary historians as "bastards" who were "always there with their pencils out."

Yet Kennedy had encouraged Schlesinger to keep his own journal and had told Sorensen he might collaborate with him. "I just wanted to make sure you got that down for the book we're going to write," Kennedy said to Sorensen at one point during the Cuban Missile Crisis.

———

Kennedy remained equally preoccupied with what Philip Graham called "the first rough draft of history"—the work of daily and weekly journalists. "The only thing I regret," David Bruce noted in his diary on February 21, 1963, "is that the President is such an omnivorous reader of newspapers, foreign and domestic. I think he takes their pontifications too seriously, not appreciating that journalists focus primarily on crises of the moment. I believe he is oversensitive to their criticism."

Coverage of Kennedy continued to be overwhelmingly adoring, which didn't diminish his focus on the critics. "At least once a night, our conversation turns to the news business," Ben Bradlee observed in late March. Kennedy's bugbear that spring was the accusation that he was cynically "managing" the news. Arthur Krock had led the charge in the March *Fortune* magazine, describing how Kennedy used "social flattery" and "selective personal patronage" with reporters. After "intimate background briefings," Krock wrote, "journalists . . . emerge in a state of protracted enchantment evoked by the President's charm and the awesome aura of his office." *New York Times* correspondent Hanson Baldwin offered a similar critique in the *Atlantic Monthly.*

Kennedy's carping to Bradlee about the charges led to a *Newsweek* cover story on "Who Manages What News?" that largely debunked the notion that the White House was orchestrating press coverage. If nothing else, the mere publication of the article showed how adept the White House had become in steering journalists in sympathetic directions. "Krock," the story noted, "deplored the way the President . . . blurred . . . critical faculties with his charm (as if he could be deliberately dull)." Both Krock and Baldwin were "outs" in Washington, declared *Newsweek,* denied the sort of "inside contacts" they had enjoyed with previous administrations.

Kennedy told Bradlee the cover story "was the best thing he had read on the subject," although the President was disappointed that *Newsweek* had not sufficiently "tucked it to Arty [Krock]." Bradlee felt they had done enough by calling the "former friend" of Kennedy "old and out of it." Kennedy also let slip to Bradlee that he no longer spoke to either Lippmann or Reston. "He said he had answered Reston's request for an interview," Bradlee noted, "by suggesting that Reston interview Krock, who was posing as an informed observer of the Kennedy Administration."

No journalist or publication had supplanted Henry Luce's Time Inc. either in its importance or its power to annoy the President. The depth of JFK's continuing irritation was clear in a phone conversation he had with Bobby in early March. Kennedy boasted that he had just blistered Luce for forty-five minutes over *Time*'s coverage only to have Luce turn around and invite the President to the magazine's fortieth birthday party in May. "They're just mean as hell up there," said JFK. "Bastards," said Bobby.

Kennedy had already cut the cord with Clare Luce following a luncheon with her in October 1962 before the missile crisis. She told him then that great men could be summed up for history in one simple sentence, and she wondered if Jack would be strong enough to "turn the world tide of communism." When Hugh Sidey arrived at the White House to retrieve her, he realized that they had finished considerably before the appointed time. Kennedy "was sore as hell," Sidey recalled. "She was lecturing him. He said, 'This is the last time I am going to see that woman.'" Clare was angry as well. "I have never been treated this way," she complained. "He wouldn't let me finish my dessert. He cut me off."

Kennedy declined the invitation to the *Time* fete. He told Sidey that people would call him a "sap" for playing up to Luce by attending. In the message he sent to be read at the dinner, JFK hailed Luce for his creativity, observed that *Time* had "instructed, entertained, confused and infuriated its readers," and ventured that the magazine in middle age showed a "mellowing of tone . . . greater tolerance of human frailty" and an "occasional hint of fallibility."

The same might well have been said of Kennedy himself. On his forty-sixth birthday several weeks later on Wednesday, May 29, his staff threw a surprise party with an array of gag gifts: a tiny rocking chair, boxing gloves "to deal with Congress," a basket of dead grass presented by Jackie on behalf of the "White House Historical Society—genuine antique grass from the antique Rose Garden." In the evening, Jackie arranged a dinner cruise on the Potomac with two dozen guests aboard the *Sequoia,* most of them family and close friends: Bobby and Ethel, Sarge and Eunice, Teddy, the Fays, Bartletts, and Bradlees, as well as Reed, Walton, and Billings. Also included were George Smathers and his wife, Rosemary, British actor David Niven and his wife, Hjordis (soigné members of "Hollywood Royalty" who had been friendly with the Kennedys since the mid-fifties when they went dancing together at Manhattan's El Morocco), Clem Norton (an old-fashioned Boston pol who came with Teddy), Fifi Fell, Mary Meyer, and Jack's new friend Enüd Sztanko, identified only as "Teacher, Georgetown U." Although they were on the guest list, Steve and Jean, Peter and Pat, and Chuck Spalding didn't appear, nor did Joan Kennedy, who was nearly seven months pregnant. None of Kennedy's intimates in the administration were invited, not even McNamara, whose birthday gift was an expensive antique engraving of Mount Vernon that Kennedy had admired.

Jackie instructed everyone to wear "yachting clothes" for an 8:01

departure, and Kennedy wore his nautical blue blazer. After drinks on the fantail, dinner was served in the cabin—beginning with roast fillet of beef and ending with 1955 Dom Pérignon champagne. It was a hot evening, with thunder, lightning, and torrential rain. The mood was raucous and boozy, especially throughout the toasts, which were greeted by jeers in typical Kennedy family style. Commanded to make a speech, Sztanko "felt absolute panic" before she said "Happy birthday" and "Best wishes" in Hungarian "as if it was a perfectly normal thing."

A three-piece band played—mostly twist music that Kennedy kept requesting for the dancers. He had been suffering from especially severe back pain, prompting Jackie to ask Janet Travell if she could give him total relief for his party. The only shot, Travell told her, would "remove all feeling below the waist." Cracked Kennedy, "We can't have that, can we, Jacqueline?" Whatever palliative Travell provided, JFK later said that he had felt "miraculously better" all evening. He even commanded the captain to take the cruiser five miles upstream four times, which kept the festivities going until 1:23 a.m.

"It was a wild party," Tony Bradlee recalled. "People were shouting and laughing." David Niven was "whispering in my ear all night, three sheets to the wind," recalled Martha Bartlett. "I loved it!" Red Fay sang his signature "Hooray for Hollywood" as well as "Me and My Shadow." Everyone was "more or less drenched," Ben Bradlee recalled. Teddy was "the wettest," and during some "fairly strenuous Kennedy games," he lost the entire left leg of his trousers—"ripped off at the crotch," Niven recalled, "with white underpants on the port side flashing." Clem Norton got so drunk he fell onto the pile of gifts, stomping on a rare engraving from Jackie showing a scene from the War of 1812. With her characteristic "veiled expression," she avoided dampening the mood by saying, "Oh, that's all right. I can get it fixed." Tony could see clearly that "Jackie was distressed."

But it was Jack himself who misbehaved in an especially reckless fashion. With Jackie nearby, not to mention Mary, Kennedy zeroed in on Tony Bradlee. "Oh, Jack, you know you always say that Tony is your ideal," Jackie had said jokingly at dinner a month earlier. "Yes, that's true," JFK had replied, pausing briefly before adding, "You're my ideal Jacqueline." Twice since then Kennedy had urged Tony to join him on a state visit to Europe at the end of June. Both times she had refused.

Several hours into the birthday cruise, as Tony made her way to the bathroom, she realized Jack was following her. "He chased me all around the boat," recalled Tony. "A couple of members of the crew were laughing. I was running and laughing as he chased me. He caught up with me in the ladies' room and made a pass. It was a pretty strenuous attack, not as if he pushed me down, but his hands wandered. I said 'That's it, so long.' I was running like mad."

By Tony's recollection, Kennedy was not drunk. "The atmosphere probably influenced Jack's chase," she said. "I guess I was pretty surprised, but I was kind of flattered, and appalled too." Tony would eventually tell Ben, but not until much later. She never told Mary, however. At the time, Kennedy's behavior "struck me as odd," Tony recalled. "But it seems odder knowing what we now know about Mary."

The next morning Kennedy marked Memorial Day by placing a wreath at Arlington Cemetery's Tomb of the Unknowns. At midday he, Jackie, the Bradlees and Nivens flew to Camp David for swimming, skeet shooting, golf on the front lawn, and conversation. Tony and Jack acted as if nothing had happened the night before—not a hint of either awkwardness or coolness.

As the group drank Bloody Marys on the terrace, Kennedy tore into his pile of birthday gifts "with the speed and attention of a four-year-old child," Bradlee noted. Kennedy laughed over Ethel's scrapbook of a chaotic Hickory Hill tour that parodied the White House guidebook. The standout gift was a pair of drawings by Bill Walton commemorating JFK's historic preservation efforts. Jackie told Walton she wished he had seen Jack's delight, adding wryly, "though Clem Norton would have probably put his foot through them." Walton's rendering of the statue of Andrew Jackson in Lafayette Square was "the most beautiful thing—a Leonardo!" wrote Jackie, and his view of the Old Executive Office Building made Washington "seem as romantic as Venice." Both would be hung in the West Sitting Hall "where we keep all the things we love most."

On Wednesday, June 5, Kennedy left Washington for a five-day trip out west. In Colorado Springs he visited a military command bunker and addressed the graduates at the U.S. Air Force Academy; in White Sands, New Mexico, he watched missiles being launched; in El Paso he conferred with Governor John Connally and Lyndon Johnson about a future fundraising trip to Texas; in San Diego he met marine recruits;

in Los Angeles he spoke at two Democratic party fundraisers; and in Honolulu he sought the help of the nation's mayors to calm their cities as civil rights unrest erupted around the country.

But the highlight was his eighteen hours aboard the aircraft carrier *Kitty Hawk* off the coast of California. The onetime lieutenant junior grade "sat in an admiral's cushioned chair on the flight deck," noted the *New York Times,* "puffing a cigar and drinking coffee, as jets roared over-head, missiles seared the sky, and the nuclear submarine *Permit* surfaced at a 20-degree angle a thousand yards to starboard."

JFK had been suffering from a flare-up of painful back spasms that may have originated during his overnight stay at the Hotel Cortez in El Paso on June 6. Hugh Sidey later heard from a woman in the presiden-tial entourage that Kennedy had hurt himself in an amorous skirmish with her. "He either came into her room or he asked her to his room," Sidey recalled. "They were sitting on the bed, and he wanted to have sex. She wrenched to pull herself away, swung her arms, pushed him against the wall and he injured his back."

On the evening of June 7, journalist Alistair Cooke watched for a full minute as Kennedy grabbed the arms of his chair to "force himself in a twisted, writhing motion to his feet" before two navy officers could help him to his quarters on the *Kitty Hawk.* In the White House several days later, documentary filmmaker Robert Drew caught JFK "moving awkwardly and pushing his knuckles into his cheek, then pressing them into his teeth, as he rocked back and forth."

———

When he returned to Washington, Kennedy gave speeches on con-secutive days that set in motion two of the most significant diplomatic and domestic achievements of his presidency. The first was deliv-ered June 10 at American University's commencement. The address, which *Newsweek* later called "historic," came to be known as Kennedy's "Peace Speech." Secretly in the works for several weeks, it was meant to break the deadlock over a nuclear test-ban treaty. As usual, Sorensen had been Kennedy's principal collaborator, but Mac Bundy, Arthur Schlesinger, Walt Rostow, Carl Kaysen (Bundy's deputy), and Tom Sorensen had chipped in ideas as well. According to Schlesinger, Ken-nedy had deliberately excluded Dean Rusk until only two days before the commencement.

Not only did Kennedy call for curbing nuclear weapons, he proposed a searching reexamination of Soviet-American relations. To that end, he announced that the United States had suspended atmospheric testing of nuclear weapons and would send a delegation to Moscow to discuss a comprehensive test ban. "In the final analysis our most basic common link is that we all inhabit this small planet," Kennedy said. "We all breathe the same air. We all cherish our children's future, and we are all mortal."

The pacifist and Unitarian imprint of Sorensen could be seen in the emphasis on mankind's ability to solve man-made problems, rather than relying on the power of the Almighty. "Probably some of my language helped commit him to the idea," said Sorensen. "I was writing some things I hoped he would share. Every speech writer knows how sentiment is expressed is as important as the sentiment itself."

Less than a month later, during an appearance on July 2 in East Berlin, Khrushchev announced he would accept a limited nuclear test ban. The Soviet leader had actually retreated from his earlier proposal for a comprehensive ban with three annual on-site inspections. After Kennedy's insistence on more frequent monitoring, Soviet hard-liners had forced Khrushchev to pull back from a total ban.

Still, the "Peace Speech" had persuaded Khrushchev that Kennedy was serious about securing a treaty and improving relations with the Soviet Union. Although Macmillan was disappointed that Khrushchev had ruled out a comprehensive ban, he told Kennedy that "even the second prize may turn out well worth having and would certainly be fatal to lose." All told, there had been 336 nuclear explosions in the atmosphere by the United States, Britain, and the Soviet Union. Banning them would reduce pollution from radiation and set a precedent by establishing a binding legal obligation. Kennedy regarded a limited ban "as more of a beginning than a culmination," wrote Sorensen. It was JFK's hope that such an accord could help curb the spread of nuclear weapons and pave the way for future disarmament.

American and British negotiating teams convened in Moscow on July 15. With no need to haggle over underground tests and on-site monitoring, they made rapid progress. The negotiators took just ten days to reach agreement on a treaty banning nuclear tests in the atmosphere, the oceans, and outer space.

On July 26, Kennedy went on television to explain the treaty and build support for its ratification by the Senate. "Yesterday a shaft of light cut into the darkness," he said. He acknowledged that nuclear stockpiles would remain intact, but said the treaty would "radically reduce the nuclear testing" that had "so alarmed mankind."

During the eventful summer of 1963, Kennedy also had to contend with the ongoing civil rights crisis. A crucial ally in developing the administration's strategy turned out to be Lyndon Johnson, who rallied to the cause after hitting bottom psychologically in his third year as vice president.

"Lyndon is fat and greyish and emotional," Katie Louchheim wrote after hearing Johnson speak at the Mayflower Hotel not long after Kennedy's buoyant State of the Union. A reporter from *Time* asked Orville Freeman what had happened to Johnson, implying that "he certainly had not lived up to expectations and almost faded away." The magazine followed up with a withering story in early February headlined "Seen, Not Heard." "Power has slipped from his grasp," *Time* concluded. While LBJ still appeared at meetings and White House functions, "he is free to speak up, but nobody really has to heed him anymore."

To Schlesinger, LBJ had become "a spectral presence at meetings in the Cabinet Room. . . . The psychological cost was evidently mounting." Johnson frequently escaped to his ranch in Texas on Thursdays, returning to Washington the following Monday, "laying low" as Charley Bartlett put it. "He would get depressed," said George Christian, one of his aides, "but he would fight his way out of it. Every now and then he would engage in self pity, but it wasn't a constant thing." Down at the ranch, Dale Malechek, Johnson's foreman, kept his boss company during long games of dominoes. LBJ was so needy that once when Malechek was milking the cows at 4 a.m. he looked up to see Johnson in his bathrobe, watching him intently.

In May 1963, Johnson and Kennedy both appeared in New York at a Democratic fundraiser. Afterwards, Earl and Flo Smith had a party at their Fifth Avenue apartment. "Like a fool I went," Johnson later told Harry McPherson. "The President was there, sitting in a big easy chair, and everyone was in a circle around him, leaning in to hear every word. I was leaning over too, and suddenly I didn't want to do that, be in the back of the circle, listening."

Johnson retreated to a spot in front of the French doors overlooking Central Park. When Flo Smith saw him standing alone, she approached a pretty young friend named Jeanne Murray Vanderbilt, who was with a group of prominent Democrats. "Will somebody go and talk to the Vice President?" Flo whispered. "I'll talk to him," Vanderbilt replied, "but what can I talk to him about?" "Don't give it a thought," said Flo. "She was right," Vanderbilt recalled. "He never stopped talking, and he was so charming." After several hours the Vice President offered Vanderbilt a ride home. As they parted, Johnson said, "I'll never forget how nice you were to me tonight." Recalled McPherson, "It was so moving to think of this massive figure, reduced in his eyes and the eyes of others."

Yet by then the equal rights issue had already begun to bring back the old Johnson. Starting in the spring, he had ventured out to North Carolina and Florida to make a series of speeches on the subject. "I want [blacks] on the platform with me," he announced to local officials. "And if you don't let them, I'm not coming, period." Under Johnson's pressure, blacks appeared with him—a moral victory.

On June 3, Johnson sprang to life during an extraordinary phone conversation with Ted Sorensen—a preview of LBJ's lightning grasp of the presidency after Kennedy's assassination six months later. With demonstrations spreading from Birmingham to other cities, Jack and Bobby had begun to fashion a framework for a new civil rights law. Not surprisingly, Johnson had been kept out of the loop. "I've never seen it," he told Sorensen. "I got it from the *New York Times*."

Now Johnson took charge, dictating a civil rights blueprint to Sorensen. "I think I have the feeling the Negro has in this country," Johnson told him. "I've been talking to a good many of them." He proposed five steps: improve the proposed legislation, have JFK talk to black leaders directly, enlist Republican support starting with Eisenhower, line up Democratic committee chairmen, take the case to the Deep South by making speeches. "We got a little pop gun," Johnson said, "and I want to pull out the cannon. The President is the cannon." Kennedy needed to "be the leader of the nation and make a moral commitment to them . . . the Negroes are tired of this patient stuff . . . this piecemeal stuff."

Johnson cautioned Sorensen that "we run the risk of touching off about a three- or four-month debate that will kill [Kennedy's] program and inflame the country and wind up with a mouse." LBJ also warned that "these risks are great and it might cost us the South" in 1964, "but those sorts of states may be lost anyway." Hearkening back to his own techniques in 1957, the Vice President said Kennedy should make his case directly in Jackson, Mississippi: "If he goes down there and looks them in the eye and states the moral issue and the Christian issue, and he does it face to face, these Southerners at least respect his courage. They feel that they're on the losing side of an issue of conscience."

Johnson had been burned too many times to take the lead publicly within the Kennedy administration. "I'm as strong for this program as you are, my friend," he told Sorensen. "I don't want to debate these things around fifteen men and then have them all go out and talk about the Vice President. . . . I haven't sat in on any of the conferences they've had up there with the senators. I think it would have been good if I had. I don't care. . . . But if at the last minute I'm supposed to give my judgment, I'm going to do it honestly as long as I'm around here, and I'm going to do it loyally."

One week later, in the hours after his Peace Speech, Kennedy faced a volatile new confrontation in the Deep South. His antagonist was Alabama governor George Wallace, who had vowed to "stand in the schoolhouse door" to prevent integration at the University of Alabama. On May 21 a federal judge had ordered the university to admit two black students, setting the stage for a showdown on June 11 between Deputy Attorney General Nicholas Katzenbach and Wallace.

The question at hand on Monday, June 10, was whether Kennedy should take to the airwaves to talk about race relations. The possibility of a nationally televised address had been debated for days. At a dinner party the previous Thursday, Ted Sorensen had emphatically declared, "He should not go on unless there is crisis." Kennedy's special counsel did not believe the President needed to educate Americans about civil rights or make an impassioned plea. "Ted wants him off," wrote Katie Louchheim.

Lyndon Johnson's exhortation to "pull out the cannon" had failed to persuade Sorensen, or for that matter the President, who shared his aide's caution about political consequences. It took Johnson's nemesis Bobby to make the difference. Bobby had been seeking the upper hand on civil rights over Johnson for several months. Most memorably, the attorney general had gone on the attack in May during a meeting of the Committee on Equal Employment Opportunity chaired by the Vice President. Although the committee had used its clout to increase black employment in the federal government, RFK had castigated Johnson for taking insufficient action. By early June, Bobby had staked out his position "on the side of the angels" in a "just cause," observed Cy Sulzberger.

As filmmaker Robert Drew rolled his cameras on Monday afternoon in the Oval Office for an ABC documentary about the integration crisis, Bobby pressed his brother to go on television. Kennedy couldn't make up his mind. The next day Katzenbach faced down the implacable Alabama governor—also in front of a Drew camera crew. Kennedy federalized the state's national guardsmen, who forced Wallace to yield, allowing the two students to register. "I want to go on television tonight," said Kennedy after watching a replay of Wallace's defiance.

So on June 11, Kennedy gave the second of his historic speeches. He, Sorensen, and Bobby scrambled to pull together the President's remarks in the five hours before airtime. In his eighteen-minute prime-time talk, Kennedy improvised brilliantly on an incomplete text. He insisted that "the rights of every man are diminished when the rights of one man are threatened. . . . We are confronted primarily with a moral issue. It is as old as the Scriptures and is as clear as the American Constitution." He said blacks could no longer be second-class citizens in a nation preaching "freedom around the world." He noted that "the fires of frustration and discord are burning in every city," but the remedy could not be "repressive police action" or "token moves" or "increased demonstrations in the streets." It was the government's obligation to pass new laws to ensure that "revolution" and "change" be "peaceful and constructive for all."

Kennedy's improvisations, Sorensen later wrote, "drew on at least three years of evolution in his thinking, on at least three months of revolution in the civil rights movement, on at least three weeks of meetings in the White House." Kennedy had exerted moral leadership at a crucial moment. "Circumstances sort of caught up with [JFK and Bobby]," said Missouri congressman Richard Bolling, a liberal ally of Kennedy's. "The political situation changed. It became clearer that there was going to be a real reaction if they didn't move."

Eight days after the speech, Kennedy submitted his promised legislation to Congress. The bill forbade any private organization that served the public—whether a school, college, hotel, restaurant, store, theater, or sports arena—to engage in discrimination based on race, religion, ethnicity, or sex. If equal access either to services or accommodations was denied, the federal government could use the courts to force compliance. The Justice Department was also given the power to order school desegregation and to mandate equal opportunity in employment. The bill incorporated as well the provisions of the more limited civil rights legislation Kennedy had submitted in February to outlaw discrimination in voting.

The violence in the cities abated, and Kennedy worked through the summer months to reach out to leaders of the equal rights movement, who were busy planning a March on Washington for Jobs and Freedom on August 28. To build support for civil rights legislation, he held a series of meetings with opinion leaders at the White House. In these sessions, Kennedy was "controlled and terse," Johnson was "evangelical and often very moving," and Bobby was "blunt and passionate," wrote Arthur Schlesinger. Katie Louchheim attended a meeting with three hundred heads of nearly one hundred women's organizations in mid-July. "I watched the President's face while the Vice President made a long good speech, even talking about how women could not go to toilets cross-country if they were colored," she wrote. In his more muted way, Kennedy asked the women to "support our legislation" and "integrate your groups."

The equal rights march turned out better than expected, both for Kennedy and for its organizers. Fearing violence, the President had initially tried to stop the march and then worked to use the event on behalf of the civil rights bill. The government chose the symbolic Lincoln Memorial as the setting, helped plan the program, and carefully coordinated security. The rally's centerpiece was Martin Luther King's "I have a dream" speech, calling for an America where individuals would "not be judged by the color of their skin but by the content of their character." Afterwards, Kennedy invited the ten leaders of the march to the White House for tea, coffee, canapés, and sandwiches during an hour-long conference in which he praised "the deep fervor and quiet dignity" of the more than 200,000 demonstrators. Kennedy said that he had watched the speeches on television and admiringly told King that now he too had "a dream."

TWENTY-SEVEN

With the announcement of her pregnancy in mid-April, Jackie had been freed from the usual springtime burden of official events, although she continued to participate selectively. On Thursday, May 2, she skipped a congressional wives' brunch that she had committed to months earlier. JFK tried to make amends for her absence by cracking that she was "engaged in increasing the gross national product in her own way." But Jackie's telegram was "most frostily received. . . . In a room of 2,000 women they didn't make much noise," wrote Katie Louchheim. The reason for their displeasure was Jackie's appearance—chronicled in all the newspapers—the evening before at a performance of the Royal Ballet at the Metropolitan Opera House in New York.

She had already done her first lady turn that week by co-hosting a white-tie state dinner on April 30 for Charlotte, the Grand Duchess of Luxembourg—an event that originally had been intended for the previous October but was scuttled by the Cuban Missile Crisis. Kennedy was "very annoyed" at the prospect of entertaining royalty from such an insignificant country, and Chief of Protocol Angier "Angie" Biddle Duke had to persuade him, arguing that Roosevelt had sheltered the Grand Duchess after the Nazis had overrun her country in World War

II. Kennedy "did go through it bravely and nobly," Duke recalled. "But he certainly didn't enjoy it much."

Among the important dinner guests was André Meyer, whom Jackie had met for the first time earlier that month at a small White House gathering. Meyer, a Wall Street financier, was a longtime client of Stéphane Boudin. "He was a great womanizer," recalled Paul Manno, Boudin's representative in New York. "Boudin and I went to see him and said, 'How would you like to meet Jacqueline Kennedy?' His eyes popped out of his head. I said, 'It will only cost you $50,000.' He said, 'For what?' I said, 'For a rug.'" Meyer obediently purchased a nineteenth-century Savonnerie carpet coveted by Jackie to complete her beloved Blue Room, and the introduction followed. After the White House years, Meyer would become her confidant and financial adviser.

The theme for the evening's entertainment was Elizabethan poetry and music played on seventeenth-century instruments. Jackie selected sonnets and other works by Marlowe, Shakespeare, Jonson, and Donne to be read by Basil Rathbone. As a surprise epilogue, she had the sonorous English actor recite the St. Crispin's Day speech from *Henry V* beloved by JFK. ("We few, we happy few, we band of brothers. For he today that sheds blood with me shall be my brother.") She told Rathbone that her husband "reminds me of [Henry V]—though I don't think he knows that." Against the strains of antique lutes, citterns, and virginals, the readings produced a "hushed melodic reflectiveness that stilled the listeners to a mood of intense concentration."

It was the second time Shakespeare had figured in a state dinner, and by then Kennedy's penchant for quoting the Bard in his public appearances was well known. That spring Kennedy reeled off passages from *Richard II, Henry IV,* and *King John.* Journalists unabashedly admired such displays of erudition, although Kennedy stumped them at a fifty-first birthday party for Dave Powers in April with an inscription on a silver mug: "There are three things which are real: God, human folly and laughter. The first two are beyond our comprehension. So we must do what we can with the third." Finally Tom Wicker of the *New York Times* discovered that the passage came from *The Ramayana,* as told by Hindu writer Aubrey Menen, and that Kennedy had rattled the words off from memory to his military aide Ted Clifton.

Jackie's next public appearance was her final one before she left for

Cape Cod: a state dinner on June 3 for President Radhakrishnan of India with a performance of an excerpt from Mozart's *Magic Flute*. After everyone was seated, Jackie came in "like a queen, but on cat's feet," commented Katie Louchheim. "All during dinner I caught her beautiful rapt look directed at the little old Indian president."

The dinner crowd was larger and more eclectic than usual. At JFK's request, Schlesinger submitted a high-toned list of suggested guests—philosophers including Paul Weiss of Yale and Morton White of Harvard, theologian Reinhold Niebuhr, and various Indologists and writers such as Pearl Buck, Christopher Isherwood, Aldous Huxley, and Nicholas Nabokov. At the same time, Kennedy reached out to Democratic contributors, mindful that the 1964 campaign was just over the horizon. Democratic party stalwart Katie Louchheim sent names to the President through Charley Bartlett. "The President gave the orders," Louchheim wrote, "but how quickly is what amazed me." Even Galbraith marveled that Kennedy was able to pay off "a phenomenal number of political debts."

Tish Baldrige left her post at the White House the following day—not "on a stretcher, because things have been so frantic," as she predicted to her friend Clare Luce, but with copious tears despite her "last tense months." "I really do love them with all my heart," Baldrige told Luce, "and I feel as strongly as I have ever felt about *anything* that he is a *great* wonderful President." Jackie gave Baldrige a warm send-off complete with champagne and the Marine Band playing as the staff sang "Arrivederci, Tish," written by Jackie to the tune of "Arrivederci, Roma." JFK spent fifteen minutes with Baldrige in the Oval Office, commenting that she was "the most emotional woman he'd ever known," and thanking her for supporting Jackie so tirelessly.

By then Jackie was well along with her last major White House restoration task. Almost a year had passed since she unveiled the redecorated room she described as a "gentleman's library." She had delegated Schlesinger to work with Yale University librarian James T. Babb as well as Bunny Mellon, an ardent bibliophile, to assemble 2,500 volumes by purchase or donation. But progress had stalled, at least in part because of Jackie's uncertainty over what the library should be.

In April, Jackie outlined her plan for a collection of "significant American" books "that have influenced American thinking," such as the memoirs of Ulysses Grant and other presidents. Jackie wanted "old books in their bindings wherever possible," but not *precious* first editions. By May 1963, Schlesinger produced a list with a suitable range, and Jackie promised to design a bookplate over the summer.

Although Jackie had originally promised a "working library," she balked at letting White House staff members borrow books. She worried that potential donors would think their books might be mistreated or stolen. Schlesinger finally turned her around by arguing, "there seems something a little sterile and artificial about a library which is not used." Jackie decided to make borrowing privileges "tacit," with someone on hand to supervise the circulation. "You can dress up in 18th century costume & sit there all day . . . reading *Civil Disobedience,*" she wrote Schlesinger.

Jackie's other project, the new house in Virginia, was completed by the end of May. Other than a few quick inspections with Jackie and various friends, Jack had given the place a wide berth. "It was a joke, that house," said Ben Bradlee. "Jack didn't want it. What was he going to do there?" The completed house was surprisingly modest and undistinguished. "There was not any size or scope," said White House curator James Ketchum. "The sight lines were wonderful, though. That was its salvation."

Jackie spent just one night at Wexford that spring, bringing Mary Gallagher to help finish the furnishing. Jackie gave the decor exotic accents with carved elephants from Pakistan, handmade chairs and tables from India, and her collection of exquisite Indian Moghul miniatures that had previously been in the West Sitting Hall. "Jack never liked them," she told Bill Walton. At Wexford, she hung them in the dining room. "Rather erotic," sniffed Mary Gallagher, who found them more suitable for a bedroom.

Gallagher was the guinea pig for the Wexford guest room, where vivid red, orange, and green paisley wallpaper covered not only the walls, but the ceiling and even the doors. When Jack Kennedy first saw the room, he likened it to "the inside of a Persian whorehouse." Paul Fout was convinced that the dizzying decor was designed to discourage long visits. "They're not going to like that ceiling," he told Jackie. "I hope you're right," she said.

Even before the house was finished, the Kennedys decided to lease it for the summer for $1,000 a month—"like renting your new mink jacket before you've even been seen in it," noted one Washington columnist. Washington stockbroker A. Dana Hodgdon took the house from June through August, followed by San Diego oilman Ogden Armour, who leased until October 1.

Once again the President and First Lady had arranged to spend their summer on Squaw Island, away from the Kennedy compound. This time they rented Brambletyde, a rambling gray shingled home belonging to wealthy Pennsylvania industrialist Louis Thun. Situated on a point of land, the house had panoramic ocean views. Jackie and the children were scheduled to arrive there on June 27, and as in previous years, they would move to Newport for the month of September. Financial problems had forced Jackie's mother and stepfather to sell Merrywood and move to a considerably smaller Georgetown home in May. But Janet Auchincloss continued to live in high style at Hammersmith Farm and was eagerly planning a debutante ball in August for Jackie's half sister Janet—an extravaganza for a thousand guests in a simulated Venetian garden with a thirty-foot red-and-black gondola brimming with flowers and the Meyer Davis orchestra dressed as gondoliers.

Whatever had transpired between JFK and Mary Meyer at the dinner dance in March, she remained in Kennedy's orbit. She had helped celebrate his birthday on the *Sequoia,* and after his American University speech on June 10, Kennedy had seen her at a Joe Alsop dinner party while Jackie was in the country. "The President . . . had said he'd like to come at the next to last minute," Alsop wrote to Evangeline Bruce, "and then at the last minute, after a female had been procured from [*sic*] him, had a bit of bother with his back caused by his taxing weekend trip to Hawaii." In the end, Kennedy opted to "come for a drink." The "female" was doubtless Meyer; the other guests were David Bruce, diplomat William Attwood, Alice Longworth, David and Sissie Gore, Oatsie Leiter, Hugh and Antonia Fraser, Bob and Marg McNamara, and Oxford don Sir Maurice Bowra.

Kennedy had been "in a gay mood" that late spring evening, engaging in the "persiflage about the Profumo case . . . and sensations still to be revealed." Kennedy's intended brief stop stretched to nearly an hour. It was during drinks in Alsop's garden, with Meyer seated between himself and Attwood, that Kennedy reminisced about the first time he had danced with her at Choate nearly three decades earlier. But the President also had time for a colloquy with the lovely thirty-year-old Antonia Fraser. As Alsop told Evangeline Bruce, he looked "rather like a small boy wondering whether to plunge a spoon into a fresh dish of peach ice cream."

Two nights later, on Wednesday, June 12, Meyer was back in the White House for dinner with Jack, Jackie, Red Fay, and Bill Walton. Among other topics, they discussed Ros Gilpatric's planned exit from government to resume his law practice in New York. Kennedy once jokingly speculated to Ben Bradlee that the handsome and charming deputy secretary of defense might be the administration's "hidden Profumo." Jackie had recently spent the day with Gilpatric at his farm on Maryland's Eastern Shore. "You could tell how constrained she was," Gilpatric recalled, "how much she wanted to break loose and yet how concerned she was about her image, how determined she was not to embarrass her husband." In Jackie's farewell letter to "dear Ros," written on June 13, she said that his departure would leave "a real void." Jackie spent the following night at Camp David, and Mary Meyer spent yet another evening with JFK at the White House.

Kennedy was set to leave on June 22 for a ten-day trip to Europe. His aim was to strengthen the Atlantic alliance by visiting Germany and Italy, and to indulge in some sentimental travel in Ireland. He purposely omitted France after de Gaulle blackballed Britain from the Common Market. At the same time he arranged a twenty-four-hour visit to Britain that he wanted to keep secret as long as possible to avoid inflaming the French. "The declared purpose for it could be thought up at the time depending on what was happening in the world," David Gore told Macmillan after a strategy session with JFK on May 3. To downplay the visit, which was announced in early June, Macmillan suggested that they meet at his country home, Birch Grove, rather than London.

Since Kennedy was then awaiting Khrushchev's reply to the Peace Speech, he wanted to discuss strategy for the test-ban treaty negotiations due to begin several weeks later. But JFK also sought to bolster

Macmillan, who was reeling from continued revelations in the Profumo affair. The Tory government's problems had intensified with Profumo's disclosure on June 4 that in March he had lied to the House of Commons when he denied sexual intimacy with Christine Keeler. Macmillan told Parliament that he had been "grossly deceived" by his war minister. Censured by his peers, Profumo left public life in disgrace—largely because "the telling of such a falsehood in the House is considered even more serious than cheating at cards in a gentleman's club," noted American ambassador David Bruce. In a telegram to Kennedy on June 18, Bruce described Macmillan's admission of ignorance as "pitiable and extremely damaging." That day in an Oval Office meeting with August Heckscher, Kennedy marveled that Macmillan had been in the dark about the affair. "But as a matter of fact, of course, nobody ever told *me* what was going on," said Kennedy. "But then, the CIA never does tell me anything."

Four days later, Bruce sent JFK an "eyes only" memo describing the "current gossip" about the Profumo affair as "of a variety and virulence almost inconceivable. I shall speak to you about some of it when I see you. Thus far, no American government official has, to my knowledge, been involved in these speculations and accusations, nor have I reason to believe any will become so unless by innuendo." From the moment the Profumo scandal broke, Kennedy "had devoured every word," according to Ben Bradlee. "It combined so many of the things that interested him: low doings in high places, the British nobility, sex, and spying."

Still, Kennedy was "very depressed," Jackie recalled, about the impact on Macmillan—"the prospect of what he considered to be a great hero brought down." As a special gesture, JFK arranged to give Macmillan's wife, Dorothy, "a golden dressing table set with her initials on it."

—————

Planning for the trip included the transport of what Macmillan described as Kennedy's "specially constructed bed . . . on which he alone could get comfort." Mac Bundy and Philip de Zulueta, Macmillan's private secretary, spent a week arranging to install the double bed for Kennedy's one night at Birch Grove.

Jackie "wished to make every detail perfect" for her husband's journey, and involved herself extensively in the logistics. Writing to Dorothy Macmillan on the eve of JFK's departure, Jackie expressed dismay that the White House chef had sent elaborate instructions for the Birch Grove visit. "*Please* think of Jack as someone David Gore is bringing down for lunch," Jackie wrote, "and just do whatever you would do in your own house—His tastes are distressingly normal—plain food—children's food—good food—He likes anything."

Kennedy prepared himself with the usual complement of briefing papers. Schlesinger weighed in against the "banality and vapidity" of drafts by State Department analysts and continued to criticize Rusk for his conventional thinking and bland personality that resulted in "authority but not command." The historian also wisely cautioned Kennedy against publicly advocating the multinational nuclear force. Sorensen was working overtime to prepare no fewer than twenty-seven public statements and speeches for his boss and girding himself for a succession of sleepless nights. At Schlesinger's suggestion, Kennedy assigned Mac Bundy to share the speechwriting burden.

Days before his departure, JFK summoned Enüd Sztanko to the White House to critique some German phrases he planned to use at the Berlin wall. "The pronunciation is terrible," she told him. "I had him repeat the phrases ten times, and I corrected his pronunciation." Although they were alone in the private quarters, Kennedy "behaved impeccably. He was like a little boy and said, 'See, I've been good.'"

Some in the press raised questions about the need for a European trip in light of more pressing domestic problems. Even David Gore warned his superiors on June 20 about the "unpropitious" timing. Kennedy, he said, would be "leaving behind a disquieting internal situation. . . . The racial crisis has reached in places an explosive stage," with talk among Negro leaders of "large-scale civil disobedience . . . nationwide." Gore noted a "marked lack of enthusiasm here for the President's journey." A Harris poll taken just before Kennedy's departure bore out Gore's instincts: JFK's popularity registered at 59 percent—a sharp drop from his high of 75 percent after the missile crisis. Harris blamed the decline on the "boiling civil rights crisis."

In a meeting with a group of national leaders before his departure, "when the civil rights riots were at their height and passions were flaring," recalled James Reston, Kennedy "tolled off the problems that beset him on every side." Then, "to the astonishment of everyone there," the President pulled a paper from his pocket and concluded by reading from Blanche of Spain's speech in *King John*:

> The sun's o'ercast with blood
> Fair day, adieu!
> Which is the side that I must go withal?
> I am with both. Each army hath a hand,
> And in their rage, I having hold of both
> They whirl asunder and dismember me.

Reston later wondered if Kennedy had felt "a premonition of tragedy—that he who had set out to temper the contrary violences of our national life would be their victim." Yet Shakespeare's play had a larger meaning that resonated in JFK's case by dramatizing the undoing of a great king by personal weakness. "More than anything else," wrote critic Irving Ribner, Shakespeare sought to affirm "the inseparability of public and private virtue, that only a good man can be a good king."

Kennedy managed to transform his European trip into great political theater. His visit to Berlin on June 26 drew 1.5 million out of the city's population of 2.2 million—Kennedy's biggest crowd ever. After showing palpable revulsion when he first caught sight of the wall, he stood before the Berlin City Hall and spoke resoundingly of freedom's power in the face of communism—an almost taunting tone that threatened to undermine his Peace Speech overture. "Freedom has many difficulties, and democracy is not perfect," he said. "But we have never had to put a *wall* up to keep our people in." To those who doubted the superiority of democracy over communism, he incanted, "Lass sie nach Berlin kommen! Let them come to Berlin," adding, "All free men, wherever they may live, are citizens of Berlin, and therefore, as a free man, I take pride in the words, 'Ich bin ein Berliner.'"

The sentiment was pure Kennedy, and Bundy had given him the German translation. "There we were on the goddamn airplane coming down on Berlin while he repeated the phrase over and over again," Bundy recalled. It turned out that Bundy's locution could also have meant "I am a doughnut," which has prompted teasing from historians who have pointed out that Kennedy should have said, "Ich bin Berliner."

But the Berliners didn't care and responded with roars of approval. Dean Rusk told David Bruce that Kennedy's reception was "the most remarkable spectacle he ever saw." Back at the White House, Jackie and Robert McNamara sat together on the second floor and watched a replay of the speech on television. It was her last night in Washington, and McNamara had invited her to dinner at Georgetown's Salle du Bois restaurant. "She and I were talking about his speaking," McNamara said. Jackie described how much her husband had improved his performance as an orator, and she gave McNamara a film of JFK during the 1950s so that he could see the difference for himself. "I was almost embarrassed to watch it," McNamara recalled.

Kennedy's next three days in Ireland offered drama on a more personal scale, with visits to relatives in New Ross and his modest "ancestral homestead" in Dunganstown, as well as an elegant garden party at the residence of Irish president Eamon de Valera. "I imagine that he was never easier, happier, more involved and detached, more completely himself" than during this "blissful interlude of homecoming," Schlesinger wrote. In his exuberance, Kennedy was also incautious: climbing out of his car and "letting two flanks of people mob him, almost crush him except for elbowing frantic Secret Service," recalled Democratic party official Matt McCloskey.

JFK had specifically invited all his staff members of Irish descent to accompany him, along with Jean, Eunice, Lee Radziwill, and Lem Billings. After touring the countryside, he bolted into the American Embassy in Dublin and ran up the stairs to greet Lee. "They love me in Ireland!" he exclaimed. "It was so wonderful," recalled Barbara Gamarekian, who witnessed the scene. "Such a joyful free spirited thing to do, running up the staircase. I had never seen him like that." To Kennedy family friend Dorothy Tubridy he said, "These were the three happiest days I've ever spent in my life."

Even so, JFK could not escape the shadow of his secret life back home. Left behind in Washington, Mimi Beardsley, now twenty and back for a second summer internship after her sophomore year, became upset when the woman in charge of the press office, Helen Gans, refused to give her the day off. Beardsley tearfully called Kennedy at the

American Embassy, raising suspicions among the presidential travel-ing party in Dublin. "Dave Powers came up to Pierre and told him the President was just furious!" recalled Gamarekian. "If the President were back in Washington, Dave said, Helen Gans would be fired this very instant . . . I thought it was utterly asinine to think that [JFK] would get upset about a little girl in the office . . . Obviously she did have sort of a special relationship with the President . . . To be able to place a call through the White House switchboard to Ireland from the United States and to get through directly to the President to make her complaint was a little unusual."

On a cold and windy day, Kennedy left Ireland promising to "see old Shannon's face again," and flew to England, where he touched down briefly at Chatsworth to visit the grave of his sister Kathleen. The Devonshires' chauffeur drove the President to the churchyard down the road from their grand house. For two minutes JFK gazed at the simple thin headstone adorned on top with scrolls and inscribed, "Joy she gave. Joy she found."

At Birch Grove, Kennedy held lengthy private meetings with Macmillan that yielded no fresh ideas or strategies. The two men effec-tively interred the already moribund multinational nuclear force, and they agreed, as Macmillan put it, to go "full steam ahead with Moscow talks." Macmillan was pleased to see that Kennedy showed "a greater degree of authority," and his staff a "lesser tendency . . . to try to impose their views upon him."

The meetings resembled "a country house party" rather than "a grave international conference," recalled Macmillan. He judged Ken-nedy to be in "the highest of spirits," his humor "puckish," his mood "mischievous." Macmillan had also glimpsed Kennedy's physical infir-mities: "very puffed up, very unhealthy," the prime minister recalled, noting that "he suffered agony" with his back problems—the sprint upstairs in Dublin notwithstanding.

Yet Kennedy evidently had pleasure in mind for his stopover on Sunday, June 30, near the Italian resort town of Bellagio following his late afternoon departure from Birch Grove. At Kennedy's request, Dean Rusk had secured overnight accommodations at the Villa Serbel-loni, a splendid seventeenth-century retreat for scholars tucked into a hillside overlooking Lake Como and distant alpine peaks. The villa was run by Rusk's former employer, the Rockefeller Foundation, and it offered a notably secluded setting, surrounded by fifty acres of terraced gardens, grottos, and woodlands crisscrossed with gravel paths. The press plane was dispatched to Rome, and Kennedy was accompanied only by Powers, O'Donnell, and a Secret Service detail.

In the early evening, Kennedy "made an unscheduled 10 minute automobile trip through the village for a quick look at Lake Como," the *Washington Post* reported. "Shopkeepers, tourists, and townsmen applauded, cheered and ran after the car. . . . He was then driven back to the villa where he dined quietly with his staff."

Rusk told biographer Richard Reeves that Kennedy had demanded that the villa's resident director as well as support staff move out to ensure complete privacy. The reason, according to Rusk, was a rendezvous Kennedy had planned with Marella Agnelli, who lived 125 miles away in Turin. Asked about the tale thirty-nine years later, she would only say, "Maybe yes, maybe no. It is impossible to say. . . . I am an old grandmother, and Gianni and I are still together very much." Her friend Countess Marina Cicogna said she had a "small suspicion" that a "brief encounter" took place at Lake Como. "A couple of times Marella said something specific about Kennedy that way," recalled Cicogna. "So I wouldn't rule it out."

In Rome the following night, Italian president Antonio Segni honored Kennedy with a dinner at the Quirinal Palace that Gianni and Marella Agnelli attended. The trip wound down after an audience with Pope Paul VI, an old friend of the Kennedy family whose coronation had taken place only the day before JFK's arrival. At Kennedy's urging, Lem Billings spent a frantic ninety minutes scouring Roman antique shops for ancient busts, statues, and jewelry that Kennedy bought for himself, Jackie, Billings, and connoisseurs such as Mary Lasker. For his Oval Office desk, Kennedy chose a small 500 B.C. figure of *Herakles and the Skin of a Lion,* and for Jackie he selected a Roman imperial head of a young satyr.

Kennedy's send-off in Naples produced "more passionate excitement than even in Berlin," noted Angie Duke. "Women absolutely threw themselves—were projected over the crowd to try and get at the President." JFK slept most of the way home, although at one point during the night he joined Jean Smith, Pierre Salinger, and Angie Duke for a drink and "kidded about it all. . . . The President had a dry manner, and he was not given to self-delusion," recalled Duke.

The President had a full schedule in the White House the next day: meeting with his cabinet for two hours, writing and recording a brief TV address reporting on his trip, and conferring with his top foreign policy advisers. After a seven-minute stroll on the South Lawn, and a swim, he went upstairs for an evening with Mary Meyer.

In the summer of 1963, Meyer had come to the rescue, ironically enough, of Helen Chavchavadze, who was pulling herself together after leaving Sibley Hospital. Chavchavadze still felt the burden of her secret liaison with Kennedy. "The double life is not in my nature," she recalled. "I told Mary about my thing with Jack. Nobody else knew about it." Meyer replied that "he had made a move in her direction, and she had been tempted for historical reasons but hadn't done it." If Mary Meyer was upset by Chavchavadze's revelation, she didn't show it. "In 1963 she was guarding her secret carefully," said Chavchavadze.

JFK gave no indication of difficulty juggling his various assignations; his mood was remarkably insouciant. Mimi Beardsley was sharing a house that summer in Georgetown with two Wheaton classmates and Farmington alumnae, Marnie Stewart and Wendy Taylor. Neither had any idea of Beardsley's involvement with Kennedy.

When Dave Powers inveigled the three interns to take a swim in the White House pool in July, Taylor was stunned when Kennedy arrived unannounced. After they had chatted while swimming and sipping wine, Kennedy "called for some minion who brought down a big box of fur pelts," Taylor recalled. Jackie had recently told Evelyn Lincoln that "the only thing she really wanted" for Christmas was an expensive fur bedspread. Kennedy took the hint and turned it into a flirtatious opportunity. "I want to ask your opinion," he told the interns. "I am having a throw made for Jackie for Christmas, and I want to know what furs you like." The three young women dried their hands, examined the pelts of squirrel, rabbit, fox, and mink, and made their recommendations. "We thought this was very amusing," recalled Taylor.

By then a situation disturbingly akin to the Profumo affair threatened the President, and Bobby was working hard to stop it. The first blip on the radar had come on Saturday, June 29, with an article in Hearst's *New York Journal-American* reporting that a "high elected American official" had been intimate with a prostitute named Suzy Chang, a friend of Christine Keeler's. On Monday, July 1, while JFK was in Rome, Bobby Kennedy interrogated Dom Frasca and James Horan, the two reporters who wrote the article. They asserted that the official in question was JFK, although the FBI could find no specific evidence of such a liaison. After their confrontation with the attorney general, Frasca and Horan abandoned the story, and no other journalists followed up.

Just two days later, J. Edgar Hoover warned Bobby more ominously that he had a report of Kennedy's sexual involvement with twenty-seven-year-old Ellen Rometsch, a fetching brunette who had emigrated from East Germany eight years earlier and was suspected of spying for the Soviets. Married to a West German air force sergeant posted to the embassy in Washington, Rometsch appeared to be an ordinary house-wife living in an affluent neighborhood of Arlington, Virginia. Her expensive lifestyle, FBI investigators concluded, "hardly could have been maintained on the pay of a German army enlisted man."

By night Rometsch was a call girl associated with Bobby Baker, sec-retary of the Senate and a longtime aide to LBJ. Among several sideline businesses, Baker ran the Quorum Club at the Carroll Arms Hotel on Capitol Hill, a "smoky and dimly lit" hideaway where congressmen and lobbyists congregated to drink and enjoy the favors of beautiful young women. Wearing a tight dress and black fishnet stockings, Rometsch worked there as "hostess" and catered to a large clientele of "impor-tantly placed politicos" for more than two years. According to Baker, Bill Thompson had taken her to the White House several times in 1962 for assignations with JFK.

Since the FBI had linked Rometsch to an employee at the Soviet Embassy, the Profumo-like implications of espionage and blackmail were unnerving. As with Suzy Chang, the FBI couldn't corroborate Kennedy's involvement with Rometsch. But the attorney general re-mained sufficiently concerned that he arranged to have her secretly deported to Germany in late August. JFK was strikingly cavalier about Rometsch, gossiping to Bradlee that Hoover told him she was charging senators "a couple of hundred dollars a night," and that judging by the photo Hoover had shown him, she was "a really beautiful woman." Yet a connection between JFK and Rometsch was every bit as dangerous as his involvement with Judith Campbell. However protected Kennedy felt by a compliant press corps, his reckless womanizing had the potential to compromise if not undo his presidency.

Helen Chavchavadze knew nothing of either Ellen Rometsch or Judith Campbell, but she did know firsthand the unsettling disjunction between Kennedy's private and public behavior. "It was a compulsion," she concluded, "a quirk in his personality. He was out of control. It may have looked like beautiful convertibles and women and sophistication, but it was the shadow destroying the self. For Mary and me it was our shadow too."

TWENTY-EIGHT

*J*ackie celebrated her thirty-fourth birthday on Sunday, July 28, during a lively weekend house party in Hyannis Port with David and Sissie Gore, Lem Billings, Chuck Spalding, and the Radziwills. They took a three-hour cruise on the *Honey Fitz* and dined that evening at Brambletyde. David Gore gave Jackie a copy of *The Fox in the Attic* by Richard Hughes, a novel Gore found "haunting," with a "historically accurate account of Hitler's first Munich 'putsch.'" Averell Harriman, the leader of Kennedy's negotiating team in Moscow, arrived that afternoon, bearing a large jar of caviar from Khrushchev. Kennedy treated the veteran diplomat like "a conquering hero," said Gore.

In the sunshine and sea breezes of Cape Cod, Kennedy couldn't have appeared more carefree that July. After a hiatus of two years he had resumed playing golf, and he was out on the course every weekend. He usually played only five holes, occasionally managing nine. Two hours was all he could endure. With Lem Billings, JFK flew kites and sailed a three-foot model schooner that Italian president Segni had sent to John Jr. On the weekend after his return from Europe, Kennedy forced family and friends to view three newsreels of the trip. "He was watching the Berlin speech, and he started clapping," Jim Reed recalled. "He was not being egotistical. He was transported outside himself to the movie image."

Jackie was equally radiant, relaxing with her children on the beach in front of Teddy and Joan's house and taking Caroline to riding lessons at a stable in Osterville. In the tranquility of Brambletyde, Jackie read from her pile of books, including Rudyard Kipling's *Kim* and *Civilization of Rome* by Pierre Grimal, painted at her easel on the second-floor sun porch overlooking the ocean, and tended to her correspondence.

She continued to send instructions to the Curator's Office as well as her East Wing staff. Nancy Tuckerman had moved into an apartment at 2500 Q Street in Georgetown, several blocks from the new Auchincloss home. Tuckerman's office, a center of "tiptoe diplomacy," featured a painting of Jackie, an orchid on the coffee table, copies of *Larousse Gastronomique,* a Betty Crocker cookbook, stacks of menus and magazines, and somewhat incongruously, a voodoo doll similar to one displayed on Ted Sorensen's desk.

Although Jackie didn't plan any official appearances for many months, she was nevertheless immersed in the details of a state dinner for the king of Afghanistan on September 5 to be hosted by Jack and Eunice. Jackie's ability to create a grand tableau for official visitors was now firmly established. Earlier in her tenure she had displayed her directorial talent when she installed a big square mirror in the front hall of the White House. "On a state evening when the color guard and procession are reflected in the mirror," she wrote to Harry du Pont, "many more people can see the ceremonies." More recently, she had told White House photographer Cecil Stoughton, "Don't make pictures of Jack and me. Make pictures of what we are looking at and what we are doing." After watching Stoughton's film of JFK's European trip, she had told the lensman to move closer to the presidential car "to capture the emotion on the faces of the people as the President passed."

Jackie also kept in touch with Bill Walton. While Arthur Schlesinger remained the "keeper of the intellectual tone of the White House," Walton had become chairman of the Fine Arts Commission. His task, in JFK's words, was to make Washington "a more beautiful and functional city." "How lovely to have you there to cope with all these charming little details," Jackie wrote to Walton in late July with her ideas for new guard boxes outside the White House: "the most classical and simple"

design "so we won't be getting Lever Brothers ones some day"—
doubtless a reference to the highly modernist Lever House office building on Park Avenue with its facade of green glass and stainless steel.

JFK applauded his wife's record as first lady in an interview with
Hearst reporter Marianne Means, pointing to Jackie's "emphasis on
creative fields, her concentration on giving historical meaning to White
House furnishings, her success as an ambassador on trips she has made
with me abroad." Although a year earlier Kennedy had bemoaned the
inability of Radcliffe graduates to use their talents sufficiently in the
working world, now he said that "by carrying out her primary responsibility to back up her husband and care for her children well, [Jackie] is
doing her real job as a woman."

Their friends observed more intimacy between Jack and Jackie as
her delivery date approached. When Jim Reed was visiting Brambletyde
in mid-July, Jackie awoke feeling unwell, prompting a frantic search for
her obstetrician, John Walsh. Jack was "extremely solicitous" of Jackie
and "very very upset" over the doctor's absence, Reed recalled. Walsh
had been out on a walk, and when he turned up, Kennedy calmed himself to ask in a "kind and gentle" way that the doctor "always tell someone where you are, how you can be reached immediately."

Two weeks later, Red Fay wandered into Jack and Jackie's bedroom
to find them "lying there in each other's arms. I said, 'Oh my God,' and
apologized. Jack said, 'Don't worry about it. We're just lying here chatting.'" That weekend Jack and Jackie were making the final selections
from the trove of sculpture Lem Billings had collected in Rome. Kennedy was drawn to the five-inch-high Herakles statuette, and Fay was
skeptical that the piece was nearly two thousand years old. Kennedy
instructed Fay to ask Jackie "any question you can think of dealing
with Roman or Greek history. Ask her about the authenticity of this
figurine." Fay posed the questions. "It was an amazing performance,"
Fay recalled. "She answered every question with ease." Afterwards,
Kennedy told Fay that of all the attractive women he had known, "there
was only one I could have married—and I married her."

During the summer of 1963, Jack also connected more deeply with the
Kennedy brother who was fifteen years his junior. When Teddy first

took his seat in the Senate the previous January, he kept his distance, at least publicly. Joan committed a faux pas in an interview with *Look* in which she revealed that Jackie sometimes wore wigs and that JFK's bad back prevented him from lifting John Jr. "They thought I should be a little more politically correct," said Joan. "They didn't get cross with me. These things were well known among everyone, but I simply said them."

The youngest Kennedy couple was "invited a lot" to the White House, Joan recalled. "Teddy thought it was better not to go. He wanted to be his own person. He didn't think politically it was a good idea. We went to only a couple of big parties, but spent a lot of time in the family quarters, having dinner, hanging out, watching movies." They visited Camp David and accompanied Jack on his tour of the Civil War battlefield at Antietam in April.

Jackie and Joan were both expecting in August, but Joan lost her baby boy at "almost full term" in June—her second miscarriage in two years. Out on Squaw Island, Jackie helped console Joan, particularly when Ethel gave birth to her eighth child on July 4. "Jackie was so wonderful," Joan recalled. "I went to her and said I felt under pressure about having more family, and she was wonderful about that." Joan and Teddy already had a three-year-old daughter and eighteen-month-old son. It would be four more years before the birth of their second son.

As "summer bachelors," Teddy and Jack would often get together at the White House. "We really enjoyed each other," Teddy told biographer Ralph Martin. ". . . What I did was to stop by on the way home from the Senate and go into the Oval Office by the back door at the end of his working day. Then we'd have a daiquiri, take a swim together, then just sit around and talk about everything. Sure I'd make him laugh. We'd gossip about the Senate. . . . The two of us would go upstairs and have dinner alone and sometimes spend the whole evening just talking and laughing."

The Shrivers had become more prominent as well. With other favored Kennedy administration initiatives stalled in Congress, Sarge's Peace Corps was the most visible program hatched by the President. Eunice used her influential position to be a persistent advocate of research into mental retardation and federal support for the mentally handicapped. In May 1963 she had the temerity to launch a "blistering attack" on the government's employment policy regarding mentally retarded workers. Speaking to the Women's Committee for the President's Committee on Employment of the Handicapped, Eunice called for a jobs program to redress the federal government's "frustrating and dismal" record. The committee itself, she said, had given "virtually no attention" to the mentally retarded while focusing on such handicaps as deafness.

"Nothing Eunice did was official," said White House aide Myer Feldman, JFK's West Wing liaison with his sister. "She was the only person who called him Jack in public. Even Bobby called him Mr. President in public." JFK knew that "when she set out to accomplish something, nothing would stand in her way," said Feldman. "She would simply overpower her opponents."

In September 1962, Eunice had written an article for the *Saturday Evening Post* revealing the congenital mental retardation of forty-four-year-old Rosemary Kennedy—the first time the family had disclosed she had not been a "childhood victim of spinal meningitis." The lobotomy ordered by Joe Kennedy, however, remained a secret. Because of Rosemary, Jack Kennedy had a natural interest in mental retardation, but Eunice educated him and pushed him to launch an array of federal programs—conferences, commissions, a new research institute—and to mention the issue prominently in speeches. "It was the beginning of treating the mentally retarded as humans and not warehousing them," said Feldman.

———

For the Kennedys, Saturday, August 3, began as a typically jolly Cape Cod day in what would become one of the saddest weeks of the Kennedy presidency. Red and Anita Fay were visiting for the weekend, and Ken Galbraith had come down from Cambridge for the afternoon. But during their cruise in Nantucket Sound on the *Honey Fitz,* Kennedy was alerted by radio telephone that Phil Graham had committed suicide. Kennedy quickly issued a statement of condolence, calling the death of the forty-eight-year-old publisher "a serious loss to all who knew and admired his integrity and ability."

"Jack was as upset as everyone else, but we couldn't dwell on it," Red Fay recalled. Jackie sat down and wrote an emotional eight-page letter that Katharine Graham described as "the most understanding and comforting of *any* I got." Bill Walton told Kennedy that Jackie's letter "knocked [the Graham family] for a loop . . . in a good sense, I mean," helping them cope with their sorrow.

In Washington on Monday the fifth, Jack spent the evening with Mary Meyer. By then Meyer was "a friendly familiar diversion," said Anne Truitt. Although with Helen Chavchavadze Kennedy had "never mentioned" his back problems, he had grown accustomed to telling Meyer about his physical pain. "He was not shy about it when he was with someone who knew him," said Anne Truitt. "He was a factual man. It is what he lived with, the root of his life. He coped in the most gallant fashion." Meyer never viewed JFK as vulnerable, but "she was very surprised by the extent of his pain. It did change her view of him, it absolutely did. It turned the relationship from what it might have been in terms of sexuality into friendship."

That day delegations from the United States, Britain, and the Soviet Union signed the test-ban treaty in Moscow. Kennedy had pressed de Gaulle to join the signatories but he had predictably refused. JFK could never dispel his disappointment over France's position. One month before his death, he would tell Hervé Alphand over dinner at the White House that he resented de Gaulle's "desire to maintain between France and the United States a relationship full of acrimony and bitterness."

On arriving at the Osterville stables with Caroline and John at 11 a.m. Wednesday morning, Jackie felt the first stabs of labor pain. Her Secret Service agent sped her back to Squaw Island where she told John Walsh, "I think I'm going to have that baby"—three weeks before the due date of August 27. They climbed into a helicopter at 11:28 and landed at the Otis Air Force Base hospital twenty minutes later. At 12:52 p.m., Patrick Bouvier Kennedy was born by cesarean section and was immediately placed in an oxygen-fed incubator. Weighing only 4 pounds, 10½ ounces, he was suffering from hyaline membrane disease, a lung condition that blocked the supply of oxygen to the bloodstream.

Seventeen minutes after he was alerted about Jackie's condition, Kennedy was en route to the Cape with Nancy Tuckerman, Pamela Turnure, and Pierre Salinger. Nobody even had time to grab a toothbrush. Kennedy "was completely withdrawn," Turnure recalled. "He just kept sitting and staring out of the window, and obviously his

thoughts were completely with her." Kennedy arrived at the hospital at
1:30 p.m. while Jackie was still in surgery. Following a conference with
doctors, he agreed to send Patrick to Children's Hospital in Boston for
treatment. Jackie was never permitted to hold her brown-haired baby.
She only glimpsed him as JFK wheeled the incubator to her bedside
before the ambulance departed. When Jack told her Patrick had to be
taken away, she was "deeply distressed."

In Boston, Kennedy shuttled between a suite at the Ritz Carlton
Hotel and the hospital, where Patrick was attended by a team of Harvard doctors. "He wanted to know what we would be doing with the
baby," said Dr. Judson Randolph, then a young resident who cared for
Patrick on his arrival. When Randolph said he needed to perform a
tracheostomy—inserting a metal tube in the infant's throat to keep
the chest pressure stabilized and prevent the lungs from collapsing—
Kennedy drilled him with questions. "He wanted to know what material the tube was made of, how I could put a tube in such a small baby's
trachea," Randolph recalled. "It dawned on me that he didn't care what
the tube was. He was measuring me. I was thirty-four years old, and he
wanted to know does this guy know what he is doing."

Kennedy flew in Dr. Sam Levine, a specialist from Cornell Medical
College in New York who had successfully treated Lee Radziwill's premature daughter, Christina, two years earlier. Bobby arrived as well and
called a physician in Michigan who had been his Harvard classmate.
"Bobby was a little nettling, running roughshod to find information
from maybe not the best sources," said Randolph. "The President was a
little steadier, taking the larger view, and Bobby subsided."

On Thursday afternoon the physicians decided to place Patrick in a
hyperbaric chamber in the basement of an adjacent Harvard Medical
School building. Thirty-one feet long and eight feet in diameter, the
pressurized (44 to 55 pounds per square inch compared to 14.7 pounds
at sea level) and oxygenated white steel chamber had been used during
surgery more than two dozen times to help patients by forcing oxygen
into their lungs. "It was a desperate move," Randolph recalled.

Kennedy and Dave Powers stayed in a fourth-floor waiting room
converted into a presidential suite with a bed, rocking chair, carpet, and
telephones. At 2 a.m., the doctors told the President that Patrick was
in critical condition. He and Powers hurried to the basement, where
Kennedy donned a white surgical gown and cap, and sat in a wooden

chair outside the chamber. Periodically he stood up to peer through a small porthole at the floodlit chamber where attendants wearing spaceman-style pressurized suits hovered around the little plastic incubator on wheels.

When it was clear that Patrick was failing, the team brought him out of the chamber to be with his father. The infant died of cardiac arrest at 4:04 a.m. on Friday, August 9, after a life of 39 hours and 12 minutes. "He put up quite a fight," Kennedy said to Powers. "He was a beautiful baby." Upstairs in his temporary quarters Kennedy "sat on the bed and wept," Powers recalled. "He didn't want anybody to see him crying, so he asked me to go outside and telephone Teddy."

Dr. Walsh broke the news to Jackie at 6:25 a.m., and JFK joined her three hours later. With Mary Gallagher's help, she dried her tears and freshened up to look "as presentable as possible." She was already in a weakened condition, having had a double blood transfusion after her surgery. Telling Jackie about the ordeal in Boston, Jack wept again. When Patrick was still struggling, Jack had said to Janet Auchincloss, "I just can't bear the effect [the infant's death] might have on Jackie." Over the next four days, he visited Jackie in her hospital room at least twice a day. Caroline came as well, clutching a bouquet of freshly picked larkspur, black-eyed susans, and pink trumpet flowers. Jackie was also consoled by her mother and Lee, who arrived on Friday after JFK located her in Greece. Lem Billings offered to cancel his vacation, saying he "couldn't care less about going to Europe," but Jack insisted he leave as planned.

On Saturday, Richard Cardinal Cushing celebrated a "Mass of the Angels" for Patrick in the chapel at his Boston residence. Joining the President were his siblings and their spouses, Lee, and a quartet of Auchinclosses: Janet, Hughdie, and their two children, Jamie and Janet. Rose Kennedy was on a holiday in Paris, and Jackie was too ill to attend.

JFK took a gold St. Christopher's medal coin clip that Jackie had given him as a wedding present and put it inside the little white casket as a relic representing them both. After the service, Kennedy wept "copious tears," and was so "overwhelmed with grief that he literally put his arm around that casket as though he was carrying it out," Cushing said. The burial took place at Holyhood Cemetery in Brookline, the first in the large family plot purchased by Joe Kennedy.

Back in Washington, Kennedy called Enüd Sztanko and asked her to come to the White House. "He was very depressed," she recalled. "I thought very hard about going, but I didn't think it was appropriate. I felt enormous empathy. We talked a long time on the phone, about why God would let a child die, and I didn't go."

Looking wan and wobbly, Jackie left the hospital hand in hand with Jack exactly a week after Patrick's birth. Before leaving she gave each of her nurses and doctors an autographed framed lithograph of the White House. She later told Ken Galbraith that she had been upset that the press had turned their tragedy into a "theatrical production." Lee stayed with her for two days at Brambletyde, Joan offered quiet sympathy deepened by her own recent loss, and Bunny Mellon sent over an exquisite basket of flowers. From afar, Harold Macmillan wrote "in the midst of all [his] troubles," Jackie recalled, to say that "private griefs are so much worse than public ones."

The rest of the month Kennedy spent more time than usual in Hyannis, making midweek overnight trips as well as his customary long weekend visits. Each time he would bring a special gift. Kennedy's "anguish for his wife and their dead son," wrote Schlesinger, "gave August a melancholy cast."

The first non-family visitor was Chuck Spalding, who diverted Jack with an early evening golf game. Bill Walton arrived the following weekend to find the house "full of sadness. . . . Jack and Jackie were very close. . . . She hung onto him and he held her in his arms." The Fays were on hand for Labor Day weekend. "It is so hard for Jackie," Kennedy told Fay. "After all the difficulties she has in bearing a child, to lose him is doubly hard. . . . It would have been nice to have another son."

During Walton's visit Jackie received a cable from Lee, who was cruising the Aegean with Aristotle Onassis and his longtime lover, the opera diva Maria Callas. Lee's affair with Onassis had begun several months earlier, and she had come aboard the *Christina,* the opulent 325-foot Onassis yacht, immediately on her return from Washington. "I was astonished she hadn't stayed with her sister," Maria Callas confided to a friend. "She repeatedly told us how undone Jackie was by the death of her baby. Both Aristo and I felt badly about it, so he extended an open invitation to the president and Mrs. Kennedy to join us on a cruise."

Kennedy clearly could not go, and he had deep misgivings about letting Jackie keep company with Onassis. As the majority owner of the

Casino in Monte Carlo, the multimillionaire Greek shipowner had been a familiar figure to the Kennedy family. Writing to her children in 1955, Rose had mentioned turning down an invitation to dine on the Onassis yacht because "your Papa" mistrusted "the Greeks and the way they do not pay any taxes." Five years later, after Rose rebuffed an attempt by Onassis to be photographed with her at a gala, he sent her four dozen red roses and an apologetic note.

When the invitation came from Lee, Kennedy "remembered something hanging over Onassis on some court case, and I was instinctively dead set against it," said Walton. Onassis had bought a fleet of ships from the U.S. government that he had illegally operated under a foreign flag; when the federal government indicted him, he paid a $7 million fine. "Onassis is a pirate. He's a crook," Kennedy said to Evelyn Lincoln.

Jackie, however, was adamant. She couldn't yet face Washington, and "she just wanted to get away." Although Walton thought that Kennedy had yielded to her wishes that weekend, the matter was far from settled. To avoid embarrassing the Kennedys, Onassis offered to stay out of the picture entirely. But Jackie said she would not accept his hospitality and then not let him come along. Her insistence, she said, was "an act of kindness."

On Labor Day, Jackie coaxed her husband into calling Franklin Roosevelt at his farm in upstate New York. "Lee wants Jackie to be her beard," Kennedy told Roosevelt. But Jack needed "someone from Washington to provide cover," said Justin Feldman, who was with the Roosevelts that weekend. "You are the only one she has agreed to have come along," Kennedy told his friend. The Roosevelts would "give an air of respect," recalled Sue Roosevelt. "I don't think Jack wanted Jackie to go. I think he was appalled by it, so he arranged for us to make it look less like the jet set."

But Roosevelt, who had finally received his appointment as under secretary of commerce the previous March, had his own concerns. The previous year, Onassis had done $4 million in shipping business with the Commerce Department through the U.S. Maritime Administration, and Roosevelt feared the appearance of a conflict of interest. "He said he was working on a new image," Jackie recalled. The President reassured FDR Jr. that his presence would be perfectly proper. To justify the trip, Roosevelt arranged to attend a trade fair in Somalia.

The next weekend in Hyannis, Kennedy was still trying to dissuade Jackie. "Jack went down on one knee, begging Jackie not to go," said houseguest Martha Bartlett. "Neither of them was giving in. When she wanted to do something, she did it." Kennedy put on the best face, defending Jackie's decision to Kenny O'Donnell and Pam Turnure, who worried about political repercussions with a reelection campaign imminent. "Well, I think it will be good for Jackie," Kennedy told Turnure, "and that's what counts."

Kennedy nevertheless decided to hide Onassis's involvement as long as he could. Early in September he fussed over a proposed press release stating Stas Radziwill had "secured" the Onassis yacht for the cruise. Kennedy explained to Stas that the choice of words was purposely "ambiguous" to suggest "you have possession of it during that period and Jackie is your guest and not Onassis'."

As it turned out, the White House announcement in late September mentioned neither the cruise nor Onassis, only that Jackie would be leaving on October 1 for a two-week holiday with her sister and brother-in-law at a rented villa in Greece. A week later, a report out of Paris said that Onassis, a "close friend" of Lee, had placed his yacht "at the disposal of the princess." On the eve of the trip, the White House said the yacht had been "secured" by Stas Radziwill. Asked if Onassis would be aboard, Pam Turnure said, "not to my knowledge."

Jack and Jackie celebrated two milestones in the month of September. The first was Joe Kennedy's seventy-fifth birthday at Hyannis on September 6. Eleven sons, daughters, and spouses (with the exception of Peter Lawford, from whom Pat was increasingly estranged) gathered in Joe Kennedy's house on a rainy and windy Friday night, along with the Bartletts and Lem Billings. Rose had just arrived home after a month-long holiday in Europe. At the beginning of the festivities, "twenty-one grandchildren trooped in with birthday gifts for 'Grampy Joe,'" *Time* recounted.

The Ambassador looked dapper in a blue dressing gown over his white shirt and tie, and he wore a red, white, and blue party hat perched at a jaunty angle. After dinner he laughed heartily as his children presented him with gag gifts and serenaded him with comic songs. The mood turned melancholy, though, when Jack sang "September Song" ("Oh the days dwindle down to a precious few: September, November, and these few precious days I'll spend with you"). "He did it so well," said Martha Bartlett. "That was a killer, the old man in a wheelchair, the son singing. You almost felt Jack knew he wasn't going to see old age."

Despite leaden skies and a chilly breeze, Jack and Jackie took the Bartletts out on the *Honey Fitz* on Saturday and Sunday. Jack and Charley talked "at some length [about] what Lyndon would be like as President. . . . He always [liked] talking about all the eventualities." JFK specifically worried that Bobby might run against Johnson in 1968. "He gave me the feeling he wasn't pleased," said Bartlett. "He wanted a record of his own. I sensed that he wanted the Kennedy administration to be Jack, and Bobby was going to turn it into a succession thing. Jack didn't want a dynasty, although I am sure his father would have wanted that."

Kennedy also mused about life after the presidency, although he bristled when Jackie joked, "I don't want to be the wife of a headmaster of a girls school." "At first it used to depress him," Bartlett recalled. But that weekend, "it depressed him less." He pondered being ambassador to Italy, because "Jackie would like it." His main concern was being out of the way when his successor took over—a sentiment he expressed to Bill Walton, who was supposed to be Kennedy's front man in buying a Georgetown home. "We may spend a couple of years in Cambridge, maybe travel some, but then we'll come back here when the heat is off," Kennedy had told Walton.

The next weekend marked Jack and Jackie's tenth anniversary, which they celebrated at the scene of their marriage, Hammersmith Farm, with a candlelit dinner for ten on Thursday the twelfth. Cocktails were served in the spacious "Deck Room," with tall French windows overlooking Narragansett Bay and high, vaulted ceilings ornamented by ribwork of dark beams. This time it was an Auchincloss crowd, and the outsiders were the Bradlees and Sylvia Whitehouse Blake, a Vassar classmate who had been a bridesmaid.

"It was a happy sort of evening," recalled Janet Auchincloss. "I felt that all their strains and stresses, which any sensitive people have in a marriage, had eased to a point where they were terribly close to each other. I almost can't think of any married couple I've ever known that had greater understanding of each other." Ben and Tony Bradlee had a similar reaction when they witnessed "by far the most affectionate embrace we had ever seen them give each other."

Jack and Jackie opened gifts during cocktail hour. She gave him a gold St. Christopher money clip from Tiffany's to replace the one buried with Patrick, and he gave her a gold ring with emerald chips—an expression of Jack's "Irish mystique"—for her to wear on her little finger in memory of Patrick. Jackie also presented Jack with a set of brass buttons for his blazer with the insignia of the Irish Brigade he had seen during his European trip, and a scrapbook of photographs chronicling Bunny Mellon's transformation of the Rose Garden, annotated by quotations on gardening, many written by Joe Alsop, which JFK read aloud.

Jack scattered an array of presents for Jackie on a large circular carved table, with a list of descriptions and prices from the Klejman antiquities dealer in New York: antique Greek and Italian bracelets, pre-Christian and Etruscan sculptures, as well as drawings by Degas and Fragonard. "Now don't forget, you can only keep one," Jack repeated. Jackie picked at least two—a drawing and a gold bracelet coiled like a serpent.

For the next three days, the Bradlees and Kennedys cruised on the *Honey Fitz* and swam at Bailey's Beach. Jack had worked himself up to thirteen holes of golf, which he played twice with Ben at the Newport Country Club. As the two couples headed to their rooms one night after dinner, Jackie grew tearful and said, "You two really are our best friends." Bradlee considered the remark "forlorn . . . almost like a lost and lonely child." It is difficult to believe that if Jackie had suspected her husband's affair with Mary Meyer, she could have voiced such sentiments.

But Jackie's most revealing comments were to Charley Bartlett in a letter written a week after the anniversary. She told him that the weekend could have been so much happier if Patrick had lived, but that it also could have been tragic. Jack made the difference, Jackie told Charley, because he had helped "re-attach me to life" and to appreciate "all the lucky things" they shared. She thanked Charley most of all for the thoughtfulness of his matchmaking a decade earlier. She said that Jack could have enjoyed "a worthwhile life without being happily married." But without Jack as her husband, she told Charley, her life would have "all been a wasteland, and I would have known it every step of the way."

$\mathcal{F}$ollowing a summer that turned from promise to tragedy, Jack Kennedy's final autumn had an uneasy drifting quality. "Somehow missing from the White House is that sense of electric excitement," *Time* observed in mid-September. "Somehow gone from the President's words, both public and private, is that man-the-barricades urgency." Even Kennedy's liegemen became more fractious—"taking turns cutting each other and their boss up," wrote Katie Louchheim.

Jack and Jackie may have reached a new level of what she described as "understanding, respect, and affection," but they were apart two thirds of the time in September, October, and November—forty-two out of sixty-three days. (The previous year they had been away from each other during the same period less than half of the time, and in 1961 less than a quarter of the time.) "I was melancholy after the death of our baby and I stayed away . . . longer than I needed to," Jackie later confessed to the Reverend Richard T. McSorley, a Catholic priest, when she was deeply despondent over her husband's assassination. "I could have made [Jack's] life so much happier, especially for the last few weeks. I could have tried harder to get over my melancholy."

Kennedy's popularity sank to a low of 57 percent in October (compared to his peak of 82 percent after the Bay of Pigs), his high-profile

tax cut and civil rights bills were stalled in Congress, and a series of missteps led to a foreign policy debacle in South Vietnam. With the help of
Bobby, he also managed to extinguish a scandal that came within days
of scorching his presidency.

After avoiding Vietnam for eighteen months, Kennedy became en-
tangled in an ominous fight between South Vietnamese factions and
essentially lost control of the situation. "No doubt he realized that Vietnam was his great failure in foreign policy," wrote Schlesinger.

South Vietnamese president Ngo Dinh Diem had long disquieted
Kennedy and his chief aides. McNamara considered Diem "autocratic,
suspicious, secretive, and insulated." The American government felt
even deeper misgivings about the Vietnamese leader's two principal
advisers, his younger brother Ngo Dinh Nhu and scheming sister-in-
law Madame Nhu—"a true sorceress," in McNamara's words. All three
were strict Catholics who stifled dissent and imposed their religious
teachings on the Vietnamese people to replace the laws of the Buddhist
majority.

Yet since the mid-fifties, the United States had supported Diem's
regime with some $300 million a year ($1.8 billion today, less than
the $3 billion the United States gave Israel in 2003, but more than the
$1.7 billion sent to Egypt, the second largest current recipient of Amer-
ican aid) and assisted his army in fighting Viet Cong guerrillas allied
with communist North Vietnam. Kennedy admired Diem for holding
South Vietnam together and maintaining its independence "under very
adverse conditions." By November 1963, Kennedy had raised the stakes
by increasing the number of American troops "advising" the South
Vietnamese forces from 2,000 to 16,000.

Within the administration, the harshest critic of this policy had been
Ken Galbraith, who had sent JFK a series of memos about Diem's in-
competence and the damaging effects of the American presence as a
"colonial military force." Back in March 1962, Galbraith had written
that the Russians "couldn't be more pleased than to have us spend our
billions in these distant jungles where it does us no good and them
no harm." Galbraith urged a political settlement even at the risk of dis-
pleasing "fighting Joe Alsop," one of Washington's most vocal hawks.
Above all, Galbraith cautioned against committing any combat troops:
"A few will mean more and more and more," he wrote. "Then the South
Vietnamese boys will go back to the farms. We will do the fighting."

But Kennedy was preoccupied with other matters, content to be guided by the optimism of his military and civilian advisers in Saigon. Vietnam was a "marginal thing . . . not much of an issue in the Kennedy years," Schlesinger recalled. In April 1963, at Kennedy's urging, Charley Bartlett had written a column saying "the experts dare at last to say that the West is winning this insidious war." Barely a month later, Diem launched a campaign of political and religious repression. During a peaceful rally by Buddhists in the provincial city of Hue, Diem's forces killed and wounded scores of demonstrators. To protest the Diem crackdown, a Buddhist monk doused his saffron robes with gasoline and ignited himself in the middle of Saigon. Two months later, on Sunday, August 4, a second monk immolated himself.

With Diem arresting protesters by the truckload, a group in the State Department led by Averell Harriman argued that the United States could no longer support his despotic leadership. On Saturday, August 24, Kennedy was in Hyannis Port still grieving over Patrick's death, and Rusk, McNamara, Bundy, and McCone were also out of town. Back at Foggy Bottom, Harriman, State Department official Roger Hilsman, and Bundy deputy Michael Forrestal drafted a cable for the new American ambassador in Vietnam, Henry Cabot Lodge. The wire authorized American support for a military coup against Diem.

Forrestal and Under Secretary of State George Ball consulted Kennedy and read him excerpts from the cable. The President gave his okay subject to agreement by Rusk and Gilpatric. But in a classic bureaucratic screwup, each of the absent officials notified by Forrestal signed off thinking everyone else had approved it. McNamara later characterized their hasty endorsement as "one of the truly pivotal decisions concerning Vietnam made during the Kennedy and Johnson administrations." Kennedy deeply regretted the cable, and in subsequent telegrams attempted to "redress the balance," as he put it. But the Vietnamese generals now had their justification for removing Diem, and they set in motion a course of action to achieve that. Averell Harriman, the hero of the nuclear test-ban talks, never regained Kennedy's confidence.

In subsequent weeks, American officials tried to press Diem to institute reforms. But they had deep differences about how involved the United States should be. "My God, my government's coming apart," Kennedy told Bartlett after one acrimonious meeting. Back in

Washington for consultations in September, David Bruce described attending a "melee over Vietnam." After still another tough session, Kennedy found himself in a meeting to promote the hat industry— a setting somewhere between incongruous and darkly comic. As he begrudgingly tried on an assortment of headgear, he asked Salinger, O'Donnell, and several other advisers to pick their favorites. Each chose a different model. "You remind me of my Vietnam advisers," JFK cracked.

JFK compounded the confusion over his Vietnam policy with two television interviews he gave in early September, the first to Walter Cronkite on CBS and the second to Chet Huntley and David Brinkley on NBC. In each he offered a mixed message about American intentions that tilted toward a stronger American commitment in Vietnam. "In the final analysis, it is their war," he told Cronkite. "They are the ones who have to win it or lose it." Yet he also pledged that the United States would continue to help. "I don't agree with those who say we should withdraw," he said. "That would be a great mistake. I know people don't like Americans to be engaged in this kind of effort. Forty-seven Americans have been killed in combat with the enemy, but this is a very important struggle even though it is far away. . . . It doesn't do us any good to say, 'Well, why don't we all just go home and leave the world to those who are our enemies.'"

To Huntley and Brinkley, Kennedy acknowledged "a kind of ambivalence in our efforts. . . . We are using our influence to persuade the government there to take steps which will win back support." And again he said, "Americans will get impatient and say because they don't like events in Southeast Asia or they don't like the government in Saigon that we should withdraw. That only makes it easy for the Communists. I think we should stay. We should use our influence in as effective a way as we can but we should not withdraw."

The Kennedy administration vacillated about whether to support Diem or an alternative leader. Lyndon Johnson, who had spent time with Diem two years earlier, spoke strongly against supporting a coup. "In Texas we say that it's better to deal with the devil you know than the devil you don't know," he said.

Kennedy rejected the idea of a coalition government incorporating communist representatives, which he concluded had not worked in Laos. Indeed, circumstances in Laos had enabled the North Vietnamese to use the Ho Chi Minh trail as a supply line to aid the Viet Cong. McNamara believed that JFK "confronted with a choice among evils . . . remained indecisive far too long" over Vietnam. It was as if Kennedy's crisp management of the missile crisis had evaporated.

In late September, Kennedy sent McNamara and Maxwell Taylor to Saigon to analyze the situation. After McNamara met for the last time with Diem, he reported that the South Vietnamese military campaign was succeeding but that Diem had to be replaced unless he moderated his policies. At least initially, the replacement regime would need to be "strongly authoritarian" to ensure order. To put pressure on Diem, McNamara recommended that financial support be withheld; to signal progress in creating Vietnamese self-sufficiency, he urged that one thousand American advisers be withdrawn at the end of the year. Kennedy accepted the recommendations, and Salinger announced the administration's intention to withdraw the troops—but stopped short of saying the plan would definitely be carried out. The unrest continued on the streets of Saigon, and the West Wing was paralyzed by indecision.

McNamara's stock remained high with Kennedy as Rusk's continued to drop. The defense secretary was so dominant at the Pentagon that the press was referring to the "McNamara monarchy." At the same time, rumors had begun to circulate in March that Rusk would be the "first to be replaced." Adding to the unrelenting criticism of the secretary of state from Schlesinger and Galbraith, Dillon offered his opinion at Kennedy's request. "In the summer of 1963 when Kennedy mentioned Rusk to me he was sort of exasperated," Dillon recalled. "He said, 'He won't do anything himself. He won't take any responsibility.' " Dillon told Kennedy that McNamara was "a good candidate to be Secretary of State."

In the White House, Bundy was jockeying for that position as well, although in early August Charley Bartlett observed to Katie Louchheim, in "one of those authoritative intonations," that Bundy would "never be Secretary." Bartlett had harsh words as well for O'Donnell, telling Louchheim's dinner guests that he was "strictly the appointments secretary and nothing else. He's the only one who has gotten too big in the head. He's really inflated."

O'Donnell was also feuding with Salinger, one of several White House insiders whose marital problems were attracting unwanted attention. In October, Ted Sorensen's divorce splashed across two columns of the *Washington Star,* along with photographs of himself and his estranged wife. "It is no fun to be the President's alter ego and get your name in the paper over a divorce," noted Louchheim. Salinger's wife had finally left him, and the press secretary was flagrantly "playing around," Louchheim reported to a friend, adding that Deputy Press Secretary Andrew Hatcher "disappeared on the President's advance trip to Europe—left Rome with a Negro model and wasn't heard from in ten days."

At Georgetown dinner parties, Walter Heller openly disparaged Douglas Dillon, who had clearly eclipsed him in Kennedy's estimation. Listening to a phone conversation with Dillon during a Hyannis Port weekend, Jim Reed was struck by Kennedy's deference: "Mr. Secretary, if you think that's what is best under all the circumstances, that's all right with me." Heller couldn't help feeling resentful and insecure, describing to friends a "typical Dillon ploy—to pin the blame on someone else." Heller also complained that Kennedy found it "difficult to give one a boost," and despaired over JFK's "chilly aloofness," even his failure to invite his economic adviser for a swim in the White House pool.

Despite Lyndon Johnson's energetic involvement in rallying support for a civil rights bill, he had slipped into another funk by the late summer of 1963. "Johnson had grown heavy and looked miserable," recalled his confidant Harry McPherson. Standing in the swimming pool at The Elms with McPherson, LBJ lamented that he had no role and said he didn't think he could remain on the ticket. "I think he really meant it," said McPherson.

In early September, Kennedy dispatched Johnson on a goodwill tour to Scandinavia. Before his departure, LBJ asked to confer with Kennedy in Hyannis Port. In typically high-handed fashion, O'Donnell turned down Johnson's request, forcing the Vice President to seek access through presidential military aide Chester Clifton.

Johnson arrived on the Saturday of Labor Day weekend, and houseguest Red Fay was struck by Johnson's apparent "uneasiness and unsureness." When Johnson asked the President to review a proposed speech, Kennedy whipped through the pages, editing quickly. "I think it is very good," Kennedy told Johnson. "I have crossed out a few short sections, which won't hurt the speech but which are better unsaid." Kennedy also vetoed Johnson's request to add Poland to the itinerary. Afterwards, Kennedy said to Fay, "The poor guy's got the lousiest job in government and just wants to make a significant contribution. . . . Unfortunately the timing isn't right. Otherwise I'd love to see him go and have a little fun."

Ten days later JFK sent a solicitous letter to Johnson during the trip. "I am sorry to hear that you are tired," Kennedy wrote, "and I want to be sure that you pay more attention to the doctors than you usually do. The rest of your trip is really not of comparable importance to what you have already accomplished." Kennedy urged Johnson to "take it easy" and praised him for his "exceptionally good" work overseas. "You have shown yourself the best of our ambassadors, with leaders and with the people."

One of the first glimmers of Jackie's recovery came in a letter to Bill Walton on August 27. "Dear Baron," she wrote (along with "Czar," one of several pet names she had for him), inquiring about the White House guard box project. She expressed her doubts about painting them green, since the sentry posts at Wexford were that color and looked like "out houses or army camouflage buildings."

The steady flow of praise for the restoration project helped rejuvenate Jackie as well. "The White House is all it should be—It is all I ever dreamed for it," she wrote to Clark Clifford, her legal consultant on the project. A few items remained on her wish list, including curtains for the East Room, curtains and upholstery for the State Dining Room, and lanterns and chandeliers in the ground floor hall. "It is marvelous what we have accomplished," she told Harry du Pont.

By September, Jackie had already begun to focus on a new round of projects: the Kennedy Library, Harvard historian Frank Freidel's book about the presidents as a companion to the White House guidebook, and a book of photo essays on the White House collection, along with a documentary on the same subject. Jackie even solicited her mother for ideas on the documentary.

The most ambitious new venture was the refurbishment of Blair House and an adjoining nineteenth-century building that the federal government had acquired to expand accommodations for the President's guests. In April, Jackie had formed a committee to preserve Blair House, but because of her pregnancy she had appointed Robin Duke, wife of protocol chief Angier Biddle Duke, to oversee the restoration. The house had been shuttered since the early summer for the installation of central air conditioning and a new kitchen.

"Now I worry about the President's guest house," she wrote to Harry du Pont on September 20, lamenting its "peeling walls, wire coat hangers, stuffed furniture and a ghastly television set." It galled Jackie that visitors to the Soviet Union "have probably just slept in gilded beds and eaten off an Ivan the Terrible gold-plated plate in the Kremlin," only to encounter "quite shocking . . . shabby rooms" across the street from the White House. Jackie asked du Pont for his help, and said she hoped Robin Duke "has not been too efficient." Jackie soon discovered that to the contrary, the committee had been "absolutely bogged down" because Duke "has a much nicer character than I do and is much less autocratic. . . . She lets everyone speak!"

She also consulted with Tuckerman about White House events in the months to come. Although Jackie didn't plan to participate until after the first of the year, there would be state dinners for Emperor Haile Selassie of Ethiopia, Irish prime minister Sean Lemass, and West German chancellor Ludwig Erhard. From Brambletyde she continued to closely supervise the state dinner on September 5. Afghanistan's King Mohammed Zahir Shah and Queen Homaira arrived during a rainstorm, and both JFK and Eunice refused to wear raincoats or hats, much less carry umbrellas, the result of "this marvelous mania for health and youth," observed Angie Duke. "The whole official party stood there in a steady downpour," Duke recalled. "I can still picture the King with the water dripping down his face and going into his collar. Of course the President, vigorous, youthful, magnificent, standing in the rain, was a marvelous figure."

Worried about the weather, Jackie called several times during the day. Although the skies cleared, she finally decided to move the dinner indoors from the Rose Garden because of the wet grass. The after-dinner entertainment proved to be spectacular. Kennedy made his own dramatic impact by requesting that the Jefferson Memorial be illuminated for the first time, so the 116 guests seated on the South Portico outside the Blue Room could see it glowing in the distance along with the Washington Monument. A marine drill organized by Jackie and Tuckerman featured some three hundred officers performing as searchlights crisscrossed their precision patterns. A fireworks finale was another White House first, prompting a flood of calls to the police from frightened citizens worried about exploding bombs.

Jackie had been somewhat subdued during Joe Kennedy's seventy-fifth birthday party and the tenth anniversary celebration, but she was positively giddy during her last weekend in Newport with Vivian Crespi and the Fays as houseguests. Crespi and her son Marcantonio flew with JFK on Friday, September 20, from New York. That afternoon JFK had addressed the United Nations General Assembly, making headlines by proposing a joint U.S.-Soviet trip to the moon. The evening before his speech he and Dave Powers had been at Earl and Flo Smith's Fifth Avenue apartment until after midnight.

Flying to Rhode Island, JFK was absorbed in his papers as Marcantonio tore around the plane. "How can you concentrate in that din?" Crespi asked. "Don't forget," Kennedy said, "I grew up in a family of nine children." On Saturday everyone went swimming and boating as usual, but Jack decided to vary the routine by making a home movie. "You will have the starring role," Kennedy said to Crespi, "and the under secretary will play your ardent suitor. All you have to do is model a bikini." After JFK had chosen "the least conservative and most colorful," he said to Crespi, "How is your running, kiddo?"

With Janet and Hughdie away in Europe, and the children safely back in the house with Secret Service agent Bob Foster, Kennedy assigned the filming to naval photographer Robert Knudsen, who along with Cecil Stoughton chronicled family events under Jackie's watchful eye. Working from a script scribbled by Fay, Kennedy, in what Chuck Spalding would later call his "Roger Vadim" role, blocked out the action: Crespi in her bikini being chased by Fay, wearing long boxer shorts and garters. Jackie gleefully chipped in: "Wouldn't the rape scene be better by moonlight?" As the camera rolled, Fay and Crespi sprinted across Hammersmith's manicured lawn while Kennedy yelled, "Crespi, give him a chance!" "We ended up horizontal in the bushes," Crespi recalled, "with a close-up of Red Fay's feet sticking out of Mrs. Auchincloss's Queen Elizabeth roses."

The second scene had Fay getting killed, ending with him lying in a boat with ketchup splattered on his chest as Crespi, Anita Fay, Jack, and

Jackie blithely stepped over him. "I was the bad guy," Fay recalled. "The Secret Service men were in it too. They came roaring up in a car." Crespi recalled the First Couple's hearty laughter as well as "scratches and thorns in my poor behind."

To the Kennedys' dismay, a press helicopter caught this "murder" sequence, and some publications ran stories on "presidential hijinks." According to Fay, after JFK's assassination, Jackie made certain that the film was locked up "so it would not get into anyone's hands."

Jackie came back to Washington with her family on Monday, September 23—the first time she had been in the capital in three months. Two days later, Caroline was scheduled to start first grade. Jackie had decided to extend the White House school for one final year before sending Caroline to Stone Ridge, a private school for girls in suburban Maryland run by the nuns of the Sacred Heart, who had educated Rose Kennedy and her daughters as well as Joan and Ethel Kennedy.

"I think Mrs. Kennedy was glad to have the privacy and quiet life for Caroline to continue as long as was practical," recalled Alice Grimes. Jackie emphasized to Grimes, "It must be a real first grade where they learn as much as you do at Chapin or Brearley." Grimes also placed Caroline in a catechism class at Georgetown Visitation, a nearby private Catholic girls school. Jackie was eager to have Caroline "religiously up with her 2nd grade comrades & ready to make her first communion with them."

The Kennedy children had become favorites around the White House. "When people spoke they listened," noted Tish Baldrige. "They did not interrupt their elders." Their mother "refused to allow them to feel they were privileged," wrote Baldrige. "Jackie said over and over that she didn't want her daughter and son to consider themselves rich or elite."

Only one day after Jackie returned to the White House, Jack left on a 10,000-mile five-day trip to eleven western states to talk about conservation issues—not ordinarily high on his agenda. The press nicknamed him "Smokey the Bear," "Paul Bunyan," and "Johnny Appleseed," which tickled rather than irritated him. The first stop was, somewhat improbably, Milford, Pennsylvania, the site of Grey Towers. The Pinchot family had given the federal government the mansion belonging to the late uncle of Tony Bradlee and Mary Meyer, former Pennsylvania governor Gifford Pinchot, to use for conservation studies.

Ordinarily the gift would not have attracted presidential attention, but Kennedy wanted to see "where his friends the Pinchot girls had grown up." Tony and Mary flew on Air Force One with the President, and then by helicopter to a pasture on the Pinchot estate. Tony noticed nothing untoward between Jack and Mary that day. "He was easy with both of us," she recalled. "There was no sexual thing evident. I always felt he liked me as much as Mary. You could say there was a little rivalry."

After a perfunctory ceremony at Grey Towers, JFK made a bee-line to the modest home of Tony and Mary's mother, Ruth Pinchot, a onetime liberal free spirit who had turned ardently right wing. "Jack got in the car, and Mary and I ran alongside," Tony said. "When we got there we showed him family pictures. He was joking and having fun." Standing on Ruth Pinchot's "ratty porch," they had their pictures taken—"one of history's most frozen shots," Ben Bradlee recorded. "Jack loved the idea of sticking it to Ruth," he recalled. "Her two daughters brought a Democratic president. The look on her face was as if she had something sour in her mouth. Jack was sort of teasing about the whole thing."

As Kennedy shuttled from state to state—Wisconsin, Minnesota, North Dakota—he droned through what the *Washington Post* described as "sometimes rambling speeches" about national parks and natural resources, and the crowds gave him a tepid response. "Kennedy seemed ill at ease in this guise," noted *Time*. But on September 24, the Senate ratified the limited test-ban treaty, prompting Kennedy to shift gears in Montana and start talking about the need to curb nuclear weapons and pursue international peace. He continued those themes on subsequent stops in Wyoming, Washington, Utah, Oregon, California, and Nevada.

"It was the subtle beginning of the presidential campaign," recalled Kennedy's secretary of the interior, Stewart Udall. "When he began talking about peace he got a wonderful response, so he essentially stopped talking about my subject. I didn't resent it. Ted Sorensen and his people were writing speeches, but Kennedy sensed he should say something about peace. People were aware how dangerous the world was. The first step was the test-ban treaty and talking about the importance of peace. He improvised this, and smart reporters saw this as the first theme of the '64 campaign."

The last weekend of the trip Kennedy spent at Bing Crosby's house in Palm Springs with O'Donnell and Powers. As she had on Kennedy's previous visit to Crosby, Pat Lawford joined her brother for Sunday mass and then spent the day with him before flying to Washington Sunday evening.

———

Jack Kennedy looked "ruddy" as he greeted Ethiopia's Haile Selassie at Washington's Union Station on Tuesday, October 1, while drumrolls and five-foot silver trumpets signaled the arrival of the seventy-one-year-old emperor's train. Standing at JFK's side was Jackie, making her first public appearance since Patrick's death. She seemed "healthy and rested," conversed in animated French with the bearded monarch and his thirty-three-year-old granddaughter, and winked at the crowd. Later in the afternoon, Jackie had tea with the royal guests, who presented her with a full-length leopard coat. "Je suis comblée! (I am overcome)," she exclaimed. She even wore her gift when she escorted Selassie to the Rose Garden. "See, Jack!" she trilled. "He brought it to me! He brought it to me!" Deadpanned Kennedy, "I had wondered why you were wearing a fur coat in the garden."

Afterwards Jackie watched the Joffrey Ballet rehearse its performance of a 1920s-style vaudeville dance for the evening's white-tie dinner. When she realized that the skimpy costumes on the women might offend the African ruler, she sent Nancy Tuckerman scurrying to rent more decorous flapper skirts and tops. As the first guests were arriving, Jackie was already en route to New York, where she caught her flight to Athens.

Once again she had her own special compartment in first class, but she was so fatigued she needed to take oxygen during the eleven-hour journey. On arrival in Athens she looked "pale and drawn," and she was whisked to the seclusion of shipowner Marcos Nomikos's villa overlooking the Saronic Gulf where she and Lee had stayed two years earlier.

She instantly came close to provoking a diplomatic incident by refusing to have lunch with Greece's King Paul and Queen Frederika. She told U.S. Ambassador Henry Labouisse she couldn't stand the queen—an opinion he had heard eight months earlier at a White House dinner party, when she twice said, "I hate her." He finally persuaded her to meet the monarchs for tea. She brought Lee but not Stas, because the queen "hates Stas," the ambassador told Cy Sulzberger that evening.

Jackie, the Radziwills, and the Roosevelts boarded the *Christina* on Friday, October 4, for their Aegean cruise to Istanbul. The Onassis "pleasure palace" had a crew of sixty, a dance band, and two coiffeurs from Athens. On the first night the guests dined on tongue meunière and roast beef, washed down with vintage champagne. During a visit to Smyrna on the Turkish coast, Onassis gave his guests a tour of the town where he had grown up. Jackie had permission from Onassis to direct the *Christina* "wherever her heart desires" through the Greek islands, fulfilling "the dream of my life," she said.

"Onassis was very courtly to Jackie, who was the guest of honor," recalled Sue Roosevelt. "He admired her, but he was not any more attentive to her than to anyone else." Jackie, in turn, found Onassis to be "an alive and vital person." The Roosevelts were fully aware that Lee was involved with Onassis. Stas stayed aboard for only the first few days, and during most of the cruise Jackie and Lee stuck together, doing "zany things" like putting heaps of nutmeg in Roosevelt's soup at lunch because they heard it was a hallucinogen. "They teased him," said Sue. "I thought they were a bit juvenile with all their giggling." Still, it was a relief to see Jackie in an upbeat mood. Onassis pampered his guests, kept everything "on a light note," and gave the women extravagant gifts: gold and diamond bracelets for Lee, a gold and diamond minaudière from Van Cleef & Arpels plus three gold bracelets for Sue Roosevelt, and a diamond and ruby necklace for Jackie.

Jack and Jackie stayed in touch by telephone, including one call from the sisters to report that the *Christina* had been overtaken by pirates, a jejune but ultimately harmless prank. Another time Kennedy mistakenly reached the wife of Moorhead Kennedy, an American consular officer, instead of Jackie.

Several years later, when William Manchester interviewed Jackie for his landmark book *The Death of a President,* she gave him a ten-page letter she had written to Kennedy. Manchester drew from the letter to emphasize "her sorrow" that she couldn't share with her husband the "tension-free atmosphere" of the Aegean cruise. But the letter was actually written by Jackie from Italy more than a year earlier; it contains references to the faulty telephone service in Ravello, to Caroline's easy adjustment, and to a future weekend in Newport with David and Sissie Gore. Manchester's mistake was amplified by other writers over the years as evidence of Jackie's "complexity" and the "authentic love" rekindled after Patrick's death.

The trip aboard the "brilliantly lighted ship . . . gay with guests, good food and drinks" sparked criticism in the press and from Kennedy's political opponents. Republican national chairman William E. Miller attacked the Kennedy administration's "lack of decorum and dignity," citing "late night parties in foreign lands." Republican congressman Oliver Bolton of Ohio denounced both Jackie and Roosevelt for consorting with Onassis. Even the *Washington Post* weighed in. When word reached the White House that the newspaper planned to run an editorial criticizing Roosevelt's conflict of interest, JFK asked Mac Bundy to call Katharine Graham, who had succeeded her husband as president of the *Post* in late September, and request that the editorial not run. She dutifully spoke to editor Russ Wiggins, but he ran it anyway.

Instead of cutting her trip short, Jackie added a second leg to Morocco, a place she had longed to visit as much as Jack had yearned for Ireland. She and Lee were invited by King Hassan II, returning the Kennedys' hospitality the previous March. The two sisters spent three days in the king's Bahia Palace in a suite decorated with white leather Moroccan and modern furniture, overlooking groves of palm trees and the Atlas Mountains. Servants in white robes and red fezzes offered them dates on brass trays and milk poured from silver ladles, and the king flew in two hairdressers and a manicurist. Jackie and Lee slept late and prowled the bazaars for exotic goods.

One afternoon, as they waited for the king, they met "almost one hundred smiling and giggling ladies dressed in golden caftans"—the harem of Hassan's late father and grandfather. When they had exhausted all conversational possibilities, Jackie announced that Lee would sing "In an Old Dutch Garden Where the Tulips Grow" and "The White Cliffs of Dover." Lee's predicament sent Jackie into "hysterical laughter."

In Jackie's absence—what Manchester later described as "a strange hiatus between tragedy and tragedy"—JFK took Caroline and John to Camp David on weekends and entertained his father at the White House. Kennedy scarcely socialized on his own. One evening he invited Vivian Crespi, Red Fay, and Teddy for supper. "Jack wanted to show me some Christmas presents he wanted to buy for Jackie," Crespi recalled. "He knew I knew her taste."

Another Christmas surprise he planned for Jackie was a new proficiency in French after secret lessons from Jacqueline Hirsh, a teacher Jackie had hired to enrich the curriculum at the White House school. During their four sessions together Kennedy "kept interrupting," Hirsh recalled, "constantly asking questions." She was struck that the President "seemed extremely self conscious, extremely. He kept fiddling with his tie and getting up and sitting down." When Hirsh asked him why he was so eager to "surprise the world," he said "Well, it's always good to improve anything you know."

For four days photographer Stanley Tretick was given free access to snap nearly a thousand pictures of Kennedy and his children in the White House and at Camp David—intrusions ordinarily frowned on by Jackie. The resulting photo spread in *Look* featured a memorable series of John Jr. peeking from under his father's desk and perched on the presidential rocking chair. During the photo shoots, Tretick's colleague Laura Bergquist found Kennedy to be unusually remote. "There wasn't the lighthearted banter, the fun and games of our early sessions with him," she said. "This was a very sober preoccupied man who was obviously beginning to look middle aged."

Jim Reed sensed the same mood at the state dinner for Irish prime minister Sean Lemass on Tuesday, October 15. Jean Smith filled in as hostess, and Kennedy organized the evening's entertainment of Air Force Bagpipers in "traditional Irish saffron kilts." The guest list was overwhelmingly Irish American. Dancer Gene Kelly called it a "four handkerchief evening," having "cried at every Irish tune." Afterwards Kennedy invited some fifteen guests upstairs for more music by bagpipers and violinists. Gene Kelly danced, and Kennedy family friend Dorothy Tubridy sang "The Boys of Wexford." "She sang it well, but it is a very sad song," Reed recalled. "I watched the President in the doorway by himself. It was a touching, poignant picture. I had never seen him that way. It was the only time I could remember a sadness that came across his countenance."

Jackie came home on Thursday night, "suntanned but exhausted," noted chief usher J. B. West. She and the children went to Wexford for the weekend, while Jack headed to New England. Kennedy's visit was as nostalgic as it was political. With Powers, O'Donnell, and O'Brien he watched the Harvard-Columbia football game but left at halftime. "I want to go to Patrick's grave," he said. For twenty minutes he stood at the headstone inscribed only with KENNEDY. "He seems so alone here," JFK finally said. After a butterscotch sundae with Powers at a nearby Schrafft's restaurant, Kennedy and his aides walked back to their hotel to prepare for the evening's event, a fundraiser for six thousand of the party faithful in Boston's Commonwealth Armory. "People were swarming around him," recalled historian James MacGregor Burns. "There was that smiling, live, electric figure. . . . It was family night in Boston, with lots of the old retainers and supporters around, including myself."

For one member of his entourage, Mimi Beardsley, it was her last presidential trip. Instead of returning to Wheaton College that September, she had been so "enthralled" by the White House, recalled her schoolmate Wendy Taylor, that she had stayed on. Beardsley left the White House shortly afterwards to prepare for her wedding to Williams graduate Anthony Fahnestock. "My mother said, 'You are coming home,'" Beardsley recalled. Beardsley and Fahnestock later divorced, and she finally received her bachelor's degree four decades after she dropped out. In May 2003, when she was working as an administrator at the Fifth Avenue Presbyterian Church in Manhattan, a long-sealed oral history at the Kennedy Library in Boston revealed her affair with Kennedy, prompting her to break her decades-long public silence and admit that "from June 1962 to November 1963 I was involved in a sexual relationship with President Kennedy." As a sixty-year-old grandmother of four, she described her disclosure as a "relief" and a "gift" to share finally with her two married daughters.

On Sunday, October 20, Kennedy traveled to Hyannis to cruise on the *Marlin* and visit with his father. As he left in his helicopter Monday morning, he kissed the old man not once but twice. Glancing back at his father in a wheelchair on the porch, Kennedy said to Powers, "He's the one who made all this possible, and look at him now."

Kennedy returned to his native Massachusetts one final time the following Saturday to dedicate the Robert Frost Library at Amherst College. The poet had died the previous January at age eighty-eight. At the time of his death, he and Kennedy had been estranged as a result of Frost's remarks on American weakness after visiting the Soviet Union. When Frost fell ill in December 1962, it was front-page news. Telegrams poured in from around the world, but no word came from the White House. "Frost was deeply offended that Kennedy hadn't communicated with him," said Stewart Udall, Frost's close friend. "I was unhappy. I thought it was cold and unfeeling."

Nevertheless, Kennedy remained a great admirer of Frost's work and decided to honor him. Flying to Amherst on Saturday, October 26, Kennedy worked over remarks written by Arthur Schlesinger for the Frost dedication. Udall warned Kennedy that Leslie Frost was furious about the President's snub at the end of her father's life. "Is there going to be a fuss?" Kennedy inquired. "I don't think so," Udall replied. "But if you see me wrestling on the ground with a woman you'll know she's there." Replied JFK, "Whatever you do, Stewart, we'll give you the benefit of the doubt."

Kennedy's speech was one of his finest, a meditation on the role of the artist in a civilized society. He called Frost "one of the granite figures of our time in America," and observed that "because he knew the midnight as well as the high noon, because he understood the ordeal as well as the triumph of the human spirit, he gave his age strength with which to overcome despair." Kennedy admired Frost for coupling "poetry and power, for he saw poetry as the means of saving power from itself. . . . When power corrupts, poetry cleanses. . . . I see little of more importance to the future of our country and our civilization than full recognition of the place of the artist. . . . I look forward to an America which will reward achievement in the arts as we reward achievement in business or statecraft."

$\mathcal{T}$he same day that Jack Kennedy spoke of the cleansing power of poetry, a tawdry political scandal rocked the administration. Investigative reporter Clark Mollenhoff had sniffed out the mysterious deportation of Ellen Rometsch and had written an article in the *Des Moines Register* headlined "U.S. Expels Girl Linked to Officials." The "part-time model and party girl" had been associating with "prominent New Frontiersmen from the executive branch of the government." The *Washington Post* simultaneously broke a story describing the activities of Bobby Baker's Quorum Club on Capitol Hill, and on Sunday, October 27, ran an even more incendiary account based on the Mollenhoff revelations under the headline "Hill Probe May Take Profumo-Type Twist."

The *Post* promised "a spicy tale of political intrigue and high level bedroom antics" involving the still unnamed Rometsch in an "upcoming Senate probe of its employees' extracurricular activities." On Tuesday the twenty-ninth, Republican senator John J. Williams of Delaware would be holding a closed-door session of the Senate Rules Committee to hear testimony on "an extremely sensitive and dangerous matter" involving "a 27 year old German woman of alluring physical proportions and some offhand braggadocio." The article referred to her hasty expulsion on August 21, but made no mention of Bobby Kennedy's role in it.

The previous week Harold Macmillan had resigned as prime minister. The proximate cause was a prostate attack in early October that had required emergency surgery. But in fact the Profumo affair had brought him down, a source of both sadness and disquiet to Jack Kennedy.

The Rometsch matter had resurfaced a month earlier when the FBI and Justice Department launched investigations into Bobby Baker's far-flung business interests after some suspicious activities were mentioned in a lawsuit against Baker by a Washington vending machine company. Investigators made allegations of kickbacks involving both cash and sexual favors for government contracts. When Bobby Baker resigned as secretary of the Senate on October 7, the news led the *Washington Post,* and Mollenhoff eagerly plumbed his contacts. According to Robert Kennedy biographer Evan Thomas, FBI sources probably tipped Mollenhoff about Rometsch, whose name was linked to both JFK and George Smathers in the newsman's diaries. Mollenhoff, in turn, told Williams about Rometsch's activities and urged the senator to issue subpoenas to unearth more details.

Kenny O'Donnell later said that JFK joked about the Baker probe while asking him to quiz White House aides about their contacts with the former secretary to the Senate majority leader. Kennedy also made light of both Rometsch and Baker to Ben Bradlee, who could see that JFK had been "briefed to his teeth" on Baker. JFK told the newsman that Baker was a "rogue, not a crook. He was always telling me he knew where he could get me the cutest little girls, but he never did." Kennedy also joked to Bradlee about the "dirt" Hoover had on certain senators. "You wouldn't believe it," said the President.

Yet it was hardly a casual matter, judging by the large volume of phone calls on both October 25 and 26 involving JFK, Bobby, O'Donnell, Hoover, Mollenhoff's publisher John Cowles, and LaVern Duffy, an investigator for Bobby who had been a lover of Rometsch and who had escorted her to West Germany in August. Bobby hurriedly dispatched Duffy back to Germany to ensure Rometsch's continued silence, and the West German government released a statement insisting that she had no dealings with East Germany. "Correspondence between

Rometsch and Duffy . . . suggests that Duffy sent her money, but does not indicate the amount or the source," Thomas wrote.

The strongest indicator of concern by the Kennedys was Bobby's meeting with Hoover on Monday, October 28. The attorney general argued that if the Williams probe linked senators to a woman suspected of spying for the communists it could create a national crisis. Later that day Hoover met with congressional leaders Mike Mansfield and Everett Dirksen. The FBI director said no evidence had turned up to prove espionage by Rometsch or her sexual activity with anyone in the executive branch—but he did document Rometsch's liaisons with senators. Whether this was the plain truth or a shrewd ploy to protect JFK is one of the many secrets that Hoover took to the grave. When Williams convened his hearings the next day, he limited his inquiries to Baker's business affairs, and the Rometsch scandal vanished.

By then, Bobby Kennedy had paid a shameful price for Hoover's help. After months of resistance, Bobby had yielded to pressure from the FBI director on October 10 to authorize extensive wiretaps on the telephones of Martin Luther King Jr. Hoover supposedly was interested in proving that the civil rights leader had ties to communists, but he primarily wanted to delve into King's extramarital sex life. Given the potential problems of the Rometsch threat at the time, Bobby had little choice but to placate Hoover, even though he knew that the wiretaps would probably be abused.

Vietnam was just then approaching a climactic moment. Throughout October, South Vietnamese generals plotted a coup while Kennedy and his men kept abreast of their progress. At the same time, Ambassador Lodge increased pressure on Diem to make changes. Finally, on October 29, Lodge cabled that a coup was "imminent," and JFK met with his national security advisers to discuss American support for the effort. As a result, Bundy sent a cable to the embassy in Saigon on October 30 saying the United States would "reject appeals for direct intervention," but he added that once a coup had begun, it was in American interests "that it should succeed."

On Friday, November 1, the generals launched their coup, and the next morning the White House Situation Room received word that

Diem and his brother had been shot in the back of the head and stabbed by bayonets. On hearing the news, Kennedy bolted from the room "with a look of shock and dismay on his face which I had never seen before," Maxwell Taylor recalled. To Schlesinger, JFK appeared "somber and shaken. I had not seen him so depressed since the Bay of Pigs." In a Dictabelt recording two days later, Kennedy pinned responsibility on the original August 24 cable, which was "badly drafted . . . should never have been sent on a Saturday," and which he should not have consented to "without a roundtable conference at which McNamara and Taylor could have presented their views."

In subsequent weeks Kennedy continued to send ambiguous signals both publicly and privately about American intentions. Because he managed to speak alternately like a hawk and a dove, JFK left plenty of evidence for partisans on both sides to argue how he would have proceeded in Vietnam had he lived. Loyalists like Kenny O'Donnell said that JFK talked of a total military withdrawal from Vietnam. "I can't do it until 1965—after I'm reelected," O'Donnell quoted him as saying. Yet Robert McNamara told Stewart Alsop that the United States "would have intervened in Vietnam with ground troops under any circumstances because the national interest demanded intervention."

Kennedy's final words on the subject—the text of the speech he intended to give in Dallas on November 22—showed his concern about the prospect of committing combat forces, but no weakening of his resolve to draw a line against communism in Vietnam. American assistance to the nations "on the periphery of the Communist world," he wrote, "can be painful, risky and costly, as is true in Southeast Asia today. But we dare not weary of the task. . . . Reducing our effort to train, equip and assist their armies can only encourage Communist penetration and require in time the increased overseas deployment of American combat forces. . . . Our adversaries have not abandoned their ambitions, our dangers have not diminished, our vigilance cannot be relaxed. . . . We in this country, in this generation, are—by destiny rather than choice—the watchmen on the walls of world freedom."

The day Diem and Nhu were assassinated, Kennedy had planned to fly to Chicago for the Army–Air Force football game. Instead, after his briefing on Vietnam, he invited Mary Meyer to the White House for the afternoon. "He was in touch when things were falling apart in Vietnam," said Anne Truitt. "It was a very natural impulse to call a friend. That is what I gathered from talking to Mary." In any event, Meyer and Kennedy never saw each other again.

After another hour-long meeting about Vietnam, Kennedy took the helicopter to Wexford that evening to join Jackie and the Fays. It was only the second weekend JFK had spent with his family at their new country retreat. The neighbors were well aware of their presence because the hilltop residence was "ablaze with lights," including giant floodlights. But according to Mary Gallagher, Kennedy was displeased that the house had insufficient closet space and guest rooms. There was already talk, she noted, of building an addition.

Jackie, however, couldn't have been happier with Wexford. She had resumed hunting on October 26, and the next morning had taken Caroline out "beagling" with Paul Fout—pursuing rabbits down a trail behind a pack of beagle hounds. Wearing blue jeans and her hair under a large kerchief, she had been spotted window-shopping in Middleburg with John Jr. and at the grocery store buying canned soups, vegetables, and magazines.

On that first weekend they had spent Sunday with Lem Billings and Princess Irene Galitzine, the Italian fashion designer who had been with Jackie for several days aboard the *Christina*. For entertainment, the Kennedys showed movies of the cruise as well as the Kennedy-Nixon debates from 1960. Galitzine noted that Kennedy was so absorbed that "he held on to my glass of champagne and drank out of it without realizing what he was doing, lost in his thoughts."

Jackie had actually invited Galitzine to stay at the White House on Friday, October 25, but JFK had objected. From Monday through Thursday that week the Kennedys had endured the ubiquitous presence and persistent questioning of Jim Bishop, who was writing a cover story for *Reader's Digest* on "A Day in the Life of President Kennedy." Kennedy consented to the project, he said, because "the way things are going for us right now, we can use anything we get. Anyway, we have the right of clearance." By day three, both Jack and Jackie were describing Bishop's various intrusions to Ben and Tony Bradlee over dinner. Jackie was upset that Bishop was "prying awfully deep into their privacy." Her session with him that day had been "chaotic, with one dog biting the other, with the children shouting and screaming up a storm, and with the telephone buzzing like mad." JFK was cross with valet George Thomas for disclosing that the President owned twenty-five pairs of shoes.

At JFK's meeting with Governor John Connally and Lyndon Johnson in El Paso the previous June, they had discussed a trip to the Lone Star State in the fall. "Kennedy had wanted to go to Texas for a long time," Charley Bartlett later told Manchester. Connally officially extended the invitation during a visit to the White House on October 4 and asked if Jackie would come along. She was away in Greece at the time, but it seemed unlikely she would agree. She had declined to campaign with her husband since the 1960 primaries, and she was not scheduled to resume her activities as first lady until early 1964.

During the cruise, Irene Galitzine had detected remorse in Jackie about the negative political fallout produced by her jet set activities. "She agonized over it," Galitzine recalled. Five days after her return, JFK played on what he called "Jackie's guilt feelings" during dinner with the Bradlees. "Maybe now you'll come with us to Texas next month," said JFK. "Sure I will, Jack," she replied. She opened her red leather engagement book with JACQUELINE KENNEDY in gold letters on the cover and scrawled TEXAS on November 21, 22, and 23.

Jackie's decision to campaign surprised Pamela Turnure. "It was significant," Turnure recalled, "the first domestic trip she had ever taken with the President as President." Turnure wanted to know what to tell the press. "Say I am going out with my husband on this trip and that it will be the first of many that I hope to make with him," Jackie instructed. "Say yes that I plan to campaign with him and that I will do anything to help my husband be elected President again."

But the White House withheld the announcement because Jackie wavered several times about going. At dinner on Friday, October 25, with Irene Galitzine, Franklin and Sue Roosevelt, and Hervé and Nicole Alphand, Jackie expressed concern about an ugly incident the previous night during Adlai Stevenson's visit to Dallas. Seventy anti-UN demonstrators had swarmed Stevenson after he gave a speech celebrating world peace. The crowd of 20,000 had given Stevenson a standing ovation, but as police escorted him from the Dallas Memorial Auditorium, the protesters jeered and spat on him, and hit him in the head with a placard. The city fathers said Dallas had been "disgraced" by such "storm trooper actions," and issued a profound apology.

The Roosevelts cautioned Jackie to be careful. She responded by saying "she wanted to take a 'pass'" on the Texas trip, citing the advice of her doctors. "But Jack wanted her at his side," Alphand noted in his diary. In the following days, Jackie continued to balk. Finally John Connally called the White House and "laid down the law," recalled George Christian, then press secretary to the governor. "He started raising hell when she wasn't coming. She was popular in Texas, and she really needed to be there."

On November 7, Turnure announced that Jackie would join her husband in Texas, a trip that would include her first visit to the Johnson Ranch in Stonewall. The Johnsons made special preparations to please their guests: a hard mattress for Jack, a supply of Poland Water, and a walking horse in readiness for Jackie. There would also be swimming, a ranch tour, and a demonstration of roping and herding at the barbecue grounds.

Connally scheduled a fundraiser at the governor's mansion in Austin on Friday night, November 22, but otherwise the President's trip consisted of speeches at "nonpartisan" events in San Antonio, Houston, Fort Worth, and Dallas. "Kennedy wanted to come to Texas for money," said George Christian. "He needed support. It was his idea, and the focal point was Austin."

The drop in JFK's popularity during 1963 had resulted mainly from his stand on civil rights. Whites, especially in the South, felt he was moving "too far and too fast," while blacks were disappointed that his legislation wasn't offering enough. According to a *Newsweek* poll in early October, Kennedy was "the most widely disliked Democratic President of this century among white Southerners," with 67 percent of them "dissatisfied with the way he has handled racial problems." As the biggest southern state, Texas was just as crucial to Kennedy's reelection in 1964 as it had been in 1960. But by the autumn of 1963 "a lot of Texas had decided Kennedy was a big eastern liberal and Johnson was his lap dog," said Christian. "Kennedy was interested in his reelection and he needed desperately to get Texas in his corner."

Polls showed that JFK's most likely opponent was conservative senator Barry Goldwater of Arizona, although New York governor Nelson Rockefeller and Michigan governor George Romney were also contenders. In trial matchups, Kennedy held comfortable leads against each of them. Surveys also showed Goldwater to be the main beneficiary of southern hostility toward Kennedy.

JFK not only welcomed a Goldwater candidacy, he actively talked it up at news conferences and in speeches. Press reports on Kennedy's Boston speech in late October noted that he took some "political pleasure" at the prospect of taking on the Arizonan. Kennedy liked Goldwater and appreciated his quick wit, but felt his extreme views would sink him.

Romney was a strict Mormon who had been a highly successful automotive executive. He posed a mild threat because he had such an impeccable reputation, although Kennedy was suspicious of a man with "no vices whatsoever." JFK believed the most formidable opponent would be fifty-five-year-old Rockefeller, whose centrist views were far more palatable than Goldwater's. The New Yorker also had a magnetic personality, a huge fortune, and the mystique of a family even more illustrious than the Kennedys. "Jack was scared stiff of Rockefeller," said Charley Bartlett. JFK told Ros Gilpatric that with Rockefeller "it would be a close contest."

Kennedy took every opportunity to buttonhole Gilpatric, who had known the Rockefellers for decades. "He endlessly questioned me about every phase of the Rockefeller family," said Gilpatric. Whenever the New York governor was coming to Washington on official business, JFK would ask his subordinates to engage in "concentrated espionage—who Rockefeller was seeing . . . what he was doing," Gilpatric recalled. During his service in Washington, Gilpatric "never saw more concentrated attention given to any political subject" than Kennedy's focus on Nelson Rockefeller.

On November 7, Rockefeller was the first to officially announce his candidacy—six months and three days after his marriage to Margaretta "Happy" Murphy. He and his new wife—the mother of four children—had both divorced their spouses, which most political professionals considered an insurmountable liability. Still, Rockefeller came out swinging, attacking Kennedy's "failures at home and abroad" as well as Goldwater's opposition to progressive ideas, including the civil rights bill.

A week later Kennedy held his first strategy session for the 1964 campaign. The White House meeting included Bobby Kennedy, Steve Smith, Ted Sorensen, Kenny O'Donnell, and Larry O'Brien. "As usual, the campaign will be run right from here," Kennedy said. Steve Smith would be in charge, and the theme of the campaign would be "peace and prosperity."

Lyndon Johnson's conspicuous absence from the session was picked up by the press, fueling speculation that he would be dumped from the ticket. "Preposterous on the face of it," Kennedy told Ben Bradlee. "We've got to carry Texas in '64 and maybe Georgia." When Bartlett quizzed the President, he "turned on me and he was furious," Bartlett recalled. "'Why would I do a thing like that? That would be absolutely crazy. It would tear up the relationship and hurt me in Texas.'"

The conjecture was prompted in part by the Baker investigation, which was widely interpreted in political and journalistic circles as Bobby Kennedy's effort to damage Johnson, Baker's former mentor. Johnson, who had a conspiratorial cast of mind, firmly believed he was the real target.

When George Smathers asked about the rumored link between the Baker probe and LBJ's future, Kennedy exploded. "Can you see me now in a terrible fight with Lyndon Johnson, which means I'll blow the South?" JFK said. "George, do you know how that would read if Bobby Baker was indicted tomorrow morning with the girl situation involved? *Life* magazine would put twenty-seven pictures of these lovely looking, buxom lasses running around with no clothes on, twenty-seven pictures of Bobby Baker and hoodlums, and then the last picture would be of *me,* and it would say, 'Mess in Washington under Kennedy Regime,' and 99 percent of the people would think I was running around with twenty-nine girls because they don't read the story, and I'm going to defeat myself. You think my brother doesn't like the attorney general's job? He wants to be out? Smathers, you just haven't got any sense, and if Lyndon thinks that, he ought to think about it. I don't want to get licked. I really don't care whether Lyndon gets licked, but I don't want to get licked, and he's going to be my vice president because he helps me!"

Still, during a Kennedy family meeting that fall, "Bobby had strongly attacked Lyndon," Agriculture Secretary Orville Freeman wrote in his journal. "This would confirm the rumors that he was doing so around town following the Bobby Baker matter." On hearing RFK's attack, "Jackie Kennedy had climbed all over Bobby, saying she wouldn't listen to this, that Lyndon had been kind, helpful and loyal, and this just wasn't fair. She wouldn't tolerate it or listen to it."

Bobby Kennedy kept after Baker, mindful that with the Rometsch matter eliminated, the prospect of "buxom lasses" linked to JFK had disappeared. Baker was eventually convicted in 1967 of theft, fraud, and income tax evasion based on his acceptance in 1962 of $100,000 that he described as "campaign donations." He served sixteen months of a three-year sentence.

In the two weeks before the Texas trip, Jack and Jackie pursued busy schedules and were apart as much as they were together. They hosted a few small dinners where Jackie played records of Moroccan dances and demonstrated some of the "bumps and grinds" she had seen in Marrakesh, and Jack spoke excitedly about the coming election. "He was looking forward to '64," said Bradlee. "There is no question he was full of confidence about it." With the Alsops, Jackie talked up their Texas plans, although Susan Mary felt her enthusiasm was forced. One evening Jack and Jackie invited Ben, Tony, Bobby, and Ethel to watch *From Russia with Love,* the latest James Bond movie. Bradlee noticed that JFK "seemed to enjoy the cool and the sex and the brutality" and that Bobby was "dressed like a Brooks Brothers beatnik."

The most diverting private dinner was on November 13 in honor of Greta Garbo. JFK had lured the reclusive Swedish actress to the White House with the help of Washington hostess Florence Mahoney, who had met Garbo at La Fiorentina, the Riviera home of philanthropist Mary Lasker. Garbo was to be accompanied by her best friend, the Russian dress designer Valentina Schlee, and husband Georges Schlee, who was the film legend's lover.

JFK also intended the dinner as a practical joke on Lem Billings. After meeting Garbo at the Lasker villa, where he was a frequent guest, Billings had boasted to Kennedy of "blithe and enchanting adventures" with the actress. His curiosity piqued, Kennedy decided it was "time to hear Garbo's side." That autumn Billings had not been much in evidence at the White House, so the invitation from JFK was especially meaningful. "I got the feeling at the end that Jackie was trying to close

Lem out," recalled Bartlett. The evening with Garbo would be the final time Billings would see his oldest and dearest friend.

Helen Chavchavadze was invited to dine as well—her second visit to the White House that day after a hiatus of nearly a year. Jackie had invited Helen to bring her daughters to the afternoon performance of the Black Watch Regiment of bagpipers on the South Lawn for 1,700 underprivileged children. The spectators sat in bleachers, while the First Family and their guests watched from the South Portico balcony outside the Blue Room.

Both invitations stirred feelings of ambivalence in Chavchavadze. Following her release from Sibley Hospital, she had spent the summer and fall rebuilding her confidence, starting a new job teaching Russian at American University, reclaiming her children, and regaining her home. She had met the man who would become her second husband and was feeling optimistic about her future. "After I had been so down, I went to the White House again," she recalled. "I did not want to be pulled back in. I was relieved that that part of my life was over."

Billings was thrilled that he would be seeing Garbo at the White House. "Greta!" he exclaimed as she walked into the dining room with Jackie. Fixing Billings with a blank stare, Garbo said to Kennedy, "I have never seen this man before"—a ruse JFK had concocted with her only moments before his friend arrived. To Billings's bewilderment, she kept the deception going until the second course. Kennedy milked the prank for every drop of amusement, watching his old friend squirm. Chavchavadze was far more intrigued by Garbo's ménage à trois and sensed that Jackie also admired the sophistication of Garbo's arrangement with the Schlees.

After dinner, Kennedy took Garbo to the Oval Office where she admired his scrimshaw and mentioned her own small collection. Impulsively he presented her with one of his intricately carved whale's teeth as a gift. Writing to Jackie afterwards, the actress thanked her for a "most unusual evening. . . . I might believe it was a dream if I did not have in my possession the President's 'tooth.'" According to Chavchavadze, "Jackie was very upset, because she had given that beautiful piece of scrimshaw to Jack."

Jack and Jackie invited the Bradlees to join them for their third weekend together at Wexford. The weather was chilly and clear, and the foursome had cocktails on the terrace. Bradlee judged the house "very swell," but took note of the "unlived-in decorator look." Kennedy confessed that the house had indeed cost more than $100,000, as Bradlee had bet it would—although JFK declined to pay off the wager.

Kennedy fretted about the Texas trip because Connally was feuding with Senator Ralph Yarborough, who also had bad blood with Lyndon Johnson. Connally and Johnson represented the conservative wing of the Texas Democratic party, and Yarborough the liberal flank—an ongoing statewide rivalry dating from Roosevelt days. Connally had infuriated Yarborough by excluding the Texas congressional delegation from the Austin fundraiser and limiting the invited politicians to Democratic state legislators. Kennedy complained to Bradlee that Johnson had become "a less viable mediator than he had once been." JFK was also concerned that the Stevenson incident in Dallas several weeks earlier had signaled that "the mood of the city was ugly."

Pat Lawford, whose estrangement from her husband had been reported in the press, showed up for Sunday lunch "looking very upset and nervous," Bradlee noted. She drank too much that afternoon, and Jackie stayed with her "literally all night talking" while everyone else went to bed.

Monday, November 11, was Veterans Day, and the group spent a leisurely morning taking walks, reading the newspapers, and watching Jackie on horseback. Kennedy left first on his helicopter with John Jr. to attend a ceremony at Arlington Cemetery. "It was the last time I ever saw him," Bradlee wrote.

At Arlington, Kennedy was "alternatively somber and smiling" during the ceremony at the Tomb of the Unknowns. Instead of leaving right afterwards as planned, he took John Jr. to the amphitheater for more music and speeches. As the President marched with military officers, the little boy broke away from his Secret Service detail to join the parade, and his father burst out laughing.

———

By mid-November, Kennedy's tax reduction bill—at the time the biggest in history—had been whittled down to $11 billion ($66 billion today) from his requested $13.5 billion. The legislation was stuck in Wilbur Mills's House Ways and Means Committee, and the Senate Finance

Committee was dragging its feet on hearings. The civil rights bill was similarly tied up in the House Judiciary Committee. Kennedy worried as well about the likelihood of a Senate filibuster on civil rights.

In foreign policy, Kennedy continued to be sorely vexed by France. Hervé Alphand had recently given a tough speech denying that France wished to "dominate" Europe and justifying his country's refusal to sign the test-ban treaty on the grounds that de Gaulle had seen "no obvious sign" of true détente. In those circumstances, Alphand said, it was vital for the French to maintain their own nuclear deterrent.

Kennedy had complained bitterly to Alphand about de Gaulle's refusal to play by the "rules of the alliance," and Alphand had shot back that France simply wanted to be "an ally without being a protégé." Yet Kennedy was eager for a visit by de Gaulle in February 1964, and he even hoped his progress with Jacqueline Hirsh would enable him to impress the French president by negotiating in his own language. JFK was pushing for a ceremonial trip to Washington, complete with a parade. Alphand insisted that de Gaulle wanted a "working trip" away from the capital "to avoid public displays." "But the Irishman would not let go of his idea," Alphand noted in his diary.

Facing the press for the sixty-fourth time at his final news conference on November 14, Kennedy was remarkably serene in the face of unusually tough questioning. Asked about congressional intransigence on the tax and civil rights bills, Kennedy declared, "The fact of the matter is that both these bills should be passed." If there was further stalling on the tax bill, he warned, "I think the economy will suffer."

Yet he also expressed his faith in the 88th Congress by quoting from Arthur Hugh Clough's poem "Say Not the Struggle Naught Availeth":

> *And not by eastern windows only,*
> *When daylight comes, comes in the light;*
> *In front the sun climbs slow, how slowly,*
> *But westward, look, the land is bright.*

Playing off the final line, he said that however dark it seemed at the moment, he was confident that by the summer of 1964 he would sign the civil rights and tax bills into law.

The Black Watch performance marked Jackie's reemergence as first lady. Two days before, the White House had announced that in addition to the Texas trip, she would resume her official duties six weeks earlier than expected by serving as the hostess of two events—the annual judicial reception on November 20 and the Erhard state dinner on the twenty-fifth.

Three months after the loss of her baby, she seemed more serene. Robin Douglas-Home, a British journalist she had gotten to know in Ravello, came to visit her at Wexford on Saturday, November 16. He intended to spend only a few hours and ended up staying for dinner. During their extended conversation, Jackie displayed a "new humility. . . . The moods were less shifting, the wit less biting." In earlier encounters, he had feared that her "merciless mockery" might be turned on him along with "other people and customs and protocols and institutions." Now he felt more relaxed in her presence.

She told him, as she had written to Charley Bartlett, that after Patrick's death JFK had helped her appreciate how fortunate they were to have Caroline and John, and that she was heartened to see "how much he valued their presence." The shared tragedy, she said, had "strengthened their self-sufficiency as a family."

Jackie also talked about the visit to Dallas the following week. "Now I'm quite firm in my decision to go to Texas," she said, "even though I know I'll hate every minute of it. But if he wants me there, then that's all that matters. It's a tiny sacrifice on my part for something that he feels is very important to him."

Kennedy was away that weekend on a five-day speechmaking trip in New York and Florida. On Thursday he had gone to a dinner party at Steve and Jean Smith's Fifth Avenue apartment. The gathering included Bobby and Ethel, Oleg Cassini, Adlai Stevenson, and the novelist William Styron. "I heard Stevenson advising the President not to go to Texas," Cassini recalled. Stevenson had been rattled by the violent mood he had encountered in Dallas three weeks earlier and had asked Schlesinger to recommend that Kennedy scuttle the trip. Schlesinger had worried that JFK would take offense and that O'Donnell would dismiss Stevenson as "a fussy old man." As Schlesinger wavered, Stevenson called back "to withdraw his objections." Now face-to-face with Kennedy, Stevenson had raised his doubts anew. "Why do you go?" Cassini asked Kennedy afterwards. "Your own people are saying you should not." Kennedy just "shrugged and smiled," Cassini recalled.

The most noteworthy part of JFK's Manhattan stopover was his decision to avoid "fuss and feathers" by dispensing with his usual motorcycle escort, which "aged his Secret Service detail ten years," reported *Time*. As the presidential limousine crawled through midtown traffic and halted at a stoplight on Madison Avenue, a woman rushed the car and fired a flash camera in JFK's face. "She might well have been an assassin," said a New York police officer.

Such fearlessness on Kennedy's part had become commonplace, and was a trait valued in his family. His mother told him she had been pleased to hear from the "proletariat" of New York—an elevator man, hairdresser, and cabdriver—who applauded him for shedding his police escort "to be just like us." She wanted Jack to know he had achieved a political "coup" with the electorate.

In the same spirit he had permitted crowds of young men in Ireland to swarm his car as he eagerly shook their hands, and the previous summer he had been mobbed on the South Lawn by more than two thousand screaming foreign students who stole his tie clasp and pocket handkerchief before he was rescued by police. "The kind of man he was made it impossible for him to take precautions, to guard against maniacs, to think of his life being in danger, to accept protection," wrote Katie Louchheim.

Kennedy spent the final weekend of his life in Florida with the ever faithful Dave Powers as well as Congressman Torbert Macdonald, the old Harvard friend and fellow "tailhound" kept on the margins by Jackie for the previous three years. They arrived at La Guerida in Palm Beach in the early evening of Friday, November 15. O'Donnell and Smathers joined them on Saturday morning at Cape Canaveral, where they watched the successful firing of a Polaris missile from a submarine and inspected the massive Saturn rocket being constructed to launch a man to the moon.

Back at Joe Kennedy's house, JFK spent the afternoon swimming and watching the Navy-Duke football game on TV. After dinner, he sang "September Song" "better than usual," Powers recalled. Sunday was another leisurely day spent watching the Chicago Bears and Green Bay Packers play on TV, followed by a screening of the bawdy new film *Tom Jones*. "Usually this time of year, the wind just blows and blows,"

Macdonald recalled. "But this time—four pleasant days, not a cloud in the sky. . . . It was like back in 1939, where there was nothing of any moment on anybody's mind. Sure there was some talk of politics . . . but it wasn't the usual tension-filled weekend."

On Monday, Kennedy and his guests took a swing through Tampa and Miami, where he pledged that the United States stood ready to help any Latin American country "to prevent the establishment of another Cuba in this hemisphere." Aboard Air Force One back to Washington, Kennedy confided to Smathers some anxiety about the Texas trip. "I wish we had this thing over with," he said, but quickly added, as he had "many, many times: 'You've got to live every day like it's your last day on earth and it damn well may be!'"

That night Jackie decided to remain in Middleburg to rest before the journey to Texas. Once again, Kennedy invited Enüd Sztanko to the White House to "just talk." "He seemed a little low," she recalled, and she was struck by "some kind of urgency" in his voice. "I was afraid if I went that evening I might get involved. I said no because Jackie wasn't there." Sztanko later "regretted not having seen him at the last possible moment" and for years afterwards "felt regret that I could not have been a friend and given some kind of comfort."

Jackie had been wavering about returning to Washington in time to make her scheduled appearance at the Judicial Reception Wednesday evening the twentieth. "It was a big crisis," Tuckerman recalled. "She hedged back and forth." On Wednesday morning Jackie took her horse Sardar out for a vigorous five-mile ride. On returning to Wexford, she instructed Clint Hill, her Secret Service agent, to notify Evelyn Lincoln that she wouldn't be coming to the reception.

It was a disappearing act Jackie had pulled repeatedly, but this time Kennedy refused to indulge her. He immediately phoned Jackie, and by Hill's tactful description, "It was decided that she would come back earlier that day." Just before 1:30 p.m. her car slipped through the Southwest Gate of the White House.

Taking his midday swim with Dave Powers, Kennedy said he was "so happy" Jackie was going to Texas. JFK had also just met with Jim Reed about a lease the following July for Brambletyde. Reed knew the owner and had negotiated the rent down from $3,000 to $2,300 for the month. As he signed the lease, "Kennedy was in great form, good cheer," Reed recalled, "but he bitched about the rent." The Kennedys had already contracted to rent Annandale Farm in Newport for August and September. It was an eighty-acre estate next to Hammersmith Farm, with a large white-columned house, equally panoramic views, and even greater privacy. Combined with a month on Squaw Island, the summer of 1964 promised to be the best yet.

At six-thirty Jack, Jackie, Bobby, and Ethel received the members of the Supreme Court in the Yellow Oval Room before greeting some seven hundred guests from the federal judiciary, Justice Department, and White House. Jackie wore a burgundy velvet evening suit and pink satin blouse with a simple strand of pearls. Kennedy was tanned from his days in Florida. As he chatted amiably with the justices and their wives, Ethel caught a slight undercurrent. "It was the only time I've ever seen him look preoccupied," she said later. "I went to say hello but he looked through me" as he never had before.

The group marched downstairs, led by the Kennedys with Chief Justice Earl Warren and his wife. JFK decided on the spot to dispense with the traditional East Room receiving line. Nancy Tuckerman had reminded him that the previous year some judges were "upset" that they never made it through the line, so this year he and Jackie would circulate through all the state rooms. After her long absence from the public spotlight, Jackie was the center of attention. Numerous guests congratulated her on looking so good. White House curator James Ketchum watched with pleasure as Jackie and Bobby "went around to the wives of the judges, keeping them happy." Spotting Douglas Dillon, JFK smiled warmly and exclaimed, "You're going off to Japan, I've got to go to Texas. I wish we could change places!"

The President and First Lady stayed less than a half hour. He ducked into his office to read some cables before joining Jackie, Bobby, and Ethel on the second floor. The younger Kennedys were off to host a party for sixty at Hickory Hill to celebrate Bobby's thirty-eighth birthday.

As the Marine Band played songs from *Camelot* and *My Fair Lady* for the dancing guests in the East Room, Jack and Jackie had dinner upstairs and packed for their trip the next morning. JFK decided he would help Jackie plan her wardrobe, with an eye toward all the "rich

Republican women" in Texas who would be "wearing mink coats and diamond bracelets"—perhaps forgetting momentarily his wife's own diamonds, couture clothes, and double-breasted mink coat. As if she needed reminding about the virtues of sartorial restraint, he advised Jackie to "be simple—show these Texans up." He made a selection of pastel outfits including a nubby pink wool Chanel suit with a navy blue collar and a matching pillbox hat to wear in Dallas. Although Cassini remained her official couturier, on the sly Jackie was still buying Parisian clothes through Lee and Letizia Mowinckel.

Janet Auchincloss and Rose Kennedy had sent notes of encouragement to Jackie that she read after dinner. "Have a wonderful time in Texas!" wrote Janet. "I am so glad you are going and I should think it would be the greatest fun even if hectic." Rose's message was more businesslike, alerting Jackie that she had sent White House guidebooks to Sacred Heart convents around the world. Jack also showed Jackie a teasing letter from Lee addressed to "Dear Chief Curley," reporting that whenever Jackie went on trips, such as the recent cruise with Onassis, she got beautiful gifts, while Lee received only "3 dinky little bracelets that Caroline wouldn't wear to her own birthday party."

With the children asleep, Jack and Jackie talked on the phone to Eunice, Peter Lawford, George Ball, and Charley Bartlett. JFK and Bartlett talked about former HEW secretary Abe Ribicoff, the new senator from Connecticut. Bartlett asked why Ribicoff had run for the Senate, and Kennedy replied, "He wants to be the first Jewish president, and that's a long alley with no cans to kick." Kennedy tried to reach Chuck Spalding, the first of three attempts before Dallas. Afterwards, Spalding figured his friend was trying to invite him to the country the following weekend, but he could only wonder about the "sort of insistence" implicit in those calls.

The feud between Connally and Yarborough had sparked newspaper stories speculating that the split could "reduce the political mileage the President can expect to make" in Texas. These accounts focused on the exclusion of Yarborough from the Austin dinner, neglecting to note that no members of Congress had been invited. To Kennedy, the Texas troubles were a "minor annoyance," not a consuming issue, according to Kenny O'Donnell. Kennedy had no intention of "going down there to patch things up." JFK understood that Texas was a "fractious place with lots of infighting," said George Christian. "Kennedy wasn't going to wave his hand and all would be fine. He tried to get along with both sides, which is all anyone should try to do."

At six-thirty on Thursday morning the twenty-first, Kenneth Battelle arrived to cut and style Jackie's hair. "She had lists of things," he recalled. "Who was going to be there, things people never think of." Kenneth had traveled to the White House many times since inauguration day 1961, but that morning was one of the rare moments he saw the President and First Lady together.

"At 7 a.m. I was sitting in the hall on the second floor," Kenneth recalled. "The President came along. He looked better than I had ever seen him—relaxed and tan, in a pale colored suit. She was very relaxed and very happy. There was something about both of them. I remember thinking it at the time."

According to Kenny O'Donnell, JFK said to him that morning, "I feel great. My back feels better than it's felt in years." Indeed, when Jackie had asked her husband what he wanted to do at the Johnson ranch, he had replied unexpectedly, "I'd like to ride." Yet underneath his shirt, Kennedy was wearing his brace of white cotton that resembled a corset and covered his midsection, buttressed by vertical stays and fastened with buckles.

Kennedy spent an hour in the Oval Office before walking back upstairs to prepare for his departure with Jackie. He was briefly irritated by a weather report forecasting warmer weather than anticipated. All Jackie's clothes were wool, and he worried about her comfort. He had also planned to take John Jr. on the helicopter to Andrews Air Force Base, but Miss Shaw was resisting because it was raining and she didn't want the boy to get wet. "I'll go dress him," JFK said, and Jackie giggled. "She saw the funniness of it in an easy, simple way," said Kenneth.

Father, mother, and son climbed into the first of three helicopters. O'Brien, O'Donnell, Powers, and Lincoln were making the trip, along with Turnure and Gallagher. At the airport, John Jr. cried as his parents boarded Air Force One. JFK kissed his son, and Secret Service agent Bob Foster tried to divert the boy with stories as the plane lifted off. En route to Texas, Kennedy quizzed Powers and O'Donnell separately about Bobby's birthday party the night before—"who was there, what did they have to say, what happened."

Jack and Jackie attracted large and friendly crowds that day in San Antonio and Houston—some 125,000 people in San Antonio alone. Jackie gave brief remarks—only seventy-three words—in Spanish that delighted her Hispanic audience. "Oh gee, she's going to do it just fine," Lady Bird said to herself.

Speaking about the space program in San Antonio, Kennedy drew from one of his favorite Irish authors, Frank O'Connor, who told a story about a boy who tossed his hat over high walls that he was afraid to climb. "This nation has tossed its cap over the wall of space," Kennedy said, "and we have no choice but to follow it."

In Houston, public relations man Jack Valenti crouched under the podium throughout Kennedy's speech and was transfixed by the President's hands "vibrating so violently at times that they seemed palsied. . . . Several times he nearly dropped his 5 x 7 cards." Valenti assumed JFK was merely nervous, but the shaking seemed more significant than the slight tremble sometimes visible in Kennedy's public performances. During an Oval Office meeting in mid-November, the FBI's White House liaison, Cartha DeLoach, had noticed an "uncontrollable tremor" in Kennedy's hands.

A few shadows darkened the first day in Texas. *The Thunderbolt,* a right-wing newsletter, carried the headline "Kennedy Keeps Mistress" for a story about Pamela Turnure based on Florence Kater's accusations. Ralph Yarborough also misbehaved on the presidential plane, telling reporters that Connally had declined to invite him to the Austin event because he is "so terribly uneducated governmentally. How could you expect anything else?" Although both Connally and Johnson shook Yarborough's hand at the San Antonio airport, the senator remained petulant, twice refusing LBJ's invitation to ride with him in the motorcade.

Meeting with Johnson in Houston's Rice Hotel, Kennedy vented about Yarborough's behavior. "The President told me that he just thought it was an outrage," Johnson recalled, "that he had told him that Yarborough had to ride with us or get out of the party." After a discussion with Larry O'Brien, Yarborough relented. Veteran Democratic congressman Albert Thomas also persuaded Connally to invite Yarborough to the Austin event.

The Kennedys spent the night in Fort Worth at the Texas Hotel, where their three-room suite had been specially adorned with $200,000 worth of paintings and sculpture—sixteen pieces including a Monet, a Picasso, a Van Gogh, and a Prendergast—lent by local collectors. But Jack and Jackie were too exhausted to notice the thoughtfully assembled exhibit that even came with a catalogue. It was already past midnight when they settled into the suite. "You were great today," Jack said as they embraced before heading to separate bedrooms for much-needed sleep.

Newspaper accounts the next morning called Jackie her husband's "secret weapon" on the campaign trail. When Jack asked for an appraisal of the crowds, Powers said, "Just about the same as they did the last time you were here, only about a hundred thousand more have come to see Jackie!"

Kennedy was scheduled to speak first at a rally in the parking lot outside the hotel, and Jackie would join him for breakfast in the ballroom with the Fort Worth Chamber of Commerce. Standing in the drizzle, Kennedy exhorted and joked with a crowd that included boisterous union workers who yelled, "Where's Jackie?" He pointed to the window of their suite and said, "Mrs. Kennedy is organizing herself. It takes her a little longer, but, of course, she looks better than we do when she does it."

As Jackie "organized herself," Mary Gallagher did an inventory of the contents of her boss's handbag: lipstick, comb, handkerchief, dark glasses, and Newport menthol cigarettes, which Jackie now smoked instead of L&Ms. Peering into the mirror, Jackie inspected her face for wrinkles, found one, and told Mary, "One day in a campaign can age a person thirty years."

Ten minutes after Jackie's scheduled 9:15 arrival, Kennedy sent word that she should come downstairs immediately. She was still undecided about her choice of gloves, finally opting for a short white pair instead of more formal long ones. She was focused on the trip to Dallas and had forgotten the breakfast. When the elevator stopped at the lobby, she said to Clint Hill, "Aren't we leaving?" and he reminded her of the breakfast. As she entered the ballroom through the kitchen, two thousand Texans burst into applause. In his remarks, Kennedy sounded a somber note. "This is a dangerous and uncertain world," he said. "No one expects our lives to be easy—not in this decade, not in this century."

Back in their suite to rest before flying to Dallas, the President and First Lady had time to inspect their personal art exhibit. At JFK's suggestion, they called Ruth Carter Johnson, the first name listed in the catalogue. Jack expressed his gratitude, and Jackie said, "They're going to have a dreadful time getting me out of here with all these wonderful works of art. We're both touched—thank you so much."

The President and First Lady worked the fence at Dallas's Love Field, shaking a multitude of extended hands. Lady Bird observed approvingly as Jackie took on "something quite new in her life and very old in ours . . . and she was doing it gracefully and sweetly and making a lot of people happy. I thought, 'How nice.'" CBS correspondent Bob Pierpoint was struck that Jackie "suddenly had decided to become the good political wife, trying very hard and even managing to make it appear that she was enjoying this political jaunt. She really looked and acted like one who was very much in love with her husband and even in love with the fact that he's a politician."

For the motorcade to the Dallas Trade Mart, the Kennedys and Connallys rode together in an open convertible. Pam Turnure had earlier suggested they use a bubbletop to shield Jackie's hair. "Never satisfactory," Kennedy said, explaining that the people needed to see the President and First Lady clearly. When Roy Kellerman, the lead Secret Service agent, had asked in Fort Worth about using a top, O'Donnell said only if there was rain in Dallas.

The sun was blazing as the motorcade pulled away, the temperature an uncomfortable 76 degrees for Jackie's wool suit. She put on her sunglasses, but Jack quickly asked her to take them off so that her face would be fully visible. She held on to them anyway, slipping them on periodically whenever the crowds were sparse. As the motorcade advanced slowly down Main Street, spectators thronged the route, screaming their approval.

"The motorcade is one of the hardest things for people to do," recalled John Connally's wife, Nellie. "All the people staring, and you have to look pleasant, and you can't be carrying on too much of a conversation in the car, so we would banter." Kennedy asked Nellie what she would do if someone in the crowd said something ugly to her husband. "If I'd get close enough I'd scratch their eyes out," she said, and he laughed. Moving at a crawl, the motorcade turned onto Elm Street and Nellie said, "Mr. President, you can't say Dallas doesn't love you." "No you can't," Kennedy replied.

Thirty seconds later, at 12:30 p.m., three shots rang out, fired by Lee Harvey Oswald from the sixth floor of the Texas School Book Depository. Within six seconds, one bullet had passed through Kennedy's back and out through his throat—not a mortal wound. A second bullet smashed into the rear of the President's head, exploding his brain and sending a piece of his skull flying. Connally was hit in the back, although not fatally. "My God, they've killed Jack," Jackie wailed. "They've killed my husband, Jack, Jack!" As the car sped to Parkland Hospital, Kennedy slumped in his wife's lap, his blood and brain fragments splattering her Chanel skirt.

Kennedy was rushed into the trauma bay within minutes. As a practical matter, he was already dead, but his heart was still beating. Doctors inserted tubes in his trachea, chest, ankle, and arm, gave him blood and fluids, administered 300 milligrams of hydrocortisone for his Addison's disease, and applied close cardiac massage. When they abandoned their efforts, Jackie approached the gurney, kissed her husband's foot, and held his hand as a priest gave him extreme unction. The doctors pronounced John Fitzgerald Kennedy dead at 1 p.m. central standard time.

Jackie asked a policeman to pull off her blood-caked gloves. She wanted to give her husband something meaningful, just as she had placed a treasured bracelet in her father's coffin and Jack had left his St. Christopher's medal with Patrick. She decided it would be the simple gold wedding band she had worn for a decade.

Jackie tugged at the blood-stained ring but couldn't pull it free. Vernon Oneal, the "squat, hairy, and professionally doleful" undertaker, came to her rescue with a jar of Lubafax, massaging her finger so that she could slip off the ring. She placed it on Kennedy's finger. Unable to push it beyond the knuckle, she let his hand drop. Kenny O'Donnell was watching from the doorway, and several other people were milling about. Wishing she could be alone with Jack, she kissed his hand and his lips and wanted to embrace him, but did not. Outside in the hallway she took O'Donnell aside. "The ring," she said. "Do you think it was right? Now I have nothing left." "Yes," O'Donnell replied. "You leave it right where it is."

THIRTY-ONE

After the horrifying six seconds on Elm Street, the Kennedy court rallied round for an extraordinary three days—grieving, comforting each other, making arrangements for Kennedy's funeral and burial on Monday, November 25. "It was like the fall of all hope and youth," Bunny Mellon said.

On the plane to Washington, O'Donnell, Powers, and O'Brien stayed with Jackie near Kennedy's body, loyal sentries who earned her gratitude and new appreciation. They told her stories about Jack. She talked of Abraham Lincoln's funeral and her need to find "the book" about it. As she spoke, Jackie had "a way of not looking at you," Powers recalled.

Bobby was first on the plane at Andrews Air Force Base. "Hey Jackie," he said, putting his arms around her. "He was so understated, as always," said Pam Turnure. "Oh Bobby," Jackie whispered. "I just can't believe Jack has gone."

Watching television at his home in McLean, Dr. Frank Finnerty, Jackie's secret therapist, realized when he saw her disembark in her blood-spattered pink suit "the degree of shock she was in . . . I had heard her say many times how fanatical she was about changing a blouse or skirt with a small spot." This time, though, Jackie had emphatically deflected suggestions that she change clothes. "No," she said. "Let them see what they've done."

Jackie and Bobby rode together in the ambulance with the casket to Bethesda Naval Hospital. In the illuminated interior, they could be seen talking nonstop—an image sadly evocative of the limousine that Jackie, Walton, and Jack had taken to the inaugural gala. ("Turn on the lights so they can see Jackie.")

At Bethesda, family and friends converged for eight hours in a suite of rooms on the seventeenth floor as doctors performed an autopsy and morticians did what they could to reconstruct Kennedy's shattered head. Joining Jackie were her mother, Hughdie, the Bradlees, McNamaras, Bartletts, Nancy Tuckerman, Ethel and Bobby, Pam Turnure, Evelyn Lincoln, Jean Smith, Kenny O'Donnell, Larry O'Brien, Mary Gallagher, and Dave Powers, who made Manhattans and scotches for anyone who needed them.

Bradlee spotted Jackie huddling with O'Donnell, talking about her wedding band. "Now [she] had decided she wanted to keep it," recalled Bradlee. "Jackie, I'm going to get that ring back for you," O'Donnell said. He found White House physician Dr. George Burkley, who retrieved the ring from the morgue and gave it to Jackie.

There had been a mixup of messages as Caroline and John were shuttled first to the Auchincloss home in Georgetown and then back to the White House at Jackie's direction "to be in their own beds." Ben and Tony had initially rushed to the White House to help with the children. Ben had been on the verge of telling Caroline and John about their father when Tony stopped him, saying, "That is not a decision for you to make." Later in the evening, Jackie would instruct Maud Shaw to break the news, which the devoted nanny did with sensitivity and sympathy. As they nodded off to sleep, she told them, "Your father has gone to look after Patrick. Patrick was so lonely in heaven. . . . Now he has the best friend anyone could have. . . . God is making your father a guardian angel over you and your mother, and his light will shine down on you always."

When she first embraced her mother, Jackie briefly broke down, but quickly righted herself. "Poor Nancy," she said, turning to Tuckerman, her oldest friend. "You came down all the way from New York to take this job. Now it's all over. It's so sad. You will stay with me a little while, won't you?" In those hours at Bethesda, "Jackie was astounding," Ethel

Kennedy recalled. "She was so warm and loving to everyone." Ethel tried to reassure her that Jack "went right to heaven, no stopovers." After Jackie told Ethel how wonderful Bobby had been, Ethel said, "I'll share him with you."

In graphic images, Jackie described the Dallas horror over and over to the intimates she greeted at the hospital. "I was so startled and shocked she could repeat in such detail how it happened," said Ethel. "I thought it was such torture, so clinical." Reflecting back, Jackie said she had been "sort of keyed up in a strange way." Her elaborate concern for those around her, she said, "was part of her masque."

When Bradlee saw Jackie, he hugged her—a "totally doomed child," he thought—and said, "Don't be too brave, cry." She sobbed but with few tears. "Oh Benny, do you want to hear what happened?" she said, followed by her instinctive wariness: "But not as a reporter for *Newsweek,* okay?" She told Ben of watching "the whole front of his head jump out," adding, "With that instinctive grace of his he reached for it, and it wasn't there." "Gallic," Ben said to Ethel, explaining that Jackie was "trying to get rid of it by talking of it, by emptying herself."

Bradlee was most impressed by Bobby's strength: "subdued, holding Jackie together." McNamara was "the second towering figure," in Bradlee's view. "No subterfuge, no special smiles. The naked strength. A man without guile." McNamara spent hours sitting on the floor of a small kitchen, listening to Jackie. "She just wanted someone to talk to," McNamara recalled. "I had to be calm for her and the hell with the others." Ethel Kennedy saw parallels between her husband and McNamara. "I was trying to think what in his philosophy made [McNamara] so strong and sympathetic," Ethel recalled.

By the time Charley and Martha Bartlett arrived late in the evening, Ben Bradlee decided, "suddenly we had been there too long." Charley's reaction to Jackie's outpouring mirrored Ben's. "That French imagination," he thought. He was also struck that Jackie was most concerned about Dave Powers and Evelyn Lincoln. "I'm not going to cry until the next three or four days are over," Jackie told Bartlett. In an effort to entertain the group, she tried to talk about the last White House dinner party she and Jack had hosted.

"Will you sleep tonight at the White House?" Jackie asked her mother, insisting she and "Uncle Coo" (Caroline and John's name for Hughdie) stay in Jack's bedroom. "Anywhere you like," Janet said, "but I felt sacrilegious." Still, Janet was "touched" that Jackie wanted her near.

Over in Georgetown, Mary Meyer asked Anne Truitt to spend the night at her house. "She was so sad," recalled Truitt. "I tried to comfort her. We cried, but we didn't talk that much." Helen Chavchavadze had been standing by her ironing board when she heard the news. "I stood there ironing and crying," she recalled. But she also had to admit, "When he was killed a tiny part of me felt freed."

When it was time to leave Bethesda at around 4 a.m., Jackie put her arms around a tearful Pam Turnure. "Poor Pam," Jackie said. "What will become of you now?" On the arrival of Jackie and the flag-draped casket at the White House gates, the driveway was lit with small flaming pots, a surprisingly dramatic and decorative touch conceived by Sarge Shriver. Inside, Walton had prepared the East Room with Nancy Tuckerman. After studying a book about Lincoln's funeral that he found in Jackie's sitting room, Walton had decided that the elaborate mid-nineteenth-century style for the catafalque was too "lachrymose and sentimental." He directed Bunny Mellon's upholsterer, Larry Arata, to create simple black swags. At Walton's instruction, vases in each corner were filled with boughs from Andrew Jackson's grand magnolia tree near the South Portico.

As Jackie passed by, Chuck Spalding caught her eye, "and we stood staring at each other. The stains of the accident were on her clothes, and the shock of the day had frozen her face in grief . . . I thought of all the things planned for, all the things fought for, all the things achieved, all the things to do, all the things suddenly lost."

***

Showing the strength of her upbringing and character, Jackie Kennedy managed to gather herself and oversee the preparations for the funeral. She drew on her knowledge of history and on her innate feel for what was tasteful and appropriate. "Jackie has a great sense of the dramatic," her mother said. "There were no wrong notes."

Jackie collected treasured items to put in Jack's casket: her first anniversary gift to him of inlaid gold cufflinks, the scrimshaw with the presidential seal she had given Jack the previous Christmas, a sapphire bracelet from Lee, the silver rosary Ethel had given Bobby at their wedding, and Bobby's PT boat tiepin.

Jackie also included three letters. Caroline neatly printed two sentences expressing her love and saying she would miss her daddy. Jackie sat on a small nursery chair and helped John Jr., who would turn three on the day of his father's funeral, make his scribbles. Her own letter began "My darling Jack," her "special salutation" that she considered a "rare endearment."

She wrote that the previous night she had slept in his bed, the hard mattress like a concrete slab, and sobbed for hours. She told him about his children and reminded him that after losing Patrick she had said that "the blow she could not bear" would be his death. As she scrawled page after page, her tears obliterated most of the words on her pale blue stationery. "She also knew it didn't matter," Manchester wrote. "She knew it would never be read by anyone."

Jackie and Bobby took the items and letters down to the East Room where they placed them with Jack. Jackie kissed her husband, caressed his hair and cut some off with J. B. West's scissors. Back in her dressing room, she divided the hair and put each half in a small ceramic frame. One she gave to Bobby, and she kept the other.

It fell to trusted friends and family to carry out her wishes. Sarge Shriver proved a master of detail and logistics, assembling guest lists, setting timetables. "Sarge had a tough job," Sorensen noted. "But it all seemed awfully efficient." Jackie wanted the Black Watch Highlander Regiment that had performed at the White House the previous week, and Tish Baldrige finally tracked them down in Knoxville, Tennessee. Another request was for the honor guard of thirty cadets of the Military College of Ireland. JFK had been impressed in Dublin by the drama of their performance, and their brass buttons—one of Jackie's anniversary gifts—now adorned his favorite blazer.

Bob McNamara strongly believed that JFK should be buried at Arlington National Cemetery, arguing his case against tough opposition from the Kennedy family and "Irish mafia." They favored Holyhood in Brookline, where Patrick had been buried just fifteen weeks before. But the defense secretary found a perfect spot, below the Custis-Lee Mansion that Jack and Charley Bartlett had visited the previous March on a Sunday afternoon. McNamara would later say that a Park Service employee told him that during the visit he had heard the President call the view "the most beautiful sight in Washington"—a remark that became mythologized as Kennedy's wish to "stay here forever." "All sorts of people are remembering all kinds of things Jack Kennedy never said," Bartlett told Katie Louchheim. "I never heard him say he'd like to stay there forever. That was *NOT* like him—out of character."

In a series of visits on Saturday in a drenching rain, McNamara persuaded Walton, Billings, Reed, Bobby, Jean, Eunice, and finally Jackie that the hillside site was the most fitting resting place. Jackie was won over by the beauty of the setting, as well as its historical importance. With his artist's eye, Walton located the precise placement for the grave that would line up with the mansion. He turned out to be only six inches off.

Bobby inherited the mantle of paterfamilias from his fallen brother and helped Jackie with all the major decisions. One of the first was whether to have an open casket. Jackie seemed to want it closed, so Bobby polled the views of various intimates. Spalding went into the East Room and peered under the lid. "The face looked like the rubber masks stores sold as novelties," Spalding recalled. "I said to close the casket." Arthur Schlesinger agreed, as did Nancy Tuckerman and Bill Walton. "One felt the face had been rebuilt," said Schlesinger. "It looked less and less like him." Walton was stunned by the "wax dummy" with the "false hair" and "silly expression."

Teddy and Eunice flew to Hyannis to tell their father. Eunice spent most of her time with Rose, taking long walks to Squaw Island. "We talked about Jack as if he were still alive," said Eunice. Joe sensed something was wrong, but they waited until Saturday night to break the news. "He had been looking out to the sea," Teddy recalled. "He looked right into my eyes. He followed every word. 'As a matter of fact, he died.'" Joe was unable to speak, but he wept. "Daddy got it," said Eunice. "He and Ted cried and that was it. He did not collapse. Twenty-five minutes later he had the TV on watching the East Room."

The White House was filled to capacity. Bobby first occupied the Lincoln Bedroom, then moved to another room when Rose arrived. Pat Lawford stayed in the Queen's Room, and Lee and Stas were assigned Jack's room. Occupying third-floor guest rooms were Peter Lawford, his agent Milt Ebbins, Lem Billings, Chuck and Betty Spalding, Steve and Jean Smith, Larry O'Brien, and Kenny O'Donnell.

"The whole family was like a bunch of shipwreck survivors," said

Billings. "I don't think they could have made it at all without Bobby. He seemed to be everywhere. He always had an arm around a friend or family member and was telling them it was okay, that it was time to move ahead." At one point on Saturday everyone sat in Bobby's room in a state of paralysis. Jack "had the most wonderful life," said Bobby. Pat Lawford was in the worst shape, her emotions already frayed by the disintegration of her marriage. Schlesinger observed that "Pat drank too much," and Bradlee noticed that Peter walked "as though he was being held up by the back of a coat."

Rose, a model of fortitude and deep faith, required less support from Bobby than the others. Janet Auchincloss thought Rose was "extraordinary," but also "felt how separate Rose was. I thought of first one son, then daughter, then husband, and of all people Jack. I had a terrible feeling Rose was alone that day, and how much faith Rose had." When Sarge Shriver remarked on Rose's admirable poise, she snapped, "What do people expect you to do? You can't just weep in a corner."

———

The Kennedy circle attended a mass by the East Room bier on Saturday morning. Walton clasped Pam Turnure, who was making "choking sounds." Ben Bradlee sobbed in spasms before retreating to the Green Room to compose himself. Red Fay hid his grief behind curtains in a corner of the East Room. "Jackie held up the longest," said David Gore. "By the time I talked to her, she was in a state of collapse," her voice a barely audible whisper. She told David and Sissie that if Patrick had lived, Sissie would have been named his godmother.

Janet and Hughdie picked up Lee at the airport on Saturday afternoon, along with Stas's sister and brother-in-law. Told of her assignment to Jack's room, Lee said, "I can't. I can just see him walking around and shouting for George in that strong voice." Replied Janet, "Yes you can. We did." Stas, who had been entertaining a shooting party in England, decided to wait one more day, "not wishing to intrude on the first meetings of the sisters."

Bunny Mellon arrived at the White House past midnight on Saturday morning after flying from Antigua through violent thunderstorms. J. B. West, tears streaming down his face, told Mellon that Jackie wanted her to arrange flowers for the Capitol, the church, and grave site. Mellon sat by Kennedy's bier in the East Room. Walton's arrangement of the room met with Mellon's discerning approval: "most dignified and not sentimental. It all went back to the simplicity, youth and dignity of Jack Kennedy." For more than an hour, "my tears would not stop," she recalled.

Mellon knew instinctively that Jackie wouldn't want "funereal" flowers, so on Saturday morning she decorated the Capitol rotunda with palm plants from the Washington Botanic Gardens. She took all the donated flower arrangements and placed them in the hallways leading to the rotunda, which remained unsullied and dignified for the arrival of Kennedy's casket to lie in state.

On Saturday afternoon, Mellon met with Jackie about flowers for the service at St. Matthew's Cathedral, a nineteenth-century landmark on Rhode Island Avenue near Eighteenth Street. "I don't want the church to look like a funeral," Jackie said. "I want it like spring. I want it not sad because Jack was not a sad man. He was a simple man. . . . He hated the funeral look of the flowers sent to Patrick. He doesn't want a funeral look, because he loved flowers." Mellon wanted to use "two simple urns," and Pam Turnure suggested blue vases from the White House that had been a gift from France.

Walking through the White House basement, Mellon encountered J. B. West, frantic because he couldn't find a full mourning veil requested by Jackie. "I racked my brain," Mellon recalled, "but I had no idea. Later he had a colored maid make it."

The Dillons also came to call on Saturday, carrying a gold basket of small white flowers that Phyllis had arranged. As they entered the White House, they spotted Larry O'Brien in the hall, sobbing. "A big man in tears," thought Doug. As she had done with others the night before at Bethesda, Jackie told them both in detail about Dallas.

Charley Bartlett busied himself with the sort of self-appointed tasks he had done so often for JFK. He combed the Library of Congress for accounts of the Lincoln funeral, and on Sunday he met Tish Baldrige, who had flown in at Sarge Shriver's request to help plan the grave site. With JFK's military aides, they mapped out where the Irish Guards would stand and the timing of a military flyover.

Sorensen broke down twice, once when he watched JFK's casket being carried off Air Force One at Andrews and again when he first used the phrase "Mr. President" with Johnson: "I hung up and wept." Sorensen's most important task was assembling remarks to be read at the funeral and graveside. Bundy did what he could to help Sorensen. "He was hit hardest," Bundy recalled. Since Johnson decided to stay away from the Oval Office until after the funeral, Bundy had many tasks to get ready for his new boss. "I was grateful for the work," said Bundy. "It kept me busy." Schlesinger observed that Bundy had "everything under iron control." As Bundy later noted, "Friday and Saturday I cried at home—after that not."

Schlesinger consulted with Bobby, Sarge, and Steve Smith about collecting Kennedy administration papers for the presidential library and promised to keep Jackie up to date. When Franklin Roosevelt Jr. comforted him, Schlesinger was touched by his "great kindness and sweetness." The historian spent the weekend drinking, although "it had no effect, except to keep me stable." Mostly Schlesinger sat in his East Wing office writing compulsively in his journal—the first deliberate words of *A Thousand Days.* He composed a eulogy for the *Saturday Evening Post,* which he sent with a note to "dearest Jackie, who was the full and inseparable partner in the most brilliant and gay and passionate adventure I shall ever know."

Jackie had dinner upstairs on Saturday. For the second night in a row, Dr. John Walsh, her personal physician, administered the tranquilizer sodium amytal to help her sleep; at Bethesda he had also injected her with Vistaril, a powerful tranquilizer, and had been amazed that she remained awake. Lee had received a tranquilizer shot from her doctor for the transatlantic trip, and she needed her own dose from Walsh of what she called blue "anti-crying pills." But composure was inbred in the Bouvier women, as it was in their mother. "I have learned to shut off something and go through it," Jackie told her friend Jessie Wood.

Down on the state floor, a dozen mourners gathered in the Family Dining Room: the Dillons, McNamaras, Shrivers, Lawfords, Bobby Kennedys, and Smiths. "Everyone was trying not to talk about what happened and succeeded quite well," said Dillon. "It was not serious. It sounds awful but it wasn't." In a moment of horseplay, Ethel took off her wig (which she wore when she didn't have time for a hairdresser) and passed it around the table, where it landed improbably on McNamara's head. "Jack would have enjoyed it," Dillon said. Afterwards, the Dillons went again to the East Room, knelt by the bier, and Dillon thought, "Goodbye Mr. President."

In the Capitol rotunda on Sunday, Mike Mansfield, Chief Justice Earl Warren, and Speaker of the House John McCormack gave eulogies. Mansfield's was the most emotional, with a repeated refrain—"And so she took a ring from her finger and placed it in his hands"—that recalled her agony at Parkland Hospital. "Bad poetry," Janet Auchincloss said to herself. "I thought if he said that once more I would scream." David Gore considered Mansfield's excesses "absolutely appalling." Afterwards, Joe Alsop penned a note on Senate Press Gallery paper to Jackie. "I love you as I loved him," he wrote. "There is only one thing I can send. . . . My thanks and congratulations. To play a high role perfectly in a great episode of history—to be always warm, always true, always yourself under the glare of history—is not an easy thing to do, to put it mildly indeed."

Charley Bartlett hastily scribbled his condolence on White House letterhead: "We had a hero for a friend. . . . He had uncommon courage, unfailing humor, a penetrating ear, curious intelligence and overall a matchless grace. He was our best. He will not be replaced, nor will he be forgotten. . . . We will remember him always, with love and sometimes as the years pass and a story is retold, with a little wonder."

Lem Billings blended into the woodwork as usual, his ebullient laugh silent, an unobtrusive participant in family decisions. When Lee arrived he provoked her ire by telling her it was nice of her to come. "How can you say that?" she exclaimed. "Do you think that I wouldn't?"

Bobby had asked Red Fay and Jim Reed to "be around, be helpful," and they did what they could at the White House on Sunday after attending mass. That evening Reed went out to McLean to have dinner with Vivian Crespi at Red and Anita Fay's house. After supper they walked and reminisced.

When Stas arrived on Sunday afternoon, he greeted Bunny Mellon with a kiss. "It was like Versailles, when the King died, when the King departed for good," he thought. Stas declined the offer to stay in Jack's bed, preferring instead to use an army cot set up in a corner. "Poor Stas," Jackie later said. As William Manchester wrote, "With his old-fashioned European dignity he stiffly insisted he would be quite comfortable there. He even refused to use the bathroom [and] wandered through the mansion for ablutions elsewhere." Stas asked only that a

Parisian rosary from his childhood be included among the treasured objects with Jack. Jackie picked a red carnation that Stas wound the rosary around. A Secret Service man placed it inside the casket.

Lyndon Johnson "looked carved in bronze those hours," Lady Bird recalled. "Very stern and very grave." He was "a different Johnson," observed Orville Freeman. "The frustration seemed gone, he seemed relaxed. The power, the confidence, the assurance of Majority Leader Johnson seemed to be there." Sorensen noted that LBJ "couldn't have been more humble and discreet in the early days of the Administration."

Yet Johnson's insecurities continued to dog him. As LBJ and Lady Bird climbed into bed on the eve of Kennedy's funeral, Johnson commanded his longtime aide Horace Busby to "stay right there till I go to sleep." Each time Busby rose, Johnson made him sit back down. It wasn't until past two in the morning that Johnson finally fell asleep and Busby extricated himself.

The word went out to selected friends on Sunday that Jackie needed their company after the midday ceremony at the rotunda. David and Sissie Gore found Jackie, Lee, and Bobby in the West Sitting Hall. Gore took Jackie aside and offered two large rooms at the British Embassy on Massachusetts Avenue for the White House school to use. She agreed it would be a perfect haven, with its beautiful enclosed grounds offering privacy to the twenty-two children. Gore later apologized to Jackie for being "weak and selfish" in showing his own sorrow. "It was more than my flesh and blood would stand to see you made to suffer so." He told Jackie that he had loved Jack "beyond words."

Chuck Spalding wandered down from his third-floor guest room, followed by Ken Galbraith, who was staying with Katharine Graham. Jackie offered Galbraith a drink, which he accepted, although he had abstained from alcohol for many months. He found her determined to uphold the "sense of pageantry" that Jack would have wanted. Jackie insisted that mourners walk in the funeral cortege because she didn't want "everybody rushed off in fat black Cadillacs."

Inspired by the Tomb of the Unknown Soldier at the Arc de Triomphe, she also asked for an eternal flame at the grave. With only one other such flame in the United States, at Gettysburg, it seemed at first an extravagant idea. Walton objected that it would be "aesthetically unfortunate," but Jackie overruled him. The Washington Gas Company supplied a propane-fed torch that could be safely lit at the burial and used until a permanent burner could be installed.

When Jackie mentioned that her parents' house in Georgetown was too small for her family, Galbraith realized she had nowhere to go after leaving the White House. He immediately asked Averell Harriman to lend Jackie his home—a large and gracious red-brick Federal-style townhouse at 3038 N Street in Georgetown that had "the particular advantage of some of the best Impressionist paintings in the world." Harriman readily agreed to move to a hotel to accommodate her.

During a discussion of funeral plans, Jackie was "very well composed," said Gore. She proposed that instead of a standard eulogy, the service include brief remarks with quotes from Jack's speeches and favorite passages from the Bible. She ruled out the 23d Psalm as "obvious" and "banal," and requested instead Ecclesiastes 3:1–8: "To everything there is a season, and a time for every purpose under heaven. . . ." (It would be two more years before "Turn, Turn, Turn," the hit song by The Byrds, would popularize those verses as a call for world peace.) "Do you think there is an English priest in Washington to read in a proper voice?" she joked to Gore. Sorensen couldn't help being amused by Jackie's Ecclesiastes request. He remembered when Jack had read the verses to her with the coda, "and a time to fish and a time to cut bait."

On Sunday night there was another boisterous gathering downstairs in the Family Dining Room, this time for Eunice, Bob McNamara, the Spaldings, Phyllis Dillon, and Dave Powers. The most incongruous presence was Aristotle Onassis, who had followed Lee to Washington. The group teased Onassis about cadging time on his yacht the following summer when he wasn't using it. (The next morning, James Ketchum, who only recently had been named White House curator, was stunned to find the Greek billionaire sleeping on a sofa in the Yellow Oval Room.)

Up on the second floor, Stas ate with Rose in the dining room while Jackie, Lee, Bobby, and Teddy dined in the West Sitting Hall. Bunny Mellon had a private visit with Jackie early in the evening and was startled to hear the grim facts of Jack's death. "Jackie told me how she couldn't believe when the thing hit," Mellon recalled. "She said it wasn't disgusting. . . . It was horrifying and not disgusting." "I wanted so much to hide, protect, take care of him," Jackie told Mellon. Clutching the mass card with Jack's picture, Jackie talked of heaven. "I believe in clouds and fields," she said. "I really believe in God, I believe in heaven, but where has God gone?"

Jackie's instructions to Mellon for Arlington were even more specific than for St. Matthew's. "Please fix a basket for Arlington, like the one you sent to the hospital when Patrick died," she said, "all from the Rose Garden." In the bottom of the basket, she told Mellon, "somewhere scrunched down, put in your own note to Jack. Stick it in with the moss and the wet." It was a brisk November evening, and Mellon doubted she would find much. She figured she would have to rely on the duplicates in her greenhouse of all the flowers she had planted during her redesign.

She went into the Rose Garden with a basket and scissors. "What was remarkable," Mellon recalled, "was there were dozens of white roses in bloom in November. It was almost pitch dark." She picked all the flowers she could find—blue salvia, chrysanthemums, and roses—as well as berries from the hawthorn and crab apple trees. From her greenhouse she added nicotiana, red geraniums, blue cornflowers, and carnations. She assembled everything at home in a fifteen-inch-long willow basket from Martinique and inserted her note: "Thank you Mr. President for your confidence and inspiration. Love, Bunny."

Bunny Mellon took her basket to Arlington on Monday morning. She had already seen to having the profusion of floral arrangements moved away from the grave site to be spread on a nearby hillside "like an enormous blanket." Bunny and Paul Mellon were among the last to arrive at the church. Only Nancy Tuckerman missed the service and burial. On duty in her East Wing office, she watched the proceedings on TV.

Before the funeral cortege departed from the White House for the eight-block walk to St. Matthew's, friends assembled in the State Dining Room. "It was 100 percent male," Walton noticed. "Not a woman there." Clustered in the southwest corner were Fay, Billings, Spalding, and Bartlett, as well as JFK's school friends Ben Smith and Rip Horton, along with David Gore, who had chosen not to walk with the diplomatic corps. Red Fay caught up with Dave Powers, who imagined Kennedy looking down and saying, "Damn it, Powers, you beat me out of a few more drinks."

Her face covered by her newly made long black veil, Jackie led the funeral procession, flanked by Teddy and Bobby, with Sarge Shriver and Steve Smith directly behind. Lem Billings walked next to Ken Galbraith, and David Gore lined up with Red Fay. Eunice, who was pregnant, had agreed to ride in a limousine, a decision she instantly regretted. Directly behind the horse-drawn caisson, a black riderless steed symbolizing the lost leader pranced and snorted along the route. He was a sixteen-year-old gelding called Black Jack—a spooky coincidence of names Jackie did not know about at the time. The Irish guards performed complex military drills as they marched, and four drummers beat out a steady cadence on eighteenth-century-style drums.

Inside the church, Bunny Mellon had created simple and elegant arrangements of daisies, white chrysanthemums, and stephanotis. Soldiers and Kennedy friends including Ben Bradlee and Hugh Sidey seated the mourners, who included sixty-two heads of state. Jackie entered, majestic and solemn, holding the hands of her two children. "She was raised correctly," Charles de Gaulle whispered to Nicole Alphand. After everyone was settled, the noon service began with the skirl of bagpipers from the Black Watch outside the open doors of the Cathedral. Richard Cardinal Cushing, a tall craggy-faced figure who had presided over so much Kennedy family celebration and sadness, said the pontifical requiem mass in traditional Latin.

The Reverend Philip Hannan, auxiliary bishop of Washington, delivered the eleven-minute talk deftly linking biblical passages to some of Kennedy's speeches, including his address only days earlier to a Houston audience: "Your old men shall dream dreams, your young men shall see visions, and where there is no vision the people perish." There were citations from the Proverbs, the prophecies of Joel, Joshua, and Isaiah, as well as the passage from Ecclesiastes Jackie had designated. Hannan ended with excerpts from the inaugural address. For the first time, Jackie lost control in public, shaking with sobs. To calm herself, she asked Clint Hill to "get me a blue pill from Lee." Hill also gave her his handkerchief because "she was having troubles."

For Eunice, the ceremony was "sad instead of hopeful . . . sadder than it should have been." She could "never remember Jack being sad in his life." Mary Meyer and Tony Bradlee sat together, and Tony was struck that her sister "didn't seem very upset. It puzzled me."

It took an hour for the motorcade to reach Arlington. When the caisson neared the graveside, fifty air force and navy jets (one for each state of the Union) flew overhead in formation, followed by Air Force One, which paid tribute by dipping one wing. At that moment, Lee burst into tears. Arthur Schlesinger would always remember "the wildly twittering birds . . . while the statesmen of the world looked on."

Following Cardinal Cushing's burial prayer to "this wonderful man, Jack Kennedy," a twenty-one-gun salute, and the folding of the American flag, Jackie and Bobby lit the eternal flame, and Jackie received the flag. Bobby and Teddy had prepared remarks in their pockets to read after the bugler had played taps, but as Cardinal Cushing started to introduce Teddy, he balked. "This great hunk of a man couldn't go on," said Joan Kennedy. The end of the Arlington service struck Mac Bundy as "the fall of a curtain, or the snapping of taut strings."

Jackie received the heads of state and other dignitaries back at the White House with great dignity, "like a Roman queen, a stone statue," observed Nicole Alphand, whose face still peered from newsstands on the previous week's cover of *Time,* which had inopportunely featured an article on Washington social life. A few high-level guests came up to the Yellow Oval Room, where Jackie had replaced the four Cézanne paintings with giant aquatints of American cities in the early nineteenth century. "I want it to be an American setting," she explained to Jim Ketchum.

Jackie spent fifteen minutes with Charles de Gaulle, who said, "He died like a soldier under fire." Echoing what she had heard her husband tell Hervé Alphand a month earlier, Jackie told the French president how much Jack wanted to be "such a good friend of France's and yours, and you never allowed it, and now it's too late." She added, however, that "Jack was never bitter." According to Jean Smith, Jackie also informed de Gaulle that "only three could be trusted—Bobby, McNamara and Mac Bundy." Jackie showed the French leader the chest of drawers he had given the Kennedys after their visit to Paris. On top was a vase filled with oxeye daisies. She took one blossom and gave it to him as "a last souvenir of President Kennedy." De Gaulle put the daisy "very tenderly, carefully," inside the pocket of his tunic.

After the funeral reception, Vivian Crespi went upstairs to find Jackie in a state of exhaustion. John, Caroline, and their cousins were in the dining room for a small celebration to mark John's birthday. "Jackie said, 'I couldn't disappoint little John,'" recalled Crespi. "There was a party with balloons and horns. It was such a shock going from a funeral to a children's party—after seeing Haile Selassie and the queen of Greece and Charles de Gaulle, then to go up and see the children hopping around. It was a macabre scene."

In the evening Jackie held an informal wake in the West Sitting Hall to reminisce and watch the funeral replayed on TV. "A Kennedy trait," Bradlee remarked. "He loved to watch himself." At times Jackie "seemed completely detached," Bradlee recalled, "as if she were someone else watching the ceremony of [another] person's grief. Sometimes she was silent, obviously torn. Often she would turn to a friend and reminisce."

Powers and Teddy sang "Heart of My Heart," and Bobby was "so choked up he had to leave the room," said Ethel. To shift the mood, Powers spun hoary tales of early campaign days for the family and intimates who lingered. In what William Manchester described as a "reedy, hearty voice . . . Dave entertained without intruding, gently reminding them that Kennedy, too, had known how to laugh when there had seemed to be no laughter left in the world." The atmosphere became "cheerful," Bradlee observed, "except Jackie, who was red eyed." As the group dispersed, Tony couldn't resist looking into Jack's room, where so many parties had wound down. Her glance caught Stas on his army cot, sound asleep.

Around midnight, Jackie said to Bobby, "Should we go visit our friend?" They drove to Arlington and stood before the grave as Jackie gently lay a bouquet of lilies of the valley on top of the boughs covering the freshly turned soil. When Jackie went to bed that night, she found a note from Lee on her pillow addressed to "Jacks" from "Pekes." It said, "Goodnight my Darling Jacks—the bravest and noblest of all. L."

Jackie lived in the White House for eleven more days until the Harriman home could be readied. Ken Galbraith visited her at midday on Tuesday and found her "rather more distraught" now that she was faced with "the barrenness of life." He encouraged her to write, and to spend time with friends. "I am like a wounded animal, I want to stay in a corner," she told Nicole Alphand. Lee and Pat remained with Jackie as she prepared for her departure. Jackie called Dr. Finnerty periodically, her words punctuated by sighs, a common signal of anxiety and depression. She fretted about living a private life and keeping the press at bay, and she spent one conversation worrying about how to dispose of Jack's clothing.

Several days after the funeral, Jackie sent her mother and Teddy Kennedy to retrieve Patrick's casket from Holyhood in Brookline, and her stillborn daughter's from a cemetery in Newport. On December 4 the remains of the infants were buried at Arlington with their father.

With her customary discipline, Jackie sat at her West Sitting Hall desk and composed thank-you notes. She told Nellie Connally that she was glad Jack had "died in the company of a man like John Connally. We could have been riding with some little mayor from somewhere— and then his death would not have been so noble." Jackie's most significant letter was to Soviet premier Nikita Khrushchev. Her handwritten message was modified by the State Department and forwarded by Mac Bundy through diplomatic channels.

She told the Russian leader that she was moved to write because Jack cared about peace. She believed that he and the Soviet premier had become allies in trying to prevent the world from being destroyed and had developed mutual respect. The danger, she wrote, was "that war might be started not so much by the big men as by the little ones." It was up to the "big men" to promote diplomacy and prevent conflict.

The excised portions added little of substance, but offered some insights into Jackie's state of mind and view of her role. She apologized for seeming "presumptuous . . . I never meddled in politics when my husband was alive. Why should I dare to write to you now that he is dead?" She worried specifically about the "next time a convoy is stopped on the autobahn, and if one of our soldiers shoots, and yours shoot back, and some general there gives an order, why there could be a war within minutes." Poignantly she added, "I don't care for myself because I don't have much to live for—but for my husband's dreams."

When Teddy White arrived at Hyannis Port on Thanksgiving weekend, he found Jackie surrounded by "the good-willed comforters": Dave Powers, Chuck Spalding, Pat Lawford, and Franklin Roosevelt Jr. "I realized that I was going to hear more than I wanted to," White wrote later.

Moving-out day was Friday, December 6 ("Don't worry," Jackie told Lady Bird, "not Pearl Harbor Day"). "Jack and I did a lot in two years,

10 months and 2 days—so I can surely move out for you in 4½ days," Jackie wrote on December 1. She gave her successor detailed instructions about the White House restoration ("Each room has all the historic pictures and furniture it can hold") and tips on living in the Executive Mansion. "You will be remembered as the one who *PRESERVED* it," Jackie wrote to Lady Bird. She emphasized the importance of the White House Historical Association and the continued need for the Smithsonian Institution to employ the White House curator, lest "some future president's wife, who didn't care about history like you do, might appoint her Aunt Nellie as curator, who ran a little curio shop on Elm Street."

The day before the move, Jackie had a joint birthday party for Caroline and John. Janet Auchincloss was there, along with Jack's three military aides and Dave Powers. The U.S. Marine Band, resplendent in red tunics, "were playing with unusual zeal to hide their sorrow," wrote Molly Thayer. Jackie wanted her children "to leave the White House in gay remembrance."

To welcome the Johnsons on Friday, Jackie left them a vase of her favorite lilies of the valley. She shook hands with the household staff in the West Sitting Hall and presented each of them with a copy of a painting of the Green Room as "a continual reminder of the President." Jackie wore a simple black dress and jacket, and the children were attired in the same powder blue coats they had worn to their father's funeral. Accompanied by Lee, Bobby, and Ethel, they walked through the Diplomatic Reception Room, out the doors under the South Portico and into a waiting limousine.

Jackie's *Camelot* interview, published in *Life* in the first week of December, had already begun reverberating, but even she didn't grasp its full impact. While Teddy White later regretted being a conduit for such romantic imagery, he had felt a need to comply with nearly everything Jackie wanted. Jack Kennedy had held the most powerful office in the world, but his thirty-four-year-old widow held the power of his memory. "She took the man she loved and made him unforgettable," said Washington diarist Katie Louchheim. "It was Jackie who created Jack Kennedy's legacy."

"The Washington landscape seemed to me to be littered with male widows," Joseph Alsop wrote. Jack Kennedy's assassination affected Alsop more profoundly than the death of his own father. Bob McNamara, Mac Bundy, and Doug Dillon confided to Alsop that they never got over losing JFK. Even CIA director John McCone, "a hard-bitten objective Republican," told Walt Rostow that he had not seen anyone in public life inspire greater affection from his closest associates. "The fact is that Jack Kennedy had an extraordinary knack for capturing people and changing them," Alsop wrote. "To me this was his most inexplicable quality."

The men and women of JFK's inner circle moved on with varying degrees of success. A few remained on close terms—Sorensen and Schlesinger, for example—and some periodically came together for academic symposiums that perpetuated the mystique of Kennedy and his administration. But most spun off in different directions. "Since he left, the glue that held us together was gone," said Sorensen.

They were touched forever by their association with Kennedy, and most believed that his violent death marked a turning point for the United States. On the Saturday night before the Kennedy funeral, journalist Mary McGrory gave a dinner for a group of friends. "We'll never laugh again," she said to Daniel Patrick Moynihan. "We will," answered the future Democratic senator from New York, "but we'll never be young again."

Jacqueline Kennedy stayed in the Harriman home for a month before buying a large brick house across the street. At one point Bobby Kennedy was so alarmed about Jackie's psychological fragility that he asked the Reverend Richard T. McSorley, a Jesuit priest who was a close friend, to give her private counseling. During their sessions in the spring and summer of 1964, Jackie confessed to suicidal thoughts, wondering, "Do you think God would separate me from my husband if I killed myself? Wouldn't God understand that I just want to be with him?" By July she had found some equilibrium, vowing to McSorley that she intended to "keep busy and to keep healthy" and devote herself to her children.

That summer she fled Washington and the hordes of tourists who crowded her sidewalk and stripped the bark off her magnolia trees for souvenirs. She moved to 1040 Fifth Avenue at Eighty-fifth Street in Manhattan, where she lived in a fifteen-room book-filled apartment reminiscent of her childhood homes before her parents divorced.

Eighteen months after her husband's assassination, Jackie told Harold Macmillan that she was determined to make Caroline and John "what he would have wanted them to be. . . . You have to have something that makes you want to live—and now I have them." She did not return to the White House until February 1971 during the presidency of Richard Nixon, when she, Caroline, and John came to see her newly unveiled official portrait by Aaron Shikler.

She shocked the world by marrying Aristotle Onassis within months of Bobby Kennedy's assassination in 1968. It was a misalliance that gave her wealth but tarnished her reputation. After several years, the marriage unraveled and they began spending more time apart. In 1975, Onassis died of the degenerative disease myasthenia gravis. Jackie resumed a quiet life in Manhattan as a respected book editor and advocate for historic preservation. Her constant companion was wealthy diamond merchant Maurice Tempelsman. Although he was a month younger than Jackie, he appeared older, and he was the married father of three children. He expertly managed Jackie's $26 million inheritance from Onassis and shared her interests in literature and French culture.

On May 19, 1994—the birthday of Black Jack Bouvier—Jackie died of cancer at age sixty-four surrounded by her closest friends and family. Seven years later, the Metropolitan Museum of Art erased her Onassis identity by naming its exhibit on her indelible style *Jacqueline Kennedy: The White House Years.*

Lyndon Johnson was solicitous and comically flirtatious with Jackie in the first months of his presidency, phoning her frequently and calling her "sweetie" and "dear" and "honey." "You just come over here and put your arm around me. . . . Let's walk around the back yard," he implored. Jackie responded coquettishly, humoring him with flattery and girlish giggles: "You're so nice to call me, Mr. President. You must be out of your mind with work piled up." But she deflected all his entreaties to return to the White House. "I'm so scared I'll start to cry again," she said. "I'll do anything I can for you, but don't make me come down there."

Johnson was forever insecure and uneasy with the Kennedy team. His friction with Bobby deepened into a "mutual contempt." "He looks at me like he's going to look a hole through me," LBJ told John Connally. But Johnson tried to placate Bobby. "I do not want to get into a fight with the family, and the aura of Kennedy is important to all of us," said LBJ.

Buoyed by a landslide victory in 1964, Johnson made history by pushing through Kennedy's agenda of tax reduction, civil rights, Medicare, and aid to education. Tapping Walter Heller on his chest, Johnson announced, "I want you to know and your liberal friends that I'm no conservative—I am a New Deal Democrat." True to his word, Johnson vastly expanded the federal role in helping the dispossessed with his Great Society program. He was ultimately crushed by America's failure in Vietnam. Johnson declined to run for reelection in 1968 after Bobby Kennedy challenged his candidacy with a stinging anti-war campaign. Afflicted by heart disease, LBJ died five years later at age sixty-four. Jackie counted *Lady Bird* as a friend and spent time with her during summers on Martha's Vineyard.

Robert F. Kennedy remained as attorney general until September 1964, when he ran successfully for the U.S. Senate from New York. He became Jackie's closest confidant and protector—a "passionate and unconquerable soul," she described him to Harold Macmillan. At Jackie's suggestion, Bobby studied the Greek tragedies in his quest for meaning. "They had a touching need for each other," said Tish Baldrige. "It was pure friendship." As Jackie herself said to William Manchester, "My adored brother in law could do no wrong in my eyes ever."

Bobby obsessively viewed Lyndon Johnson as his brother's usurper—"as though a ruling family had been displaced by unjust fortune," Joe Alsop said. In his upstart campaign for the presidency in 1968, RFK scored a crucial win in the California primary on June 4. Leaving a hotel ballroom after his victory speech, he was shot in the head by Sirhan Sirhan, a Palestinian immigrant. Bobby Kennedy died twenty-six hours later at age forty-two. To Jackie, Bobby's death brought "a great suffocating fog." She told Joe Alsop that grief had become "an element one lives in—like sea or sky or earth." *Ethel* remained at Hickory Hill, and gave birth to their eleventh child, Rory, on December 12, 1968—six months after her father's assassination.

Joseph P. Kennedy declined steadily in the years after JFK's death. On hearing of Bobby's assassination, Joe Kennedy "wept uncontrollably." Jackie remained devoted to her father-in law, visiting him often at Hyannis Port. He died at age eighty-one in November 1969, after eight years of spending his waking hours in a wheelchair, unable to speak.

Rose Kennedy kept up her routines well into her eighties—daily three-mile walks rain or shine, swimming in the cold surf, mass each morning. In addition to summers on the Cape and winters in Palm Beach, she remained an intrepid traveler. She also grew closer to Jackie, who treated her to dinner at Maxim's during Rose's twice yearly visits to the Parisian couture houses. "There was a natural affection between Jackie and Rose," said Jessie Wood, who dined with them in Paris. On Easter Sunday in 1983, Rose had a massive stroke at age ninety-three. Speechless and confined to a wheelchair, Rose survived another decade before dying in 1995 at age 104.

Edward M. Kennedy took over as the head of the Kennedy family after Bobby's assassination, and barely a year later caused a scandal when he drove a car off a bridge in Martha's Vineyard into a pond, killing his passenger, a young woman who had been with him at a party that evening. He failed in a run for the presidency in 1980, and the following year was divorced from *Joan,* who had coped with his womanizing by finding refuge in drinking. With the help of Alcoholics Anonymous, she managed her addiction, and she went on to earn a master's degree in education. Teddy later remarried and redeemed his reputation as a hard-working and effective U.S. senator.

Patricia Lawford "was in a bad way before the tragedy," Jackie said six months after the assassination. "She has been worse since." Pat and *Peter* were divorced in 1966, and she battled drinking problems for many years. She moved to New York City to live a quieter life than her ex-husband, who stayed in California. His acting career stalled out, and he succumbed to drug and alcohol abuse. He died of liver and kidney failure in 1984 at age sixty-one.

Eunice Shriver expanded her work with the mentally and physically handicapped into the Special Olympics, a worldwide organization. *Sarge* worked for Lyndon Johnson first as the head of the War on Poverty and later as ambassador to France. In 1972, George McGovern chose Sargent Shriver as his running mate, and their ticket suffered a crushing defeat by Jack Kennedy's old nemesis, Richard Nixon.

Jean and Stephen Smith continued to live in New York, where he managed the Kennedy family's business enterprises. His womanizing strained their marriage, but they remained together. In 1974, Jean founded Very Special Arts to provide arts education and programs for people with disabilities. Steve died of cancer in 1990 at age sixty-two. Three years later President Bill Clinton named Jean ambassador to Ireland, where she served for five years.

Joseph Alsop spent considerable time consoling Jackie. When she moved into her Georgetown home he gave her a Japanese lacquered box in black and gold, "the colors of love and death," she noted. "People always say time makes everything better," Jackie wrote Alsop nine months after the assassination. It wasn't true about Jack, she said—"just the reverse for me—and the same for you . . . How awful when the best in you is not called upon anymore."

Alsop saw his influence as a columnist wane after Jack's death, and he directed his energy to writing books about art and antiquities that were praised for their erudition. After a three-year battle with cancer, Joe's brother Stewart died in 1974 at age sixty. A year later Joe and *Susan Mary* were divorced. To finance his retirement, Alsop sold the Dumbarton Avenue house and rented a friend's home nearby, where he kept his position as the *über*-host of Georgetown until he died of lung cancer at seventy-eight in 1989.

Janet Auchincloss had the presence of mind on the weekend after the funeral to tell Jackie's maid, Provie, not to clean the pink Chanel suit Jackie had worn the day Jack was shot. "I had a feeling that this was the last link. I felt this precious blood not wash out," she said. She placed the suit in a box marked "worn by Jackie 11-22-63" in the attic of her Georgetown home alongside the box containing Jackie's wedding dress. (The pink suit eventually went to the National Archives to be kept in storage for one hundred years.) Jackie and her children continued to spend holidays at Hammersmith Farm. As Janet and *Hughdie*'s fortunes shrank, Jackie gave them financial support. A decade after Hughdie's death in 1976, Janet was diagnosed with Alzheimer's disease. Jackie set up a $1 million trust fund for nursing care and traveled frequently to Newport in the last four years of her mother's life. When Janet died in 1989 at age eighty-one, Jackie was at her bedside at Hammersmith Farm.

Letitia Baldrige worked for six years at the Kennedy family's Merchandise Mart in Chicago and wrote a best-selling memoir. She married at age thirty-eight, had two children, and moved to New York City, where she built a thriving public relations business. Baldrige made a name for herself as a lecturer and writer on etiquette, teaching comportment to bank tellers as well as business executives. She returned to Washington with her husband in 1988.

Charles and Martha Bartlett continued to see Jackie intermittently and kept up with John, who was Martha's godson. In 1967 the Bartletts traveled to Cambodia with Jackie, but their times together were never the same: they seemed to remind Jackie of a past she didn't wish to think about. Charley moved his column to the *Washington Star*, and for a time teamed with Cord Meyer, but his audience dwindled. Eventually Bartlett shifted to writing a weekly political newsletter that had a respectable circulation among opinion makers.

Lem Billings was probably the saddest of the Kennedy "widows." "In many ways Lem thought of his life being over after Jack died," said Bobby Kennedy Jr. Billings occupied himself at first raising money for Washington's Cultural Center, which was renamed the Kennedy Center for the Performing Arts. Jackie kept aloof from Billings, however. Through the next generation of Kennedys he tried to keep the family spirit alive as a one-man oral history—"a link to our dead fathers," said Bobby Kennedy Jr. Kennedy youngsters flocked to Billings's art- and antique-filled townhouse in New York. While spinning tales for them, Billings also shared their indulgence in alcohol and illicit drugs. On May 28, 1981—the day before JFK's sixty-fourth birthday—he died of a heart attack at age sixty-five.

Ben and Tony Bradlee saw Jackie a few times after Jack's death, but they quickly lost touch. "The relationship of four was not going to work as a relationship of three," Ben concluded. Tony felt that she and Ben "brought back sad memories." Ben and Tony split in 1973, and five years later he married writer Sally Quinn. In 1975, Ben published *Conversations with Kennedy* based on his journals. Jackie considered the book a violation of her privacy and disliked the inclusion of Jack's profanity. She never spoke to Ben again. Bradlee achieved fame as editor of the *Washington Post,* overseeing the newspaper's Watergate investigations that eventually toppled Richard Nixon from power.

McGeorge Bundy stayed on as Lyndon Johnson's national security adviser for more than two years. Along with Robert McNamara, Bundy presided over the escalation of the American involvement in Vietnam. Bundy left Washington in March 1966 to head the Ford Foundation. After his retirement in 1979, he taught history at New York University and authored *Danger and Survival,* an analysis of American nuclear policy in the Cold War. He died of a heart attack in 1996 at age seventy-seven.

Oleg Cassini prospered as a dress designer on the strength of his Kennedy association, making mass-produced clothing. He worked out of an elegant Manhattan townhouse and spent weekends on a fifty-acre estate on Long Island.

Vivian Crespi remained close to Jackie, sharing her New York life and coincidentally living in the building where Jack Bouvier had spent his later years. For more than a decade Crespi had a romance with Italian writer Luigi Barzini, and they spent time with Jackie and Tempelsman, who brought Jackie "peace of mind" in Crespi's view.

Douglas Dillon was Johnson's Treasury secretary until 1965. He returned to Wall Street and served as president of the Metropolitan Museum of Art from 1970 to 1978 and chairman for five more years. Shuttling among his homes in Manhattan; Hobe Sound, Florida; and Isleboro, Maine, he lived as a consummate gentleman. He remained active into his nineties; only weeks before his death in 2003 at ninety-three he was making decisions on acquisitions for the Met from his hospital bed.

Paul Fay returned to California and rejoined the family business. In 1966, Fay wrote *The Pleasure of His Company,* an affectionate memoir of his friendship with Jack. At Jackie's request, Bobby Kennedy, who had been nearly as close to Fay as Jack was, reviewed the manuscript. Jackie was incensed about Fay's "locker room humor," and she objected that the book would "diminish" his brother. Bobby demanded that Fay cut two thirds of the book. Fay made some excisions, but kept most of the personal material that had offended the Kennedys.

Eve and Paul Fout saw Jackie frequently when she resumed hunting in Virginia in 1984 after many years spending her weekends in the horse country of Far Hills, New Jersey. Eve had started Caroline in a pony club when she was in kindergarten, and in later years Caroline brought her own children to ride with the Fouts as well.

John Kenneth Galbraith continued to teach economics at Harvard and write books. Jackie maintained an affectionate relationship with him and relied on him for advice. By leaving the administration when he did, Galbraith had already broken free and moved forward. As he wrote years later, the death of Roosevelt "meant a world come to an end. The loss of Kennedy was that of a well-loved friend. Life went on."

David Ormsby Gore became Lord Harlech when his father died in 1964. He deeply admired Jackie's "proud, independent spirit" and considered her personality "a sacred thing . . . not to be tampered with or displayed to all . . . No one has a right to see into the inner recesses of one's heart." David Gore finished his term as ambassador in 1965, and two years later *Sissie* was killed at age forty-five in an automobile accident. He and Jackie had a romance for several months, even traveling together to Cambodia and Thailand late in 1967. In 1969, he married Pamela Colin, and sixteen years later, at age sixty-six, he too died in a car crash.

Robert McNamara stayed on for five years as Johnson's defense secretary, but LBJ always suspected him of leaking information to Bobby Kennedy. Johnson was intimidated by McNamara's intellect and actively courted his approval. Yet Johnson periodically turned on his defense secretary in meetings, where he "squeezed him like an orange." As the principal architect of the Johnson administration's failed Vietnam policy, McNamara was haunted by that legacy. After leaving the government in 1968, he ran the World Bank for thirteen years and wrote two books, *In Retrospect* and *Argument Without End,* seeking to explain his views on Vietnam.

Bunny Mellon grew closer to Jackie even as she herself withdrew further from the social world. After Jackie sold Wexford for $225,000 in 1964, she abandoned Virginia as a regular retreat for two decades. But she saw the Mellons in New York, on the Cape, and in Antigua. When Jackie embraced the Virginia hunt country again, she became a permanent houseguest at Oak Spring, where she stabled her horses and rode in privacy. Jackie sought Bunny's help on a number of projects, from the final landscaping scheme for JFK's Arlington grave to the house Jackie built on Martha's Vineyard. Bunny also redesigned the East Garden at the White House, although Jackie declined to return for its dedication as the Jacqueline Kennedy Garden by Lady Bird Johnson in April 1965. The associations with the past were too painful, she explained to Lady Bird. "I will always think it was [JFK's] garden because he planned it," Jackie wrote.

Mary Meyer "sort of picked up and went on," said Cicely Angleton. Meyer continued to paint, working in a studio behind the Bradlees' house in Georgetown. Her work was exhibited, and she seemed reasonably contented. Although Meyer and her friend *Helen Chavchavadze* stayed in touch, Meyer never shared her secret about JFK. Chavchavadze remarried in 1964 and devoted herself to writing poetry, splitting her time between Key West and Cape Cod.

On October 12, 1964, Meyer took one of her customary walks on the towpath of the Chesapeake & Ohio Canal along the Potomac River. There, in the middle of the day, she was shot twice in the head at point-blank range—a chilling repetition of her former lover's fate—and died instantly, just two days before her forty-fourth birthday. Raymond Crump Jr., an African-American drifter, was charged with the murder. Crump gave a confused account of his behavior that day, but no murder weapon was ever found, and Crump's lawyer raised doubts about the account of a witness who saw, from some distance, a black man standing over Meyer's body. After deliberating eleven hours, a racially mixed jury acquitted Crump of first-degree murder. Like Kennedy's assassination a year earlier, Meyer's shocking death spawned its share of conspiracy theorists who speculated that she was killed because she knew too much about Kennedy.

Lawrence O'Brien had always maintained cordiality with LBJ, which made him the most compatible New Frontiersman in the Johnson administration. "O'Brien knew he was working with the best legislative mind and operator in the modern era," said Johnson aide Harry McPherson. "It was like a race car driver who gets to drive a Ferrari. When LBJ was vice president Larry was not authorized to use this Ferrari. Now O'Brien could really use this guy." Johnson rewarded him by naming him to the cabinet as postmaster general, and O'Brien went on to lead the Democratic National Committee. In 1972 it was his office at the DNC in the Watergate building that Republican operatives burglarized to obtain political intelligence—the beginning of the scandal that led to Richard Nixon's resignation two years later. O'Brien died in 1990 at age seventy-three.

Kenneth O'Donnell reacted to Kennedy's death initially by seeking to comfort Jackie on many afternoons with Bobby, although he acknowledged "she probably was more consoling to us than we were helpful to her." Kenny O'Donnell stayed in Johnson's West Wing until Bobby

Kennedy won his Senate seat. O'Donnell ran twice for governor of Massachusetts without the blessing of the Kennedys. On the campaign trail, he was an awkward candidate who had "no political presence," said William Manchester. "He lived for Jack."

By then, O'Donnell had fallen into a self-destructive spiral that Manchester first glimpsed in the bar of the Mayflower Hotel in the spring of 1964: "He had eleven screwdrivers lined up and drank them all." Even O'Donnell's daughter Helen acknowledged the terrible toll of his alcoholism—and her mother's as well. "They died long before their last breath," Helen O'Donnell wrote. O'Donnell and his wife (also named *Helen*) got divorced and both died in 1977. He was fifty-three.

David Powers trekked to the Harriman home each day to have lunch and play with John Jr. For months Powers endured "violent pains . . . confined to the back of his skull . . . where he had seen the last bullet strike." The headaches subsided, and Powers remained with the Lyndon Johnson White House until early 1965. In 1970, Powers and Kenny O'Donnell published an affectionate memoir about JFK titled *"Johnny, We Hardly Knew Ye."* Until his death at age eighty-five in 1998, Powers devoted himself to Jack Kennedy's memory as curator of the John F. Kennedy Library, a majestic building designed by I. M. Pei with a sweeping view of the Boston harbor.

Lee Radziwill remained with Jackie for weeks at the Harriman house, where they received regular visits by Jack's friends and aides. In her anguish, Jackie lashed out at Lee. "She hits me across the face," Lee told Cecil Beaton. "I've done nothing." Lee's romance with Onassis didn't last, but in 1973 she and *Stas* split up, and he died of a heart attack two years later. Lee moved to New York, tried her hand at interior design and acting, suffered financial decline and drinking problems, and had highly publicized romances with photographer Peter Beard and attorney Peter Tufo. Jackie helped Lee financially, but the marriage to Onassis led to a long estrangement between the sisters. Lee gave up drinking and was reconciled with her sister during Jackie's illness from cancer.

James Reed attended Jackie's first dinner party in Georgetown, along with Bobby, Red Fay, and Bob McNamara. "Red was singing and dancing," Reed recalled. "Jackie was withdrawn, cordial, and lovely. We never talked of the President." Reed practiced law and ran a financial consulting business for five years in New York City, and afterwards in Maine. "I never really worked for anyone, and I never retired," he said. Still, his ex-wife *Jewel* recalled, "He never stopped looking at the Kennedy years as the zenith of his career."

Franklin D. Roosevelt Jr. and his wife *Suzanne* were divorced in 1969, and he married three more times. In the months after JFK's death, Roosevelt was one of Jackie's faithful visitors in Georgetown. After leaving the Commerce Department in 1965, he served Johnson as chairman of the Equal Employment Opportunity Commission for its first year. FDR Jr. returned to New York and ran unsuccessfully for the Democratic nomination for governor. He spent the following years working for several organizations dedicated to the legacy of his parents and raising cattle on his farm in upstate New York. When he died at age seventy-four in 1988, Jackie told his widow, Tobie, "Oh how I loved your Franklin. He was such a gentleman."

Arthur Schlesinger left the White House at the end of January 1964, and he and *Marian* divorced the following year. "Life in the White House was a pressure cooker," he explained. "I think the shock of Dallas suddenly made people examine their lives and decide if a marriage wasn't working. Mine wasn't working then." He moved to New York and became an acclaimed writer. "I had spent forty years in Cambridge," he said. "I decided I had other lives to live." Noted Marian, "Arthur became a celebrity, and for a while he was even a playboy." With *A Thousand Days* and a subsequent biography of Robert Kennedy, Schlesinger found a role far more important than what he ever did in the White House: creating an essential record of the Kennedy years, which formed the bedrock of the enduring Kennedy mythology.

Florence Smith was suffering from leukemia through the latter part of the Kennedy administration, a fact that *Earl* concealed from her as well as their friends. When Flo died at age forty-five in November 1965, Jackie wrote to "Dearest Dearest Earl" of "so many memories—so much of all our happy times gone now with dearest loving Flo—Who ever thought you and I would be the ones left." Earl moved permanently to Palm Beach, where he was elected to numerous terms as mayor. He died in 1991 at age eighty-eight.

Theodore Sorensen never entirely recovered from the assassination of Jack Kennedy. Sorensen "lived this man's life, thought with him and spoke the same words," said Katie Louchheim. Afterwards, Louchheim noted, Sorensen was "not morose but stilled. He was often bitter."

Sorensen was the first to leave Johnson's White House, in mid-January 1964, and he moved to New York where he joined the prestigious law firm of Paul Weiss Rifkind Wharton & Garrison. Sorensen's biography of Kennedy came out in 1965 along with Schlesinger's. Like his colleague, he presented a proudly partisan account. He became one of the Kennedy family's closest advisers, and he wrote speeches for Bobby's senatorial and presidential campaigns. In later years he worked for the Democratic party, lectured, and wrote opinion pieces about issues of the day. Jackie came to rely on Sorensen as a trusted counselor. The better he knew her, he said, the more he "lived in awe of Jackie."

Charles and Betty Spalding were divorced, and he moved to California. She stayed in Connecticut with their children and became an ardent feminist. "She had a difficult divorce, and she made that a cause—cases of bigamy, lack of child support," said Nancy Tenney Coleman. At age seventy-one Betty received her bachelor's degree from Yale. Chuck married twice more, both times to wealthy women. His principal contact with the Kennedy crowd was Red Fay, with whom he occasionally played golf in San Francisco. Chuck died at eighty-one in 1999, and Betty two years later.

Adlai Stevenson reached out tenderly to Jackie after Kennedy's death. "I love you (which clarifies but doesn't identify)," he wrote. "I *know* there is much joy and peace and fulfillment for you. As Fra Lianni said, there is a radiance and glory in the darkness, could one but see. And *you can see.*" He continued to serve as U.S. ambassador to the United Nations and maintained his flock of female admirers. Walking with the closest of them, Marietta Tree, through Grosvenor Square in London on a late July afternoon in 1965, he collapsed and died of a heart attack at age sixty-five. Shortly before his death, Stevenson had confided to CBS correspondent Eric Sevareid that he wished to leave his post at the UN. "For a while," Stevenson said, "I would just like to sit in the shade with a glass of wine in my hands and watch people dance."

Nancy Tuckerman followed Jackie to New York, where she worked for her old friend for many years, handling her business affairs and dealing with the press. They remained confidantes until Jackie's death, when "Tucky" retired to Connecticut.

Pamela Turnure worked for Jackie for several years in New York before marrying a wealthy Canadian businessman named Robert Timmins. She ran a decorating business, and after the death of her husband moved to Colorado where she spent her time selling real estate and skiing.

William Walton continued to pursue his career as an artist. Tony Bradlee recalled "an abstract painting with a big splash of red. I knew immediately it represented the assassination." He also returned to writing. In 1966 he wrote *The Evidence of Washington,* an elegant book about the capital city. He grew even closer to Jackie, serving as her escort and confidant. In 1980 as an editor at Doubleday, she published Walton's first novel, *A Civil War Courtship,* which his friend Teddy White called a "marvelous roaring tender story." Walton died in 1994 at age eighty-five.

Jayne Wrightsman reigned as one of New York's renowned collectors, donating priceless French furniture and old master paintings (including a Vermeer, Tiepolo, El Greco, and Poussin) to the Metropolitan Museum of Art, where she served on the board for decades. After *Charles* Wrightsman's death in 1986 at ninety-one, she became an arbiter of Manhattan society, cultivating an aura of mystery and remaining aloof from the world outside her rarefied circle. "I think she learned rather a lot from Jackie Kennedy," said one of her friends. "The less you're available, the more exclusive you become."

Source Notes

The story of the Kennedy administration is now four decades old and has shifted from contemporary politics into the realm of American history. As a result, nearly everyone I interviewed spoke for the record. However, several individuals requested anonymity. Any quotations not specifically cited have come from these few confidential sources.

I interviewed 142 people who were participants and observers during the Kennedy administration. Whenever possible, I spoke to those with firsthand knowledge. The cast of characters at the beginning of the book includes spouses whose intimacy with Jack or Jackie Kennedy gave them a special place in the court life of the Kennedy years. Of the twenty-eight listed principals who were alive during my research, I interviewed twenty, plus five spouses not included on the list.

Of the numerous books written about the Kennedys, I read and analyzed more than a hundred that were pertinent to my inquiry. Complete information on these works, plus others about members of the Kennedy circle, is cited in the accompanying bibliography. The most frequently mentioned in the notes are given abbreviations below. In a number of cases, one author has written several books, or two authors share the same surname. I have added Roman numerals to these citations to ensure clarity. For example:

Stewart Alsop, *The Center* (Alsop I)
Joseph W. Alsop, *"I've Seen the Best of It": Memoirs* (Alsop II)

Laurence Leamer, *The Kennedy Women* (Leamer I)
Laurence Leamer, *The Kennedy Men: 1901–1963* (Leamer II)

Also listed below are abbreviations for frequently cited individuals, publications, archives, and manuscript collections.

Between its oral histories and collections of personal papers, the John F. Kennedy Library was an invaluable resource. Most of the oral history citations in the notes are from the Kennedy Library. Oral histories from Columbia University are specifically cited by an abbreviation indicated below.

In the first reference to an oral history or an interview, the full name appears;

subsequent references cite only the last name, except in the case of spouses or siblings, where the full name is repeated.

Unless otherwise indicated, all references to the dates, times, and participants in meetings and social engagements are drawn from "The President's Appointments," the official schedule of John F. Kennedy, as well as the Sanford Fox Social Files at the Kennedy Library. References to phone calls are drawn from desk diaries kept by John F. Kennedy's secretary, Evelyn Lincoln, and found in her collection at the library. Details on the comings and goings of White House guests come from the gate logs kept by the Secret Service, also at the Kennedy Library. Other archival sources are indicated below, with abbreviations.

Frequently Cited Books
TCY: Michael R. Beschloss, *The Crisis Years: Kennedy and Khrushchev, 1960–1963*
CWK: Benjamin C. Bradlee, *Conversations with Kennedy*
AJ: John Kenneth Galbraith, *Ambassador's Journal: A Personal Account of the Kennedy Years*
DOAP: William Manchester, *The Death of a President*
AH: Ralph Martin, *A Hero for Our Time*
KT: Ernest R. May and Philip D. Zelikow, eds., *The Kennedy Tapes: Inside the White House During the Cuban Missile Crisis*
PR-JFK: Ernest May, Timothy Naftali, and Philip Zelikow, eds., *The Presidential Recordings: John F. Kennedy: The Great Crises*. Vol. 1, July 30–August 1962; Vol. 2, September 4– October 21, 1962; Vol. 3, October 22–28, 1962
JWH: Kenneth P. O'Donnell and David Powers, *"Johnny, We Hardly Knew Ye"*
PK: Richard Reeves, *President Kennedy: Profile of Power*
ATD: Arthur M. Schlesinger Jr., *A Thousand Days: John F. Kennedy in the White House*
HTF: Amanda Smith, ed., *Hostage to Fortune: The Letters of Joseph P. Kennedy*
KE: Theodore C. Sorensen, *Kennedy*
LG: C. L. Sulzberger, *The Last of the Giants*
JKWH: Mary Van Rensselaer Thayer, *Jacqueline Kennedy: The White House Years*
RKHL: Evan Thomas, *Robert Kennedy: His Life*

Archives
JFKL: John Fitzgerald Kennedy Library
JPKP: Joseph P. Kennedy Papers, John F. Kennedy Library
JCBC: Joan and Clay Blair Collection, University of Wyoming (taped interviews for *The Search for JFK,* by Joan and Clay Blair Jr.)
DBD: The Diaries of David Bruce, Richmond Historical Society
OH-CU: Oral History from the Columbia University Oral History Project
WMP: William Manchester Papers, JFKL
LBJL: Lyndon Baines Johnson Library
KSLP: Katie S. Louchheim Papers, Library of Congress (1957–63)
LOC: Library of Congress
HMA: Harold Macmillan Archive, Bodleian Library, Oxford University
PRO: Public Record Office, Kew, Prime Minister's Files 1961–64

Publications
NYT: *The New York Times*
NYHT: *The New York Herald Tribune*
WP: *The Washington Post*
WS: *The Washington Star* (*The Evening Star* and *The Sunday Star*)

Selected Individuals
JFK: John Fitzgerald Kennedy
JBK: Jacqueline Bouvier Kennedy

JPK: Joseph Patrick Kennedy
RK: Rose Fitzgerald Kennedy
RFK: Robert Francis Kennedy
EMK: Edward M. Kennedy
LBJ: Lyndon Baines Johnson

Organization
FBI: Federal Bureau of Investigation

The Kennedy Court: January 1961

xii "harpies": Letitia Baldrige, *A Lady First: My Life in the Kennedy White House and the American Embassies of Paris and Rome* (Baldrige I), p. 175.

xii he kept a set of clothing: Lem Billings OH.

xii "a complete liberation of the spirit": David Michaelis, *The Best of Friends: Profiles of Extraordinary Friendships*, p. 175.

xii "dazzling clarity and speed": *ATD*, p. 208.

xii "strut sitting down": Joan Dillon, la Duchesse de Mouchy, interview.

xiii "full of the old malarky": Rowland Evans interview.

xiii "impertinent cables": Mary Barelli Gallagher, *My Life with Jacqueline Kennedy*, p. 165.

xiii Friend since college days: Lord Harlech OH. (During the Kennedy administration, he was known as David Ormsby Gore.)

xiii brainpower that JFK felt exceeded: *ATD*, p. 208.

xiii with whom he read poetry aloud: Robert McNamara interview.

xiii "very motherly figure": Lee Radziwill interview.

xiv "talk the balls off a brass monkey": *RKHL*, p. 353.

xiv "Wolfhound": *AH*, p. 318.

xiv "Cobra": Helen O'Donnell, *A Common Good*, p. 256.

xiv "Iceman": Patrick Anderson, *The Presidents' Men*, p. 240.

xiv "Good night, pal": *JWH*, p. 264.

xiv fondness for poetry of: James Reed interview.

xiv "court philosopher": Anderson, p. 213.

xv "intellectual blood bank": Laura Bergquist Knebel OH.

xv "Billy Boy": *JKWH*, p. 51.

Preface

xvii "They certainly have acquired": *JKWH*, p. 247; Oleg Cassini, *A Thousand Days of Magic* (Cassini I), p. 53.

xvii On November 29, 1963: Four-paragraph description of JBK interview with Theodore H. White is based on "The Camelot Documents," 1963–1964, Papers of Theodore H. White, JFKL.

xviii At an exhibit: author's observation.

xviii "devour [stories of] the knights": "The Camelot Documents," JFKL.

xviii As an adult he had been: *DOAP*, p. 623.

xviii middlebrow fondness: *AH*, p. 563, quoting Charles Spalding: "He *loved* to play the song ['Camelot']."

xviii in May 1962 Jackie invited Frederick Loewe: Edward McDermott OH.

xix "overdone": John Kenneth Galbraith interview.

xix "myth turned into a cliché": Arthur M. Schlesinger Jr. interview.

xix "her most mischievous interview": JFKL seminar on JBK exhibit at the Metropolitan Museum, New York City, Feb. 3, 2002, C-SPAN.

xix "magic": *WP*, May 29, 1995.

xix "overly sentimental" . . . "right" . . . "brief shining moment": JBK to Harold Macmillan, Jan. 31, 1964, HMA.

xix   "life-affirming, life-enhancing zest": *ATD,* p. 1030.

xx   "Bonapartist": Isaiah Berlin OH.

xx   "Tudor Court": David Ormsby Gore, "The Centres of Power in the Kennedy Administration," Jan. 23, 1962, PRO.

xx   "court life": Harlech OH. The reference was made by Richard Neustadt in one of his questions.

xxi   "The place is lousy with courtiers": Stewart Alsop to Martin Sommers, Dec. 21, 1961, Joseph and Stewart Alsop Papers, LOC.

xxi   "Jackie wanted to do Versailles": Oleg Cassini interview.

xxi   In particular Jackie admired: Sarah Bradford, *America's Queen,* p. 55.

xxi   "My life here which I dreaded": JBK to William Walton, June 8, 1962, Walton Papers, JFKL.

xxi   "the cockiest crowd": *AH,* p. 300.

xxi   "the Harlem Globetrotters": Peter Collier and David Horowitz, *The Kennedys,* p. 266.

xxi   heated to 90 degrees: David Powers OH.

xxi   grilled cheese, cold beef: Jim Bishop, *A Day in the Life of President Kennedy,* p. 56.

xxi   Jackie, meanwhile, might be: Gallagher, p. 130; Memo, ND: "Mrs. Kennedy smokes L&M cigarettes, filter, soft pack," Godfrey McHugh Papers, JFKL.

xxi   Perhaps she would be bouncing: Letitia Baldrige interview; Bishop, p. 38.

xxii   curled up with Marcus Cheke's: Cassini I, p. 52.

xxii   ducking into the White House school: Carl Sferrazza Anthony, *The Kennedy White House: Family Life & Pictures, 1961–1963,* pp. 175–79, 183–84.

xxii   "new face": *JKWH,* p. 249.

xxii   Italian songs played softly: *LG,* p. 808.

xxii   "nothing but a busy-body": Theodore H. White memo on dinner at the White House, Feb. 13, 1963, Theodore White Papers, Harvard University.

xxii   the origin of the French ambassador's: Hervé Alphand, *L'étonnement d'être: Journal (1939–1973),* pp. 409–11.

xxii   "nice fellow in private": *LG,* p. 927. JFK also told Ben Bradlee that Nixon was "a cheap bastard; that's all there is to it" (*CWK,* p. 75).

xxii   "Europe wants a free ride": *LG,* p. 928.

xxii   waiters carried large trays: Henry Koehler interview.

xxii   "They served the drinks in enormous": George Plimpton interview.

xxii   "It was Irish, which made it": Nancy Dickerson, *Among Those Present: A Reporter's View of Twenty-five Years in Washington,* p. 67.

xxii   "great guns": Marian Schlesinger OH.

xxii   "Not so": Elspeth Rostow interview.

xxii   "But St. Thomas said": ibid.

xxiii   The sober atmosphere collapsed: ibid.

xxiii   Jackie knew what was: Cecil Beaton unpublished diary, June 1968, Beaton Collection, St. John's College, Cambridge, copyright, The Literary Executors of the late Sir Cecil Beaton.

xxiii   Some, like her friend: Eve Fout interview.

xxiii   "All Kennedy men are like that": Joan Kennedy interview.

xxiii   "She had made a bargain": Jessie Wood interview.

xxiii   "smart life": Alistair Horne, *Macmillan,* vol. 2, 1957–1986, p. 307.

xxiv   "adopted a comical air": Betty Beale, *Power at Play: A Memoir of Parties, Politicians and the Presidents in My Bedroom,* p. 64.

xxiv   "very few really had much": Charles Bartlett OH. (Since Charles Bartlett's wife, Martha, did not give an oral history to the JFKL, subsequent references to this oral history will cite last name only; both Bartletts gave interviews to the author and will be cited separately in those instances.)

xxiv   Only two personal friends: Charles Bartlett, Paul "Red" Fay, Kenneth O'Donnell, David Powers, and Lawrence O'Brien were Catholics.

xxiv   five personal friends and three: Lem Billings, Red Fay, Charles Bartlett, James Reed, Earl E.T. Smith, McGeorge Bundy, Douglas Dillon, and Robert McNamara were Republicans.

xxiv   including her stepsister Nina: Jan Pottker, *Jack and Jackie: The Story of a Mother and Her Daughter, Jacqueline Kennedy Onassis,* p. 168.

xxiv   "an elegant, mandarin tone": William Manchester, *Portrait of a President: John F. Kennedy in Profile* (Manchester II), p. 106.

xxiv   "cheerful, amusing, energetic": *KE,* p. 378.

xxiv   Nearly everyone in the Kennedy court: *JWH,* p. 111: "All of the Kennedys, and especially Jack, judged people by their appearance"; Jewel Reed interview.

xxiv   "enjoyed . . . almost anyone from": *KE,* p. 386.

xxiv   "hated the suburbia-type existence": James Reed OH. (James Reed's wife, Jewel, did not give an oral history to the JFKL, so subsequent references to this oral history will cite last name only; both Reeds gave interviews to the author and will be cited separately in those instances.)

xxiv   Even as a teenager: Jacqueline Bouvier to Lee Bouvier, ND (probably 1950), "The Way It Was," book proposal by Lee Radziwill.

xxiv   "real ping pong": Fred Holborn interview, WMP.

xxv   "terror" of boring JFK: Katharine Graham, *Personal History,* p. 290.

xxv   "My God, I said something": Suzanne Roosevelt Kloman interview.

xxv   "hated dimness": Berlin OH.

xxv   "The Kennedys were pretty tough eggs": Marian Schlesinger OH.

xxv   routinely performed "Hooray": Paul Fay, *The Pleasure of His Company,* pp. 83–84.

xxv   Oleg Cassini would launch: Oleg Cassini, *In My Own Fashion* (Cassini II), p. 325.

xxv   "Kennedy knew he was a potentate": Cassini interview.

xxv   "to an exceptional degree": *ATD,* p. 78.

xxv   "friends came in layers": ibid.

xxv   "each had a certain role": James Reed interview.

xxv   "alter ego": Ted Sorensen interview; Lester Tanzer, ed., *The Kennedy Circle,* pp. 7, 24.

xxv   "That man [Sorensen] never knows": Katie Louchheim journal, Aug. 5, 1963. All further references from Louchheim are found in this journal, KSLP.

xxv   "No one—no single aide": *KE,* p. 5.

xxvi   Kennedy didn't talk about women: William Walton interview, JCBC.

xxvi   "determined, unrelenting and profane": *ATD,* p. 92.

xxvi   "prismatic": Laura Bergquist Knebel OH.

xxvi   Kennedy disliked being alone: Benjamin Bradlee interview; Jewel Reed interview; Baldrige interview.

xxvi   "You'd never bleed": Walton interview, JCBC.

xxvi   "wasn't a cozy friend": Bartlett OH.

xxvi   "He didn't like to be with": *AH,* p. 372.

xxvi   Everyone in Kennedy's circle: *KE,* p. 379; Ben Bradlee interview.

xxvi   "his own private information network": David Ormsby Gore, "Centres of Power" memorandum, Jan. 23, 1962, PRO. In many accounts of the period, the British ambassador's name has been hyphenated as Ormsby-Gore. But in official documents, he appeared as "Sir David Ormsby Gore," without a hyphen (see Sir David Ormsby Gore to Lord Home, Oct. 27, 1961). His friends referred to him simply as "David Gore" (see Harold Macmillan to JFK, Mar. 10, 1962, reference to "David Gore").

xxvi   "consistent patter of asking": James Reed interview.

xxvi   "Women never have any effect": JPK to Lucius Ordway, Nov. 17, 1950, JPKP.

xxvii   "happiness compartment": Richard Neustadt interview, Arthur M. Schlesinger Jr. Papers, JFKL.

xxvii   "Whatever his waywardness": Arthur Schlesinger interview.

xxvii   He was intrigued by what women: Walton interview, JCBC.

xxvii   "It drove him wild": Walton OH.

xxvii   "capacity to state problems": Arthur Schlesinger interview.

xxvii   "She was an intellectual": Marian Schlesinger interview.

xxvii   "I don't think she found": Radziwill interview.

xxvii   "she did keep in touch": Baldrige e-mail to author, July 11, 2002.

xxvii   "She would cozy up": Patricia Hass interview.

xxvii   "confidante of an important": Bradford, p. 55.

xxviii   "She enjoyed the thoughts": McNamara interview.

xxviii   Jackie Kennedy prized loyalty: Interviews with Suzanne Wilson, Hugh D. "Yusha"
         Auchincloss III, Martha Bartlett, Vivian Crespi, Solange Herter, Jessie Wood, and
         Letitia Baldrige on JBK's views of friendship.

xxviii   "She didn't like empty-headed": Herter interview.

xxviii   "pushy creature": JBK to Walton, June 8, 1962, Walton Papers, JFKL.

xxviii   "She liked women who were feminine": Herter interview.

xxviii   "Jackie didn't enjoy superficial": Deeda Blair interview.

xxviii   She had high standards: Cassini II, p. 304; Crespi interview.

xxviii   "ran hot and cold": Herter interview.

xxviii   "hermetic periods": Cassini II, p. 304.

xxviii   "She would have enthusiasms": Baldrige interview. In her application for *Vogue*
         magazine's Prix de Paris (May 21, 1951) when she was twenty-one years old, Jackie
         wrote in "Feature-Question 1": "One of my most annoying faults is getting very
         enthusiastic over something at the beginning and then tiring of it halfway through.
         I am trying to counteract this by not getting too enthusiastic over too many things
         at once." *Vogue* Materials, JFKL.

xxviii   "gave a great impression of affection": Arthur Schlesinger interview.

xxviii   "a source of his fascination and power": *ATD*, p. 78.

xxviii   "unto herself": Baldrige interview.

xxviii   "Jack Kennedy enjoyed his friends": Arthur Schlesinger interview.

xxviii   "I doubt life would have been": ibid.

xxix   "I was writing some things": Theodore Sorensen interview.

xxix   "great man" theory: Arthur Schlesinger interview; Berlin OH.

Chapter One

3   "Where's Jackie?": Leo Damore, *The Cape Cod Years of John Fitzgerald Kennedy,*
     p. 226; Theodore H. White, *The Making of the President 1960* (White I), p. 379;
     NYHT, Nov. 11, 1960.

3   nerve center for thirty-five years: *HTF,* p. 64.

3   her cheery white and yellow: Apple Parish Bartlett and Susan Bartlett Crater, *Sister:
     The Life of Legendary American Interior Decorator Mrs. Henry Parish II,* p. 79; *AH,* p. 241.

3   "pixie things": Liz Carpenter interview.

3   droll watercolors: Laura Bergquist manuscript for profile of Jackie Kennedy, ND,
     Laura Bergquist Papers, the Howard Gotlieb Archival Research Center at Boston
     University.

4   her artistic mentor Ludwig Bemelmans: Thomas Guinzburg OH-CU.

4   "fairly important young executive": Norman Mailer, "An Evening with Jackie
     Kennedy: Being an Essay in Three Acts," *Esquire,* July 1962.

4   Jack, however, had: *AH,* p. 241; White I, pp. 6, 16.

4   "He's lost another state": *AH,* p. 235.

4   The Washington artist Bill Walton: White I, p. 19.

4   "Oh, Bunny, you're President": ibid., p. 20.

4   Jackie went to bed before: *NYHT,* Nov. 11, 1960.

4   "the heat and crowds": *NYT,* Sept. 15, 1960.

4   She had awakened: White I, pp. 378–79.

5   "unusually large": *JKWH,* p. 63.

5   a source of vanity: Hugh Sidey interview; *KE,* p. 24.

5   "it would be unendurable": *Sunday Standard-Times* (Cape Cod), Feb. 28, 1954.

5   "the look of a beautiful lion": *NYT,* July 15, 1960.

5   "unfortunately far apart": Jacqueline Bouvier essay, "Feature-Question 1," *Vogue* Materials, JFKL.

5   "bouffant purple coat": *NYHT,* Nov. 10, 1960.

5   "It was involuntary": *ATD,* p. 114.

5   "a very naughty eight-year-old": Mailer, *Esquire,* July 1962.

5   the French phrase spelled out: Mini Rhea, *I Was Jacqueline Kennedy's Dressmaker,* p. 79.

6   "Love me, love my dog": ibid.

6   "The coat of arms for this Administration": *NYT,* Jan. 30, 1961. In her unpublished manuscript on Jackie, Laura Bergquist attributes this quote to JBK. Laura Bergquist Papers, Boston University.

6   "All I ask is someone with": Jacqueline Bouvier to Lee Bouvier, ND (probably 1950), Lee Radziwill book proposal.

6   Their Newport wedding: *Newport Daily News,* Sept. 12, 1953; Sept. 13, 1953.

6   "humiliation she would suffer": Doris Kearns Goodwin, *The Fitzgeralds and the Kennedys* (Goodwin I), p. 774. This is the definitive work on the Kennedy family, ending with the election of JFK to the presidency.

6   "You're pretty much in love": Peter Davis, *Jack,* a documentary on CBS, Nov. 17, 1993.

6   "really drove him out": Lem Billings OH. The Billings oral history was originally intended to be off-limits to historians for fifty years after his death. However, it has been opened to some writers, and copies are now available outside the Kennedy Library.

7   "She breathes all the": Donald Wilson, "John Kennedy's Lovely Lady," *Life,* Aug. 24, 1959.

7   "a vegetable wife": *Cape Cod Times,* Feb. 28, 1954.

7   "things of the spirit": Wilson, *Life,* Aug. 24, 1959.

7   "direct, energetic types": Laura Bergquist Knebel OH.

7   "curious inquiring mind": Wilson, *Life,* Aug. 24, 1959.

7   "fascinated by the way he thinks": Rhea, p. 171.

7   "imperturbable self-confidence": *KE,* p. 120.

7   "exchanged eyes": *DOAP,* p. 84.

7   "Jackie was the only woman": Crespi interview.

7   "mesmerized": Iris Turner Kelso OH-CU.

7   "We loved them in every way": Nellie Connally, *From Love Field: My Final Hours with President John F. Kennedy,* p. 85, quoting from JBK to Nellie Connally, Dec. 1, 1963.

7   "Jack's love had certain": Robin Chandler Duke interview.

7   "I would describe Jack": JBK to Fletcher Knebel, ND, for use in Knebel's article "What You Don't Know About Kennedy," *Look,* Jan. 17, 1961, Fletcher Knebel Papers, Boston University.

8   trembling hands: According to Robert Kennedy biographer Evan Thomas, John, Robert, and Edward Kennedy were periodically affected by what Eunice Shriver described as a "family tremor" (*RKHL,* p. 398).

8   "My wife and I prepare": *NYHT,* Nov. 10, 1960.

8   "Hard-hearted Jack": Mary McGrory to Theodore H. White, Nov. 12, 1960, Theodore White Papers, Harvard University.

8   "all made out of the same clay": Philip Ziegler, *Diana Cooper,* p. 308.

8   cared for by nuns since: Laurence Leamer, *The Kennedy Women* (Leamer I),
     pp. 319–23; 412–13. As of this writing, Rosemary at age eighty-five is still living at the
     St. Coletta School for Exceptional Children in Jefferson, Wisconsin.
8   "childhood victim": *Time*, July 11, 1960.
8   Almost twenty years earlier: Goodwin I, p. 614; *HTF*, p. 511.
9   But this time Jack Kennedy: Damore, p. 227.
9   "grim and pale": ibid.
9   "awkward moment": Theodore White notes on the day after JFK's election, ND,
     Theodore White Papers, Harvard University.

Chapter Two

10   Excluded from their group: *CWK*, p. 34.
10   "Lem couldn't stand me": Ben Bradlee interview.
10   "a dud": *AH*, p. 275.
10   "Okay, girls, you can take": *CWK*, p. 32.
10   "Do you think I should stuff": Bergquist manuscript for profile of Jackie Kennedy,
     ND, Laura Bergquist Papers, Boston University.
11   Bradlee said Kennedy should: *CWK*, p. 33.
11   when the newspapers announced: *ATD*, p. 125.
11   For more than a year: Nigel Hamilton, *JFK: Reckless Youth*, p. 435; Joan and Clay
     Blair Jr., *The Search for JFK*, p. 151; Goodwin I, p. 632.
11   "not evil as he is depicted": Hamilton, pp. 431–32.
11   Even after JFK had been: Hamilton, pp. 438, 489; Goodwin I, p. 633.
11   JFK's defiance was: Hamilton, p. 458.
11   "He's got a lot to learn": ibid., p. 423, quoting from an interview with John White,
     recalling Arvad's comments.
11   Kennedy knew that Hoover: ibid., p. 489.
11   But JFK was unaware: Confidential Airtel to J. Edgar Hoover from SAC, Los
     Angeles, Apr. 1, 1960, FBI, mentioned JFK's "association with SINATRA . . . the
     Senator is vulnerable to bad publicity. . . . Sex activities by Kennedy . . . involving the
     Senator and Sinatra occurred in Palm Springs, Las Vegas, and New York City"; FBI,
     J. Edgar Hoover O&C Files #96 (Kennedy, John Fitzgerald) memorandum July 13,
     1960 alleged "immoral activities" by JFK including the possibility that he "was
     'compromised' with a woman in Las Vegas and that Kennedy and Frank Sinatra in
     the recent past have been involved in parties in Palm Springs, Las Vegas, and New
     York."
11   because he thought her resemblance: Garry Wills, *The Kennedy Imprisonment*, p. 22.
11   they had been friends since: Walton OH.
11   The son of an Illinois: ibid.
12   "gloriously florid": *JKWH*, p. 51.
12   "rather like a clever": Martha Gellhorn to Adlai Stevenson, Aug. 15, 1960, Adlai E.
     Stevenson Papers, Princeton University.
12   Walton was forthright: Nancy White Hector interview; Anne Truitt interview.
12   "glorious fun": Gellhorn to Stevenson, Aug. 15, 1960, Stevenson Papers, Princeton
     University.
12   Bradlee had entered: Benjamin C. Bradlee, *A Good Life* (Bradlee II), p. 204.
12   a love affair that began: ibid., pp. 158–60.
12   Bradlee's family mingled: ibid., pp. 21–23.
12   "the private lives and public postures": *CWK*, p. 21.
12   "nineteenth-century court gossip": *KE*, p. 373.
12   He was unconventional enough: Bradlee II, p. 53.
12   "You had to have a light touch": Ben Bradlee interview.
12   "I married a whirlwind": Deane and David Heller, *Jacqueline Kennedy*, p. 92.

13 Anthony Trollope's *The Warden*: Anne Truitt interview; Manchester II, p. 92.

13 cast for bluefish: *Time,* Nov. 28, 1960.

13 saw a play (Gore Vidal's): Fred Kaplan, *Gore Vidal: A Biography,* p. 486.

13 "a city upon a hill": *WP,* Jan. 10, 1961.

13 "We'll kill a deer": *NYHT,* Nov. 12, 1960.

13 more recently had shot quail: *WS,* Apr. 17, 1961.

13 Johnson pressed him: *CWK,* p. 212; Collier and Horowitz, p. 251; *Newsweek,* Nov. 28, 1960.

13 "Lyndon, I thank you": Lloyd Hand interview.

13 "whale" . . . "minnow": Harry McPherson, *A Political Education: A Washington Memoir,* p. 48.

13 "To Johnson . . . [JFK] was": ibid., p. 42.

14 four inches taller, he could: Carpenter interview.

14 Johnson had been born: Robert Caro, *The Years of Lyndon Johnson: Master of the Senate,* p. 115.

14 "Lyndon was a powerhouse": Ben Bradlee interview.

14 "He'd suck your guts out": Orville Freeman Reminiscence, Nov. 23, 1963, WMP.

14 rarely read a book and tended: Hand interview; Harry McPherson interview.

14 many of Kennedy's acolytes: Stewart Alsop, *The Center* (Alsop I), p. 38.

14 LBJ's simple words and colorful locutions: Many of these appeared in the extensive tape recordings Johnson made of his telephone conversations during his presidency. On Aug. 16, 1965, for example, Johnson told Senator Richard Russell, Democrat of Georgia, "You can be poor and ignorant all your life. Then you take a few drinks, and you'll be rich and smart in an hour." LBJ Tapes, LBJL.

14 Kennedy cringed at: Alsop I, p. 47; Otto Fuerbringer interview; Caro, pp. 121–22.

14 "uncouth and somewhat of an oaf": George Smathers Senate OH.

14 Yet he admired: ibid.; McPherson, p. 42.

15 While LBJ did not actively: Newton Minow OH-CU; *ATD,* p. 19.

15 take "the Catholic flavor": *AJ,* p. 112.

15 "the smartest thing": *ATD,* p.58.

15 "collaborator . . . than": ibid., p. 50.

15 "I'm not going to die": *AH,* p. 178.

15 "significant assignments": *ATD,* p. 49.

15 For his part: Bill Moyers interview, Schlesinger Papers, JFKL.

15 because Kennedy would take credit: McPherson, p. 179.

15 "I looked it up": Ralph G. Martin, *Henry and Clare: An Intimate Portrait of the Luces* (Martin II), p. 363.

15 Her instinct was to surround: *WP,* Jan. 8, 1961; Gallagher, pp. 29–31.

15 For her social secretary: Baldrige I, p. 68.

16 Baldrige had acquired discipline: ibid., p. 13.

16 Having grown to six foot one: ibid., p. 19.

16 "commando from the White House": Letitia Baldrige, *Of Diamonds and Diplomats* (Baldrige II), p. 248.

16 "that floorflusher Kennedy": Letitia Baldrige to Clare Boothe Luce, Feb. 17, 1959, Clare Boothe Luce Papers, LOC.

16 "Vixen for Nixon": Clare Luce to Baldrige, May 20, 1963, Clare Luce Papers, LOC.

16 "Jack Kennedy has shown": Baldrige to Clare Luce, July 25, 1960, Clare Luce Papers, LOC.

16 "a complete makeover of": Baldrige I, p. 182.

16 "redecorate" . . . "a word I hate": *ATD,* p. 670.

16 "Jackie was suddenly on fire": Baldrige I, p. 165.

16 "a showcase for great American": *NYHT,* Nov. 23, 1960; *JKWH,* p. 15; Baldrige II, p. 158.

16   "I've learned lesson number one": Baldrige to Clare Luce, Dec. 16, 1960, Clare Luce
      Papers, LOC.

17   "a very inexperienced, beautiful": Baldrige I, p. 168.

17   this petite twenty-three-year-old: J. B. West, *Upstairs at the White House,* p. 205.

17   "learn the duties gradually": Gallagher, p. 106.

17   "notably aggressive feminine": *JKWH,* p. 30.

17   The choice mystified: Beale, p. 87.

17   Turnure's landlady: "Allegation Against John F. Kennedy, President of the United
      States," April 19, 1963, FBI; D. C. Morrell to Cartha DeLoach, April 11, 1963, FBI;
      A. Rosen to Belmont, May 24, 1963, FBI.

17   "This lady claimed he was having": Fletcher Knebel OH.

17   "The rumors were rampant": Barbara Gamarekian interview.

17   "asked me if I knew [Jack] was": *AH,* p. 314.

17   "heroines": Hamish Bowles, "Defining Style: Jacqueline Kennedy's White House
      Years," *Jacqueline Kennedy: The White House Years,* Metropolitan Museum of Art
      (hereafter referred to as *Met Catalogue*), p. 17.

18   cool and laconic: Arthur Schlesinger interview.

18   "small, fine-boned brunette": *JKWH,* p. 30.

18   "could almost be taken for": Gallagher, p. 147.

18   she was the daughter of: *NYT,* Jan. 12, 1961; *WP,* Jan. 12, 1961; Louise Drake
      interview.

18   "proved efficient": *JKWH,* p. 30.

18   "Pam was always very quiet": Drake interview.

18   Jack and Jackie spent: *NYHT,* Nov. 25, 1960.

18   dinner that included caviar: *Newsweek,* Dec. 5, 1960.

18   Jackie's due date was still: *NYHT,* Nov. 25, 1960; *JKWH,* p. x.

18   "because of all the excitement": Jacqueline Kennedy Onassis OH, John Sherman
      Cooper Oral History Project, University of Kentucky.

18   The ambulance driver found: *WP,* Nov. 25, 1960; *NYT,* Nov. 26, 1960.

18   "She was smiling": *NYT,* Nov. 25, 1960.

18   But her anxiety showed: *NYHT,* Nov. 26, 1960.

18   The scenario was alarmingly similar: United Press International (UPI), Aug. 26,
      1956; *JKWH,* p. 107.

18   In 1956 she had returned: *UPI,* Aug. 26, 1956. Laurence Leamer, in *The Kennedy Men:
      1901–1963* (Leamer II), p. 358, describes JFK's secrecy surrounding the yacht rental.
      In March 1956, Kennedy had directed William Thompson, a railroad lobbyist, to
      secure the eighty-five-foot yacht for $1,750 for two weeks. JFK could have paid
      himself, but asked the yacht broker to omit his name from the transaction. In his
      letter to the agent in Cannes, Kennedy wrote, "Do not wish . . . in any way
      connected with the hiring of the boat" for the rental beginning Aug. 21, 1956.

19   "Oh no, not that!": *NYT,* Nov. 25, 1960.

19   Teddy Roosevelt, who had six: Edmund Morris, *Theodore Rex,* p. 251.

19   "If you bungle raising": Heller, p. 118.

Chapter Three

20   For two weeks she worked: Baldrige I, p. 165.

20   While Baldrige and other: *ATD,* pp. 669–70.

20   At 55,000 square feet: *NYT,* Feb. 15, 1962.

20   By comparison, the Seattle: *WP,* May 17, 2003.

20   Completed in 1802: Betty C. Monkman, *The White House: Its Historic Furnishings and
      First Families,* pp. 10–11.

20   Jackie consulted forty books: *JKWH,* p. 281.

20   including the January 1946 issue: ibid., p. 116.

20   After examining fabric: *JKWH*, p. 111; Monkman, pp. 224–26; James A. Abbott and Elaine M. Rice, *Designing Camelot: The Kennedy White House Restoration*, pp. 16–17.
21   a quick refurbishment: *JKWH*, p. 15.
21   using $50,000 designated: Abbott and Rice, p. 17.
21   "a woman of quality and taste": Bartlett and Crater, p. 88.
21   Room after room: Bowles, *Met Catalogue*, p. 22.
21   "seasick green": West, p. 200.
21   the ambiance was as cold: JBK to Henry du Pont, Oct. 10, 1961, Courtesy Henry Francis du Pont Winterthur Museum, Winterthur Archives.
21   "so sad": *JKWH*, p. 281.
21   "Jackie did not have two big": Bartlett and Crater, p. 82.
21   a number of twentieth-century presidents: James Ketchum interview; Abbott and Rice, pp. 13–17.
21   Jackie had grown up: West, p. 209.
21   "a bit Henry Jamesian": Bergquist manuscript for profile of Jackie Kennedy, ND, Laura Bergquist Papers, Boston University.
22   "Our background was influential": Radziwill interview.
22   "Every library . . . had chintz": William Norwich, "A New Balance: Lee Radziwill Finds Serenity in Paris," *NYT Magazine*, Oct. 22, 2000.
22   Jackie was determined: Yusha Auchincloss interview.
22   "I felt like a moth": *AH*, p. 282.
22   Only days after her son's: *NYT*, Dec. 13, 1960; Cassini II, pp. 305–307.
22   "on the Paris Couture fashion ticket": *Women's Wear Daily*, July 13, 1960.
22   "a Fifth Avenue store": *NYT*, Sept. 15, 1960.
22   "A newspaper reported": ibid.
22   "Put Jackie and Joan back": Bergquist manuscript for profile of Jackie Kennedy, ND, Laura Bergquist Papers, Boston University.
22   The ladies' garment workers union: Bowles, *Met Catalogue*, p. 27.
22   "gotten so vulgarly out of hand": Cassini II, p. 310, citing letter from JBK on Dec. 13, 1960.
22   "a single person, an American": *JKWH*, p. 21.
23   "Veronese green": Cassini I, p. 31.
23   a first in White House history: Cassini II, pp. 298–99, 308.
23   He was the scion: ibid., pp. 16, 20, 139.
23   "wise-cracking ladies' man": *WP*, Dec. 9, 1960.
23   "fantasy life": Cassini II, pp. 146–48.
23   Cassini became friendly with: ibid., p. 300.
23   "Don't bother them": ibid., p. 308.
23   "sophisticated simplicity": *JKWH*, p. 22.
23   He in turn could: Cassini interview.
24   Jackie had been intrigued: Bowles, *Met Catalogue*, p. 32.
24   For nearly a decade: Wilson, *Life*, Aug. 24, 1959; Bowles, *Met Catalogue*, p. 20.
24   "excellent cut and unobtrusive": Jacqueline Bouvier, "Fashion-Question 1," *Vogue* Prix de Paris application, May 21, 1951, JFKL.
24   "look delicious in front of": ibid.
24   At a time when: Rhea, p. 36; Bowles, *Met Catalogue*, p. 44.
24   "Just remember I like": Bowles, *Met Catalogue*, p. 28, citing JBK to Vreeland, Aug. 1, 1960.
24   "a pace setter who has worn": *NYT*, July 15, 1960.
24   "a great dip brimmed": Jacqueline Bouvier, "Thesis-Topic I, IV, for the girl with more taste than money, NOSTALGIA HAS NINE LIVES," *Vogue* Prix de Paris application, May 21, 1951, JFKL.
24   "an American Versailles": Cassini II, p. 306.

24 "continue to dress": *JKWH,* pp. 22–23.

24 "that I would wear if": Cassini II, p. 309, citing JBK to Cassini, Dec. 13, 1960.

24 "fat little women hopping": ibid., p. 310.

25 "Whenever I was upset": *AH,* p. 221.

25 "Mors tua vita mea est": Cassini I, p. 152.

25 "demeaning and vulgar": Leamer I, p. 434, citing Robert Coughlan interview with Rose Kennedy.

25 "Women are very idealistic": *NYHT,* Nov. 11, 1960; *U.S. News & World Report,* July 25, 1960.

25 "I'd love to get to know": *Sunday Standard-Times,* Feb. 28, 1954.

25 "I don't think Jack has changed": *AH,* p. 227.

25 "skittish and edgy": Bergquist manuscript for Jackie Kennedy profile, ND, Laura Bergquist Papers, Boston University.

25 "curled up on the campaign plane": ibid.

25 "Don't ask Jack mean questions": Dickerson, p. 65.

25 "looking daggers": Peter Lisagor OH; Collier and Horowitz, p. 237.

25 she had worked for fifteen months: *JKWH,* p. 97.

25 "You could make the column": Heller, p. 71.

26 "an old man's darling": Rhea, p. 100.

26 "What makes little boys": ibid., p. 118.

26 "Are wives a luxury": ibid., p. 68.

26 "the candybox spillings": Jacqueline Bouvier, "Feature-Question 3," *Vogue* Prix de Paris application, May 21, 1951, JFKL.

26 "vague little dreams": JBK to Mary E. Campbell, May 1, 1951, *Vogue* Materials, JFKL.

26 "there was no routine": *WP,* Jan. 19, 1961.

26 "field course in psychology": Rhea, p. 167.

26 "to learn how people thought": ibid., p. 168.

26 Within two days of Kennedy's election: *JKWH,* p. x.

26 Molly Thayer was no ordinary: Baldrige interview; Eugenie Rahim interview.

26 Jackie and Thayer agreed: Bruce and Beatrice Gould OH-CU.

27 "Jackie did a lot of the writing": Mary Bass Gibson OH-CU.

27 Thayer sent the completed: *JKWH,* pp. x–xi.

27 "complete sellout": Gould OH-CU.

27 "exactly how Jackie wanted": Baldrige interview.

27 "the best legal mind" . . . "the most devout": Mary Van Rensselaer Thayer, *Jacqueline Bouvier Kennedy* (Thayer II), pp. 102–104.

27 "a rock . . . I lean on him": ibid., p. 113.

27 "many-faceted character": ibid., p. 115.

27 It was an account of: ibid., p. 88; Jacqueline and Lee Bouvier, in *One Special Summer,* wrote that they set sail on June 6, 1951.

27 "looked into Jack's laughingly aroused": Thayer II, p. 95.

Chapter Four

29 "long, white, vaguely Spanish": *AJ,* p. 5.

29 had been designed: John Castle interview; Leo Racine interview.

29 "Bastard-Spanish-Moorish": *WP,* Mar. 30, 1995.

29 he sunbathed in the nude: Collier and Horowitz, p. 212.

29 "like a Stradivarius": ibid.

30 After his election, JFK declined: Racine interview.

30 "relishing the mob scenes": *JKWH,* p. 11.

30 with whom he was frequently confused: *The Billings Collection,* ed. Nan Richardson, p. 94, Nigel Hamilton Research Collection, Massachusetts Historical Society.

30 But Billings had a loud raspy: ibid., pp. 22, 57, 178.

30 "among hundreds of others": ibid., p. 181.

30 The Billings voice: ibid., p. 23.

30 "a mystifying relic": ibid., p. 188.

30 sharing a sandwich: *NYT,* Jan. 3, 1961.

30 Another time he might: ibid., Jan. 2, 1961.

30 "I thought, 'Jesus, this is strange' ": Fletcher Knebel OH.

30 "a stable pony": Charles Bartlett interview.

30 Jack and Lem met: Lem Billings interview, JCBC.

30 Lem's mother was from: Blair, p. 35.

31 An Episcopalian descended: Richardson, p. 50; Billings interview, JCBC.

31 "Jack had the self-assurance": Michaelis, p. 134.

31 They had countless nicknames: Richardson, p. 48.

31 "Muckers": Goodwin I, p. 488.

31 A poignant measure: Peter Kaplan interview.

31 Billings even pretended: Michaelis, p. 141.

31 Jack and Lem enrolled: *HTF,* p. 187.

31 "Lem and his battered": Richardson, p. 67.

31 Billings's full-time mission: ibid., pp. 19, 26.

31 "Lem had the ability to": Michaelis, p. 144.

31 Joe Kennedy often subsidized: Blair, p. 62; Richardson, pp. 74, 119.

31 After college Billings received: Richardson, p. 68.

31 "Fizzies": ibid., p. 158.

31 Finally in 1960 he moved: ibid., pp. 134, 158, 209.

31 In the White House, Billings came: Billings OH.

32 Before Jack and Jackie were: ibid.; Bradford, p. 69.

32 "I thought it was a challenge": Billings OH.

32 "Lem was a bridge": Kaplan interview.

32 "I didn't see anything overtly": Paul Fay interview.

32 "idolatrous": Ben Bradlee interview.

32 "Can you imagine": Michaelis, p. 172.

32 "superb physical condition": *NYT,* Jan. 17, 1961, quoting *Today's Health.*

33 The report was guilty of: Hamilton, p. 655.

33 Nor were there references: Robert Dallek, "The Medical Ordeals of JFK," *Atlantic Monthly,* December 2002.

33 The second and third: Evelyn Lincoln, *My Twelve Years with John F. Kennedy* (Lincoln I), p. 69.

33 Addison's disease, diagnosed: Blair, pp. 640–41.

33 "rather like a bad portrait": Joseph W. Alsop, *"I've Seen the Best of It": Memoirs* (Alsop II), p. 411.

33 His critical illness: Blair, pp. 641, 646.

33 "doomed to die": Arthur Krock interview, JCBC.

33 he could be treated with: Blair, pp. 643–44.

33 side effects including insomnia: Dallek, *Atlantic Monthly,* December 2002.

34 "looked like a spavined hunchback": *CWK,* p. 68.

34 "adrenal insufficiency": *NYT,* Jan. 17, 1961.

34 "I don't have Addison's": Pierre Salinger OH.

34 "hard knot": Billings OH.

34 family friend Kay Halle recalled: Kay Halle OH.

34 "set him somewhat apart": *ATD,* p. 80.

34 "the face . . . a little whiter": *AH,* p. 97.

34 "I've always said he's a child": JPK to JBK, Aug. 25, 1957, JPKP.

35　"It was so crowded": *JKWH*, p. 11.

35　She had arrived in a state: ibid., p. 9.

35　largely kept to herself: Lady Bird Johnson OH.

35　"she was not feeling well": *AJ*, p. 5.

35　Occasionally she ventured: *WP*, Dec. 26, 1960; *NYT*, Dec. 31, 1960. The JPKP
　　contain letters JPK wrote proposing candidates for membership in the Everglades on
　　Jan. 2, 1946, and the Bath and Tennis on Dec. 27, 1945.

35　"a sort of family home": Alphand, p. 411.

35　"as a threat": Goodwin I, p. 771.

35　"unbroken Shetland pony look": Stewart Alsop to Martin Sommers, Sept. 27, 1961,
　　Alsop Papers, LOC.

35　"called her 'the Deb' ": Goodwin I, p. 771.

35　"why worry if you're not": ibid., pp. 771–72.

35　"If only she had realized": ibid., p. 771.

35　"last will & testament": JBK last will and testament, Jan. 11, 1960, on stationery of
　　Half Moon Hotel, Montego Bay, Jamaica, *Documents and Artifacts Relating to the Life
　　and Career of John F. Kennedy,* Guernsey's, Mar. 18–19, 1998.

36　five foot three: Hamilton, p. 74.

36　Bright and inquisitive: Goodwin I, pp. 132, 145.

36　"greatest regret": ibid., p. 144.

36　Rose had raised her nine: Nancy Tenney Coleman interview; Eunice Shriver
　　interview.

36　"great on self improvement": Leamer I, p. 499.

36　Rose's own father: Goodwin I, pp. 248–49.

36　"She was never there": *AH,* p. 31.

36　she was a daily communicant: Coleman interview.

36　"I have spent a long happy": RK to JBK, June 9, 1958, JPKP.

36　"It might be noticed": Oatsie Leiter Charles interview.

36　Jackie admired Rose's faith: Yusha Auchincloss interview.

37　"there was just nothing afterwards": JBK to Harold Macmillan, Jan. 31, 1964, HMA.

37　the daily ocean swims: Dorothy Tubridy OH; *Standard-Times,* Jan. 8, 1961.

37　"to live in a disorganized": JBK to Walton, June 8, 1962, Walton Papers, JFKL.

37　She often slept: Gallagher, pp. 75–76; Goodwin I, p. 772.

37　When Rose pushed: John Corry, *The Golden Clan,* p. 74.

37　irreverence that shocked: Gallagher, p. 76.

37　Jackie recognized the pressures: Goodwin I, p. 772; *HTF,* p. 662.

37　"you don't reveal yourself": Leamer I, p. 433, citing Robert Coughlan interview with
　　RK.

37　"It must have been difficult": ibid.

37　happened to be Jackie's favorite: *AH,* p. 98.

37　"the glue" that held : ibid., p. 32.

37　"architect of our lives": Rose Kennedy, *Times to Remember,* p. 57.

37　"We don't want any losers": ibid., p. 143.

37　"living in an intellectual": Kay Halle, unpublished article on JPK, Halle Papers,
　　JFKL.

37　"one of his Emperor Augustus": *AH,* p. 91.

38　"I used to tell him": Goodwin I, p. 772.

38　"they would talk about everything": *AH,* p. 91.

38　"the Gibbon": Manchester II, p. 83.

38　"Joseph Kennedy told me": *AH,* p. 128.

38　"very quiet and beautiful": JBK to JPK, Aug. 15, 1957, JPKP.

38　a horde of Kennedy family: Bergquist manuscript for profile of Jackie Kennedy, ND,
　　Laura Bergquist Papers, Boston University.

Chapter Five

39   Yet with the exception: *RKHL*, p. 109.

39   Only one senator: Arthur M. Schlesinger Jr., *Robert Kennedy and His Times* (Schlesinger II), p. 236.

39   Washington reporters were so: Pierpoint OH.

40   "I just wanted to give": *RKHL*, pp. 110–11.

40   Joe Kennedy suggested the move: George Smathers OH; Fay interview.

40   Bobby at the Justice Department: *RKHL*, p. 109; Wills, pp. 34–37; Bartlett OH.

40   Jack could speak candidly: Walt Rostow OH.

40   "the unvarnished truth": *RKHL*, p. 110.

40   until Jack ran for: *ATD*, p. 694.

40   Bobby had grown up: *RKHL*, pp. 31–32, 59.

40   He often made a poor: Schlesinger II, p. 589; *LG*, p. 852; *RKHL*, p. 23; *HTF*, p. 635.

40   His salient trait: *RKHL*, p. 45.

40   "He reminds me of a little donkey": Joe Kane to JPK, March 14, 1945, JPKP.

40   "One had the impression": *ATD*, p. 692.

40   Bobby muddled through: *RKHL*, p. 35.

40   Joe Kennedy was nearly sixty: Goodwin I, pp. 328, 339, 421; Richard J. Whalen, *The Founding Father: The Story of Joseph P. Kennedy*, p. 170.

41   "I thought money would give": *AH*, p. 37.

41   "It would take a very great": Robert T. Elson, *The World of Time, Inc.: The Intimate History of a Publishing Enterprise*, vol. 2, *1941–1960*, p. 471.

41   Joe Kennedy's grand political: Joe Kane to JPK, Mar. 20, 1944: "Both boys are lashed to the mast for this election," JPKP.

41   "buying *The Boston Post*": JPK to Willard Kiplinger, June 30, 1961, JPKP.

41   "not because it was natural": JPK to John McCormack, Aug. 8, 1951, JPKP.

41   He had finally attracted: *RKHL*, p. 59; Goodwin I, p. 761.

41   When the call came: David Powers OH; *RKHL*, p. 62.

41   "new generation of leadership": John F. Kennedy, "Acceptance Speech at the 1960 Democratic Convention," July 15, 1960, *The Greatest Speeches of President John F. Kennedy* (Kennedy II), p. 7.

41   "unknown opportunities": ibid.

41   His team had an overtly: *KE*, pp. 255–56.

41   a plurality of only: White I, pp. 336, 382–83.

42   "so thin as to be": ibid., p. 382.

42   "The election of 1960 . . . totally devoid": Theodore H. White, *In Search of History* (White II), p. 479.

42   Only anxiety about Soviet: *PR-JFK*, vol. I, p. xxxiii.

42   "just a member of": Smathers OH.

42   "in the interests of national": *LG*, p. 696.

42   Kennedy relied heavily: Walter Isaacson and Evan Thomas, *The Wise Men: Six Friends and the World They Made*, pp. 593–95.

42   "If I string along": *JWH*, p. 236.

42   Only Dillon was a partisan: *KE*, p. 251.

42   "basic thinking . . . close": *LG*, p. 696.

42   McNamara had been president: Tanzer, p. 161.

43   "range of issues which [JFK]": McNamara interview.

43   McNamara was a rare: Tanzer, p. 178.

43   In keeping with Kennedy-style: McNamara interview.

43   "striking gifts": *ATD*, p. 312.

43   "the blotched pink": *DOAP*, p. 506.

43   a temperament of intense: Tanzer, p. 178; Deborah Shapley, *Promise and Power: The Life and Times of Robert McNamara*, p. 216.

43   He was a year older: Robert McNamara, *In Retrospect,* p. 6; Robert McNamara interview, *Booknotes,* Apr. 23, 1995, C-SPAN.

43   "The things that most men": Tanzer, p. 178.

43   "a faintly quizzical expression": *Newsweek,* Mar. 4, 1963.

43   a household that prized: ibid.

44   "sly of wit and with": Kai Bird, *The Color of Truth: McGeorge Bundy and William Bundy: Brothers in Arms,* p. 58.

44   "Mahatma Bundy": ibid., p. 59.

44   By the time Bundy rose: ibid., pp. 101, 110; Tanzer, pp. 34–36.

44   Bundy's wife, Bostonian: Bird, p. 108; Ben Bradlee interview.

44   Bundy had been a wartime friend: Kathleen Kennedy to family, Jan. 2, 1943; Kathleen Kennedy to family, Jan. 12, 1944, in which she mentioned "Mac Bundy, who Joe says is the smartest guy he ever met and who is going to be my master of ceremonies at a truth and consequences program which I am running on Friday." JPKP.

44   Bundy and Kennedy had renewed: Lincoln, p. 107; Bird, p. 151.

44   "there weren't any Democrats": Charles Bartlett interview.

45   Dillon's paternal grandfather: Tanzer, p. 143.

45   an indignity also suffered: Whalen, pp. 12–13.

45   Similarly, both JFK and Doug: Goodwin I, p. 477.

45   made a $190 million: *Time,* Aug. 18, 1961.

45   Douglas Dillon was born: Douglas Dillon interview; *Time,* Aug. 18, 1961.

45   With six residences: Tanzer, p. 145.

45   "patrician reserve and almost": ibid., p. 140.

45   Through Kennedy's membership: ibid.

45   "We both had rather rapid": Dillon interview.

46   "Liberal governments have foundered": ibid.

46   The U.S. balance of payments: Douglas Dillon OH.

46   "Kennedy was a deeply conservative": Dillon OH-CU.

46   "His father had tremendous": Dillon interview.

46   "lack of confidence": *ATD,* p. 623.

46   "pacifist father": Galbraith interview.

47   "Along with people who like": John Kenneth Galbraith, *Letters to Kennedy* (Galbraith II), citing Galbraith to JFK, Nov. 13, 1960.

47   "I don't see why": *AJ,* p. 44.

47   "a government of the rich": *LG,* p. 700.

47   "suicides on Wall Street": ibid.

47   "He's a fine novelist": Isaacson and Thomas, p. 594.

47   Ironically, Galbraith would: *TCY,* pp. 248, 712.

47   a prestigious post where: Dillon interview.

47   To Dillon, Galbraith would: ibid.

47   "kinetic Democrats": Arthur Schlesinger to JFK, Aug. 26, 1960, Schlesinger Papers, JFKL.

48   Schlesinger was willing: *KE,* p. 49; Anderson, p. 281.

48   To Schlesinger, Jack was: Arthur Schlesinger interview.

48   "skeptical mind": *ATD,* p. 91.

48   "inward and reflective quality": ibid., p. 77.

48   "brawling Irishmen": Hugh Sidey interview.

49   One after another: Arthur Schlesinger to JFK, Nov. 14, 1960, Schlesinger Papers, JFKL; *LG,* p. 700.

49   "We'll have to go along": *ATD,* p. 143.

49   "profoundly realistic mind": ibid., p. 479.

49   "would have loved": Marian Schlesinger OH.

49   "a good address but no clear": *AJ,* p. 24.

49 "I am not sure what": *ATD*, p. 162.
49 "that no American historian": Arthur Schlesinger to Eleanor Roosevelt, Mar. 14, 1961, Franklin D. Roosevelt Library, Hyde Park, NY.
49 "In Jack's mind he must": William vanden Heuvel interview.
49 "I'll write my own official": *JWH*, p. 243.
49 "Adlai was not in": Arthur Schlesinger interview.
50 "same mood and tempo": *ATD*, p. 23.
50 "became sort of prissy": Arthur Schlesinger interview.
50 "never saw Stevenson": *ATD*, p. 463.
50 Behind Stevenson's back: Smathers OH; *RKHL*, p. 134.
50 "They're not queer": John Monagan OH.
50 "a certain amount of arrogance": Elizabeth Ives OH-CU.
50 Kennedy lobbied hard: Newton Minow OH-CU; Arthur Schlesinger to Adlai Stevenson, May 16, 1960, Stevenson Papers, Princeton University.
50 As an inducement: Adlai Stevenson to Arthur Schlesinger, June 7, 1960, Stevenson Papers, Princeton University.
50 "Had [Adlai] come out": Arthur Schlesinger OH-CU.
50 He felt that he: In his letter to Arthur Schlesinger on June 7, 1960, Stevenson wrote: "I have always felt in a way responsible for Jack's recent political progress. . . . In short, I have felt that I launched him." Stevenson Papers, Princeton University.
50 Stevenson still hoped: William Blair interview.
50 "I don't have a cult": Charles Bartlett interview.
50 "I do not feel he's the right": Barbara Ward OH.
51 "You've got twenty-four hours": William Blair interview.
51 "wild demonstration": Dickerson, p. 38.
51 "behaved indecisively and stupidly": Pierre Salinger to Theodore White on JFK in Hyannis from July 27, 1960, to Aug. 8, 1960, Theodore White Papers, Harvard University.
51 Still, Stevenson pined: Agnes Meyer to Adlai Stevenson, Sept. 16, 1960, Stevenson Papers, Princeton University; *LG*, p. 692, quoting David Bruce; Arthur Schlesinger to JFK, Nov. 14, 1960, Schlesinger Papers, JFKL.
51 But Kennedy didn't want: John Sharon OH-CU; John Kenneth Galbraith, *Name-Dropping* (Galbraith III), pp. 99–100.
51 "second-rate job": Marietta Tree OH.
51 "You must never again": Agnes Meyer to Adlai Stevenson, Dec. 14, 1960, Stevenson Papers, Princeton University.
51 "on the phone between the two": Marietta Tree OH.

Chapter Six
52 "Kennedys were everywhere": *ATD*, p. 166.
52 The occasion was: *WP*, Jan. 18, 1961.
52 with the rest of the family: Beale, p. 55.
52 "had all the glamour of": *WP*, Jan. 18, 1961.
52 "Where do you come from": ibid.
52 Her friend Deeda: Deeda Blair interview.
53 "the beautiful nymphets": Marian Schlesinger OH.
53 "the agreeable enthusiasm": *AJ*, p. 104.
53 A graduate of: Leamer I, p. 388.
53 the Kennedy sister most: Arthur Schlesinger interview.
53 Jean's husband, Steve: Leamer I, p. 457.
53 "Listening to the Kennedy brothers": Arthur Schlesinger interview.
53 "He rowed to his objective": Laura Bergquist to James Ellison, ND, "Kennedy—Very Casually," Laura Bergquist Papers, Boston University.

53   In the new administration: *NYHT,* Mar. 10, 1961.
53   Jack came alone: *WP,* Jan. 18, 1961.
53   The President-elect was beaming: Fay, pp. 82–83.
53   "people were having too much": ibid., p. 86.
53   When Jackie flew north: *WP,* Jan. 18, 1961.
53   "almost unnoticed": ibid., Jan. 19, 1961.
54   Nobody came to the airport: ibid.; *NYT,* Jan. 19, 1961.
54   "womenfolk": ibid.
54   "curtail her activities": *JKWH,* p. 43.
54   In fact, her time: Janet Travell, *Office Hours: Day and Night: The Autobiography of Janet Travell, M.D.,* p. 44.
54   The place was swarming: Lincoln, p. 108; *JKWH,* p. 49.
54   For weeks Jack Kennedy had: *KE,* p. 239.
54   "I had heard it in bits": *JKWH,* p. 76.
54   "less daring": *AJ,* p. 14.
54   Kennedy had also sought: *ATD,* p. 163.
54   "adversary" . . . "enemy": Ronald Steel, *Walter Lippmann and the American Century,* p. 525.
54   "square, wintry, bespectacled": Anderson, p. 298.
55   After signing on: ibid., p. 285; Tanzer, p. 8.
55   Sorensen even developed: Sorensen interview.
55   "I could predict": ibid.
55   Sorensen routinely used: Louchheim Journal, July 12, 1959, KSLP.
55   "never have two people": Richard Neustadt interview, Schlesinger Papers, JFKL.
55   He had never seen a finger bowl: Sorensen interview.
55   His father, the son: Tanzer, pp. 10–11.
55   When Sorensen joined: Anderson, p. 277.
55   "spoke easily but almost": *KE,* p. 11.
55   "disliked shows of emotion": ibid., p. 14, quoting John Buchan in *Pilgrim's Way,* JFK's "favorite book," according to Sorensen.
56   "free man" . . . "free mind": ibid., p. 21.
56   Kennedy had many: Frank Morrissey to JPK, July 15, 1955, JPKP.
56   at least once took a $5,000: *HTF,* pp. 114, 186.
56   They contributed research: *PR-JFK,* vol. I, p. xlix; Wills, p. 136; Anderson, p. 282; Charles Spalding OH.
56   "for his invaluable": John F. Kennedy, *Profiles in Courage* (Kennedy I), p. xiv.
56   "log roll": Arthur Krock interview, JCBC.
56   "I worked as hard as": ibid.
56   "sole responsibility": *KE,* p. 69.
56   he asked directly if: McNamara OH.
56   "I am not sure precisely": McNamara interview.
56   "write prose of equal quality": McNamara OH.
57   When Schlesinger wrote: *KE,* pp. 22, 117; *ATD,* p. 69.
57   "tended to resent": *ATD,* p. 70.
57   "Ted is such a little": *AH,* p. 148.
57   "indispensable": *ATD,* p. 70.
57   The title had added: Tanzer, p. 21.
57   "Once Ted got the title": Neustadt interview, Schlesinger Papers, JFKL.
57   By 1961 their writing: *KE,* p. 241.
57   "I don't want people to think": ibid., p. 242.
58   Instead of his predecessor's: *JKWH,* p. 67.
58   "He recognized that even": Goodwin I, p. 813.
58   On Thursday, January 19: *NYT,* Jan. 21, 1961.

58   Earlier in the day: *WP,* Jan. 19, 1961.
58   "If you stay in": Walton OH.
58   "camped out": Truitt interview.
58   Kennedy conducted meetings: *JKWH,* pp. iii, 50, 55.
58   A small task force: John Sharon OH-CU.
58   "understanding of the world": *ATD,* p. 126.
58   "Aren't you excited": *JKWH,* p. 49.
58   "Not in love but": Chiquita Astor interview, Nigel Hamilton Research Collection,
     Massachusetts Historical Society. In the transcript of this taped interview, Chiquita
     Astor recalled her days in New York working for *Vogue,* when JFK "used to ring up at
     odd times" to have "long conversations about everything under the sun." She told
     Hamilton that in one such talk ("I did it on the telephone, not in a car"), "I just asked
     him, I said, 'Have you ever been in love,' this is such a private thing. And he said [*sic*]
     sort of silent for a while and he thought and he thought and he said, 'No, not in love
     but very very interested,' he said. He used the word interested. Very very
     interested . . . I think it wasn't an only woman. I think he was very interested with
     lots of women." Curiously enough, on p. 714 of his book, Hamilton described this
     conversation as having occurred toward the end of Kennedy's life while riding in a
     car: JFK "looked out of the window," and said "No," then "smiled, as he turned back
     to face her" and said, "though often *very* interested."
58   Kennedy called "Billy Boy": *JKWH,* p 60.
58   not only was white her favorite: Cassini I, p. 31.
59   "most ceremonial": Bowles, *Met Catalogue,* p. 59.
59   "a sort of Overall Art Director": Jacqueline Bouvier, "Feature-Question 3," *Vogue*
     Prix de Paris application, May 21, 1951, *Vogue* Materials, JFKL.
59   "the night journey was eerie": *JKWH,* p. 3.
59   "Turn on the lights": ibid., p. 62.
59   The gala, a fundraiser: ibid., p. 63.
59   It was 3:48 a.m.: *NYT,* Jan. 21, 1961.
59   Actresses such as Angie: *JKWH,* pp. 87–88.
59   Dickinson's lifelong friend: Arthur Schlesinger interview.
59   Six years earlier: Leamer I, pp. 446–47.
59   Like her sisters: ibid., pp. 330, 382.
59   The son of Sir Sydney: ibid., p. 446.
60   "Peter was good fun": Sargent Shriver interview.
60   "the worst kind": Cassini II, p. 264.
60   Lawford compensated for: Kurt Niklas, *The Corner Table,* pp. 204–205.
60   By the time of: Leamer I, pp. 487, 523, 542.
60   Jack Kennedy visited: ibid., p. 482; Niklas, pp. 204–207.
60   The Kennedy family grew: Coleman interview; Betty Spalding interview, JCBC.
60   "Why did [Gary] Cooper": Blair, p. 548.
60   "OK now it's time to turn": ibid., p. 160.
60   "enjoyed the game": Gore Vidal, "The Holy Family: The Gospel According to
     Arthur, Paul, Pierre, and William and Several Minor Apostles," *Esquire,* April 1967.

Chapter Seven
61   "We went to the ceremony": Diana Vreeland, *D.V.,* p. 224.
61   "shining young couple": William Walton, *The Evidence of Washington,* p. 51.
61   "greige": Bowles, *Met Catalogue,* p. 55.
61   "I thought she was going to freeze": Vreeland, p. 224.
61   "were coated in mink": *WP,* Jan. 21, 1961.
61   "I just didn't want": *JKWH,* p. 67.
62   22-degree chill: *NYT,* Jan. 21, 1961.

62   JFK removed his: *JKWH,* p. 73; Dickerson, p. 60.
62   "he whistled and rocked": Dickerson, p. 60.
62   The poet had agreed to read: *NYT,* Jan. 15 and 21, 1961.
62   "a poet's benediction": Stewart Udall interview.
62   "It's a good idea": ibid.
62   Instead, he recited: *NYT,* Jan. 21, 1961.
62   it was backed up by: August Heckscher OH; *ATD,* p. 731.
62   Jack Kennedy took only: *WP,* Jan. 21, 1961; *NYT,* Jan. 21, 1961.
62   "with shaking hands and": *WS,* Jan. 21, 1961.
63   The *New York Times* drew: *NYT,* Jan. 21, 1961.
63   "remarkable . . . a revival": ibid., Jan. 22, 1961.
63   "so pure and beautiful": *JKWH,* p. 75.
63   "It was short, to the point": ibid., p. 100.
63   Jack didn't kiss: Bergquist manuscript for profile of Jackie Kennedy, ND, Laura
     Bergquist Papers, Boston University.
63   "Mrs. Truman sat stolidly": ibid.
63   "old kitchen chairs": *WP,* Jan. 19, 1961.
63   "a prisoner of the Secret Service": ibid.
63   TV viewers wrote letters: Bergquist manuscript for profile of Jackie Kennedy, ND,
     Laura Bergquist Papers, Boston University.
63   "I was so proud of Jack": *JKWH,* p. 75.
63   Three District of Columbia: *WP,* Jan. 21, 1961.
63   "It was an extraordinary": Goodwin I, pp. 815–16.
64   In his exuberance: *NYT,* Jan. 21, 1961.
64   "the first members of British": Goodwin I, p. 812.
64   "a blow to the family": *HTF,* p. 584.
64   although Joe had accepted: ibid., p. 581.
64   Three months later: Goodwin I, pp. 622, 686; Hamilton, p. 660.
64   She was buried: Goodwin, pp. 740–41.
64   On inauguration day: Duchess of Devonshire interview; Duke of Devonshire
     interview.
64   JFK could scarcely contain: *JKWH,* p. 81.
64   Reflecting the intermingled themes: *NYT,* Jan. 21, 1961.
64   "like a beatnik": ibid.
64   headed for the reviewing: *NYHT,* Jan. 21, 1961.
65   His heroism had resulted: Hamilton, pp. 556, 559.
65   "pitch black night": ibid., p. 569.
65   Despite the force: ibid., p. 577; Goodwin I, p. 655.
65   They were marooned: Hamilton, pp. 590, 594.
65   Lost in the myth: ibid., p. 567.
65   "give him a medal": ibid., p. 637.
65   The famous coconut, encased: Manchester II, p. 156.
65   When the PT boat display: *NYT,* Jan. 21, 1961.
65   He came from a West Coast: Fay interview.
65   "Kennedy liked people who": Evans interview.
66   "His laugh kind of exploded": Fay interview.
66   "coldly serious man": Fay, p. 74.
66   Fay lacked the necessary experience: ibid., pp. 77, 107.
66   "It was the only appointment": Roswell Gilpatric OH.
66   "it was good to show the President": Fay interview.
66   "You're my pal": ibid.
66   Reed was a Harvard-educated: James Reed interview.
66   "Jack had so many": Jewel Reed interview.

66 During the Depression: James Reed interview.

67 "We had enormous rapport": ibid.

67 Jackie left the inaugural: *JKWH,* p. 84.

67 "I'm not leaving": ibid.

67 Inside the White House: ibid., p. 86.

67 "Lawzy, we sho' is": Richardson, p. 257; Michaelis, p. 173.

67 eight-foot-high headboard: Monkman, pp. 125, 291.

67 "who had drunk a little": Alphand, pp. 349–50.

67 The only absentee: *NYT,* June 6, 1961.

68 "Janet never pushed herself": Jane Ridgeway interview.

68 "the guardians of tradition": Walton, p. 81.

68 The irony was that: Pottker, pp. 7, 53.

68 "She is just lace curtain": Wood interview.

68 Yet Jackie was more of: Molly Nicoll interview.

68 He was a tough-minded tyrant: Pottker, p. 40.

68 "the smartest old rooster": JPK to Bernard Gimbel, July 13, 1953; JPKP.

68 A governess taught her: Pottker, pp. 45, 53.

68 The Bouviers had their own: *JKWH,* pp. 39–41.

69 In fact, the first: Pottker, p. 9.

69 Janet insisted that: ibid., p. 86.

69 Like Jack Bouvier, he was: Yusha Auchincloss interview.

69 Frequently disparaged as: Bradford, pp. 21–22; Kaplan, pp. 65, 495.

69 Auchincloss was actually: Yusha Auchincloss interview; Ridgeway interview.

69 "be famous": JBK to Yusha Auchincloss, Jan. 15, 1945, courtesy of Yusha Auchincloss.

69 "take short rest periods": *NYT,* Jan. 18, 1961.

69 She and Jack had been: ibid., Jan. 21, 1961.

69 "I couldn't get out": *JKWH,* p. 85.

70 "breathlessly, in a gentle": ibid., p. 90.

70 once more intended: Rhea, p. 134; Bowles, *Met Catalogue,* p. 66.

70 The Kennedys followed: *JKWH,* pp. 92–93.

70 "I just crumpled": ibid., p. 94.

70 In Kennedy's restless: *NYT,* Jan. 21, 1961.

70 Earlier in the week: Alsop II, p. 432.

70 "If the lights are on": ibid.

70 "Over a long period": Blair, p. 362.

70 "the fascinating people": Duke interview.

70 Flo had been: Earl E.T. Smith Jr. interview.

70 a wealthy and solidly: ibid.

71 "Man is by nature": Florence Pritchett Smith, *These Entertaining People* (Smith I), p. 1.

71 "very keen": Duke interview.

71 "Send Diamonds!": Blair, p. 632.

71 Flo grew close: Smith interview.

71 "the best collection of English": *New York Journal-American,* Nov. 2, 1960.

71 "Why don't you jump in": Fay, p. 94.

71 "Neither Angie nor Kim Novak": Fay interview.

71 "there were no Hollywood stars there": Peter Duchin interview.

72 Helen Chavchavadze, a twenty-seven-year-old: Helen Chavchavadze interview.

72 "She was just gorgeous": Ben Bradlee interview.

72 "a role model of freedom": Chavchavadze interview.

72 "He was not at that point": ibid.

72 "He followed me home": ibid.

72   "One of the reasons is": JFK to Helen Chavchavadze, ND, courtesy of Helen
      Chavchavadze.
72   "A little innuendo": Chavchavadze interview.
72   "he was cold and negative": ibid.
73   "By his appearance": ibid.
73   "I never knew if Jackie": ibid.
73   "almost an artifact": Hector interview.
73   Savile Row suits and waistcoats: Edwin M. Yoder Jr., *Joe Alsop's Cold War,* p. 29.
73   "weirdly shaped and more": Philip Graham fiftieth birthday toast to Joseph Alsop,
      Oct. 11, 1960, Alsop Papers, LOC.
73   "dear boy" . . . "darling": Robert W. Merry, *Taking On the World: Joseph and Stewart
      Alsop—Guardians of the American Century,* p. xxiv.
73   During a trip to the Soviet: ibid., pp. 362–63.
74   "Joe was gay": Ben Bradlee interview.
74   "exaggerated WASP": ibid.
74   "cousin Eleanor": Joseph Alsop to JBK, Aug. 4, 1960, Alsop Papers, LOC.
74   she entered the marriage: Merry, p. 365.
74   commanded "general conversation": ibid., p. 367.
74   Alsop had never liked: Joseph Alsop OH.
74   "made my flesh crawl": Alsop II, p. 406.
74   "I am not like [Jack] who": *HTF,* p. xxiii.
74   Alsop had dismissed: Alsop II, pp. 410–11.
74   It was only when Alsop: Merry, p. 341.
74   "wears gloom like a toga": *Time,* July 25, 1960.
75   But their partnership: Merry, p. xvii.
75   "stuffy and self-satisfied": Yoder, p. 147.
75   "Joe Alsop was a fawner": Tom Braden interview.
75   By cultivating Alsop: James Symington interview.
75   "a voluptuous daydream": JBK to Joseph Alsop, ND (probably April 1960), Alsop
      Papers, LOC.
75   Alsop assumed an avuncular: Elizabeth Winthrop interview.
75   "when to put a touch": ibid.
75   "Jackie was a Bouvier": Ben Bradlee interview.
75   Kennedy relished Alsop's acerbic: Joseph Alsop OH; Yoder, p. 168.
75   Like other prominent journalists: Merry, p. 357; Joseph Alsop OH.
75   "enjoyed pleasure": Joseph Alsop OH.
76   "All the lights on the outside": ibid.; Alsop II, p. 434.
76   "in the bright light": Joseph Alsop OH.
76   "like something on the stage": ibid.
76   "made a small, almost imperceptible": *JKWH,* p. 96.
76   Alsop offered a bowl: Alsop II, pp. 94, 435.
76   Kennedy mingled for: Merry, p. 358.
76   "the greatest of American delicacies": Alsop II, p. 435.

Chapter Eight

77   "let's get this country": Anderson, p. 29; Walt Rostow OH.
77   "The atmosphere bubbles": Isaacson and Thomas, p. 601.
77   The economy, however, had slid: *PK,* p. 37; Merry, p. 340.
78   "The glow of the White House": *ATD,* p. 207.
78   Jack Kennedy had a deep: *KE,* pp. 260, 278, 281; Arthur Schlesinger interview.
78   "an idealist without illusions": John Morton Blum, "Kennedy's Ten-Foot Shelf,"
      NYT Magazine, Mar. 12, 1961; *KE,* p. 22.
78   "on action, not philosophy": *KE,* p. 386.

78 The Eisenhower White House: Dillon interview.
78 "President Kennedy was under": ibid.
78 "ministry of talent": *KE*, p. 254.
78 He slashed the size: Sorensen interview.
78 "I can't afford only": Neustadt interview, Schlesinger Papers, JFKL.
78 "to get information in his mind": *KE*, p. 259.
78 "unimpressed by the emotional": Neustadt interview, Schlesinger Papers, JFKL.
78 "clash of ideas": Tanzer, p. xvii.
79 "deal up and down the line": Richard Helms interview.
79 "enormous energy to maintain": Walt Rostow OH.
79 "on the phone more than 50": *KE*, p. 371.
79 "great man" theory: Berlin OH.
79 JFK had studied: Halle OH.
79 "astonishing" list: White II, p. 469.
79 "read and reread": Jacqueline Kennedy, "Kennedy Memorabilia: These Are the
     Things I Hope Will Show How He Really Was," *Life*, May 29, 1964.
79 The first book JFK gave: *ATD*, p. 105. Four decades later, President George W. Bush
     would name *The Raven* as his favorite book (*WP*, Mar. 9, 2003).
79 "was dubious about the theory": Sorensen interview.
79 "Kennedy felt individuals": Arthur Schlesinger interview.
80 "the reception room in a Radcliffe dorm": *AJ*, p. 210.
80 On white linen tablecloths: *NYT*, May 20, 1963.
80 "snow" a visitor: Baldrige interview.
80 She always ate: *Newsweek*, Jan. 7, 1963.
80 "complex little area": Gamarekian OH.
80 "headlong into a closet": *AJ*, p. 17.
80 For display in the Oval: *Newsweek*, Feb. 6, 1961.
80 "hanging pictures": JBK to LBJ, Nov. 26, 1963, LBJL.
80 "setting out his collection": ibid.
80 "austere formality": *NYT*, Jan. 29, 1961; Abbott and Rice, p. 212.
80 "still restless" . . . "He paces": Salinger to White, Mar. 6, 1961, White Papers, Harvard
     University.
80 "opening letters himself": *Time*, Mar. 3, 1961.
80 Kennedy would stroll: Barbara Gamarekian interview.
80 "sort of floating on": Gamarekian OH.
81 Kennedy fostered an almost: *WS*, Jan. 20, 1961; Reed OH; Bartlett OH; Anderson,
     p. 197.
81 "how Kennedy generated love": Rostow OH.
81 "was like being Alice": *JKWH*, p. 99.
81 Stamped by his privileged: David Powers interview, JCBC.
81 Powers's parents had been: ibid.
81 for whom Joe Alsop served: Yoder, p. 49.
81 "irrepressible leprechaun": *Newsweek*, Apr. 23, 1962.
81 He knew nearly every detail: *JWH*, p. 252; *LG*, p. 808.
81 "always had someone": *HTF*, p. 694.
81 they underestimated his savvy: Galbraith interview.
82 "aggressively shy": Powers interview, JCBC.
82 "tub talk": *JWH*, p. 291.
82 "Irish on his chauffeur's": White memo, Jan. 13, 1963, White Papers, Harvard
     University.
82 tales of Chinese peasants: Powers interview, JCBC; *JWH*, p. 252.
82 "my kind of Shah": *Newsweek*, Apr. 23, 1962.
82 "a nice employee": Billings OH.

82 "He was a perennial": Gamarekian interview.
82 "thought he was crude": Baldrige interview.
82 "friends from the past": ibid.
82 Few knew that he carried: O'Donnell, p. 295; Anderson, p. 230.
82 "quiet almost fanatical": *DOAP,* p. 120.
83 "A lot of noise, huh?": O'Donnell, p. 210.
83 He was the varsity quarterback: Evan Thomas interview; O'Donnell, p. 32.
83 O'Donnell had grown: O'Donnell, p. 38.
83 "Kenny's genius was simply": ibid., p. 193.
83 Not only did the thirty-six-year-old: Nancy Dutton interview; *JWH,* p. 226;
     O'Donnell, p. 271.
83 "hovering, grim-faced": Bartlett OH.
83 He was decisive and crisp: *KE,* p. 263; Anderson, p. 240.
83 "with his gut": Nancy Dutton interview.
83 plenty of friends and aides: Dillon interview.
84 But in her disarming fashion: *Newsweek,* Jan. 7, 1963.
84 "I thought I fired her": Sorensen interview.
84 she was one of the few: Anderson, p. 106.
84 O'Donnell considered Lincoln's: ibid., p. 206.
84 "to talk about leaks": Sorensen interview.
84 staff meetings only stirred: Anderson, p. 201.
84 disbanded the council's: Dillon interview; *PK,* p. 53.
84 "a waste of time": Arthur Schlesinger interview; *KE,* p. 283.
84 When Kennedy did call: *KE,* p. 283.
84 "curious dim figures": Stewart Alsop to Martin Sommers, Sept. 7, 1961, Alsop
     Papers, LOC.
84 "We didn't even have": Udall interview.
84 "hard driving but easy": *KE,* p. 372.
84 With the exception: *PR-JFK,* vol. I, p. liv.
84 "Miz Lincoln": Anderson, p. 106.
85 "enough of a remoteness": Gamarekian OH.
85 A handful of key aides: *KE,* p. 374.
85 "quick, tough, laconic": *ATD,* p. 438.
85 "more than thirty seconds": Marcus Raskin interview.
85 ideological, earnest, or: Walt Rostow interview.
85 His preferred time frame: *KE,* p. 372.
85 "was terribly taut": Berlin OH.
85 "a stimulant": Ward OH.
85 "He often cut short": *KE,* p. 372.
85 "lean forward, his eyes": *ATD,* p. 673.
85 he would betray his impatience: ibid., p. 672; Rostow OH.
85 "exactly what the words": Berlin OH.
85 He had little tolerance: Charles Bartlett interview.
85 "Never even in conversation": *AJ,* pp. 554–55.
85 on the assumption that if: *ATD,* p. 673; Smathers OH.
85 "contrary arguments, sometimes": Harlech OH.
86 "It was his habit": Joseph Alsop OH.
86 "beautiful mind": Curtis Prendergast, with Geoffrey Colvin, *The World of Time Inc.:
     The Intimate History of a Changing Enterprise, 1960–1980,* p. 22.
86 "acute" . . . "penetrating": Andrei Gromyko to Comrade N. S. Khrushchev, "John
     Fitzgerald Kennedy—Political Character Sketch," Aug. 3, 1960, Cold War
     International History Project, Woodrow Wilson International Center for Scholars.
86 "aptitude for facts": Joseph Alsop OH.

86   "a good catalyst": Gromyko memo, Aug. 3, 1960.
86   "a city of southern efficiency": Sorensen interview.
86   "Kennedy's genius": ibid.
86   a small black leather volume: Ben Bradlee, "He Had That Special Grace," *Newsweek*, Dec. 2, 1963.
86   "I'll read [an article]": *AH*, p. 101.
86   although not profoundly: Joseph Alsop OH.
86   propping up a book: *ATD*, p. 105.
86   sometimes taking a volume: Horne, p. 289.
86   "information, comparison, insight": Arthur Schlesinger interview.
86   an exploration of economic dissent: John Kenneth Galbraith interview with Harry Kreisler, UC Berkeley, Mar. 27, 1986.
86   "two or three once-famous": Henry Luce OH.
87   "did not go out": Neustadt interview, Schlesinger Papers, JFKL.
87   When he hired Dillon: Dillon interview.
87   "to protect myself": ibid.
87   a necessary "counterweight": *PK*, p. 27.
87   "Heller was supposed to": Dillon interview.
87   Kennedy wouldn't put up: *KE*, pp. 55, 374.
87   "all the eggheads": Harold Macmillan, *Pointing the Way: 1959–1961* (Macmillan I), p. 352.
87   "When Bundy passed": Anderson, p. 207.
87   Sorensen and his deputy: Leamer II, p. 477.
87   "political buccaneers": *AJ*, p. 19.
87   "an incompetent long-winded": DBD, Mar. 28, 1961.
87   "should be spanked": Rowe to White, May 25, 1961, White Papers, Harvard University.
88   "aggressive individualists": *KE*, p. 260. Arthur Schlesinger also spoke of the "jostling and body checks" among Kennedy's top aides (Arthur Schlesinger interview).
88   "soft jackets and easy shoes": Tanzer, p. xvi.
88   "You have to understand": Anderson, p. 217.
88   Jackie actually spent: Baldrige interview.
88   "unhappy and uncertain": *AJ*, p. 23.
88   "Arthur was always worried": Ben Bradlee interview.
88   "There were frustrating moments": Arthur Schlesinger interview.
88   "bivouacking in his chair": Halle OH.
88   "that wonderfully spare": Rostow OH.
88   "They were meditations": Arthur Schlesinger interview.

Chapter Nine

89   "dark and dreary": JBK to Henry du Pont, June 8, 1962, Winterthur Archives.
89   "propped up in the enormous": *JKWH*, p. 101.
89   "I couldn't get out of bed": Jacqueline Kennedy Onassis OH, John Sherman Cooper Oral History Project, University of Kentucky.
89   She often made such: Jewel Reed interview; Baldrige interview.
89   In fact, Jackie left: West, p. 208.
89   She took walks: ibid., p. 198.
89   "We've got a lot of work": ibid., p. 197.
90   "the conflict between what": Joseph Alsop to JBK, Aug. 4, 1960, Alsop Papers, LOC.
90   "the most stylish and most effective": ibid.
90   "very perceptive": JBK to Joseph Alsop, ND (probably mid-August 1960), Alsop Papers, LOC.

90   "veil of lovely inconsequence": Arthur M. Schlesinger Jr., "Jacqueline Kennedy in the White House," *Met Catalogue,* p. 3.

90   "caught in this maw": Louchheim Journal, Mar. 21, 1959, KSLP.

90   "57-year-old grandmother": *NYT,* Oct. 1, 1961.

90   She had been educated: *WP,* Jan. 13, 1961; *NYT,* Oct. 1, 1961.

90   "I was tired & I wanted": JBK to Walton, June 8, 1962, Walton Papers, JFKL.

91   "ninety-nine things that I had to do": Gallagher, p. 159.

91   "where a woman's place is": JBK to Nellie Connally, Dec. 1, 1963, courtesy of Nellie Connally.

91   "compassion for women": Hugh Sidey, *John F. Kennedy, President* (Sidey I), p. 97; Sidey interview.

91   "great presence and control": *NYT,* Nov. 26, 1960.

91   "I really don't think I am better": Jacqueline Bouvier to Yusha Auchincloss, Jan. 15, 1945, courtesy of Yusha Auchincloss.

91   wishing she had gone to Radcliffe: *LG,* p. 914.

91   "I did not want to live like": Wilson, *Life,* Aug. 24, 1959.

91   "Jackie had a certain quality": Cassini interview.

91   "you know everything": Jacqueline Bouvier to Yusha Auchincloss, Nov. 20, 1945, courtesy of Yusha Auchincloss.

91   "make you feel quite secretly": Jacqueline Bouvier, "Thesis-Topic 1," *Vogue* Prix de Paris application, May 21, 1951, *Vogue* Materials, JFKL.

91   "sphinxlike": Cassini II, p. 305.

91   Jackie's favorite statue: Pierre-Marie Rudelle to author, May 28, 2001; Radziwill interview.

92   "A sphinx is rather what": JBK to Adlai Stevenson, Feb. 4, 1963, Stevenson Papers, Princeton University.

92   "She has a great deal": *Newsweek,* Feb. 6, 1961.

92   As a general's wife: Beale, p. 39.

92   "a woman's place in public": ibid.

92   Yet Bess also went: *AH,* p. 278; Michael Beschloss on *The NewsHour with Jim Lehrer,* July 31, 2000; Beale, p. 39.

92   "she kept her family": Bowles, *Met Catalogue,* p. 84; Bergquist manuscript for profile of Jackie Kennedy, ND, Laura Bergquist Papers, Boston University.

92   "it is very silly to try": Janet Auchincloss OH.

92   "organizing things as well": JBK to Walton, June 8, 1962, Walton Papers, JFKL.

92   "overall unified supervision": *JKWH,* p. 320.

92   "the use of power that": JBK to Walton, June 8, 1962, Walton Papers, JFKL.

92   "charismatic presence": Nancy Tuckerman, "A Personal Reminiscence," *The Estate of Jacqueline Kennedy Onassis Catalogue,* Sotheby's, 1996, p. 15.

93   "all the accepted games": *WP,* Feb. 23, 1963.

93   "distinctive looks": Tuckerman, Sotheby's catalogue, p. 16.

93   "a special bond": ibid.

93   "Nancy knew everything": Janet Felton Cooper interview.

93   Quiet and somewhat withdrawn: Audrey Koehler interview; Elizabeth Boyd interview.

93   "intelligence, wit, and sense": Tuckerman, Sotheby's catalogue, p. 15.

93   At Farmington they would sneak: Jacqueline Bouvier to Yusha Auchincloss, Jan. 14, 1943, April 20, 1945, courtesy of Yusha Auchincloss. Jackie told her stepbrother that she and Tucky would often stare out the window of their dorm, pretending that their pencils were cigarettes.

93   "she had me walk under": Tuckerman, Sotheby's catalogue, p. 19.

93   When the Kennedy administration: Cooper interview.

93   "diabolically figure out": JBK to Walton, June 8, 1962, Walton Papers, JFKL.

93   "for the very reason that": *JKWH,* p. 33.
94   "Jackie Kennedy put a little": Vreeland, p. 223.
94   "the stage on which the drama": Abbott and Rice, p. 5.
94   Jackie had decided: *NYT,* Feb. 24, 1961.
94   "had such wonderful taste": *NYHT,* Apr. 12, 1961.
94   Jackie moved quickly: Abbott and Rice, p. 18.
94   the suggestion of Wilmarth: Bradford, pp. 26, 29.
94   a trustee of Winterthur: Ruth Lord, *Henry F. du Pont and Winterthur: A Daughter's Portrait,* p. 225.
94   Du Pont was shy: West, p. 243.
94   "snap the whip": Cooper interview.
95   "my cozy little Rolls": Henry du Pont to Jayne Wrightsman, Nov. 22, 1961, Winterthur Archives.
95   "He would leave and we would": Cooper interview.
95   "reflect so eloquently": Lord, p. 225.
95   "a symbol of cultural": Henry du Pont to JBK, Mar. 9, 1961, Winterthur Archives.
95   But after *Life* magazine: *JKWH,* p. 284; Schlesinger, *Met Catalogue,* p. 4.
95   "monotonous" . . . "present living": Julian Boyd and Lyman Butterfield, "The White House as a Symbol," Apr. 24, 1961, Winterthur Archives.
95   "would come flying in": JBK to Henry du Pont, Sept. 20, 1963, JFKL.
95   they would exchange more than: Lord, p. 226.
95   "That hall was getting so": JBK to Henry du Pont, Oct. 10, 1961, Winterthur Archives.
95   "purely a creation of": JBK to Lady Bird Johnson, Dec. 1, 1963, LBJL.
95   "Jackie had everyone's number": Cooper interview.
95   "talked with me for hours": *WP,* Sept. 5, 1962.
96   Jackie would eventually pull: Mary Lasker OH-CU.
96   "everything Jefferson was": *JKWH,* p. 339.
96   "stood above all of them": Edith Wharton, *The Age of Innocence,* p. 33.
96   "The Mellons didn't have to": Charles interview.
96   By 1961, Paul and Bunny: Paul Mellon, *Reflections in a Silver Spoon,* p. 381.
96   "the man who used to own Listerine": RK to children, Jan. 7, 1950, JPKP.
96   "where girls didn't go to college": Burton Hersh, *The Mellon Family: A Fortune in History* (Hersh I), p. 406; Eve Fout interview.
96   She was educated at: Eve Fout interview.
97   outfits for gardening: Cooper interview.
97   "Bunny was kind of a star": Duchess of Devonshire interview.
97   In 1948, Bunny married: Mellon, pp. 224–25.
97   "Having known each other": ibid., p. 225.
97   "We became partners to help": Hersh I, p. 407.
97   Both Paul and Bunny stayed: Janet Grayson Whitehouse interview; Eve Fout interview.
97   Paul Mellon was a gentleman: Mellon, pp. 270, 322.
97   she helped Joe Alsop devise: Paul Richard interview; Yoder, p. 29.
97   "interior landscapes": Mellon, p. 271.
97   The spacious and perfectly: Charles interview; Richard interview.
97   She spent her days: Mellon, p. 226.
97   small vase of buttercups: Oliver Murray interview.
97   Shortly after the birth: Rachel Lambert Mellon, "Jacqueline Bouvier Kennedy: A Reminiscence," *Met Catalogue,* p. 13.
97   "Marvelous woman, frightfully": Duke of Devonshire interview.
97   "Lady Foulmouth": Sally Bedell Smith, *Reflected Glory: The Life of Pamela Churchill Harriman* (Smith III), p. 101.

98   "I loved your house": Mellon, *Met Catalogue,* p. 13.
98   "I even loved the stale": ibid.
98   "It never bothered Mrs. Kennedy": James Roe Ketchum interview.
98   "Bunny was pleased": Baldrige interview.
98   Bunny shared Jackie's: Paul Manno interview; Whitehouse interview; Kenneth Battelle interview.
98   "I'm not scholarly myself": Hersh I, p. 406.
98   "What appealed to Jackie": Radziwill interview.
98   "true to her self": Mellon, *Met Catalogue,* p. 14.
98   Less obvious was the model: Mellon, p. 225.
98   Although Paul was naturally: Richard interview; Mellon, p. 270; Paul Fout interview.
98   "She has a moat": Baldrige interview.
98   Both Paul and Bunny consulted: Mellon, pp. 342–43.
98   "fluffs and frills": Whitehouse interview.
98   "At dinner they would talk": Murray interview.
99   "You don't need to shout": Charles interview. Oatsie Leiter Charles noted that the friendship of Paul Mellon and Dorcas Hardin "went on for years. Dorcas was one of my closest friends, but we never talked about it."
99   "What does Bunny use": JBK to Janet Felton, ND, courtesy of Janet Felton Cooper.
99   Bunny worked with Jackie: *JKWH,* pp. 138–40; Bowles, *Met Catalogue,* p. 22.
99   "lugubrious Victorian palms": Bowles, *Met Catalogue,* p. 22.
99   She often supplied: Bunny Mellon interview, WMP; Crespi interview.
99   "six different sets": Cooper interview.
99   Bunny installed her favorite: Lawrence Arata OH.
99   In this instance, she looked: Baldrige interview; Crespi interview.
99   "it was a cultural friendship": Marella Agnelli interview.
99   "Little Egypt": Francesca Stanfill, "Jayne's World," *Vanity Fair,* January 2003.
100 "the most immaculate man": Thomas Hoving, *Making the Mummies Dance,* p. 90.
100 A polo-playing ladies' man: Stanfill, *Vanity Fair,* January 2003.
100 With a net worth of: RK to Helene Arpels, June 2, 1952, JPKP.
100 "Jayne, come over here": Manno interview.
100 "her face twitches": Cecil Beaton, *The Unexpurgated Beaton: The Cecil Beaton Diaries as He Wrote Them* (Beaton I), p. 84.
100 Boudin headed Jansen: *NYT,* Apr. 1, 1961; Bowles, *Met Catalogue,* p. 24.
100 "Jayne consulted Boudin": Manno interview.
100 Jayne first met: Khoi Nguyen, "Gilt Complex," *Connoisseur,* September 1991.
100 a pound of caviar: Lucius Ordway to JPK, Nov. 26 (no year given), JPKP.
100 "Jaynie" once helped: RK to children, Aug. 18, 1955; Jayne Wrightsman to JPK, Mar. 31 (probably 1946), JPKP.
101 when Joe was about: Charles Wrightsman to JPK, Jan. 13, 1958, JPKP.
101 "who knows—she may": *NYT,* Apr. 1, 1961.
101 During his visit: Manno interview.
101 "I'm still in a glow": JBK to Jayne Wrightsman, May 1959, JFKL.
101 Having worked on: Bowles, *Met Catalogue,* p. 24; Abbott and Rice, p. 53.
101 "trained as an interior": Martin Filler, "A Clash of Tastes at the White House," *NYT Magazine,* Nov. 2, 1980.
101 "eye for placement": Bowles, *Met Catalogue,* p. 25.
101 "to represent the United States": *NYT,* Apr. 1, 1961.
101 "friendship": ibid.
101 "primary visionary": Bowles, *Met Catalogue,* p. 24.
101 Chattering and sharing: West, p. 243; Manno interview.
101 "a wife in name only": Manno interview.
102 "La Maison Blanche": Wrightsman to JBK, Apr. 5, 1961, JFKL.

102   "stroke of genius": du Pont to JBK, Oct. 5, 1961, Winterthur Archives.

102   Even so, Parish threatened: Abbott and Rice, pp. 83, 157, 163; Cooper interview.

102   "say this tactfully": Cooper interview.

102   Du Pont was irked: Abbott and Rice, p. 35.

102   "I shudder to think": du Pont to Wrightsman, Nov. 22, 1961, Winterthur Archives.

102   During his White House: Cooper interview.

102   he took placement: Docent's commentary, Winterthur.

102   "fresh and vigorous": Lorraine Pearce to du Pont, Dec. 13, 1961, Winterthur Archives.

102   to undo du Pont's scheme: ibid.

102   Jackie often rearranged: Abbott and Rice, p. 39; Lord, p. 231.

102   "Mr. du Pont was rigid": Susan Mary Alsop interview.

102   "You are a wonder man": Wrightsman to du Pont, July 7, 1961, Winterthur Archives.

102   "each 'little touch'": JBK to du Pont, April 1962, Winterthur Archives.

102   "Mrs. Kennedy juggled": Ketchum interview.

102   "As the elder statesman": Lord, p. 231.

103   "that could survive the marauding": Cassini II, p. 304.

103   Joe Kennedy bought: Janet Des Rosiers to John Ford, Dec. 5, 1952, JPKP.

103   "They didn't even own": Walton interview, JCBC.

103   whose passion for art: Richardson, p. 120, quoting publisher Charles Scribner III, a fellow Princetonian, who read Billings's senior thesis on Tintoretto: "That familiar enthusiasm was matched by solid scholarship, elegant and altogether passionate prose, and an extraordinary degree of art historical sophistication and range of insight from an undergraduate. . . . It might easily have been written by a young Bernard Berenson or Kenneth Clark. It revealed a genuine talent and dimension in Lem that I found deeply moving."

103   "he really had no idea": Harlech OH.

103   "he liked the door knocker": Janet Auchincloss OH. The observation was made by the interlocutor, Joan Braden.

103   "Do you think we're prisoners": ibid.

103   "paintings of water": JBK to Fletcher Knebel, ND (for use in Knebel, Look, Jan. 17, 1961), Fletcher Knebel Papers, Boston University.

103   At Jackie's urging: Knebel, Look, Jan. 17, 1961; AH, p. 98.

103   "did a lot of terrible": AH, p. 99.

103   "he had no gift": ibid.

103   "he was really very visual": Mary Lasker OH-CU.

103   "You can tell by the boards": Halle OH.

103   "Furniture classes sprung up": Dickerson, p. 68.

104   JFK took to stopping: Lorraine Pearce interview with Steven O'Connor, University of Delaware, summer 1994.

104   "John F. Kennedy's feeling": Walton, p. 51.

104   "every morning for something": Walton OH.

104   Together Walton and Kennedy: ibid.; JKWH, p. 104.

104   a Citizens Committee to Save: WS, May 10, 1961.

104   "I want you to remember": Walton OH.

Chapter Ten

106   who had been with: DOAP, p. 409.

106   "She won't need much": West, p. 198.

106   "with words alone": Gallagher, p. 209.

106   "a little puffed up": Truitt interview.

106   "Mommy," not "Mummy": Bergquist manuscript for profile of Jackie Kennedy, ND, Laura Bergquist Papers, Boston University.

106   "She usually had": Ketchum interview.

106 "She was a remarkable mother": Wilson interview.

106 As a surprise for: Caroline Kennedy, *The Best Loved Poems of Jacqueline Kennedy Onassis*, p. 31.

106 "a tremendous sense": Ketchum interview.

106 "Let's go kiss": Bergquist manuscript for profile of Jackie Kennedy, Laura Bergquist Papers, Boston University.

106 "so happy, so abandoned": West, p. 217.

106 "a quality that seems to": Bergquist manuscript for profile of Jackie Kennedy, Laura Bergquist Papers, Boston University.

106 In her quest to: Truitt interview; Elizabeth Boyd interview; Hass interview; Wilson interview.

107 "Jackie thought it would be more": Wilson interview.

107 But JFK promised: Hass interview.

107 For the first four months: *WP,* Sept. 8, 1961; Anne Mayfield interview.

107 the following fall she was joined: *NYT,* Sept. 20, 1962; Jaclin Marlin interview.

107 Jackie designed: West, pp. 217–18; Gallagher, p. 132.

107 "as the average medium- to high": Sidey I, p. 96.

107 "Jack Kennedy with children": Truitt interview.

107 three-clap summons: Bishop, p. 38.

107 "a man who all his life": Rostow OH.

108 "with an air of businesslike": Charles Heckscher memo, June 19, 1963, Schlesinger Papers, JFKL.

108 "I always heard back": Baldrige I, p. 180.

108 "a slender butterfly": Hugh Sidey, Chester V. Clifton, and Cecil Stoughton, *The Memories: JFK, 1961–1963* (Sidey II), p. 83.

108 She continued to keep: West, p. 202.

108 "She was determined": Baldrige interview.

108 Jackie had breakfast: Gallagher, p. 99; *AH,* p. 279; *JKWH,* p. 239.

108 After pushing John: *JKWH,* p. 23; Cooper interview; Bishop, p. 38; West, p. 217; *AH,* p. 521.

108 She avoided the White House pool: Baldrige interview.

108 she believed that she: *JKWH,* p. 231.

108 At first she had toyed: Ketchum interview.

108 But like her predecessors: ibid.; *JKWH,* p. 232; Gallagher, p. 130.

109 eleven rooms including: William G. Allman, White House Curator, to author, Apr. 1, 2003; Abbott and Rice, p. 146; Manchester II, p. 5.

109 "an average Park Avenue tycoon": *ATD,* p. 665.

109 At the west end: Bishop, p. 58; Abbott and Rice, pp. 146–48; *DOAP,* p. 547; Manchester II, p. 6.

109 specially designed Tiffany bookplates: Gallagher, p. 181.

109 A door on the north side: Abbott and Rice, pp. 152, 155–56.

109 The Kennedys had their own: Traphes Bryant, *Dog Days at the White House,* p. 45, for a diagram of the White House second-floor layout.

109 The immediacy of: *ATD,* p. 665; *DOAP,* p. 619.

109 "without the slightest embarrassment": *CWK,* p. 151.

109 "the last guests [were] bidding": *DOAP,* p. 619.

109 "like the Lubianka!": *JKWH,* p. 100.

110 "a way of letting sunlight": Wilson interview.

110 "the heart of the White House": *JKWH,* p. 251.

110 Jackie usually spent: Baldrige I, p. 185.

110 "I want to live my life": Jacqueline Kennedy Onassis OH, John Sherman Cooper Oral History Project, University of Kentucky.

110 She had a light lunch: *JKWH,* p. 232; Gallagher, p. 103; West, p. 203.

110 "fifty to one hundred": Jacqueline Bouvier, "Fashion-Question 2," *Vogue* Prix de Paris application, May 21, 1951, *Vogue* Materials, JFKL.

110 120 pounds, according to Oleg: Cassini interview. At first Cassini balked when asked the weight of his most famous client, whose measurements he meticulously recorded. But when Tish Baldrige—who was six inches taller than Jackie—guessed 140 pounds, Cassini replied, "With all due respect, that is ridiculous. Jackie was at most 120 pounds."

110 "She was very slim": ibid.

110 "with the rigor of a diamond": Baldrige I, p. 182.

110 If Jackie added: ibid.

110 a barrel-shaped gold cigarette case: *NYHT,* Apr. 12, 1961.

110 "She was always smoking": Crespi interview; Walton OH.

110 The landmark surgeon general's: *CWK,* p. 234.

110 Few outside the Kennedy circle: Bishop, p. 99.

110 "newly lit cigarettes": Gallagher, p. 233.

111 "take furtive puffs": Lawrence O'Brien, *No Final Victories,* p. 56.

111 Afternoons for Jackie: Bishop, p. 101; Gallagher, p. 174.

111 Camouflaged by a head scarf: Baldrige I, p. 179.

111 "she had a way of rendering": Truitt interview.

111 Jackie rarely held: Baldrige I, p. 185; Ketchum interview; Cooper interview.

111 "For others she insisted": West, p. 195.

111 "never saw her dealing": Lady Bird Johnson to author, June 7, 2001.

111 Tish Baldrige never accepted: Baldrige I, p. 186.

111 "ears pinned back": Heckscher OH.

111 "The President came": Ymelda Dixon interview.

112 "Saint Bird": Baldrige I, p. 183.

112 "little-girl quality": Lady Bird Johnson to author, June 7, 2001.

112 "to reinvent the White House": Baldrige I, p. 185.

112 "I was lying through": Gamarekian interview.

112 when he told June Havoc: *NYT,* Feb. 28, 1961; *WP,* Mar. 1, 1961.

112 For all of Jackie's surface: Gallagher, p. 120.

112 "She gets pressured": Baldrige interview.

112 "I want Jackie to feel": Baldrige I, p. 186.

112 "stiffness, even shyness": Bergquist manuscript for profile of Jackie Kennedy, ND, Laura Bergquist Papers, Boston University.

112 the nails that she would pick: Crespi interview; Baldrige interview.

112 "She would get terribly down": Baldrige interview.

112 It took vigorous physical: Eve Fout interview.

112 "great steep hills": *NYT,* Jan. 14, 1962.

112 "watch the water": Jacqueline Bouvier to Yusha Auchincloss, Jan. 14, 1943, courtesy of Yusha Auchincloss.

112 "I love them both": ibid.

113 "People would pull up stakes": Ketchum interview.

113 "the most private place": JBK to Eve Fout, July 1962, courtesy of Eve Fout.

113 Glen Ora: *JKWH,* p. 225.

113 Jackie preferred the verdant: JBK to Roswell Gilpatric, June 13, 1963, quoted in *WP,* Feb. 10, 1970.

113 "comfortable and unpolished": *AJ,* p. 294.

113 Jackie and Sister Parish organized: *JKWH,* p. 226.

113 Jackie belatedly discovered: Cassini I, p. 49, quoting JBK to Cassini, Feb. 17, 1961.

113 Bit of Irish: *NYHT,* Mar. 25, 1961; *Time,* Jan. 26, 1962; Eve Fout interview.

113 tourists peered through: West, p. 216.

113 "Jackie wanted her kids": Eve Fout interview.

113   "giving them baths": JBK to Eve Fout, ND (probably July 1962), courtesy of Eve
      Fout.

113   She could buy a cup: Eve Fout interview; Whitehouse interview; *Time,* Mar. 24, 1961.

114   "I do not consider myself": JBK to Eve Fout, ND (probably July 1962), courtesy of
      Eve Fout.

114   The two weekdays: Baldrige interview; Eve Fout interview.

114   "to be out with people": Eve Fout interview.

114   "There isn't anything to do": JBK to JPK, Aug. 15, 1957, JPKP.

114   Jackie was passionate: Eve Fout interview; Nicoll interview; Whitehouse interview.

114   "There is a kind of religious": Cassini interview.

114   "very, very good": Whitehouse interview.

114   "knocked unconscious": Kitty Slater, *The Hunt Country of America,* p. 145.

114   Jackie had known Eve: Eve Fout interview.

115   "she walked like a duck": Paul Fout interview.

115   "sticking your neck out": JBK to Eve Fout, Sept. 17, 1960, courtesy of Eve Fout.

115   "She liked homework": Ketchum interview.

115   "freshened her up": Eve Fout interview.

115   "hunt country hangers-on": Ben Bradlee interview.

115   JFK liked to visit the Mellons: Billings OH.

115   "The whole reason for Glen Ora": Paul Fout interview.

115   "He looked like Ichabod": Ben Bradlee interview.

116   he had an array of specialists: Dallek, *Atlantic Monthly,* December 2002.

116   JFK's regimen of strong: ibid.

116   Kennedy's day began: *ATD,* p. 664; *KE,* p. 371; *Newsweek,* Feb. 27, 1961; Bishop,
      pp. 6–7.

116   "a short soak": *Newsweek,* Feb. 27, 1961.

116   He ate a hearty: *JKWH,* p. 63.

116   One morning when Ken Galbraith: *AJ,* p. 44.

116   Following a round: *Newsweek,* Feb. 27, 1961.

116   "He was a slow starter": Ward OH. The comment was made by Walt Rostow, the
      interlocutor.

116   "It was part of his therapy": Powers OH.

117   his black fifty-three-year-old valet: Bishop, p. 4.

117   "the stumpy walk": ibid.

117   After changing into: Bishop, p. 57; *ATD,* p. 665; *AH,* p. 267.

117   "changed Jack's whole life": LBJ phone conversation with JBK, WH 6401.01, Jan. 9,
      1964, LBJL.

117   specially made from cattle-tail hair: Janet Travell OH.

117   Heads of state had to: Philip de Zulueta to Harold Macmillan, June 13, 1963; de
      Zulueta to McGeorge Bundy, June 19, 1963; Bundy to de Zulueta, June 20, 1963,
      PRO.

117   "Such a chair": *NYT,* Mar. 22, 1961.

117   Sometimes JFK instructed: *AJ,* p. 334.

117   "most restless man": Nancy White memo, Feb. 14, 1963, Theodore White Papers,
      Harvard University.

118   "seems to have a life": Manchester II, p. 9.

118   "his gingerly walking": Sorensen interview.

118   "bend to pick up": Alphand, p. 373.

118   "asked me to pick up": ibid., p. 382.

118   Kennedy asked her to crack: *CWK,* p. 169.

118   "strange sitting positions": Fay, p. 111.

118   finally he instructed: *CWK,* pp. 99–100, 128.

118   He was similarly incapable: *NYT,* Feb. 20, 1961; *CWK,* pp. 209–10.

118   changing his shirt: *AH,* p. 267.

118   In the evenings: *CWK,* p. 52; *KE,* p. 29.

118   His major indulgence: Charley Bartlett to JFK, ND, recommended "small Dutch Upmann cigars," Bartlett Papers, JFKL; Holborn interview, WMP; Cassini II, p. 324; *KE,* p. 28; *AH,* p. 188.

118   "He could chain smoke": Ben Bradlee, *Newsweek,* Dec. 2, 1963.

118   Kennedy enjoyed small-stakes: Billings OH.

118   "I've got some reading": *JKWH,* p. 248.

118   "All our family are light": JPK interview, WMP; Manchester II, p. 95.

Chapter Eleven

119   When he was a senator, his: *KE,* p. 66.

119   "Kennedy takes printer's": Manchester II, p. 38.

119   JFK read so many: ibid., p. 82; *KE,* pp. 310–11; Sidey II, p. 3.

119   "as though they were his": Holborn interview, WMP.

120   "What happened to Snowball?": Laura Bergquist to James Ellison, ND, "Kennedy— Very Casually," Laura Bergquist Papers, Boston University.

120   "play editor": ibid.

120   "You ought to cut Rocky's": *CWK,* p. 74.

120   gave him tidbits: ibid., p. 134.

120   "read leaks": Sidey interview.

120   "spot special prejudices": Sidey II, p. 3.

120   "The American ship": Stewart Alsop to Martin Sommers, Jan. 16, 1962, Alsop Papers, LOC.

120   "That's a great thing": *CWK,* p. 224.

120   "thumbnail sketch": White to RFK, Mar. 17, 1961, White Papers, Harvard University.

120   unlike the Eisenhower White House: Salinger OH.

120   But one staff member: Nancy Dutton interview.

120   "intellectual politician": ibid.

120   "God's angry woman": Bradlee II, p. 198.

120   "to make [JFK] growl": Manchester II, p. 32.

120   "Fred didn't do it on purpose": Nancy Dutton interview.

121   "the court publicist": Anderson, p. 213.

121   He ran a chaotic: Gamarekian interview.

121   "In the tradition of": *NYHT,* Feb. 3, 1961.

121   "Pierre would poke": Sidey II, p. 4.

121   The Irish mafia: Laura Bergquist Knebel OH.

121   "Kenny thought he was a foppish": John Reilly interview.

121   "Get back into long pants": Anderson, p. 231.

121   Underneath the banter: ibid., p. 233.

121   Growing up in San Francisco: ibid., p. 230.

121   he pushed JFK to conduct: ibid., p. 233.

121   "It's really crazy": Salinger interview, *Booknotes,* Nov. 12, 1995, C-SPAN.

122   "We were simply there": Peter Lisagor OH.

122   "elaborately serious": *NYT,* Jan. 26, 1961.

122   "sometimes gets lost in a fog": *NYHT,* Mar. 16, 1961.

122   "It was hard to find a verb": Howard K. Smith OH.

122   "He was always in control": Pierpoint OH.

122   "When it comes to evasion": Galbraith interview.

122   "Our presidents are selected": Joe Kane to JPK, Apr. 6, 1944, JPKP.

122   "remember, reporters are not": *RKHL,* p. 114.

122   "kind reference": JPK to JFK, Oct. 1, 1945, JPKP.

122   to use influential contacts: ibid., July 23, 1956.

122   "of great political import": JPK to Enrico Galeazzi, Apr. 15, 1958, JPKP.

122   the Ambassador made a $500,000: Whalen, pp. 429–31.

123   "You know we had to": Laura Bergquist Knebel OH.

123   "It was studied and calculated": Smathers OH.

123   "was fascinated that I had": Otis Chandler interview.

123   "Protect me": *LG,* p. 759.

123   Unbeknownst to: John F. Stacks, *Scotty: James B. Reston and the Rise and Fall of American Journalism,* pp. 196–99.

123   "I always had the feeling": Alsop I, p. 192.

123   JFK granted reporters: Laura Bergquist Knebel OH; Sidey I, pp. 98–99.

123   "both of us were naked": Sidey interview.

123   "typically, when Jackie surprised": Stewart Alsop to Martin Sommers, Jan. 16, 1962, Alsop Papers, LOC.

124   "unbelievable private candor": Laura Bergquist Knebel OH.

124   "a total shit": *CWK,* p. 84.

124   "bastard": ibid., p. 104.

124   "probably illegal": ibid., p. 218.

124   Sometimes Kennedy stipulated: Sidey OH.

124   "He put you on your mettle": Henry Brandon OH.

124   Cy Sulzberger suggesting: *LG,* p. 760.

124   Teddy White arguing: White to JFK, Aug. 9, 1961, White Papers, Harvard University.

124   CBS correspondent David Schoenbrun: *CWK,* p. 158.

124   "playing the game": Pierpoint OH.

124   JFK had met Bartlett: Charles Bartlett interview.

124   "Chicago industrial aristocracy": Krock interview, JCBC.

124   The family had made: Charles Bartlett interview.

125   "kind of classy": Louchheim Journal, Nov. 22, 1962, KSLP.

125   "cosy, conspicuous way": ibid.

125   "kind of cheerful lightning": Charles Bartlett tribute to JFK, November 1963, WMP.

125   "had the same view": Charles Bartlett interview.

125   Like Walton, Bartlett had: ibid.

125   "intellectual beau": Yusha Auchincloss interview.

125   with "foreigners": JBK to Lee Bouvier, ND, 1950, Lee Radziwill book proposal.

125   "became so dull": Salinger OH.

125   "nothing mattered to me": Charles Bartlett interview.

125   "Ben had a different": ibid.

125   "without embarrassment": Ben Bradlee interview.

126   "got pleasure and reward": ibid.

126   "could never make it": Ben Bradlee to JFK, ND, Charles Bartlett Papers, JFKL.

126   "I am a little stuffy": Charles Bartlett interview.

126   "a dweeb": Ben Bradlee interview.

126   "cast no shadow": ibid.

126   Bartlett had written: Charles Bartlett interview; *Chattanooga Times,* July 13, 15, 21–24, 26–29, 1955; Aug. 2, 1955.

126   "make it tough": Charles Bartlett interview.

126   "Bartlettisms": *KE,* p. 315.

126   "Spartan diet": Charles Bartlett to JFK, Dec. 29, 1961, Bartlett Papers, JFKL.

126   "Are you trying to change": Bartlett OH.

126   "I'd shoot things in": Charles Bartlett interview.

127   Jack Kennedy relied on: Gore, "The Centres of Power in the Kennedy Administration," Jan. 23, 1962, PRO.

127   "need to know something about": *LG,* p. 762.

127   "We told him everything": Walton OHCU.

127 "started boasting how": ibid.

127 "Mr. Facing Both Ways": Merry, p. 356.

127 "guy from Iowa": Sidey interview.

127 "impeccable Arthur Krock": Manchester II, p. 84.

127 It was Krock who had suggested: Blair, p. 138.

127 "the single major influence": James Rousmanière OH-CU.

127 Krock had seen the commercial: Krock OH; *HTF,* p. 417.

127 "work over": Krock OH; Goodwin I, p. 605.

127 "gave [JFK] my house man": Krock interview, JCBC.

127 the only black Kennedy knew: Krock OH.

127 "natural conservatism": ibid.

128 Krock had written favorable: *HTF,* pp. 228, 255.

128 Although Krock was Jewish: Beale, p. 68.

128 Krock had accepted his $5,000: *HTF,* p. 114.

128 "a kind of bribe": Krock interview, JCBC.

128 "the racial question": Krock OH.

128 "come out for Jack": ibid.

128 "Probably he never liked": Krock interview, JCBC.

128 "Mr. Krock": Krock OH.

128 "Bust it off": *CWK,* p. 141.

128 "his easy domination": *ATD,* p. 214.

128 "How does such a benign-looking": Charles Bartlett interview.

128 Krock continued to "jab": *KE,* p. 317.

128 "It was very very hard": Billings OH.

128 "rarely saw": *KE,* p. 314.

128 the most influential: JFK to Henry Luce, Aug. 8, 1961, including Ted Sorensen's memo on press bias, Aug. 4, 1961, JFKL.

128 "I read that damn magazine": Sidey interview.

129 "swing opinion": Prendergast and Colvin, p. 31.

129 "JPK in bedroom": Sylvia Jukes Morris, *Rage for Fame: The Ascent of Clare Boothe Luce,* p. 372.

129 "political power relationship": Baldrige interview.

129 "Give me a half an hour's": JPK to Clare Luce, Dec. 10, 1947, JPKP.

129 "devastating remark": RK to Joseph P. Kennedy Jr., June 15, 1942, JPKP.

129 "considerable national figure": Elson, p. 469.

129 Putting his Republican principles: ibid., p. 465.

129 "He seduces me": Martin II, p. 361.

129 "like a cricket": *ATD,* p. 63.

130 "no doubt my feminine weakness": Clare Luce to Baldrige, May 20, 1963, Clare Luce Collection, LOC.

130 "sacred medal": Blair, p. 198.

130 "They liked each other": *AH,* p. 359.

130 "mean and bitter": Billings OH.

130 Each Sunday night JFK: Sidey interview.

130 "in cheerfully profane style": Martin II, p. 380.

130 "who lived in Greenwich": Prendergast and Colvin, p. 32.

130 "file the Bible": *CWK,* p. 141.

130 "slanted, unfair": *KE,* p. 316.

130 "never worried about *Newsweek*": Fuerbringer interview.

130 "We were never anti-Kennedy": ibid.

130 "Has anybody been": ibid.

130 "paid attention": ibid.

131 "was groping": White II, pp. 496, 498, 499.

Chapter Twelve

132 "Here they were in that house": Kloman interview.
132 "Jack missed things": Crespi interview.
132 "historians are great gossips": Marian Schlesinger interview.
132 "took the opinion": Alsop OH.
132 "what people were thinking": Hass interview.
133 "It was light, but not idle": Battelle interview.
133 "liked to meet friends": *CWK,* p. 96.
133 "Liz Taylor would scream": Herter interview.
133 He dutifully inquired: Spalding OH.
133 "all-time favorite subjects": *CWK,* p. 73.
133 "Who does Castro sleep with": Laura Bergquist Knebel OH.
133 Jackie's approach: Herter interview; Crespi interview.
133 "Jackie would say disparaging": Hass interview.
133 "She liked to hear things": Radziwill interview.
133 "He was seldom sure": *JKWH,* p. 248.
133 Jackie would signal Evelyn: *CWK,* p. 161.
133 "the pizza palace": ibid., p. 110.
134 For example, Bill Walton: Charles Bartlett interview; Ben Bradlee interview; Walton interview, JCBC.
134 "There was underground jealousy": Laura Bergquist Knebel OH.
134 "stimulating people": *JKWH,* p. 249.
134 the names often supplied: Arthur Schlesinger interview; Cassini interview.
134 "social treadmill": Jacqueline Kennedy Onassis OH, John Sherman Cooper Oral History Project, University of Kentucky.
134 "men can talk to": ibid.
134 "intense concentration": Graham, p. 290.
134 "hit-and-run": Marian Schlesinger interview.
134 "social samurai": Cassini II, p. 321.
134 "the conversation jumped": *CWK,* p. 123.
134 "relaxed but scattered": ibid., p. 129.
134 "He used 'prick' ": ibid., p. 135.
134 Yet Kennedy scarcely swore: Charles Bartlett interview; James Reed interview.
134 "an eclectic blend": Manchester II, p. 86.
135 Jackie discouraged "gen con": Marian Schlesinger OH.
135 "extremely sensitive and high-strung": Spalding OH.
135 "She conceived it right": Harlech OH.
135 "to talk about parties": Earl E.T. Smith Jr. interview.
135 "sybarites in ancient Egypt": Smith I, p. 50.
135 "Old-fashioned Washington": Elizabeth Burton interview.
135 "historian of *le tout monde*": Cassini II, p. 321.
135 Another favorite was Arkady: RK to children, Aug. 18, 1955, JPKP.
135 "Arkady was very close": Herter interview.
135 she wore a size 10A: *Time,* March 23, 1962. When Jackie shed her shoes to enter a shrine in India, Keyes Beech of the *Chicago Daily News* looked inside and reported, "I can state with absolute certainty that she wears 10A and not 10AA."
136 "stable-companion": Walton, p. 26.
136 "Adams managed to be": ibid., p. 25.
136 "a size too small": JBK to Walton, Dec. 31, 1960, Walton Papers, JFKL.
136 "charmingly ugly": Nuala Pell interview.
136 "against a million smiles": JBK collage, ND, Walton Papers, JFKL.
136 He played bridge: Katharine Graham interview.
136 "slightly crumbling mansion": Walton, p. 46.

136 "He was at once": Hector interview.

136 "gay as a goose": Ben Bradlee interview.

136 Walton had gone through: Truitt interview; *JKWH*, p. 51; Walton interview, JCBC.

137 The furniture was draped: Kloman interview.

137 "enormous gold bucket": Alsop II, p. 437; *JKWH*, p. 101.

137 a fifty-something widow: Rudy Abramson, *Spanning the Century: The Life of W. Averell Harriman, 1891–1986*, p. 677.

137 The third of FDR's: Ted Morgan, *FDR: A Biography*, p. 457.

137 Young Roosevelt had been the son: Doris Kearns Goodwin, *No Ordinary Time: Franklin and Eleanor Roosevelt: The Home Front in World War II* (Goodwin II), p. 386.

137 As a girl, Jackie had: Justin Feldman interview.

137 "He didn't do his homework": Kloman interview.

137 Like his siblings, Franklin: Goodwin II, p. 178; Morgan, p. 454.

137 FDR Jr. intrigued Kennedy: Arthur Schlesinger interview.

138 "a little pathetic": FDR to John Boettiger, Mar. 3, 1941, Franklin D. Roosevelt Library.

138 "cold and calculating person": Eleanor Roosevelt to Adlai Stevenson, Aug. 11, 1960, Franklin D. Roosevelt Library.

138 "did a lot to win her over": Charles Bartlett interview.

138 "Jack honestly didn't like": Walton OH.

138 "huge fun": Charles Bartlett interview.

138 Early in 1960: White notes, Feb. 28, 1960–Mar. 6, 1960, White Papers, Harvard University.

138 "In a certain sense he was": Charles Peters OH.

138 Under intense pressure: *RKHL*, p. 95; Leamer II, p. 426, citing Franklin D. Roosevelt Jr. interview, Schlesinger Papers, JFKL: "Bobby had been bringing pressure on me to mention it. He kept calling—five or six calls a day."

138 It was the turning point: *Poughkeepsie Journal*, Sept. 16, 1988, quoting Jacqueline Kennedy Onassis on the occasion of FDR Jr.'s death: "You know, President Kennedy could not have been President without Franklin."

138 But McNamara rejected: McNamara interview; Tobie Roosevelt interview.

138 "Jack Kennedy owed Franklin": Kloman interview.

139 "didn't dare give one": *CWK*, p. 147.

139 The first of these honorees: *Time*, Sept. 14, 1962; Diana DuBois, *In Her Sister's Shadow: An Intimate Biography of Lee Radziwill*, p. 79.

139 She had been married: *Time*, Mar. 19, 1959, and Sept. 14, 1962.

139 "Why he is nothing but": Lee Radziwill, *Happy Times*, p. 72.

139 "gold-brown like a glass": ibid.

139 At five foot six: DuBois, p. 30.

139 "have twelve children": Radziwill, p. 135.

139 Horses frightened Lee: Radziwill interview, *Larry King Live*, Mar. 27, 2001, CNN.

140 Both girls received: Radziwill, p. 135.

140 "be the best": ibid., p. 34.

140 Their mother prodded: ibid., p. 24.

140 "where she cried": Radziwill, *Larry King Live*, Mar. 27, 2001.

140 a crooked seam: Jacqueline Bouvier, "Feature-Question 1," *Vogue* Prix de Paris application, May 21, 1951, *Vogue* Materials, JFKL.

140 "She was overbearingly proper": Herter interview.

140 "was always grateful": Bradford, p. 24.

140 the crisp gabardine suits: Lee Radziwill, "Opening Chapters," *Ladies' Home Journal*, January 1973.

140 "To be with him when": Radziwill, p. 133.

140 Jackie and Lee were caught: Bradford, p. 13.

140   Lee was hit especially: DuBois, p. 2; Gloria Steinem, "And Starring . . . Lee Bouvier!" *McCall's,* February 1968.

140   "to press the button": Bradford, p. 13.

140   He was reduced: Crespi interview.

140   "If I didn't come in": Radziwill, p. 134.

141   "They were like little orphans": Chavchavadze interview.

141   Their mother had a soft: Kay Meehan interview.

141   "could never tell us apart": Radziwill interview, *Larry King Live,* Mar. 27, 2001.

141   "galloping tongue": Pell interview.

141   "the odd habit of halting": *LG,* p. 914.

141   "My voice cracked": Jacqueline and Lee Bouvier, p. 30.

141   "We jitterbugged": ibid., p. 52.

141   Lacking Jackie's intellectual: DuBois, pp. 46–47.

141   "I often thought": Symington interview.

142   He was difficult to miss: *Time,* Sept. 14, 1962.

142   Stas had helped: *LG,* p. 696; DuBois, p. 107.

142   Jack and Jackie enjoyed: Radziwill, p. 44; DuBois, pp. 110, 247.

142   "In a way, Jackie": Agnelli interview.

142   "the one person with whom": Gallagher, p. 46.

142   Letters flew back: Bradford, p. 172. Radziwill told Bradford that in her letters, Jackie was "imploring me to come over, what pleased Jack or didn't please him, what would make him happy and a lot about our children and trying to keep them together and seeing each other every summer. Those letters showed great anxiety to keep us together and the children together as often as possible."

142   "Lee wanted to be": Baldrige interview.

142   "There was drama": Charles interview.

142   Jackie was warmer: Crespi interview.

142   When Lee arrived at the White: Ketchum interview.

142   Jackie and Lee embraced: *WP,* Mar. 9, 1961.

143   Accompanied by two: ibid.

143   who had been keeping JFK: *WP,* Mar. 6, 1961.

143   Lee occupied the Queen's: West, p. 234.

143   To the delight of: *WP,* Mar. 13 and 14, 1961; *NYT,* Mar. 26, 1961.

143   "JK 102": *NYT,* Mar. 22, 1961.

143   Jackie brought ten suitcases: ibid.; *WP,* Mar. 24, 1961.

143   a duplex on the top: *NYT,* Mar. 26, 1961; *WP,* Jan. 10, 1961.

143   It was said that: *AH,* p. 402.

143   "very precious": Baldrige e-mail to author, July 11, 2002.

143   "Jackie was in charge": Chavchavadze interview.

144   "no *New York Times,* no Luce": Stewart Alsop to Martin Sommers, Mar. 28, 1961, Alsop Papers, LOC.

144   "From that moment the city's": Sidey I, p. 92.

144   Guests mingled first: *WS,* Mar. 17, 1961; *WP,* Mar. 17, 1961.

144   After a dinner of *saumon*: Merry, p. xvi; *WS,* Mar. 17, 1961.

144   "dramatic white sheath": *WP,* Mar. 17, 1961.

144   "moved from one group": *ATD,* p. 215.

144   "champagne flowing": Stewart Alsop to Martin Sommers, Mar. 28, 1961, Alsop Papers, LOC.

144   "full Johnson treatment": ibid.

144   "the Beautiful People": Bradlee II, p. 232; Ben Bradlee interview.

145   "Jack was always so complimentary": Tony Bradlee interview.

145   "the sense of possibility": *ATD,* p. 215.

145   "Well, girls, what did": Truitt interview.

Chapter Thirteen

146 Marilyn Monroe, with whom: Niklas, p. 210.

146 "Billy said, 'Hugh, this'": Sidey interview.

146 "Jack Kennedy is down": Billy Brammer to Hazel Foshee, July 19, 1961, courtesy of
     Harry McPherson.

147 "You heard there was a special": Gamarekian interview.

147 upper-class New Yorker: Raskin interview.

147 in a strange coincidence: The Shaw-Parkman Family Tree of Col. Robert Gould
     Shaw and BG Henry Sturgis Russell (website). Robert Gould Shaw had two sisters.
     Susannah Shaw and her husband, Robert Minturn, were the great-grandparents of
     Mary and Tony Pinchot. The other sister was Ellen Shaw, who married Francis
     Canning Barlow. Their great-granddaughter is Diana de Vegh.

147 "There was an empty": Davis, CBS, Nov. 17, 1993.

147 Mac Bundy, then dean: Raskin interview.

147 "Bundy said to Kennedy": ibid.

147 "We would have dinner": Davis, CBS, Nov. 17, 1993.

147 "a way to get even": Raskin interview.

147 "She was put to work for me": Leamer II, p. 478.

148 Her work involved: Raskin interview.

148 afterwards JFK and de Vegh: Davis, CBS, Nov. 17, 1993.

148 "the kind of peace": Sidey I, p. 279.

148 "I never did experience John": Davis, CBS, Nov. 17, 1993.

148 "of his time" . . . "He was limited": ibid.

148 "There were a couple of the girls": Gamarekian OH.

149 The most conspicuous: Gamarekian interview; Lincoln I, pp. 229–30.

149 "The President said to Fiddle": Phyllis Mills Wyeth interview.

149 "these girls would go on": Gamarekian interview.

149 "doing his hair": ibid.; Sorensen, p. 24, also described JFK's "regular scalp massages"
     by a "succession of secretaries," a "habit acquired from his father."

149 "I said I didn't think": AH, p. 300.

149 "long-legged, tawny": Gamarekian interview.

149 "joking, warm, easygoing": Wendy Taylor Foulke interview.

149 "They would go off": Gamarekian interview.

149 "swimming and cavorting": ibid.

150 "The President came in": Foulke interview.

150 "that gal needs": Hamilton, p. 215.

150 With Billings in tow: ibid., p. 121; Blair, p. 34.

150 "was a sensuous man": Krock interview, JCBC.

150 "Look around and see how": Walton interview, JCBC.

150 "Jack wanted more": Cassini interview.

150 "Most women have no influence": Louchheim Journal, July 12, 1959, KSLP.

150 longtime labor organizer: WP, Jan. 13, 1961; NYT, Oct. 1, 1961.

151 "I was the only woman": Liz Carpenter interview.

151 "compounded of grit": AH, p. 401.

151 "the girl for Jack": Kathleen Kennedy to family, Sept. 23, 1943, JPKP.

151 "a leading Catholic": ibid., Mar. 24, 1945.

151 "As usual, he was absolutely": Ward OH.

151 "one of the rare and unexpected": AJ, p. 28.

151 "vivandière": Ward OH.

151 "On the whole he had little": ibid.

151 "They treat one in quite": Kathleen Kennedy to JFK, July 29, 1943, JPKP.

151 "vibrated sympathetically": Arthur Schlesinger interview.

151 "to make the most of": David Cecil, Melbourne, pp. 20, 23.

152   "The chase is more fun": Crespi interview.

152   According to Judith Campbell: Leamer II, p. 523.

152   "lousy lover": *AH*, p. 56.

152   "He was such a warm, lovable": Blair, p. 599.

152   "Jack was caring": Chavchavadze interview (and following quotes).

153   Still, the extent: Jewel Reed interview.

153   "disease": Charles Bartlett interview; Leamer II, p. 407.

153   "I haven't seen those beautiful": JPK to EMK, Aug. 15, 1955, JPKP.

153   "I think Jack had better": Krock interview, JCBC.

153   "there's a lot of life": Kathleen Kennedy to family, Jan. 12, 1944, JPKP.

153   "He was totally open": Walton interview, JCBC.

154   "underlying sexual tension": Barbara Gamarekian, "My Turn," *Newsweek,* June 16,
      1997.

154   "license in the air": Marian Schlesinger OH.

154   the love affair of: Nancy Hogan Dutton interview.

154   "There are more votes": ibid.

154   "like a God": *PK*, p. 291.

154   The romance between: Nancy Dutton interview.

154   "She kept getting heavier": Gamarekian interview.

154   Shortly afterwards, Kennedy transferred: Nancy Dutton interview.

155   "the rich are different": ibid.

155   "nomadic lives": Sidey I, p. 94.

155   "While in the White House": Salinger interview, *Booknotes,* Nov. 12, 1995, C-SPAN.

155   "Kennedy is doing for sex": Nancy Mitford, *Love from Nancy: The Letters of Nancy
      Mitford,* p. 393 (Nancy Mitford to Jessica Truehaft, Dec. 18, 1961); Duke of
      Devonshire interview.

155   "if the First Lord doesn't": Mitford, p. 393 (Nancy Mitford to Duchess of
      Devonshire, July 3, 1961).

155   to symbolize "integration": "In Memoriam: Frances Scott Fitzgerald Smith,
      1921–1986," eulogy by Mary M. Chewning.

155   "Magnolia, you're the only": Charles interview.

155   "The President made a request": Thomas Guinzburg OH-CU.

155   "decent person": Dillon interview.

155   "Didn't you know all about": Kaplan, p. 575.

156   "the stories in circulation": Schlesinger to Stevenson, Jan. 4, 1960, Stevenson Papers,
      Princeton University.

156   "just a bull": Ives OH-CU.

156   "I'm going to keep": Charles Bartlett interview.

156   "a President is watched": Walton, p. 120.

156   "Like everyone else": Bradlee II, p, 268.

156   "Lem didn't want to know": Peter Kaplan interview.

157   "He gave a lightning look": Kaplan, p. 488.

157   Kennedy had first met: Goodwin I, p. 582.

157   "wasn't that attractive": Coleman interview.

157   The son of a stockbroker: Blair, pp. 98–99, 143; Charles Bartlett interview; Betty
      Spalding interview, JCBC.

157   "Brune" for Brunhilde: Coleman interview.

157   "the most engaging person": Spalding OH.

157   By the time Kennedy entered: Betty Spalding interview, JCBC.

157   "to keep a totally abnormal": Spalding OH.

157   he would escape: Betty Spalding interview, JCBC; Charles Bartlett interview.

157   "Betty was in Greenwich": Coleman interview.

157   "would talk to me": Betty Spalding interview, JCBC.

158 "always on the outside": Dick Spalding interview.

158 "She was not given": Coleman interview.

158 "got White House fever": Charles Bartlett interview.

158 "hunting expeditions": Collier and Horowitz, p. 147.

158 "Chuck would serve as a beard": Betty Spalding interview, JCBC.

158 "He knew how to take precautions": Charles Spalding OH.

158 When he expected: Bryant, p. 18.

158 "has even been known": WP, May 11, 1963.

158 Secret Service agents rarely: Alvin Shuster, "The Forty Watchdogs of the President," NYT Magazine, Oct. 21, 1962; Bryant, p. 18.

158 "naked blonde office girl": Bryant, p. 18.

159 "a slightly mussed bed": Time, Dec. 19, 1960.

159 Newsweek further revealed: Newsweek, Dec. 19, 1960.

159 Kennedy and his guests: WP, Jan. 10, 1961.

159 "It was kind of a weird": AH, p. 402.

159 "The fact is a lot of reporters": Seymour Hersh, The Dark Side of Camelot (Hersh II), pp. 23–24.

159 "the woman disappeared": AH, p. 475.

159 "The affairs that I knew about": Pierpoint OH.

159 "it was hearsay": Sidey interview.

159 "there sitting on the sofa": Fuerbringer interview.

159 "We knew about his affairs": Ruth Montgomery OH-CU.

160 "very swinging sexual animal": Laura Bergquist to James Ellison, ND, "Kennedy— Very Casually," Laura Bergquist Papers, Boston University.

160 "entertained other women": Dickerson, p. 67.

160 "reciprocal forbearance": Arthur Schlesinger interview.

160 "marvelous self-control": Janet Auchincloss OH.

160 "I knew exactly what [Jack] was": Cecil Beaton, Beaton in the Sixties: More Unexpurgated Diaries (Beaton III), pp. 246–47.

161 "in her bare feet": Gamarekian interview.

161 "walked into Mrs. Lincoln's": Gamarekian OH. The reporter was probably Mathias Polakovitz, a friend of Jackie and Lee who knew everyone in the international set.

161 "What is going on here?": Gamarekian interview.

161 "And of course my reaction too": Gamarekian OH.

161 Vivian Stokes Crespi was two: Crespi interview.

161 "creatures of their time": ibid. (and following quotes and biographical facts).

162 "She told me she knew": Tony Bradlee interview.

162 "She was very dignified": Bradford, p. 205.

162 "The men she liked were all": Radziwill interview.

162 Robert McNamara periodically: McNamara interview.

162 McNamara sensed that the poem: ibid.

162 "You say he was cruel?": Gabriela Mistral, "Prayer," translated by Langston Hughes, copy courtesy of Robert McNamara.

163 "he was very quick": Radziwill interview.

163 "Men can't understand": CWK, p. 230.

163 "She was flirtatious": McNamara interview.

163 "insidious slim little volume": JBK to Gilpatric, June 13, 1963, quoted in WP, Feb. 10, 1970.

163 Gilpatric fielded her questions: AH, p. 319.

163 "force and kindness": JBK to Gilpatric, June 13, 1963.

163 "happy for one whole": ibid.

163 "my little friend Jackie": Ives OH-CU.

163 For Valentine's Day: ibid.

163   "There was real rapport": Sharon OH-CU.

163   "had troubles that she liked": Ives OH-CU.

163   "Look, I may not be": Graham, p. 291.

164   "I always push": JBK to Gilpatric, June 13, 1963.

165   Because of her position: Frank Finnerty interview; Frank Finnerty unpublished
       memoir. The following quotations and facts of Dr. Finnerty's friendship with Jackie
       Kennedy were from these accounts, backed up by an earlier interview of Finnerty
       conducted by his cousin by marriage, veteran journalist Clare Crawford Mason.

166   "the sex symbol": Kaplan, p. 494; Gore Vidal, *Palimpsest: A Memoir*, p. 380.

166   "Kennedy never thought she": Finnerty interview.

Chapter Fourteen

167   "The Ambassador was never": *AH*, p. 137.

167   Joe had entertained Democratic: *HTF*, p. 688, citing RK Diary on June 23, 1960;
       White I, p. 153; *RKHL*, p. 104.

167   "If Jack had known": *AH*, p. 171.

167   "Joe Kennedy would use indirection": Carmine de Sapio interview.

168   "tyrannical old man": *NYT*, Jan. 8, 1961; *Time*, July 11, 1960.

168   "sometimes four or five": JPK interview, WMP.

168   "It was another one": Charles Bartlett interview.

168   The baby of the Kennedy family: Adam Clymer, *Edward M. Kennedy*, p. 32.

168   He graduated from: Phyllis Macdonald interview, JCBC.

168   "they were tailhounds": Ben Bradlee interview.

168   "chased everything": Richard Krolik interview.

169   "the latest backroom word": Clymer, p. 32.

169   Almost immediately: Garrett Byrne OH; Collier and Horowitz, pp. 285–86.

169   at age twelve: JPK to Kathleen Kennedy, Apr. 6, 1944, JPKP.

169   "used to say he wished": Tubridy OH.

169   "Teddy on the hoof": Duke of Devonshire interview.

169   "the scapegrace younger brother": Arthur Schlesinger interview.

169   After he was kicked: Collier and Horowitz, p. 216.

169   "would mention him": Thomas Winship OH.

169   "Ted had no real choice": Joan Kennedy interview.

169   During the presidential: Winship OH.

169   As president, Jack continued: Clymer, p. 32.

169   JFK's choice created: *KE*, p. 355; JPK interview, WMP. In the interview, conducted
       on Oct. 20, 1961, Joe Kennedy told William Manchester, "Teddy is going to win.
       McCormack's son [*sic*] has no more chance than you have."

170   "Without Johnson, Kennedy would": *ATD*, p. 703.

170   a mutual mistrust that had begun: McPherson interview; Kenneth O'Donnell OH;
       RKHL, p. 96.

170   "sealed their enmity": George Christian interview.

170   With JFK's narrow election: Sorensen interview.

170   The southerners controlled: *PR-JFK*, vol. 1, p. liii.

170   Although Johnson had been: *ATD*, p. 42; Dillon OH.

170   "likable man": Alsop I, p. 297.

170   When Mansfield was elected: Caro, pp. 1035–1036.

170   "the place I know best": ibid., p. 1036.

170   Mansfield supported: McPherson interview; Caro, p. 1038.

171   When Mansfield said: *Time*, Feb. 23, 1962.

171   But the unexpectedly large: Caro, p. 1039.

171   "The steam really went": *CWK*, p. 226.

171   "Johnson beat an angry": Sorensen interview.

171 "tactful and courteous": Carpenter interview.

171 But Johnson mostly limited: Caro, p. 1039; McPherson, p. 184.

171 a graduate of Northeastern University: Sidney Hyman, "Inside the Kennedy Kitchen Cabinet," *NYT Magazine,* Mar. 5, 1961; *Time,* Sept. 1, 1961; Anderson, p. 251.

171 "ovoid torso": *DOAP,* p. 306.

171 He first worked: O'Brien, p. 6; Anderson, p. 215.

171 Both of O'Brien's parents: O'Brien, p. 16.

171 During the 1952 campaign: Anderson, p. 247.

171 "audacity": O'Brien, p. 17.

172 "Once he came to my cafe": ibid., p. 21.

172 Since Kennedy's first: ibid., p. 112.

172 On weekends: Sidey interview; Sander Vanocur interview.

172 "winning mixture of blarney": Anderson, p. 251.

172 New Deal liberal: *ATD,* p. 93.

172 "always used less power": John Kenneth Galbraith interview with Harry Kreisler, UC Berkeley, Mar. 27, 1986.

172 "he would have found": McPherson interview.

172 "frustrated force of nature": Ziegler, p. 307.

172 "powerless obscurity": Alsop I, p. 46.

172 "a proud and imperious": *ATD,* p. 705.

172 "a doomed relationship": ibid., p. 703.

172 issuing edicts: Baldrige interview; Rostow OH.

173 At the dance in March: Crespi interview.

173 "the young beauties exuding": Louchheim Journal, Dec. 22, 1963, KSLP.

173 "They were laughing": McPherson interview.

173 "You know what he does": ibid.

173 McPherson suspected that: ibid.

173 "J. Edgar Hoover has": *PK,* p. 288, citing confidential dispatch in *Time* archives.

173 "Johnson said he was waiting": Frank Stanton interview.

173 "poking fun at him": Gilpatric OH.

174 "really likes [LBJ's] roguish": *CWK,* p. 92.

174 "a strange figure": Alsop OH.

174 "not on the take": *CWK,* p. 216.

174 "whom he loved to tease": Alsop OH.

174 During his time: *ATD,* p. 705.

174 "errands": Pierpoint OH.

174 "Johnson would have to be": Hand interview.

174 "I can't stand Johnson's": Smathers OH.

174 "I know he didn't do": Alsop OH, Robert F. Kennedy Oral History Project, JFKL.

174 O'Donnell kept in daily touch: *AH,* p. 265.

174 "Oh that": Evans interview; O'Donnell, pp. 270–71.

174 "gilded impotence": *RKHL,* p. 97.

174 "Bobby saw him as": vanden Heuvel interview.

175 "that little shitass": *RKHL,* p. 99; Collier and Horowitz, p. 243, quoting Bobby Baker.

175 "was a kind of chemical thing": Alsop OH.

175 "squats to piss": William Manchester interview.

175 Responding to her pleas: *WP,* June 29, 1962; *JKWH,* p. 260.

175 Since her husband disliked: Carpenter interview.

175 "the greatest act": JBK to LBJ, Nov. 26, 1963, LBJL.

175 "was always nicer to me": Michael Beschloss, ed., *Reaching for Glory: Lyndon Johnson's Secret White House Tapes, 1964–1965* (Beschloss II), p. 19, quoting from a telephone conversation with Pierre Salinger on Dec. 23, 1963.

175   Jackie found little: Dickerson, p. 35; Lady Bird Johnson OH; Carpenter interview.

175   "willingness to assume": JBK to LBJ, Nov. 26, 1963, LBJL.

175   "It was a disappointment": David Gore, "Annual Review for 1961," Jan. 1, 1962,
      PRO.

175   Dillon convinced JFK: *Time,* Aug. 18, 1961.

176   Behind the scenes: Dillon interview; Richard Bolling OH-CU.

176   "one of the greatest obstacles": Douglas Dillon, "Remembering JFK," speech at the
      Century Association, Oct. 20, 1996.

176   Both men were also willing: Dillon interview.

176   "I think Kennedy is trapped": Rowe to White, Mar. 28, 1961, White Papers, Harvard
      University.

176   "The Soviets were on the move": Rostow OH.

177   "ambassadors of peace": Robert A. Liston, *Sargent Shriver: A Candid Portrait,* p. 112.

177   "at the same level as the citizens": *PK,* p. 69.

177   "Jack never uttered": Sargent Shriver interview.

177   It was Shriver who: Liston, p. 130.

177   "it would be easier": ibid., p. 111.

177   Eunice was the only: JPK to JFK, Oct. 15, 1943, describing Eunice's transfer to
      Radcliffe to complete course work for her Stanford degree, JPKP; Leamer I,
      pp. 201, 323.

178   "wild originality of countenance": Ziegler, p. 308.

178   she was even diagnosed: Blair, p. 661.

178   "Eunice and Jack were": Sargent Shriver interview.

178   "If that girl had been born": Collier and Horowitz, p. 159.

178   Eunice had been an avid: Smathers interview, JCBC.

178   "Eunice can hardly wait": RK to JBK, Jan. 4, 1960, JPKP.

178   "she was direct": Deeda Blair interview.

178   "make Jack laugh": *AH,* p. 429.

178   "fantastically dogged": Liston, p. 55.

178   "It was not an easy": Sargent Shriver interview.

178   The handsome scion of: Liston, pp. 14–36.

178   Sarge and Eunice were married: ibid., pp. 53, 63–66.

179   "boy scout": ibid., p. 71.

179   "unruffled courtesy": *ATD,* p. 146.

179   a successful program that: ibid., p. 607.

179   "you never get the feeling": Liston, p. 176.

179   "a person capable of penetrating": Sargent Shriver interview.

179   "I never saw Jack act": Eunice Shriver interview.

Chapter Fifteen

180   The first flashpoint: *ATD,* p. 329; Horne, p. 290.

180   "The President was watching": Rostow OH; Ward OH.

181   "a special relationship": Brandon OH.

181   "rather have [David's] judgment": *AH,* p. 504.

181   "David belonged to all three": Horne, p. 307.

181   Not only was Gore's: *HTF,* p. 563.

181   "English political society": *ATD,* p. 83.

181   At Oxford, Gore lost: *The Times,* Jan. 28, 1985.

181   They shared a sense: Pamela Harlech interview.

181   Both men were sons: ibid.; Duke of Devonshire interview.

181   "I think he had deep": Harlech OH.

182   A member of Parliament: *HTF,* p. 563.

182   "He took a very keen interest": *The Sunday Times,* March 28, 1965.

182   During the campaign: *Evening Standard,* June 4, 1968.

182   When Gore met with Kennedy: *Daily Mail,* Jan. 9, 1962.

182   "must come to Washington": *ATD,* p. 424.

182   By that time: ibid., p. 423; *HTF,* p. 563.

182   "David fitted exactly": Duchess of Devonshire interview.

182   "Speaking with the bluntness": *ATD,* p. 335.

182   The British government opposed: Horne, pp. 291–92.

182   "deepest anxiety": Macmillan, p. 329.

182   "languid Edwardian": *ATD,* p. 375.

182   "a sharp, disillusioned": ibid., p. 376.

183   "elegance, information": *AJ,* p. 8.

183   "common experiences": Horne, p. 288.

183   Macmillan disliked Joe: ibid., p. 280.

183   "I 'fell' for him": Harold Macmillan to JBK, Feb. 18, 1964, HMA.

183   "They were astonished": Duchess of Devonshire interview.

183   Kennedy's bond with Macmillan: *KE,* p. 558; *ATD,* p. 376.

183   The President had already: *ATD,* p. 333; Harold Macmillan Journal, Mar. 26, 1961, HMA.

183   "pressed very hard": Macmillan Journal, Mar. 26, 1961, HMA.

183   "Kennedy obviously thought": Brandon OH.

184   "in order not to be": Macmillan Journal, Mar. 26, 1961, HMA.

184   "worthy of engaging": *ATD,* p. 329.

184   "Kennedy was ready": Rostow OH.

184   Operation Pluto: Alsop I, p. 221.

184   "He tried to keep": Dillon interview.

184   Kennedy considered several options: Macmillan, p. 353; *ATD,* p. 232; Rostow OH.

184   "a complete muddle": Macmillan, p. 353.

185   As originally conceived: *ATD,* pp. 237, 243.

185   "Boss, it checks out": Dickerson, p. 72.

185   "We were led to believe": McNamara OH.

185   Arthur Schlesinger expressed: *ATD,* pp. 240, 255.

185   "curious atmosphere": ibid., p. 250.

185   Rusk seemed dubious but: *PK,* p. 80; *ATD,* p. 250; *Newsweek,* May 1, 1961.

185   he questioned the likelihood: *ATD,* pp. 247–49.

185   "He couldn't quite bring": Alsop I, p. 226.

185   "the issue forever": Rostow OH.

185   "The President was quite passive": Sorensen interview.

185   "frankly for a vacation": *TCY,* p. 99.

185   They stayed at: Earl E.T. Smith, *The Fourth Floor: An Account of the Castro Communist Revolution* (Smith II), p. 222; Julia Amory interview.

186   "Kennedy wasn't a great": *TCY,* p. 99.

186   "He loved Earl": Charles Bartlett interview.

186   A graduate of Yale: Smith II, pp. 4, 5, 7.

186   For the next eighteen months: ibid., pp. 20, 30, 174.

186   "Castro's own boy": Charley Bartlett to JFK, ND (probably April 1961), Bartlett Papers, JFKL.

186   Shortly after Batista: Smith II, pp. 230–34; *KT,* p. xxxvi.

186   continued to belittle: Schlesinger interview; Laura Bergquist Knebel OH.

186   "the pro-Castro elements": Earl E.T. Smith to JFK, Feb. 21, 1961, Evelyn Lincoln Papers, JFKL.

187   "My father said": Earl E.T. Smith Jr. interview.

187   But Mac Bundy and Schlesinger: *TCY,* pp. 107–108.

187   "What the hell has happened": ibid., p. 107.

187   "He told me . . . he expected": Spalding OH.
187   Ben and Tony Bradlee, who were: Ben Bradlee interview.
187   Although there had been: Fuerbringer interview.
187   With the assistance of: *ATD*, p. 261.
187   A similar article: *TCY*, p. 109; *PK*, p. 83.
187   "In Miami everyone is talking": Charles Bartlett interview.
188   "did not land on Khrushchev's desk": Aleksandr Fursenko and Timothy Naftali,
      "One Hell of a Gamble": The Secret History of the Cuban Missile Crisis, p. 91.
188   However, neither the Soviets: ibid., p. 93.
188   Out at Glen Ora: Paul Fout interview; Eve Fout interview.
188   "striding suddenly into": Slater, p. 79.
188   The initial air assault: *ATD*, p. 270; *PK*, p. 90.
188   He lied unintentionally: Arthur Schlesinger OH-CU; *ATD*, p. 271.
188   When the cover story: *TCY*, p. 115; *ATD*, pp. 272–73.
188   At 2 p.m. on Sunday: *PK*, p. 92; Spalding OH.
188   "menacing the field mice": *Time*, Apr. 14, 1961.
188   Late that afternoon: *PK*, p. 91.
188   "sat on in silence": *ATD*, p. 273; *TCY*, p. 116, cites Schlesinger interview with JBK as
      well as Lem Billings Diary for Apr. 29, 1961.
189   "Kennedy understood part": Dillon interview.
189   After a day of fighting: *PK*, p. 92.
189   "an impish look": *Time*, Apr. 28, 1961.
189   Jackie twirled: Beale, p. 63.
189   After the First Couple left: *PK*, p. 93; *Time*, Jan. 5, 1962; *ATD*, p. 279; *JWH*, pp. 270,
      272.
189   "his normal quota": *Time*, Apr. 28, 1961.
189   Jackie later told Arthur: *TCY*, pp. 123–24, citing draft for *ATD* at JFKL.
189   "so upset all day": *HTF*, pp. 697–98.
189   "That's the only time": Spalding OH.
189   "He had this golf club": *AH*, p. 336.
189   "a crime which has revolted": *Newsweek*, May 1, 1961.
190   "suffered heavily in prestige": DBD, Apr. 28, 1961.
190   Harold Macmillan privately: Horne, p. 296.
190   "should have committed": ibid., p. 300.
190   In all likelihood: *ATD*, p. 295.
190   "sour fog of failure": *Time*, Apr. 28, 1961.
190   "sadder and wiser": *NYT*, Apr. 21, 1961.
190   "against the advice of Rusk and Bowles": ibid.
190   "had serious misgivings": *NYT*, Apr. 28, 1961.
190   "I think a public panel": Charley Bartlett to JFK, ND (probably April 1961), Bartlett
      Papers, JFKL.
190   Instead, Kennedy appointed: *ATD*, p. 292.
190   "admirable, nice figure": *PR-JFK*, vol. 1, p. 49.
190   "It's just like Eisenhower": *ATD*, p. 292.
190   "I would have been impeached": *Time*, Jan. 5, 1962.
190   "Before the Bay of Pigs": *AH*, p. 336.
191   "that the odds would break": Alsop OH.
191   "somewhat deviously": *Time*, Apr. 28, 1961.
191   "soft" Stevenson man: *RKHL*, p. 122; DBD, Mar. 28, 1961.
191   "that will look pretty good": *ATD*, p. 289.
191   "certain mistrust": Richard Davies OH-CU.
191   McNamara emphatically: McNamara interview.
191   "do your intellectual": ibid.

191   "became so disenchanted": Gilpatric OH.
191   Stricken with guilt: *TCY,* p. 146.
191   moving his office: Anderson, p. 264; *PK,* p. 114; Dickerson, p. 72.
191   Bobby had appeared: *ATD,* p. 238.
191   "I need someone who knows": Sorensen interview.
192   "Bobby *was* the only": Collier and Horowitz, pp. 271–72.
192   Beneath the radar: *TCY,* p. 134.
192   According to Richard Bissell: ibid.
192   "people would be gratified": *RKHL,* p. 155.
192   "given to believe": *TCY,* p. 139.
192   Instead of shutting: *RKHL,* p. 123.
192   "some very naïve questions": Laura Bergquist Knebel OH.
192   "Bobby became very anti-Castro": Davies OH-CU.
193   "If we don't want": *TCY,* p. 124.
193   "espionage, sabotage": ibid., p. 375, citing RFK's statement in November 1961.
193   "the failure of the covert": Macmillan I, p. 353.
193   "I was ready to go": Sidey I, p. 228.
193   "Vietnam would be next": *TCY,* p. 161, citing Billings diary for May 7, 1961.
193   "we began to talk": *LG,* p. 935.
193   Kennedy was asking: Alsop I, p. 148.
193   "I just don't think": *ATD,* p. 337.
194   For public consumption: ibid., p. 339.
194   But he also pushed: *ATD,* p. 335; Macmillan I, pp. 346–47; Rostow OH; *PK,* p. 112.

Chapter Sixteen
195   "a lithe young diver": *Newsweek,* Apr. 10, 1961.
195   "second State of the Union address": *NYT,* May 26, 1961.
195   This time Kennedy grabbed attention: ibid.
195   Kennedy changed his mind: *PK,* pp. 85, 118.
196   Astronaut Alan Shepard Jr.: *NYT,* May 6 and 9, 1961; *ATD,* p. 343.
196   scientists had estimated: *PK,* p. 118.
196   "With Shepard rode the hopes": *Time,* May 12, 1961.
196   Otherwise the speech failed: *NYT,* May 26, 1961.
196   Press accounts speculated: *WS,* Apr. 3, 1961; *WP,* Apr. 4, 1961.
196   "about one out of every five": *WS,* Feb. 9, 1961.
196   "tied up in other official": *NYHT,* Apr. 4, 1961.
196   "strange Frenchmen": Jacqueline Bouvier to Yusha Auchincloss, ND (probably
       1950), courtesy of Yusha Auchincloss.
196   "an Existentialist night club": Jacqueline Bouvier to Lee Bouvier, ND (probably
       1950), book proposal by Lee Radziwill.
197   "drunken dazzled adoration": Jacqueline Bouvier to Yusha Auchincloss, ND
       (probably 1950), courtesy of Yusha Auchincloss.
197   "come out of a museum": Jacqueline Bouvier to Lee Bouvier, ND (probably 1950),
       book proposal by Lee Radziwill.
197   when she had named her poodle Gaullie: Hugh D. Auchincloss III, "Growing Up
       with Jackie," *Palm Beach Journal,* winter 2001.
197   Later she read de Gaulle's: *ATD,* p. 103.
197   during a primary campaign: Heller, p. 135.
197   "The only thing I want": *NYHT,* Apr. 4, 1961.
197   Jackie brushed up: Finnerty interview.
197   "sumptuous fabric": Cassini I, p. 69.
197   "She didn't plan to outshine": McNamara interview.
197   "great and gloomy figure": *ATD,* p. 358.

197   "irritating, intransigent": *KE*, p. 561.

197   "bottomless military and political quagmire": *TCY*, p. 185.

198   "wild with fury": Tree OH.

198   "He promised me not to pursue": Alphand, pp. 349–50.

198   "You'll be out of the woods": JPK to JFK, Aug. 7, 1957, JPKP.

198   He studied a translation: Sidey I, pp. 167–68.

198   Bundy and Sorensen counseled: Alphand, pp. 354–55.

198   "prepare a favorable atmosphere": *LG*, p. 760.

198   "the little pinhead": Horne, p. 319.

198   "my dear friend" de Gaulle: Macmillan to de Gaulle, Apr. 14, 1961, PRO.

198   "pride, his inherited hatred": Horne, p. 319.

198   "conversations with de Gaulle": Macmillan I, p. 428.

198   "sometimes puts his thoughts": Macmillan to JFK, Apr. 28, 1961, PRO.

198   whom Kennedy had met fleetingly: *TCY*, p. 15; *Time*, June 16, 1961.

198   The first overtures: *TCY*, p. 78.

199   but the Bay of Pigs seemed: *LG*, p. 757; *TCY*, pp. 151, 162.

199   Bobby Kennedy met secretly: *TCY*, p. 152; *RKHL*, p. 132.

199   "missile gap": *KT*, p. xxx.

199   18,000 nuclear weapons: ibid.

199   Spurred on by David Gore: *TCY*, p. 84; *KT*, p. xlv.

199   "a man of exceedingly fast responses": *AJ*, p. 109.

199   observed that Khrushchev: Sidey I, p. 195; *PK*, p. 157.

199   "is more aggressive": *PK*, p. 158.

199   Sixty-nine-year-old: Isaacson and Thomas, p. 268.

199   Rather, Kennedy should try: *AH*, p. 351.

200   Lasker gave Jackie $10,000: Lasker OH.

200   "more Parisian than American": *WP*, Oct. 8, 1961.

200   "under a hair dryer": Adlai Stevenson to Marietta Tree, Mar. 10, 1963, Marietta Tree
       Papers, Radcliffe Institute, Harvard University.

200   Jackie wore a dramatic: Cassini I, p. 57.

200   For entertainment, she organized: *WS*, May 4, 1961.

200   "Prince Reindeer": Baldrige interview.

200   "had nurtured crushes": Baldrige, *In the Kennedy Style: Magical Evenings in the Kennedy
       White House* (Baldrige III), p. 43.

200   "never failed to amuse": Cassini II, p. 264.

200   "I suspect [Jackie] got": Baldrige III, p. 43.

201   JFK engaged Princess Grace: ibid.

201   But while the prince: *NYT*, May 25, 1961.

201   "She was so scared": *AH*, p. 363.

201   "rather long & difficult": JBK to Paul Fout, ND (spring 1961), courtesy of Eve Fout.

201   "9,000 square yards": *CWK*, p. 211.

201   With its seventeenth-century: Cassini I, p. 93; Stanfill, *Vanity Fair*, January 2003.

201   "the giant French chauffeur": Beaton I, p. 358.

201   "I think she realized how important": Baldrige interview.

202   In Palm Beach, Jackie's complaints: Dr. Max Jacobson, unpublished manuscript,
       "General Practice," p. 16, "John F. Kennedy," pp. 6–7.

202   A disheveled figure: *TCY*, pp. 189, 191; *PK*, p. 684.

202   Among Jacobson's patients: Jacobson manuscript, "John F. Kennedy," pp. 1–2.

202   "interfered with his concentration": ibid.

202   "periodic depression": ibid., p. 6.

202   "her mood changed": ibid., p. 7.

202   He had been adhering: *WP*, Feb. 19, 1961; Dallek, *Atlantic Monthly*, December 2002.

202   "bone tired": *AJ*, p. 32.

202   "normally blasé": *NYT,* May 16, 1961.

202   Jackie smiled sweetly: *NYT,* May 20, 1961; *WS,* May 17, 1961.

203   "major triumph": ibid., May 18, 1961.

203   While Jackie politely turned: ibid., May 17, 1961.

203   He felt stabbing pain: ibid., June 8, 1961.

203   "to relieve his local": Jacobson manuscript, p. 8.

203   "comparatively good spirits": ibid.

203   "Can't you get your goddamned friends": *PK,* p. 125.

203   JFK had authorized Bobby: Schlesinger II, pp. 320–25.

204   "not retreat a single inch": *NYT,* May 30, 1961.

204   "Zhack-ee": *Time,* June 9, 1961; *NYT,* June 1, 1961.

204   "I am the man": *NYT,* June 3, 1961; *Time,* June 9, 1961.

204   "serene": *WS,* June 1, 1961.

204   "very commendable": *NYT,* May 31 and June 2, 1961.

204   At every opportunity: *JWH,* p. 290; Baldrige II, pp. 38–39.

204   Kennedy had arranged: Jacobson manuscript, "John F. Kennedy," p. 10.

204   "Why is he here?": Sorensen interview.

204   "slimy person": Baldrige interview.

204   "do-it-yourself nuclear arms": *Time,* June 9, 1961.

205   "anti-American feeling": *LG,* p. 762.

205   Kennedy rebuffed: *PK,* pp. 144–50.

205   "fictitious" country: *TCY,* p. 184.

205   "fear of communist contamination": Alphand OH.

205   "méchanceté": *LG,* p. 758.

205   "intelligence, lucidity": Anthony Rumbold to Earl of Home, June 7, 1961, PRO.

205   "Roosevelt and [de Gaulle] had hated": Alphand, pp. 354–55.

205   "I have more confidence": *LG,* p. 761.

205   "low slow French": *Time,* June 9, 1961.

205   "Louis XVI, the Duc d'Angoulême": *ATD,* p. 350.

205   Jackie further endeared: Cassini I, p. 69.

205   "There is tremendous value": *LG,* p. 718.

205   Only days earlier, Malraux's sons: *ATD,* p. 352.

206   Jackie had been intrigued: Wood interview; *East Hampton Star,* Nov. 21, 1996.

206   Jackie was well versed: *AH,* p. 348.

206   "What did you do before": Crespi interview.

206   "intellectual crush": Baldrige interview.

206   her favorite was Manet's: *NYT,* June 3, 1961.

206   "extremely jealous": *NYT,* June 3, 1961.

206   Jackie was particularly interested in Malmaison: Monkman, pp. 242, 245, 58–61.

206   The entourage included: Tony Bradlee interview; *WS,* June 2, 1961.

206   "bevy of lesser ladies": *Time,* June 9, 1961.

206   "There wasn't anything": Collier and Horowitz, p. 275.

206   toting two thick black notebooks: Baldrige II, pp. 33, 42.

207   Jackie escaped just once: Sidey I, pp. 177, 182–86.

207   The highlight of the visit: Baldrige II, p. 43; Baldrige interview.

207   "I thought I was in heaven": *Time,* June 9, 1961.

207   "a fairy-like air": *NYT,* June 2, 1961.

207   She earned raves: *Newsweek,* June 12, 1961; *Time,* June 9, 1961.

207   "more valuable to United States": DBD, June 7, 1961.

207   "to make the atmosphere": Billings OH.

207   "tub talk": *JWH,* p. 291.

207   The Kennedys had barely: *WS,* June 4, 1961.

207   "The meeting may last": Jacobson manuscript, p. 14.

207   "like a broncobuster": *Time,* June 9, 1961.
208   "I was damned if I": La Duchesse de Mouchy interview.
208   "combination of external jocosity": *ATD,* p. 367.
208   "quiet and understated": Davies OH-CU.
208   "was a mistake": *PK,* p. 163.
208   "intent upon . . . gaining": Davies OH-CU.
208   "like a smitten schoolboy": *WS,* June 4, 1961.
208   "mermaid dress": Cassini I, pp. 72, 75.
208   "Oh, Mr. Chairman": *ATD,* p. 367.
208   "she threw back her head": *WS,* June 4, 1961.
208   "almost cozy": *ATD,* p. 367.
208   "She didn't impress me": Nikita Khrushchev, *Khrushchev Remembers: The Last Testament, 1974,* pp. 498–99.
209   "bone in my throat": *PK,* p. 168; *Time,* June 16, 1961; Isaacson and Thomas, p. 609. In a speech delivered on January 6, 1961, Khrushchev had called Berlin "a splinter from the heart of Europe" that he intended to "eradicate" (*KE,* p. 584).
209   Since 1958, Khrushchev: *NYT,* June 4, 1961.
209   Now Khrushchev announced: *PK,* p. 168.
209   "If the United States wants war": ibid., p. 171; *TCY,* pp. 217–18, 223.
209   "split on Berlin": *NYT,* June 5, 1961.
210   "worst thing in my life": *PK,* p. 172, citing an interview with Reston.
210   "did it because of the Bay of Pigs": *TCY,* p. 225.
210   "asked him for surrender": Alsop OH.
210   "too intelligent and too weak": *TCY,* p. 228.
210   "a modern man not cluttered": *LG,* p. 762.
210   "a worthy partner": ibid., p. 800.
210   The doctor entered: Jacobson manuscript, "John F. Kennedy," pp. 17–18.
210   "ebullient": DBD, June 5, 1961.
210   "stunned" . . . "baffled": Macmillan I, pp. 356–58.
210   "no progress was made": ibid., p. 356.
211   "completely overwhelmed": Horne, p. 303.
211   "like a bull being teased": Macmillan I, p. 397.
211   "for the first time in his life": ibid., p. 400.
211   "a very gay luncheon": ibid., p. 358.
211   "How would you react": Horne, p. 304, quoting from a lecture by Nicholas Henderson on March 6, 1981.
211   "Our friendship seemed confirmed": Macmillan I, p. 359.
211   "I feel at home": Horne, p. 305.
211   Still wearing his tuxedo: Sidey I, p. 203; *Time,* Jan. 3, 1962.
211   "He remembered little things": Sidey OH.
211   "invaluable": Sidey I, p. 204.
211   "helps me make up my mind": *LG,* p. 762.
211   "appalling moral burden": Alsop OH.

Chapter Seventeen
212   "surrounded by enthusiastic": DBD, June 6, 1961.
212   "outspoken and impolitic": Cecil Beaton, *Self Portrait with Friends: The Selected Diaries of Cecil Beaton* (Beaton II), p. 341.
212   "a huge mouth, flat Mongolian features": ibid., p. 262.
212   The previous fall she had postponed: Bowles, *Met Catalogue,* p. 29.
212   "affected": Beaton II, p. 341.
213   Since the Greek leader lived: *Time,* June 16, 1961; Baldrige II, p. 247; *AH,* p. 355; *WS,* June 11–13, 1961.

213 "Jackie invited us": Letizia Mowinckel interview.
213 Jackie's friend from Paris: Herter interview; Radziwill interview; *WS*, June 13, 1961.
213 Tish Baldrige was on hand: Baldrige I, p. 199.
213 "I could only describe it": ibid.
213 "chief tattler": ibid., p. 200.
213 "Jackie was a very complex person": Mowinckel interview.
213 "a momentary lapse of selfishness": Baldrige interview.
214 "First Lady Dances Till 1": *WS*, June 13, 1961.
214 After dinner one evening: ibid.; Mowinckel interview; *Time*, June 16, 1961.
214 "in a Mercedes": *Time*, June 23, 1961.
214 "She was on the phone": Mowinckel interview.
214 "in passing": *NYT*, June 15, 1961.
214 he was forced to use: *WS*, June 12, 1961.
214 "complete rest": *NYT*, June 9 and 13, 1961.
214 Kennedy needed to soak: Sidey I, p. 206.
214 "kept a sharp vigil": *WS*, June 10, 1961.
214 slept nearly twelve hours: *Time*, June 16, 1961; *Newsweek*, June 19, 1961.
214 He also consulted: *WS*, June 12, 1961.
214 "a weird night": Sidey interview.
215 "I said to myself, 'Hugh, you stupid guy' ": ibid.
215 "just a bit upsetting": *Newsweek*, June 26, 1961.
215 "I think he is suffering": *AJ*, p. 116.
215 "badly formed": de Zulueta to Macmillan, June 16, 1961, PRO.
216 JFK was driven to National Airport: *NYT*, June 16, 1961.
216 "tanned and radiant": *Time*, June 23, 1961.
216 "flew into the arms": *Newsweek*, June 26, 1961.
216 "very fresh, gay and beautiful": *AJ*, p. 116.
216 The all-night dance was held: ibid., pp. 117–18.
216 "Someone said an entire vintage year": Graham, p. 286.
216 "a huge star": Baldrige interview.
216 "All the men are in love": Stewart Alsop to Martin Sommers, June 5, 1961, Alsop Collection, LOC.
216 "She liked the excitement": Martha Bartlett interview.
216 "for the things I care about": JBK to Joseph Alsop, ND (probably mid-August 1960), Alsop Papers, LOC.
216 "use power with tact": Susan Mary Alsop interview.
216 "without mixing in politics": Leamer II, p. 535.
216 Nor did Jackie have any illusions: Sidey I, p. 97, quotes Jackie telling the author that she felt "compassion for women who could not find enough in their husbands to stimulate them and interest them so that they themselves had to seek power and dominance"; Sidey interview.
216 "I was an observer": JBK to Macmillan, Jan. 31, 1964, HMA.
217 "deeper purpose": Galbraith III, pp. 127–28.
217 Jackie applied her new: Baldrige I, p. 196.
217 Because Ayub had been such a staunch: Sidey I, pp. 84–85.
217 "at your disposal": *JKWH*, p. 199.
217 "native *fête champêtre*": *Time*, July 21, 1961.
217 Designers from Tiffany's: Anne H. Lincoln, *The Kennedy White House Parties* (Lincoln II), pp. 28–33; *NYT*, July 11, 1961; Baldrige II, p. 182; *JKWH*, p. 199; *Time*, July 21, 1961.
218 The weather was clear: Baldrige II, p. 184; *Time*, July 21, 1961.
218 "Not Jack's type": Crespi interview.
218 "Veronese green": Cassini I, pp. 78–79.

218   All the men sported: *Time,* July 21, 1961; Baldrige I, p. 197; Baldrige II, p. 184; *NYT,* July 12, 1961.

218   When a cameraman waved: Baldrige II, p. 185.

218   Following the dinner: *Time,* July 21, 1961; *NYT,* July 11, 1961.

218   "It was done meticulously": Baldrige interview.

218   "too fancy and costly": *NYT,* July 13, 1961.

218   "grandeur of the French court": Richard Kluger, *The Paper: The Life and Death of the New York Herald Tribune,* p. 629.

219   "starchy strongman": *Time,* July 21, 1961.

219   "People think he's thinking": ibid.

219   Lem Billings was usually: Richardson, pp. 256–58; *WP,* Aug. 12 and Sept. 4, 1961.

219   Throughout the summer: *Newsweek,* July 10, 1961; *WP,* Sept. 2, 1961; Sidey I, p. 219; *TCY,* p. 271; *ATD,* p. 481.

219   "He never relaxes in the house": JBK to Janet Auchincloss, Oct. 2, 1961, Nigel Hamilton Collection, Massachusetts Historical Society.

220   "It was curiously moving": Noël Coward, *The Noël Coward Diaries,* p. 478.

220   Weekends were a halcyon time: Joan Kennedy interview.

220   Jackie even took golf: *WP,* Aug. 14 and Sept. 4, 1961.

220   During one demonstration: Sidey I, p. 247.

220   "enthralled": JBK to Arthur Schlesinger, July 24, 1961, Schlesinger Papers, JFKL.

220   She traveled incognito: Susan Sheehan, "The Happy Jackie, the Sad Jackie, the Bad Jackie, the Good Jackie," *NYT Magazine,* May 31, 1970.

220   "bounced up and down on the bed": Kaplan, p. 493.

220   once she went to Boston: *WP,* Aug. 18, 1961.

220   "was sweet to the whole": Coward, p. 476.

220   "liked Hyannis Port because": Joan Kennedy interview.

220   After returning from Greece: Baldrige I, pp. 200–201.

220   "She was wonderful again": Baldrige interview.

221   For the inaugural concert: *WP,* Aug. 23, 1961.

221   "brilliant and full of energy": *JKWH,* p. 318.

221   "difficult situation": James Biddle to Henry du Pont, June 2, 1961, Winterthur Archives.

221   Among the patrons: *Time,* July 14, 1961.

221   "van load of treasures": JBK to Bernice Garbisch, July 27, 1961, courtesy of White House Curator's Office.

221   "Shall we have a little statue": *JKWH,* p. 252.

221   "One time I sat for three days": Sidey interview. "The First Lady Brings History and Beauty to the White House" appeared in the Sept. 1, 1961, issue of *Life.*

222   "was like dealing with Dad": Collier and Horowitz, p. 278.

222   "For weeks after he returned": *CWK,* p. 125.

222   "Tears came into his eyes": Sidey interview.

222   "he sometimes ceases to listen": *Time,* July 21, 1961.

222   "suddenly . . . hard to get close to": Manchester II, p. 36.

222   "Whoever is flailed": DBD, Dec. 21, 1963.

222   "this impatient snapping": Isaacson and Thomas, p. 590.

222   Not long after the book: ibid., pp. 589–90.

223   "how one capable of such": JBK to Acheson, March 1958, quoted in ibid., p. 590.

223   "The Olympians seem to me": Acheson to JBK, March 1958, quoted in ibid.

223   "in politics you don't": *Time,* Sept. 1, 1961.

223   The recommendations Acheson forcefully presented: *PK,* pp. 183, 190–91; *TCY,* pp. 242–43.

223   "Berlin Book": *Time,* July 21, 1961.

223 "consumed in vanity and bitterness": Schlesinger to JFK, Nov. 14, 1960, Schlesinger Papers, JFKL.
223 "rather bloodcurdling": *ATD*, p. 380.
223 "asking only that we advertise": *AJ*, p. 132.
223 "We should not engage": *PK*, p. 194.
223 At Bobby's urging: ibid., pp. 183, 191; *NYT*, June 27, 1961; *Time*, Feb. 16, 1962.
223 "We need a man like Taylor": *Time*, July 28, 1961.
223 At Sorensen's suggestion: *TCY*, pp. 257–59; *KE*, pp. 589–91.
223 The President's July 25 address: *NYT*, July 26, 1961.
224 Defense spending represented: ibid. Comparisons to current figures were drawn from *WP*, Jan. 6 and 31, 2003.
224 when he first read about it: Evan Thomas OH-CU recounts how he sent galleys of the book to JFK in November 1960.
224 "holocaust and humiliation": *TCY*, p. 256.
224 "an attack upon that city": ibid., p. 260.
224 But Kennedy also signaled: *NYT*, July 26, 1961; *Time*, July 28, 1961.
224 In his peroration: *KE*, p. 591; Tanzer, p. 41.
224 "there is no quick and easy solution": *TCY*, p. 261.
224 Khrushchev's response barely: ibid., p. 264.
224 nearly thirty thousand in the month: *ATD*, p. 394.
224 "Kennedy wasn't the type": Philip Zelikow interview.
225 "The Russians are going to block": Rostow OH.
225 By various winks and nods: *TCY*, pp. 269, 271, 279; *PK*, p. 209.
225 "Why would Khrushchev put": *JWH*, p. 303.
225 "This island does not stand alone!": *TCY*, p. 284.
225 "It was where he was in charge": Carpenter interview.
225 "Come and see us, heah?": *Time*, Oct. 27, 1961.
226 "conventional toughness": Rostow OH.
226 the Vice President helped engineer: *WP*, Sept. 20, 1961; *NYT*, May 9, 1961.
226 "He is sort of an Indian snake charmer": *AH*, p. 453.
226 "who made sense": Dillon interview.
226 "a tremendous amount of work": *Newsweek*, Mar. 4, 1963.
227 "iron faith in the definitiveness": Sidney Hyman, "When Bundy Says, 'The President Wants—,'" *NYT Magazine*, Dec. 2, 1962.
227 "the Buddha": Isaacson and Thomas, p. 611.
227 "Rusk plays his cards": Louchheim Journal, Mar. 31, 1963, KSLP.
227 "very correct": Schlesinger interview.
227 "one of those Italian palaces": Jewel Reed to her father, Feb. 9, 1962, courtesy of Jewel Reed.
227 In the days before JFK's Berlin speech: *Time*, Aug. 18, 1961.
227 "a brilliant bureaucratic infighter": Stewart Alsop to Martin Sommers, Sept. 7, 1960, Alsop Papers, LOC.
227 "obdurate Republican": *AJ*, p. 1.
227 "excellent operator": ibid., p. 116.
227 "Galbraith would come back": Dillon interview.
228 "Indo-Talleyrand Series": Galbraith to JFK, Apr. 17, 1961, Galbraith II, p. 65.
228 "tedium": *AJ*, p. xiv.
228 "Saigon . . . has the most stylish": ibid., p. 232.
228 "gave the most brilliantly argued": Sorensen interview; *KE*, p. 590.
228 "Ted can look at you in silence": Theodore White memo for Chapter Nine, *The Making of the President 1960*, White Papers, Harvard University.
228 "I probably was abrupt": Sorensen interview.

229   Ethel set the exuberant: *Time,* Feb. 16, 1962.

229   concocting pranks such as: Beale, p. 65.

229   "subdued . . . peppy": Gallagher, p. 191.

229   "never seemed to need any release": Schlesinger II, p. 599.

229   "With Bobby there were no belly laughs": Fay interview.

229   "Bobby would just tell him": *AJ,* p. 32.

229   "He was like a human drill": La Duchesse de Mouchy interview.

229   "Lord Root of the Matter": Schlesinger interview.

229   "Bobby knew instantly": Symington interview.

230   "Get Rusk on the phone": *Time,* Feb. 16, 1962.

230   "Jack has traveled": Schlesinger II, p. 601.

230   "He didn't have to be nice": Rostow OH.

230   Bobby's most conspicuous assignment: *PK,* pp. 140, 151; *Time,* Feb. 16, 1962.

230   The most effective treatment: *NYT,* Oct. 21, 1961.

230   According to Jacobson's expense records: Leamer II, p. 543.

230   "You cannot be permitted": ibid., p. 545.

231   "roundering": Billy Brammer to Hazel Foshee, July 19, 1961, courtesy of Harry
        McPherson.

231   a railroad executive from Florida: Hersh, p. 301.

231   "Jack would just take them": *RKHL,* p. 255.

231   "lighthearted": Chavchavadze interview.

231   For several weeks in September: *WP,* Sept. 18, 1961.

231   "Cinderella story": *NYT,* Oct. 30, 1961.

231   "He got so excited": Laura Bergquist Knebel OH.

231   "showing off": Chavchavadze interview.

232   "John's other wife": *JWH,* p. 264.

232   "Beyond the Blue Horizon": ibid., p. 375.

232   "pepper-pot tower": *WP,* Sept. 18, 1961; *Time,* Oct. 6, 1961.

232   "stood on deck like an old sea dog": Sidey I, p. 257.

232   "a lapful at a time": *Time,* Oct. 6, 1961.

232   "a great book": Sidey I, p. 247.

232   "We sit for hours": JBK to Janet Auchincloss, Oct. 2, 1961, Hamilton Collection,
        Massachusetts Historical Society.

Chapter Eighteen

233   "seemed extremely well": *LG,* p. 809.

233   "has grown thinner": *WP,* Oct. 13, 1961.

233   "much softer": *LG,* p. 810.

233   "very confused": ibid., p. 812.

233   Meyer's confidante Anne Truitt: Truitt interview.

234   Mary Pinchot Meyer and her younger: Nina Burleigh, *A Very Private Woman: The Life
        and Unsolved Murder of Presidential Mistress Mary Meyer,* pp. 32–33, 38.

234   "happily recalled having cut": William Attwood, *The Reds and the Blacks: A Personal
        Adventure,* pp. 133–34.

234   Mary went on to work: Burleigh, pp. 81–84, 89.

234   As an idealistic advocate: *WP,* Mar. 15, 2001; Harris Wofford, *Of Kennedys and Kings,*
        p. 29.

234   Jack and Cord took an instant: Burleigh, p. 92.

234   Their marriage began unraveling: ibid., p. 145.

234   "She was probably affected": Kenneth Noland interview.

234   Mary worked hard at her art: Truitt interview; Chavchavadze interview.

234   She also underwent psychotherapy: Noland interview. Wilhelm Reich encouraged
        his patients to scream and flail to release their inhibitions. His follower in

Philadelphia was Dr. Charles Oller. But according to Noland, "Mary only went a few times. She tried it, but she resisted that form of therapy. Conventional talk therapy suited her purposes."

235   When Tony and Ben Bradlee returned: Tony Bradlee interview.
235   the sort who reduced a cocktail party: Truitt interview.
235   "She was extremely feminine": Ben Bradlee interview.
235   "She had an eager charm": Truitt interview.
235   "The secret to Mary's personality": Cicely Angleton interview.
235   "she was a little out": Ben Bradlee interview.
235   "Jack Kennedy once said to Mary": Angleton interview.
236   "She crawled on the floor": Sidey I, p. 276.
236   "The 2 times I've seen": JBK notation on guest list for Nov. 13, 1961 state dinner for the Governor of Puerto Rico and Mrs. Muñoz Marín, JFKL.
236   "Standing is determined": Stewart Alsop to Martin Sommers, Dec. 21, 1961, Alsop Papers, LOC.
236   "Let's go": Duchess of Devonshire interview.
236   "Jackie didn't look the least": Slater, p. 146.
237   "the polite drawing room evenings": NYT, Oct. 6, 1961.
237   "a concert led by Haydn": Time, Nov. 24, 1961.
237   "English royalty entertains": ibid.
237   "a willowy medieval princess": Cleveland Plain Dealer, Nov. 18, 1961.
237   The Kennedys had met: Agnelli interview.
237   "In some things they were similar": ibid.
237   "intense conversation with the beautiful": Dickerson, p. 85.
237   "looked to me extremely like Carlo": Agnelli interview.
238   "had spent hours and days": AJ, p. 222.
238   Oleg Cassini introduced the twist: WP, Nov. 13, 1961; NYT, Feb. 19, 1962.
238   The twist, which originated: WP, Dec. 11, 1962.
238   Pierre Salinger denied: ibid., Dec. 19, 1961.
238   "That crowd has been getting": Charley Bartlett to JFK, ND, Bartlett Papers, JFKL.
238   "He slid to the floor": Piedy Lumet (Mary Bailey Gimbel) interview.
238   New Yorker Heyward Isham: Chavchavadze interview.
238   During an after-dinner toast: Kloman interview; Plimpton interview.
238   "went over his desk three times": AJ, p. 222.
238   "filled with charm and malice": Schlesinger II, p. 594.
238   After an unsuccessful run: Kaplan, p. 494.
238   "We are old-fashioned observant": Gore Vidal interview.
239   "Jackie dragged us all": ibid.
239   "admired the President's pragmatic": Kaplan, p. 495.
239   "rigidly Catholic": Schlesinger II, p. 595.
239   "Mad Hatter evening": Gore Vidal interview.
239   Wandering into the Red Room: Kaplan, pp. 498–99; Vidal, pp. 392–95.
239   "He had been working late": Kloman interview.
239   "Don't ever do that": Schlesinger II, p. 594; Kaplan, p. 499.
239   "Gore went after him": Plimpton interview.
239   "I'd like to wring your brother's neck": Kaplan, p. 499.
239   "someone . . . perhaps Jacqueline": Schlesinger II, p. 595.
239   "Gore was having a terrible": Plimpton interview.
239   Vidal tried to justify: Schlesinger II, p. 595.
239   "irritated": ibid.
240   Anne Truitt's husband, James: National Enquirer, Mar. 2, 1976.
240   "very intelligent . . . rather rude": JFK Travel Journal, 1951, JFKL; ATD, p. 522.
240   "It's like trying": AH, p. 428.

240   Just before Nehru's arrival: *AJ*, p. 207.

240   Nehru had asked: *ATD*, p. 524.

240   "interest and vivacity": ibid., p. 525.

240   Both Jackie and Billings found Indira: Billings OH.

240   "Jack Kennedy did see": Arthur Schlesinger interview.

241   Indira incongruously flipped: *AJ*, p. 214.

241   "a brilliant monologue": ibid., p. 216.

241   "the light of love": ibid.

241   "wobbly and fuzzy": Marietta Tree OH.

241   "a disaster . . . the worst": *ATD*, p. 526.

241   JFK did manage to inject: Michaelis, p. 177.

241   "Madame Gandhi's passion": ibid.

241   "That fucking liar": *PK*, p. 223.

241   the most massive and dirty: Sidey I, pp. 245, 333; Macmillan I, pp. 396, 400; *PK*, pp. 226, 228.

241   Beginning with a twenty-six-page: *KT*, p. xlvi; Harold Macmillan, *At the End of the Day: 1961–1963* (Macmillan II), pp. 143, 145; *TCY*, pp. 326, 336.

242   On returning from his Asian: *ATD*, pp. 541–43.

242   "We have to confront": *PK*, p. 173.

242   They reported that despite problems: *ATD*, pp. 546–47; *TCY*, p. 338.

242   "a real bastard to solve": White to JFK, Oct. 11, 1961, White Papers, Harvard University.

242   "much to the irritation": Schlesinger to White, Oct. 14, 1961, White Papers, Harvard University.

242   "a can of snakes": *AJ*, p. 231.

242   "a ground war in Asia": Sidey interview; Powers OH; *NYT*, July 21, 1961.

242   Kennedy felt he couldn't: *ATD*, p. 548.

242   "Kennedy was stringing out Vietnam": Sidey interview.

243   In October he replaced: *Time*, Oct. 6, 1961.

243   "the first head to roll": ibid., July 28, 1961.

243   "very smart counterploy": Stewart Alsop to Martin Sommers, July 25, 1961, Alsop Papers, LOC.

243   "more and more out of things": *AJ*, p. 210.

243   In a Thanksgiving weekend shuffle: *Time*, Dec. 8, 1961; Alsop OH; Sidey I, p. 285.

243   Dean Rusk, fifty-two, displeased: Stewart Alsop to Martin Sommers, Sept. 7, 1961, Alsop Papers, LOC.

243   "force and fertility": *ATD*, p. 150.

243   "Chester Bowles with machine guns": ibid., p. 422. Sidney Hyman in the *NYT Magazine* on Dec. 2, 1962, described Mac Bundy as "Harry Hopkins with hand grenades."

243   The plump and balding: Rostow interview; Bird, pp. 63, 186.

244   In part, Harriman was being rewarded: *WP*, Jan. 22, 1962.

244   "instinct for the care": Schlesinger interview.

244   "the supreme centre of power": Gore, "The Centres of Power in the Kennedy Administration," Jan. 23, 1962, PRO.

244   "first class men . . . clearly not yet": Gore, "Annual Review for 1961," Jan. 1, 1962, PRO.

244   "giddy with power": Rowe to White, May 25, 1961, White Papers, Harvard University.

244   "peered over the brink": Gore, "Annual Review for 1961," Jan. 1, 1962, PRO.

244   Inspired by two weeks: Schlesinger II, p. 592; Collier and Horowitz, p. 284.

244   Regulars included: Elspeth Rostow interview.

244   "particularly undaunted questioners": *ATD*, p. 695.

244   "precious": Schlesinger II, p. 592.

244   "a sort of intellectual quick fix": Marian Schlesinger OH.

244   his discussion at the White House: Ros Gilpatric to Chadbourne Gilpatric, Feb. 20, 1961, Gilpatric Papers, JFKL.

245   "who seemed to have an extraordinarily": David Donald to Ros Gilpatric, Feb. 24, 1962, Gilpatric Papers, JFKL.

245   "How word of such affairs": Gilpatric to Donald, Feb. 27, 1962, Gilpatric Papers, JFKL.

245   "It is inconceivable to me": *NYT,* Sept. 21, 1961.

245   Charley Bartlett also resigned: ibid.; *NYT,* Oct. 12, 1961; *Boston Globe,* Apr. 26, 1962.

245   "up to the consciences of his aides": *NYT,* Oct. 12, 1961.

245   Privately, JFK liked to bait: Bird, p. 190.

245   What Bundy didn't know: The Brook membership book, 2002, p. 62: John F. Kennedy, 1957–1963.

245   Through his friendship: Earl E.T. Smith Jr. interview.

246   "impossible for an Irish Catholic": Fay, p. 124.

246   "This is the first and probably": Thomas OH-CU.

246   even held a strategy session: White notes for *The Making of the President 1960,* Dec. 28, 1960, White Papers, Harvard University.

246   "persistent and not always gentle needling": *DOAP,* p. 581.

246   "I always felt sorry": Charles Bartlett interview.

246   "more a schmalzfest": *Time,* Dec. 22, 1961.

246   "Viva Miss America": *NYT,* Dec. 19, 1961.

246   While Kennedy was "moved": *WP,* Dec. 24, 1961.

246   "it was almost like a family": *Sunday Times,* March 28, 1965.

246   Kennedy showed Khrushchev's secret: Macmillan II, p. 145.

246   "on the wider issues he seems": Macmillan Journal, Dec. 23, 1961, HMA.

246   "very easily pleased": Macmillan II, p. 148.

247   "I wonder how it is": Horne, p. 290.

247   "the sixty-seven-year-old monogamous": ibid.

247   Kennedy had hurt his back: *PK,* p. 273.

247   "difficult to sit": Macmillan II, p. 148.

247   "pick up a book or paper": Macmillan Journal, Dec. 23, 1961, HMA.

247   "excellent general health": *NYT,* Dec. 28, 1961.

247   eight-bedroom Regency-style: *WP,* Dec. 2, 1961; *NYT,* Dec. 25, 1961; DBD, Dec. 20, 1961.

247   Jack had planned: *WP,* Dec. 19, 1961; *NYT,* Dec. 19, 1961.

247   Dressed in shorts: *NYT,* Dec. 20, 1961; *WP,* Dec. 20, 1961; *Time,* Dec. 29, 1961.

247   As he was teeing off: Rose Kennedy, p. 417.

248   "Don't call any doctors!": *Time,* Dec. 29, 1961.

248   When Ann looked in: Rose Kennedy, p. 418.

248   Joe had suffered: *WP,* Dec. 21, 1961; *NYT,* Dec. 23, 1961.

248   "might have hopefully interpreted": *NYT,* Dec. 23, 1961.

248   Other than "nooo": Rita Dallas, *The Kennedy Case,* p. 32.

248   "Jackie probably likes": *HTF,* p. 698, Rose Kennedy diary, Nov. 23, 1961.

248   As the President smoked: Fay, p. 261.

248   "big derrière": *HTF,* p. 699, Rose Kennedy diary, Nov. 23, 1961.

248   "an attack": ibid.

248   "had chucked them away": *LG,* p. 915.

248   "the possibility of a stroke": *NYT,* Dec. 22, 1961.

248   "I get awfully blue": Leamer I, p. 546, based on an interview with Frank Waldrop. In *RKHL* (p. 164), Evan Thomas recounts that on December 11, FBI director J. Edgar Hoover sent Bobby Kennedy a memo about the agency's investigation of the Mafia

that included a "reference to Joseph Kennedy Sr. and [Sam] Giancana's alleged role in the 1960 election. . . . Robert Kennedy's reaction has gone unrecorded. Nor is it known if RFK spoke to his father. If he did, it was one of their last conversations."

249 "The President will have": Jack Warner to JPK, Dec. 8, 1961, JPKP.
249 Joe had replied enthusiastically: JPK to Warner, Dec. 14, 1961, JPKP.
249 On Christmas Eve they spent: *NYT,* Dec. 26, 1961.
249 Otherwise, life went on: ibid.
249 The loss of Joe's everyday: Charles Bartlett interview; Sorensen interview.
249 "Holy cow, fella": Racine interview.
249 "Old age is a shipwreck": Charles Bartlett interview.

Chapter Nineteen
250 The tony gathering turned raucous: *WP,* Feb. 3, 1962.
250 "a rare signed pair": Cassini I, p. 95.
250 "rarely took her eyes off him": *WP,* Jan. 13, 1962.
251 Kennedy sought support: ibid., Jan. 11, 1962; *NYT,* Jan. 14, 1962.
251 popularity ratings that had held: *WP,* Mar. 3, 1962.
251 "wiser, more mature": *Time,* Jan. 5, 1962.
251 "made the world safe for brunettes": *NYT,* Jan. 20, 1962.
251 On Monday, January 15: *WP,* Jan. 17, 1962; *JKWH,* pp. 325–30.
251 "I thought a couple of handsome men": Perry Wolff interview.
251 Jackie committed all the facts: ibid.
251 On the day of the taping: ibid.; *JKWH,* p. 328.
251 Deferring to "Mr. Schaffner": Wolff interview.
251 "but I had to rest my feet": *AH,* p. 392.
251 "shy manner": ibid., pp. 392–93.
252 Jackie gave him what Farmington girls: Wolff interview.
252 "She knew her stuff": ibid.
252 "she smoked all the time": ibid.
252 "chamber of horrors": Perry Wolff, *A Tour of the White House with Mrs. John F. Kennedy,* p. 222.
252 "who now sit in the hall": ibid., p. 226.
252 At the Kennedys' request: Wolff interview.
252 "When the lights went up": Perry Wolff speech, Jan. 10, 2002.
253 Amid all the "Russian kissing": Leonard Bernstein OH.
253 "weary" from a day of rehearsals: *WP,* Jan. 20, 1962.
253 In fact, Stravinsky had gotten: Chavchavadze interview.
253 "My God, how jealous": Truman Capote to Cecil Beaton, Feb. 9, 1962, Beaton Collection, St. John's College, Cambridge.
253 Their send-off: *CWK,* pp. 53–54.
253 Because the Kennedys were obliged: *WP,* Feb. 11, 1962.
253 "We were so out": *CWK,* p. 49.
253 Oleg Cassini performed a solo: *WP,* Feb. 11, 1962.
253 "much to the distress": McNamara interview; *CWK,* p. 55.
253 During another twist: *CWK,* p. 55.
253 JFK found time to tip: ibid., pp. 49–51; *WP,* Feb. 11, 1962.
254 "By that time": *CWK,* p. 52.
254 "Mary would be rough": ibid., p. 54.
254 "Mary was not easy because": Angleton interview.
254 Less than three weeks earlier: *National Enquirer,* Mar. 2, 1976.
254 "She told me she had fallen": Truitt interview.
254 "Bill was a friend of the marriage": Chavchavadze interview.
254 "She and Jack understood": Truitt interview.

255   "amitié amoreuse": ibid.

255   "I think the real key": Ben Bradlee interview.

255   "great woman": Charles Bartlett interview.

255   "we knew Mary was a pal": Baldrige interview.

255   On Valentine's Day, America fell: *NYT,* Feb. 16, 1962; *JKWH,* p. 330.

255   "English clubhouse": *NYT,* Feb. 15, 1962: broadcast transcript.

256   "impressed with Jackie's knowledge": *CWK,* p. 57.

256   "over my performance": ibid., p. 58.

256   "verve and pleasure": *NYT,* Feb. 15, 1962.

256   In the three days following: *WP,* Feb. 18, 1962.

256   "scathing neurotic attack": *Newsweek,* July 16, 1962.

256   "odd public voice": Mailer, *Esquire,* July 1962.

256   "so gentle": Alphand, p. 373.

257   insisted it was genuine: Wood interview.

257   "really intelligent things": Marina Sulzberger, *Marina: Letters and Diaries of Marina Sulzberger* (Sulzberger II), p. 274.

257   "it was a voice that kept": Wilson interview.

257   "was part of her intimacy": Plimpton interview.

257   "too full of herself": Cooper interview.

257   "desperately important": JBK to Schlesinger, March 1962, Schlesinger Papers, JFKL.

257   she needed its revenue: ibid., Feb. 14, 1962.

257   "She wanted a story": Ketchum interview.

257   Jackie spent many hours: ibid.; Cooper interview.

257   "some stirring phrases": JBK to Schlesinger, Feb. 14, 1962, Schlesinger Papers, JFKL.

257   most notably when he took into account: Isaacson and Thomas, p. 611.

257   Yet Kennedy ignored: Anderson, p, 216.

258   "relied on him a lot": Ben Bradlee interview.

258   "He was pulling strings": Jean Friendly interview.

258   Schlesinger proposed August Heckscher: *ATD,* p. 734; *NYT,* Feb. 22, 1962; Heckscher OH.

258   As a part-time film reviewer: *Time,* June 29, 1962.

258   Schlesinger would also alert: Schlesinger to JBK, Jan. 17, 1963, Schlesinger Papers, JFKL.

258   The President found *L'Avventura: NYT Magazine,* Jan. 29, 1962.

258   "the puzzle aspect": Arthur Schlesinger interview.

258   "chanelish chiffons": Cassini I, p. 108.

258   "I am sorry to impose": JBK to Schlesinger, Feb. 14, 1962, Schlesinger Papers, JFKL.

258   "ghastly": ibid., March 1962.

258   "something to take away": ibid.

258   "imperishable memories": Schlesinger, draft introduction to White House Guidebook, Schlesinger Papers, JFKL.

259   "lively, even controversial": JBK to Schlesinger, April 1962, Schlesinger Papers, JFKL.

259   "If you can do all this": ibid.

259   "certain jobs to do": Arthur Schlesinger interview.

259   Jackie and Lee's goodwill trip: *NYT,* Feb. 26, 1962.

259   "low-grade sinus infection": ibid., Feb. 27, 1962.

259   Only the day before the announcement: *WP,* Feb. 26, 1962; *Time,* Mar. 9, 1962.

259   "John Kennedy's pique": *Time,* Mar. 9, 1962.

259   "Jackie now hates the idea": Stewart Alsop to Martin Sommers, Feb. 19, 1962, Alsop Papers, LOC.

259   Jackie was hardly an intimate: Joan Braden, *Just Enough Rope* (Braden I), pp. 108–11; *WP,* June 19, 1962; Heller, p. 45; Democratic National Committee News Release, Nov. 1, 1960.

259 "She has a remarkable talent": Stewart Alsop to Martin Sommers, May 25, 1962, Alsop Papers, LOC.

260 "a unique combination": ibid., May 1, 1962.

260 "that little freckle-faced girl": Tom Braden, *Eight Is Enough* (Braden II), p. 182.

260 "total freedom—just enough rope": Braden I, p. 48.

260 Joan's most noted liaison: ibid., p. 43.

260 "fix it up": Stewart Alsop to Martin Sommers, Feb. 19, 1962, Alsop Papers, LOC.

260 "inside story": ibid.

260 "Che bella": *WP*, Mar. 11, 1962.

260 She was scheduled to have: DuBois, p. 100.

260 Jackie saw the pope alone: *WP*, Mar. 12, 1962.

260 Afterwards, Jackie consulted: *NYT*, Mar. 12, 1962; DuBois, p. 100; Joan Braden, "An Exclusive Chat with Jackie Kennedy, *Saturday Evening Post*, May 12, 1962.

260 The Kennedys had deep connections: *HTF*, p. 135.

260 "Papal Countess": *WP*, Mar. 5, 1962.

260 "most magic two weeks": *NYT*, Mar. 27, 1962.

260 "maladjusted and vagrant boys": *WP*, Mar. 15, 1962.

260 "mass and symmetry": *WP*, Mar. 16, 1962; *Time*, Mar. 23, 1962.

260 Jackie wore Ayub Khan's Astrakhan: Braden, *Saturday Evening Post*, May 12, 1962.

260 The sisters stayed: *WP*, Mar. 18 and 21, 1962; *NYT*, Mar. 15, 1962.

261 "fantastic gaits": *NYT*, Mar. 23, 1962.

261 After some initial unease: *NYT*, Mar. 18 and 23, 1962.

261 "makes an elephant feel": *WP*, Mar. 26, 1962.

261 "Both the First Lady": ibid.

261 Nehru was so bewitched: *WP*, Mar. 12 and 14, 1962.

261 "We never talked of serious things": Braden, *Saturday Evening Post*, May 12, 1962.

261 "they talked about what they were reading": Galbraith interview.

261 "magnificent": Braden, *Saturday Evening Post*, May 12, 1962.

261 "fine character": Macmillan II, p. 130.

261 "like Jack—tough and brave": Braden, *Saturday Evening Post*, May 12, 1962.

261 "There will be a lot of sun": Cassini I, p. 112.

261 "queenly white": *AJ*, p. 287.

262 "excellent sense of theater": ibid., p. 281.

262 The sisters brought: Cassini I, p. 112.

262 Jackie wore twenty different: *NYT*, Mar. 18, 1962.

262 Jackie dropped nearly $600: *AJ*, p. 289.

262 "Only an economist": Braden, *Saturday Evening Post*, May 12, 1962.

262 "He makes Tish look reticent": JBK to JFK from Delhi, Mar. 13, 1962, WMP.

262 "told me that the care": *AJ*, p. 288.

262 As with the previous year: Baldrige I, p. 251.

262 One hundred pages: *NYT*, Mar. 11, 1961.

262 "exactly like a drugstore": *AJ*, p. 531: an account written by Catherine A. Galbraith, May 1963.

262 "One must be adamant": JBK to Averell Harriman, Oct. 13, 1967, Harriman Collection, LOC.

262 "It was not easy for me": Baldrige interview.

262 Midway through the trip: Baldrige I, p. 265.

262 "slightly alarming report": *AJ*, p. 286.

262 Jackie bounced back: *WP*, March 28, 1962.

262 "le hully gully": Cassini I, p. 142.

262 The two friends draped: ibid., p. 144.

263 Jackie's trip had no specific: *NYT*, Mar. 27, 1962.

263 "took all the bitterness": *CWK*, p. 69.

263 "the charm of her personality": *NYT,* Mar. 22, 1962.
263 "psychological pull": ibid.
263 "everyone loved": *WP,* Mar. 24, 1962.
263 Indira's mood brightened: *NYT,* Mar. 27, 1962.
263 "She gave him sugar": *AH,* p. 424.

Chapter Twenty
264 meeting her only hours: *WP,* Mar. 16, 1962.
264 On Thursday, March 22: *PK,* pp. 288–90.
264 "freelance artist": Courtney Evans memo, Mar. 20, 1962, J. Edgar Hoover Official and Confidential File 96 (John F. Kennedy), FBI. According to a Senate investigation in 1975, there had been seventy phone calls in all. (*Alleged Assassination Plots Involving Foreign Leaders: An Interim Report,* Washington, DC: 94th Congress, 1st Session, Report No. 94-465, November 1975: Report of the Church Committee, pp. 129–30.)
264 That afternoon, Kennedy called: *PK,* p. 290.
265 Over the weekend he stayed: Tina Sinatra, *My Father's Daughter,* p. 79; *RKHL,* pp. 166–70.
265 "shacking up with John Kennedy": Evans memo, Mar. 20, 1962, J. Edgar Hoover Official and Confidential File 96 (John F. Kennedy), FBI.
265 Sinatra's relationship with the Kennedys: Braden I, p. 110.
265 "he got in to see Jack": Sinatra, p. 78.
265 "personified a page": ibid.
265 "mob-infested unions": ibid., p. 72; *TCY,* pp. 140–43, also details FBI allegations about JPK's links with mobsters during the 1960 campaign.
265 "Dad was stunned": Sinatra, p. 77.
265 Under those circumstances: ibid., p. 79; *PK,* p. 293.
265 On the weekend of March 24: *RKHL,* p. 191; *TCY,* p. 367.
266 "something about the difficulties": *WP,* Jan. 13, 1962.
266 "nutty schemes": *TCY,* p. 376.
266 "There was nothing Bobby did": Helms interview.
266 The Cuban intelligence service: *TCY,* pp. 370, 371, 375.
266 Kennedy's resumption: ibid., p. 369.
266 These shared apprehensions: *PR-JFK,* p. li; *TCY,* pp. 380–83, 387; *KT,* p. 460.
267 "It feels unnatural": *NYT,* Mar. 30, 1962.
267 "well-televised": *AJ,* p. 294.
267 It was a relaxed evening: *ATD,* p. 530.
267 "general political grace": *AJ,* p. 295.
267 "acute observations about Nehru": Arthur Schlesinger interview.
267 "a bit tired": *AJ,* p. 294.
267 "I don't even care": JBK to Cooper, ND, courtesy of Janet Felton Cooper.
267 The President had to serve: Evelyn Lincoln Diary, Apr. 6, 1962, Evelyn Lincoln Papers, JFKL; *WP,* Apr. 3, 1962.
267 In his spare time: *WP,* Apr. 5, 1962; Lincoln Diary, Apr. 7, 1962, Lincoln Papers, JFKL; *NYT,* Apr. 10, 1962.
268 Jackie considered the White House swimming pool: Gallagher, p. 134; Abbott and Rice, p. 209; *Time,* Dec. 7, 1962; *WP,* Apr. 3, 1962.
268 At one point, LaMotte: *WP,* Apr. 29, 1962.
268 "brains dinner": Baldrige III, p. 88.
268 "blindingly impressive": *WP,* Apr. 12, 1962.
268 "one of the most stimulating": ibid., Apr. 30, 1962.
268 "appeared to be self-conscious": Diana Trilling, "A Visit to Camelot," *The New Yorker,* June 2, 1997.
269 "When you were at Vassar": *Newsweek,* May 14, 1962.

269   a chapter from an unpublished novel: *Time,* May 11, 1962.

269   "so poor that one was pained": Trilling, *The New Yorker,* June 2, 1997.

269   "the biggest bore I've had": Walton interview, JCBC.

269   "I am so happy to get out": Walton OH.

269   "at once had the place": Trilling, *The New Yorker,* June 2, 1997.

269   "Jackie's personal part": ibid.

269   "filled with cigar smokers": William Styron, "Havanas in Camelot," *Vanity Fair,* July 1996.

269   "health rocker": Trilling, *The New Yorker,* June 2, 1997.

269   "wreathed in smoke": Styron, *Vanity Fair,* July 1996.

269   "Jackie spoke very openly": Trilling, *The New Yorker,* June 2, 1997.

270   "Think of the headlines": ibid.

270   By the time of the Nobel dinner: *ATD,* p. 634; *PK,* pp. 294–95; *Newsweek,* Apr. 23, 1962.

270   "the best settlement": Memo of Conversation (Memcon), Dillon and Roger Blough, Apr. 3, 1962, Dillon Papers, JFKL.

270   "only one slant": Gilpatric OH.

270   "Many of his questions": ibid.

270   On Tuesday, April 10: Sidey I, pp. 292–93; *ATD,* p. 635.

270   "They kicked us": *CWK,* p. 76.

270   Kennedy felt particularly betrayed: Sidey I, p. 291; *Time,* Apr. 20, 1962.

270   "My father always told me": *ATD,* p. 635.

271   The previous Friday: Bartlett OH.

271   "a stiff or conciliatory": ibid.

271   "irresponsible defiance": *Time,* Apr. 20, 1962.

271   His anger barely contained: *CWK,* p. 77; *RKHL,* pp. 170–71; *PK,* p. 298.

271   Bobby Kennedy rashly dispatched: Roger Blough OH-CU.

271   "It was highly overdone": Bartlett OH.

271   "it was a tough way to operate": *AH,* p. 414.

271   "The steel people made": Dillon interview.

271   "ready to make peace": Bartlett OH.

271   "understood the workings": ibid.

272   "We're going to tuck it to them": *CWK,* p. 78.

272   As the secret talks proceeded: *Time,* Apr. 20, 1962; Sidey I, p. 302.

272   "began to realize that there": Blough OH-CU.

272   "had been smart enough to wait": Bartlett OH.

272   A year later when the steel: Blough OH-CU.

272   Kennedy's stance played well: *NYT,* May 30, 1962; *WP,* June 23, 1962.

272   "almost totalitarian": *Time,* Apr. 20, 1962.

272   caused a breach: Blough OH-CU.

272   "modest and intelligent man": Macmillan Journal, Apr. 25, 1962, HMA.

272   Kennedy tried to retract: *WP,* May 10, 1962.

272   In a speech to the U.S. Chamber: *Time,* May 11, 1962.

272   "watched him work over": Bartlett OH.

272   "this fixation": ibid.

272   "He seems to want advice": Macmillan Journal, May 6, 1962, HMA.

272   "bitterness of his feeling": Macmillan, "Note by the Prime Minister of his conversation with President Kennedy on the morning of Saturday, April 28, 1962, at the White House," PRO.

273   "de Gaulle's rudeness": Macmillan Journal, May 6, 1962, HMA.

273   "being cynical": ibid.

273   "the same humorous view": Macmillan note, Apr. 28, 1962, PRO.

273   Much of their conversation focused: Harlech OH.

273   More than ever, Macmillan recognized: Macmillan Journal, May 6, 1962, HMA.

273 "a Plantagenet, with a strong": *Evening Standard,* May 31, 1967.

273 Sissie had a fey: Charles interview; Wilson interview; Ben Bradlee interview.

273 "a certain puritan streak": Lord Jenkins of Hillhead interview.

273 "the worst two weeks": JBK to Harry du Pont, May 3, 1962, Winterthur Archives.

273 she occupied herself by mouthing: *WP,* May 4, 1962.

273 She gave a tea: ibid.

273 "Je vous baptise": *WP,* May 9, 1962.

273 On the way to the ceremony: ibid., May 7, 1962.

273 "While the others pretended": Dallas, p. 81.

274 During her two-hour visit: *WP,* May 7, 1962.

274 "the little blunders": Dallas, p. 82.

274 Before the social season ended: Edward McDermott OH; *CWK,* pp. 78–79; Chavchavadze interview.

274 "How do you go about": McDermott OH.

274 Walter Sohier, a handsome favorite: Wendy Morgan interview.

274 "good and sometimes sultry": *AJ,* p. 329.

274 "I know the National Gallery": *WP,* May 11, 1962.

274 "strode through": ibid., May 12, 1962.

274 Jackie welcomed the French statesman: Gallagher, p. 227.

275 She wore a luminous: Cassini I, pp. 152–53.

275 To match Malraux's varied: *WP,* May 11, 1962; Baldrige III, p. 103.

275 who nearly was turned away: *WP,* May 12, 1962.

275 "great Americans": Baldrige III, p. 103.

275 "landed in France": Bowles, *Met Catalogue,* p. 99.

275 Malraux spoke little: Elspeth Rostow interview.

275 "wanted to talk to Arthur": ibid.

275 "Her manners were perfect": ibid.

275 she murmured to him: *Time,* May 18, 1962.

275 "un peu gaga": *ATD,* p. 671.

275 As the evening came: Bowles, *Met Catalogue,* p. 99.

275 "above all on political": *LG,* p. 927.

276 "the management of industrial": *ATD,* p. 644.

276 "to look at things": *WP,* May 25, 1962.

276 "give-away": Dillon OH; Dillon and Blough, Memcon, May 10, 1962, Dillon Papers, JFKL.

276 Throughout the fall: *PK,* p. 318; Dillon OH.

276 "the government was going to try": Dillon interview.

276 As confidence dimmed: Sidey I, p. 308; *PK,* p. 318.

276 "Thucydides of the 1929 crash": *AJ,* p. 328.

276 "a psychological occurrence": Dillon OH.

276 The Treasury secretary made: Dillon and JFK, Memcon, May 28, 1962, Dillon Papers, JFKL; Sidey I, p. 310.

276 When Jack Kennedy turned forty-five: *PK,* p. 320; Dillon OH; Dillon and Phil Graham, Memcon, July 3, 1962, Dillon Papers, JFKL; Dillon interview.

277 Chef René Verdon prepared: *WP,* May 30, 1962.

277 The President never saw: ibid.

277 "The amazing thing to me": *Time,* June 1, 1962.

277 "The figure was famous": ibid.

277 "making love to the President": Bradford, p. 224.

277 Afterwards, Kennedy attended: O'Brien, p. 151; Walton OH; *NYT,* May 19, 1962.

277 "skin and beads": Schlesinger II, p. 590.

277 "I didn't see the beads!": Stevenson to Mary Lasker, May 21, 1962, Stevenson Papers, Princeton University.

278   "was not the mistress of any Kennedy": Walton OH.
278   "Marilyn started making passes": ibid.
278   "enchanted by her manner": Schlesinger II, pp. 590–91.
278   "She was an exhibitionist": Walton OH.
278   "surprise participant": *NYT,* May 20, 1962; Eve Fout interview.
278   *It is a sign of pride:* TCY, p. 251, citing Bundy-JFK, ND, JFKL, and Bundy interview in *WP,* Jan. 25, 1974.
279   He had enlisted: Rachel Lambert Mellon, "President Kennedy's Rose Garden," *White House History: Journal of the White House Historical Association,* 1983.
279   "to appeal to the most discriminating": ibid.
279   "Bunny, where is my garden": ibid.
279   "tapestry of flowers": ibid.
279   Mellon dug up the old: *WP,* May 8, 1962.
279   The President designed: Mellon, *Journal of the White House Historical Association,* 1983.
279   "gaily striped pavilion": DBD, Apr. 27, 1962.
279   "changing and pruning": Mellon, *Journal of the White House Historical Association,* 1983.
279   "bookish": *WP,* June 22, 1962.
279   The room bore the strong: Abbott and Rice, pp. 122–26; Cornelia Conger to Henry du Pont, June 6, 1961, Winterthur Archives.
280   "working library": *WP,* June 22, 1962.
280   "the most historic": ibid., June 29, 1962.
280   "rather ugly charm": *JKWH,* p. 346.
280   Most of the ponderous relics: *WP,* June 29, 1961, and Sept. 8, 1962.
280   a dramatic design conceived: Abbott and Rice, pp. 190–91.
280   "adults and scholars also": *WP,* June 29, 1962.

Chapter Twenty-one
281   During his second summer: *WP,* Oct. 10 and Sept. 21, 1962.
281   "sun colors": Bowles, *Met Catalogue,* p. 166.
281   Betraying slight nervousness: *WP,* July 1, 1962.
281   "the profound faith": ibid.
282   "change in the attitude": ibid., July 2, 1962.
282   For greater privacy: *Time,* July 13, 1962; Joan Kennedy interview.
282   "She became more remote": Cooper interview.
282   "tense and apprehensive": Max Jacobson unpublished manuscript, "John F. Kennedy," p. 26.
282   In May the President's special bed: *CWK,* pp. 99–100.
282   A month later he needed: *AJ,* p. 334; *CWK,* pp. 110–11.
283   "back still bothers him": *LG,* p. 895.
283   secret taping system: *PR-JFK,* vol. I, p. xviii; Michael Beschloss, ed., *Taking Charge: The Johnson White House Tapes, 1963–1964* (Beschloss III), pp. 547–50.
283   "a power-drunk dictator": *Newsweek,* July 16, 1962.
283   "cherished": *Time,* July 27, 1962.
283   "quickie" tax cut: *WP,* July 22, 1962.
284   The shaky coalition government: *PR-JFK,* vol. 1, p. 420; vol. 2, pp. 178–79.
284   "don't seem to have cojones": *PR-JFK,* vol. 1, p. 48.
284   "languid" . . . "hard and tough": ibid., p. 49.
284   "an old lady if you ever": ibid., p. 50.
284   Later that day he shifted: ibid., p. 105.
284   Kennedy effectively synthesized: ibid., p. 126.
285   "a lovely way about her": James Reed interview.
285   James Truitt later claimed: *National Enquirer,* Mar. 2, 1976; *WP,* Feb. 23, 1976.
285   Truitt had been suffering: Truitt interview.

285   "drunk and out of control": ibid.

285   "Mary was a risk taker": Noland interview.

285   But Noland—and the Bradlees: ibid.; Ben Bradlee interview.

286   "was devastated": Ben Bradlee interview.

286   "little notebook with a pretty cover": Truitt interview.

286   Only about ten pages were devoted: ibid.; Ben Bradlee interview; Tony Bradlee interview.

286   "just floored": Truitt interview.

286   "very cryptic": Tony Bradlee interview.

286   "No entry was more": Ben Bradlee interview.

286   After James Truitt's interviews: Anne Truitt interview; Tony Bradlee interview.

286   "Everyone thought it was full": Tony Bradlee interview.

286   In June 1962, Jack Kennedy gave: WP, May 24, 1962. (The program was taped on April 18 for broadcast on June 2, 1962.)

286   "curve of academic excellence": ibid.

286   After more than a year: Raskin interview.

287   As the editor of the newspaper: Marion Beardsley Fahnestock interview.

287   "was brought over and met": Gamarekian interview.

287   "a sexual relationship": Associated Press, May 15, 2003.

287   "She wasn't in the office very long": Gamarekian OH.

287   Finally, at the insistence: Fahnestock interview.

287   "in this way that people know": Raskin interview.

288   Monroe began telling: PK, p. 332; Hersh II, p. 106.

288   "Phone records show": Evan Thomas interview, C-SPAN, July 13, 2002.

288   "damage control": RKHL, p. 192.

288   Fearful that the Monroe stories: Hersh, pp. 104–105; Bradford, p. 221.

288   "You think, 'By God, I'll sing'": Richard Meryman, "Marilyn Monroe Lets Her Hair Down About Being Famous," Life, Aug. 3, 1962.

288   "I felt as though I had": NYT, July 22, 1962; Gallagher, p. 146.

288   The next day, Monroe called: Leamer I, p. 568.

288   Washington Post's banner headline: WP, Aug. 6, 1962.

289   His last meeting of the day: PR-JFK, vol. 1, pp. 234–59.

289   They stayed in Villa Episcopio: Time, Aug. 30, 1962; LG, pp. 914–16; NYT, Aug. 9, 1962; Radziwill, pp. 10–11.

289   who were with Jackie for the entire: Benno Graziani interview.

289   "We went sightseeing": Agnelli interview.

289   For several days: WP, Aug. 15, 1962; Radziwill, p. 11.

290   "angry faces": WP, Aug. 14, 1962.

290   Dining at the villa: Bradford, p. 230; WP, Aug. 14, 1962.

290   they giddily sang "Volare": Radziwill, p. 11.

290   When the group returned: WP, Aug. 15, 1962.

290   Over the years, a number: Edward Klein, All Too Human: The Love Story of Jack and Jackie Kennedy, pp. 315–17.

290   But Marella was also aboard: Agnelli interview; Graziani interview.

290   "was notable for a fair amount": Judy Bachrach, "La Vita Agnelli," Vanity Fair, May 2003.

290   indeed no such photographs: Ann Schneider interview.

290   "There was nothing between": Graziani interview.

290   "Obviously there is no truth": Radziwill interview.

290   "It was not like Gianni": Countess Marina Cicogna interview.

290   "Dearest dearest Jack . . . I miss you very much": JBK to JFK, ND, letterhead: "L'Episcopio, Ravello, Prov Di Salerno," August 1962, WMP.

291   He eventually got through—several times: LG, p. 914.

291   "Jackie was very quiet": Graziani interview.

291   "immensely ambitious": *LG,* p. 915.

291   "the most controlled person": ibid.

291   By the end of her sojourn: *Time,* Sept. 7, 1962.

291   renamed by the town council: *NYT,* Aug. 26, 1962.

292   "JACKIE'S BIG NIGHT": Bradford, p. 231.

292   "why Mrs. Kennedy had to go": Louchheim Journal, Aug. 12, 1962, KSLP.

292   In early August, Kennedy had sent: *PR-JFK,* vol. 1, p. 131.

292   When Khrushchev made no immediate: ibid., p. 328; vol. 2, pp. 73–75.

292   Bobby Kennedy's Operation Mongoose: ibid., vol. 1, p. 482.

292   "if it became known": ibid., p. 488.

292   Two days later: ibid., pp. 482, 593, 599–602.

293   Nevertheless Kennedy asked: ibid., p. 607.

293   "an act of war": ibid., vol. 2, p. 62.

293   "No one would desire more": ibid., p. 71.

293   Kennedy also requested a review: ibid., vol. 1, pp. 422, 458, 460, 607.

293   "I will say that the Soviet Union": ibid., vol. 2, p. 64.

293   On August 31 aerial: ibid., vol. I, p. 650; vol. 2, p. 33.

293   "gravest issues would arise": ibid., vol. 2, p. 80.

293   "We've got the Monroe Doctrine": ibid., vol. 2, p. 29.

293   "creating a kind of panic": ibid.

293   "making a threat": ibid., vol. 2, p. 40.

293   "You have to understand": ibid., p. 39.

293   In the end, Rusk: ibid., pp. 41, 80.

293   Khrushchev responded: *TCY,* pp. 421, 426.

293   Stewart Udall had been: Udall interview.

293   "go to war or sign": *PR-JFK,* vol. 2, pp. 111, 147.

293   "were too liberal to fight": ibid., p. 111.

293   It was a statement: Udall interview.

294   "summer bachelor": *Time,* Aug. 3, 1962.

294   "absolutely boiling hot": Janet Auchincloss OH.

294   They stayed at the home: *WP,* Aug. 11 and 12, 1962.

294   With Kennedy at the tiller: James Reed interview.

294   Reed, now working: Reed OH.

294   "They swooned": *Time,* Aug. 31, 1962.

294   "in perfect form": *WP,* Aug. 20, 1962.

294   "likes pleasure and women": Alphand, p. 382.

295   "if you want more special": JBK to JFK, ND, August 1962, WMP.

295   The one prominent absentee: *CWK,* pp. 23–25.

295   "It's almost impossible": ibid., p. 23.

295   "dinner at the White House": ibid., p. 25.

295   "to present the semblance": Jewel Reed interview.

295   Ben Bradlee made a cameo: *CWK,* pp. 114–17.

295   "No. He's not coming": ibid., p. 117.

295   Dressed in a blue yachting blazer: *NYT,* Sept. 23, 1962.

296   "the great unfinished business": *WP,* Sept. 23, 1962.

296   "quiet and proud determination": ibid.

296   "the political and social elite": *NYT,* Sept. 26, 1962.

296   While Jackie and their guests: Smith III, p. 230.

296   Broadway producer Leland: *WP,* Sept. 27, 1962.

297   "Was the first act as bad": Louchheim Journal, Sept. 28, 1962, KSLP.

297   "Dismal, corny": DBD, Sept. 26, 1962.

297   a lavish midnight champagne supper: *WP,* Sept. 27, 1962; *NYT,* Sept. 26, 1962.

297   "Everyone ogled everyone": Louchheim Journal, Sept. 28, 1962, KSLP.
297   Jackie wore an exquisite: Bowles, *Met Catalogue,* p. 110.
297   She chose Hervé Alphand: *Time,* Oct. 5, 1962.
297   "danced vigorously": DBD, Sept. 26, 1962.
297   "it was an evening to remove": *WP,* Sept. 27, 1962.
297   "were still hot footing": DBD, Sept. 26, 1962.
297   "The only thing that had intruded": *Time,* Oct. 5, 1962.

Chapter Twenty-two
298   The trouble stemmed from: *PR-JFK,* vol. 2, pp. 222–25.
298   At that stage, JFK canceled: *WP,* Sept. 29, 1962.
298   For the next forty-eight hours: *PR-JFK,* vol. 2, pp. 237–319.
299   "You don't want to have a lynching": ibid., p. 287.
299   "Where is Nick?": ibid., p. 268.
299   "I haven't had such an interesting": ibid., p. 274.
299   "Did he break his back?": ibid., p. 277.
299   But despite the attacks: ibid., p. 276. When the idea of retaliation was raised, JFK
       replied, "You see, once some one fellow starts firing, everybody starts firing. That's
       what concerns me." Later, Bobby Kennedy turned down a request to fire back,
       although when asked specifically about an attack on Meredith, RFK said, "Oh, I
       think that they can fire to save *him*" (p. 292). In his biography of RFK, Arthur
       Schlesinger described "the President's personal order not to shoot except to protect
       Meredith's life" (Schlesinger II, p. 323).
299   "I would think they'd be": *PR-JFK,* vol. 2, p. 294.
299   "I have a hunch that Khrushchev": ibid., p. 300.
299   "Your daughter's car": ibid., p. 303.
300   "If you ever made a chronological": ibid.
300   Yet Kennedy paid no political penalty: *PK,* p. 364.
300   With the protection: *PR-JFK,* vol. 2, p. 319.
300   "transform the White House": *WP,* Sept. 5, 1962.
300   The worst part was: ibid., Sept. 6, 1962.
300   "mustached and dapper": ibid., Sept. 9, 1962.
300   "Boudin's Boudoir": ibid.
300   "play down the French influence": ibid.
301   "Oh, Doris, what in the world": Dickerson, p. 64.
301   "wouldn't even recognize": Laura Bergquist Knebel OH.
301   "harpies": Baldrige I, p. 175.
301   "If you were appalled": JBK to du Pont, Sept. 28, 1962, Winterthur Archives.
302   "The room will remain blue": Charles Roberts to Kermit Lansner, ND, with note
       to Turnure scrawled by Roberts: "Pam, All these corrections were made in the text,"
       White House Files, JFKL.
302   Months earlier Jayne: Abbott and Rice, p. 108.
302   On its doors were images: ibid., pp. 204–205.
302   "mes objets adorés": JBK to Stéphane Boudin, ND (September 1962), written from
       Hammersmith Farm, courtesy of Pierre-Marie Rudelle.
302   The idea for the wardrobe: Pierre-Marie Rudelle to author, May 28, 2001; *WP,* Sept.
       9, 1962. Rudelle couldn't make room for two other images of Jackie's "adored
       objects": a gingerbread house and *Anthologie de l'amour sublime,* by Benjamin Peret, an
       essayist and surrealist poet known for his wild imagination and irreverence. In the
       anthology, Peret explores themes of sublime love through works by writers from
       Apollonius of Rhodes to Baudelaire and Breton.
302   "poets and idealists who could paint": Jacqueline Bouvier, "Feature-Question 3,"
       Vogue Prix de Paris application, May 21, 1951, *Vogue* Materials, JFKL.

302   "I am flabbergasted!!!!!": JBK to Stéphane Boudin, September 1962, courtesy of Pierre-Marie Rudelle.

303   Jackie wanted to keep her: Alice Grimes Gaither interview; Elizabeth Boyd interview; *WP*, Sept. 20, 1962.

303   "Jackie, you're pregnant": Jaclin Marlin interview

303   The two new teachers: Gaither interview; Boyd interview.

303   "it was a given": Gaither interview.

303   "We were very private": Boyd interview.

303   On the eve of: *WP*, Sept. 20, 1962.

304   On Wednesday, October 10: Truitt interview.

304   Since the early days: *ATD*, p. 737; *WP*, Oct. 18, 1962.

304   "The wreckers haven't started": *WP*, May 26, 1994, quoting JBK letter to Bernard Boutin, March 1962, noting, "Unfortunately last summer the President okayed some plans for the building."

304   By coincidence, Red Fay brought: Fay, pp. 214–15.

304   Warnecke came up with: *WP*, Oct. 18, 1962.

304   "conservative taste": Heckscher OH.

304   "some State School": Gallagher, p. 189.

304   Jackie twice found JFK: Walton OH.

304   "played a key part": ibid.

304   Warnecke had come to town: *WP*, Oct. 18, 1962.

305   James Truitt was included: Truitt interview.

305   At a hastily scheduled meeting: *PR-JFK*, vol. 2, p. 381.

305   Kennedy had been so rattled: *KT*, p. 166.

305   Schlesinger in particular: *KE*, p. 353.

305   To help the campaign, he had committed: *Time*, Oct. 19, 1962.

305   "polite and plain": Truitt interview.

305   "I think I was corrupt": ibid.

306   Using Paul Fout as a front: Paul Fout interview.

306   even when Jackie christened: *JKWH*, p. 229.

306   "hates Virginia and Glen Ora": *LG*, p. 895.

306   "rather liked it": ibid.

306   Situated on 125 wooded acres: "The History of Camp David" website.

306   "motel shacks": JBK to Ros Gilpatric, June 13, 1963, quoted in *WP*, Feb. 10, 1970.

306   "I always knew he would call": Louchheim Journal, Dec. 9, 1962, KSLP.

306   "I myself do not like": *WP*, Dec. 14, 1962.

306   But Jackie was determined: *Newsweek*, Nov. 12, 1962; *WP*, Nov. 3, 1962, and Apr. 28, 1963.

306   Jackie sketched out: Paul Fout interview; *WP*, Nov. 3 and 11, 1962; Slater, p. 148.

307   "She wanted a practical house": Paul Fout interview.

307   The estimated cost was $45,000: *WP*, Nov. 11, 1962.

307   "Jackie was immersed": Paul Fout interview.

307   The President had just finished: *PR-JFK*, vol. 2, p. 390; *PK*, p. 368.

307   Several days earlier: *PR-JFK*, vol. 2, p. 355; *ATD*, p. 651.

307   "Attention!": *WP*, Oct. 16, 1962.

307   "It was really charming": JBK to Alice Grimes, ND, courtesy of Alice Grimes Gaither.

308   Later in the day Joe Kennedy came: *WP*, Oct. 16, 1962; *JKWH*, pp. 135–36, quoting JBK to West, ND.

308   "make-believe cocktails": *JKWH*, p. 136.

308   While Joe was visiting: *PK*, p. 368; *Who's Who in America*, 1962.

308   Across town in Kalorama: McNamara interview; Elspeth Rostow interview.

308   All afternoon, analysts: *KT*, p. 31.

308   "There we all were": Elspeth Rostow interview.
308   "a strenuous campaign weekend": McGeorge Bundy, *Danger and Survival: Choices About the Bomb in the First Fifty Years,* p. 684: "Memorandum for the President," Mar. 4, 1963.
308   "It was a hell of a secret": ibid.

Chapter Twenty-three

310   "increased amounts of hydrocortisone": Robert Dallek, *An Unfinished Life: John F. Kennedy 1917–1963,* p. 576.
310   Besides JFK, the dozen: *KT,* p. 151.
310   "We're going to take out": ibid., p. 50.
310   From the start he worried: ibid., p. 62.
310   "he's probably going to grab": ibid., p. 91.
310   Kennedy was also constantly aware: ibid., pp. 41, 56, 95, 422.
310   "The only offer we would make": ibid., p. 90. See also JFK on p. 86: "If we said to Khrushchev that: 'We have to take action against it. But if you begin to pull them out, we'll take ours out of Turkey.'"
310   In the first week, Robert McNamara: ibid., p. 442.
310   The NSC adviser initially: ibid., p. 122.
311   including Kennedy's touchstone book: ibid., p. 79.
311   Sorensen (who continued to be plagued): Anderson, p. 295; *KT,* pp. 102, 442.
311   Thompson was the first: *KT,* p. 88.
311   "Just frightens the hell": ibid., p. 71.
311   "the kind of conduct": ibid., p. 91.
311   "the mark of Cain": ibid., p. 96.
311   "I am depending on you": Powers OH.
311   "He kept it from going back": *Newsweek,* Mar. 18, 1963.
311   "score sheet": Gilpatric OH.
311   At one point he proposed: *KT,* p. 68.
311   "not in our traditions": ibid., p. 124.
311   By Thursday evening: ibid., p. 108.
311   "appeasement at Munich": ibid., p. 113.
311   "You're in a pretty bad fix": ibid., p. 117.
311   The hawkish views: ibid., p. 125.
311   When Kennedy rejoined: ibid., p. 130.
312   "minimum price": ibid., p. 103.
312   Sorensen favored McNamara's: ibid., p. 126.
312   "evacuation of Guantánamo": ibid., p. 133.
312   "sharply rejected": ibid., p. 136.
312   "You have to admire Adlai": *KE,* p. 2.
312   JFK ultimately ruled out: *KT,* pp. 125, 130, 134, 139.
312   "at an appropriate time": ibid., pp. 132, 134.
312   He understood that the Jupiter: ibid., pp. 140, 460.
312   "so that we don't take the cover": ibid., p. 108.
312   "Not a happy man": Louchheim Journal, Oct. 21, 1962, KSLP.
312   That evening Jack and Jackie: Merry, p. 385.
312   It was a warm Indian summer: Susan Mary Alsop interview; Merry, p. 386.
313   Kennedy was urging Bohlen: *KT,* p. 459.
313   "The sangfroid": Berlin OH.
313   The men gathered: Merry, p. 386.
313   "when their backs were against": *PK,* p. 377.
313   "as a cross examiner": Berlin OH.
313   "sought [Jackie's] company": *KE,* p. 705.

313 She too kept her schedule: *WP*, Oct. 16, 1962.
313 Adlai Stevenson confided: Tree OH.
313 "his shoulders sort of caved": Bartlett OH.
313 "He'd find me, wherever": *AH*, p. 468.
314 Jack headed to Cleveland: *KT*, p. 109.
314 "A slight upper respiratory": *WP*, Oct. 21, 1962.
314 "If you tell I'll shoot you": Hand interview.
314 "couldn't hide his anguish": Alphand, p. 387.
314 Reporters and columnists buzzed: *JWH*, p. 327.
314 "they think it's Cuba": Louchheim Journal, Oct. 21, 1962.
314 Kenny O'Donnell called: *JWH*, p. 326.
314 Kennedy phoned *New York Times* publisher: *ATD*, p. 809.
314 "would probably have taken out": Graham interview.
314 "MARINE MOVES IN SOUTH": *WP*, Oct. 21, 1962; *JWH*, p. 326.
314 In meetings with his advisers: *KT*, p. 153.
314 "I can't say that strongly": ibid., p. 161.
314 "doing nothing . . . would imperil": ibid., p. 171.
315 "flexibility": ibid.
315 "There's no use in waiting": *KT*, p. 183.
315 "most difficult meeting": ibid.
315 "Aggressive conduct": ibid., p. 186.
315 "often sounded rather vapid": Horne, p. 367.
315 He had earlier urged: ibid., p. 368.
315 "played a double game": *KT*, p. 192.
315 moved into the Queen's Bedroom: Gallagher, p. 239.
315 Helen watched the speech: Chavchavadze interview.
315 "just listening and praying": Graham, p. 298.
315 She began to sob: Chavchavadze interview.
315 "Jackie tried to be cheerful": Cassini interview.
315 "refused to seem depressed": Cassini II, p. 323.
316 In a series of meetings: *KT*, p. 203.
316 JFK gave a background briefing: Fuerbringer interview.
316 "Our troops are ready": Henry Luce OH.
316 Meanwhile, Bobby dispatched: *KT*, pp. 468–69; *RKHL*, pp. 133–34.
316 "The conditions of such a trade": *KT*, p. 469.
316 At 7:10 that evening: ibid., pp. 218–22.
317 "Oh Christ, about the dinner": ibid., p. 219.
317 In a gesture of reciprocal: *WP*, Oct. 26, 1962.
317 They were invited to dinner along with: Graziani interview; Cassini interview.
317 Jack, in turn, had invited: Duchess of Devonshire interview.
317 "unfailing good humor": *KE*, p. 705.
317 "squatting on the floor": Horne, p. 373.
317 To help build the American case: Harlech OH; *Sunday Times*, Mar. 28, 1965.
317 *Time* was still able to run: Fuerbringer interview.
317 "The Soviet Union had some": *Sunday Times*, Mar. 28, 1965.
317 Kennedy had earlier dispatched: *RKHL*, p. 224.
317 "in a state of agitation": Anatoly Dobrynin, *In Confidence*, p. 81.
318 Unlike his emissaries: *RKHL*, p. 224.
318 "the time of greatest worry": Schlesinger II, p. 514.
318 "We are eyeball to eyeball": *KT*, p. 232.
318 "straight out": Macmillan II, p. 204; Macmillan Journal, Oct. 24, 1962, HMA.
318 "I think the pressure": Charles Bartlett interview.
318 "I should think you'd feel": Bartlett OH.

318   "You'd be interested": ibid.

318   Kennedy responded: *KT,* p. 257.

318   The *Washington Post* sent: *WP,* Oct. 25, 1962.

318   It was a leak, most likely: Sorensen interview; Philip Zelikow interview.

318   Throughout that day's meetings: *KT,* pp. 254–55, 266, 273; Robert F. Kennedy, *Thirteen Days,* pp. 76–78.

319   "Don't wait for the translation": *Newsweek,* Nov. 5, 1962.

319   "I never knew Adlai had": *JWH,* p. 334.

319   "Roses are red": Ethel Kennedy valentine, Feb. 14, 2001, courtesy of Douglas Dillon.

319   "to watch and listen": *JWH,* p. 312.

319   On Friday the twenty-sixth: *KT,* p. 245.

319   a position that diminished: ibid., p. 441.

319   "hesitant and frightened": Alphand, p. 388.

319   "territorial integrity": *KT,* p. 282.

319   "pointed at our hearts": ibid., p. 283.

320   Continuing surveillance: ibid., pp. 288, 290, 444.

320   "much more serious undertaking": ibid., pp. 291, 425.

320   At the same time, Kennedy received: ibid., pp. 292, 294.

320   Early that evening: ibid., pp. 298–99.

320   She had bowed out: *WP,* Oct. 26, 1962.

320   As she was chasing the hounds: *NYT,* Nov. 2, 1962; *WP,* Nov. 3, 1962.

320   Khrushchev had followed: *KT,* pp. 303–87.

320   Not knowing about the Bartlett: ibid., pp. 375–76, 383.

320   "It's too complicated": ibid., p. 316.

320   "A lot of Jack's close advisers": Duke of Devonshire interview.

320   Kennedy was unwilling: *KT,* p. 323.

320   "a radical decline": ibid., p. 330.

321   "Bobby's formula": ibid., p. 350.

321   Bundy had initiated: ibid., p. 306.

321   Sorensen, Thompson, and McCone: ibid., pp. 346, 348.

321   Bobby refined it: ibid., p. 350.

321   "the Trollope ploy": In "The White House in the Cuban Crisis" (*Saturday Evening Post,* Dec. 8, 1962), Charley Bartlett and Stewart Alsop first revealed the "Trollope ploy" coinage, describing it as a "standard scene" by "the Victorian novelist": "a young man with no marital intentions makes some imprudent gesture toward a marriage-hungry maiden—he squeezes her hand, even kisses her. The lady instantly seizes the opportunity by shyly accepting what she chooses to interpret as a proposal of marriage." While the authors wrongly credited Bobby Kennedy with originating the strategy for the Khrushchev letter, they provided no clue about who dreamed up the Trollope allusion. As a reader of Trollope, JFK might have done so, although RFK biographer Evan Thomas suggested that Bundy may have been responsible (*RKHL,* p. 438).

321   "take out that SAM site": *KT,* p. 359.

321   "violent protest": ibid., p. 357.

321   Kennedy held them both: ibid., pp. 360, 444.

321   "the uncertainty": *JWH,* p. 312.

321   It was there that Dean Rusk: *KT,* pp. 388–89. In Dobrynin, pp. 86–88, the Soviet ambassador vividly described RFK's secret report on the Turkish missile trade. "Throughout the whole meeting he was very nervous," Dobrynin recalled. "Indeed, it was the first time I saw him in such a state."

321   Only on that Saturday: *KT,* pp. 370–81, 436.

321   "I'd like to take Cuba back": ibid., p. 400.

322   "Dave, are you sure your wife": *JWH,* p. 340.

322   After a late dinner: *KT*, p. 401; *JWH*, pp. 339–41.*

322   "I saved Cuba": *KT*, p. 348.

322   "Today was the day of the doves": ibid., p. 405.

322   "without a trace of excitement": *KE*, p. 717.

322   The discovery of the missiles: *KT*, p. 429.

322   "fuel to the conflict": ibid., p. 431.

322   Kennedy's unanticipated firmness: ibid., p. 433.

322   Negotiations over the withdrawal: ibid., pp. 410, 438, 444.

323   "When the crunch came": Rostow OH.

323   "mystery": Macmillan II, p. 217.

323   "a cynical piece of statesmanship": *Time*, Nov. 2, 1962.

323   "would be hard to accept": *Newsweek*, Nov. 5, 1962.

323   "could not have thought": *LG*, p. 928.

323   "It occurs to me": Charles Bartlett to JFK, Oct. 29, 1962, Bartlett Papers, JFKL.

323   Kennedy encouraged Bartlett: *Time*, Dec. 14, 1962.

323   "It obviously was going to entail": Charles Bartlett interview.

323   "He gave us a story": ibid.

324   "so I gave the manuscript to Jack": ibid.

324   "threw it in the fire": ibid.

324   "He was ready to give in": Louchheim Journal, Nov. 22, 1962, KSLP.

324   "It will be better": ibid.

324   "wanted a Munich": Alsop and Bartlett, *Saturday Evening Post*, Dec. 8, 1962.

324   in fact, Forrestal: Charles Bartlett interview.

324   "Stevenson was strong during the UN debate": Alsop and Bartlett, *Saturday Evening Post*, Dec. 8, 1962.

324   "wrong in literally every detail": *Time*, Dec. 14, 1962.

324   The article triggered a burst: Charles Bartlett interview.

324   "it was promptly and widely": *Time*, Dec. 14, 1962.

324   "All right, cease fire": Marietta Tree OH.

325   "I had nothing whatever": Minow OH-CU.

325   "The fact that Charley Bartlett": JFK to Stevenson, Dec. 5, 1962, Stevenson Papers, Princeton University.

325   "regret": JFK to Stevenson, Dec. 5, 1962 (public version), Stevenson Papers, Princeton University.

325   Stevenson stayed in his job: Tree OH.

325   "We had the illusion": Charles Bartlett interview.

Chapter Twenty-four

326   Election day on November 6: Clymer, p. 42; *PK*, p. 429.

326   "The family could not quite": Thomas Winship OH.

327   Less than a month later: Clymer, pp. 37, 39; *PK*, p. 324.

327   When Massachusetts Democrats: Clymer, p. 39.

327   "For fledgling politician": *CWK*, p. 109.

327   Teddy's margin: Clymer, p. 42.

327   Teddy was one of six new Democratic: *ATD*, p. 833; *PK*, pp. 429, 431, 460.

327   Still, Kennedy's popularity: *WP*, Mar. 27, 1963; *PK*, p. 473.

327   "keep the evening light": Arthur Schlesinger interview.

327   "extremely informal": *LG*, p. 926.

328   "very pretty young blonde": ibid.

328   "wanted to talk only": ibid.

328   "It is better to 'go' fast": ibid., p. 928.

328   "as excited and nervous": Sulzberger II, p. 273.

328   "the sexiest and most irresistible": ibid., p. 274.

328 "absolute happiness": Berlin OH.

328 "a little ill at ease": *LG*, p. 928.

328 "Cy was very deaf": Arthur Schlesinger interview.

328 "exciting tension": Berlin OH.

328 "Jackie seems to know": *LG*, p. 928.

328 The next night the Kennedys threw: *CWK*, p. 118.

329 "special dance": ibid.

329 "had a long session": ibid.

329 "extremely pretty": Chavchavadze interview.

329 Sztanko had left Hungary: Enüd Sztanko McGiffert interview.

329 "I hope you're not a spy:" ibid.

330 "made it very clear": ibid.

330 After raising his dosages: Dallek, p. 576.

330 Kennedy suffered a flare-up: Gallagher, p. 240.

330 His back problems also worsened: *CWK*, p. 128.

330 Most worrying of all: Dallek, *Atlantic Monthly,* December 2002.

330 Only later did a journalist tell: Gamarekian OH.

330 Berlin was more nervous than ever: Elspeth Rostow interview.

330 "Not at all a way to treat": Berlin OH.

330 But Berlin was taken aback: ibid.

331 The next day: Dallek, *Atlantic Monthly,* December 2002.

331 "tanned and brisk": *AJ*, p. 452.

331 "she was trembling": Louchheim Journal, Dec. 9, 1962 (referring to an event on Nov. 29, 1962), KSLP.

331 Two weeks later as she left: Gallagher, p. 243.

331 "boiling" about all day: *CWK*, p. 119.

331 Even her indulgent father: Radziwill book proposal, pp. 36–37.

331 "She didn't shop all the time": Tony Bradlee interview.

331 "If Jackie liked something": Gallagher, p. 214.

331 "clothing scouts": ibid., p. 48; *AH*, p. 380.

332 "art scouts": Gallagher, p. 135.

332 In the autumn of 1962: ibid., p. 238.

332 But by the end of his second year: *CWK*, p. 119.

332 In 1962, Jackie's spending: Gallagher, p. 223.

332 all of which he gave: *CWK*, p. 118.

332 With trust funds worth: *Newsweek,* Nov. 23, 1962.

332 "would agree with almost anything": Gallagher, p. 172.

332 Lem Billings believed: Billings OH.

332 For Christmas JFK bought: Gallagher, p. 247; Lincoln Diary, Dec. 22, 1962, Lincoln Papers, JFKL.

332 Jackie's gift to Jack: *Time,* Jan. 4, 1963.

332 *The First Family,* a phonograph: *Time,* Nov. 30, 1962.

333 "cheap jokes": Gallagher, p. 172.

333 Jack quite enjoyed: *CWK,* pp. 123–24.

333 When a reporter queried him: *NYT,* Dec. 19, 1962.

333 "far out of contact": ibid., Dec. 18, 1962.

333 "long period of peace": *Time,* Dec. 28, 1962.

333 JFK also briefly mentioned: ibid.

333 The United States and Britain had invested: *PK,* p. 438; *ATD,* pp. 857–58; *NYT,* Dec. 19, 1962.

333 With a tin ear: Horne, p. 434.

334 "lethal damage": ibid., p. 433.

334 "urgent summons": DBD, Dec. 16, 1962.

334   They decided to offer: *Time,* Dec. 28, 1962; Horne, p. 442.
334   The purpose would be: *PR-JFK,* vol. 3, pp. 134, 462.
334   The aides were assigned: DBD, Dec. 18, 1962; *Sunday Times,* March 28, 1965.
334   "acute, quick and comprehensive": DBD, Dec. 19, 1962.
334   "almost hesitant": ibid.
334   "a compromise which": Gore, "Annual Review for 1962," Jan. 1, 1963, PRO.
334   "As the entourage of cars": Gamarekian OH.
335   "What in heaven's name": McGiffert interview.
335   Besides the daily cruises: Lincoln Diary, Jan. 3, 1963, Lincoln Papers, JFKL.
335   Unlike the gray soggy: *NYT,* Dec. 26, 1962.
335   "peculiar little white corset": Alphand, p. 391.
335   "was very agitated": ibid.
335   There he addressed 50,000 Cubans: *Time,* Dec. 28, 1962; Lincoln Diary, Dec. 28,
        1962, Lincoln Papers, JFKL; *PK,* p. 445.
336   The price for the prisoners': *RKHL,* pp. 236–37.
336   "all but ordered drug": *Time,* Dec. 28, 1962.
336   "You knew from the moment": Radziwill, p. 28.
336   "I don't know that my social skills": Sorensen interview.
336   "Not since the fall of Rome": Sidey interview.
336   "He was shaking": ibid.
337   "more or less at the front": Marian Schlesinger OH.
337   "Arthur is not one": Louchheim Journal, May 1963, KSLP.
337   "I didn't mind": Marian Schlesinger interview.
337   Salinger's antics: Louchheim Journal, Oct. 13, 1963, KSLP.
337   "He was in the hotel": Gamarekian interview.
337   That autumn Jewel Reed had returned: Jewel Reed interview.
337   Chuck Spalding had moved: Spalding OH.
337   "Without the White House": Coleman interview.
337   Betty turned bitter: Charles Bartlett interview; Dick Spalding interview.
337   "colored her view": Coleman interview.
337   "She said, 'You must be kidding'": Charles Bartlett interview.
337   *Time* had inadvertently hit: *Time,* Sept. 14, 1962.
337   "The President was bitter": Prendergast and Colvin, p. 29.
338   "I think I need a drink": ibid., p. 30.
338   Besides frequently traveling: *Time,* Sept. 14, 1962.
338   "a little flirtation and friendship": Agnelli interview.
338   In 1963, Lee would begin: DuBois, pp. 124–25.
338   she was equally intrigued: Radziwill book proposal, p. 64.
338   "frankly there wasn't": Baldrige II, p. 267.
338   That commitment contributed: Louchheim Journal, Nov. 4, 1962, KSLP.
338   Tom Sorensen, who worked: Sidey interview.
338   "a genius . . . not a fond husband": Louchheim Journal, July 11, 1963, KSLP.
338   "Sorensen, [James] Rowe reports": ibid., Jan. 25, 1963.
338   "shy with perspiring palms": ibid., Nov. 22, 1962.
338   "a winning blonde who stood": ibid., Mar. 31, 1963.
338   future feminist writer: ibid., Oct. 13, 1963.
339   "He never lets me feel": ibid., July 11, 1963.
339   "It was very sad": Sorensen interview.
339   "He apologized once": ibid.

Chapter Twenty-five
340   "I am taking the veil": Gallagher, pp. 93, 251.
340   Gallagher and White House maid: ibid., p. 251.

340   "at an age": *WP,* Jan. 21, 1963.

340   "All I beg of you": JBK to Arthur Schlesinger, Jan. 18, 1963, Schlesinger Papers, JFKL.

340   Scarcely a month later: *NYT,* Feb. 21, 1963.

341   "genius in joviality": DBD, Feb. 21, 1963.

341   "social stuff": O'Donnell, p. 281.

341   "ears pinned back": Heckscher OH.

341   "It was a change in the climate": Baldrige interview.

341   suffered spasms: Baldrige I, p. 206.

341   "to resent press clips": ibid.

341   "prefer frenzy": JBK to Walton, June 8, 1962, Walton Papers, JFKL.

341   "Their relationship had frayed": Ketchum interview.

341   "You need to learn": Baldrige interview.

341   "Nancy is ripe to come and work": Cooper interview.

341   She had occasionally helped: *NYT,* Feb. 21, 1963; *WP,* Feb. 23, 1963.

341   "She was the opposite": Baldrige I, p. 208.

342   "cotillion ball gown": JBK to Cooper, ND, courtesy of Janet Felton Cooper.

342   "convinced Nancy that after": Ketchum interview.

342   "Linky" was another veteran: *JKWH,* pp. 154–55.

342   "She knows how I want cigarette boxes": West, p. 211.

342   "show off" the First Lady's: Cassini I, p. 181.

342   The preview at the National Gallery: *WP,* Jan. 10, 1963; *JKWH,* p. 189.

342   "You mustn't brood": *JKWH,* pp. 198–99.

342   Several days later she displayed: *WP,* Jan. 15, 1963.

342   "I don't want a fight": Lincoln Diary, Jan. 14, 1963, Lincoln Papers, JFKL.

343   "You girls must be crazy": ibid., Jan. 19, 1963.

343   In late January, Jackie unveiled: *NYT,* Jan. 22, 1963; *WP,* Jan. 23, 1963.

343   "mysterious . . . Think of people": JBK to Averell and Marie Harriman, June 22, 1962, Harriman Papers, LOC.

343   "mutually attracted": DBD, Feb. 14, 1963.

343   "vigorous animal . . . What a woman": Ziegler, p. 309.

343   "I found Jackie more beautiful": ibid., p. 308.

344   "near-divorce mood": ibid.

344   "If you are in political life": JBK to du Pont, Mar. 7, 1963, Winterthur Archives.

344   While the bulk of Jackie's: Gallagher, p. 254.

344   During the first week: *NYT,* Feb. 11, 1963.

344   Throughout his missile crisis: Berlin OH; *CWK,* p. 121.

344   He saluted her friendship: Teddy White memo, Feb. 4, 1963, White Papers, Harvard University.

344   Jackie's presence proved so unnerving: ibid.

344   "ran the gamut": JBK to Stevenson, Feb. 4, 1963, Stevenson Papers, Princeton University.

344   Later in the week Jackie: *WP,* Feb. 9, 1963.

344   "undercurrents and tension": JBK to Stevenson, Feb. 9, 1963, Stevenson Papers, Princeton University.

344   They made a merry band: *NYT,* Feb. 11, 1963; *WP,* Feb. 11, 1963.

345   On their return to Washington: *WP,* Feb. 11, 1963.

345   on Monday she slept: *CWK,* p. 129.

345   Jackie had also slept for twelve hours: JBK to Stevenson, Feb. 9, 1963, Stevenson Papers, Princeton University.

345   "relaxed but scattered": *CWK,* p. 129.

345   "fitness fever": *WP,* Feb. 11, 1963.

345   On the weekend JFK was tramping: ibid.; Schlesinger II, p. 586.

345   "always looks well": DBD, Feb. 20, 1963.
345   "he felt at that minute": *CWK,* p. 150.
345   During Christmas in Palm Beach: Radziwill, p. 54.
346   "looked as if he hadn't seen": *CWK,* p. 149.
346   "with a look of fierce determination": Radziwill, p. 54.
346   Accompanying Stas, forty-eight: Jacobson manuscript, "John F. Kennedy," p. 29.
346   "I don't care if it's horse piss.": *RKHL,* p. 191.
346   he acknowledges giving pure oxygen: Jacobson manuscript, "John F. Kennedy," p. 31.
346   The men set out at 2:05 a.m.: ibid.; Radziwill, p. 54; *WP,* Feb. 25, 1963.
346   "like an English grenadier": Jacobson manuscript, "John F. Kennedy," p. 31.
346   They reached the finish line: *WP,* Feb. 25, 1963; Jacobson manuscript, "John F. Kennedy," p. 32; *CWK,* pp. 149–50.
346   Jackie immortalized: Radziwill, p. 46.
347   They walked up the Mall: Bartlett OH; *WP,* Mar. 5, 1963.
347   Jack loved the view across: *DOAP,* p. 497.
347   "Maybe we'd better move": Louchheim Journal, Dec. 2, 1963, KSLP.
347   "He said, 'I guess I'll have to go' ": Bartlett OH.
347   Graham had met JFK: Graham, p. 259; Walton interview, JCBC.
347   "a strong and wise": Philip Graham to JFK, Dec. 13, 1960, President's Special Correspondence, JFKL.
347   "natural friend": *CWK,* p. 139.
347   "friends of a certain kind": Graham interview.
347   "cut him off terribly": Truitt interview.
347   "erratic, often brilliant": *CWK,* p. 139.
347   "seemed well and in balance": Graham, p. 292.
348   "out of control, hectic": Arthur Schlesinger eulogy: Katharine Graham Memorial Service, July 23, 2001.
348   Graham turned abusive: Graham, pp. 299, 301.
348   "quite wild": Rostow OH.
348   During a trip to Paris: Graham, p. 301.
348   His mood aggravated: ibid., pp. 308–309.
348   "was in a high mood": Chandler interview.
348   "wanted me to ask Curtis LeMay": Lincoln Diary, Jan. 17, 1963, Lincoln Papers, JFKL.
348   As soon as Ben McKelway: Chandler interview; Bernard Ridder interview.
348   "his buddy": Chandler interview.
348   "Phil is out of control": ibid.
348   The *Post* executive called: Truitt interview.
349   "who in Washington was sleeping": Deborah Davis, *Katharine the Great: Katharine Graham and the Washington Post,* p. 165.
349   "rude and critical": Ridder interview.
349   "Phil was roaming from one": Chandler interview.
349   After being tranquilized: Graham, pp. 311–12.
349   "would die at the thought": ibid., p. 311.
349   "No one present that night": ibid., p. 310.
349   She knew only that her husband's "wild remarks": Graham interview.
349   "We heard Phil flipped out": Ben Bradlee interview.
349   "James would have told me": Truitt interview.
349   "the story of the week": Louchheim Journal, Jan. 25, 1963, KSLP.
349   Graham had barely been released: Graham, p. 313.
350   "peculiar absentmindedness": Blair, p. 20.
350   "hardly a briefcase of 'national crises'": *CWK,* p. 139.

350   Shortly after his visit: Graham, pp. 317, 322.
350   Jackie betrayed no change: Tony Bradlee interview; Ben Bradlee interview.
350   He had not intended: Tony Bradlee interview.
350   "would not write anything": CWK, p. 153.
350   didn't understand his role: ibid., p. 137.
350   "uninvite": ibid., p. 147.
350   "gently and wildly Viennese": Stevenson to Tree, Mar. 10, 1963, Tree Papers, Schlesinger Library, Radcliffe Institute, Harvard University.
350   "the lights were shut off": ibid.
351   Ninety-four guests consumed "only": CWK, p. 148.
351   The girlfriend of Godfrey McHugh: ibid., p. 147.
351   "spent a large portion": Stevenson to Tree, Mar. 10, 1963, Tree Papers, Harvard University.
351   Gore was famous in the House of Lords: Peter McKay interview.
351   "Where's McNamara?": WP, Mar. 16, 1963.
351   "lighthearted mood": Stevenson to Tree, Mar. 10, 1963, Tree Papers, Harvard University.
351   Despite the chill: Truitt interview.
351   "simply disappeared for a half hour": AH, p. 398.
351   "people talking about": Tony Bradlee interview.
351   "unhappy": Truitt interview.
351   Bobby Kennedy called: ibid.
351   "Mary said Bobby had been nice": Angleton interview.
352   "females imported from New York": CWK, p. 147.
352   "always talked about divorce": Stevenson to Tree, Mar. 10, 1963, Tree Papers, Harvard University.
352   "I don't care how many": ibid.
352   In addition to the likelihood: McPherson interview.
352   There were rumors in later years: Burleigh, p. 201.
352   "the nuttiest thing": Angleton interview.
352   "indicated a knowledge": Helms interview.
352   Helen Chavchavadze had also come under: Chavchavadze interview.
353   "They were interrogating me": ibid.
353   "You look like a frightened rabbit": ibid.
353   Kennedy interceded: ibid.
353   "I think he was interested": ibid.
353   "the conspiracy of silence": ibid.
354   who gave the President a gold sword: CWK, p. 166.
354   Jackie wrote the king: ibid.
354   "my bust is bigger": ibid., p. 147.
354   She denied it, but the Bradlees: ibid., p. 165.
354   Jackie's unwillingness: ibid., p. 186.
354   Jackie devoted herself: Newsweek, Mar. 25, 1963; NYT, Mar. 15, 1963; WP, Mar. 20, 1963.
354   Jackie used the presidential retreat: NYT, Apr. 1, 1963.
354   "I was getting divorced": James Reed interview.
355   "waited for her husband at a spot": WP, Apr. 12, 1963.
355   he interrupted a Honey Fitz cruise: NYT, Apr. 15, 1963.
355   The next day, Monday: NYT, Apr. 16, 1963.

Chapter Twenty-six
356   "theatrical quality of grandeur": Louchheim Journal, Jan. 14, 1963, KSLP.
356   "the tide of events": NYT, Jan. 15, 1963.

357   "buoyantly hopeful": ibid.

357   The French leader had rejected: *PK*, p. 451; Alphand OH; *WP*, Jan. 17, 1963.

357   "From a strictly economic viewpoint": *ATD*, p. 871.

357   Nor was Kennedy enthusiastic: ibid., p. 872.

357   "gave an evasive answer": *CWK*, pp. 134–35.

357   Kennedy declined to confront: Gore, "Annual Review for 1963," Jan. 2, 1964, PRO.

357   "What can you do with a man": *ATD*, p. 871.

357   "we have to live with": *PK*, p. 454.

357   "During official dinners": Alphand, p. 401.

357   "bitter and emotionally anti-British": *LG*, p. 990.

357   "He even uses the same phrases": ibid.

357   "The French have now been": Gore to Macmillan, May 24, 1963, PRO.

358   "a remarkable position": Macmillan II, p. 469.

358   "the most important step": Macmillan to JFK, Mar. 16, 1963, PRO.

358   "very deep personal obligation": ibid.

358   the "rats" in the Kennedy administration: Macmillan II, p. 465.

358   Yet for all Macmillan's pushing: ibid., p. 464.

358   "devastating blow": Horne, p. 447.

358   "the gravest failure": ibid., p. 450.

358   In late March: ibid., p. 472.

358   "girl of doubtful reputation": Macmillan II, p. 440.

358   where David Bruce's office: Tom Corbally and Alfred Wells, U.S. Embassy, Memcon, Jan. 29, 1963, David Bruce Papers, Virginia Historical Society.

358   "sort of fashionable London call girl": JFK and Schlesinger, telephone recording transcript, Mar. 22, 1963, Presidential Papers, Office Files, Presidential Recordings, JFKL.

358   "frivolous and decadent": Schlesinger to JFK, "The British Political Situation," Mar. 25, 1963, Harriman Papers, LOC.

358   "intelligence, self-control": ibid.

359   "the best memo": *CWK*, p. 158.

359   "The papers have rather": *AJ*, p. 452.

359   Kennedy had asked him to extend: ibid., p. 452.

359   "high and mighty ways": *LG*, p. 953.

359   "full of Republican clichés": *AJ*, p. 453.

359   It came as no surprise: *WP*, Apr. 7, 1963.

359   "What is interesting about Ken": Marian Schlesinger interview.

359   As Jack Kennedy was happily: *NYT*, Apr. 15, 1963.

359   Kennedy had finally submitted: *ATD*, p. 950.

360   On April 3 the Reverend: *PK*, p. 486.

360   When few adults agreed: White II, p. 506.

360   Evening newscasts and the front pages: *PK*, p. 487.

360   While Kennedy pressed: *ATD*, p. 959.

360   "maintain standards": *PK*, p. 495.

360   he had put federal troops: *WP*, May 13, 1963.

360   Kennedy's aides, Bobby in particular: *RKHL*, p. 246.

360   The previous day he had toured: *NYT*, May 12, 1963.

360   "major episodes in your administration": Schlesinger to JFK, Jan. 29, 1963, President's Office Files, JFKL.

361   "made the gathering of history": *NYT*, Nov. 23, 1963.

361   "house historian could become": Schlesinger to JFK, Jan. 29, 1963, President's Office Files, JFKL.

361   Kennedy agreed, and shot down: ibid., Feb. 20, 1963.

361   "ad hoc specialists": ibid.

361   "I plead for you to consider": ibid., June 8, 1963.

361   "Don't worry, I have enough": Charles Bartlett interview.

361   "always there with their pencils": *CWK*, p. 152.

361   Yet Kennedy had encouraged: Anderson, p. 215; *KE*, p. 5.

361   "I just wanted to make sure": *KE*, p. 3.

361   "the first rough draft": Ben Bradlee interview.

361   "The only thing I regret": DBD, Feb. 21, 1963.

361   "At least once a night": *CWK*, p. 153.

362   "social flattery": *WP*, Feb. 24, 1963.

362   *New York Times* correspondent Hanson: ibid.

362   "Krock deplored the way": *Newsweek,* Apr. 8, 1963.

362   "was the best thing": *CWK*, pp. 163–64.

362   "former friend": ibid., p. 164.

362   "They're just mean as hell": JFK and RFK, telephone recording transcript, Mar. 11, 1963, Presidential Papers, Office Files, Presidential Recordings, JFKL.

362   "turn the world tide": Clare Luce to JFK, Oct. 4, 1962 (letter evidently not sent), Clare Luce Papers, LOC.

363   "was sore as hell": Sidey interview.

363   people would call him a "sap": Martin II, p. 386.

363   "instructed, entertained": Elson, p. 478.

363   "to deal with Congress": Gallagher, p. 268.

363   "White House Historical": *AH,* p. 473.

363   In the evening, Jackie arranged: Ben Bradlee interview; Tony Bradlee interview; Fay interview; James Reed interview; Charles Bartlett interview; Martha Bartlett interview.

363   soigné members of "Hollywood Royalty": David Niven, *The Moon's a Balloon,* p. 320.

363   whose birthday gift was an expensive: *CWK*, p. 188.

363   "yachting clothes": ibid., p. 196.

364   Kennedy wore his nautical: Reed OH; *CWK*, p. 197.

364   "felt absolute panic." McGiffert interview.

364   A three-piece band: *CWK*, pp. 197–98.

364   "remove all feeling": ibid., p. 200.

364   "It was a wild party": Tony Bradlee interview.

364   "whispering in my ear all night": Martha Bartlett interview.

364   Red Fay sang his signature: Fay interview.

364   "more or less drenched": *CWK*, p. 198.

364   "the wettest": ibid.

364   "ripped off at the crotch . . . white underpants": Niven, pp. 328–29.

364   Clem Norton got so drunk: *CWK*, p. 197; Gallagher, p. 259.

364   "veiled expression": *CWK*, p. 197.

364   "Jackie was distressed": Tony Bradlee interview.

364   "Oh, Jack, you know": *CWK*, p. 187.

364   Twice since then: ibid., p. 192.

365   "He chased me all around": Tony Bradlee interview.

365   "The atmosphere probably influenced": ibid.

365   Tony would eventually tell Ben: ibid.; Ben Bradlee interview.

365   "struck me as odd": Tony Bradlee interview.

365   Tony and Jack acted: ibid.; Ben Bradlee interview.

365   "with the speed and attention": *CWK*, p. 202.

365   "though Clem Norton would have probably": JBK to Walton, June 2, 1963, Walton Papers, JFKL.

365   "the most beautiful thing": ibid.

366   "sat in an admiral's cushioned": *NYT,* June 8, 1963.

366   "He either came into her room": Sidey interview.
366   "force himself in a twisted": Goddard Lieberson and Joan Meyers, eds., *John Fitzgerald Kennedy . . . As We Remember Him*, Alistair Cooke reminiscence, p. 196.
366   "moving awkwardly": *PK*, p. 515.
366   "historic": *Newsweek*, Dec. 2, 1963.
366   Secretly in the works: *ATD*, p. 900.
366   According to Schlesinger: ibid.
367   "In the final analysis": Lieberson and Meyers, p. 194.
367   "Probably some of my language": Sorensen interview.
367   Less than a month later: *TCY*, p. 618.
367   The Soviet leader had actually: ibid., pp. 596, 618.
367   After Kennedy's insistence: Macmillan II, p. 475.
367   Still, the "Peace Speech": *TCY*, pp. 600–601.
367   "even the second prize": Macmillan to JFK, July 4, 1963, PRO. Two decades later, speaking to biographer Alistair Horne, the elderly statesman blamed JFK's "weakness" (p. 525) for failing to achieve a total weapons ban. Macmillan said Kennedy could have taken up the offer of three inspections if he had not been "weakened by constantly having all those girls, every day." The prime minister had voiced no such reservations at the time, and indeed had known of JFK's womanizing since Jock Whitney briefed him in November 1960. Historian Michael Beschloss speculated that a more plausible reason for Kennedy's intransigence on inspections was his worry that political opponents might accuse him of accepting Khrushchev's proposal as a "secret concession" linked to the Cuban Missile Crisis (*TCY*, p. 637).
367   All told, there had been: *KE*, p. 740.
367   Banning them would reduce: Kennedy II, p. 54.
367   "as more of a beginning": *KE*, p. 740.
368   "Yesterday a shaft of light": Kennedy II, p. 51.
368   "Lyndon is fat and greyish": Louchheim Journal, Jan. 20, 1963, KSLP.
368   "he certainly had not lived up": Freeman Journal, WMP.
368   "Power has slipped": *Time*, Feb. 1, 1963.
368   "a spectral presence": *ATD*, p. 1018.
368   "laying low": Charles Bartlett interview.
368   "He would get depressed": Christian interview.
368   "Like a fool I went": McPherson interview.
369   "Will somebody go and talk": Jeanne Murray Vanderbilt interview.
369   "It was so moving to think": McPherson interview.
369   "I want [blacks] on the platform": LBJ and Sorensen, transcript of telephone conversation, June 3, 1963, LBJL.
369   "I've never seen it": ibid.
369   "I think I have the feeling": ibid.
369   "we run the risk of touching": ibid.
370   "I'm as strong for this": ibid.
370   On May 21 a federal judge: *ATD*, p. 964.
370   "He should not go on": Louchheim Journal, June 8, 1963, KSLP.
370   Bobby had been seeking: *RKHL*, p. 245.
371   "on the side of the angels": *LG*, p. 987.
371   As filmmaker Robert Drew rolled: *RKHL*, pp. 247–48.
371   "I want to go on television": *PK*, p. 521.
371   He, Sorensen, and Bobby: ibid.
371   "the rights of every man": Kennedy II, pp. 43–44.
371   "drew on at least three years": *KE*, p. 495.
371   "Circumstances sort of caught up": Richard Bolling OH-CU.
371   Eight days after the speech: White II, pp. 507–10; *ATD*, p. 967.

372 March on Washington: *WP,* July 18 and Aug. 29, 1963.

372 To build support: *ATD,* pp. 968–69.

372 "controlled and terse": ibid., p. 967.

372 Katie Louchheim attended: *WP,* July 11, 1963.

372 "I watched the President's face": Louchheim Journal, July 11, 1963, KSLP.

372 Fearing violence, the President: *PK,* pp. 580–81; John Reilly interview.

372 "not be judged by the color": *PK,* p. 584.

372 "the deep fervor": *WP,* Aug. 29, 1963.

372 he too had "a dream": *NYT,* Aug. 29, 1963.

Chapter Twenty-seven

373 "engaged in increasing": *WP,* May 3, 1963.

373 "most frostily received": Louchheim Journal, May 1963, KSLP.

373 The reason for their displeasure: *WP,* May 3, 1963; *NYT,* May 3, 1963.

373 "very annoyed": Angier Biddle Duke OH.

374 "He was a great womanizer": Manno interview.

374 The theme for the evening's: Lincoln II, pp. 152–55.

374 "reminds me of [Henry V]": Bradford, p. 249, citing JBK to Basil Rathbone, Basil Rathbone Papers, Boston University.

374 "hushed melodic reflectiveness": *WP,* May 2, 1963.

374 It was the second time Shakespeare: The first was the state dinner for President Abboud of the Sudan on Oct. 4, 1961, when the American Shakespeare Festival Theatre performed excerpts from *Henry V, Macbeth, As You Like It, Troilus and Cressida,* and *The Tempest* (Lincoln II, p. 40).

374 That spring Kennedy reeled off: *Time,* Mar. 15, 1963; *PK,* p. 491; *NYT,* Nov. 23, 1963.

374 Kennedy stumped them: Schlesinger II, p. 602.

375 "like a queen, but on cat's feet": Louchheim Journal, June 17, 1963, KSLP.

375 Schlesinger submitted a high-toned: Schlesinger to JBK, May 8, 1963, Schlesinger Papers, JFKL.

375 "The President gave the orders": Louchheim Journal, May 8, 1963, KSLP.

375 "a phenomenal number of political debts": *AJ,* p. 506.

375 Tish Baldrige left her post: *NYT,* June 5, 1963.

375 "on a stretcher": Baldrige to Clare Luce, ND (May 1963), Luce Papers, LOC.

375 "last tense months": Baldrige I, p. 108.

375 "I really do love them": Baldrige to Luce, ND (May 1963), Luce Papers, LOC.

375 "Arrivaderci, Tish": Baldrige I, p. 207; Baldrige III, p. 137.

375 "the most emotional woman": Baldrige III, p. 137.

375 "gentleman's library": JBK to James T. Babb, Apr. 30, 1963, Schlesinger Papers, JFKL.

375 She had delegated: James T. Babb to JBK (c.c. to Mrs. Paul Mellon, Mr. William V. Elder III), Apr. 24, 1963, Schlesinger Papers, JFKL.

375 "significant American": JBK to Babb, Apr. 30, 1963, Schlesinger Papers, JFKL.

376 By May 1963, Schlesinger produced: Schlesinger to JBK, May 9, 1963, Schlesinger Papers, JFKL.

376 "working library": *WP,* June 22, 1962.

376 she balked at letting: JBK to Babb, Apr. 30, 1963; JBK to Schlesinger, ND (May 1963), Schlesinger Papers, JFKL.

376 "there seems something a little sterile": Schlesinger to JBK, May 9, 1963, Schlesinger Papers, JFKL.

376 "tacit . . . You can dress up": JBK to Schlesinger, ND (May 1963), Schlesinger Papers, JFKL.

376 "It was a joke": Ben Bradlee interview.

376 "There was not any size or scope": Ketchum interview.

376   Jackie spent just one night: Gallagher, p. 263.

376   Jackie gave the decor exotic: *WP,* July 22, 1963.

376   "Jack never liked them": JBK to Walton, June 2, 1963, Walton Papers, JFKL.

376   "Rather erotic": Gallagher, p. 264.

376   "the inside of a Persian whorehouse": Slater, p. 148.

376   "They're not going to like": Paul Fout interview.

376   Even before the house: *WP,* Apr. 25, 1963.

376   "like renting your new mink": *AH,* p. 483.

377   Washington stockbroker: *NYT,* May 11, 1963; *WP,* Sept. 20, 1963.

377   This time they rented: *NYT,* Apr. 6 and May 26, 1963; *DOAP,* p. 14; Gallagher, p. 276.

377   Financial problems had forced: *WP,* May 15 and 28, 1963.

377   an extravaganza for a thousand: *NYT,* Aug. 18, 1963.

377   "The President . . . had said": Alsop to Evangeline Bruce, June 12, 1963, Alsop Papers, LOC.

377   the other guests were David Bruce: DBD, June 10, 1963.

377   "in a gay mood": ibid.

377   Kennedy's intended brief stop: Alsop to Bruce, June 12, 1963, Alsop Papers, LOC.

377   It was during drinks: Attwood, p. 133.

378   "rather like a small boy": Alsop to Bruce, June 12, 1963, Alsop Papers, LOC.

378   Among other topics: JBK to Gilpatric, June 13, 1963, quoted in *WP,* Feb. 10, 1970.

378   "hidden Profumo": *CWK,* p. 230.

378   "You could tell how constrained": *AH,* p. 320.

378   "dear Ros": JBK to Gilpatric, June 13, 1962, quoted in *WP,* Feb. 10, 1970.

378   His aim was to strengthen: *WP,* Apr. 17, 1963.

378   "The declared purpose": Gore to Macmillan, May 3, 1963, PRO.

378   To downplay the visit: de Zulueta to Gore, May, 12, 1963, PRO.

379   The Tory government's problems: DBD, June 6, 1963; Macmillan II, p. 441; Horne, p. 478.

379   "grossly deceived": DBD, June 17, 1963.

379   "the telling of such a falsehood": ibid., June 6, 1963.

379   "pitiable and extremely damaging": Horne, p. 483, quoting Bruce cable to Dean Rusk, June 18, 1963.

379   "But as a matter of fact": Heckscher OH.

379   "eyes only": Bruce to JFK, June 22, 1963, DBD.

379   "had devoured every word": *CWK,* p. 230.

379   "very depressed": Horne, p. 514, quoting interview with Jacqueline Kennedy Onassis.

379   "specially constructed bed": Macmillan II, p. 474.

379   Mac Bundy and Philip de Zulueta: de Zulueta to Macmillan, June 13, 1963; de Zulueta to Bundy, June 19, 1963; Bundy to de Zulueta, June 20, 1963, PRO.

379   "wished to make every detail": *JKWH,* p. 269.

380   "*Please* think of Jack": Horne, p. 513, quoting JBK to Dorothy Macmillan, June 22, 1963.

380   "banality and vapidity": Schlesinger to JFK, June 8, 1963, Harriman Papers, LOC.

380   "authority but not command": *ATD,* p. 435.

380   Sorensen was working overtime: Louchheim Journal, June 17 and July 11, 1963, KSLP; *ATD,* p. 884.

380   At Schlesinger's suggestion, Kennedy assigned: Schlesinger to JFK, June 8, 1963, Harriman Papers, LOC.

380   "The pronunciation is terrible": McGiffert interview.

380   Some in the press raised questions: *Newsweek,* June 17, 1963.

380   "unpropitious": Gore to Foreign Office, June 20, 1963, PRO.

380 A Harris poll taken: *WP,* July 1, 1963.

380 "when the civil rights riots": *NYT,* Nov. 23, 1963.

381 "More than anything else": Irving Ribner, Introduction, *The Life and Death of King John,* William Shakespeare, *The Complete Works,* p. 601.

381 His visit to Berlin: DBD, June 26, 1963.

381 After showing palpable revulsion: *PK,* p. 535, quoting Sidey's observation that Kennedy looked "like a man who just glimpsed Hell."

381 "Freedom has many difficulties": Kennedy II, p. 49.

381 "All free men": ibid., II, p. 50.

381 "There we were on the goddamn airplane": *TCY,* p. 605.

381 It turned out that: ibid., p. 606. Kennedy's purported solecism has caused much comment over the years. "Ich bin ein Berliner" is not wrong idiomatically. It can mean "I am a person who lives in Berlin" or "I am a doughnut." "Ich bin Berliner" technically means "I am from Berlin" in the sense of being born and raised there. According to Agnes Langdon, a longtime professor of German at Colgate University, the full name of the doughnut in question is Berliner Pfannkuchen, which may be one reason the crowd didn't laugh at Kennedy's words. "If he had been in Frankfurt and said, 'Ich bin ein Frankfurter,' or in Hamburg and said, 'Ich bin ein Hamburger,' they would have laughed," Langdon explained.

382 "the most remarkable spectacle": DBD, June 26, 1963.

382 "She and I were talking about": McNamara interview.

382 "ancestral homestead": "The President's Appointments," Thursday, June 27, 1963.

382 "I imagine that he was never easier": *ATD,* p. 885.

382 "letting two flanks of people": Louchheim Journal, Dec. 22, 1963, KSLP.

382 JFK had specifically invited: O'Brien, p. 15; Duke OH; *NYT,* June 30, 1963; *AH,* p. 491.

382 "They love me in Ireland!": Gamarekian interview.

382 "These were the three happiest": Tubridy OH.

382 Left behind in Washington: Gamarekian OH.

383 "Dave Powers came up to Pierre": ibid.

383 "see old Shannon's face": *NYT,* June 30, 1963.

383 The Devonshires' chauffeur: John Oliver interview.

383 "full steam ahead": Macmillan Journal, July 7, 1963, HMA.

383 "a greater degree of authority": Macmillan memorandum, July 1, 1963, PRO.

383 "a country house party": Macmillan II, p. 473.

383 "very puffed up": Horne, p. 514.

383 The villa was run: Rockefeller Foundation website.

384 "made an unscheduled": *WP,* July 1, 1963; *JWH,* pp. 372–73.

384 Rusk told biographer Richard Reeves: *PK,* p. 539.

384 The reason, according to Rusk: Kati Marton, *Hidden Power: Presidential Marriages That Shaped Our Recent History,* p. 128. Biographer Reeves told Marton that Rusk had revealed that Agnelli was the woman in question.

384 "Maybe yes, maybe no": Agnelli interview.

384 "small suspicion": Cicogna interview.

384 In Rome the following night: Agnelli interview; *NYT,* June 30, 1963.

384 The trip wound down after: *ATD,* p. 886.

384 At Kennedy's urging: *PK,* p. 540.

384 For his Oval Office desk: Jacqueline Kennedy, *Life,* May 29, 1964.

384 "more passionate excitement": Duke OH.

385 "The double life is not": Chavchavadze interview.

385 Mimi Beardsley was sharing: Foulke interview.

385 "called for some minion": ibid.

385 "the only thing she really wanted": Gallagher, p. 278.

385   "I want to ask your opinion": Foulke interview.
385   The first blip on the radar: *RKHL*, p. 254; *TCY*, pp. 610–11; Hoover Official and
       Confidential Files, memo of meeting, July 2, 1963, Courtney Evans forwarded to
       Hoover, July 3, 1963, FBI.
386   Just two days later: *RKHL*, p. 255.
386   "hardly could have been maintained": *WP*, Oct. 27, 1963.
386   By night Rometsch was a call girl: *RKHL*, p. 255.
386   "smoky and dimly lit": *WP*, Oct. 26, 1963.
386   "importantly placed politicos": ibid., Oct. 27, 1963.
386   According to Baker, Bill Thompson: *RKHL*, p. 255.
386   Since the FBI had linked: *TCY*, p. 616; *RKHL*, p. 256.
386   "a couple of hundred dollars": *CWK*, p. 228.
386   "a really beautiful woman": ibid.
387   "It was a compulsion": Chavchavadze interview.

Chapter Twenty-eight
388   "haunting": Gore to JFK, Aug. 2, 1963, Presidential Office Files, JFKL.
388   "a conquering hero": Harlech OH.
388   After a hiatus of two years: Reed OH; *JWH*, p. 375; *WP*, July 14, 1963.
388   With Lem Billings, JFK flew: *WP*, July 18 and 21, 1963.
388   "He was watching the Berlin speech": Reed interview.
389   Jackie was equally radiant: Joan Kennedy interview.
389   In the tranquility of Brambletyde: Gallagher, pp. 265, 276; *NYT*, Aug. 18, 1963.
389   Nancy Tuckerman had moved: *WP*, Apr. 11, 1963.
389   "tiptoe diplomacy": Bishop, p. 22.
389   somewhat incongruously, a voodoo doll: ibid., p. 27.
389   "On a state evening": JBK to du Pont, May 17, 1962, Winterthur Archives.
389   "Don't make pictures of Jack and me": Sidey II, p. 160.
389   "to capture the emotion": ibid.
389   "keeper of the intellectual tone": Heckscher OH.
389   "a more beautiful and functional": JFK to Walton, Jan. 23, 1963, Walton Papers,
       JFKL.
389   "How lovely to have you there": JBK to Walton, July 29, 1963, Walton Papers, JFKL.
390   "emphasis on creative fields": *WP*, July 20, 1963.
390   Their friends observed more intimacy: James Reed interview.
390   "extremely solicitous": Reed OH.
390   "lying there in each other's arms": Fay interview.
390   "any question you can think of": Fay, p. 182.
390   "there was only one I could have married": ibid., p. 183.
391   Joan committed a faux pas: *NYT*, Feb. 12, 1963.
391   "They thought I should be a little": Joan Kennedy interview.
391   "invited a lot": ibid.
391   "almost full term" in June: ibid.
391   "Jackie was so wonderful": ibid.
391   "We really enjoyed": *AH*, pp. 446–47.
391   "blistering attack": *WP*, May 11, 1963.
392   "Nothing Eunice did was official": Myer Feldman interview.
392   Because of Rosemary: Eunice Shriver OH.
392   "It was the beginning": Myer Feldman interview.
392   "a serious loss to all": *WP*, Aug. 4, 1963.
392   "Jack was as upset as everyone": Fay interview.
392   "the most understanding": Katharine Graham to JFK, Wednesday, ND (August
       1963), President's Special Correspondence, JFKL; Graham, p. 337.

393 "knocked [the Graham family]": Walton to JFK, August 1963, Walton Papers, JFKL.

393 "a friendly familiar diversion": Truitt interview.

393 "never mentioned": Chavchavadze interview.

393 "He was not shy about it": Truitt interview.

393 Kennedy had pressed de Gaulle: *TCY,* p. 626.

393 JFK could never dispel: *ATD,* p. 914. Schlesinger records that JFK told David Brinkley, "Charles de Gaulle will be remembered for one thing only, his refusal to take that treaty."

393 "desire to maintain": Alphand, p. 410.

393 On arriving at the Osterville stables: *Time,* Aug. 16, 1963; *WP,* Aug. 8 and 9, 1963.

393 Seventeen minutes after: *NYT,* Aug. 8, 1963; notes by Pamela Turnure, ND, Pierre Salinger Papers, JFKL; Gallagher, pp. 283–86.

393 "completely withdrawn": Turnure OH.

394 Jackie was never permitted: *WP,* Aug. 10, 1963.

394 "deeply distressed": *WP,* Aug. 8, 1963.

394 "He wanted to know": Dr. Judson Randolph interview.

394 Kennedy flew in Dr. Sam Levine: *NYT,* Aug. 10, 1963.

394 "Bobby was a little nettling": Randolph interview.

394 On Thursday afternoon the physicians: ibid.; *WP,* Aug. 9, 1963; *NYT,* Aug. 10, 1963.

394 "It was a desperate move": Randolph interview.

394 Kennedy and Dave Powers stayed: ibid.; *JWH,* pp. 376–77; *Newsweek,* Aug. 19, 1963; *Time,* Aug. 16, 1963.

395 When it was clear: Randolph interview.

395 "He put up quite a fight": *JWH,* p. 377. "Babies don't die of hyaline membrane disease anymore," said Dr. Judson Randolph four decades later. An afflicted baby is given medications that "dissolve the hyaline membrane so it can be flushed out or coughed out."

395 "as presentable as possible": Gallagher, p. 289.

395 She was already in a weakened: *WP,* Aug. 9, 1963.

395 Telling Jackie about the ordeal: *DOAP,* p. 8.

395 "I just can't bear": Janet Auchincloss OH.

395 Caroline came as well: *WP,* Aug. 12, 1963.

395 Jackie was also consoled: ibid., Aug. 10, 1963.

395 "couldn't care less": Lincoln Diary, Aug. 8, 1963, Lincoln Papers, JFKL.

395 On Saturday: Richard Cardinal Cushing OH.

395 JFK took a gold St. Christopher's: *JWH,* p. 378.

395 "copious tears": Cushing OH.

395 the first in the large family plot: *WP,* Aug. 10, 1963; *JWH,* pp. 378–79.

396 "He was very depressed": McGiffert interview.

396 Before leaving she gave: *WP,* Aug. 16, 1963.

396 "theatrical production": *AJ,* p. 525.

396 Joan offered quiet sympathy: Joan Kennedy interview.

396 Bunny Mellon sent over: Mellon interview, WMP.

396 "in the midst of all": JBK to Macmillan, Jan. 13, 1964, HMA.

396 Each time he would bring: Lincoln I, p. 355.

396 "anguish for his wife": *ATD,* p. 978.

396 "full of sadness": *AH,* p. 528.

396 "It is so hard for Jackie": Fay, p. 235.

396 Lee's affair with Onassis: DuBois, pp. 124–25.

396 "I was astonished": Nicholas Gage, *Greek Fire: The Story of Maria Callas and Aristotle Onassis,* p. 234.

397 "your Papa": RK to children, Aug. 18, 1955, JPKP.

397 Five years later: *HTF,* p. 691.

397 "remembered something hanging": *AH*, p. 529.

397 "Onassis is a pirate": Leamer I, p. 587, citing interview with Evelyn Lincoln.

397 "she just wanted to get away": *AH*, p. 529.

397 she would not accept: *CWK*, p. 219.

397 "Lee wants Jackie to be her beard": Justin Feldman interview.

397 "air of respect": Kloman interview.

397 But Roosevelt, who had finally: *NYT,* Mar. 22, 1963.

397 The previous year, Onassis: *Newsweek,* Oct. 28, 1963.

397 "He said he was working on": *AH*, p. 530.

397 The President reassured: Justin Feldman interview; Kloman interview.

398 "Jack went down on one knee": Martha Bartlett interview.

398 "Well, I think it will be good": Turnure OH.

398 Stas Radziwill had "secured": JFK to Stas Radziwill, Sept. 3, 1963, courtesy of Robert White.

398 "you have possession of it": ibid.

398 As it turned out: *WP,* Sept. 22, 1963.

398 Onassis, a "close friend": ibid., Sept. 28, 1963.

398 "not to my knowledge": ibid., Oct. 1, 1963.

398 "twenty-one grandchildren trooped": *Time,* Sept. 13, 1963.

399 "He did it so well": Martha Bartlett interview.

399 "at some length [about] what Lyndon": Bartlett OH.

399 "He gave me the feeling": Charles Bartlett interview.

399 "I don't want to be the wife": Bartlett OH.

399 "At first it used to depress": Charles Bartlett interview.

399 "We may spend a couple of years": Walton, p. 51.

399 which they celebrated at the scene: *Newsweek,* Sept. 23, 1963; *WP,* Sept. 18, 1963.

399 "It was a happy sort": Auchincloss OH.

400 "by far the most affectionate": *CWK*, p. 206.

400 She gave him a gold: Gallagher, pp. 289, 290; *NYT,* Dec. 5, 1963; "The Camelot Documents," JFKL; *DOAP,* p. 293.

400 Jackie also presented Jack: Gallagher, p. 277; *CWK*, pp. 207–208.

400 Jack scattered an array: *CWK*, p. 207; Auchincloss OH.

400 "Now don't forget": Auchincloss OH.

400 Jackie picked at least two: ibid.; *CWK*, p. 207.

400 "You two really are": *CWK*, p. 208.

400 She told him that the weekend: JBK to Charles Bartlett, Sept. 19, 1963, courtesy of Charles Bartlett.

Chapter Twenty-nine

401 "Somehow missing from the White House": *Time,* Sept. 20, 1963.

401 "taking turns cutting each other": Louchheim Journal, Aug. 4, 1963, KSLP.

401 "understanding, respect, and affection": Robin Douglas-Home, "The Private Thoughts of Jackie Kennedy," *News of the World,* Mar. 12, 1967.

401 "I was melancholy": *WP,* Nov. 13, 2003, quoting the Reverend Richard T. McSorley's diary based on counseling sessions with Jackie Kennedy in the spring and summer of 1964.

401 Kennedy's popularity sank: *WP,* Nov. 10, 1963.

402 "No doubt he realized": *ATD,* p. 997.

402 "autocratic, suspicious": McNamara, p. 42.

402 "a true sorceress": ibid.

402 All three were strict Catholics: *ATD,* p. 986; *TCY,* p. 651.

402 Yet since the mid-fifties: *ATD,* p. 539.

402   less than the $3 billion: *Statistical Abstract of the U.S., 2002,* charts 1275 and 484;
      Jerusalem Post, July 8, 2003.

402   "under very adverse conditions": Leamer II, p. 728, quoting from JFK's Dictaphone
      recording on Monday, Nov. 4, 1963.

402   By November 1963, Kennedy had raised: *ATD,* p. 998.

402   "colonial military force": *AJ,* p. 270.

402   "couldn't be more pleased": ibid.

402   "fighting Joe Alsop": ibid., p. 271.

402   "A few will mean more": ibid., p. 270.

403   But Kennedy was preoccupied: *ATD,* p. 997.

403   "marginal thing": Schlesinger OH-CU.

403   "the experts dare at last": Bartlett to JFK, Apr. 7, 1963: "Thank you for this idea,"
      enclosing Bartlett "News Focus" column, Apr. 7, 1963, Bartlett Papers, JFKL.

403   Barely a month later: Rostow OH; *ATD,* p. 986; *TCY,* p. 651.

403   Two months later: *WP,* Aug. 5, 1963.

403   With Diem arresting protesters: *PK,* p. 557.

403   On Saturday, August 24: ibid., pp. 560–63.

403   "one of the truly pivotal": McNamara, p. 52.

403   "redress the balance": Leamer II, p. 727, quoting from JFK's Dictaphone recording
      on Monday, Nov. 4, 1963.

403   Averell Harriman, the hero: Smith III, p. 258.

403   "My God, my government's coming apart": Charles Bartlett interview.

404   "melee over Vietnam": DBD, Sept. 17, 1963.

404   "You remind me of my Vietnam advisers": Louchheim Journal, Oct. 6, 1963, KSLP.

404   "In the final analysis": *WP,* Sept. 3, 1963.

404   "a kind of ambivalence": ibid., Sept. 10, 1963.

404   The Kennedy administration vacillated: McNamara, p. 63.

404   "In Texas we say": David Halberstam, *The Best and the Brightest,* p. 292.

404   Kennedy rejected the idea: McNamara, p. 62.

405   "confronted with a choice": ibid., p. 70.

405   "strongly authoritarian": ibid., p. 78.

405   To put pressure on: ibid., pp. 78, 80; *PK,* pp. 611–12, 614.

405   "McNamara monarchy": *WP,* Mar. 13, 1963.

405   "first to be replaced": *Time,* Mar. 15, 1963.

405   "In the summer of 1963": Dillon interview.

405   "one of those authoritative": Louchheim Journal, Aug. 4, 1963, KSLP.

406   "It is no fun to be": ibid., Oct. 13, 1963.

406   "playing around": ibid.

406   "Mr. Secretary, if you think": Reed OH.

406   "typical Dillon ploy": Louchheim Journal, Aug. 5, 1963, KSLP.

406   "difficult to give one a boost": ibid.

406   "Johnson had grown heavy": McPherson, p. 200.

406   "I think he really meant it": McPherson interview.

406   In typically high-handed: Anderson, p. 240.

406   "uneasiness and unsureness": Fay, p. 2.

406   "I think it is very good": ibid., p. 4.

407   "The poor guy's got the lousiest job": ibid., p. 5.

407   "I am sorry to hear": JFK to LBJ, Sept. 13, 1963, President's Special Correspondence,
      JFKL.

407   "Dear Baron": JBK to Walton, Aug. 27, 1963, Walton Papers, JFKL.

407   "The White House is all": *JKWH,* p. 291.

407   A few items remained: ibid., pp. 346–47.

407 "It is marvelous what we have": ibid., p. 347.

407 By September, Jackie had: Ketchum interview.

408 In April, Jackie had formed: *NYT,* Apr. 18, 1963; *WP,* July 15, 1963; Gallagher, p. 302.

408 "Now I worry about": JBK to du Pont, Sept. 20, 1963, JFKL.

408 "absolutely bogged down": JBK to Lady Bird Johnson, Dec. 1, 1963, LBJL.

408 Although Jackie didn't plan: *WP,* Sept. 20. 1963.

408 Afghanistan's King: ibid., Sept. 6, 1963.

408 "this marvelous mania": Duke OH.

408 Worried about the weather: *WP,* Sept. 7, 1963.

408 Kennedy made his own dramatic: ibid.

409 Jackie had been somewhat: Charles Bartlett interview; Ben Bradlee interview.

409 That afternoon JFK had addressed: *WP,* Sept. 21, 1963.

409 "How can you concentrate": Crespi interview.

409 "You will have the starring": ibid.

409 Working from a script: Fay interview.

409 "Wouldn't the rape scene": Crespi interview.

410 "I was the bad guy": Fay interview.

410 "scratches and thorns": Crespi interview.

410 "presidential hijinks": ibid.; *AH,* p. 545, noted the film's "grisly kind of humor."

410 "so it would not get": Fay interview. James B. Hill, the audiovisual archives specialist at the Kennedy Library, said he had heard of the film but to his knowledge it was not part of the library's collection.

410 "I think Mrs. Kennedy was glad": Gaither interview.

410 "It must be a real first grade": JBK to Grimes, Dec. 29, 1962, courtesy of Alice Grimes Gaither.

410 "religiously up with her 2nd grade": ibid.

410 "When people spoke they listened": Baldrige I, p. 180.

410 "refused to allow them": ibid., p. 179.

410 The press nicknamed him: *Time,* Oct. 4, 1963; Bradlee, *Newsweek,* Dec. 2, 1963.

411 "where his friends the Pinchot girls": *CWK,* p. 213.

411 "He was easy with both": Tony Bradlee interview.

411 "Jack got in the car": ibid.

411 "ratty porch": Ben Bradlee interview.

411 "one of history's most frozen shots": *CWK,* p. 214.

411 "Jack loved the idea": Ben Bradlee interview.

411 "sometimes rambling speeches": *WP,* Sept. 29, 1963.

411 "Kennedy seemed ill at ease": *Time,* Oct. 4, 1963.

411 But on September 24: Udall interview; Lieberson and Meyers, p. 216.

411 "It was the subtle beginning": Udall interview.

412 The last weekend of the trip: *JWH,* p. 379.

412 "ruddy": *WP,* Oct. 2, 1963.

412 "healthy and rested": ibid.

412 "Je suis comblée!": *Time,* Oct. 11, 1963.

412 When she realized: Tuckerman OH; *WP,* Oct. 3, 1963.

412 she was so fatigued: *NYT,* Oct. 3, 1963.

412 "pale and drawn": ibid.

413 She told U.S. Ambassador: *LG,* p. 1011.

413 "I hate her": Nancy White account of dinner party, Feb. 12, 1963, White Papers, Harvard University.

413 "hates Stas": *LG,* p. 1011.

413 "pleasure palace": *Time,* Oct. 11, 1963.

413 On the first night: *WP,* Oct. 5, 1963.

413 "wherever her heart desires": ibid., Oct. 10, 1963.

413 "Onassis was very courtly": Kloman interview.
413 "an alive and vital person": *CWK*, p. 219.
413 "zany things": Kloman interview.
413 "They teased him": ibid.
413 extravagant gifts: ibid.
413 Jack and Jackie stayed: *WP*, Oct. 5, 1963; Kloman interview.
413 Another time Kennedy mistakenly: *WP*, Oct. 12, 1963.
413 "her sorrow": *DOAP*, p. 9.
414 it contains references: JBK to JFK, August 1962, WMP.
414 "complexity . . . authentic love": Marton, p. 132.
414 "brilliantly lighted ship": *WP*, Oct. 5, 1963.
414 "lack of decorum": ibid., Oct. 16, 1963.
414 Republican congressman Oliver Bolton: *Newsweek*, Oct. 28, 1963.
414 When word reached the White House: Graham, pp. 350–51.
414 The two sisters spent three days: *Time*, Oct. 25, 1963; *WP*, Oct. 14 and 15, 1963.
414 "almost one hundred smiling": Radziwill, p. 142.
415 "a strange hiatus": *DOAP*, p. 9.
415 "Jack wanted to show me": Crespi interview.
415 "kept interrupting": Jacqueline Hirsh OH.
415 For four days photographer: Laura Bergquist Knebel OH.
415 "There wasn't the lighthearted": Laura Bergquist to James Ellison, ND, "Kennedy—Very Casually," Laura Bergquist Papers, Boston University.
415 "traditional Irish saffron kilts": Lincoln II, p. 172.
415 "four handkerchief evening": *WP*, Oct. 16, 1963.
415 "She sang it well": James Reed interview.
416 "suntanned but exhausted": West, p. 272.
416 "I want to go to Patrick's grave": *JWH*, p. 378.
416 "He seems so alone": ibid., p. 379.
416 "People were swarming": Lieberson and Meyers, p. 216.
416 "enthralled": Foulke interview.
416 "My mother said": Fahnestock interview.
416 "from June 1962": *New York Daily News*, May 15 and 16, 2003.
416 "He's the one who made": *JWH*, p. 39.
417 "Frost was deeply offended": Udall interview.
417 "Is there going to be a fuss?": ibid.
417 "one of the granite figures": Lieberson and Meyers, pp. 214–15.

Chapter Thirty
418 Investigative reporter Clark: *RKHL*, p. 266.
418 "prominent New Frontiersmen": ibid.
418 "a spicy tale": *WP*, Oct. 27, 1963.
419 The previous week Harold: Macmillan II, p. 507.
419 The Rometsch matter had resurfaced: *WP*, Oct. 8, 1963.
419 According to Robert Kennedy biographer: *RKHL*, p. 265.
419 Kenny O'Donnell later said: ibid., p. 266.
419 "briefed to his teeth": *CWK*, p. 217.
419 "rogue, not a crook": ibid., p. 215.
419 "dirt" Hoover had: ibid., p. 228.
419 Yet it was hardly a casual: *RKHL*, p. 267; *TCY*, p. 616.
419 "Correspondence between Rometsch": *RKHL*, p. 267.
420 The strongest indicator of concern: ibid., pp. 267–68.
420 By then, Bobby Kennedy had paid: ibid., p. 264.
420 Vietnam was just then approaching: *PK*, pp. 639–40.

420   "reject appeals for direct": ibid., p. 643.

421   "with a look of shock": *AH*, p. 498.

421   "somber and shaken": *ATD*, p. 997.

421   "badly drafted . . . should never": Dallek, p. 685.

421   In subsequent weeks: *PK*, p. 660.

421   "I can't do it": *JWH*, p. 16.

421   "would have intervened": Alsop, p. 150.

421   "on the periphery of the Communist world": *Public Papers of the Presidents of the United States: John F. Kennedy 1963*, "Remarks Prepared for Delivery at the Trade Mart in Dallas, November 22, 1963," pp. 892–94.

422   "He was in touch when things": Truitt interview.

422   "ablaze with lights": *WP*, Nov. 1, 1963.

422   But according to Mary: Gallagher, p. 300.

422   "beagling" with Paul Fout: *WP*, Nov. 1, 1963.

422   "he held on to my glass": Bradford, p. 261, quoting from Irene Galitzine with Cinzia Tani, *Dalla Russia alla Russia*, p. 173.

422   "the way things are going for us right now": *CWK*, p. 224.

423   "chaotic, with one dog": ibid., p. 223.

423   "Kennedy had wanted to go": Charles Bartlett interview, WMP.

423   Connally officially extended: *WP*, Oct. 5, 1963.

423   it seemed unlikely she would agree: *DOAP*, p. 8.

423   "She agonized over it": Bradford, p. 258.

423   "Jackie's guilt feelings": *CWK*, p. 219. Evidently that guilt intensified after JFK's death. In interviews with William Manchester for *The Death of a President*, she turned the facts around and insisted that Jack had forced her to take the Aegean cruise to "forget herself in other lands. . . . His mind was made up," she said (*DOAP*, pp. 8–9).

423   "Maybe now you'll come": *CWK*, p. 220.

423   She opened her red leather: Manchester notes for *DOAP*, WMP; *DOAP*, p. 9.

423   "It was significant": Turnure OH.

423   But the White House withheld: *WP*, Nov. 8, 1963.

423   At dinner on Friday, October 25: Alphand, p. 410.

423   Seventy anti-UN: *WP*, Oct. 25, 1963.

424   "disgraced": ibid.

424   "she wanted to take a 'pass' ": Alphand, p. 410.

424   "laid down the law": Christian interview.

424   On November 7, Turnure announced: *WP*, Nov. 8, 1963.

424   The Johnsons made special: Lady Bird Johnson interview, WMP.

424   Connally scheduled a fundraiser: *AH*, p. 546; *DOAP*, p. 21.

424   "Kennedy wanted to come to Texas": Christian interview.

424   The drop in JFK's popularity: *WP*, Oct. 12, 1963.

424   "too far and too fast": *NYT*, Oct. 21, 1963.

424   "the most widely disliked": *Newsweek*, Oct. 14, 1963.

424   "a lot of Texas had decided": Christian interview.

425   Polls showed that JFK's most: *PK*, p. 655; *WP*, Oct. 17, 1963.

425   JFK not only welcomed: *WP*, Oct. 20, 1963.

425   "political pleasure": *NYT*, Oct. 21, 1963.

425   Kennedy liked Goldwater: *CWK*, p. 190.

425   "no vices whatsoever": Fay, p. 259.

425   JFK believed the most formidable: Charles Bartlett interview.

425   "Jack was scared stiff": ibid.

425   "it would be a close contest": Gilpatric OH.

425   "He endlessly questioned": ibid.

425   On November 7, Rockefeller was the first: *WP*, Nov. 8, 1963.

425   He and his new wife: *Newsweek,* June 3, 1963.

425   "failures at home and abroad": *WP,* Nov. 8, 1963.

426   "As usual, the campaign will be run": *JWH,* p. 386.

426   Steve Smith would be: Schlesinger II, p. 604; *PK,* p. 656.

426   "Preposterous on the face": Schlesinger II, p. 605.

426   "turned on me": *AH,* p. 566.

426   The conjecture was prompted: Schlesinger II, p. 604; *WP,* Nov. 1, 1963; *JWH,* p. 37.

426   "Can you see me now": O'Donnell OH.

426   "Bobby had strongly attacked": Freeman Journal, WMP.

427   Baker was eventually convicted: Caro, p. 408.

427   In the two weeks before: Out of fourteen days, they were together for seven and apart for seven.

427   "bumps and grinds": *CWK,* p. 222.

427   "He was looking forward": Ben Bradlee interview.

427   With the Alsops, Jackie talked: Susan Mary Alsop interview.

427   "seemed to enjoy the cool": *CWK,* p. 227.

427   JFK had lured the reclusive: Martha Bartlett interview.

427   After meeting Garbo at the Lasker: Deeda Blair interview.

427   "time to hear Garbo's side": Michaelis, p. 177.

427   That autumn Billings had not: Martha Bartlett interview; Ketchum interview.

427   "I got the feeling at the end": Charles Bartlett interview.

428   Helen Chavchavadze was invited: Chavchavadze interview; *Time,* Nov. 22, 1963; *WP,* Nov. 8, 1963.

428   Following her release: Chavchavadze interview.

428   "After I had been so down": ibid.

428   "Greta!" he exclaimed: Michaelis, pp. 177–78.

428   Chavchavadze was far more intrigued: Chavchavadze interview.

428   "most unusual evening": Garbo to JBK, Nov. 18, 1963, JFKL; JFKL press release, May 10, 2000.

428   "Jackie was very upset": Chavchavadze interview.

429   "very swell": *CWK,* p. 236.

429   Kennedy confessed: ibid.

429   Kennedy fretted about the Texas trip: Christian interview.

429   "a less viable mediator": *CWK,* p. 237.

429   "the mood of the city was ugly": ibid.

429   "looking very upset": ibid., p. 239.

429   "It was the last time": ibid.

429   "alternatively somber and smiling": *NYT,* Nov. 24, 1963.

429   As the President marched: *Time,* Nov. 22, 1963.

429   By mid-November, Kennedy's: ibid., Sept. 20 and Nov. 22, 1963; *Newsweek,* Aug. 26, 1963; *WP,* Nov. 15, 1963; *PK,* p. 658.

430   France wished to "dominate": *WP,* Oct. 23, 1963.

430   "rules of the alliance": Alphand, p. 410.

430   "an ally without being a protégé": ibid.

430   Yet Kennedy was eager: *ATD,* p. 1016.

430   "working trip": Alphand, p. 411.

430   "The fact of the matter is": *Time,* Nov. 22, 1963.

430   "Say Not the Struggle": *WP,* Nov. 15, 1963.

431   The Black Watch performance: ibid., Nov. 11, 1963.

431   "new humility": Robin Douglas-Home, *News of the World,* Mar. 12, 1967.

431   On Thursday he had gone: *JWH,* p. 387.

431   "I heard Stevenson advising": Cassini I, p. 198.

431   "a fussy old man": *DOAP,* p. 38.

431   "to withdraw his objections": ibid.

431   "Why do you go?": Cassini I, p. 198.

432   "fuss and feathers": *Time,* Nov. 22, 1963.

432   the "proletariat" of New York: RK to JBK, Nov. 20, 1963, WMP.

432   In the same spirit: Sidey interview.

432   the previous summer he had been: *WP,* July 19, 1963.

432   "The kind of man he was": Louchheim Journal, Thanksgiving Eve, 1963, KSLP.

432   fellow "tailhound" kept on the margins: Ben Bradlee interview; Krolik interview;
       Frank Thompson Jr. OH-CU.

432   they watched the successful: *NYT,* Nov. 17, 1963.

432   "better than usual": *JWH,* p. 388.

432   "Usually this time of year": Lieberson and Meyers, p. 217.

433   On Monday, Kennedy and his guests: *WP,* Nov. 19, 1963.

433   "I wish we had this thing": *AH,* p. 539.

433   That night Jackie decided: *DOAP,* p. 15.

433   "just talk . . . He seemed a little": McGiffert interview.

433   "It was a big crisis": Tuckerman interview, WMP.

433   On Wednesday morning Jackie: John Walsh interview, WMP.

433   On returning to Wexford: Clint Hill interview, WMP.

433   "It was decided that she": ibid.

433   Just before 1:30 p.m.: *DOAP,* p. 15.

433   "so happy": Powers interview, WMP.

434   "Kennedy was in great form": James Reed interview, WMP.

434   The Kennedys had already contracted: *NYT,* Oct. 31, 1963; *WP,* Nov. 1, 1963.

434   At six-thirty Jack, Jackie: *WP,* Nov. 22, 1963; *DOAP,* pp. 15–18.

434   "It was the only time": Ethel Kennedy interview, WMP.

434   some judges were "upset": Tuckerman to JFK, ND, WMP.

434   After her long absence: *WP,* Nov. 22, 1963; Walsh interview, WMP.

434   "went around to the wives": Ketchum interview.

434   "You're going off to Japan": Dillon interview, WMP.

434   The President and First Lady: *DOAP,* pp. 28, 33.

434   As the Marine Band played: ibid., p. 29.

434   "rich Republican women": ibid., p. 10.

435   "be simple—show these Texans": original manuscript for *Look* excerpts of *DOAP,*
       Part One, Galley Two, Myrick Land Papers, Boston University.

435   "Have a wonderful time": Janet Auchincloss to JBK, Nov. 20, 1963, WMP.

435   Rose's message was more: RK to JBK, Nov. 20, 1963, WMP.

435   "Dear Chief Curley": Lee Radziwill to JFK, Nov. 14, 1963, WMP.

435   "He wants to be the first": Charles Bartlett interview.

435   "sort of insistence": *AH,* p. 552.

435   "reduce the political mileage": *WP,* Nov. 20, 1963.

435   neglecting to note: Christian interview.

435   "minor annoyance": *JWH,* p. 4.

435   "going down there to patch": ibid., p. 3.

436   "fractious place": Christian interview.

436   "She had lists of things": Battelle interview.

436   "I feel great": *JWH,* p. 4.

436   "I'd like to ride": *DOAP,* p. 118.

436   Yet underneath his shirt: *The Warren Commission Report: The Official Report of the
       President's Commission on the Assassination of President John F. Kennedy,* Testimony of Dr.
       Charles James Carrico, p. 359.

436   He was briefly irritated: *JKWH,* p. 48; *DOAP,* p. 58.

436   "I'll go dress him": Battelle interview.

436   Father, mother, and son: *DOAP*, pp. 59–60, 63–64.

437   "who was there": *JWH*, p. 18.

437   Jack and Jackie attracted: ibid., pp. 21–22; *JKWH* pp. 351–53; *NYT*, Nov. 22, 1963.

437   "Oh gee, she's going": Lady Bird Johnson OH.

437   Speaking about the space: *JWH*, p. 21.

437   "This nation has tossed": Sidey interview.

437   "vibrating so violently": *DOAP*, p. 85.

437   "uncontrollable tremor": Leamer II, p. 730.

437   *The Thunderbolt*, a right-wing: *AH*, p. 549. To Kenny O'Donnell at least, the headline
        was old news. On May 29, 1963, J. Edgar Hoover wrote to O'Donnell, enclosing
        "the latest issue of *The Thunderbolt* . . . which carries an article on the front page
        captioned 'JFK Accused of Adultery.'" Hoover noted that the article reflected "the
        accusations of Florence Kater" regarding Turnure. FBI FOIA Kennedy Documents.

437   "so terribly uneducated": *NYT*, Nov. 22, 1963; *WP*, Nov. 22, 1963.

437   "The President told me": Beschloss III, p. 13.

437   After a discussion: *JWH*, pp. 23, 25.

438   The Kennedys spent the night: *DOAP*, p. 121; *AH*, p. 552.

438   "You were great today": *DOAP*, p. 87.

438   they embraced before heading: ibid.; *AH*, p. 552.

438   "secret weapon": *JKWH*, p. 351.

438   "Just about the same": ibid.

438   Kennedy was scheduled: *ATD*, p. 1024; *JWH*, p. 23.

438   "Where's Jackie?" *DOAP*, p. 114.

438   Mary Gallagher did an inventory: manuscript for *Look* excerpt of *DOAP*, Part Two,
        Galley Two, Myrick Land Papers, Boston University.

438   "One day in a campaign": Gallagher, p. 319; *DOAP*, p. 114.

438   Ten minutes after Jackie's: *DOAP*, p. 117.

438   "Aren't we leaving?": Hill interview, WMP.

438   "This is a dangerous and uncertain": *Newsweek*, Dec. 2, 1963.

439   "They're going to have a dreadful": *DOAP*, p. 121.

439   "something quite new": Lady Bird Johnson OH.

439   "suddenly had decided": Pierpoint OH.

439   Pam Turnure had earlier suggested: *DOAP*, p. 10.

439   "Never satisfactory": Turnure interview, WMP.

439   When Roy Kellerman, the lead: *JWH*, p. 25.

439   The sun was blazing: *Newsweek*, Dec. 2, 1963; *DOAP*, pp. 135, 137; *JWH*, p. 26.

439   "The motorcade is one of the hardest": Nellie Connally interview.

440   "If I'd get close enough": ibid.

440   "Mr. President, you can't": ibid.

440   Thirty seconds later: ibid.

440   Within six seconds: *The Warren Commission Report*, Carrico Testimony, p. 362; "The
        Camelot Documents," White Papers, JFKL; *JWH*, p. 27.

440   "My God, they've killed Jack": *DOAP*, p. 160.

440   Kennedy was rushed: *The Warren Commission Report*, Carrico Testimony, pp. 359–61,
        365.

440   Jackie approached the gurney: "The Camelot Documents," White Papers, JFKL.

440   The doctors pronounced: *DOAP*, p. 188.

440   Jackie asked a policeman: ibid., p. 294.

440   She wanted to give: ibid., pp. 290, 293–94.

440   "squat, hairy": ibid., p. 291.

440   came to her rescue: manuscript for *Look* excerpt of *DOAP*, Part Three, Galley Seven,
        Myrick Land Papers, Boston University.

440   Wishing she could be alone: ibid.

440   "The ring" . . . "Do you think": "The Camelot Documents," White Papers, JFKL;
       DOAP, p. 294; *NYT,* Dec. 5, 1963.

Chapter Thirty-one
441   "It was like the fall": Bunny Mellon interview, WMP.
441   On the plane to Washington: O'Brien, p. 160.
441   "a way of not looking": Dave Powers interview, WMP.
441   "Hey Jackie" . . . "He was so understated": Turnure interview, WMP.
441   "Oh Bobby. I just can't believe": *DOAP,* p. 391.
441   "the degree of shock": Finnerty interview.
442   "No. Let them see": *DOAP,* p. 348.
442   In the illuminated interior: Walsh interview, WMP. Dr. Walsh, who rode in the car
       directly behind the ambulance, told Manchester of the "light on in the ambulance.
       Jackie and the Attorney General were talking constantly, leaning over the coffin."
442   At Bethesda, family and friends: *CWK,* p. 240; Tuckerman interview, WMP; Charles
       Bartlett interview, WMP.
442   "Now [she] had decided": *CWK,* p. 243.
442   "Jackie, I'm going to get": *DOAP,* p. 427.
442   "to be in their own beds": Janet Auchincloss interview, WMP.
442   "That is not a decision": Ben Bradlee interview, WMP.
442   Jackie would instruct: Tuckerman interview, WMP.
442   "Your father has gone": *DOAP,* p. 409.
442   "Poor Nancy . . . You came down": Tuckerman interview, WMP.
442   "Jackie was astounding": Ethel Kennedy interview, WMP.
443   "I'll share him with you": Ben Bradlee interview, WMP.
443   "I was so startled": ibid.
443   "sort of keyed up": *DOAP,* p. 415.
443   "was part of her masque": manuscript for *Look* excerpt of *DOAP,* Part Four, Galley
       Two, Myrick Land Papers, Boston University.
443   "totally doomed child": *DOAP,* p. 406.
443   "Don't be too brave, cry": Ben Bradlee interview, WMP.
443   She sobbed but with few: ibid.
443   "Oh Benny, do you want": *CWK,* p. 242.
443   "the whole front of his head": Ben Bradlee interview, WMP.
443   "Gallic," Ben said: Ethel Kennedy interview, WMP.
443   "trying to get rid": Ben Bradlee interview, WMP.
443   "subdued, holding": *DOAP,* p. 407.
443   "the second towering figure": ibid., p. 417.
443   "She just wanted someone": McNamara interview, WMP.
443   "I was trying to think what": Ethel Kennedy interview, WMP.
443   "suddenly we had been there": Ben Bradlee interview, WMP.
443   "That French imagination": Charles Bartlett interview, WMP.
443   "Will you sleep tonight": Auchincloss interview, WMP.
444   "touched" that Jackie wanted: Auchincloss OH.
444   "She was so sad": Truitt interview.
444   "I stood there ironing and crying": Chavchavadze interview.
444   "Poor Pam": Turnure interview, WMP.
444   the driveway was lit: ibid., p. 438.
444   "lachrymose and sentimental": Walton interview, WMP.
444   He directed Bunny Mellon's upholsterer: Arata OH; *JKWH,* p. 353.
444   "and we stood staring": Spalding to Manchester, Sept. 28, 1964, WMP.
444   "Jackie has a great sense": Auchincloss interview, WMP.
444   Jackie gathered treasured: *DOAP,* pp. 516–17; Ben Bradlee interview, WMP.

445 Caroline neatly printed: manuscript for *Look* excerpt of *DOAP,* Part Four, Galley Nineteen, Myrick Land Papers, Boston University.

445 "My darling Jack": ibid., Galley Eight.

445 She wrote that the previous night: ibid.

445 "the blow she could not bear": ibid., Galley Eighteen.

445 "She also knew it didn't matter": ibid.

445 Jackie and Bobby took: ibid., Galley Nineteen.

445 Back in her dressing room: ibid., Galley Twenty.

445 "Sarge had a tough job": Sorensen interview, WMP.

445 Tish Baldrige finally tracked: Baldrige interview, WMP.

445 Another request was for: *DOAP,* p. 488; EMK interview, WMP.

445 Bob McNamara strongly believed: *DOAP,* pp. 490–97.

445 "the most beautiful sight": ibid., p. 497.

445 "stay here forever": ibid., p. 17; Bradford, p. 262.

446 "All sorts of people": Louchheim Journal, Dec. 2, 1963, KSLP.

446 In a series of visits: McNamara interview, WMP; Reed OH.

446 With his artist's eye: *DOAP,* p. 496.

446 "The face looked like": Spalding to Manchester, Sept. 28, 1964, WMP.

446 "One felt the face": Arthur Schlesinger interview, WMP.

446 "wax dummy": Walton interview, WMP.

446 "We talked about Jack as if": Eunice Shriver interview, WMP.

446 "He had been looking out": EMK interview, WMP.

446 "Daddy got it": Eunice Shriver interview, WMP.

446 The White House was filled: Stas Radziwill interview and Steve Smith interview, WMP.

446 "The whole family was like": Collier and Horowitz, p. 314.

447 "had the most wonderful life": Ethel Kennedy interview, WMP.

447 "Pat drank too much": Arthur Schlesinger interview, WMP.

447 "as though he was being held up": Ben Bradlee interview, WMP.

447 "extraordinary": Auchincloss interview, WMP.

447 "What do people expect": *DOAP,* p. 554.

447 "choking sounds": ibid., p. 462.

447 "Jackie held up the longest": David Ormsby Gore interview, WMP.

447 "I can't. I can just see": Auchincloss interview, WMP.

447 "not wishing to intrude": DBD, Nov. 23, 1963.

448 "most dignified and not sentimental": Mellon interview, WMP.

448 Mellon knew instinctively: *DOAP,* p. 515.

448 "I don't want the church": Mellon interview, WMP.

448 "I racked my brain": ibid.

448 "A big man in tears": Dillon interview, WMP.

448 Charley Bartlett busied: Charles Bartlett interview, WMP; Baldrige interview, WMP.

448 "I hung up and wept": Sorensen interview, WMP.

449 "He was hit hardest": Bundy interview, WMP.

449 "I was grateful for the work": ibid.

449 "Friday and Saturday I cried": *DOAP,* p. 445.

449 "great kindness and sweetness": Schlesinger interview, WMP.

449 "dearest Jackie, who was": Schlesinger to JBK, ND, WMP.

449 For the second night: *DOAP,* p. 510; Walsh interview, WMP; Stas Radziwill interview, WMP.

449 blue "anti-crying pills": *DOAP,* p. 576.

449 "I have learned to shut off": Jessie Wood interview.

449 "Everyone was trying not to talk": Dillon interview, WMP.

450 "And so she took a ring": Mike Mansfield Tribute, Nov. 24, 1963, WMP.

450   "Bad poetry": Auchincloss interview, WMP.

450   "absolutely appalling": Gore interview, WMP.

450   "I love you as I loved": Joe Alsop to JBK, ND, WMP.

450   "We had a hero": Bartlett to JBK, ND, WMP.

450   "How can you say that": *DOAP,* p. 503.

450   "be around, be helpful": Fay interview, WMP.

450   That evening Reed went: Reed interview, WMP; Crespi interview.

450   "It was like Versailles": Stas Radziwill interview, WMP.

450   "With his old-fashioned": *DOAP,* p. 547.

450   Stas asked only: Stas Radziwill interview, WMP.

451   "looked carved in bronze": Lady Bird Johnson interview, WMP.

451   "a different Johnson": Freeman Journal, WMP.

451   "couldn't have been more humble": Sorensen interview, WMP.

451   "stay right there till I go": Alsop I, p. 34.

451   David and Sissie Gore found: Gore interview, WMP.

451   "weak and selfish": Gore to JBK, Nov. 26, 1963, WMP.

451   Chuck Spalding wandered: Stas Radziwill interview, WMP; Gore interview, WMP.

451   "sense of pageantry": *AJ,* p. 521.

451   "everybody rushed off": Galbraith interview, WMP.

451   "aesthetically unfortunate": *DOAP,* p. 551.

452   "the particular advantage": *AJ,* p. 523.

452   "very well composed": Gore interview, WMP.

452   "obvious" . . . "banal": ibid.

452   "Do you think there is": ibid.

452   "and a time to fish": Sorensen interview, WMP.

452   On Sunday night there was: EMK interview, WMP.

452   The next morning, James Ketchum, who: Ketchum interview.

452   Up on the second floor: EMK interview, WMP.

452   "Jackie told me how she": Mellon interview, WMP.

453   "Please fix a basket": ibid.

453   "What was remarkable": ibid.

453   "like an enormous blanket": ibid.

453   Only Nancy Tuckerman missed: Tuckerman interview, WMP.

453   "It was 100 percent male": Walton interview, WMP.

453   "Damn it, Powers": Fay interview, WMP.

454   Eunice, who was pregnant: Eunice Shriver interview, WMP.

454   Directly behind the horse-drawn: *DOAP,* p. 490; *NYT,* Nov. 26, 1963.

454   Inside the church: Mellon interview, WMP; *NYT,* Nov. 26, 1963.

454   "She was raised correctly": Nicole Alphand interview, WMP.

454   "Your old men shall dream": *NYT,* Nov. 26, 1963.

454   For the first time, Jackie lost: *DOAP,* p. 587.

454   "get me a blue pill": Clint Hill interview, WMP.

454   "sad instead of hopeful": Eunice Shriver interview, WMP.

454   "didn't seem very upset": Tony Bradlee interview.

454   When the caisson neared: *NYT,* Nov. 26, 1963.

455   Lee burst into tears: *DOAP,* p. 597.

455   "the wildly twittering birds": *ATD,* p. 1030.

455   "this wonderful man": *NYT,* Nov. 26, 1963.

455   Bobby and Teddy had prepared: RFK interview, WMP; EMK interview, WMP.

455   "This great hunk of a man": Joan Kennedy interview, WMP.

455   "the fall of a curtain": *DOAP,* p. 603.

455   "like a Roman queen": Nicole Alphand interview, WMP.

455   whose face still peered: *Time,* Nov. 22, 1963.

455   "I want it to be an American": Ketchum interview.
455   "He died like a soldier": Nicole Alphand interview, WMP.
455   "such a good friend": Steve Smith interview, WMP.
455   "Jack was never bitter": *DOAP,* p. 608.
455   "only three could be trusted": Jean Smith notes, WMP.
455   "a last souvenir" . . . "very tenderly": Nicole Alphand interview, WMP.
455   John, Caroline, and their cousins: *DOAP,* p. 617.
455   "Jackie said, 'I couldn't disappoint'": Crespi interview.
456   "A Kennedy trait": Ben Bradlee interview, WMP.
456   "seemed completely detached": *CWK,* p. 244.
456   "so choked up he had to leave": Ethel Kennedy interview, WMP.
456   "reedy, hearty voice": *DOAP,* p. 617.
456   "cheerful . . . except Jackie": Ben Bradlee interview, WMP.
456   Her glance caught Stas: Tony Bradlee interview, WMP.
456   "Should we go visit": *DOAP,* p. 619.
456   "Goodnight my Darling Jacks": Lee Radziwill to JBK, ND, WMP.
456   "rather more distraught": *AJ,* p. 524.
456   "I am like a wounded": Nicole Alphand interview, WMP.
456   Jackie called Dr. Finnerty: Finnerty interview.
457   Several days after the funeral: Auchincloss interview, WMP.
457   "died in the company of a man": JBK to Nellie Connally, Dec. 1, 1963, courtesy of
      Nellie Connally.
457   "that war might be started": JBK to Nikita Khrushchev, Dec. 1, 1963, WMP.
457   "presumptuous . . . I never meddled": ibid.
457   "the good-willed comforters": White II, p. 520.
457   "Don't worry, not Pearl Harbor Day": JBK to Lady Bird Johnson, Dec. 1, 1963,
      LBJL.
458   The day before the move: Auchincloss interview, WMP.
458   "were playing with unusual zeal": *JKWH,* pp. 353–54.
458   To welcome the Johnsons: Liz Carpenter interview; *DOAP,* p. 629.
458   "a continual reminder": *NYT,* Dec. 7, 1963.
458   Accompanied by Lee, Bobby, and Ethel: ibid.
458   While Teddy White later regretted: White II, p. 520.
458   "She took the man she loved": Louchheim Journal, November 1963, KSLP.

Epilogue
459   "The Washington landscape": Alsop II, p. 464.
459   "a hard-bitten objective Republican": Rostow OH.
459   "The fact is that Jack Kennedy": Alsop II, p. 463.
459   "Since he left, the glue": Sorensen interview.
459   "We'll never laugh again": Daniel Patrick Moynihan interview, WMP.
460   Jacqueline Kennedy stayed: *DOAP,* p. 642; DBD, Dec. 21, 1963.
460   At one point Bobby Kennedy: *WP,* Nov. 13, 2003.
460   "Do you think God": ibid., quoting from McSorley's Apr. 28, 1964, diary.
460   "keep busy and to keep healthy": ibid., quoting from JBK to McSorley, July 15, 1964.
460   hordes of tourists: Gaither interview.
460   She moved to 1040 Fifth Avenue: *NYT,* May 31, 1970.
460   "what he would have wanted them": JBK to Macmillan, May 17, 1965, HMA.
460   She did not return: Monkman interview.
460   After several years, the marriage unraveled: Sorensen interview.
461   "You just come over here": LBJ and JBK, Dec. 2, 1963, Beschloss II, pp. 12–13.
461   "You're so nice to call me": ibid., Dec. 23, 1963, p. 18.
461   "I'm so scared I'll start to cry": ibid., Jan. 9, 1964, p. 22.

461   "I'll do anything I can": ibid.

461   "He looks at me like he's going": LBJ and John Connally, July 23, 1964, Beschloss III, p. 468.

461   "I do not want to get": Freeman Journal, WMP.

461   "I want you to know": ibid.

461   a "passionate and unconquerable": JBK to Macmillan, Sept. 14, 1965, HMA.

461   At Jackie's suggestion: *RKHL,* pp. 285–87.

462   "They had a touching need": Baldrige interview.

462   "My adored brother-in-law": JBK to Manchester, June 17, 1968, courtesy of William Manchester.

462   "as though a ruling family": Alsop OH, Robert F. Kennedy Oral History Project, JFKL.

462   On the way to a hotel ballroom: *RKHL,* pp. 390–92.

462   "a great suffocating fog": JBK to Manchester, June 17, 1968, courtesy of William Manchester.

462   "an element one lives in": JBK to Alsop, Sept. 8, 1968, Alsop Papers, LOC.

462   "wept uncontrollably": *RKHL,* p. 392.

462   Jackie remained devoted: Whalen, p. 495.

462   Rose Kennedy kept up: Leamer I, pp. 684–85, 690.

462   "There was a natural affection": Wood interview.

463   With the help of Alcoholics Anonymous: *Boston Globe Magazine,* July 9, 2000.

463   "was in a bad way": JBK interview, WMP.

463   Pat and Peter were divorced: Leamer I, p. 610.

463   she battled drinking problems: ibid., p. 750.

463   His womanizing strained: ibid., p. 721.

463   In 1974, Jean founded: Jean Kennedy Smith biography, U.S. Department of State; *Business Week,* Aug. 15, 2001.

463   "the colors of love and death": JBK to Alsop, Sept. 8, 1968, Alsop Papers, LOC.

463   "People always say time": ibid., Aug. 31, 1964.

464   A year later Joe and Susan Mary: Alsop II, p. 469.

464   "I had a feeling that this": Auchincloss interview, WMP.

464   She placed the suit: *DOAP,* p. 646.

464   (The pink suit eventually went: Newhouse News Service, Nov. 12, 2003.

464   As Janet and Hughdie's fortunes: Yusha Auchincloss interview.

464   Jackie set up a $1 million: Pottker, p. 307.

464   Letitia Baldrige worked: Baldrige interview.

464   In 1967 the Bartletts: Charles Bartlett interview; Martha Bartlett interview.

465   "In many ways Lem thought": Michaelis, p. 182.

465   Billings occupied himself: Bartlett interview; Lasker OH-CU.

465   "a link to our dead fathers": Michaelis, p. 183.

465   "The relationship of four": Ben Bradlee interview.

465   "brought back sad memories": Tony Bradlee interview.

465   Jackie considered the book: Ben Bradlee interview.

465   After his retirement in 1979: *Harvard University Gazette* website.

465   Oleg Cassini prospered: Cassini interview.

466   Vivian Crespi remained close: Crespi interview.

466   "peace of mind": ibid.

466   He returned to Wall Street: Dillon interview.

466   only weeks before his death: *NYT,* Jan. 12, 2003.

466   At Jackie's request, Bobby: Fay interview.

466   "locker room humor": Collier and Horowitz, p. 333.

466   Eve and Paul Fout saw Jackie: Eve Fout interview; Paul Fout interview.

466   "meant a world come to an end": Galbraith III, p. 115.

467 "proud, independent spirit": Gore to JBK, Nov. 26, 1963, WMP.

467 two years later Sissie was killed: *Daily Express,* May 31, 1967.

467 He and Jackie had a romance: Pamela Harlech interview.

467 "squeezed him like an orange": Shapley, p. 278, quoting Dean Acheson.

467 After Jackie sold Wexford: *CWK,* p. 153.

467 Jackie sought Bunny's help: Bradford, p. 321.

467 although Jackie declined: JBK to Lady Bird Johnson, Mar. 15, 1965, LBJL.

467 "I will always think it was": JBK to Lady Bird Johnson, Apr. 25, 1965, LBJL.

467 "sort of picked up": Angleton interview.

468 Although Meyer and her friend: Chavchavadze interview.

468 On October 12, 1964: Burleigh, pp. 9, 231, 244; Katie McCabe, "She Had a Dream," *Washingtonian,* March 2002.

468 "O'Brien knew he was working": McPherson interview.

468 "she probably was more consoling": *JWH,* p. 390.

469 "no political presence": Manchester interview.

469 "He had eleven screwdrivers": ibid.

469 "They died long before": O'Donnell, p. xiv.

469 David Powers trekked: Powers OH; *JWH,* p. 390.

469 "violent pains": *DOAP,* p. 617.

469 Until his death: JFKL Newsletter, spring/summer 1998.

469 "She hits me across": Cecil Beaton unpublished diary, June 1968, Beaton Collection, St. John's College, Cambridge, copyright, The Literary Executors of the late Sir Cecil Beaton.

469 "Red was singing": James Reed interview.

470 "I never really worked for anyone": ibid.

470 "He never stopped looking": Jewel Reed interview.

470 In the months after JFK's death: Kloman interview.

470 "Oh how I loved your Franklin": Tobie Roosevelt interview.

470 Arthur Schlesinger left: Marian Schlesinger interview.

470 "Life in the White House was a pressure": Arthur Schlesinger interview.

470 "Arthur became a celebrity": Marian Schlesinger interview.

470 Florence Smith was suffering: Earl E.T. Smith Jr. interview.

470 "Dearest Dearest Earl": JBK to Earl E.T. Smith, Nov. 9, 1965, courtesy of Earl Smith Jr.

471 "lived this man's life": Louchheim Journal, Thanksgiving Eve, 1963, KSLP.

471 Sorensen was the first: Anderson, pp. 296–97; *KE,* p. 5.

471 "lived in awe of Jackie": Sorensen interview.

471 "She had a difficult divorce": Coleman interview.

471 Chuck married twice more: Betty Spalding interview, JCBC; Charles Bartlett interview.

471 His principal contact: Fay interview.

471 "I love you": Stevenson to JBK, ND, Stevenson Papers, JFKL.

472 "For a while, I would just like to sit": Graham, p. 378.

472 Nancy Tuckerman followed Jackie: Bradford, p. 410.

472 She ran a decorating business: Baldrige interview.

472 "an abstract painting with": Tony Bradlee interview.

472 "marvelous roaring tender story": White to JBK, April 14, 1980, White Papers, Harvard University.

472 Jayne Wrightsman reigned: Stanfill, *Vanity Fair,* January 2003.

472 "I think she learned rather": ibid.

BIBLIOGRAPHY

Books

Abbott, James A., and Elaine M. Rice. *Designing Camelot: The Kennedy White House Restoration*. New York: Van Nostrand Reinhold, 1998.

Abramson, Rudy. *Spanning the Century: The Life of W. Averell Harriman, 1891–1986*. New York: Morrow, 1992.

Alphand, Hervé. *L'étonnement d'être: Journal (1939–1973)*. Paris: Fayard, 1977.

Alsop, Joseph W. *"I've Seen the Best of It": Memoirs*. New York: Norton, 1992.

Alsop, Stewart. *The Center: People and Power in Political Washington*. New York: Harper & Row, 1968.

Anderson, Patrick. *The Presidents' Men: White House Assistants of Franklin D. Roosevelt, Harry S. Truman, Dwight D. Eisenhower, John F. Kennedy, and Lyndon B. Johnson*. Garden City, N.Y.: Doubleday, 1968.

Anthony, Carl Sferrazza. *The Kennedy White House: Family Life & Pictures, 1961–1963*. New York: Simon & Schuster, 2001.

Attwood, William. *The Reds and the Blacks: A Personal Adventure*. New York: Harper & Row, 1967.

Baldrige, Letitia. *In the Kennedy Style: Magical Evenings in the Kennedy White House,* with recipes by White House Chef René Verdon. New York: Doubleday, 1998.

———. *A Lady First: My Life in the Kennedy White House and the American Embassies of Paris and Rome*. New York: Viking Penguin, 2001.

———. *Of Diamonds and Diplomats*. Boston: Houghton Mifflin, 1968.

Bartlett, Apple Parish, and Susan Bartlett Crater. *Sister: The Life of Legendary American Interior Decorator Mrs. Henry Parish II*. New York: St. Martin's, 2000.

Beale, Betty. *Power at Play: A Memoir of Parties, Politicians and the Presidents in My Bedroom*. Washington, D.C.: Regnery Gateway, 1993.

Beaton, Cecil. *Self Portrait with Friends: The Selected Diaries of Cecil Beaton,* ed. Richard Buckle. London: Pimlico, 1991.

——— (Introduced by Hugo Vickers). *The Unexpurgated Beaton: The Cecil Beaton Diaries as He Wrote Them*. London: Weidenfeld & Nicolson, 2002.

———— (Introduced by Hugo Vickers). *Beaton in the Sixties: More Unexpurgated Diaries.* London: Weidenfeld & Nicolson, 2003.

Beschloss, Michael R. *The Crisis Years: Kennedy and Khrushchev, 1960–1963.* New York: HarperCollins, 1991.

————, ed. *Reaching for Glory: Lyndon Johnson's Secret White House Tapes, 1964–1965.* New York: Simon & Schuster, 2001.

————, ed. *Taking Charge: The Johnson White House Tapes, 1963–1964.* New York: Simon & Schuster, 1997.

Bird, Kai. *The Color of Truth: McGeorge Bundy and William Bundy: Brothers in Arms.* New York: Simon & Schuster, 1998.

Bishop, Jim. *A Day in the Life of President Kennedy.* New York: Random House, 1964.

Blair, Joan, and Clay Blair Jr. *The Search for JFK.* New York: Berkeley, 1976.

Bouvier, Jacqueline, and Lee Bouvier. *One Special Summer.* New York: Delacorte, 1974.

Bowles, Hamish. *Jacqueline Kennedy: The White House Years: Selections from the John F. Kennedy Library and Museum.* New York: Metropolitan Museum of Art/Little, Brown, 2001.

Braden, Joan. *Just Enough Rope: An Intimate Memoir.* New York: Villard, 1989.

Braden, Tom. *Eight Is Enough.* New York: Random House, 1975.

Bradford, Sarah. *America's Queen: The Life of Jacqueline Kennedy Onassis.* New York: Viking, 2000.

Bradlee, Benjamin C. *Conversations with Kennedy.* New York: Norton, 1975.

————. *A Good Life: Newspapering and Other Adventures.* New York: Simon & Schuster, 1995.

Brammer, Billy Lee. *The Gay Place.* Austin: University of Texas Press, 1995.

Bryant, Traphes, with Frances Spatz Leighton. *Dog Days at the White House: The Outrageous Memoirs of the Presidential Kennel Keeper.* New York: Pocket Books, 1976.

Buchan, John (Lord Tweedsmuir). *Pilgrim's Way: An Essay in Recollection.* Cambridge, Mass.: Riverside, 1940.

Bundy, McGeorge. *Danger and Survival: Choices About the Bomb in the First Fifty Years.* New York: Random House, 1988.

Burleigh, Nina. *A Very Private Woman: The Life and Unsolved Murder of Presidential Mistress Mary Meyer.* New York: Bantam, 1999.

Caro, Robert. *The Years of Lyndon Johnson: Master of the Senate.* New York: Knopf, 2002.

Cassini, Oleg. *In My Own Fashion: An Autobiography.* New York: Simon & Schuster, 1987.

————. *A Thousand Days of Magic: Dressing Jacqueline Kennedy for the White House.* New York: Rizzoli, 1995.

Cecil, David. *Melbourne.* New York: Bobbs-Merrill, 1954.

Clymer, Adam. *Edward M. Kennedy: A Biography.* New York: Morrow, 1999.

Collier, Peter, and David Horowitz. *The Kennedys: An American Drama.* New York: Summit, 1984.

Connally, Nellie, and Mickey Herskowitz. *From Love Field: My Final Hours with President John F. Kennedy.* New York: Rugged Land, 2003.

Corry, John. *The Golden Clan: The Murrays, the McDonnells and the Irish American Aristocracy.* Boston: Houghton Mifflin, 1977.

Coward, Noël. *The Noël Coward Diaries,* eds. Graham Payn and Sheridan Morley. London: Papermac, 1982.

Dallas, Rita, R.N., with Jeanira Ratcliffe. *The Kennedy Case.* New York: Putnam, 1973.

Dallek, Robert. *An Unfinished Life: John F. Kennedy, 1917–1963.* Boston: Little, Brown, 2003.

Damore, Leo. *The Cape Cod Years of John Fitzgerald Kennedy.* Englewood Cliffs, N.J.: Prentice-Hall, 1967.

Davis, Deborah. *Katharine the Great: Katharine Graham and the Washington Post.* Bethesda, Md.: National Press/Zenith, 1987.

Dickerson, Nancy. *Among Those Present: A Reporter's View of Twenty-five Years in Washington*. New York: Random House, 1976.

Dobrynin, Anatoly. *In Confidence: Moscow's Ambassador to America's Six Cold War Presidents*. New York: Times Books, 1995.

DuBois, Diana. *In Her Sister's Shadow: An Intimate Biography of Lee Radziwill*. New York: St. Martin's Paperbacks, 1997.

Elson, Robert T. *The World of Time, Inc.: The Intimate History of a Publishing Enterprise,* vol. 2, *1941–1960*. New York: Atheneum, 1973.

Fay, Paul. *The Pleasure of His Company*. New York: Harper & Row, 1966.

Fursenko, Aleksandr, and Timothy Naftali. *"One Hell of a Gamble": The Secret History of the Cuban Missile Crisis*. New York: Norton, 1997.

Gage, Nicholas. *Greek Fire: The Story of Maria Callas and Aristotle Onassis*. New York: Knopf, 2000.

Galbraith, John Kenneth. *Ambassador's Journal: A Personal Account of the Kennedy Years*. Boston: Houghton Mifflin, 1969.

———. *Letters to Kennedy*. Cambridge, Mass.: Harvard University Press, 1998.

———. *Name-Dropping: From FDR On*. Boston: Houghton Mifflin, 1999.

Gallagher, Mary Barelli, with Frances Spatz Leighton. *My Life with Jacqueline Kennedy*. New York: McKay, 1969.

Goodwin, Doris Kearns. *The Fitzgeralds and the Kennedys: An American Saga*. New York: Simon & Schuster, 1987.

———. *No Ordinary Time: Franklin and Eleanor Roosevelt: The Home Front in World War II*. New York: Touchstone/Simon & Schuster, 1995.

Graham, Katharine. *Personal History*. New York: Knopf, 1997.

Halberstam, David. *The Best and the Brightest*. New York: Random House, 1972.

Hamilton, Nigel. *JFK: Reckless Youth*. New York: Random House, 1992.

Heller, Deane, and David Heller. *Jacqueline Kennedy*. Derby, Ct.: Monarch, 1963.

Hersh, Burton. *The Mellon Family: A Fortune in History*. New York: Morrow, 1978.

Hersh, Seymour M. *The Dark Side of Camelot*. Boston: Little, Brown, 1998.

Horne, Alistair. *Macmillan*, vol. 2, *1957–1986*. New York: Viking, 1989.

Hoving, Thomas. *Making the Mummies Dance: Inside the Metropolitan Museum of Art*. New York: Touchstone/Simon & Schuster, 1994.

Isaacson, Walter, and Evan Thomas. *The Wise Men: Six Friends and the World They Made*. New York: Simon & Schuster, 1986.

Kaplan, Fred. *Gore Vidal: A Biography*. New York: Doubleday, 1999.

Kennedy, Caroline. *The Best Loved Poems of Jacqueline Kennedy Onassis*. New York: Hyperion, 2001.

Kennedy, John F. *The Greatest Speeches of President John F. Kennedy*. Bellingham, Wash.: Titan, 2001.

———. *Profiles in Courage*. New York: Perennial Classics, 2000.

Kennedy, Robert F. *Thirteen Days: A Memoir of the Cuban Missile Crisis*. New York: New American Library, 1969.

Kennedy, Rose. *Times to Remember*. Garden City, N.Y.: Doubleday, 1974.

Khrushchev, Nikita. *Khrushchev Remembers: The Last Testament, 1974*. tr. and ed. Strobe Talbott. Boston: Little, Brown, 1974.

Klein, Edward. *All Too Human: The Love Story of Jack and Jackie Kennedy*. New York: Pocket Books, 1996.

Kluger, Richard. *The Paper: The Life and Death of the New York Herald Tribune*. New York: Knopf, 1986.

Leamer, Laurence. *The Kennedy Men: 1901–1963: The Laws of the Father*. New York: Morrow, 2001.

———. *The Kennedy Women: The Saga of an American Family*. New York: Villard, 1994.

Lieberson, Goddard, and Joan Meyers, eds. *John Fitzgerald Kennedy . . . As We Remember Him*. New York: Atheneum, 1965.

Lincoln, Anne H. *The Kennedy White House Parties*. New York: Viking, 1967.

Lincoln, Evelyn. *My Twelve Years with John F. Kennedy*. New York: McKay, 1965.

Liston, Robert A. *Sargent Shriver: A Candid Portrait*. New York: Farrar, Straus, 1964.

Lord, Ruth. *Henry F. du Pont and Winterthur: A Daughter's Portrait*. New Haven, Conn.: Yale University Press, 1999.

Macmillan, Harold. *At the End of the Day: 1961–1963*. London: Macmillan, 1973.

———. *Pointing the Way: 1959–1961*. London: Macmillan, 1972.

Malraux, André. *Anti-Memoirs*. New York: Holt, Rinehart and Winston, 1968.

Manchester, William. *The Death of a President: November 20–November 25, 1963*. New York: Harper & Row, 1967.

———. *Portrait of a President: John F. Kennedy in Profile*. Boston: Little, Brown, 1962.

Martin, Ralph G. *Henry and Clare: An Intimate Portrait of the Luces*. New York: Putnam, 1991.

———. *A Hero for Our Time: An Intimate Story of the Kennedy Years*. New York: Macmillan, 1983.

Marton, Kati. *Hidden Power: Presidential Marriages That Shaped Our Recent History*. New York: Pantheon, 2001.

May, Ernest R., Timothy Naftali, and Philip Zelikow, eds. *The Presidential Recordings: John F. Kennedy: The Great Crises*, vol. 1, *July 30–August 1962*; vol. 2, *September–October 21, 1962*; vol. 3, *October 22–28, 1962*. New York: Norton, 2001.

May, Ernest R., and Philip D. Zelikow, eds. *The Kennedy Tapes: Inside the White House During the Cuban Missile Crisis*. New York: Norton, 2001.

McNamara, Robert S., with Brian VanDeMark. *In Retrospect: The Tragedy and Lessons of Vietnam*. New York: Vintage, 1996.

McPherson, Harry. *A Political Education: A Washington Memoir*. Boston: Houghton Mifflin, 1988.

Mellon, Paul, with John Baskett. *Reflections in a Silver Spoon*. New York: Morrow, 1992.

Merry, Robert W. *Taking On the World: Joseph and Stewart Alsop—Guardians of the American Century*. New York: Viking, 1996.

Michaelis, David. *The Best of Friends: Profiles of Extraordinary Friendships*. New York: Morrow, 1983.

Mitford, Nancy. *Love from Nancy: The Letters of Nancy Mitford*, ed. Charlotte Mosley. Boston: Houghton Mifflin, 1993.

Monkman, Betty C. *The White House: Its Historic Furnishings and First Families*. New York: Abbeville, 2000.

Morgan, Ted. *FDR: A Biography*. New York: Simon & Schuster, 1985.

Morris, Edmund. *Theodore Rex*. New York: Random House, 2001.

Morris, Sylvia Jukes. *Rage for Fame: The Ascent of Clare Boothe Luce*. New York: Random House, 1997.

Niklas, Kurt. *The Corner Table: From Cabbages to Caviar, Sixty Years in the Celebrity Restaurant Trade*. Los Angeles: Tuxedo Press, 2000.

Niven, David. *The Moon's a Balloon*. New York: Putnam, 1972.

O'Brien, Lawrence F. *No Final Victories: A Life in Politics—from John F. Kennedy to Watergate*. Garden City, N.Y.: Doubleday, 1974.

O'Donnell, Helen. *A Common Good: The Friendship of Robert F. Kennedy and Kenneth P. O'Donnell*. New York: Morrow, 1998.

O'Donnell, Kenneth P., and David Powers, with Joe McCarthy. *"Johnny, We Hardly Knew Ye": Memories of John Fitzgerald Kennedy*. Boston: Little, Brown, 1970.

Pottker, Jan. *Janet and Jackie: The Story of a Mother and Her Daughter, Jacqueline Kennedy Onassis*. New York: St. Martin's, 2001.

Prendergast, Curtis, with Geoffrey Colvin. *The World of Time Inc.: The Intimate History of a Changing Enterprise, 1960–1980*. New York: Atheneum, 1986.

Radziwill, Lee. *Happy Times*. New York: Assouline, 2000.

Reeves, Richard. *President Kennedy: Profile of Power*. New York: Simon & Schuster, 1993.

Rhea, Mini, with Frances Spatz Leighton. *I Was Jacqueline Kennedy's Dressmaker*. New York: Fleet, 1962.

Richardson, Nan, ed. *The Billings Collection*. Boston: John F. Kennedy Library Foundation, 1991.

Schlesinger, Arthur M., Jr. *Robert Kennedy and His Times*. Boston: Houghton Mifflin, 1978.

———. *A Thousand Days: John F. Kennedy in the White House*. Boston: Houghton Mifflin, 1965.

Shakespeare, William. *William Shakespeare: The Complete Works: The Pelican Text Revised*, ed. Alfred Harbage. Baltimore: Penguin, 1969.

Shapley, Deborah. *Promise and Power: The Life and Times of Robert McNamara*. Boston: Little, Brown, 1993.

Sidey, Hugh. *John F. Kennedy, President*. New York: Atheneum, 1963.

———, Chester V. Clifton, and Cecil Stoughton. *The Memories: JFK, 1961–1963*. New York: Norton, 1973.

Sinatra, Tina, with Jeff Coplon. *My Father's Daughter: A Memoir*. New York: Simon & Schuster, 2000.

Slater, Kitty. *The Hunt Country of America: Then and Now*. Upperville, Va.: Virginia Reel, 1997.

Smith, Amanda, ed. *Hostage to Fortune: The Letters of Joseph P. Kennedy*. New York: Penguin, 2002.

Smith, Earl E.T. *The Fourth Floor: An Account of the Castro Communist Revolution*. New York: Random House, 1962.

Smith, Florence Pritchett. *These Entertaining People: A Guide for the Elegant Hostess*. New York: Macmillan, 1966.

Smith, Sally Bedell. *Reflected Glory: The Life of Pamela Churchill Harriman*. New York: Simon & Schuster, 1996.

Sorensen, Theodore C. *Kennedy*. New York: Harper & Row, 1965.

Stacks, John F. *Scotty: James B. Reston and the Rise and Fall of American Journalism*. Boston: Little, Brown, 2003.

Steel, Ronald. *Walter Lippmann and the American Century*. Boston: Little, Brown, 1980.

Sulzberger, C. L. *The Last of the Giants*. New York: Macmillan, 1970.

Sulzberger, Marina. *Marina: Letters and Diaries of Marina Sulzberger*, ed. C. L. Sulzberger. New York: Crown, 1978.

Tanzer, Lester, ed. *The Kennedy Circle: The New Men in Washington*. Washington, D.C.: Luce, 1961.

Thayer, Mary Van Rensselaer. *Jacqueline Bouvier Kennedy*. Garden City, N.Y.: Doubleday, 1961.

———. *Jacqueline Kennedy: The White House Years*. Boston: Little, Brown, 1971.

Thomas, Evan. *Robert Kennedy: His Life*. New York: Simon & Schuster, 2000.

Travell, Janet, M.D. *Office Hours: Day and Night: The Autobiography of Janet Travell, M.D.* New York: World, 1968.

Vidal, Gore. *Palimpsest: A Memoir*. New York: Penguin, 1996.

Vreeland, Diana. *D.V.*, eds. George Plimpton and Christopher Hemphill. New York: Vintage, 1985.

Walton, William. *The Evidence of Washington*. New York: Harper & Row, 1966.

West, J. B., with Mary Lynn Kotz. *Upstairs at the White House: My Life with the First Ladies*. New York: Coward, McCann & Geoghegan, 1973.

Whalen, Richard J. *The Founding Father: The Story of Joseph P. Kennedy*. Washington, D.C.: Regnery Gateway, 1993.

Wharton, Edith. *The Age of Innocence*. New York: Barnes and Noble Classics, 1996.
White, Theodore H. *In Search of History: A Personal Adventure*. New York: Harper & Row, 1978.
———. *The Making of the President 1960*. New York: Atheneum, 1961.
Wills, Garry. *The Kennedy Imprisonment: A Meditation on Power*. Boston: Little, Brown, 1982.
Wofford, Harris. *Of Kennedys and Kings*. New York: Farrar, Straus, & Giroux, 1980.
Wolff, Perry. *A Tour of the White House with Mrs. John F. Kennedy*. Garden City, N.Y.: Doubleday, 1962.
Yoder, Edwin M., Jr. *Joe Alsop's Cold War: A Study of Journalistic Influence and Intrigue*. Chapel Hill: The University of North Carolina Press, 1995.
Ziegler, Philip. *Diana Cooper*. London: Hamish Hamilton, 1981.

Documents

Alleged Assassination Plots Involving Foreign Leaders: An Interim Report. Washington, D.C.: 94th Congress, 1st Session, Report No. 94-465, November 1975: Report of the Church Committee, U.S. Government Printing Office, 1975.
Documents and Artifacts Relating to the Life and Career of John F. Kennedy, Guernsey's, March 18–19, 1998.
The Estate of Jacqueline Kennedy Onassis Catalogue. New York: Sotheby's, 1996.
Public Papers of the Presidents of the United States: John F. Kennedy 1963.
Statistical Abstract of the United States: 2002. U.S. Census Bureau, December 2002.
The Warren Commission Report: The Official Report of the President's Commission on the Assassination of President John F. Kennedy.

Archives

John Fitzgerald Kennedy Library. ORAL HISTORIES: Hervé Alphand, Joseph Alsop, Lawrence Arata, Janet Auchincloss, Charles Bartlett, Sir Isaiah Berlin, Leonard Bernstein, Lem Billings, Henry Brandon, Garrett Byrne, Richard Cardinal Cushing, Douglas Dillon, Angier Biddle Duke, Barbara Gamarekian, Roswell Gilpatric, Kay Halle, Lord Harlech (David Ormsby Gore), August Heckscher, Jacqueline Hirsh, Lady Bird Johnson, Fletcher Knebel, Laura Bergquist Knebel, Arthur Krock, Peter Lisagor, Henry Luce, Edward McDermott, Robert McNamara, John Monagan, Kenneth O'Donnell, Charles Peters, Robert Pierpoint, David Powers, James Reed, Walt Rostow, Pierre Salinger, Marian Schlesinger, Hugh Sidey, George Smathers, Theodore Sorensen, Charles Spalding, Janet Travell, Marietta Tree, Dorothy Tubridy, Nancy Tuckerman and Pamela Turnure, William Walton, Barbara Ward (Lady Jackson), Thomas Winship.

    COLLECTIONS: JFK Personal Papers, President's Office Files, Presidential Recordings, President's Special Correspondence Files, White House Social Files, Secret Service White House Gate Logs, Charles Bartlett Papers, Chester Clifton Papers, Douglas Dillon Papers, Sanford L. Fox Papers, Roswell Gilpatric Papers, Kay Halle Papers, August Heckscher Papers, Joseph Patrick Kennedy Papers, Evelyn Lincoln Papers, William Manchester Papers, Godfrey McHugh Papers, Richard E. Neustadt Papers, Pierre Salinger Papers, Arthur M. Schlesinger Papers, Theodore Sorensen Papers, *Vogue* Materials, William Walton Papers, Theodore White Papers.
Bodleian Library, Oxford University. Harold Macmillan Archive.
Howard Gotlieb Archival Research Center at Boston University. Laura Bergquist Papers, Fletcher Knebel Papers, Myrick Land Collection.
St. John's College, Cambridge. Cecil Beaton Collection, Diaries and Correspondence.
Columbia University. Oral History Project ORAL HISTORIES: Roger Blough, Richard Bolling, Richard Davies, Douglas Dillon, Mary Bass Gibson, Bruce and Beatrice Gould, Thomas Guinzburg, Elizabeth Ives, Iris Turner Kelso, Mary Lasker, Newton Minow,

Ruth Montgomery, David Powers, James Rousmanière, Arthur M. Schlesinger Jr., John Sharon, Evan Thomas, Frank Thompson Jr.

Federal Bureau of Investigation. J. Edgar Hoover Official and Confidential Files, FOIA Kennedy documents, FOIA Joseph Alsop file.

Harvard University. Theodore White Papers.

Harvard University, The Arthur and Elizabeth Schlesinger Library on The History of Women in America, Radcliffe Institute for Advanced Study. Gloria Emerson Papers, Marietta Tree Papers.

Herbert Hoover Library. Correspondence between JBK and Herbert Hoover.

Lyndon Baines Johnson Library. JBK Correspondence with Lyndon and Lady Bird Johnson.

University of Kentucky. The John Sherman Cooper Oral History Project. Interview with Jacqueline Kennedy Onassis.

Library of Congress. Joseph and Stewart Alsop Papers, Bess Furman Papers, W. Averell Harriman Papers, Clare Boothe Luce Papers, Katie S. Louchheim Papers, Agnes Meyer Papers.

Massachusetts Historical Society. Nigel Hamilton Research Collection.

Princeton University, Seeley G. Mudd Manuscript Library. Arthur Krock Papers, Adlai E. Stevenson Papers, John Bartlow Martin Papers.

Public Record Office, Kew. Prime Minister's Files, 1961–1964.

Richmond Historical Society. David Bruce Papers.

Franklin D. Roosevelt Presidential Library. Correspondence of Franklin and Eleanor Roosevelt, and Franklin Roosevelt Jr. with the Kennedys and several friends.

Henry Francis du Pont Winterthur Museum. Winterthur Archives.

University of Wyoming, American Heritage Center. Joan and Clay Blair Collection.

U.S. Senate Historical Office. George Smathers Oral History.

ACKNOWLEDGMENTS

Biographers are accustomed to sifting and cross-checking facts, but writing about Jack and Jackie Kennedy also requires separating fact from myth—what might be called the Camelot variations. Whether in hagiographies or attack biographies, the Kennedys are often unrecognizable. Researching and writing this book was like restoring an old photograph: filling in the missing pieces, sharpening the blurred lines, removing the discolorations. I was helped in this effort by a wide spectrum of people. The most prominent members of the Kennedy circle provided the contours of the photograph and the traits of its central characters. Many of the details came from people on the fringe of the Kennedys' world. They supplied missing bits and pieces, which they recalled with the vividness of people watching history for the first time. I tested one memory against another—and against interviews, diaries and correspondence from the period, memoirs written in the decades after JFK died, and the most reliable accounts of historians and biographers.

Several dozen of the people I interviewed about their experiences during the Kennedy administration had not discussed them publicly before, and I am deeply grateful for their candor and willingness to relive events that were sometimes painful. Others had previously spoken about those years, and I thank them for their patience as I nudged them to dig even further into their memories for fresh anecdotes and insights. If I have overlooked anyone, I beg forgiveness in advance:

Marella Agnelli; Howard Allen; Susan Mary Alsop; Charles and Julia Amory; Cicely Angleton; Hugh D. Auchincloss III; Letitia Baldrige; Charles and Martha Bartlett; Kenneth Battelle; James Bellows; William and Deeda Blair; Elizabeth Boyd; Tom Braden; Benjamin Bradlee; Tony Bradlee; Elizabeth Burton; Liz Carpenter; Oleg Cassini; Otis Chandler; Marion Leiter Charles; Helen Chavchavadze; George Christian; Countess Marina Cicogna; John Coleman; Nancy Tenney Coleman; Nellie Connally; Janet Felton Cooper; Vivian Crespi; Walter Curley; Lloyd Cutler; Carmine De Sapio; The Duke and Duchess of Devonshire; Wyatt Dickerson; Douglas Dillon; Joan Dillon, la Duchesse de Mouchy; Ymelda Dixon; Louise Drake; Joseph Dryer; Peter Duchin; Robin Chandler Duke; Nancy Hogan Dutton; Rowland Evans; Mimi Beardsley Fahnestock; Paul Fay; Justin Feldman; Myer Feldman; Dr. Frank Finnerty; Wendy Taylor Foulke; Paul and Eve

Fout; Jean Friendly; Otto Fuerbringer; Alice Grimes Gaither; John Kenneth and Catherine Galbraith; Barbara Gamarekian; Katharine Graham; Gilbert "Benno" Graziani; George Griffin; Thomas Guinzburg; Lloyd Hand; Barbara Harbach; Patricia Hass; Nancy White Hector; Richard Helms; Reinaldo Herrera; Solange Herter; Lord Jenkins of Hillhead; Lady Bird Johnson; Horace Kelland; Joan Kennedy; James and Barbara Ketchum; Suzanne Roosevelt Kloman; Henry and Audrey Koehler; Polly Kraft; Richard Krolik; Wendy Vanderbilt Lehman; Piedy Lumet; William Manchester; Paul Manno; Jaclin Marlin; Anne Mayfield; Nan McEvoy; Enüd Sztanko McGiffert; Robert McNamara; Harry McPherson; Kay Meehan; Starke Meyer; Tom Monroe; Wendy Morgan; Letizia Mowinckel; Molly Vere Nicoll; Paul Nitze; Kenneth Noland; Lorraine Pearce; Scott Peek; Claiborne and Nuala Pell; Walter Pincus; George Plimpton; Leo and June Racine; Lee Radziwill; Dr. Judson Randolph; Marcus Raskin; James Reed; Jewel Reed; John Reilly; Bernard Ridder; Jane Ridgeway; Walt and Elspeth Rostow; Pierre-Marie Rudelle; Arthur M. Schlesinger Jr.; Marian Cannon Schlesinger; Sargent and Eunice Shriver; Hugh Sidey; Earl E. T. Smith Jr.; Theodore Sorensen; Richard Spalding; Natalie Spencer; Frank Stanton; James Symington; Anne Truitt; Stewart Udall; William vanden Heuvel; Jeanne Murray Vanderbilt; Sander Vanocur; Gore Vidal; Sue Vogelsinger; Janet Whitehouse; Sue Wilson; Perry Wolff; Jessie Wood; and Phyllis Wyeth.

I relied as well on numerous individuals who helped me in ways large and small with their suggestions and support: Jonathan Alter, Andy Athy, Andrea Ball, Peter and Amy Bernstein, Michael Beschloss, Kai Bird, Terry Bracy, Sarah Bradford, Tom Brokaw, Brock Brower, Sam Butler, Bernard and Joan Carl, Sasha Chavchavadze, Frank Chopin, Joanna Clark, Tim Clark, Payson and Kim Coleman, David Patrick Columbia, Bill and Pat Compton, Mary Copeland, Richard Craven, Robert Dallek, Peter Davis, Susan Sage Dillon, Dominick Dunne, Jim Dunning, Pat Dunnington, Joseph J. Ellis, Alex Forger, Mimi Gilpatric, David and Patty Goodrich, Ginny Grenham, Ed Grosvenor, Louise Grunwald, Selina Hastings, Gale Hayman, George Herrick, Jane Hitchcock, Walter Isaacson, Robert Isabell, Dorothy Jackson, Liz Johnson, Peter Kaplan, Penne Korth, Jonathan Larsen, Griffin Lesher, Susan Magrino, Kinsey Marable, Kati Marton, Clare Crawford Mason, Alyne Massey, Bonnie Matheson, Chris Matthews, William McCue, Charlie and Meriwether McGettigan, Robert Merry, Sir Christopher Meyer, Melody Miller, Linda Mortimer, Oliver Murray, Sheila Mutcher, Al Neuharth, Jeffrey O'Connell, Maryann O'Donnell, John Oliver, Rich Oppel, Maureen Orth, Patricia Patterson, Daune Peckham, Jean Perin, Tammy Pittman, Leezee Porter, Bill Powers, Delina Pryce, Sally Quinn, Carole Radziwill, Eugenie Rahim, Paul Richard, Terri Robinson, Tobie Roosevelt, James Rowe III, Ann Schneider, Aniko Gaal Schott, Tim Sellers, Martha Sherrill, Dolph Simons, Evelyn Small, Hamilton South, Francesca Stanfill, Jean Stein, Strobe and Brooke Talbott, Lane Taylor, Evan Thomas, Betty Tilson, Peter Tufo, Karen Vaughan, Hugo Vickers, Robin West, Heyden White, Robert White, Rosalyn Whitehead, Elizabeth Winthrop, Linden Wise, and Philip Zelikow.

Understanding the look and feel of the White House was essential for my narrative, and Betty Monkman, the White House curator, gave several hours of her time to take me on an extensive tour. Barbara McMillan of the curator's office provided additional help, as did William Allman, Ms. Monkman's successor. John Castle, the current owner of La Guerida, Joe Kennedy's Palm Beach villa, showed me his beautifully restored house and gardens, with Leo Racine, a longtime Kennedy family employee, adding valuable details. Jackie Kennedy's stepbrother Yusha Auchincloss took me around Hammersmith Farm in Newport as he reminisced about visits by Jack and Jackie Kennedy during the presidency.

I am particularly indebted to William Manchester for graciously granting me exclusive access to his interview notes and other documents, which he used when writing *Death of a President* and *Portrait of a President*. These papers, which are stored at the John Fitzgerald Kennedy Library, had been sealed for nearly four decades. They contain striking new details, especially about Jack Kennedy's last days and the thoughts and actions of his widow, friends, and associates after the assassination. My thanks to Joseph G. Lynch and James C. Stearns for introducing me to Mr. Manchester, a masterly historian whose work I have long admired.

I am also grateful for permission from the Joseph P. Kennedy Papers Donor Committee to use material from the Joseph P. Kennedy Collection at the Kennedy Library, which provided essential background and perspective on members of the Kennedy family. Paul Kirk, Joann S. Nestor, Tracy Goyette Cote, and Jennifer Quan all helped to expedite access to those papers. For expert guidance on the JPK papers and many other collections in the library, I am thankful to Deborah Leff, Megan Desnoyers, Sharon Kelly, Allan Goodrich, Maura Porter, Michael Desmond, Ron Whealan, James Hill, and others on the library's dedicated staff.

My thanks as well to the trustees of the Harold Macmillan Book Trust for permission to quote from the former British prime minister's letters and journals at the Bodleian Library at Oxford University. Helen Langley, Philippa Blake-Roberts, Caroline Mackenzie, and the Earl of Stockton smoothed the way for my use of this valuable archive.

Howard Gotlieb of the Howard Gotlieb Archival Research Center at Boston University also kindly granted me permission to use material from the Myrick Land Collection.

Two largely unknown accounts of the period that offered fresh information about the Kennedys and their circle were the journals of Katie Louchheim, a Democratic party activist and State Department appointee, and the diaries of diplomat David Bruce, ambassador to Britain during the Kennedy years. My thanks to David Wigdor and Mary Wolfskill of the Library of Congress, site of the Louchheim diaries, and Nelson Lankford of the Virginia Historical Society, which houses the Bruce diaries.

Other skilled archivists who helped were Chris Carberry and Peter Drummie at the Massachusetts Historical Society; Linda Seelke and Claudia Anderson at the Lyndon Baines Johnson Library; Caroline Preston, who catalogued the Theodore White Papers at Harvard University; Jeffrey Suchanek at the University of Kentucky Wendell Ford Research Center; and Christine Sears and Kenneth Cohen at the Winterthur Archives.

Assembling and digesting this research would have been impossible without the generous assistance of Mike Hill, a man of enormous enthusiasm and amazing resourcefulness. His ability to navigate the Kennedy Library and other archives helped me focus my investigations; his meticulously organized binders filled with clippings, letters, journals, and memos provided vital details to enrich my account of the Kennedy years. His cheerful optimism gave me a lift whenever I felt defeated by mountains of information. He even enlisted his wife, Becky, to help out from time to time. Above all, he became a close and trusted friend.

In London, Jacqueline Williams was my intrepid proxy in combing through the Macmillan Archive as well as the prime minister's files at the Public Record Office in Kew. As she had on previous research projects, she exercised keen judgment in finding precisely what I needed. Edda Tasiemka again supplied me with clippings from her unrivaled archives. Abigail Pickus unearthed illuminating correspondence from the Alsop Papers at the Library of Congress, and I was fortunate that my daughter, Lisa Bedell, could gather letters from the Adlai Stevenson Collection while she was a senior at Princeton. Also assisting with research were Virginie Grolleau and Timea Bana. Cherryl Maddox transcribed tapes, and Lillie Trent and Agnes Langdon did stellar translations for me.

As he did for my previous book, my friend Peter Bernstein provided the inspiration for *Grace and Power.* This time, he passed his idea along to Ann Godoff, then publisher and editor in chief of Random House, and my editor, Jonathan Karp. Over breakfast at a midtown Manhattan hotel, Ann and Jon briefly described the book they envisioned, and I eagerly embraced the project. Having worked with Jon before, I knew I could rely on his excellent judgment. When I was ready to write, Jon patiently and perceptively helped me frame my approach, saving me from scurrying down the wrong path. I was grateful for his willingness to trust me as I disappeared for more than a year without showing him anything I had written. He edited the manuscript with sensitivity, asking insightful questions and making constructive suggestions. I simply could not ask for a better advocate for my work.

My thanks as well to Random House president and publisher Gina Centrello and editor in chief Dan Menaker for their enthusiastic support. I am deeply grateful to Jon Karp's assistant, Jonathan Jao, who took care of so many details and offered helpful ideas, especially on the photo section; Charlotte Gross for her impeccable copy editing; production editor Steve Messina; Laura Goldin for her rigorous legal review; publicity directors Carol Schneider and Tom Perry; publicists Elizabeth Fogarty and Todd Doughty; associate publishers Elizabeth McGuire and Anthony Ziccardi; creative director Gene Mydlowski; art director Allison Saltzman; sales director Janet Cooke; rights director Claire Tisne; and rights manager Rachel Bernstein.

My photo researcher, Sarah Longacre, applied imagination and determination to the task of assembling hundreds of photographs for me to choose from. She was always on the lookout for the best possible image, and she diligently fielded my queries about all sorts of obscure sources. I am also grateful to my talented website designer, Shannon Swenson of Stream Studio Web Architects.

Thanks also to Katherine Lambert for her terrific skill with a camera, and to Patti McFarland and Gloria Interiano-Piedra, who prepared me for my photo session.

I have benefited from the wise counsel of Amanda Urban, my agent for nearly twenty years, who once again energetically represented my interests and championed my work.

My family, as always, gave me endless love and support at every step. With my three children out of the nest, this was my most solitary book project, as I faced my work days without the bustle of parenting activities. But Kirk, Lisa, and David sustained me with their constant encouragement and inspired me when I was downhearted.

The contribution of my beloved husband, Stephen, throughout my three years of research and writing was incalculable. Whenever I felt daunted by a deadline, he urged me to push my way through. When I struggled with organization, he helped clarify my thinking. When I made exciting discoveries, he happily shared my joy. As he did with my previous book, he came up with the title. And when I finished my manuscript, he devoted hours to editing it sentence by sentence—challenging, trimming, refining, and always improving. Perhaps Camelot is too much with me, but after more than two decades of observing his extraordinary gifts as an editor, I consider him nothing less than magical.

INDEX

PHOTOGRAPH CREDITS

ABOUT THE TYPE

This book was set in Bembo, a typeface based on an old-style Roman face that was used for Cardinal Bembo's tract *De Aetna* in 1495. Bembo was cut by Francisco Griffo in the early sixteenth century. The Lanston Monotype Machine Company of Philadelphia brought the well-proportioned letter forms of Bembo to the United States in the 1930s.